HEALTH CARE

FRAUD *and* ABUSE:

Practical Perspectives

2004 Cumulative Supplement

Publications From BNA Books on Related Topics

Codes of Professional Responsibility: Ethics Standards in Business, Health, and Law

E-Health Business & Transactional Law

Health Care Fraud and Abuse: Practical Perspectives

Medical Ethics: Analysis of the Issues Raised by the Codes, Opinions, and Statements

Medical Ethics: Codes, Opinions, and Statements

Occupational Safety and Health Law

Prosecuting and Defending Health Care Fraud Cases

HEALTH CARE

FRAUD *and* ABUSE:

Practical Perspectives

2004 *Cumulative Supplement*

Editor-in-Chief

Linda A. Baumann

Reed Smith LLP
Washington, D.C.

The American Bar Association
Health Law Section

The Bureau of National Affairs, Inc., Washington, D.C.

Library of Congress Cataloging-in-Publication Data

Health care fraud and abuse : practical perspectives / editor-in-chief, Linda A. Baumann.
    p. cm.
"The American Bar Association, Health Law Section."
ISBN 1-57018-124-1
   1. Insurance, Health--Law and Legislation--United States--Criminal provisions. 2. Medical care--Law and legislation--United States--Criminal provisions. 3. Medicare fraud. 4. Medicaid fraud. I. Baumann, Linda A. II. American Bar Association. Health Law Section.

KF3605 .H43 2002
345.73'0263--dc21

2002066476

The materials contained in this work represent the opinions of the individual authors and should not be construed to be those of either the American Bar Association (ABA) or the ABA Health Law Section, or any other person or entity. The authors expressly reserve the right to freely advocate other positions on behalf of clients. Nothing contained herein is to be considered the rendering of legal advice for specific cases, and readers are responsible for obtaining such advice from their own legal counsel. These materials are intended for educational and informational purposes only.

Published by BNA Books
1231 25th St., N.W., Washington, D.C. 20037
http://www.bnabooks.com

International Standard Book Number: 1-57018-479-8
Printed in the United States of America

Contributing Authors

Linda A. Baumann
Reed Smith LLP
Washington, D.C.

Thomas S. Crane
Mintz, Levin, Cohn, Ferris,
Glovsky, and Popeo, P.C.
Boston, Massachusetts

Robert Salcido
Akin, Gump, Strauss, Hauer
& Feld, L.L.P.
Washington, D.C.

Patric Hooper
Hooper, Lundy & Bookman, Inc.
Los Angeles, California

Stacy Rummel Bratcher
Hooper, Lundy & Bookman, Inc.
Los Angeles, California

Robert L. Roth
Crowell & Moring, LLP
Washington, D.C.

Dennis M. Barry
Vinson & Elkins, L.L.P.
Washington, D.C.

Nancy S. Jones
Bass Berry & Sims PLC
Nashville, Tennessee

Alicia J. Palmer
Coventry Health Care, Inc.
Bethesda, Maryland

Jennifer L. Weaver
Waller Lansden Dortch & Davis
Nashville, Tennessee

Nora L. Liggett
Waller Lansden Dortch & Davis
Nashville, Tennessee

William W. Horton
Haskell Slaughter
Young & Rediker, LLC
Birmingham, Alabama

George E. McDavid
Reed Smith LLP
Princeton, New Jersey

Monty G. Humble
Vinson & Elkins L.L.P.
Dallas, Texas

Foreword

The American Bar Association (ABA) Health Law Section is proud to continue its book series with the publication of the 2004 Cumulative Supplement to *Health Care Fraud and Abuse: Practical Perspectives*, published in cooperation with BNA Books, a Division of The Bureau of National Affairs, Inc. We are pleased to have added to this BNA Books series with our second book, *E-Health Business and Transactional Law*, for which we have also just published the 2004 Supplement.

Health Care Fraud and Abuse: Practical Perspectives continues to provide practical guidance on fraud and abuse issues, both for those who are new to health law and for those who have expertise in this area. Each chapter contains valuable resources and up to date insights to this dynamic and crucially important area of the law affecting the health care industry.

The Section wishes to express its continuing appreciation to Editor-in-Chief Linda A. Baumann, who has been exceptionally dedicated to keeping this book up to date and relevant to the health law bar. She has gone "above and beyond" in shepherding the original book and each Supplement to completion. Many others have given dedicated service to this effort, including James Fattibene and Ann Gerster at BNA Books and, particularly, the Supplement authors, who have given of their time and expertise for the benefit of the profession. Thank you all on behalf of the Section for this job well done.

We are confident that you will continue to find this book and its Supplements to be a useful and practical reference source. We would welcome your thoughts as to how the Section's BNA Books series can further address your practice needs.

J. A. (TONY) PATTERSON, JR.
SECTION CHAIR

GREGORY L. PEMBERTON
CHAIR-ELECT

MICHAEL E. CLARK
CHAIR
PUBLICATIONS COMMITTEE

HEALTH LAW SECTION
AMERICAN BAR ASSOCIATION

October 2004

The American Bar Association
Health Law Section
2004–2005 Officers & Council

Preface

The enactment of the Medicare Prescription Drug, Improvement, and Modernization Act (MMA) has led to dramatic changes throughout the health care industry. These changes directly (and indirectly) impact the fraud and abuse laws, which themselves continue to evolve at an extremely rapid pace. In addition, government enforcement activities against perceived instances of fraud and abuse in the health care industry continue to expand into new areas of investigation, often leading to record-breaking settlements. Moreover, the purportedly fraudulent practices of companies in other industries have changed the enforcement landscape for health care organizations as well. As a result, corporate entities, their directors and officers, and their lawyers are facing greatly heightened scrutiny and potential liability. In light of these many new developments, I am very pleased that the ABA and BNA Books have collaborated to publish the 2004 Supplement to *Health Care Fraud and Abuse: Practical Perspectives*.

The 2004 Supplement, in addition to updating and expanding the contents of the original chapters in the Main Volume, contains a new Chapter 2 on "Federal Physician Self-Referral Restrictions," by Thomas Crane, which has been completely rewritten to reflect the new Stark II/Phase II regulations. There is also a comprehensive new Chapter 9 on "The Disclosure Dilemma: How, When, and What to Tell Stockholders and Stakeholders About Your *Qui Tam* Suit or Investigation," by William Horton and Monty Humble. In the post-Enron era, this topic is extremely timely, and the new chapter contains a wealth of practical guidance. Similarly, Chapter 8 on "Potential Liabilities for Directors and Officers of Health Care Organizations" contains a new section on "The Sarbanes-Oxley Act and Related Developments" with a checklist of Recommendations for Board Members. Both Chapter 7 and Chapter 8 analyze significant new aspects of the Sentencing Guidelines. Chapter 4 on "Practical Considerations for Defending Health Care Fraud and Abuse Cases" has been substantially expanded to address several new topics, including the multiple types of enforcement actions currently facing the pharmaceutical industry, and Chapter 5 on "Legal Issues Surrounding Hospital and Physician Relationships" has been revised to cover various new developments in this area, from Stark II/Phase II to economic credentialing. Chapter 3 of the 2004 Supplement contains extensive analysis of new False Claims Act jurisprudence, including a detailed discussion of *United States* ex rel. *Mikes v. Straus* and other implied certification cases, while Chapter 7 provides readers with information on the OIG's Compliance Program Guidance for Pharmaceutical Manufacturers as well as the important new draft Supplemental Compliance Program Guidance for Hospitals. In addition, Chapter 6 provides updated information and insights on fraud and abuse in the managed care arena. The Appendices have also been extensively revised to reflect recent changes in the fraud and abuse laws and regulations.

The 2004 Supplement is current through June 1, 2004. (The Main Volume contained citations through June 2001.) References to certain more recent, major developments have also been included in an effort to make the book as practical as possible. As noted in the Main Volume, the content of this book is designed for general informational purposes only, and should not be construed as legal advice or an opinion on any specific facts or circumstances. The views expressed in the chapters are those of the individual authors, and do not reflect the views of their firms or the firms' clients, myself, or the other authors of this volume.

Many people contributed to the success of this Supplement. While the chapter authors are very busy practitioners, they all graciously agreed to share their expertise and devote uncounted hours to this project. The current leadership and staff of the ABA Health Law Section have also been extremely supportive in these efforts. In addition, BNA Books has provided invaluable guidance to all. I also want to take this opportunity to thank my family for their patience and support throughout the writing and publication process.

The risks of exposure for health care companies and their counsel continue to be high. In light of the resignation of Inspector General Janet Rehnquist in 2003, and the appointment of a new Inspector General (who has yet to be confirmed as of this date), there is a great deal of uncertainty with regard to the OIG's future priorities and approach to enforcement. We hope readers will find that the Supplement continues to serve them well in navigating this volatile area of the law.

LINDA A. BAUMANN
EDITOR-IN-CHIEF
Reed Smith LLP
Washington, D.C.

October 2004

About the Authors

Linda A. Baumann (Chapter 1: An Introduction to Health Care Fraud and Abuse; Chapter 8: Potential Liabilities for Directors and Officers of Health Care Organizations)

Linda Baumann serves as editor-in-chief of this volume and also is the author of two of the chapters. Ms. Baumann is a partner at Reed Smith LLP, in Washington, D.C., and has extensive experience in health care regulatory matters, particularly those relating to fraud and abuse. She has worked with clients throughout the industry ranging from Fortune 50 companies to community providers, including hospitals, skilled nursing facilities, pharmaceutical companies, distributors, diagnostic testing facilities, clinical laboratories, DME suppliers, management companies, and many other types of entities involved in the health care industry. She helps clients develop strategies to promote business objectives while ensuring compliance with applicable laws and regulations, and has designed corporate compliance programs, handled government investigations (from the initial audit through negotiation and settlement), and served as outside regulatory counsel on a wide variety of legal issues. She was recently named one of the 12 Outstanding Fraud and Compliance Lawyers–2004 in the country by Nightingale's *Healthcare News*. She has experience in the federal government, in private practice, and in academia, having taught at Princeton University. She frequently speaks before national groups of health care organizations as well as attorneys, and has published numerous articles on various health care topics. Ms. Baumann also serves on the Governing Council of the ABA Health Law Section. She received her J.D. from Columbia University, where she was an editor of the *Columbia University Law Review* and an International Fellow. She received her undergraduate degree, magna cum laude, from Brown University.

Thomas S. Crane (Chapter 2: Federal Physician Self-Referral Restrictions)

Tom Crane is a member at Mintz, Levin, Cohn, Ferris, Glovsky, and Popeo, P.C., where he co-coordinates the firm's Health Care Fraud and Abuse and Corporate Compliance practice group. Mr. Crane is nationally recognized as an authority on fraud and abuse, and provides comprehensive fraud and abuse services to clients, from defense to compliance advice to compliance programs. His work in defending clients against false claims, whistleblower, and anti-kickback allegations includes internal investigations, voluntary disclosures, and negotiating settlements and corporate integrity agreements (CIAs). He also provides compliance advice to clients in structuring complex transactions to comply with fraud and abuse laws and the variety of regulatory requirements that must be met. He received his undergraduate degree from Harvard College (1972), a Masters degree in health administration from the University of Michigan (1976), and his law degree from Antioch School of Law in Washington, D.C. (1983).

Robert Salcido (Chapter 3: The False Claims Act in Health Care Prosecutions: Application of the Substantive, *Qui Tam*, and Voluntary Disclosure Provisions)

Robert Salcido is a partner at Akin, Gump, Strauss, Hauer & Feld, L.L.P., in its Washington, D.C. office. Mr. Salcido has practiced extensively in the area of the False Claims Act (FCA), having previously been a trial attorney with the Civil Fraud Unit of the Civil Division of the U.S. Department of Justice (DOJ), which has nationwide jurisdiction over FCA actions. At the DOJ, he prosecuted actions under the FCA, handled actions under the FCA's voluntary disclosure provisions, and specialized in whistleblower actions brought under the *qui tam* provisions of the FCA. Mr. Salcido is the author of the books *False Claims Act & The Healthcare Industry: Counseling & Litigation* (Amer. Health Lawyers 1999), and *False Claims Act & The Healthcare Industry: Counseling & Litigation: November 2000 Supplement* (Am. Health Lawyers 2000). He is a graduate of Harvard Law School and received his Bachelor of Arts degree summa cum laude from Claremont McKenna College.

Patric Hooper (Chapter 4: Practical Considerations for Defending Health Care Fraud and Abuse Cases)

Patric Hooper is a founding principal of Hooper, Lundy & Bookman, Inc., a health law specialty firm with a national practice. Mr. Hooper has practiced in the health law field for nearly 30 years, and has been involved in many high profile health law cases. In addition to his involvement in resolving disputes, Mr. Hooper regularly advises nonprofit and for-profit health care organizations regarding reimbursement, certification, and licensure issues associated with business transactions and combinations. He continuously advises health care providers on Medicare, Medicaid, and Tricare fraud and abuse issues and on state anti-kickback and referral issues. Mr. Hooper is a frequent writer and lecturer on fraud and abuse issues and was the first chairman of the Fraud and Self-Referral interest group of the American Bar Association (ABA) Health Law Section. He received his J.D. from the University of San Diego in 1973 and his A.B. from the University of California, Los Angeles in 1970.

Stacy Rummel Bratcher (Chapter 4: Practical Considerations for Defending Health Care Fraud and Abuse Cases)

Stacy Rummel Bratcher has been an associate with the health care law firm, Hooper, Lundy & Bookman, Inc., since September 2000. Ms. Bratcher practices in the firm's regulatory and litigation departments where she handles fraud and abuse defense, Medicare & Medicaid reimbursement cases, and managed care litigation for a variety of health care providers. Outside of her work with Hooper Lundy, Ms. Bratcher is heavily involved in Los Angeles' health care community. In July of 2003, she was appointed by the Los Angeles County Board of Supervisors to the County's Hospital and Healthcare Delivery Commission. She also serves on the Los Angeles County Bar Association's Bioethics Committee.

Dennis M. Barry (Chapter 5: Legal Issues Surrounding Hospital and Physician Relationships)

Dennis Barry is a partner in the Washington, D.C., office of Vinson & Elkins L.L.P. He leads his firm's health care practice in that office, and is co-chair of the firm's Health Section. His practice deals exclusively with health care clients whom he represents on a broad range of issues, and he spends the majority of his time on Medicare payment and compliance issues. Since 1989, Mr. Barry has served as the editor and principal author of *Dennis Barry's Reimbursement Advisor*, a monthly newsletter published by Aspen Publishing. Mr. Barry serves as co-chair of the Medicare & Medicaid Institute, an annual 3-day program sponsored by the American Health Lawyers Association (AHLA). Mr. Barry is listed in *Best Lawyers in America*. He has been active in a number of professional associations including the Healthcare Financial Management Association, and he has received the Follmer, Reeves, and Muncie, and Medal of Honor awards from that organization. He received his J.D. from the University of Virginia in 1975.

Robert L. Roth (Chapter 6: Managed Care Fraud and Abuse: Risk Areas for Government Program Participants)

Robert Roth is a partner in the Health Care Group at Crowell & Moring, LLP, in Washington, D.C., and has been in private practice since 1993. Previously, Mr. Roth represented the Health Care Financing Administration (now the Centers for Medicare & Medicaid Services) as a member of the Office of the General Counsel of the U.S. Department of Health and Human Services, served as an Assistant Attorney General assigned to Maryland's Department of Health and Mental Hygiene, and counseled the Maryland General Assembly. Mr. Roth is an adjunct professor of law at the University of Baltimore School of Law and has been active in the leadership of the ABA's Health Law Section, serving as Section Chair for 2001–2002. He also serves on the Advisory Board of *BNA's Health Law Reporter* and *BNA's Health Care Fraud Report*. He received his undergraduate degree from Lehigh University and his Juris Doctor degree from Syracuse University College of Law.

Alicia J. Palmer (Chapter 6: Managed Care Fraud and Abuse: Risk Areas for Government Program Participants)

Alicia Palmer joined Coventry Health Care as a Senior Attorney in October 2002. Prior to joining Coventry Health Care, Ms. Palmer was an associate with Crowell & Moring and Michaels & Bonner, both in Washington, D.C., and in-house counsel at Blue Cross and Blue Shield of the National Capital Area (now CareFirst Blue Cross Blue Shield). While in private practice, Ms. Palmer focused primarily on federal and state regulatory issues affecting managed care plans and health insurers, particularly issues related to the Medicare+Choice program, the Federal Employees Health Benefit Program, federal health care data bank reporting requirements, and state licensure and operating requirements for managed care plans. Ms. Palmer is a 1995 graduate of the American University, Washington College of Law, and she obtained her undergraduate degree in Human Resources at Indiana University of Pennsylvania in 1988.

Nancy Jones (Chapter 7: Corporate Compliance Programs)

Nancy Jones is a partner at Bass Berry & Sims PLC, in Nashville, Tennessee. Ms. Jones has extensive experience in general commercial litigation (both plaintiff and defendant), health care litigation and securities class actions, and corporate criminal defense. Ms. Jones received her Bachelor of Arts degree, with Honors, from the University of Missouri in 1971. In 1978, she received her Juris Doctor degree from Syracuse University. Prior to joining Bass Berry & Sims, Ms. Jones was an Assistant U.S. Attorney for the Middle District of Tennessee, from 1991 to 1993. From 1987 to 1991, she was an Assistant U.S. Attorney for the Western District of Oklahoma; from 1980 to 1987, she served as Assistant U.S. Attorney for the Northern District of New York. Ms. Jones has participated in many seminars and has written for the *Journal of the Tennessee Society of Certified Public Accountants*. Ms. Jones is an adjunct professor of law at the Vanderbilt University School of Law. She is a member of the ABA, New York, Tennessee, and Nashville Bar Associations.

Nora L. Liggett (Chapter 7: Corporate Compliance Programs)

Nora Liggett is a member of Waller Lansden Dortch & Davis, in Nashville, Tennessee. Ms. Liggett has extensive experience in the area of health care operations and regulatory issues. She advises health care providers and hospital and physician practice-management companies on a variety of health care related issues, including Medicare fraud and abuse, physician self-referral prohibitions, third-party reimbursement, managed care contracting and development, and related health care operations issues. Ms. Liggett received her

Bachelor of Arts degree, cum laude, from the University of the South in 1986, and her Juris Doctor degree from Washington and Lee University in 1989. She is a frequent contributor to health law publications, speaks regularly at health law seminars, and is the co-editor of Waller Lansden's *Health Law Newsletter*. Ms. Liggett is active in the Health Law Sections of the Nashville and Tennessee Bar Associations and is a member of the AHLA, and the Antitrust and Health Law Sections of the ABA.

Jennifer L. Weaver (Chapter 7: Corporate Compliance Programs)

Jennifer Weaver is an associate with Waller Lansden Dortch & Davis in Nashville, Tennessee. Ms. Weaver's practice focuses on health care litigation, securities litigation, and white-collar criminal defense. Ms. Weaver has extensive experience in False Claims Act litigation and health care fraud and abuse issues. Ms. Weaver received her Bachelor of Fine Arts degree with highest honors from New York University in 1993. In 1997, Ms. Weaver received her Juris Doctor degree from Columbia University, where she graduated as a Harlan Fiske Stone Scholar. Prior to joining Waller Lansden, Ms. Weaver was an associate with O'Melveny & Myers in Los Angeles, California, and served as a law clerk to U.S. District Judge Joseph R. Goodwin (Southern District of West Virginia). She is a member of the ABA Health Law Section, the American Health Lawyers Association, and the California, Tennessee, and Nashville Bar Associations.

Linda A. Baumann (Chapter 8: Potential Liabilities for Directors and Officers of Health Care Organizations)

See entry for Linda A. Baumann at Chapter 1, above.

George E. McDavid (Chapter 8: Potential Liabilities for Directors and Officers of Health Care Organizations)

George McDavid is a partner with Reed Smith LLP in the firm's Princeton, New Jersey office. His national practice focuses on complex commercial litigation, including representation of pharmaceutical manufacturers and distributors, hospitals, and other health care providers. His experience also includes products liability and toxic tort defense work. Mr. McDavid has extensive experience defending and counseling health care companies in respect of their decisions concerning the marketing of drugs and medical devices. Since his admission to the bar in 1982, he has maintained an extremely active trial practice and tried to verdict over 30 cases before juries. He has tried cases before administrative law tribunals, arbitration panels, and state and federal courts. Mr. McDavid earned his J.D. from Case Western Reserve University in 1982 and his A.B. from Dartmouth College in 1978.

xviii *Health Care Fraud and Abuse—2004 Supplement*

William W. Horton (Chapter 9: the Disclosure Dilemma: How, When, and What to Tell Stockholders and Stakeholders About Your *Qui Tam* Suit or Investigation)

Bill Horton is Of Counsel to Haskell Slaughter Young & Rediker, LLC, Birmingham, Alabama. His practice focuses on the representation of health care enterprises and other businesses in securities and corporate finance matters, mergers and acquisitions, and general health care and corporate matters. Mr. Horton has served as lead counsel on some of the largest corporate finance and acquisition transactions in the health care services industry. He currently holds leadership positions with the American Bar Association's Health Law Section and the American Health Lawyers Association, and he is a frequent speaker and author on health care, corporate, and securities law topics. A graduate of Vanderbilt University and the Duke University School of Law, Mr. Horton served in 1985–1986 as a law clerk to United States District Judge James H. Hancock (Northern District of Alabama), and was general counsel of HEALTHSOUTH Corporation, one of the nation's largest health care services providers, from 1994 through 2003.

Monty G. Humble (Chapter 9: the Disclosure Dilemma: How, When, and What to Tell Stockholders and Stakeholders About Your *Qui Tam* Suit or Investigation)

Monty Humble is a partner in the Dallas, Texas office of Vinson & Elkins, LLP. His practice is focused on public debt offerings and other business transactions, particularly those related to the health care industry. He devotes a substantial portion of his time to representing borrowers and underwriters in connection with public offerings of tax-exempt bonds. He also provides advice and counsel in other areas related to finance, such as acquisitions and reorganizations. Mr. Humble is listed in *Best Lawyers in America*. He has been active in a number of professional associations, and currently serves as Treasurer of the National Association of Bond Lawyers; he is a Fellow of the Dallas Bar Foundation. He received his J.D. from The University of Texas School of Law with honors in 1976.

Summary Table of Contents

Detailed Table of Contents

1

An Introduction to Health Care Fraud and Abuse*

---

*Linda A. Baumann, Reed Smith LLP, Washington, D.C.

I. INTRODUCTION

A. The Potential Risks

Government enforcement activities related to health care fraud and abuse have continued to accelerate in recent years, and the dollar amounts of the settlements seem to be increasing especially now that the government has targeted the pharmaceutical industry as well as those who do business with them. The statistics tell part of the story. In September 2003, the Department of Health and Human Services (HHS) and the Department of Justice (DOJ) announced that, as a result of the Health Care Fraud and Abuse Control Program created under the Health Insurance Portability and Accountability Act of 1996 (HIPAA), the federal government won or negotiated more than $1.8 billion in judgments, settlements, and administrative impositions in health care fraud cases in 2002. An additional $59 million was recovered as the federal share of Medicaid restitution. These amounts constitute the largest return for the government since the inception of the program.

Criminal prosecutions continue as federal prosecutors filed 361 criminal indictments in health care fraud cases, and 480 defendants were convicted for health care fraud–related crimes during the year. Further, in addition to the 1,529 pending civil matters, 221 civil cases were filed in 2002, and HHS excluded 3,448 individuals and entities from participating in Medicare, Medicaid, and other federally-sponsored health care programs.[1] In the six-month period from October 2003 to March 2004 alone, the HHS Office of the Inspector General (OIG) reported exclusions of 1,544 individuals and entities for fraud or abuse of federal health care programs and/or beneficiaries; 234 convictions of individuals or entities that engaged in crimes against departmental programs; and 107 civil actions, which includes all False Claims Act (FCA) and unjust enrichment suits filed in district court, Civil Monetary Penalties Law (CMP) settlements, and self-disclosure administrative recoveries.[2] Moreover, for several years health care fraud has accounted for the largest proportion of the federal government's total civil recoveries. For example, in fiscal year 2003, the federal government recovered $1.7 billion in health care fraud cases (including both whistleblower claims and those initiated by the United States in independent fraud investigations) out of $2.1 billion in total civil fraud recoveries.[3]

---

[1] U.S. DEP'T OF HEALTH & HUMAN SERVS. & DEP'T OF JUSTICE, HEALTH CARE FRAUD AND ABUSE CONTROL PROGRAM ANNUAL REPORT FOR FY 2002, at 2 (Sept. 2003), *available at* http://oig. hhs.gov/publications/docs/hcfac/HCFAC%20Annual%20Report%20FY%202002.htm. [REPORT FOR FY 2002].

[2] U.S. DEP'T OF HEALTH & HUMAN SERVS., OIG SEMIANNUAL REPORT, OCTOBER 1, 2003–MARCH 31, 2004, at 7 (2004), *available at* http://www.oig.hhs.gov/publications/docs/semiannual/2004/ semiannualSpring04.pdf [hereinafter OIG MARCH 2004].

[3] Press Release, U.S. Dep't of Justice, Justice Dept. Civil Fraud Recoveries Total $2.1 Billion for FY 2003; False Claims Act Recoveries Exceed $12 Billion Since 1986 (Nov. 10, 2003), *available at* http://www.usdoj.gov/opa/pr/2003/November/03_civ_613.htm.

Significant health fraud cases resolved during 2003 and 2004 include the following:

- In June 2003, following an OIG audit and investigation, HCA, Inc., formerly known as Columbia/HCA Healthcare Corporation (HCA) agreed to enter a settlement and pay $631 million, plus interest. The settlement resolved allegations that HCA knowingly submitted false cost reports to Medicare; entered into improper referral arrangements with physicians that violated the anti-kickback statute and the Stark law; and submitted false claims for wound care services provided at 56 HCA hospitals. HCA also agreed to pay the government $5 million to resolve its civil and administrative liability related to allegations concerning claims for patients transferred to other facilities. In a separate administrative settlement, HCA agreed to pay the Centers for Medicare and Medicaid Services (CMS) $250 million to resolve administrative overpayments in connection with its cost reports. Previously, in December 2000, HCA paid approximately $840 million in criminal fines, civil restitution, and penalties to resolve a separate set of allegations and entered into a comprehensive eight-year corporate integrity agreement. The total amount of criminal, civil, and administrative sanctions and penalties imposed on HCA as a result of this investigation represents the largest health care fraud recovery ever obtained by the government from a single provider.[4]
- In August 2003, Integrated Health Services, Inc. (IHS), a nationwide chain of nursing homes, long-term care hospitals, and providers of ancillary services to nursing homes, entered into a global settlement to resolve False Claims Act liability and administrative claims. Because the firm is currently in bankruptcy and unable to pay more, the chain agreed to pay $19.1 million. The settlement covered five whistleblower lawsuits and two other fraud cases involving numerous allegations, including billing for unnecessary services or services never provided and wrongfully depreciating equipment on its cost report. The company also agreed to enter into two five-year corporate integrity agreements (CIAs); one for its long-term care division and one for its mobile diagnostic division, both of which are being sold to other companies as part of the IHS bankruptcy reorganization.[5]
- In July 2004, a federal jury acquitted eight current and former employees of TAP Pharmaceutical Products Inc. of all charges that they defrauded the federal government and paid kickbacks to promote the sale of the company's drugs. According to prosecutors, the defendants, TAP sales and account managers,

---

[4] OIG MARCH 2004, at 22.
[5] *Id.* at 24.

defrauded Medicaid and Medicare in the late 1990s by conspiring to have doctors bill free samples of the drug Lupron to the government for reimbursement and offering illegal inducements—including free samples, fees, educational grants, travel, forgiveness of debt, and entertainment—to persuade doctors to prescribe their products.[6]

- In June 2003, Zeneca, Inc., and AstraZeneca Pharmaceuticals LP (AstraZeneca) agreed to pay almost $355 million plus interest to settle criminal and civil liabilities relating to the marketing and pricing of its prostate cancer drug Zoladex. Specifically, the settlement resolved allegations that the company improperly set average wholesale price and marketed the spread between reimbursement and cost, causing Medicaid to overpay for Zoladex. The company also allegedly paid illegal remuneration to induce the purchase of Zoladex and failed to pay full Medicaid drug rebates to the states. AstraZeneca also pleaded guilty to conspiring to cause the submission of claims for payment for samples of Zoladex that had been provided free of charge to urologists. As part of the settlement, AstraZeneca also entered a comprehensive five-year CIA.[7]

- In August 2003, Redding Medical Center, Inc. (RMC), a wholly-owned subsidiary of Tenet HealthSystems Hospitals, Inc., and its parent corporation Tenet Healthcare Corporation, Inc., agreed to pay $54 million to settle allegations that RMC performed and billed medically unnecessary cardiac services at the hospital.[8]

- In December 2003, Community Residences, Inc., a nonprofit provider for community-based physical disability, mental health, and mental retardation services in Virginia, self-disclosed to the OIG that it had engaged an excluded individual as the medical director for two of its facilities, and was able to resolve the matter for $25,000.[9]

- In August 2003, Good Samaritan Hospital in Nebraska agreed to pay the government $1.2 million and entered a five-year CIA to settle alleged violations of the statutory prohibition on physician self-referrals (the Stark law) and the federal anti-kickback

---

[6]*See, e.g.,* United States v. MacKenzie, Crim. No. 01-CR-10350 (D. Mass. July 14, 2004). In October 2001, as part of the government's focus on fraud and abuse in the pharmaceutical industry, TAP Pharmaceutical Products, Inc. agreed to pay $875 million to settle certain criminal and civil liabilities. The company pleaded guilty to conspiring to violate the Prescription Drug Marketing Act (PDMA) and agreed to pay a $290 million fine to resolve these criminal charges. The settlement also included $560 million in connection with civil FCA claims and $25.5 million relating to state civil claims. The alleged false claims included fraudulent pricing schemes, sales and marketing misconduct, failure to provide TAP's best price to the government under the Medicaid rebate program, and falsely advising customers to report inflated prices rather than their real discounted price for the drug Lupron.

[7]U.S. DEP'T OF HEALTH & HUMAN SERVS., OIG SEMIANNUAL REPORT APRIL–SEPTEMBER 2003, at 19 (2003), *available at* http://oig.hhs.gov/publications/docs/semiannual/2003/03fallsemi.pdf [hereinafter OIG SEPTEMBER 2003].

[8]*Id.* at 22.

[9]OIG MARCH 2004, at 18.

statute. The hospital allegedly provided a cardiologist with inducements, including underwriting a loan, paying practice consultants, and providing free or reduced-price drugs and medical equipment, in exchange for patient referrals. The cardiologist had been previously sentenced to one year in prison for health care fraud.[10]

- In July 2003, Abbott Laboratories and Abbott's Ross Products Division entered a global criminal, civil, and administrative settlement totaling $615 million with the government as a result of the "Operation Headwaters" sting. The settlement resolved allegations that Ross paid kickbacks to purchasers of enteral nutrition items and services by: conditioning the sale of enteral nutrition sets on the purchase of enteral nutrition feeding pumps; failing to collect rental payments for the sets and pumps; and paying "conversion bonuses" that bore no relation to the actual cost of converting from one manufacturer to another. As part of the settlement, CG Nutritionals, Inc., an Abbott subsidiary, pleaded guilty to obstructing a health care fraud investigation and agreed to be permanently excluded. While the permanent exclusion affected only this one Abbott subsidiary, Abbott agreed to enter into a company-wide, comprehensive five-year CIA as part of the settlement.[11]

Numerous other settlements are listed on the OIG's website and indicate the wide range of government enforcement efforts.[12]

B. Exposure for Attorneys

Attorneys who represent publicly-traded health care companies now have additional obligations under the Sarbanes-Oxley Act of 2002 (Sarbanes-Oxley),[13] which required the Securities and Exchange Commission (SEC) to adopt rules prescribing minimum standards of professional conduct for attorneys appearing or practicing before the SEC, in any way, in the representation of public companies.

On February 6, 2003, the SEC published final rules codified in 17 C.F.R. Part 205. These rules cover all attorneys providing legal services to an issuer,[14] and who have notice that documents they are preparing, or assisting in preparing, will be filed with or submitted to

---

[10]*Id.*

[11]*Id.* at 20.

[12]Previous significant settlements include a 2001 settlement with Vencor, a nationwide nursing home chain, for $219 million involving quality of care allegations, and an $87 million settlement with Quorum Health Group, Inc., the owner and manager of numerous hospitals, concerning "reserve" cost reports.

[13]Sarbanes-Oxley Act of 2002, Pub. L. No. 107-204, 116 Stat. 745 (2002) [Sarbanes-Oxley].

[14]Sarbanes-Oxley defines "issuer" as an "issuer (as defined in Section 3 of the Securities Exchange Act of 1934 (15 U.S.C. §78(c)), the securities of which are registered under Section 12 of that Act (15 U.S.C. §78l), or that is required to file reports under Section 15(d) or that files or has filed a registration statement that has not yet become effective under the Securities Act of 1933 (15 U.S.C. §77a et seq.), and that it has not withdrawn." *See* Sarbanes-Oxley Act §2.

the SEC. The regulations contain numerous new standards for such attorneys, including:

- Evidence of a material violation, determined according to an objective standard, must be reported "up-the-ladder" to the issuer's Chief Legal Counsel or the Chief Executive Officer or equivalent;[15]
- If the Chief Legal Counsel or the Chief Executive Officer of the company does not respond appropriately to the evidence, the attorney must report the evidence to the Audit Committee, another committee of independent directors, or the full Board of Directors;[16]
- An attorney may, without the consent of an issuer client, reveal confidential information related to his or her representation to the extent the attorney reasonably believes it necessary: (1) to prevent the issuer from committing a material violation likely to cause substantial financial injury to the financial interests or property of the issuer or investors; (2) to prevent the issuer from committing an illegal act; or (3) to rectify the consequences of a material violation or illegal act in which the attorney's services have been used; and
- An attorney supervising or directing another attorney who is appearing and practicing before the SEC must make reasonable efforts to ensure that the subordinate attorney conforms to the regulations and must comply with reporting requirements when the subordinate attorney reports evidence of a material violation.[17]

The SEC regulations generally preempt state laws except that a state may impose on attorneys more rigorous obligations that are not inconsistent with the federal rules. However, the regulations further clarify that these regulations do not create a private cause of action, and authority to enforce compliance is vested exclusively with the SEC.[18] The scope of liability for attorneys and the companies they represent that are not subject to Sarbanes-Oxley is less clear. To minimize the risk of massive exposure, numerous organizations are adopting some form of "best practices" based on

---

[15]"Evidence of a material violation" is defined as "credible evidence, based upon which it would be unreasonable, under the circumstances, for a prudent and competent attorney not to conclude that it is reasonably likely that a material violation has occurred, is ongoing, or is about to occur." SEC Standards of Professional Conduct, 17 C.F.R. § 205.2(e) (2003).

[16]If an issuer establishes a "qualified legal compliance committee" (QLCC), an attorney could satisfy his or her obligation by reporting evidence of a material violation to the QLCC. 17 C.F.R. §205.3(b)(7) (2003).

[17]*See* 17 C.F.R. §205.4.

[18]*See* 17 C.F.R. §205.7. Note that foreign attorneys who are not admitted in the United States, and who do not advise clients regarding U.S. law, would not be covered by these regulations. Nevertheless, foreign attorneys who provide legal advice regarding U.S. law would be covered to the extent they are appearing and practicing before the SEC, unless they provide such advice in consultation with U.S. counsel. *See* 17 C.F.R. §205.2(j).

Sarbanes-Oxley, which may also help protect attorneys to a certain extent. Lawyers should also be alert to applicable (and evolving) standards in the American Bar Association (ABA) and state rules of professional conduct.[19]

C. Likelihood of Increased Enforcement Efforts in the Future

In light of the events of September 11, 2001, certain government agencies and personnel turned some of their attention from health care fraud to terrorism. Nevertheless, there are numerous indications (such as the statistics cited in Section I.A.) that health care fraud continues to be an important law enforcement priority of the federal government generally. Moreover, many of the resources devoted to the fight against health care fraud and abuse are required by law, and thus may not be diverted to the fight against terrorism.

Health care fraud investigations remain a priority at the Federal Bureau of Investigation (FBI). The FBI works many health care fraud cases on a joint basis with other federal agencies, including the HHS/OIG. Under HIPAA, the FBI was given $101 million in 2002 for health care fraud enforcement. As the FBI has increased the number of agents assigned to health care fraud investigations, the number of pending investigations has increased over 400 percent, rising from 591 cases in 1992 to 2,418 cases through 2002. Federal and state criminal health care fraud convictions resulting from FBI investigations have risen from 116 in 1992, to 549 through 2002. Numerous training programs related to health care fraud have been developed and are provided to new FBI agents and other agency personnel.[20]

FBI pilot projects also have developed new techniques to identify health care fraud, such as the Medicare/Medicaid Data Analysis Center developed in cooperation with CMS. This program is analyzing claims made to both the federal Medicare and state Medicaid programs by the same providers in order to identify aberrant billing patterns, unusual growth in billings and/or utilization of services or treatments, billing for unusual time frames (i.e., more than 24 hours a day), and other indicia of potential fraud against both programs.[21]

The government's approach to health care fraud and abuse investigations remains very "high profile," as evidenced by the October 30, 2002, raid at Tenet Healthcare Corporation's Redding Medical Center. This event made headlines in the national press for days, with reports of 40 agents and inspectors from the FBI, HHS, Internal Rev-

---

[19]*See, e.g.,* ABA Task Force Final Report on Corporate Responsibility, *available at* http://www.abanet.org/buslaw/corporateresponsibility/home.html. These issues are discussed in more detail in Chapter 8 of this volume.

[20]REPORT FOR FY 2002.

[21]*Id.*

enue Service (IRS), and other agencies executing search warrants on the hospital and the offices of two of its physicians.[22] Current enforcement efforts seem to be heavily focused on the pharmaceutical industry often leading to very large settlements.

- In May 2004, Warner-Lambert agreed to pay $430 million to resolve criminal charges and civil liabilities in connection with the Parke-Davis division's illegal and fraudulent promotion of unapproved uses for one of its drug products.[23]
- Also in May 2004, Schering Corporation, Schering-Plough Corporation, and Warrick Pharmaceuticals Corporation agreed to pay the United States and the state of Texas $27 million to settle allegations of health care fraud. The government alleged that Warrick, a division of Schering-Plough, submitted false pricing information and caused providers to submit fraudulently inflated reimbursement claims to the state and federally funded Texas Medicaid program.[24]
- In April 2003, Bayer Corporation (Bayer) paid $257 million plus interest as part of a global criminal and civil settlement related to its sales of Cipro and Adalat to a health maintenance organization. Bayer pleaded guilty to a violation of certain Food and Drug Administration (FDA) reporting requirements. The settlement also resolved allegations that Bayer significantly underpaid its Medicaid drug rebates and overcharged 340B program covered entities for the drugs because the company failed to report accurate best prices. Bayer agreed to a three-year extension of an earlier CIA.[25]
- In October 2002, Pfizer Corporation and its subsidiaries, Warner-Lambert and Parke-Davis, agreed to pay $49 million to settle allegations that the company violated the False Claims Act. The government alleged that the defendants fraudulently avoided paying fully the rebates owed to the state and federal governments under the national drug Medicaid rebate program for the cholesterol-lowering drug Lipitor.[26]
- In April 2003, SmithKline Beecham Corporation, doing business as GlaxoSmithKline, agreed to pay $88 million to settle claims

---

[22] Mark Taylor, *Tenet Calif. Hospital Subject of Government Raid,* MODERN HEALTHCARE'S DAILY DOSE, Oct. 31, 2002; Rhonda L. Rundle, *Tenet Healthcare Shares Fall 26% Amid Probe of Two Physicians,* WALL ST. J., Nov. 1, 2002, at A6.

[23] Press Release, U.S. Dep't of Justice, Warner-Lambert to Pay $430 Million to Resolve Criminal & Civil Health Care Liability Relating to Off-label Promotion (May 13, 2004), *available at* http://www.usdoj.gov/opa/pr/2004/May/04_civ_322.htm.

[24] Press Release, U.S. Dep't of Justice, Schering-Plough to Pay U.S. & Texas $27 Million to Settle Medicaid Fraud Allegations (May 13, 2004), *available at* http://www.usdoj.gov/opa/pr/2004/May/04_civ_292.htm.

[25] OIG SEPTEMBER 2003, at 19–20.

[26] Press Release, U.S. Dep't of Justice, Drug Giant Pfizer & Two Subsidiaries to Pay $49 Million for Defrauding Drug Medicaid Rebate Program (Oct. 28, 2002), *available at* http://www.usdoj.gov/opa/pr/2002/October/02_civ_622.htm.

that it violated Medicaid drug rebate program requirements in connection with two of its drugs, Flonase and Paxil. Glaxo-SmithKline allegedly failed to report accurate best price information, resulting in allegedly underpaid Medicaid rebates owed to the states and overcharges to 340B program covered entities. GlaxoSmithKline agreed to a comprehensive CIA with the OIG as part of the settlement.[27]

The sweeping Medicare Prescription Drug, Improvement, and Modernization Act,[28] or MMA, expands Medicare prescription drug coverage under a new Medicare Part D program, modifies payments to virtually every type of Medicare provider, replaces the current Medicare+Choice program with a new Medicare Advantage program offering additional health plan options, establishes a controversial demonstration project to test direct competition between managed care plans and traditional fee-for-service plans, and institutes administrative reforms to improve Medicare program operations, among many other provisions. In the fraud and abuse context, the MMA is notable primarily because it gives the OIG responsibility for conducting studies and becoming directly involved in certain payment issues pertaining to durable medical equipment (DME) and drugs, particularly those for cancer and end-stage renal disease (ESRD) patients. The MMA also potentially raises new enforcement issues, since the implementation of its many new and revised programs will likely lead to additional fraud and abuse concerns. For example, before the MMA's discount drug card program began on June 1, 2004, the government announced steps it was taking to prevent drug card fraud,[29] and also issued guidance addressing payment arrangements between discount drug card sponsors and their network pharmacies in connection with education, outreach, and enrollment[30] because of concerns under the anti-kickback statute. However, the OIG and several legislators have warned that the OIG's enforcement efforts may actually decrease because the agency was given numerous new duties under the MMA but no additional resources to perform them.

The appointment of a new Inspector General may also result in shifting OIG priorities.[31] Nevertheless, the federal and state governments, as well as private payors, will likely continue to devote

---

[27]OIG SEPTEMBER 2003, at 20.

[28]Medicare Prescription Drug, Improvement, and Modernization Act of 2003, Pub. L. No. 108-173, 117 Stat. 2066.

[29]*See* Press Release, CMS, OIG Protecting Drug Card Program From Fraud (May 18, 2004), *available at* http://www.cms.hhs.gov/media/press/release.asp?Counter=1051.

[30]U.S. DEP'T OF HEALTH & HUMAN SERVS., EDUCATION AND OUTREACH ARRANGEMENTS BETWEEN MEDICARE-ENDORSED DISCOUNT DRUG CARD SPONSORS AND THEIR NETWORK PHARMACIES UNDER THE ANTI-KICKBACK STATUTE (Apr. 8, 2004), *available at* http://oig.hhs.gov/fraud/docs/alertsandbulletins/2004/FA040904.pdf.

[31]On June 19, 2004, Daniel R. Levinson was nominated to be the HHS Inspector General, to replace Acting Principal Deputy Inspector General Dara Corrigan. *See* http://www.whitehouse.gov/news/releases/2004/07/20040719-11.html.

substantial efforts to fighting health care fraud and abuse in the future.

II. The Federal Fraud and Abuse Laws

A. The Anti-Kickback Statute

2. *Exceptions and Safe Harbors*

The OIG finalized the safe harbor for ambulance restocking arrangements in December 2001.[32] A safe harbor that would expand the existing safe harbor for certain waivers of beneficiary coinsurance and deductibles to Medicare SELECT policyholders was proposed in 2002 and is still under consideration by the OIG.[33] However, a proposed safe harbor for transfers of remuneration between entities under common ownership or control was rejected by the OIG in favor of considering such arrangements on a case by case basis.[34] Also, although a proposed safe harbor for the payment of Medicare Part B or Medigap premium payments for financially needy ESRD patients was proposed by the OIG, the OIG subsequently determined that it would not promulgate that proposed regulation.[35]

3. *Special Fraud Alerts*

In March 2003, the OIG issued a Special Fraud Alert entitled Telemarketing By Durable Medical Equipment Suppliers.[36] This Special Fraud Alert reemphasized the statutory prohibition on making unsolicited telephone calls to Medicare beneficiaries regarding the furnishing of a covered item except in specific situations, and stated that the prohibition could not be circumvented by engaging third-party marketing companies. The Special Fraud Alert also emphasized a DME supplier's duty to ensure that a third-party marketer does not engage in prohibited activity on the supplier's behalf, noting that both the DME supplier and the marketer could be subject to criminal, civil, and administrative penalties under the False Claims Act if a claim, generated by a prohibited solicitation, was submitted.[37]

4. *Office of Inspector General Advisory Opinions*

Numerous advisory opinions have been issued since 2001, including those related to:

---

[32] Ambulance Replenishing Safe Harbor Under the Anti-Kickback Statute, 66 Fed. Reg. 62,979 (Dec. 4, 2001), reprinted as Appendix A-2 at the end of this Supplement.

[33] OIG September 2003, at 92.

[34] *Id.*

[35] *See* 67 Fed. Reg. 72,896 (Dec. 9, 2002).

[36] U.S. Dep't of Health & Human Servs., Telemarketing by Durable Medical Equipment Suppliers (March 2003), *available at* http://www.oig.hhs.gov/fraud/docs/alertsandbulletins/Telemarketingdme.pdf.

[37] *Id.*

- ambulatory surgery centers (ASCs);[38]
- managed care arrangements;[39]
- discounts;[40]
- swapping;[41]
- employment of an excluded individual;[42]
- donations and free goods or services;[43]
- physician recruitment;[44]
- warranties;[45]
- ambulance restocking arrangements;[46]
- waivers of deductibles, copayments, or premiums;[47]
- joint ventures;[48]
- beneficiary inducement;[49]
- management agreements;[50]
- transfers of physician practices;[51] and
- advertising.[52]

5. *Other Guidance*

The OIG issued a Special Advisory Bulletin on "Offering Gifts and Other Inducements to Beneficiaries" in August 2002, which is discussed in more detail later in this chapter.[53] This and other guidance documents related to health care fraud and abuse can be located via the OIG's Web site, at http://oig.hhs.gov, as well as in the appendix materials in the Main Volume and in this Supplement.

With regard to contractual joint ventures, on April 23, 2003, the OIG issued a Special Advisory Bulletin highlighting the agency's concerns about certain types of "contractual joint venture" arrangements (Contractual Joint Venture Bulletin).[54] According to the OIG, certain

---

[38]*E.g.,* OIG Advisory Op. Nos. 01-17, 01-21, 02-9, and 03-05.

[39]*E.g.,* Advisory Op. Nos. 01-13, 01-15, 01-16, and 02-12.

[40]*E.g.,* Advisory Op. Nos. 01-8, 02-6, 02-7, 02-8, and 02-10.

[41]*E.g.,* Advisory Op. Nos. 01-8 and 02-12.

[42]*E.g.,* Advisory Op. Nos. 01-16 and 03-01.

[43]*E.g.,* Advisory Op. Nos. 01-2, 01-19, 02-11 (academic medical center), 02-14, 03-04, 03-06, 03-07, 03-14, 04-04, and 04-05.

[44]*E.g.,* Advisory Op. No. 01-4.

[45]*E.g.,* Advisory Op. Nos. 01-8 and 02-6.

[46]*E.g.,* Advisory Op. Nos. 02-2 and 02-3.

[47]*E.g.,* Advisory Op. Nos. 01-10, 01-11, 01-12, 01-14, 01-15, 01-18, 02-1, 02-7, 02-8, 02-13, 02-15, 02-16, 03-03, 03-09, 03-10, 03-11, 04-01, 04-02, and 04-06.

[48]*E.g.,* Advisory Op. Nos. 01-17, 01-21, 03-02, 03-05, 03-12, and 03-13.

[49]*E.g.,* Advisory Op. Nos. 01-7, 01-11, 01-14, 01-15, 01-18, 02-1, 02-12, and 02-14.

[50]*E.g.,* Advisory Op. No. 03-08.

[51]*E.g.,* Advisory Op. No. 03-15.

[52]*E.g.,* Advisory Op. Nos. 02-12 and 04-03.

[53]67 Fed. Reg. 55,855 (Aug. 30, 2002), reproduced in Appendix F-18 at the end of this Supplement; *see infra* Section II.D.3.

[54]U.S. DEP'T OF HEALTH & HUMAN SERVS., CONTRACTUAL JOINT VENTURES (Apr. 2003), *available at* http://www.oig.hhs.gov/fraud/docs/alertsandbulletins/042303SABJointVentures.pdf. As used by the OIG, the term "contractual joint venture" refers to a provider's contractual arrangements with a manager or supplier, as distinguished from legal co-ownership of an entity, such as a partnership.

of these arrangements "use a combination of 'shell' entities and sub-contracting arrangements with freestanding providers of related health services, such as durable medical equipment (DME) or home oxygen suppliers, to disguise illegal kickbacks."[55]

In the Contractual Joint Venture Bulletin, the OIG focuses on those arrangements in which a health care provider (the Owner) expands into a related health care business by contracting with an existing provider or supplier of a related item or service (the Manager/Supplier). According to the OIG, the owner's ability to make patient referrals to the new business is problematic and the agency offers several examples of suspect contractual arrangements that it maintains "could provide the basis for law enforcement action." Such suspect arrangements include, but are not limited to, arrangements whereby: (1) the Owner (referral source) is expanding into a related "new" business that is itself dependent on patient referrals from, or other business generated by, the existing business; (2) the Owner neither operates nor commits substantial resources to the new business; (3) absent the contractual arrangement, the Manager/Supplier would be a competitor; and (4) the Owner and Manager/Supplier share the economic benefits of the Owner's new business.

The Contractual Joint Venture Bulletin describes numerous characteristics that potentially indicate a prohibited arrangement, including:

- *New Line of Business.* The Owner typically seeks to expand into a health care service that can be provided to its existing patients;
- *Captive Referral Base.* The new business predominantly serves the Owner's existing patients, making little effort to expand the business to serve new customers;
- *Little or No Bona Fide Business Risk.* The Owner's primary contribution to the venture is referrals, rather than a financial or other investment. The Owner delegates the operation of the venture to the Manager/Supplier while retaining profits generated from its referral base;
- *Status of the Manager/Supplier.* The Manager normally would compete with the Owner since it has the ability to provide virtually identical services and bill insurers and patients under its own name;
- *Scope of Services Provided by the Manager/Supplier.* The Manager/Supplier often provides a "turn key" type operation, which often includes the provision of: (i) day-to-day management; (ii) billing services; (iii) equipment; (iv) personnel and related services; (v) office space; (vi) training; and (vii) health care items, supplies, and services;

---

[55]*See* Press Release, Advisory Bulletin Targets Suspect Contractual Joint Ventures (Apr. 23, 2003), *available at* http://oig.hhs.gov/publications/docs/press/2003/042303release.pdf.

- *Remuneration.* The practical effect of the arrangement is to provide the Owner with the opportunity to bill for business otherwise provided by the Manager/Supplier. The Owner's profits from the venture take into account the value and volume of business the Owner generates; and
- *Exclusivity.* The parties may adopt a non-compete clause prohibiting the Owner from providing items or services to patients other than those referred by the Owner, and/or barring the Manager/Supplier from providing services in its own right to the Owner's patients.

Joint ventures that contain one or more of the suspect factors listed in the Contractual Joint Venture Bulletin are not necessarily illegal, nor are Owners (such as hospitals) prohibited from establishing and funding their own new independent subsidiary businesses in certain cases. Nevertheless, arrangements containing "questionable" characteristics, as identified in the Contractual Joint Venture Bulletin, may be subject to increased OIG scrutiny. This Bulletin also contains an important warning that even if various component agreements individually fit all the criteria of various safe harbors, the overall arrangement may, nevertheless, violate the anti-kickback statute.

Over the past several years, the OIG has issued guidance in various forms, such as "OIG Alerts," responses to inquiries (with the parties' names redacted), and other types of documents addressing a specified subject. These materials address a broad range of fraud and abuse issues.

- *Malpractice Insurance Subsidies.* In January 2003, the OIG issued a letter addressing a hospital corporation's medical malpractice insurance assistance program subsidizing the malpractice insurance premiums of its staff physicians.[56] Although the letter did not opine on whether the particular proposal would be subject to penalties under the anti-kickback statute, it did note some features of the arrangement that would be considered to be "safeguards."
- *Misuse of HHS Words and Symbols.* An "OIG Alert" warning against the misuse of HHS words, symbols, and emblems was issued, apparently prompted by a demand letter seeking over $1,000,000 for the misuse of the term "Medicare" in a company's marketing practices.[57]
- *Charges for the Uninsured.* Class action lawsuits have been filed against hospitals nationwide alleging that the rates charged, and other measures taken in regard to underinsured

---

[56] Letter From Lewis Morris, Chief Counsel to the Inspector Gen., Dep't of Health & Human Servs. (Jan. 15, 2003), *available at* http://www.oig.hhs.gov/fraud/docs/alertsandbulletins/MalpracticeProgram.pdf.

[57] U.S. Dep't of Health & Human Servs., OIG Warns against Misuse of HHS Words, Symbols, Emblems (Apr. 8, 2003), *available at* http://www.oig.hhs.gov/fraud/docs/alertsandbulletins/040803MisuseofHHSSymbols.pdf.

or uninsured patients, were illegal based on several legal theories. Hearings on this issue have also been held in Congress. On February 19, 2004, the OIG issued three documents emphasizing a hospital's ability to take various measures, including the provision of discounts or the waiver of copayment amounts, for underinsured or uninsured patients under certain circumstances, without violating the federal fraud and abuse laws. Useful guidance on related topics such as collection efforts, criteria for indigency determinations, and treatment as bad debt are also discussed.[58]

- *Concierge Physician Practices.* In response to the new and increasing creation of "concierge physician practices," an OIG alert was issued on March 31, 2004, warning physicians that charging Medicare beneficiaries more than the Medicare-authorized coinsurance and deductible amounts can potentially lead to a violation of the assignment regulations.[59]

- *Discount Drug Card Programs.* In response to perceived abuses arising in connection with the implementation of the MMA's Discount Drug Card Program, the OIG issued a guidance document on "Education and Outreach Arrangements Between Medicare-Endorsed Discount Drug Card Sponsors and their Network Pharmacies." The OIG indicates that these arrangements should be reviewed carefully since payment arrangements between drug card sponsors and their network pharmacies in connection with education, outreach, and enrollment services may raise concerns under the anti-kickback statute.[60]

OIG audit reports often indicate topic(s) the OIG intends to investigate further in the future. For example, dozens of audit reports related to the provision of outpatient cardiac rehabilitation services at hospitals across the country were published in 2003 and 2004.[61] There

---

[58]*See* U.S. DEP'T OF HEALTH & HUMAN SERVS., HOSPITAL DISCOUNTS OFFERED TO PATIENTS WHO CANNOT AFFORD TO PAY THEIR HOSPITAL BILLS, *available at* http://www.oig.hhs.gov/fraud/docs/alertsandbulletins/2004/FA021904hospitaldiscounts.pdf; *see also* U.S. DEP'T OF HEALTH & HUMAN SERVS., QUESTIONS ON CHARGES FOR THE UNINSURED: CMS DOCUMENT, *available at* http://www.cms.hhs.gov/FAQ_Uninsured.pdf; *see also* Letter From Tommy G. Thompson, Secretary of Health & Human Servs., to Richard J. Davidson, President, American Hospital Ass'n Concerning Charges for the Uninsured (Feb. 19, 2004), *available at* http://www.hhs.gov/news/press/2004pres/20040219.html.

[59]*See* Press Release, OIG Alerts Physicians About Added Charges for Covered Services (Mar. 31, 2004), *available at* http://www.oig.hhs.gov/fraud/docs/alertsandbulletins/2004/FA033104AssignViolationI.pdf.

[60]U.S. DEP'T OF HEALTH & HUMAN SERVS., EDUCATION AND OUTREACH ARRANGEMENTS BETWEEN MEDICARE-ENDORSED DISCOUNT DRUG CARD SPONSORS AND THEIR NETWORK PHARMACIES UNDER THE ANTI-KICKBACK STATUTE (Apr. 8, 2004), *available at* http://www.oig.hhs.gov/fraud/docs/alertsandbulletins/2004/FA040904.pdf.

[61]*See, e.g.,* U.S. DEP'T OF HEALTH & HUMAN SERVS., REVIEW OF CARDIAC REHABILITATION SERVICES AT COMMUNITY MEMORIAL HEALTHCARE, INC., MARYSVILLE, KANSAS, REPORT NO. A-07-03-00156 (Feb. 4, 2004), *available at* http://www.oig.hhs.gov/oas/reports/region7/70300156.htm; U.S. DEP'T OF HEALTH & HUMAN SERVS., REVIEW OF CARDIAC REHABILITATION SERVICES AT SPENCER MUNICIPAL HOSPITAL, SPENCER, IOWA, Report No. A-07-03-00158 (Jan. 30, 2004), *available at* http://www.oig.hhs.gov/oas/reports/region7/70300158.htm; U.S. DEP'T OF HEALTH & HUMAN SERVS., REVIEW OF OUTPATIENT CARDIAC REHABILITATION SERVICES AT THE COOLEY DICKINSON HOSPITAL [NORTHAMPTON, MASSACHUSETTS], REPORT NO. A-01-03-00516 (Dec. 26, 2003).

have also been numerous audits on various issues related to rebates paid to states by manufacturers of pharmaceuticals.[62]

6. Enforcement [New Topic]

There are some reported decisions in recent years that relate to the anti-kickback statute involving remuneration such as loans and leases.[63] However, it is more often the case that anti-kickback allegations are settled without a trial, often under the rubric of False Claims Act allegations.[64]

B. The Stark Law

1. The Prohibitions

On March 26, 2004, CMS published an interim final rule with comment period (Phase II)[65] implementing certain provisions of the "Stark II" physician self-referral statute that were not addressed in the January 4, 2001, "Phase I" regulations.[66] The Final Rule became effective on July 26, 2004. The Phase II regulations appear to provide much needed additional flexibility in a number of respects. This more pragmatic approach will be welcomed by providers since enforcement of the Stark statute, both by whistleblowers and the government, will likely increase now that the Phase II regulations have been promulgated.[67]

In summary, the Phase II regulations:[68]

- Revise and/or clarify several important terms including:
  - "set in advance";
  - "same building";
  - "consultation"; and
  - "referral";
- Clarify the meaning of direct and indirect ownership and affirm that common ownership of an entity does not create an

---

[62]*See, e.g.,* U.S. DEP'T OF HEALTH & HUMAN SERVS., 6-STATE ROLLUP REVIEW OF MEDICAID DRUG REBATE COLLECTIONS, REPORT NO. A-07-04-04030 (Feb. 26, 2004), *available at* http://www.oig.hhs.gov/oas/reports/region7/70404030.pdf; U.S. DEP'T OF HEALTH & HUMAN SERVS., RESULTS OF OUR SELF-INITIATED AUDITS OF MEDICAID DRUG REBATE PROGRAMS OPERATED BY THE STATE AGENCIES OF ARKANSAS, LOUISIANA, NEW MEXICO, AND OKLAHOMA, AS WELL AS THE TEXAS STATE AUDITOR'S REPORT ON THE TEXAS MEDICAID DRUG REBATE PROGRAM, REPORT NO. A-06-03-00043 (Jan. 30, 2004), *available at* http://www.oig.hhs.gov/oas/reports/region6/60300043.htm.

[63]United States *ex rel.* Perales v. St. Margaret's Hosp., 243 F. Supp. 2d 843 (C.D. Ill. Feb 7, 2003); United States *ex rel.* Pogue v. Diabetes Treatment Ctrs. of Am., Inc., 238 F. Supp. 2d 258 (D.D.C. Dec. 18, 2002); United States *ex rel.* Obert-Hong v. Advocate Health Care, 211 F. Supp. 2d 1045 (N.D. Ill. Jan. 30, 2002).

[64]*See e.g.,* Press Release, U.S. Dep't of Justice, Grand Rapids' Metropolitan Hospital & Related Entities to Pay U.S. $6.25 million to Resolve False Claims Allegations (Dec. 10, 2003), *available at* http://www.usdoj.gov/opa/pr/2003/December/03_civ_679.htm. (The anti-kickback allegations involved compensation and leases to, and purchases of practices from, referring physicians that were not commensurate with fair market value and commercial reasonableness.)

[65]69 Fed. Reg. 16,054 (Mar. 26, 2004), *available at* http://a257.g.akamaitech.net/7/257/2422/14mar20010800/edocket.access.gpo.gov/2004/pdf/04-6668.pdf.

[66]66 Fed. Reg. 856 (Jan. 4, 2001).

[67]The Stark law and its regulations are addressed in detail in Chapter 2 (Crane, Federal Physician Self-Referral Restrictions), in the Main Volume and this Supplement.

[68]*See generally,* Linda Baumann, *Learning to Live with Stark II/Phase II Regulations,* REIMBURSEMENT ADVISOR (June 2004).

ownership interest by one investor in another (although an indirect compensation analysis still must be performed);
- Explain the relationship between the definition and the exception for indirect compensation arrangements and the related "volume or value" and "other business generated" standards;
- Provide several types of additional flexibility for rural arrangements;
- Limit a provider's ability to require referrals;
- Add flexibility to standards in various exceptions by allowing "without cause" termination of contracts under certain conditions;
- Ease the Stark law's reporting requirements to eliminate mandatory annual data submission;
- Create new Stark "safe harbors" with regard to physician compensation and academic medical centers;
- Eliminate the proposed restrictions on productivity bonuses; and
- Modify various designated health services (DHS) including lithotripsy and those that are defined by current procedural terminology (CPT-4) code.

Another important change in Phase II involved certain common percentage compensation arrangements that were prohibited by the definition of "set in advance" in Phase I. Although Phase I largely went into effect on January 4, 2002, implementation of this prohibition was delayed repeatedly through issuance of interim final rules.[69] This limitation was eliminated in the Phase II regulations.

In the Phase I regulations, CMS stated that lithotripsy was a DHS. This position was rejected by a federal district court in *American Lithotripsy Society v. Thompson.*[70] In the Phase II preamble, CMS concedes that lithotripsy itself is not a DHS.[71]

2. *The Exceptions*

In some of the pre-Phase II decisions applying the Stark law, federal district courts in Michigan and Illinois provided guidance or discussion on applying the "fair market value" requirement contained in many of the exceptions to the Stark law,[72] as well as the physician recruitment exception.[73]

Phase II interprets the Stark statutory exceptions that were not previously addressed and revises some exceptions in response to com-

---

[69]*E.g.,* 66 Fed. Reg. 60,154 (Dec. 3, 2001).

[70]*See* American Lithotripsy Society v. Thompson, 215 F. Supp. 2d 23 (D.D.C. 2002), *appeal dismissed,* 2003 WL 115257 (D.C. Cir. Jan 10, 2003).

[71]*See* 69 Fed. Reg. 16,054, 16,106 (Mar. 26, 2004).

[72]*See* United States *ex rel.* Goodstein v. McLaren Reg'l Med. Ctr., 202 F. Supp. 2d 671 (E.D. Mich. 2002).

[73]*See* United States *ex rel.* Obert-Hong v. Advocate Health Care, 211 F. Supp. 2d 1045 (N.D. Ill. 2002).

ments received on Phase I. Some of the more significant revisions/
clarifications relate to the exceptions for:

- Ownership in publicly-traded securities;
- In-office ancillary services;
- Academic medical centers;
- Hospital ownership;
- Physician recruitment;[74]
- Personal services;
- Space and equipment leases;
- Risk sharing arrangements;
- Isolated transactions;
- Payments made by a physician;
- Remuneration unrelated to the provision of DHS;
- Compliance training;
- Non-monetary compensation up to $300 and medical staff inci-
  dental benefits; and
- Erythropoietin (EPO) and other dialysis-related drugs furnished
  in or by an end-stage renal disease (ESRD) facility.

In addition, Phase II creates several new exceptions to protect certain practices, including those related to:

- Arrangements involving temporary noncompliance;
- Retention payments in underserved areas;
- Intra-family referrals in rural areas;
- Professional courtesy;
- Charitable donations by a physician;
- Community-wide information systems;
- Referral services; and
- Obstetrical malpractice insurance subsidies.

3. Advisory Opinions

No Stark law advisory opinions were issued from November 1998
until June 2004. However, in implementing MMA provisions imposing
a temporary moratorium on physician ownership of certain new specialty hospitals, CMS suggested that specialty hospitals trying to determine whether they were subject to the moratorium should submit
advisory opinion requests.[75] Accordingly, in June 2004, CMS issued
an advisory opinion addressing whether a particular hospital was
subject to the specialty hospital moratorium described more fully in
Section II.B.4.[76] The Phase II regulations also suggest that providers
with further questions on the regulations submit advisory opinion

---

[74]This exception's applicability to arrangements that predate the effective date of the Phase
II regulations was confirmed in an FAQ on the CMS web site. *See* http://questions.cms.hhs.gov.

[75]*See* Press Release, CMS Issues Guidance for Exceptions to Specialty Hospital Moratorium
(Mar. 19, 2004), *available at* http://www.cms.hhs.gov/media/press/release.asp?Counter=982.

[76]*See* Advisory Opinion AO-SH-2004-06-01, *available at* http://www.cms.hhs.gov/medlearn/
ao-sh-2004-06-01.pdf.

requests, so it is likely that CMS will be issuing advisory opinions on a variety of topics much more frequently in the future.

4. Specialty Hospitals [New Topic]

The MMA modified the Stark law by providing that for an 18-month period beginning on December 8, 2003, a provider would not qualify for the Stark law's rural provider or "whole hospital" exceptions if it was a "specialty hospital." The MMA restrictions were implemented in the Phase II regulations, which now include the MMA's definition of a specialty hospital, i.e., a hospital that is primarily or exclusively engaged in the care and treatment of patients: (i) with a cardiac condition; (ii) with an orthopedic condition; (iii) receiving a surgical procedure; or (iv) receiving any other specialized category of services designated by the Secretary of HHS.[77] "Specialty hospital" does not include a hospital in operation before or "under development" on November 18, 2003, as long as the hospital has not increased the number of physician investors, changed the categories of specialty services provided, or increased the number of beds on the hospital's main campus by more than 50 percent of the number of beds as of November 19, 2003, or by five beds, whichever is greater.

5. Enforcement [New Topic]

Few Stark law decisions have been issued to date, but recent settlements involve the resolution of Stark law allegations, often brought in the context of FCA litigation. For example, Tenet Healthcare Corporation recently agreed to pay the United States $22.5 million to resolve allegations that one of its facilities improperly billed Medicare for referrals provided by doctors with whom the hospital had prohibited financial arrangements.[78] This settlement constitutes the largest False Claims Act recovery the United States has obtained from a single hospital arising out of alleged violations of the Stark law.

C. False Claims Statutes

1. The False Claims Act

In what may represent an OIG decision to rely on other enforcement methods rather than the "national project" model, the OIG Semiannual Report for the first half of 2002 contained a relatively brief section under

---

[77]No additional categories of specialty hospital were specified in Phase II. The Secretary's ability to add certain types of specialty hospitals is constrained by the MMA's legislative history, which states that certain types of hospitals, such as long-term acute care, rehabilitation, psychiatric, cancer, and children's hospitals, are not "specialty" hospitals for these purposes. Medicare Prescription Drug, Improvement, and Modernization Act of 2003, CONF. REP. No. 108-391 to H.R. 1 (Nov. 21, 2003), at 658.

[78]Press Release, U.S. Dep't of Justice, Tenet Healthcare to Pay U.S. $22.5 Million for Improperly Billing Medicare (Mar. 24, 2004), *available at* http://www.usdoj.gov/opa/pr/2004/March/04_civ_183.htm; *see also* HHS OIG CMP settlements related to physician self-referral, *available at* http://www.oig.hhs.gov/fraud/enforcement/administrative/cmp/cmpitems.html#3.

"Hospital Investigations," which did not mention any current or previous national projects.[79] Nevertheless, government investigations and settlements continue to be reported in connection with various "national project" topics including pneumonia upcoding and reimbursement to physicians at teaching hospitals (PATH). The Ohio Hospital Association settled a major case related to the Hospital Outpatient Laboratory national project in *Ohio Hospital Ass'n v. Thompson.*[80]

Although *United States* ex rel. *Goodstein v. McLaren Regional Medical Center*[81] was dismissed on other grounds, various other cases attempting to use the Stark law as the basis for an FCA violation continue to be brought.[82] Although these cases did not contain findings of liability, they also do not preclude the use of a Stark law allegation as the basis for an FCA allegation.

More generally, in the six months ending March 31, 2004, the Government negotiated more than $995 million in FCA civil settlements related to the Medicare and Medicaid programs.[83] During 2003 and 2004, some of the major FCA developments included the following:

First, HCA reached a second settlement with DOJ in June 2003, which was nearly as large as the previous settlement. Taken together, these two settlements resolved the largest and most comprehensive fraud investigation ever undertaken by DOJ. When combined with payments made to CMS for overpayments, HCA paid $1.7 billion to the government in connection with the investigation.

Second, courts have continued to address "implied certification" and other "quality of care" theories put forth by DOJ and *qui tam* relators in health care FCA cases. Many of these "quality of care" certification theories seek to impose FCA liability where payment is sought for goods or services that were delivered or rendered in a manner that violated applicable statutes or regulations notwithstanding an implicit or general certification to the contrary. Courts have begun to grapple with these theories and have generally allowed for FCA liability only in situations where the alleged regulatory violation has a specific and direct impact on the government's reimbursement decision.[84]

---

[79] U.S. DEP'T OF HEALTH & HUMAN SERVS., OFFICE OF INSPECTOR GEN., SEMIANNUAL REPORT OCTOBER 2001–MARCH 2002, *available at* http://www.oig.hhs.gov/reading/semiannual.html [hereinafter OIG MARCH 2002].

[80] No. 1:96 CV 2165 (N.D. Ohio, settlement agreement Aug. 6, 2001).

[81] 202 F. Supp. 2d 671 (E.D. Mich. 2002).

[82] *See, e.g.,* United States *ex rel.* Perales v. St. Margaret's Hosp., 243 F. Supp. 2d 843 (C.D. Ill. 2003); Peterson v. Community Gen. Hosp., 2003 WL 262515 (N.D. Ill. Feb. 7, 2003); United States *ex rel.* Pogue v. Diabetes Treatment Ctrs. of Am., Inc., 238 F. Supp. 2d 258 (D.D.C. 2002).

[83] OIG MARCH 2004, at 34.

[84] *See, e.g.,* United States *ex rel.* Cooper v. Gentiva Health Servs., No. 01-508, 2003 WL 22495607 (W.D. Pa. Nov. 4, 2003) (setting forth federal court treatment of implied certification and other quality of care issues); United States *ex rel.* Swan v. Covenant Care, Inc., 279 F. Supp. 2d 1212 (E.D. Cal. 2002) (rejecting implied certification theory in nursing home setting because regulations that were purportedly violated were conditions of participation, not conditions of payment).

Third, the Supreme Court definitively answered the question as to whether municipal corporations and other local entities could be subject to suit under the FCA. In *Cook County, Illinois v. United States ex rel. Chandler,* the Supreme Court resolved a circuit split: the Seventh Circuit had held that local governments, like state governments, were immune from suit under the FCA, while the Third and Fifth Circuits had held that those entities enjoyed no immunity. The Supreme Court reversed the Seventh Circuit in *Chandler,* and held that municipal corporations and other entities were "persons" for purposes of the FCA, and were therefore subject to suit.[85]

D. Civil Monetary Penalties

3. Special Advisory Bulletin on Beneficiary Inducement [New Topic]

On August 30, 2002, the OIG issued a Special Advisory Bulletin, "Offering Gifts and Other Inducements to Beneficiaries," which provides guidance on the civil monetary penalty (CMP) provision that prohibits certain beneficiary inducements.[86] In the Special Advisory Bulletin, the OIG confirms its position that providers may not offer any gifts or "free" services to beneficiaries that exceed $10 per item (with a $50 annual limit) unless the incentives fit within a statutory or regulatory exception or are the subject of a favorable advisory opinion. Nevertheless, the OIG officially acknowledges for the first time that incentives offered by drug manufacturers in connection with product selection generally are exempt from the statutory prohibition unless the manufacturers own or operate, directly or indirectly, other entities that file Medicare or Medicaid claims.

In addition, the OIG notes that it may solicit public comment on the possibility of creating regulatory "safe harbors" for certain complimentary local transportation and for free goods and services provided in connection with government-sponsored clinical trials. However, these safe harbors would apply only to the CMP. In this connection, the OIG notes that arrangements that do not violate the CMP may nevertheless implicate the anti-kickback statute under certain circumstances.

The Bulletin contains definitions and interpretations of key concepts within the CMP, which bars offering remuneration to Medicare or Medicaid beneficiaries where the person offering the remuneration "knows or should know" that the "remuneration" is likely to influence the beneficiary to order or receive items or services from a particular provider. The OIG notes that the term "remuneration" has been broadly interpreted to include "anything of value" in the context of various

---

[85] 538 U.S. 119 (2003). Recent FCA developments are discussed in detail in Chapter 3 (Salcido, The False Claims Act in Health Care Prosecutions: Application of the Substantive, *Qui Tam,* and Voluntary Disclosure Provisions) of this Supplement.

[86] *See* 42 U.S.C. §1320a-7a(a)(5).

health care fraud and abuse statutes and affirms this broad definition in connection with the beneficiary inducement prohibition. The "should know" standard is met if a provider acts with deliberate ignorance or reckless disregard; no proof of specific intent is required.

The "inducement" element encompasses any offer of valuable goods and services as part of a marketing or promotional activity, regardless of whether the marketing or promotional activity is active or passive. Thus, even if a provider does not directly advertise or promote the benefit to beneficiaries, exposure can result from indirect marketing or promotional efforts or informal channels of disseminating information, such as "word of mouth" promotion by practitioners or patient support groups. The OIG further considers providing free goods or services to existing customers who have an ongoing relationship with a provider as conduct that is likely to influence those customers' future purchases. Thus, the practice, common in other industries, of rewarding customers for their loyalty can violate the law in the health care context under certain circumstances.

With respect to the "beneficiaries" covered by the provision, the OIG states that inducements may not be offered to Medicare and Medicaid beneficiaries, regardless of the beneficiary's medical condition. The OIG notes that some specialty providers offer valuable gifts to beneficiaries with specific chronic conditions. However, the OIG states that there is no meaningful basis under the statute for creating an exemption based on a beneficiary's medical condition or the condition's severity, particularly because providers have more incentive to offer gifts to chronically ill beneficiaries who, as a result of their condition, are likely to generate substantially more business. Moreover, the prohibition applies regardless of whether the incentive provides therapeutic as well as financial benefits to the beneficiary. Similarly, the OIG finds no statutory basis for an exemption based on the financial need of a category of patients, because Congress expressly included the Medicaid program within the prohibition and created only a narrow exception for nonroutine waivers of copayments and deductibles based on individual financial need.

The OIG also discusses the application of the CMP to providers, practitioners, and suppliers. The OIG has interpreted this element to exclude health plans that offer incentives to Medicare and Medicaid beneficiaries to enroll in a plan, although incentives provided to influence an already enrolled beneficiary to select a particular provider, practitioner, or supplier within the plan are subject to the statutory proscription (other than copayment differentials that are part of a health plan design).

The OIG states that it will apply the beneficiary inducement CMP according to certain principles, including the following:

- Medicare or Medicaid providers may offer beneficiaries inexpensive gifts (other than cash or cash equivalents) or services without violating the statute.

- Providers may offer beneficiaries more expensive items or services that fit within one of the five statutory exceptions: (1) waivers of cost-sharing amounts based on financial need; (2) properly disclosed copayment differentials in health plans; (3) incentives to promote the delivery of certain preventive care services; (4) any practice permitted under the federal anti-kickback statute pursuant to 42 C.F.R. Section 1001.952; or (5) waivers of hospital outpatient copayments in excess of the minimum copayment amounts.
- The OIG will continue to accept requests for advisory opinions related to the prohibition on inducements to beneficiaries, although favorable opinions will likely be limited to situations involving practices that are very close to an existing statutory or regulatory exception.

The Bulletin also discusses the OIG's interpretation of the CMP, establishing an important exception that permits valuable services or other remuneration to be furnished to financially needy beneficiaries by an independent entity, even if the benefits are funded by providers, as long as (1) the independent entity makes an independent determination of need; and (2) the beneficiary's receipt of the remuneration does not depend, directly or indirectly, on the beneficiary's use of any particular provider.

Finally, although the OIG indicates that it does not currently expect to propose additional regulatory exceptions related to unadvertised waivers of copayments and deductibles, the agency encourages providers to bring such situations to the OIG's attention through the advisory opinion process.

In December 2002, the OIG issued a letter clarifying the provision of complimentary local transportation for program beneficiaries.[87] The letter states that local transportation valued at no more than $10 per trip and $50 per patient in the aggregate on an annual basis is permissible under the beneficiary inducement/CMP statute. However, because the OIG has under consideration a safe harbor for such transportation that is worth more than $10 per trip and $50 per patient in the aggregate on an annual basis, the OIG states that it will not impose administrative sanctions on such a transportation program if it is hospital based and meets the following criteria: (i) the program was in existence prior to August 30, 2002; (ii) transportation is offered uniformly and without charge or at reduced charge to all patients of the hospital or hospital-owned ambulatory surgical center (ASC) (and may also be made available to their families); (iii) the transportation is only provided to and from the hospital or a hospital-owned ASC and is for the purpose of receiving hospital or ASC services (or, in the case of family members, accompanying or visiting hospital or ASC patients);

---

[87] Letter From Kevin McAnaney, Chief, Industry Guidance Branch, to OIG (2002), *available at* http://www.oig.hhs.gov/fraud/docs/alertsandbulletins/LocalTransportation.pdf.

(iv) the transportation is provided only within the hospital's or ASC's primary service area; (v) the costs of the transportation are not claimed directly or indirectly on any federal health care program cost report or claim and are not otherwise shifted to any federal health care program; and (vi) the transportation does not include ambulance transportation.

4. *Gainsharing [New Topic]*

One CMP prohibition is for direct or indirect payment as an inducement by certain hospitals to physicians to limit or reduce services to Medicare or Medicaid beneficiaries who are under the direct care of the physician.[88] Despite strong OIG language questioning the legality of gainsharing arrangements in a Special Advisory Bulletin,[89] the OIG stated that it would not impose sanctions on the arrangements described in Advisory Opinion No. 01-01, indicating that not all gainsharing arrangements violate the anti-kickback statute or the applicable CMP. Nevertheless, a recent federal district court case in New Jersey involved a challenge to a CMS demonstration project in New Jersey to test the efficacy of a "gainsharing" arrangement, whereby physicians would receive incentive payments to help contain hospital costs.[90] In an unpublished opinion the court found that the demonstration project did not violate the anti-kickback statute and that the Stark law was inapplicable in this context. The court granted the requested enjoinment of the demonstration project based on finding that it violated the CMP absent further proceedings to cure its defects, such as receipt of a favorable advisory opinion from the OIG. However, the OIG's subsequent discussion of gainsharing in the OIG Draft Supplemental Compliance Program Guidance for Hospitals[91] emphasized the fact that gainsharing arrangements could implicate the anti-kickback statute and the Stark law as well as the CMP.

5. *CMP Enforcement [New Topic]*

OIG officials have indicated their intention to increase CMP enforcement for the past several years. This type of sanction can be imposed by the Secretary initially without a hearing. Accordingly, there have been numerous recent OIG enforcement actions under various types of CMPs, including those related to false and fraudulent claims,[92]

---

[88] 42 U.S.C. §1320a-7a(b). This prohibition is discussed in more detail in Section II.A.5.

[89] *See* Advisory Bulletin, Special Advisory Bulletin: Gainsharing Arrangements and CMPs for Hospital Payments to Physicians to Reduce or Limit Services to Beneficiaries (July 1999), *available at* http://www.oig.hhs.gov/fraud/docs/alertsandbulletins/gainsh.htm.

[90] *See* Robert Wood Johnson Univ. Hosp., Inc. v. Thompson, Civil Action No. 04-142 (JWB), 2004 U.S. Dist LEXIS 8498 (D.N.J. Apr. 15, 2004) (not for publication).

[91] 69 Fed. Reg. 32,012, 32,024 (June 8, 2004).

[92] *E.g.,* physicians submitting claims for services provided by an unlicensed person, hospitals employing or contracting with excluded persons, DME suppliers not having adequate documentation for claims such as physician signatures or determinations of medical necessity, clinics billing for services not furnished at the indicated location, and physicians billing for services not rendered. *See* http://www.oig.hhs.gov/fraud/enforcement/administrative/cmp/cmpitems.html#2.

kickbacks and self-referrals,[93] managed care,[94] patient dumping (violations of the Emergency Medical Treatment and Active Labor Act),[95] and overcharging beneficiaries.[96]

III. STATE LAWS

Even before the Stark II regulations were finalized, some states largely incorporated the Stark law and regulations into their own statutes.[97] Now that the Stark II/Phase II regulations have been finalized, this trend will likely expand to other states.

With regard to state kickback prohibitions, a Florida appellate court held in March 2004 that the state's Medicaid Provider Fraud Statute impliedly conflicted with the federal anti-kickback statute, and thus was preempted under the Supremacy Clause of the Constitution.[98] The opinion reasoned that the Florida statute, which generally had the same objectives as the federal anti-kickback statute, was an obstacle to the execution and accomplishment of the objectives and purpose of the federal anti-kickback statute. This decision is good news for providers, since many state laws contain stringent prohibitions, which do not require improper intent for a violation; often contain few, if any, exceptions; and provide little additional guidance.

IV. OTHER RESOURCES

The CMS Web site[99] also contains numerous guidance materials that can help clarify the agency's underlying regulations, in turn helping to prevent the errors that can lead to subsequent allegations of fraud and abuse. In particular, the CMS Quarterly Provider Update is an excellent source of information on changing Medicare requirements.[100] Moreover, as the agency charged with implementing the Stark law, guidance materials relating to this statute may often be located on the CMS, rather than the OIG, web site.

In those instances where the OIG resolves allegations against an entity by settlement, the corporate integrity agreements that address

---

[93]*E.g.*, physicians referring patients to entities with which they had lease agreements, physicians receiving payments greater than fair market value in return for referrals, nursing facilities billing for services referred by a medical director of the nursing facility in violation of the Stark law, physicians receiving lease payments from hospitals for unused space, physicians billing for free drug samples, physicians making greater than fair market value payments for lithotripsy services, ambulance swapping arrangements with hospitals, loans to physicians in return for referrals, termination of nonreferring physicians, and free devices from DME suppliers to physicians. *See* http://www.oig.hhs.gov/fraud/enforcement/administrative/cmp/cmpitems.html#3.

[94]*See, e.g.,* http://www.oig.hhs.gov/fraud/enforcement/administrative/cmp/cmpitems.html#4.

[95]*See, e.g.,* http://www.oig.hhs.gov/fraud/enforcement/administrative/cmp/cmpitemspd.html.

[96]*See, e.g.,* http://www.oig.hhs.gov/fraud/enforcement/administrative/cmp/cmpitems.html#5.

[97]*See* KY. REV. STAT. ANN. §205.8461 (West 2004); MONT. CODE ANN. §45-6-313 (West 2004); *see also* MICH. COMP. LAWS ANN. §333.16221 (West 2004); TEX. HEALTH & SAFETY CODE §142.019 (West 2004).

[98]*See* State v. Harden, 873 So. 2d 352, 2004 WL 444154 (Fla. Dist. Ct. App. 2004).

[99]The CMS Web site can be found at http://www.cms.hhs.gov/.

[100]*Available at* http://www.cms.hhs.gov/providerupdate/.

the perceived regulatory issues are available for general review and may provide useful guidance.[101]

A. Compliance Program Guidance

Thus far, the OIG has developed and released a total of 11 compliance program guidance documents (CPGs) for: clinical laboratories; hospitals; home health agencies; third-party billing companies; the durable medical equipment, prosthetics, orthotics and supply industry; hospices; Medicare+Choice organizations that offer coordinated care plans; nursing homes; individual and small group physician practices; ambulance service providers;[102] and pharmaceutical manufacturers.

The OIG published the long-awaited final Compliance Program Guidance for Pharmaceutical Manufacturers in 2003.[103] The final guidance retains many of the policies and principles set forth in the draft CPG.[104] At the same time, the OIG added clarifications and additional discussion in a number of areas, including the relationship between pharmaceutical manufacturers and pharmacy benefits managers, the practice of "preceptorship" or shadowing and other consulting arrangements, and manufacturer influence on formulary decisions. Further, the OIG notes that the compliance program elements and potential risk areas identified in the final guidance "may have application to manufacturers of other products that may be reimbursed by federal health care programs, such as medical devices and infant nutritional products."[105]

In September 2003, the OIG issued a notice announcing the development of compliance program guidance for recipients of National Institutes of Health (NIH) extramural research grant and cooperative agreement awards.[106] Specifically, the OIG is soliciting comments and recommendations from interested parties on the value and fundamental principles of compliance programs for colleges, universities, and other recipients of NIH grants, along with the specific elements that these grant recipients should consider when developing and implementing an effective compliance program.

In June 2004, the OIG published a draft Supplemental Compliance Program Guidance for Hospitals (Hospital CPG Supplement).[107] When the final version of this document is published, it will supplement the OIG's prior CPG, which was issued in 1998.[108] The Hospital CPG Supplement is intended to emphasize risk areas that have emerged since

---

[101] *See* http://www.oig.hhs.gov/fraud/cias.html.

[102] The draft CPG for ambulance service providers was published on June 6, 2002 (67 Fed. Reg. 39,015), and finalized on March 24, 2003 (68 Fed. Reg. 14,245).

[103] *See* 68 Fed. Reg. 23,731 (May 5, 2003); *see also* PhRMA Code on Interactions with Healthcare Professionals (Apr. 2002), *available at* http://www.phrma.org/publications/policy//2004-01-19.391.pdf.

[104] 67 Fed. Reg. 62,057 (Oct. 3, 2002).

[105] 68 Fed. Reg. 23,742 n.5 (May 5, 2003).

[106] 68 Fed. Reg. 52,783 (Sept. 5, 2003).

[107] 69 Fed. Reg. 32,012 (June 8, 2004).

[108] 63 Fed. Reg. 8,987 (Feb. 23, 1998).

1998, and it specifically highlights numerous aspects of outpatient procedure coding, admissions and discharges, supplemental payment considerations, and the efficient use of information technology. There is a detailed discussion of various fraud and abuse topics including gainsharing, joint ventures, compensation arrangements with physicians, malpractice insurance subsidies, recruitment practices, cost-sharing waivers, gifts and gratuities, and the offer of free transportation to federal health care program beneficiaries. In addition, the Supplemental Guidance provides advice regarding areas of recent concern to hospitals, including discounts to uninsured patients, preventive care services, and professional courtesy practices. The Hospital CPG Supplement also provides numerous detailed benchmarks that hospitals are encouraged to use in evaluating the effectiveness of their compliance programs.

B. The Office of Inspector General Work Plan

The OIG Work Plan for Fiscal Year 2004[109] summarizes the major projects the OIG intends to pursue in each of HHS's major operating areas and lists numerous projects under various categories, including hospitals, home health care, nursing home care, physician services, DME and supplies, drug reimbursement, Medicare managed care, other Medicare services,[110] Medicare contractor operations,[111] various Medicaid services, general administration, investigations, and legal counsel.[112] Within each of these areas, the OIG lists numerous issues planned for review.

For 2004, with regard to hospitals, the Work Plan list includes the following items, among others:

- hospital quality oversight;
- medical education payments;
- inpatient capital payments;
- long-term-care hospital payments;
- consecutive inpatient stays;
- medical necessity of and prospective payment for inpatient rehabilitation facility stays;
- medical necessity of inpatient psychiatric stays;
- payments and coding patterns for certain diagnostic related groups (DRGs);
- outlier payments;
- excessive payments for outpatient services;

---

[109] OFFICE OF INSPECTOR GEN., U.S. DEP'T OF HEALTH & HUMAN SERVS., WORK PLAN, FISCAL YEAR 2004, *available at* http://oig.hhs.gov/publications/workplan.html [hereinafter OIG WORK PLAN FY 2004].

[110] This category includes topics such as inpatient rehabilitation payments, ASCs, independent diagnostic testing facilities (IDTFs), comprehensive outpatient rehabilitation facilities (CORFs), rural health clinics, laboratory services, dialysis services, and ambulance services.

[111] This section covers topics ranging from suspension of payments to contractors' administrative costs. *See* OIG WORK PLAN FY 2004, at 21–24.

[112] This section includes references to many fraud and abuse topics, including integrity agreements, advisory opinions, safe harbors, exclusions, and CMPs. *See* OIG WORK PLAN FY 2004, at 42–44.

- outpatient cardiac rehabilitation services;
- critical access hospital home office costs;
- hospital reporting of restraint-related deaths; and
- diagnostic testing in emergency rooms.[113]

Home health issues include the impact of the prospective payment system (PPS) on quality of care, PPS system controls, home health outlier payments, enhanced payments for home health therapy, and home health agencies' arrangements with other facilities.[114]

With regard to nursing homes, the OIG will be reviewing several issues, including those related to:

- access to skilled nursing facilities (SNFs) under the SNF PPS;
- nurses aide registries;
- nursing home minimum data set reporting;
- nursing home payment system controls;
- SNF involvement in consecutive inpatient stays;
- Part B payments for nursing home beneficiaries;
- imaging and laboratory services in nursing homes;
- state compliance with complaint investigation guidelines; and
- nursing home informal dispute resolution trends.[115]

Physician reviews will include billing for consultations; services and supplies "incident to" physician's services; coding of evaluation and management services; "long distance" physician claims (i.e., claims for face-to-face physician encounters where the practice setting is a significant distance from the beneficiary's location); use of billing modifiers; care plan oversight; billing for diagnostic tests; and radiation therapy services; among others.[116]

The DME reviews will include the use and maintenance of certificates of medical necessity for DME, the medical necessity of Medicare payments for certain DME (including power wheelchairs and therapeutic footwear), and Medicare payments for items such as wheelchairs, enteral nutrition, oxygen equipment, and oxygen supplies.[117] In connection with Medicare drug reimbursement, the OIG will examine Medicare reimbursement for prescription drugs compared with costs incurred by the Department of Veterans Affairs, the physician/supplier community, and Medicaid; the appropriateness of Medicare payments for epoetin alfa used by beneficiaries who have not been diagnosed with ESRD; and the medical necessity of allergy treatments.[118]

The managed care issues to be examined in 2004 include, among others:

- the adjusted community rate proposal process;
- cost-based managed care plans;

---

[113]*See* OIG WORK PLAN FY 2004, at 1–6.
[114]*Id.* at 6–7.
[115]*Id.* at 8–10.
[116]*Id.* at 11–13.
[117]*Id.* at 14.
[118]*Id.*

- enhanced managed care payments;
- managed care excessive medical costs;
- prompt payments to noncontracting providers;
- managed care encounter data; and
- marketing practices.

The many Medicaid services to be reviewed include payments to hospitals and nursing homes, drug pricing and rebates, contingency fee payment arrangements, coding of Medicaid physician services, and Medicaid payments for Medicare-covered services.

The Work Plan for Fiscal Year 2004 also notes pharmaceutical fraud and quality of care issues for nursing facility residents as two specific investigative initiatives being conducted in cooperation with other federal and state agencies. In addition, the 2004 Work Plan indicates that the OIG will continue CMP enforcement activities.

C. The OIG Semiannual Report

In the *Semiannual Report to the Congress October 2001–March 2002,*[119] the OIG notes several recent initiatives involving consultants, including a $9 million settlement with KPMG Peat Marwick to resolve allegations of submitting false hospital cost reports to the federal government. KPMG allegedly made claims that were false, exaggerated, or ineligible for payment; concealed errors from the government; and prepared improper "reserve" cost reports.[120] In another case reported in the Semiannual Report, a hospital was liable for a $5 million overpayment because the hospital relied on a consultant to prepare its bad debt listing but did not verify the accuracy of the work.[121] These items indicate the need for providers to review their relationships with consultants, particularly in light of the OIG's Special Advisory Bulletin on this topic.[122] A July 2004 settlement between the United States and Ernst & Young emphasizes this issue. In this settlement Ernst & Young agreed to pay $1.5 million to resolve a False Claims Act complaint filed by the government charging the health care consulting division of Ernst & Young with knowingly causing nine hospitals to submit fraudulent claims for payment under the Medicare program.[123] Some of the more recent semiannual reports are discussed in Section I.A., above.

It is important to remember that although each OIG semiannual report focuses on previous enforcement activities, the numerous topics

---

[119] OIG MARCH 2002.

[120] *Id.* at 18.

[121] *Id.* at 19.

[122] OIG Special Advisory Bulletin on Practices of Business Consultants, 66 Fed. Reg. 36,583 (July 12, 2001), discussed in Main Volume Chapter 1, at Section I.B. The full text of the Advisory Bulletin is available in Appendix F-12 in the Main Volume (on disk).

[123] *See* United States v. Ernst & Young LLP, No. 04-cv-00041 (E.D. Pa. settlement announced July 20, 2004), *available at* http://www.usdoj.gov/usao/pae/News/Pr/2004/jul/EYSettlement%20Agrmnt.pdf.

discussed therein may indicate areas the OIG is likely to investigate in the same or other settings during subsequent time periods.[124] In the past several years, OIG semiannual reports have focused in part on cases of fraud in the use, distribution, or billing for prescription drugs;[125] cost reporting fraud; [126] and failure to pay Medicaid drug rebates.[127]

D. Miscellaneous

1. *The Inspector General's Open Letter on the CIA Process [New Topic]*

On November 20, 2001, Inspector General Janet Rehnquist issued an "An Open Letter to Health Care Providers" announcing several new initiatives intended to modify various aspects of the corporate integrity agreement (CIA) process and terms.[128] "A Summary of New CIA Claims Review Procedures" and "Frequently Asked Questions Regarding the OIG's New Corporate Integrity Agreement (CIA) Claims Review Requirement" were attached to the open letter. These materials indicate several important developments, including the fact that resolution of a FCA case now may proceed separately from resolution of the provider's permissive exclusion liability. In addition, when determining whether to require a CIA, the OIG has indicated that it will consider the following factors:

- whether the provider self-disclosed the alleged misconduct;
- the monetary damage to federal health care programs;
- whether the case involves successor liability;
- whether the provider is still participating in federal health care programs or is still in the line of business that gave rise to the fraudulent conduct;
- whether the alleged conduct is capable of repetition;
- the age of the conduct;
- whether the provider has an effective compliance program and would agree to limited compliance or integrity measures and would annually certify such compliance to the OIG; and
- other circumstances, as appropriate.

The new CIA claims review procedures contained several notable features:

- Full statistically valid random samples are now required only when initial claims review (the discovery sample) reveals a high error rate.

---

[124] All OIG semiannual reports are *available at* http:/www.oig.hhs.gov/publications/semi-annual.html.

[125] OIG SEPTEMBER 2002, at v.

[126] OIG MARCH 2003, at ii.

[127] OIG SEPTEMBER 2002, at ii.

[128] An Open Letter, Janet Rehnquist, Inspector General, to Health Care Providers (Nov. 20, 2001), *available at* http://www.oig.hhs.gov/fraud/docs/openletters/openletter111901.htm; *see also* http://www.oig.hhs.gov/fraud/cias.html for various other guidance documents related to CIAs.

- Discovery samples will consist of 50 randomly selected paid claims from each relevant universe and may be validated by the OIG.
- No further audit work for the year is required if the error rate in the discovery sample is below 5 percent.
- The error rate is calculated by dividing *net* overpayments by the total dollar amount associated with sample items.
- If the error rate is 5 percent or more over the reimbursement received for all sampled claims, an independent review organization (IRO) must conduct a statistically valid random sample (SVRS) (90 percent confidence/25 percent precision level) for that time period.
- Identified overpayments must be repaid pursuant to payor policies.
- Providers must conduct a systems review related to the identified errors in the discovery sample concurrently with the SVRS.
- Providers currently operating under a CIA may be allowed to use the new claims review requirements; existing CIAs will be reviewed on an individual basis.
- IROs will still be required for certain billing reviews if required under an existing CIA.
- Compliance Engagement requirements may be waived.

In her CIA open letter, Inspector General Rehnquist also indicates that the OIG is exploring ways to increase reliance on providers' internal audit capabilities and provide more flexibility related to employee training. In light of Inspector General Rehnquist's resignation, it is too early to tell how and whether this initiative will be pursued by the new Inspector General.

2. Other Types of Resources [New Topic]

CMS periodically holds town hall meetings on various topics that also furnish guidance on regulatory issues. Such guidance can be critical in the fraud and abuse context since regulatory violations often are the basis for subsequent fraud allegations. In addition, materials published by trade associations and others in the industry, although not legally binding, can be helpful. For example, the Code on Interactions with Healthcare Professionals, published by the Pharmaceutical Research and Manufacturers of America (PhRMA Code)[129] was referenced in the OIG's Pharmaceutical Compliance Guidance, which recommended using the PhRMA Code standards as a minimum baseline in order to achieve compliance with the fraud and abuse laws.[130]

---

[129] PHARMACEUTICAL RESEARCH & MFRS. OF AM., PHRMA CODE ON INTERACTIONS WITH HEALTHCARE PROFESSIONALS (July 1, 2002). The PhRMA Code is reprinted as Appendix I-3.2 at the end of this Supplement. For further information, see PhRMA's website: http://www.phrma.org.

[130] 67 Fed. Reg. 62,063 (Oct. 3, 2002).

2

Federal Physician Self-Referral Restrictions* [Substitute Text]†

---

*Thomas S. Crane, J.D., M.H.S.A. The author gratefully acknowledges the substantial assistance provided by his colleagues, Theresa C. Carnegie, J.D., Io C. Cyrus, J.D., Karen S. Lovitch, J.D., Sarah L. Whipple, J.D., Jennifer E. Williams J.D., and David L. Cusano, Law Clerk, Northeastern University School of Law.

The views expressed in this chapter are the personal views of the author and do not represent the formal position of Mintz, Levin, Cohn, Ferris, Glovsky and Popeo, P.C., any other individual attorneys at the firm, or any of its clients. The author expressly reserves the right to advocate freely other positions on behalf of clients.

†**Substitute Text:** This chapter replaces Chapter 2 in the Main Volume and the prior Supplement.

I. INTRODUCTION

For over two decades, the Social Security Act has criminalized physician self-referral through the federal health care program anti-kickback statute.[1] Congress's original concern in enacting the anti-kickback statute was to prevent fraud and abuse that might result from a variety of business and professional arrangements involving individuals in a position to influence patient referrals. In 1989, however, Congress developed another approach to the problem by enacting a sweeping, targeted federal restriction on physician self-referrals. Specifically, the federal Medicare/Medicaid self-referral statute prohibits a physician from referring Medicare/Medicaid patients for designated health services (DHS) to entities with which the physician (or an immediate family member) has a financial relationship, unless the relationship is permitted by one of the enumerated exceptions to the statute.[2]

From its inception to the present, the federal Medicare/Medicaid self-referral statute has undergone considerable change and has been subject to volumes of interpretative writings. Proponents of self-referral restrictions maintain that physicians' medical judgments as to where and when to refer patients are corrupted, however subtly, by their financial relationships with referral sources, thereby negatively affecting the quality and price of health care services and patient care. Among the many deleterious effects of self-referral, according to these proponents of restrictions, is that physicians with financial arrangements will order unnecessary services that result in increased costs to third-party payers.

Conversely, critics of restrictions on physician self-referral argue that self-referral arrangements may improve the quality of patient care because the financial arrangement fosters a stronger working relationship between the physician and the entity providing the item or service. This relationship works to ensure that the entity provides superior health care services because entities with a reputation for providing substandard services are likely to lose money. In addition, critics argue that prohibiting a physician from referring patients to an entity may make physicians hesitant to invest their own time and money in certain projects. Accordingly, certain necessary medical items and services may not become available, and a vital source of funding no longer will be available in the health care market. Regardless of this ongoing debate, the federal Medicare/Medicaid self-referral statute will continue to have a significant impact on the delivery and structure of health care in the United States.[3]

---

[1] Social Security Amendments of 1972, Pub. L. No. 92-603, 86 Stat. 1329 (1972) (originally codified at 42 U.S.C. §1395h (1972); presently codified at 42 U.S.C. §1320a-7b(b) (1987)). See Appendix A-1 for full text of the anti-kickback statute.

[2] Omnibus Budget Reconciliation Act of 1989 (OBRA 1989), Pub. L. No 101-239, §6204, 103 Stat. 2106 (1989), *codified at* 42 U.S.C. §1395nn. See Appendix B-1 for full text of the physician self-referral statute.

[3] In addition, certain states have enacted laws that prohibit or restrict physician self-referrals. These state laws are outside the scope of this chapter. Because these laws vary considerably as to their scope and penalties, however, practitioners need to review them closely.

The author's approach in this chapter has been to discuss various sections of the statute and its implementing regulations thematically and to devote separate sections to important exceptions. For example, Section VI groups together all of the exceptions that relate to physician compensation even though, in some cases (for example with group practices and academic medical centers), only the compensation provisions of those exceptions are discussed, leaving the discussion of other aspects of these exceptions for other sections. Next, Section VII covers the exception for indirect compensation, which is combined with a discussion of the definition of that term.

Even a brief reading of this chapter will make abundantly clear the complex nature of the Medicare/Medicaid self-referral statute and its implementing regulations. This chapter is intended to aid providers and their counsel in obtaining a preliminary overview of the issues raised in the Medicare/Medicaid self-referral statute and the implementing regulations, but **none of the information or analysis contained herein should be construed as providing legal advice. Readers should consult counsel familiar with the statute when questions arise.**

II. HISTORICAL BACKGROUND

A. Self-Referral Studies

Congress recognized the need for the federal Medicare/Medicaid self-referral statute after reviewing the findings of numerous studies regarding financial arrangements between physicians and health care entities.

1. *Medicare Catastrophic Coverage Act of 1988*

In 1988, Congress enacted the Medicare Catastrophic Coverage Act of 1988.[4] Although subsequently repealed by Congress,[5] the Catastrophic Coverage Act would have expanded Medicare coverage of intravenous (IV) drug therapies while simultaneously prohibiting home IV providers from providing services to Medicare or Medicaid beneficiaries referred by physicians who had ownership interests in, or received compensation from, the home IV provider. The Catastrophic Coverage Act also required the Office of Inspector General (OIG) of the Department of Health and Human Services (HHS) to perform a study of ownership or compensation arrangements between physicians and entities providing Medicare covered services (the OIG Study). The conference report for the Catastrophic Coverage Act revealed that Congress sought the OIG Study to address concerns regarding physician self-referral arrangements that might have existed beyond the scope of home IV therapy benefits.[6]

---

[4]Medicare Catastrophic Coverage Act of 1988, Pub. L. No. 100-360, 102 Stat. 683 (1988).

[5]Medicare Catastrophic Coverage Repeal Act of 1989, Pub. L. No. 101-234, 103 Stat. 1979 (1989).

[6]H.R. CONF. REP. NO. 100-661 (1988), *reprinted in* 1988 U.S.C.C.A.N. 923.

2. *The OIG Study*

The OIG Study was issued on April 30, 1989, and it contained findings on numerous issues, including the variety and scope of self-referral arrangements and the potential for such arrangements to lead to overutilization of health care services.[7] After providing an overview of several other studies regarding physician ownership,[8] the OIG Study focused on physician investments in independent clinical laboratories, independent physiological laboratories, and durable medical equipment (DME) suppliers. Overall, the OIG Study found that 12 percent of the physicians who billed the Medicare program had ownership or investment interests in entities to which they made patient referrals.[9] The OIG Study found a prevalence of physician investments in a wide range of health-related businesses other than the independent clinical and physiological laboratories and DME suppliers that were the focus of the OIG Study, including home health agencies, hospitals, nursing homes, ambulatory surgical centers, and health maintenance organizations.[10] Moreover, the OIG Study found that, nationally, at least 25 percent of independent clinical laboratories, 27 percent of independent physiological laboratories, and 8 percent of DME suppliers were owned in whole or in part by referring physicians.

Regarding utilization, the OIG Study stated that patients of physician-owned independent clinical laboratories received 45 percent more clinical laboratory services than all Medicare patients in general.[11] The OIG estimated that this increased utilization of clinical laboratory services by patients of physician-owners cost the Medicare program $28 million in 1987. Patients of physician-owned independent physiological laboratories received 13 percent more physiological laboratory services than the national Medicare average. Patients of physicians who owned or invested in DME suppliers, however, did not use any more DME than all Medicare patients in general.

Of note is that neither the OIG Study, nor the vast majority of subsequent studies, attempted to evaluate the effects of physician ownership on the quality of care or outcomes. However, many researchers

---

[7]Office of Inspector Gen., U.S. Dep't of Health & Human Servs., Report to Congress, *Financial Arrangements Between Physicians and Health Care Businesses,* No. OA-12-88-01410, *reprinted in* Medicare & Medicaid Guide (CCH) ¶37,838, at 19,925–19,938 [hereinafter OIG Study].

[8]*Id.* at 19,927. The OIG Study cited to the following studies: Mich. Dep't of Social Servs., Med. Servs. Admin., *Utilization of Medicaid Laboratory Services by Physicians With/Without Ownership Interest in Clinical Laboratories: A Comparative Analysis* (June 9, 1981) (finding that Michigan Medicaid recipients referred by physician-owners averaged 41% more tests than those referred by non-owners); Division of Health Standards & Quality, Region V, Health Care Fin. Admin., Dep't of Health & Human Servs., *Diagnostic Clinical Laboratory Services in Region V,* #2-05-2004-11 (May 1983) (finding that patients of practice-related laboratories have a higher incidence of service per patient than patients of non-practice-related laboratories); Med. Affairs Div., Blue Cross & Blue Shield of Mich., *A Comparison of Laboratory Utilization and Payout to Ownership* (May 9, 1984) (finding that laboratories owned by physicians provided 20% more services than the average for all laboratories and 40% more services than non-physician-owned laboratories).

[9]OIG Study at 19,931.

[10]*Id.* at 19,931–32.

[11]*Id.* at 19,933–34.

used the utilization variable as a proxy for quality. Thus, an inference exists that quality of care may be suspect where utilization disparities appear to be explained only by self-referral. Of course, such inferences may well be rebutted by other patient care measures.

In what remains the only reported study that examines self-referrals related to compensation arrangements, as opposed to ownership interests, the OIG Study also found that 8 percent of Medicare physicians had compensation arrangements with entities to which they referred patients.[12] These compensation arrangements varied from space rental agreements and consulting agreements to management service contracts. The OIG did not attempt to examine the effects of such compensation arrangements on the utilization of services.

Based on the results of the OIG Study, the OIG recommended that the Health Care Financing Administration (HCFA), now the Centers for Medicare and Medicaid Services (CMS),[13] pursue the legislative and regulatory changes necessary to require entities billing Medicare to disclose to the program the names of physician-owners and -investors, and to require claims submitted by all entities providing services under Medicare Part B to include the names and provider numbers of referring physicians.[14] To address overutilization problems by physician-owners and -investors, the OIG Study also urged legislators and administrators to pursue the following six options:

1. implement a post-payment utilization review program by carriers directed at physicians who own or invest in other health care entities;
2. require physicians to disclose financial interests to patients;
3. improve enforcement of the federal health care programs anti-kickback statute;
4. institute a private right of action for anti-kickback cases;
5. prohibit self-referral arrangements involving specific types of health care entities in which physicians have a financial interest; and
6. prohibit physicians from referring to any entity in which they have a financial interest.

3. The Florida Study

In the same year that the OIG Study was released, the Florida legislature required the Florida Health Care Cost Containment Board (HCCB) to conduct a special study of joint venture arrangements between health care providers. The Florida legislature required the HCCB to conduct specific studies that would identify, analyze, and evaluate the impact of ownership and compensation interests on referrals

---

[12] OIG Study at 19,932.

[13] As of July 1, 2001, the former Health Care Financing Administration (HCFA) was renamed the Centers for Medicare and Medicaid Services (CMS). For the purposes of this chapter, references will be to CMS.

[14] OIG Study at 19,936–37.

by persons who provide health care. Moreover, the HCCB was required to submit recommendations that would work to strengthen enforcement of Florida anti-kickback laws and coordinate interagency regulation of joint venture relationships in the health care industry. The HCCB issued a series of three final reports detailing the results of its study (collectively, the Florida Report).[15]

In 1991, Volume I of the Florida Report stated that "[o]f the eight states covered by the [OIG] study, Florida had the highest percentage of physicians involved in joint ventures. Medicare patients of physician owners in Florida received 40 percent more lab tests and 12 percent more diagnostic imaging tests, and utilized 16 percent more durable medical equipment than the general population of Florida Medicare beneficiaries."[16] In general, the HCCB's findings revealed that physician ownership of health care businesses providing diagnostic testing or similar ancillary services was common in Florida. The HCCB reported:

> [M]ore than three-fourths of the responding ambulatory surgical facilities and about 93 percent of the diagnostic imaging centers are owned either wholly or in part by physicians. Almost 80 percent of the responding radiation therapy centers, more than 60 percent of the responding clinical laboratories and nearly 40 percent of the responding physical therapy and/or rehabilitation facilities also report physician owners. Furthermore, about 20 percent of the responding durable medical equipment businesses, as well as close to 13 percent of the home health agencies, are owned by physicians.[17]

The HCCB also reported that a high percentage of patients who were referred to a physician-owned health care facility were sent there by the physician-owner. As a result of its findings, the HCCB recommended that the Florida legislature consider prohibiting physician owners from referring patients to the four specific facility types that the HCCB identified as being problematic—clinical laboratories, diagnostic imaging centers, physician therapy/rehabilitation centers, and radiation therapy centers.[18]

B. Legislative History

On August 10, 1988, Congressman Fortney "Pete" Stark (D-Cal.) addressed the issue of physician self-referrals by introducing a bill, H.R. 5198, "to amend Title XVIII of the Social Security Act to provide civil monetary penalties and other remedies for certain improper referral arrangements for services provided under the Medicare

---

[15]Fla. Health Care Cost Containment Bd., Joint Ventures Among Health Care Providers in Florida, Vol. I (Jan. 1991), Vol. II (Sept. 1991), Vol. III (Oct. 1991).

[16]*Id.*, Vol. I, at iv–v.

[17]*Id.*

[18]*Id.*, Vol. III, at 23. The Florida legislature subsequently enacted the Florida Patient Self-Referral Act of 1992, which prohibits a health care provider from referring a patient for "designated health services" (clinical laboratory services, physical therapy services, comprehensive rehabilitative services, diagnostic imaging services, and radiation therapy services) to an entity in which the health care provider is an investor or has an investment interest. *See* Fla. Stat. Ann. §456.653.

program."[19] This bill would have barred physician referrals for all Medicare covered services; the bill ultimately formed the basis for the Ethics in Patient Referrals Act of 1988, which was introduced by Congressman Stark, and enacted on December 19, 1989.[20] Partially as a result of the OIG Study that found elevated numbers of referrals only for clinical laboratory services, subsequent congressional negotiations in 1989 narrowed the scope of the legislation to apply only to referrals for clinical laboratory services.

In his remarks to the House of Representatives in 1988, when his original bill was introduced, Congressman Stark described his frustration with the failure of the anti-kickback statute to stop physician self-referrals even though the anti-kickback statute is a "sweeping law prohibiting payment of kickbacks for patient referrals under Medicare . . . [that] is clear on its face[.]"[21] He noted that providers of medical services, in spite of the anti-kickback statute, had continued to develop and promote "a variety of new forms of business organization specifically intended to secure patient referrals from physicians."[22] With respect to joint ventures with physicians, in particular, Congressman Stark complained that "lawyers advising health care clients have recognized that joint ventures with physicians are potentially within the scope of Medicare's anti-kickback law, but have argued that such ventures are nonetheless permissible if (i) there is no explicit requirement that physician investors make referrals and (ii) dividend payments do not vary in proportion to the number of referrals made by the physician investor."[23]

Finally, in support of the bill, Congressman Stark explained the two major shortcomings of the anti-kickback statute as being "the enormous difficulty involved in proving to the satisfaction of a judge in a criminal or civil enforcement action that a particular arrangement is deliberately structured to induce referrals[,]"[24] and the OIG's inability to adequately enforce the anti-kickback statute due to a severe lack of resources and shortage of investigators.

Congressman Stark's solution was the Ethics in Patient Referrals Act. On introducing the bill in 1998, he remarked that

> what is needed is what lawyers call a bright-line rule to give providers and physicians unequivocal guidance as to the types of arrangements that are permissible and the types that are prohibited. If the law is clear and the penalties are severe, we can rely on self-enforcement in the great majority of the cases.
>
> [My bill] provides this bright-line rule.[25]

---

[19] Ethics in Patient Referrals Act of 1988, H.R. 5198, 100th Cong. (1988).

[20] OBRA 1989, Pub. L. No. 101-239, §6204, *codified at* 42 U.S.C. §1395nn.

[21] 134 Cong. Rec. E2724-02 (daily ed. Aug. 11, 1988) (statement of Rep. Stark).

[22] *Id.*

[23] *Id.*

[24] *Id.*

[25] *Id.*

As a result of Congressman Stark's dedication to the issue of physician self-referral, the federal Medicare/Medicaid self-referral statute is commonly referred to as the "Stark law," and the initial legislation enacted in 1989 became known as "Stark I."[26] Stark I provided that, for services furnished on or after January 1, 1992, a physician who has a financial relationship with an entity that furnishes clinical laboratory services (or a physician with an immediate family member who has such a relationship) may not make a referral to that entity for clinical laboratory services that are reimbursable by Medicare unless certain exceptions are met.

In 1993, Congress significantly amended the Stark law as part of the Omnibus Budget Reconciliation Act of 1993 (OBRA 1993),[27] and the legislation became known as "Stark II." Specifically, Stark II expanded the scope of Stark I to cover referrals for numerous DHS in addition to clinical laboratory services, and included referrals for services payable under the Medicaid program. In addition, Stark II significantly amended many of the statutory definitions and exceptions enacted in Stark I.

Stark II, applicable to DHS other than clinical laboratory services, generally went into effect for referrals made after December 31, 1994. The effective date for those provisions of Stark II that amended the definitions and exceptions contained in Stark I, however, was generally made retroactive to January 1, 1992.

C. Regulatory History

1. Sanctions

The OIG is delegated with the authority to impose civil monetary penalties under the Stark law. The regulations implementing these provisions were issued by the OIG on March 31, 1995.[28]

2. Stark I

HCFA, now CMS, published a proposed regulation implementing Stark I on March 11, 1992.[29] The final Stark I regulation was published on August 14, 1995, and became effective on September 13, 1995.[30]

---

[26] Stark I was amended by §4207(e) of the Omnibus Budget Reconciliation Act of 1990 (OBRA 1990) to clarify certain definitions and reporting requirements regarding physician ownership and referral and to provide an additional exception to the prohibition. *See generally* Pub. L. No. 101-508, 104 Stat. 1388 (1990).

[27] Omnibus Budget Reconciliation Act of 1993, Pub. L. No. 103-66, §13562, 107 Stat. 312 (1993).

[28] Civil Money Penalties for Referrals to Entities and for Prohibited Arrangements and Schemes, 60 Fed. Reg. 16,580 (Mar. 31, 1995), *codified at* 42 C.F.R. §1003.102(a)(5) (2004).

[29] Medicare Program; Physician Ownership of, and Referrals to, Health Care Entities that Furnish Clinical Laboratory Services, 57 Fed. Reg. 8588 (Mar. 11, 1992), *codified at* 42 C.F.R. pt. 411 (2004).

[30] Medicare Program; Physician Ownership of, and Referrals to, Health Care Entities that Furnish Clinical Laboratory Services, 60 Fed. Reg. 41,914 (Aug. 14, 1995), *codified at* 42 C.F.R. pt. 411.

3. *Stark II Proposed Rule*

On January 9, 1998, CMS issued a proposed rule (the "Proposed Rule"), Medicare and Medicaid Programs: Physicians' Referrals to Health Care Entities With Which They Have Financial Relationships.[31] On January 9, 1998, CMS also published a final rule to implement the Stark law advisory opinion process.[32] This rule was promulgated pursuant to the Balanced Budget Act of 1997 (BBA), which required the Secretary of HHS to issue written advisory opinions regarding whether a particular referral relating to a DHS (other than clinical laboratory services) is prohibited by the Stark law.[33] The BBA directed the Secretary to apply to the Stark advisory opinion process, to the extent practicable, the rules governing advisory opinions interpreting the anti-kickback, civil monetary penalty, and Medicare exclusion statutes promulgated by the OIG pursuant to the Health Insurance Portability and Accountability Act of 1996[34] in February 1997.[35]

4. *Stark II Final Rules*

a. *Phase I and II*

CMS implemented Stark II in two phases. All final regulations are now codified at 42 C.F.R. part 411, subpart J (Sections 411.350–411.361) (collectively "the Final Rules").

Phase I was published on January 4, 2001, as an interim final rule subject to notice and comment (Phase I Final Rule).[36] The Phase I Final Rule provided a comprehensive review of the statutory history of the Stark law and implemented: (1) the general statutory prohibition on referrals; (2) statutory and regulatory definitions, including definitions of direct and indirect ownership or investment interests, direct and indirect compensation arrangements, and group practice; (3) the statutory exceptions for ownership and compensation arrangements, including in-office ancillary services; (4) new regulatory exceptions for ownership and compensation arrangements, such as academic medical centers; and (5) new regulatory compensation exceptions, for example, for fair market value and indirect compensation arrangements.[37] This rule only addresses the applicability of the Stark law to the Medicare program.

---

[31]63 Fed. Reg. 1659 (Jan. 9, 1998), *codified at* 42 C.F.R. pts. 411, 424, 435 & 455 (2004).

[32]Medicare Program; Physicians' Referrals; Issuance of Advisory Opinions, 63 Fed. Reg. 1646 (Jan. 9, 1998), *codified at* 42 C.F.R. §§411.370–.389.

[33]Pub. L. No. 105-33, §4314, 111 Stat. 251, *codified at* 42 U.S.C. §1395nn(g)(6).

[34]Pub. L. No. 104-191, §205, 100 Stat. 1936, *codified at* 42 U.S.C. §1320a-7d(b).

[35]Medicare Program; Physicians' Referrals; Issuance of Advisory Opinions, 63 Fed. Reg. 38,311 (July 16, 1998), *codified at* 42 C.F.R. pt. 1008.

[36]Medicare and Medicaid Programs; Physicians' Referrals to Health Care Entities With Which They Have Financial Relationships (Phase I), 66 Fed. Reg. 856 (Jan. 4, 2001), *codified at* 42 C.F.R. pts. 411 & 424.

[37]According to CMS, these provisions implement subsections (a), (b), and (h) of the statute. 66 Fed. Reg. at 856.

The Phase I Final Rule did not address the statutory Sections 1877(c), (d), and (e) providing exceptions for ownership and compensation (e.g., the employee and personal services exceptions), as well as Section 1877(f) related to reporting requirements.

On March 26, 2004, CMS released the second phase of the final regulation (Phase II Final Rule), providing responses to comments and changes to the Phase I Final Rule and implementing the remaining statutory exceptions and new regulatory definitions and exceptions as well as the reporting requirements of the law.[38] The Phase II Final Rule also implemented the moratorium on physician ownership of specialty hospitals enacted as part of the Medicare Prescription Drug, Improvement, and Modernization Act of 2003 (MMA).[39]

CMS will issue a subsequent rule responding to comments and making changes to the Phase II Final Rule. In addition, because both rules only implement Stark II as related to Medicare services, the implementation of Stark II related to Medicaid services will be subject to future rulemaking.

The Health Law Section of the American Bar Association filed detailed comments on both phases of the final rule.[40]

b. *CMS's Approach to Drafting the Final Rules*

In drafting the Final Rules, HHS clearly sought to re-examine the Stark law's statutory language and legislative history, to reconsider the Proposed Rule, and to respond to the industry's concerns about the Phase I Rule, the Proposed Rule, and the Stark law itself. HHS stated that it wanted to "reduce the burden and prescriptive nature"[41] of the Stark law and to avoid the "undue disruption" of common financial arrangements, yet not adversely impact the delivery of services to Medicare beneficiaries.[42] In addition, CMS used its limited statutory authority to create new exceptions, but only where it determined that there was "no risk of abuse."[43] CMS also sought to balance the provider community's need for clear "bright line" rules against the competing need for flexibility and practicality in application of the statute's restrictions. Toward these goals, HHS tried to interpret the prohibitions narrowly and the exceptions broadly, focusing on financial relationships that may result in overutilization.[44] By interpreting the Stark law in

---

[38] Medicare and Medicaid Programs; Physicians' Referrals to Health Care Entities With Which They Have Financial Relationships (Phase II), 69 Fed. Reg. 16,054 (Mar. 26, 2004), *codified at* 42 C.F.R. pts. 411 & 424.

[39] Medicare Prescription Drug, Improvement, and Modernization Act of 2003 (MMA), Pub. L. No. 108-173, §507, 117 Stat. 2066 (2003).

[40] Andrew B. Wachler et al., *Stark II Phase II: The Final Voyage,* 16 HEALTH LAW. (No. 4) (Apr. 2004) (Special Edition); Patricia T. Meador et al., *ABA Health Law Section Comments to Stark II, Phase I,* 14 HEALTH LAW. (Sept. 2001) (Special Edition).

[41] 69 Fed. Reg. at 16,055.

[42] 66 Fed. Reg. at 860.

[43] 42 U.S.C. §1395nn(b)(4).

[44] 66 Fed. Reg. at 860.

this manner, HHS interpreted the Stark law's reach as narrowly as possible, consistent with the statutory language and congressional intent.

Of note, although not publicly acknowledged, is that the OIG provided substantial technical assistance to CMS in drafting the Final Rules, as evidenced by the fact that they contain many indications of OIG policies and enforcement concerns. The OIG's role became even clearer during the implementation of the physician recruitment exception from the Phase II Final Rule. In a July 14, 2004, posting on CMS's website, published in response to frequently asked questions, CMS addressed various issues of concern raised about the physician recruitment exception, and stated that, "[i]nquiries with respect to the [Stark law] should be directed to the Office of Inspector General."[45]

Taken together, the Final Rules inject a substantial dose of common sense and an understanding of the realities of the Stark law's effect on the enormously complex health care market. On balance, HHS appears to have taken providers' concerns into account and has introduced a variety of adjustments and amendments offering greater clarity and, in several instances, increased protections for legitimate arrangements.

Finally, practitioners must bear in mind that, when researching a particular Stark law issue, one often must review both the Phase I and Phase II Final Rules unless confident that the particular issue at hand is addressed in only one of these rulemakings. The general rule as stated by CMS is to read the two rules "together as a unified whole."[46]

5. Effective Dates

On the one hand, the Stark law provides generally that it covers referrals for clinical laboratory services made on or after January 1, 1992, and referrals for all other covered services made after December 31, 1994.[47] On the other hand, the Phase I Final Rule provides an effective date of January 4, 2002, except for one section relating to physician referrals to home health agencies, which became effective February 5, 2001.[48] In addition, in several subsequent notices, CMS extended the effective date of the Phase I Final Rule regulating percentage compensation arrangements until the promulgation of the Phase II Final Rule.[49] The Phase II Final Rule became effective on July 26, 2004.[50]

Practitioners may be faced with determining which of these three dates is the applicable effective date. The problem may arise in the context of an enforcement action under the *qui tam* provisions of the False

---

[45] No. 3163 of the Frequently Asked Questions posted on CMS's website on July 14, 2004, *available at* http://www.cms.hhs.gov/faqsearch/faqfull.asp?faq_id=3163.

[46] 69 Fed. Reg. at 16,056.

[47] OBRA 1993, Pub. L. No. 103-66, §13562(b)(1).

[48] 66 Fed. Reg. at 856.

[49] *See, e.g., id.* at 959; Medicare and Medicaid Programs; Physicians' Referrals to Health Care Entities With Which They Have Financial Relationships: Partial Delay of Effective Date, 66 Fed. Reg. 60,154, 60,155 (Dec. 3, 2001), *codified at* 42 C.F.R. pt. 411.

[50] 69 Fed. Reg. at 16,054.

Claims Act (FCA)[51] where the services at issue were rendered sometime between January 1, 1995 and July 26, 2004. For example, in a September 29, 2000, letter to Congressman Stark, the Department of Justice (DOJ) announced that it had over 50 matters under investigation involving possible violations of the Stark law that were brought by whistleblowers under the FCA. Presumably, such actions are premised on the theory that Stark II became effective in January 1998.

In determining whether liability should be imposed for referrals made prior to the effective date of the Phase II Final Rule, CMS provided the following useful guidance in the frequently asked questions section of its website. It stated that while it believes providers have had an obligation to comply with the Stark law as of its statutory effective dates, "[i]n the absence of final regulations for a particular exception, parties must have complied with a reasonable interpretation of the statute."[52] This common sense statement comports with notions of fair play and the fundamental tenets of the Administrative Procedures Act that matters addressed in "legislative" or substantive rules become effective only prospectively.[53]

The foregoing amply demonstrates that this massive regulatory history is a clear indication of the failure of the promise for clear, bright-line rules, and that many issues have only been resolved through the rulemaking process.

III. Highlights of the Final Rules

The two rules taken together make important contributions to one's understanding of the Stark law. To ease in the identification of specific issues, the highlights of each rule are discussed in turn.

A. Phase I Final Rule Highlights

1. Significant Interpretations/Exceptions

The Phase I Final Rule contained several new provisions or revised interpretations of the Stark law, including four significant interpretations and/or exceptions that, taken together, provide significant relief and flexibility to providers.

- HHS introduced a knowledge standard that limits the enforcement of the Stark law to "knowing" violations as defined in the final rule.[54] This standard prevents unfair enforcement of the statute where noncompliance with an exception is de minimis or

---

[51]The False Claims Act is discussed extensively in Chapter 3 (Salcido, The False Claims Act in Health Care Prosecutions: Application of the Substantive, *Qui Tam,* and Voluntary Disclosure Provisions). The *qui tam* provisions appear at 31 U.S.C. §3730. See Appendix C-1 for full text of the False Claims Act.

[52]No. 3163 of the Frequently Asked Questions posted on CMS's website on July 14, 2004, *available at* http://www.cms.hhs.gov/faqsearch/faqfull.asp?faq_id=3163.

[53]Administrative Procedures Act, ch. 324, 60 Stat. 237 (1946) (codified as amended in scattered sections of 5 U.S.C.).

[54]66 Fed. Reg. at 864–65, 958–59; *see also* 42 C.F.R. §411.353(e).

unintended. The consequence of this approach is to introduce uncertainty because an examination of intent is now required. Ironically, HHS has determined that Congressman Stark's promise of clear, bright-line rules appears to be illusory and ultimately not achievable.[55] (See Section IV.C.7., below.)

- In a sweeping new interpretation, HHS determined that a "referral" does not take place when physicians refer patients for services the physicians personally perform.[56] This elimination of "pure self-referrals" can apply to services physicians perform anywhere, e.g., in their offices or as part of the professional component of a hospital service. (See Section IV.C.1., below.)

- HHS introduced a fair market value exception and related definition that generally allows (under certain guidelines) payments based on a per-use, per-service, per-click, or per-time-period basis, but does not permit many common percentage compensation arrangements because they violate the requirement that payments be set in advance.[57] In addition, the requirements for this exception were significantly relaxed from the Proposed Rule. (See Sections VI.C. and D., below.)

- HHS also defined "indirect compensation arrangements" and created a related exception.[58] The concept of indirect compensation could apply to a large number of arrangements that must be analyzed to determine compliance with the definition and the exception. (See Section VII., below.)

2. New Exceptions

The Phase I Final Rule also created regulatory exceptions in the following areas (see Sections IX., X., XI.B., and XIV.C., below):

- managed care;
- academic medical centers;
- erythropoietin (EPO) or other prescription drugs furnished by end-stage renal disease (ESRD) facilities; and
- non-cash gifts or benefits of minimal value.

3. Key Statutory Terms

The Phase I Final Rule also addressed key statutory terms and definitions of DHS including the following (see Sections IV.C. and V., below):

- A person or entity is generally considered to be furnishing DHS if it is the person or entity to which CMS makes payment for the DHS.[59]

---

[55] 66 Fed. Reg. at 864–65.
[56] 42 C.F.R. §411.351 (definition of "referral").
[57] *Id.* §411.354(d).
[58] *Id.* §411.354(c)(2).
[59] *Id.* §411.351 (definition of "entity").

- Unexercised stock options and unsecured loans are not ownership interests.[60]
- "Under arrangement" services provided by physician-owned providers need only comply with the compensation exceptions.[61]
- Under certain rules, a compensation arrangement may be conditioned on referrals.[62]
- Many DHS are clearly defined by Current Procedural Terminology (CPT) or CMS Common Procedure Coding System (HCPCS) codes.[63]
- Included within radiology and other imaging services are the technical and professional components of the service, but excluded are invasive procedures.[64]
- Outpatient prescription drugs include all such drugs covered under Medicare Part B.[65]

B. Phase II Final Rule Highlights

1. Significant Interpretations / Exceptions

- CMS attempted to dissipate confusion regarding the interplay of the indirect compensation definition and time- or unit-based compensation arrangements by making clear that even if a time- or unit-based arrangement meets the special rules for such arrangements, the arrangement is nevertheless an indirect compensation arrangement that must meet an exception. (See Section VII., below.)
- CMS took significant steps toward minimizing the differences in the various rules applicable to physician compensation arrangements and modified these rules so as to more accurately reflect industry practices. (See Section VI., below.)
  - ○ CMS expanded the definition of fair market value to include a provision deeming hourly compensation for a physician's personal services to be fair market value if the hourly payment is established using one of two specified methodologies.
  - ○ In the wake of a great deal of controversy regarding CMS's interpretation of the term "set in advance" in the Phase I Final Rules, CMS modified this definition to permit certain percentage compensation arrangements.
  - ○ CMS clarified the circumstances under which the exception for group practice profit shares and productivity bonuses apply.

---

[60] *Id.* §411.354(b)(3).
[61] *Id.* §411.354(c).
[62] *Id.* §411.354(d)(4).
[63] *Id.* §411.351 (definition of "list of CPT/HCPCS codes").
[64] *Id.* §411.351 (definition of "radiology and certain other imaging services").
[65] *Id.* §411.351 (definition of "outpatient prescription drugs").

    ○ DHS entities can only direct referrals from physicians under significantly narrow circumstances.

2. Statutory Exceptions

- For purposes of the in-office ancillary service exception, CMS introduced a clearer, more flexible test for determining whether services are furnished in the "same building," and, further, created three new alternative tests that are available to solo practitioners as well as group practices. All three tests require the office to be open for a specified number of hours each week with the referring physician regularly practicing medicine at the site. (See Section VIII., below.)

- CMS implemented the moratorium for ownership of specialty hospitals adopted in the MMA, which essentially modifies the so-called "whole hospital" exception to the prohibition on physician ownership. (See Section XII.B.3., below.)

- CMS significantly eased the requirements for structuring arrangements to fit within the space and equipment rental exceptions. (See Section XIII.A., below.) The following are now permitted:

    ○ termination without cause provisions within one-year lease terms;

    ○ month-to-month holdovers for up to six months;

    ○ subleases; and

    ○ capital leases.

- CMS implemented the Stark law exception for physician recruitment arrangements. (See Section XIII.B., below.)

    ○ Recruitment payments from federally qualified health centers are now permitted.

    ○ Hospital residents and new physicians need not relocate to qualify for the exception.

    ○ Indirect payments to medical groups are permitted, but under tight restrictions; for example, requiring both the group and recruited physician to sign the agreement and *not permitting:*

        —A group's costs under an income guarantee to be allocated to the recruited physician for amounts above the group's "actual incremental costs"; and

        —The group to impose additional requirements on the recruited physician, such as a non-compete clause.

These requirements, where payments flow to the existing medical practice, will likely require a significant number of existing physician recruitment arrangements to be renegotiated.

3. New Exceptions

- Based on comments received from the Phase I rulemaking, in Phase II CMS revised some of the regulatory exceptions it created, including those under the Academic Medical Centers (AMC) exception. CMS liberalized the rules for the components of a qualifying AMC and for the requirements to document the affiliations among the components of the AMC, expanded the rules for the teaching hospital to meet the admissions and faculty requirements, created deeming rules for the requirement that the referring physician devote substantial time to academic services or teaching, and eliminated the requirement that faculty practice plans be tax-exempt. (See Section X., below.)

- CMS created new additional regulatory exceptions not tied to any of the exceptions based in the statute. (See Sections IV.B., XI.E., and XIV., below.) For most of these exceptions, CMS requires compliance with the anti-kickback statute as a condition for qualifying under certain exceptions. In addition, two of these exceptions base qualification under the exception exclusively on complying with an OIG anti-kickback statute safe harbor.

  o Arrangements that have temporarily fallen out of compliance with a Stark law exception due to events beyond the provider's control;

  o Intra-family referrals in rural areas;

  o Charitable donations by physicians;

  o Referral services;

  o Obstetrical and malpractice insurance subsidies;

  o Professional courtesy;

  o Retention payments to physicians practicing in:

    —health practitioner shortage areas (HPSA), and

    —areas of "demonstrated need" as determined on a case-by-case basis through an advisory opinion.

This advisory opinion process is the first indication by CMS that it will allow this process to be used like the OIG's advisory opinion program to permit arrangements determined to be of low risk of abuse, and either innocuous or beneficial, but not otherwise permitted by the statute or regulation. With CMS soon to be arbitrating on community need for services, this suggests the federal health planning program may be rising again like the Phoenix, after being presumed long ago dead and buried since the early 1980s.

  o Community-wide health information systems.

4. Key Statutory Terms

- As a result of enactment of MMA, CMS indicated that it would revisit the definition of "outpatient prescription drug" in a future rulemaking, and stated that it was interested in receiving comments regarding potential approaches for expanding the definition to reflect the MMA's definition of "covered Part D drug." (See Section V.D., below.)

5. *Other*

- CMS eased the reporting requirements imposed on providers with a reportable financial relationship and indicated that it does not intend to issue reporting forms. (See Section XV.A., below.)
- CMS clarified that, under the Stark law, physicians are not liable for payment recoupments for claims submitted in violation of the statute, but are liable only for civil monetary penalties (CMPs) and only where the government can prove the physicians acted with knowledge of the violation. (See Section XV.B., below.)
- Regarding the relationship between the anti-kickback statute and the safe harbors to the Stark law, CMS maintained its position that the two statutes are distinct, and thus a separate analysis is required to determine compliance with each. (Section XVI., below.)

IV. GENERAL PROHIBITION AND KEY STATUTORY TERMS

A. The General Prohibition

The Stark law[66] provides that, unless certain enumerated exceptions are met:

if a physician (or an immediate family member of such physician) has a financial relationship with an entity specified in paragraph (2) [of the Stark law], then—

(A) the physician may not make a referral to the entity for the furnishing of designated health services for which payment otherwise may be made under [the Medicare program], and

(B) the entity may not present or cause to be presented a claim under [the Medicare program] or bill to any individual, third-party payer, or other entity for designated health services furnished pursuant to a referral prohibited under [this provision].[67]

The Stark law further specifies that:

a financial relationship of a physician (or an immediate family member of such physician) with an entity specified in this paragraph [(2)] is—

---

[66] Unless otherwise noted, all references will be to the Stark law as currently enacted. Practitioners must note that if they are analyzing physician relationships with clinical laboratory service providers, for which the Stark I regulation is final and binding, they may need to consult the provisions of the Stark I law. This analysis is especially important if the conduct in question occurred prior to 1995. If the conduct occurred subsequent to January 1, 1995, practitioners may want to analyze the arrangement under both the Stark I regulation and the Stark II law and regulation.

[67] 42 U.S.C. §1395nn(a)(1).

(A) except as provided in [the exceptions applicable to both owner-ship and compensation arrangements and to only ownership or invest-ments interests], an ownership or investment interest in the entity, or

(B) except as provided in [the exceptions applicable to compensation arrangements], a compensation arrangement . . . between the physician (or an immediate family member of such physician) and the entity.

An ownership or investment interest . . . may be through equity, debt, or other means and includes an interest in any entity that holds an ownership or investment interest in an entity providing the desig-nated health service.[68]

B. Temporary Noncompliance Exception

In response to commenters' requests for a "grace period" to accom-modate temporary noncompliance with the Stark law, the Phase II Final Rule created a regulatory exception to the general referral pro-hibition in Section 411.353 for entities that temporarily fall out of compliance with the statute due to events beyond their control. The exception provides that an entity that is not currently in compliance with the Stark law may nonetheless submit claims for DHS provided three conditions are met.[69]

First, the financial relationship between the entity and the refer-ring physician must have fully complied with an exception under the statute for at least 180 consecutive calendar days immediately prior to the date on which the financial relationship became noncompliant with the applicable exception.[70]

Second, the financial relationship must have fallen out of com-pliance with the exception due to reasons beyond the control of the entity, and the entity must promptly take steps to rectify the non-compliance.[71]

Third, the financial relationship must not violate the anti-kick-back statute, and the claim or bill for services must otherwise comply with all applicable federal and state laws, rules, and regulations.[72]

An entity may avail itself of this exception only during the period of time it takes the entity to rectify the noncompliance, which may not exceed 90 consecutive calendar days following the date on which the financial relationship became noncompliant with the exception.[73] For instance, if a provider's geographic area is reclassified from rural to non-rural, the rural provider ownership exception will continue for 90 days, giving the entity time to restructure its financial arrangement or take other measures so as not to disrupt the continuity of patient care.

---

[68]*Id.* §1395nn(a)(2).
[69]42 C.F.R. §411.353(f)(1).
[70]*Id.* §411.353(f)(1)(i).
[71]*Id.* §411.353(f)(1)(ii).
[72]*Id.* §411.353(f)(1)(iii).
[73]*Id.* §411.353(f)(2).

Finally, an entity may seek protection under this exception only once every three years with respect to the same referring physician. This limitation does not apply to an entity that falls out of compliance with the nonmonetary compensation or the medical staff incidental benefits exceptions because these exceptions are renewed annually.[74]

C. Key Statutory Terms

The Stark law contains a definitions section that further clarifies many statutory terms and provides special definitional rules. This section includes the terms "referral," "entity," "financial relationship," "ownership or investment interest," "compensation arrangement," and "remuneration."[75] In addition, CMS introduced a "knowledge" or scienter element.

1. Referral

The term "referral" is broadly defined. A referral can be direct or indirect, meaning that physicians would be considered to have made referrals if they caused, directed, or controlled referrals made by others.[76] A referral can be in any form, including—but not limited to—any written, oral, or electronic means of communication. A referral can also be made in a plan of care and does not require that physicians send patients to particular entities or indicate in a plan of care that DHS should be performed by particular entities.[77]

Although the term "referral" generally includes services performed by physicians' employees and group practice members, CMS determined that the term "referral" or "referring physician" excludes services personally performed by the referring physician, and referrals to a physician's wholly owned professional corporation.[78] (Similarly, CMS revised the definition of "entity" to clarify that the referring physician is not an entity for purposes of the statute.)[79] Because there are so many situations where one component of a referral involves a pure self-referral for services personally performed by the referring physician, this interpretation removes a substantial amount of conduct from the ambit of the Stark law. For example, any personally performed service a physician provides in his or her office or at a hospital is not covered by the Stark law under this interpretation. Examples of personally performed services at a hospital include the professional component of cardiac catheterization and lithotripsy. For the most part, these services are physician services, although, as discussed below, the professional

---

[74]42 C.F.R. §411.353(f)(3) & (4).
[75]*See generally* 42 U.S.C. §1395nn(h).
[76]42 C.F.R. §411.351.
[77]*Id.*
[78]*Id.*
[79]*Id.*

component of a radiology service is deemed to be a DHS. Referrals still take place when physicians refer patients to other members of their group practices or to other entities for DHS, including technical components of radiology services or hospital services themselves.

The definition of "referral" includes DHS provided in accordance with a "consultation" with another physician, including DHS performed or supervised by the consulting physician or any DHS ordered by the consulting physician.[80] However, certain requests pursuant to a "consultation" by pathologists, radiologists, and radiation oncologists are statutorily excluded from the definition of "referral."[81] To accommodate concerns raised by consulting physicians in group practices, and by radiation oncologists who furnish services that are ancillary and integral to radiation therapy services, the Phase II Final Rule allowed DHS to be supervised by a pathologist, radiologist, or radiation oncologist in the same group practice as the consulting pathologist, radiologist, or radiation oncologist, and includes those services that are necessary and integral to a course of radiation therapy treatment within the definition of "consultation."[82]

2. Entity

To fall within the scope of the Stark law, a referral must be to an "entity" furnishing DHS. An "entity" is the party to which CMS makes payment for the DHS, either directly, upon assignment on the patient's behalf, or upon reassignment pursuant to CMS's reassignment rules. Neither medical device manufacturers nor drug manufacturers are "entities" for purposes of the statute because they do not furnish prescription drugs. However, a pharmacy that delivers outpatient prescription drugs directly to patients would be an entity for such purposes.[83]

3. Financial Relationship

A "financial relationship" can occur through either a direct or indirect ownership or investment interest, or a direct or indirect compensation arrangement.[84] Surprisingly, CMS took the position that an ownership or investment interest is a subset or type of compensation arrangement.[85] However, a financial arrangement qualifying under an ownership exception need not also qualify under a compensation exception. Both ownership interests and compensation arrangements may be either direct or indirect.[86]

---

[80]*Id.*
[81]42 C.F.R. §411.351.
[82]*Id.*
[83]*Id.*
[84]*Id.* §411.354(a).
[85]66 Fed. Reg. at 870.
[86]42 C.F.R. §411.354(a).

4. Ownership or Investment Interest

a. Direct Ownership or Investment Interest

An ownership or investment interest may be through equity, debt, or "other means," and includes an interest in an entity that holds an ownership or investment interest in any entity that furnishes DHS.[87] However, an ownership or investment interest in a subsidiary is neither ownership nor investment in the parent company or in any other subsidiary, unless the subsidiary company itself holds an interest in the parent or such other subsidiary. An ownership or investment interest also includes stock, partnership shares, and limited liability company memberships as well as loans, bonds, or other financial instruments that are secured by an entity's property or revenue.

Ownership or investment interests do not include: interests in retirement plans, stock options and convertible securities received as compensation until the options are exercised or the securities converted to equity, unsecured loans, or "under arrangements" contracts between a hospital and an entity owned by a physician or physician group.[88] Many of these are defined as compensation arrangements.

The Phase II Final Rule makes clear that common ownership does not establish an ownership or investment interest by one common investor in another common investor.[89]

b. Indirect Ownership or Investment Interest

In the Final Rules, CMS substantially revised its approach to indirect financial relationships. The Final Rules articulate tests for when an indirect relationship will trigger the Stark law prohibition. The Final Rules also established a knowledge requirement, to avoid unfair application of the statute's sanctions when an entity has no reason to know that a DHS referral is tainted. The final rule provides:

(i) An indirect ownership or investment interest exists if—

(A) Between the referring physician (or immediate family member) and the entity furnishing DHS there exists an unbroken chain of any number (but no fewer than 1) of persons or entities having ownership or investment interests; and

(B) The entity furnishing DHS has actual knowledge of, or acts in reckless disregard or deliberate ignorance of, the fact that the referring physician (or immediate family member) has some ownership or investment interest (through any number of intermediary ownership or investment interests) in the entity furnishing the DHS.

(ii) An indirect ownership or investment interest exists even though the entity furnishing DHS need not know, or act in reckless disregard or deliberate ignorance of, the precise composition of the unbroken chain or the specific terms of the ownership or investment interests that form the links in the chain.

---

[87] *Id.* §411.354(b).

[88] *Id.* §411.354(b)(3).

[89] 69 Fed. Reg. at 16,061.

(iii) Notwithstanding anything in this paragraph (b)(5), common ownership or investment in an entity does not, in and of itself, establish an indirect ownership or investment interest by one common owner or investor in another common owner or investor.

(iv) An indirect ownership or investment interest requires an unbroken chain of ownership interests between the referring physician and the entity furnishing DHS such that the referring physician has an indirect ownership or investment interest in the entity furnishing the DHS.[90]

5. Compensation Arrangement

A "compensation arrangement" is any arrangement involving remuneration, direct or indirect, between a physician (or an immediate family member) and an entity.[91] Thus, the definition of a compensation arrangement is very broad, and virtually any exchange of remuneration between a physician and an entity qualifies.

Many of the Stark law compensation arrangement exceptions require that the compensation be "set in advance" (the "set in advance" test), not take into account the "volume or value of referrals" (the "volume or value" test) and, in some cases, that the compensation not take into account "other business generated between the parties" (the "other business generated" test). CMS clarified the meaning of these often-used phrases in a section of the regulations entitled "Special Rules on Compensation." In Section VI., below, we discuss direct compensation arrangements, these three tests, and the rules that apply where compensation is conditioned on referrals. In Section VII., below, we discuss the definition of "indirect compensation arrangement" together with the indirect compensation exception.

6. Remuneration

Remuneration is broadly defined as "any payment or other benefit made directly or indirectly, overtly or covertly, in cash or in kind."[92] The following, however, are excepted from this definition: the forgiveness of amounts owed for inaccurate or mistakenly performed tests or procedures or the correction of minor billing errors; the furnishing of items, devices, or supplies used solely to collect, transport, process or store specimens for the entity furnishing the items or to order or communicate the results of tests or procedures for the entity; and certain payments made by insurers or self-insured plans, or subcontractors of the insurers or plans, to physicians.[93]

7. Knowledge Standard

CMS recognized the draconian effect of denying payments when there were unintentional or technical violations of one of its complicated rules. For example, a minor compensation arrangement with a referring physician could require a hospital to repay *all* Medicare

---

[90] 42 C.F.R. §411.354 (b)(5).

[91] *Id.* §411.354(c).

[92] *Id.* §411.351 (definition of "remuneration").

[93] *Id.*

revenues related to that physician's admissions or services for the period of noncompliance. Consequently, the Final Rules include a scienter or knowledge requirement. Payment may be made for a service provided pursuant to an otherwise prohibited referral if the entity did not have actual knowledge or act in reckless disregard or deliberate ignorance of the identity of the referring physician, and the claim otherwise complies with all applicable laws.[94] Similar knowledge standards are imposed elsewhere in the Final Rules to prevent the application of the statute unless the person or entity submitting the claim knew or should have known of the situation.[95] CMS clarified that the knowledge element used in the statute is the same as in the FCA and the Civil Monetary Penalty Law.[96]

This knowledge standard generally does not impose an affirmative obligation on providers, absent some information that would alert a reasonable person to inquire or investigate whether an indirect financial relationship with a referring physician exists. Instead, providers are required to make reasonable inquiries when possessing facts that could lead a reasonable person to suspect the existence of an indirect financial relationship. The reasonable steps to be taken, the Phase I Final Rule contends, will depend on the circumstances.[97]

Many practitioners hope that, as the Stark law is enforced, the addition of this knowledge standard will provide welcome relief by preventing the law from being applied unfairly. Nonetheless, the knowledge standard represents the ultimate repudiation of Congressman Stark's original promise of regulating physician self-referrals throughout the health care landscape with bright-line rules. However alluring such a concept might have been, CMS appears to have recognized that bright-line rules could bring arbitrary enforcement with significant financial consequences to providers. In contrast, most will agree that CMS's approach preserves the underlying principles of the statute, and will achieve more effective enforcement, although at the expense of bright-line rules, in that Stark law compliance analysis will involve subjective inquiry into the parties' state of mind.

V. DEFINITIONS OF DESIGNATED HEALTH SERVICES

A. Listed Designated Health Services

The Stark law lists the following DHS:

1. clinical laboratory services;
2. physical therapy, occupational therapy, and speech-language pathology services;

---

[94] *Id.* §411.353(e)(1).

[95] *Id.* §411.354(b)(5) & (c)(2).

[96] 69 Fed. Reg. at 16,062. The knowledge or scienter requirement is expressed in both the False Claims Act, 31 U.S.C. §§3729, 3733 and the Civil Monetary Penalty Law, 42 U.S.C. §1320a-7a(a), as "knows or should know." See Appendix C-1 for full text of the False Claims Act, 31 U.S.C. §§3729, 3733; and see Appendix D-1 for full text of the Civil Penalty Law, 42 U.S.C. §1320a-7a(a).

[97] 69 Fed. Reg. at 16,062.

3. radiology and certain other imaging services;

4. radiation therapy services and supplies;

5. durable medical equipment and supplies;

6. parenteral and enteral nutrients, equipment, and supplies;

7. prosthetics, orthotics, and prosthetic devices and supplies;

8. home health services;

9. outpatient prescription drugs; and

10. inpatient and outpatient hospital services.[98]

B. General Principles

CMS defines the entire scope of a number of DHS according to the CPT and HCPCS codes that are commonly associated with those DHS and are familiar to the provider community.[99] Those DHS that are defined by CPT and HCPCS codes are: clinical laboratory services, physical therapy, occupational therapy, and speech-language pathology services, radiology and certain other imaging services, and radiation therapy services and supplies.[100] The specific list of CPT and HCPCS codes that qualify as DHS are updated annually. Since the publication of Phase I Final Rule, CMS has provided these updates as part of the annual physician fee schedule regulations. The remaining DHS are not amenable to definition through codes.

Certain DHS definitions, such as the definition of "radiology and certain other imaging services," specifically include both the professional and technical components of a service.[101] Other DHS definitions, such as those for inpatient and outpatient hospital services, specifically exclude the professional component,[102] while services such as physical and occupational therapy are inherently professional in nature.

C. Radiology and Certain Other Imaging Services

Providers have continued to advocate for special exceptions for certain radiological procedures, claiming either that the specified procedures were subject to little or no overutilization or abuse, or that beneficiaries would benefit from the exception. However, CMS declined the opportunity to create any new exceptions.[103] In the Phase II Final Rule, CMS noted its belief that the definition of "referral" and the exceptions for in-office ancillary services and physician services sufficiently address many of the commenters' concerns.[104] CMS continues to exclude nuclear medicine procedures, despite concerns raised by commenters

---

[98] 42 C.F.R. §411.351 (definition of "designated health services").

[99] *Id.* (definition of "list of CPT/HCPCS codes").

[100] *Id.*

[101] *Id.* (definition of "radiology" and "certain other imaging services").

[102] *Id.* (definition of "inpatient hospital services" and "outpatient hospital services").

[103] 69 Fed. Reg. at 16,103–05.

[104] *Id.* at 16,103.

that excluding this service increases the risk of program abuse.[105] CMS also stated that it will continue to consider the application of the Stark law to nuclear medicine procedures.

Excluded from this DHS term are X-ray, fluoroscopy, and ultrasound services that are themselves invasive procedures and integral to a nonradiology procedure, such as cardiac catheterizations and endoscopies requiring insertion of a needle, catheter, tube, or probe.[106] Because invasive radiologists are often referring physicians, this exclusion effectively removed this subspecialty from the ambit of the Stark law.

D. Outpatient Prescription Drugs

In the Phase II Final Rule, CMS noted that due to enactment of the MMA, as of January 1, 2006, many additional outpatient prescription drugs will be covered under Medicare Part D and indicated that it therefore will revisit the definition of "outpatient prescription drugs" in a future rulemaking.[107] CMS stated that it is interested in receiving comments regarding potential approaches to expanding this definition to reflect the definition of "covered Part D drug" in the MMA. CMS also clarified that drugs administered in the physician office setting fall within the definition of "outpatient prescription drugs" and noted that, typically, such drugs either will fall within the in-office ancillary services exception or will not constitute a referral when administered personally by the referring physician.

E. Inpatient and Outpatient Hospital Services

Referencing the "unique legislative history" surrounding the application of the Stark law to lithotripsy, CMS stated in the Phase II Final Rule that, while it is not revising the regulatory definition, it no longer considers lithotripsy an "inpatient or outpatient service" for purposes of the Stark law. This change follows an opinion of the U.S. District Court for the District of Columbia, where the court held that the legislative history of the Stark law demonstrated that Congress never regarded lithotripsy as part of the self-referral problem and has consistently acted to exclude it from the regulation of self-referrals.[108] CMS noted however, that contractual arrangements between hospitals and physicians or physician practices regarding lithotripsy nevertheless constitute a "financial relationship" for purposes of the Stark law.[109] As such, these contractual arrangements must comply with an exception if the physician will refer Medicare patients to the hospital for services that otherwise fall within the definition of "inpatient or out-

---

[105] *Id.* at 16,104.

[106] 42 C.F.R. §411.351.

[107] 69 Fed. Reg. at 16,106.

[108] *See* American Lithotripsy Soc'y & Urology Soc'y of Am. v. Thompson, 215 F. Supp. 2d 23 (D.D.C. 2002).

[109] 69 Fed. Reg. at 16,106.

patient hospital services" or another DHS. This approach serves to undermine any gains that providers of lithotripsy thought they may have made based on the district court's opinion, because the lithotripsy contract still must satisfy one of the exceptions if the physicians refer any other patients to the hospital.

VI. Exceptions Related to Physician Compensation

A. Introduction

There is no better example of the reach of the Stark law than its regulation of physician compensation. In the Phase II Final Rule, CMS attempted to minimize the differences among the various rules applicable to physician compensation arrangements. Although a number of differences still exist, depending on whether the physician is an employee, member of a group practice or independent contractor, CMS narrowed these differences in the Phase II Final Rule. In addition, CMS attempted to simplify any analysis of physician compensation arrangements by inserting into the Phase II Final Rule a chart summarizing the various compensation rules.[110] This CMS chart follows as Table 2-A.

Despite CMS's attempts at simplifying the requirements for those physician compensation arrangements that do not violate the Stark law, legal practitioners providing advice on physician compensation arrangements still must review carefully the special rules on compensation and the individual exceptions for employees, personal services, fair market value, and academic medical centers, as well as the rules for group practices and the definitions of fair market value and physician incentive plans.

B. Volume or Value, Other Business Generated, and Set-in-Advance Tests

Numerous exceptions under the Stark law provide that compensation paid to a referring physician must be "set in advance" and must not take into account "the volume or value of referrals or other business generated between the parties." We discuss below each of these special rules on compensation.

1. Volume or Value of Referrals

The Stark law regulations provide guidance as to what types of payment methodologies do not take into account the volume or value of referrals:

> Unit-based compensation (including time-based or per unit of service based compensation) will be deemed not to take into account the "volume or value of referrals" if the compensation is fair market value for services or items actually provided and does not vary during the course

---

[110]*Id.* at 16,067–68.

Table 2-A TERMS OF EXCEPTION	Group Practice Physicians [1877(h)(4); 411.352]	Bona Fide Employment [1877(e)(2); 411.357(c)]	Personal Service Arrangements [1877(e)(3); 411.357(d)]	Fair Market [411.357(l)]	Academic Medical Centers
Must compensation be "fair market value"?	no	yes—1877(e)(2)(B)(i)	yes—1877(e)(3)(A)(v)	yes—411.357(l)(3)	yes—411.355(e)(1)(ii)
Must compensation be "set in advance"?	no	no	yes—1877(e)(3)(A)(v)	yes—411.357(l)(3)	yes—411.355(e)(1)(ii)
Scope of "volume or value" restriction	DHS referrals—1877(h)(4)(A)(iv)	DHS referrals—1877(e)(2)(B)(ii)	DHS referrals or other business—1877(e)(3)(A)(v)	DHS referrals or other business—411.357(l)(3)	DHS referrals or other business—411.355(e)(1)(ii)
Scope of productivity bonuses allowed	personally performed services and "incident to," plus indirect—1877(h)(4)(B)(i)	personally performed services—1877(e)(2)	personally performed services—411.351 ("referral") and 411.354(d)(3)	personally performed services—411.351 ("referral") and 411.354(d)(3)	personally performed services—411.351 ("referral") and 411.354(d)(3)

Are overall profit shares allowed?	yes—1877(h)(4)(B)(i)	no	no	no	no
Written agreement required?	no	no	yes, minimum 1-year term	yes (except for employment), no minimum term	Yes, written agreement(s) or other document(s)
Physician incentive plan (PIP) exception for services to plan enrollees?	no, but risk-sharing arrangement exception at 411.357(n) may apply	no, but risk-sharing arrangement exception at 411.357(n) may apply	yes, and risk-sharing arrangement exception at 411.357 may also apply	no, but risk-sharing arrangement exception at 411.357(n) may apply	no, but risk-sharing arrangement exception at 411.357(n) may apply

Source: CMS

of the compensation agreement in any manner that takes into account referrals of DHS.[111]

The Final Rules permit per click or unit-of-service payments, even when the physician receiving the payment has generated the payment through a DHS referral, as long as the individual payment is set at fair market value at the inception of the arrangement and does not subsequently change during the term of the arrangement in any manner that takes into account *DHS referrals*. Thus, a physician may lease equipment to a hospital and receive "per use" rental payments, even on procedures performed on patients referred by the physician-owner, provided that the per use rental payments are fair market value, do not vary over the term of the lease, and meet the other requirements of the lease exception.

2. Other Business Generated

In addition to the volume or value standard, some compensation arrangement exceptions require that compensation meet the "other business generated" test. The final rules set forth the test as follows:

> Unit-based compensation (including time-based or per unit of service based compensation) will be deemed to not take into account "other business generated between the parties" as long as the compensation is fair market value for items and services actually provided and does not vary during the course of the compensation arrangement in any manner that takes into account referrals or other business generated by the referring physician, including private pay health care business (except for services personally performed by the referring physician, which will not be considered "other business generated" by the referring physician).[112]

Thus, where an exception requires compliance with the other business generated test (as in the fair market value exception), the compensation (including any per service payments) may not vary over the term of the agreement in any manner that takes into account *referrals or other business generated by the referring physician, including private pay health care business.*[113] CMS does not consider "other business generated" to include personally performed services, but the technical component corresponding to a physician's personally performed service is considered to be other business generated for the entity in certain circumstances.[114] Note that the other business generated restriction applies only to those exceptions in which it expressly appears.

3. Set-in-Advance Test

a. Percentage-Based Compensation and Productivity Bonuses

The personal services, fair market value, and AMC exceptions have provided invaluable protection to physicians and those entities

---

[111] 42 C.F.R. §411.354(d)(2).

[112] *Id.* §411.354(d)(3).

[113] *Id.* §411.354(d)(2) & (3).

[114] 69 Fed. Reg. at 16,068.

to which they refer, especially hospitals. All three exceptions require that the physician's compensation meet the "set in advance" test in addition to the volume or value and other business generated tests.

Despite CMS's efforts in the Phase I Final Rule to interpret the exceptions broadly and to avoid the "unintended disruption of common financial relationships,"[115] the Phase I Final Rule generated a great deal of controversy with its interpretation of the "set in advance" requirement, especially as applied to percentage based compensation. The Phase I Final Rule provided that percentage compensation arrangements in which compensation is based on fluctuating or indeterminate measures, or in which the arrangement results in the seller receiving different payment amounts for the same services from the same purchaser, do not constitute compensation that is set in advance.[116] Just prior to the January 2002 effective date of the Phase I Final Rule, CMS delayed the effective date of this percentage compensation provision. On three additional occasions, CMS further delayed the effective date of this provision. Finally, as part of the Phase II Final Rule, CMS responded to the criticism voiced by physicians and the entities with which they contract and eliminated this controversial provision. In doing so, CMS agreed that its original position was "overly restrictive." Now, under the personal services, fair market value and AMC exceptions, physicians can be paid a percent of revenues for personally performed services or receive a productivity bonus.

b. *Specific Formula*

Compensation will be considered "set in advance" if the aggregate compensation, a time-based or per unit of service-based (whether per-use or per-service) amount, or a specific formula for calculating the compensation is set in advance in sufficient detail in the initial agreement between the parties so that the amount can be objectively verified.[117] The payment amount must be fair market value compensation for services or items actually provided, not taking into account the volume or value of referrals or other business generated by the referring physician at the time of the initial agreement or during the term of the agreement.

C. Fair Market Value Definition

The overarching principle running through most of the Stark law physician compensation rules is that the compensation must be consistent with fair market value. The Stark law regulations define "fair market value" as the value in an arm's-length transaction that is consistent with the price that would result from bona fide bargaining between well-informed parties who are not otherwise in a position to generate

---

[115] 66 Fed. Reg. at 860.
[116] *Id.* at 959.
[117] 42 C.F.R. §411.354(d)(1).

business with each other. The definition also specifies that the fair market price usually will be the price at which other, similar bona fide sales have been consummated in the same market.[118]

The preamble to the Phase I Final Rule made clear that the contracting parties bear the burden of establishing the fairness of any agreement.[119] That stated, CMS is willing to accept any commercially reasonable valuation method. A list of comparable transactions in the marketplace or an appraisal from a qualified independent expert should be satisfactory. CMS noted, however, that the fair market value standard indicates that compensation may not take into account the volume or value of referrals or other business between the parties. CMS asserted that this volume or value restriction may preclude the use of comparables involving entities or other physicians in a position to refer patients or generate business. As a practical matter, this restriction would seem to prohibit using almost all comparables from the health care industry. Thus, at least in the case of rural communities, CMS recognized that this restriction may require the use of alternative valuation methodologies.[120]

Fair market value in the context of a lease of office space or equipment is defined as the value of rental property for general commercial purposes without taking into account the intended use of the property.[121] The definition further specifies that a lease of office space may account for the lessor's cost of developing, upgrading, or maintaining the property, but may not take into account any potential additional value that may result from the proximity between the lessor and lessee and the resulting convenience of making patient referrals from the lessor to the lessee. Although CMS did not change the definition of fair market value to exclude space leases, the preamble takes the unusual position that the term "items and services" does not include space leases. This exception therefore is not available for such arrangements.[122] While the practical effect of this interpretation may not be important, CMS's interpretation of this term is new and not consistent with the OIG's definitions.

Responding to requests to provide more bright-line rules, in the Phase II Final Rule CMS added to the definition of fair market value a provision deeming hourly compensation for a physician's personal services to be fair market value if the payment is established using either of two specified methodologies.[123] The first is tied to the average hourly rate for emergency room physician services in the relevant market, and the second is tied to the average compensation level for physicians in the same specialty area using established national physician compen-

---

[118]*Id.* §411.351.
[119]66 Fed. Reg. at 944–45.
[120]*Id.* at 944.
[121]42 C.F.R. §411.351.
[122]69 Fed. Reg. at 16,107.
[123]*Id.*

sation surveys that are listed in the rule itself. To qualify for deemed status, payment must be for the physician's personal services and not for services performed by the physician's employees, contractors, or others. The Phase II Final Rule makes clear that these are merely deeming standards, not mandatory requirements.[124]

D. Fair Market Value Exception

The fair market value compensation exception, which was created under HHS's statutory authority to promulgate new exceptions that do not pose a risk of program abuse, is very valuable to physicians and entities seeking to set up a business relationship.[125] The exception itself is relatively straightforward, and incorporates the volume or value, other business generated, and "set in advance" tests discussed in Section VI.B., above. As with several other Stark law exceptions, the arrangement must involve a transaction that is commercially reasonable.

Under the fair market value compensation exception, the parties must enter into a written contract, the form of which need not be for one year, as long as the parties enter into only one arrangement for the same items or services during the course of the year. An arrangement made for less than one year may be renewed any number of times if the terms and compensation do not change.[126] Additionally, the fair market value exception requires parties to ensure anti-kickback compliance either by meeting a safe harbor, by receiving specific approval under an advisory opinion, or by otherwise not violating the statute.[127] Considering the narrowness of the safe harbors and the stringent rules for obtaining a favorable advisory opinion, most arrangements seeking the protection of this or other exceptions requiring anti-kickback compliance will need to be subjected to a full analysis under the anti-kickback statute, particularly in regard to the parties' intent.

E. Commercially Reasonable

Several of the compensation exceptions, including the fair market value exception, require that an arrangement be "commercially reasonable." Responding to concerns that CMS was injecting too much subjectivity into the term "commercially reasonable," the preamble to the Phase II Final Rule noted that "an arrangement will be considered 'commercially reasonable' in the absence of referrals if the arrangement would make commercial sense if entered into by a reasonable entity of similar type and size and a reasonable physician . . . of similar scope and specialty even if there were no potential DHS referrals."[128]

---

[124]*Id.* at 16,092.
[125]42 C.F.R. §411.357(*l*).
[126]*Id.* §411.357(*l*)(2).
[127]*Id.* §411.351 (definition of "does not violate the anti-kickback statute").
[128]69 Fed. Reg. at 16,093.

F. Directed Referrals

The Final Rules contained a series of special compensation rules, one of which was for compensation arrangements that are conditioned on the physician's referral of patients to a particular provider or supplier where the compensation is paid by a bona fide employer or under a managed care or other contract.[129] As a result of changes in the Phase II Final Rule, such arrangements must meet the following conditions:

a. the arrangement must be in writing;

b. the compensation must be set in advance and consistent with fair market value;

c. the arrangement must comply with an exception for ownership/investment interests or compensation arrangements;

d. the referral requirement may not apply when the patient expresses a different choice of provider, the patient's insurance determines the provider, or the referral in the physician's judgment is not in the best medical interest of the patient; and

e. the directed referrals must relate *solely* to the physician's services under his or her employment or the contract and must be reasonably necessary to "effectuate the legitimate business purposes of the compensation relationship."[130]

These Phase II changes are a logical attempt to close what appeared to be a large loophole from Phase I that permitted a direct link of payment and referrals, raising serious questions regarding potential anti-kickback statute violations.

G. Compensation to Physicians in a Group Practice

The Stark law provides group practices with greater latitude than other entities furnishing DHS in determining how to allocate or divide revenues among their physicians. Under the statute, group practices receive favored treatment with respect to physician compensation in that group practices may pay their physicians both productivity bonuses and shares of profits.[131]

Based on the unique status of group practices under the statute, CMS created special compensation rules in these areas.[132] The Phase II Final Rule made clear that a group practice may pay a productivity bonus or profit share not *directly* related to the volume or value of referrals of DHS. Based on CMS's determination regarding personally performed services not constituting a referral, a group may compensate its physicians *directly* based on personally performed services.

---

[129] 42 C.F.R. §411.354(d)(4).

[130] *Id.*

[131] 42 U.S.C. §1395nn(h)(4)(B)(i).

[132] *Id.*

Responding to inquiries about whether a group practice may pay profit shares and productivity bonuses to employees and independent contractors, CMS reiterated in the Phase II Final Rule that a group practice may do so provided that the employee or independent contractor qualifies as a "physician in the group practice."[133] Otherwise, to protect referrals from an independent contractor to a group practice, another exception must be met. This important change narrowed much of the distinction found in Phase I between members of a group and physicians in a group.

The Final Rules provide examples or deeming rules for permissible profit shares and productivity bonuses.[134] In the Phase II Final Rule, CMS clarified that these safe harbors serve as deeming provisions, that group practices are not required to use these compensation formulae, and that other methods are acceptable provided they meet the fundamental requirements that the bonuses and shares are reasonable, objectively verifiable, and not directly related to referrals.[135] The group practice must maintain, and make available to the Secretary upon request, supporting documentation regarding the methodology used to calculate productivity bonuses and profit shares.[136]

In the Phase II Final Rule, CMS clarified that there is nothing in the statute or regulations that would prohibit or restrict group practice bonuses or incentives based on criteria that do not take into account the volume or value of DHS referrals.[137]

As a result of the Phase II Final Rule changes to the "set in advance" and "other business generated" requirements, the rules for physician compensation outside the group practice context now more closely resemble the broad rules for productivity bonuses in the group practice setting with one key distinction. Unlike physicians in a group practice, physician employees, physician independent contractors, and AMC physicians (who must be employees of a component of the AMC) may receive a productivity bonus based on personally performed services only, and not based on "incident to" services. In addition, such non-group practice physicians may not receive an overall profit share. Allowable compensation for each type of physician is discussed in greater detail below.

H. Compensation to Physician Employees

1. *The Bona Fide Employment Exception*

The Stark law permits bona fide employment arrangements with physicians using familiar concepts previously discussed. The arrangement must be in writing and meet the requirements and tests for fair

---

[133] 69 Fed. Reg. at 16,077–78.

[134] 42 C.F.R. §411.352(i)(2) & (3).

[135] 69 Fed. Reg. at 16,077.

[136] 42 C.F.R. §411.352(i)(4).

[137] 69 Fed. Reg. at 16,081.

market value, volume or value, and commercial reasonableness.[138] In addition, the Stark law contains special rules allowing DHS entities to pay productivity bonuses to its employees so long as the bonus is based on services personally performed by the physician, including personally performed DHS. The Final Rules track the statutory exception almost word for word.[139] Of note, elsewhere in the Final Rules, CMS takes the position that personally performed services are not referrals for purposes of the Stark law.[140] As to referrals for DHS services that are not personally performed services, such as supervision services, these payments must meet the fair market value exception.[141] CMS is concerned that payments for supervision services "may merely be a proxy for having generated the DHS being supervised . . . [and] could mask improper cross-referral or circumvention schemes."[142]

2. Leased Employees

CMS has consistently refused to expand the definition of the term "employee" to include leased employees as defined by state law. CMS's concern is that incorporation of state law definitions of employment would be inconsistent with the statute, which is based on the Internal Revenue Service (IRS) definition of employee.[143] However, to the extent that a leased employee is a bona fide employee of the DHS entity under IRS rules, remuneration paid to that employee would be eligible under the bona fide employment exception.[144]

I. Compensation to Physician Independent Contractors

For physicians who are not employees or part of a group practice, the statutory personal services exception is one of the most commonly used.[145] As implemented by CMS in the Final Rules, the arrangement must be in writing and meet the requirements and tests for fair market value, set in advance, and, except for permissible physician incentive plans (see discussion below), volume or value or other business generated.[146] This exception also has a slightly differently worded commercially reasonableness standard in that the aggregate services under the agreement must be reasonable and necessary for the legitimate purposes of the arrangement. Other provisions of the exception are discussed below.

---

[138] 42 U.S.C. §1395nn(e)(2).

[139] 42 C.F.R. §411.357(c).

[140] *Id.* §411.351 (definition of referral); *see also* 69 Fed. Reg. at 16,087.

[141] 69 Fed. Reg. at 16,088. Note that the exception does not preclude a productivity bonus based solely on personally performed supervision of services that are not DHS, since the bonus would not take into account the volume or value of DHS referrals. *See* 69 Fed. Reg. at 16,087.

[142] *Id.* at 16,088.

[143] *Id.* at 16,087.

[144] 42 C.F.R. §411.351 (definition of "employee" and definition of "member of a group").

[145] 42 U.S.C. §1395nn(e)(3).

[146] 42 C.F.R. §411.357(d).

CMS notes that this exception is the applicable exception for most foundation-model physician practices.[147] The Phase II Final Rule changes to the "set in advance" requirements, the definition of referral as excluding personally performed services, and the fair market value definition for hourly payments for physicians, all discussed above, will give physicians and providers more flexibility when crafting an arrangement to fit within the personal services exception. Nevertheless, because of some of the statutory restrictions in this exception, practitioners may find the fair market value exception to be more flexible and easier to meet.

1. Termination

Due to Phase II Final Rule changes, the personal services exception now grants providers more leeway with regard to termination of contracts prior to the end of the required one-year term. The term of the arrangement must still be at least one year, but the parties can meet the requirements of the exception even if the arrangement is terminated during the term with *or without* cause, as long as the parties do not "enter into the same or substantially the same arrangement during the first year of the original term of the arrangement."[148]

2. Master List of Contracts

The personal services exception also requires that the arrangement cover all of the services to be furnished by the physician to the entity.[149] A contract can meet this requirement if all separate arrangements between the entity and the physician incorporate each other by reference or if they cross-reference a master list of contracts.[150] This master list of contracts must be maintained and updated centrally and be available for review by the Secretary upon request.

3. "Furnishing Services"

In the Phase II Final Rule, CMS added another clarification to the personal services exception that goes a long way toward acknowledging the practical realities of a physician's practice. Under the personal services exception, physicians can "furnish" services through locum tenens and a wholly owned entity, in addition to furnishing services through employees.[151]

4. Physician Incentive Plan Exception

The personal services exception's requirement that the compensation not take into account the volume or value of any referrals or

---

[147] 69 Fed. Reg. at 16,090.
[148] 42 C.F.R. §411.357(d)(1)(iv).
[149] *Id.* §411.357(d)(1)(ii).
[150] *Id.*
[151] *Id.*

other business generated between the parties does not apply to a physician incentive plan (PIP).[152] To meet the PIP exception, no payments can be made as an inducement to reduce or limit medically necessary services.[153] In addition, where a physician or physician group is at substantial financial risk, the PIP must comply with the general PIP regulations promulgated by CMS.[154] The Phase II Final Rule expanded the definition of a PIP to include arrangements involving downstream subcontractors of the entity.[155]

J. Compensation to Physicians in Academic Medical Centers

Although an AMC physician must be an employee of a component of the AMC, this exception permits the academic physician to receive compensation from all components of the AMC, and the focus of the analysis is on the total compensation rather than on each form of remuneration from the AMC components.[156]

One of the principal nagging issues facing CMS from Phase I was how to deal with the "set in advance" rules regarding percentage-based compensation arrangements, especially in the context of faculty practice plans. The Phase II Final Rule changes to the definitions of fair market value and set in advance discussed above relate equally to AMCs, because the AMC exception requires that compensation be fair market value and set in advance. Accordingly, like bona fide employees and independent contractors, AMC physicians may receive productivity bonuses based solely on personally performed services.[157]

Importantly, in the Phase II Final Rule CMS also clarified that when an AMC is examining salary comparables to determine fair market value, it is free to look at salary information for either academic physicians or for private practice physicians.[158] This change removes any lingering questions regarding whether an AMC is allowed to match a private practice salary offer in order to retain a top-level physician.

Finally, CMS clarified in the Phase II Final Rule that any monies paid by an AMC to a physician for research under this exception may also be used for teaching and must be consistent with the grant purposes, but may not be used for indigent care or community service. In all likelihood, other exceptions would be available for such expenditures.[159] See the discussion of other provisions of the AMC exception found at Section X., below.

---

[152]*Id.* §411.357(2).
[153]*Id.* §411.357(2)(i).
[154]*Id.* §411.357(2)(iii).
[155]*Id.* §411.351.
[156]*Id.* §411.355(e)(i)(C) & (ii).
[157]69 Fed. Reg. at 16,066–67.
[158]*Id.* at 16,110.
[159]*Id.*

VII. INDIRECT COMPENSATION DEFINITION AND EXCEPTION

One of the more significant features of the Final Rules is CMS's recognition that the Stark law either does not reach or does not adequately protect indirect compensation arrangements. As a result, under its rulemaking authority under the Stark law, CMS created an exception for indirect compensation, as well as a parallel definition of this term.

A. Definitions of Indirect Compensation, Volume or Value, and Other Business Generated

The definition of indirect compensation contains a three-part test: (1) there is an unbroken chain of financial arrangements (either ownership or compensation) linking the referring physician to the entity furnishing DHS; (2) when focusing on the last financial arrangement in the chain that involves a direct payment to the physician, the *aggregate* compensation paid to the referring physician varies with, or otherwise takes into account the volume or value of referrals to, or business generated for the DHS entity; and (3) the DHS entity has knowledge that the *aggregate* compensation varies in this manner.[160]

1. Unbroken Chain Test

The first element requires, as between the referring physician and the entity furnishing DHS, "an unbroken chain of any number (but not fewer than one) of persons or entities that have financial relationships between them."[161] This first element is met if there is an unbroken chain of any type of financial relationship from the DHS entity to the referring physician, regardless of the form or purpose of the payments or their relationship to the DHS referrals.

2. Volume or Value or Other Business Generated Test

The second element in the definition is the volume or value or other business generated test, which reads:

> The referring physician . . . receives aggregate compensation from the person or entity in the chain with which the physician . . . has a direct financial relationship that varies with, or otherwise reflects, the volume or value of referrals or other business generated by the referring physician for the entity furnishing the DHS, *regardless of whether the individual unit of compensation satisfies the special rules on unit-based compensation.* . . . If the financial relationship between the physician . . . and the person or entity in the chain with which the referring physician . . . has a direct financial relationship is an ownership or investment interest, the determination whether the aggregate compensation varies with, or

---

[160] 42 C.F.R. §411.354(c)(2).
[161] *Id.* §411.354(c)(2)(i).

otherwise reflects, the volume or value of referrals or other business generated by the referring physician for the entity furnishing the DHS will be measured by the nonownership or noninvestment interest closest to the referring physician. . . . (For example, if a referring physician has an ownership interest in company A, which owns company B, which has a compensation arrangement with company C, we would look to the aggregate compensation between company B and company C for purposes of this paragraph[]).[162]

The focus of this second test is the direct financial relationship with the referring physician, i.e., the last financial relationship in the chain. The only exception occurs when the direct financial arrangement with the referring physician is an ownership or investment interest; in that case the analysis moves up the chain until the first compensation arrangement is found. In the example of a group practice's medical director contract with a hospital, one must first look to the direct financial arrangement with the physician, in this case the physician's financial interest in the group practice. If that relationship is an ownership interest, the analysis moves upstream to the hospital's compensation arrangement with the group practice.[163]

Once the reference point of the direct financial arrangement is found, the next step in the analysis is to determine whether that compensation arrangement involves aggregate compensation that varies with or otherwise reflects the volume or value of referrals or business otherwise generated. If total payments under the arrangement rise or fall based on the volume or value of referrals, and the other definitional elements are met, it is an indirect compensation arrangement that will trigger the referral prohibition. The italicized part of this rule was added in the Phase II Final Rule to clarify that with respect to time-based or unit-of-service compensation (such as "per click" fees), the aggregate compensation always takes into account the volume or value of referrals, irrespective of compliance with these special rules, and so an indirect compensation arrangement exists that would require compliance with one of the exceptions.

CMS also made clear in the Phase II Final Rule that a physician stands in the shoes of his or her professional corporation if the physician is the sole owner, and therefore such arrangements appear to be direct compensation.

3. Knowledge

The third element is a knowledge requirement similar to the one that applies to the overall regulation. For an indirect compensation relationship to exist, the entity furnishing DHS must have "knowledge" that the referring physician's compensation "varies with, or otherwise

---

[162] *Id.* §411.354(c)(2)(ii) (emphasis added).

[163] Similarly, in the case of "under arrangement" services between hospitals and physician-owned service providers, the analysis is of the compensation between the hospital and the service provider. The regulation elsewhere makes clear that physician-owned "under arrangement" providers do not have an ownership interest in the hospital, and need only comply with a compensation exception.

reflects, the value or volume of referrals or other business generated by the referring physician for the entity furnishing the DHS."[164] CMS's intent with this third element is to prevent the unfairness of imposing what would be draconian sanctions when the DHS provider is not aware of the nature of the indirect compensation arrangement. As noted above, the knowledge element here does not impose an affirmative duty on providers to investigate.[165] CMS maintains, however, that the DHS entity must make a reasonable inquiry when it has reason to suspect a financial relationship exists. The nature of such an inquiry is undefined, but CMS suggests that reasonable inquiry by the DHS entity may include obtaining, in good faith, a written assurance from the referring physician or the entity from which the referring physician receives direct compensation, that the physician's aggregate compensation is not based on the volume or value of referrals to the DHS entity.[166]

B. Exception for Indirect Compensation Arrangements

If an arrangement constitutes an indirect compensation arrangement under the indirect compensation definition, the arrangement must satisfy the indirect compensation exception. This regulation-created exception generally requires that: (1) the compensation must be set at fair market value not taking into account the volume or value of referrals or business generated; (2) the arrangement must be a signed written agreement specifying the services covered; and (3) the compensation does not violate the anti-kickback statute.[167] See the discussion of the Stark law's relationship to the anti-kickback statute in Section XVI., below.

Under this exception a fair market value indirect compensation arrangement is permitted if the compensation (not necessarily the aggregate compensation) does not take into account the volume or value of referrals or business generated, and the other standards discussed above are met. It is important to note that while some exceptions contain the standard requiring that the compensation must be set in advance (as discussed in Section VI.B above), this exception does not include such a standard.

VIII. DEFINITION OF GROUP PRACTICE AND EXCEPTIONS FOR IN-OFFICE ANCILLARY SERVICES AND PHYSICIAN SERVICES

The in-office ancillary services exception and the related definition of a group practice are among the most difficult provisions to understand and to apply, and yet they are among the most important. The importance of the in-office ancillary services exception lies in the

---

[164] 42 C.F.R. §411.354(c)(2)(iii).
[165] 66 Fed. Reg. at 866.
[166] *Id.*
[167] 42 C.F.R. §411.355(d)(4).

fact that it permits arrangements that may be barred under other exceptions, most notably, the ownership exceptions. Because the definition of group practice is relevant to the physician services exception, we will discuss that exception in this section as well.

A. Group Practice Definition

The Stark law requires a group practice to meet five requirements, as well as a predicate, definitional requirement. The Stark law defines a group practice as "a group of 2 or more physicians legally organized as a partnership, professional corporation, foundation, not-for-profit corporation, faculty practice plan, or similar association" in which each group physician:

- provides substantially the full range of services that he or she routinely provides utilizing the resources of the group;
- provides, bills, and collects for substantially all services through the group;
- shares expenses and income from the practice, which are distributed in accordance with pre-determined methods;
- does not receive, directly or indirectly, compensation based on the volume or value of the physician's referrals, except through a permitted profit-sharing or productivity bonus arrangement;
- personally conducts at least 75 percent of the group's physician-patient encounters; and
- meets other regulatory standards.[168]

These requirements fall into six functional categories, as discussed below.

1. Single Legal Entity

A group practice must consist of a single legal entity formed primarily for the purpose of being a physician group practice.[169]

The entity may be organized by physicians, health care entities, or other persons or entities (including, but not limited to, physicians individually incorporated as professional corporations).[170] Thus, although hospitals may organize a group practice, they must do so through a separate group entity. A group of hospital-employed physicians does not otherwise qualify as a group practice because, in CMS's view, such an interpretation would allow the exception to protect virtually all hospital services and contravene Congress's intent. Where hospitals merely employ physicians, such arrangements need to be structured to fit within the employment exception.

CMS also clarified in the Phase II Final Rule that a physician practice consisting of multiple legal entities operating in more than one

---

[168]42 U.S.C. §1395nn(h)(4); *see also* 42 C.F.R. §411.352.
[169]42 C.F.R. §411.352.
[170]*Id.* §411.352(a).

state may qualify as a single legal entity, but only if certain conditions are met.[171] First, the states of operation must be contiguous as a whole (but each need not be contiguous to the other). Second, the legal entities must be absolutely identical as to ownership, governance, and operation. Third, the operation of multiple entities must be necessary under the applicable jurisdictional licensing laws.

The entity may not be organized or owned by another medical practice that is an operating physician practice, even if the medical practice otherwise meets the requirements for a group practice.[172] However if a medical group is defunct or no longer furnishing medical services it can own or operate a group practice. Furthermore, a single legal entity does not include informal affiliations of physicians formed to share profits for referrals, or separate group practices under common ownership or control through another entity.

The single-legal-entity test also includes entities owned by a single physician; provided, however, that the group must have at least two physicians who are members, whether as employees or as direct or indirect owners.[173]

In the Phase II Final Rule CMS addressed a concern raised by a number of commenters regarding the Phase I requirement that the single legal entity be formed primarily for the purpose of being a physician group practice.[174] CMS agreed with commenters that the relevant inquiry is not the group's intent at the time of formation, but rather whether the group is currently operating primarily for the purpose of being a physician practice. CMS also clarified that an entity with any substantial purpose other than operating as a physician practice, such as running a hospital, cannot meet this standard.

CMS also has noted that many foundation-model practices do not meet the single legal entity test and therefore need to rely on the personal services arrangement exception.

2. Members of the Group

The term "members of the group" is a component of various group practice prerequisites, one of which requires a group practice to have at least two physicians who are "members of the group."[175] Physicians employed part-time may qualify as members of the group for purposes of the two or more physicians requirement.[176]

Significantly, in the Phase II Final Rule, CMS modified the definition of employee to include a leased employee if he or she is a bona fide employee under IRS rules.[177]

---

[171]*Id.* §411.352(a)(1)–(3).

[172]*Id.* §411.352(a).

[173]*Id.* §411.352(b).

[174]69 Fed. Reg. at 16,076–77.

[175]42 C.F.R. §411.352(b).

[176]*Id., citing* 42 C.F.R. §411.351 (definition of "employee").

[177]42 C.F.R. §411.351 (definition of "member of the group").

While independent contractor physicians may supervise tests performed in a group, they do not qualify as group practice members. CMS expressed its view that to allow non-member physicians to qualify under the "two or more physicians" test would expand the group practice definition to groups that have no physician members, a result that would be entirely inconsistent with the statutory language and would render meaningless many of the provisions relating to group practices.[178]

3. *The "Full Range of Services" Test*

The "full range of services" test requires each member of the group to furnish substantially all of the full range of patient services that the physician routinely furnishes through the joint use of shared office space, facilities, equipment, and personnel.[179] Patient care services include all services a physician performs that address the medical needs of specific patients or patients in general or benefit the group practice.[180] This test measures whether a member of a group practice provides substantially the same scope of patient care services within the group context as he or she would outside of that group; it does not require absolute identity of services.[181] If donated services are within the same scope of services that are provided as part of the group, then the group still should meet the full range of services test as well as the "substantially all" test, which is discussed below. A group practice may structure the donated services so that they are billed through the group even though the group need not actually send or collect on the bill.

4. *The "Substantially All" Test*

The "substantially all" test requires that 75 percent of the patient care services provided by members of the group must be furnished through the group and billed under the group's billing number, and payments must be treated as receipts of the group.[182] This test does not apply to group practices located in HPSAs or to services provided in HPSAs (irrespective of the location of the group practice). The Final Rules establish criteria for measuring compliance. In the Phase II Final Rule, CMS provided a number of other clarifications and changes in response to numerous comments it received.

In response to comments pointing out that the addition of a new physician can jeopardize group practice status because of delays in obtaining Medicare billing numbers, CMS added a twelve-month grace period for group practices to come into compliance with this requirement where a recruited physician has relocated his or her practice.[183] This grace period applies only if the new member has relo-

---

[178] 69 Fed. Reg. at 16,077.

[179] 42 C.F.R. §411.352(d).

[180] *Id.* §411.351 (definition of "patient care services").

[181] 66 Fed. Reg. at 955.

[182] 42 C.F.R. §411.352(d).

[183] *Id.* §411.352(d)(6)(i)(A).

cated a medical practice as defined in the physician recruitment exception (see Section XIII.B.), the group practice otherwise meets the "substantially all" test, and the new members' employment with or ownership interest in the group is documented at the inception of the relationship. Contrary to commenters' suggestions, the grace period, however, will not apply in the event of reorganization.

Group practices with members who provide substantial patient care services at AMCs must still meet the "substantially all" test.[184] To the extent such groups have difficulty doing so, they may arrange to bill the care through the group and treat amounts received as group receipts. CMS cautioned that although a medical school group practice may qualify for the in-office ancillary services exception, it may use the exception to protect referrals within the group practice, but not referrals to other components of the AMC.

In addition, CMS explained that a physician who provides substantial services through an independent practice association does not necessarily jeopardize the group's compliance with the "substantially all" test.[185] Again, this arrangement does not pose a risk for the group as long as patient care services provided through the independent practice association are not governed by an employment or contractual arrangement unrelated to the group. CMS further declined to adopt the commenter's suggested test that would only count fee for service (excluding managed care services) or Medicare and Medicaid services as "patient care services," on the grounds that this test was too narrow to achieve the purpose of the "substantially all" test.[186]

CMS also declined to accept a commenter's suggestion that it allow group practices to elect to treat independent contractors as members of the group for purposes of the "substantially all" and the physician-patient encounters tests.[187] CMS opined that such a change is unnecessary and infeasible and contrary to the expressed desire for ease of compliance, and instead, expressed its preference for the current bright-line tests. Instead, CMS suggested that the group restructure its hiring practices to integrate the physicians into the group as employees or owners or to fit into another, separate exception. Also of note, CMS agreed with a commenter that independent contractor physicians in a group practice, similar to group practice members, are in a position to make referrals of DHS to a group practice, provided that an exception applies for those referrals, such as the personal services or fair market value exceptions.[188]

CMS further declined to amend both the "substantially all" and the "full range of services" tests to exclude volunteer patient services

---

[184] 69 Fed. Reg. at 16,079.
[185] *Id.*
[186] *Id.* at 16,080.
[187] *Id.* at 16,078.
[188] *Id.* at 16,078–79.

provided in a free clinic by physicians in HPSAs.[189] As explained above, donated services would not prevent a group from qualifying for the exception under the "full range" of services test. Similarly, to the extent that the physician donates services that are different from those he provides for the group, the donated services would not hinder the group from satisfying the "substantially all" test.

Finally, CMS rejected a commenter's claim that the documentation requirement under the substantially all test is actually a "back door attestation requirement."[190] In response, CMS pointed to the distinction between a documentation requirement and an attestation, and upheld the requirement.

5. *The Unified Business Test*

To meet this test, a group practice must also be organized and operated on a bona fide basis as a single integrated business enterprise with legal and organizational integration.[191] Essential elements are: (1) centralized decision making by a body representative of the practice that maintains effective control over the group's assets and liabilities, and (2) consolidated billing, accounting, and financial reporting.

The Final Rules generally permit a group practice to use cost-center and location-based accounting with respect to services that are not DHS, provided that the compensation formulas with respect to DHS revenues otherwise meet the requirements of the Stark law.[192]

The group's overhead expenses and income must be distributed in accordance with methods "previously determined." The Final Rules treat the distribution method as "previously determined" (or determined in advance) if it is determined prior to receipt of payment for the services giving rise to the overhead expense or the production of income.[193] This approach permits groups to adjust their methodologies prospectively as often as they deem appropriate. A compensation method that directly relates to the volume or value of DHS referrals, or is retroactively adjusted, would violate the statute.

In the Phase II Final Rule, CMS responded to a concern of a commenter seeking clarification regarding the need for the test's requirement that a body representative of the group practice that maintains control over the group's assets and liabilities be responsible for the decision making within the group practice. Specifically, the commenter asked whether the test could be satisfied when individual group practice locations devise their own budgets and submit them to the board for approval. In response, CMS clarified that the "unified business" test is not supposed to dictate specific business practices, but instead is intended to be flexible in order that it may accommodate a variety of

---

[189] 69 Fed. Reg. at 16,079.

[190] *Id.* at 16,080.

[191] 42 C.F.R. §411.352(a).

[192] *Id.* §411.352(f).

[193] *Id.* §411.352(e).

group practice arrangements.[194] However, CMS cautioned that substantial group level management and operation must occur. In other words, those responsible for maintaining control over the group's assets and liabilities cannot simply "rubber stamp" decisions based on the various cost centers or locations.

6. Profit Shares and Productivity Bonuses

The rules for compensating group practice physicians are discussed in Section VI., above.

B. In-Office Ancillary Services Exception

Under the Stark law, certain DHS services are excluded from the in-office ancillary services exception. The exception itself imposes requirements on supervision, location (the "building requirements"), and billing.

1. Scope of DHS That Can Be In-Office Ancillary Services

The Final Rules permit certain DME, specifically crutches, canes, walkers, and folding manual wheelchairs, and blood glucose monitors to be furnished, provided they meet certain conditions.[195] Blood glucose monitors include a starter set of strips and lancets if the practitioners furnish outpatient diabetes self-management training to patients receiving such monitors. In addition, CMS allows external ambulatory infusion pumps (other than pumps that are PEN equipment or supplies) to be provided under this exception. CMS also explained that a physician billing Medicare for the DME at issue must have a supplier number from the National Supplier Clearinghouse.

2. Building Requirements

Generally, in-office ancillary services must be furnished in either the "same building" where the referring physician or his or her group practice provides professional services, or in a "centralized building" used to provide off-site DHS.[196] Although group practices may have more than one centralized facility, the group practice must have full-time, exclusive ownership or occupancy of the centralized space.[197] According to CMS, this requirement helps to ensure that DHS qualifying for the exception are truly ancillary and are not provided as part of a separate business enterprise.[198]

In the Phase II Final Rule, CMS significantly revised the "same building" requirement. CMS introduced three new alternative tests—available to both solo practitioners and group practices—for deter-

---

[194] 69 Fed. Reg. at 16,080.
[195] 42 C.F.R. §411.355(b)(4).
[196] *Id.* §411.355(b)(2).
[197] *Id.* §411.351 (definition of "centralized building").
[198] 69 Fed. Reg. at 16,072.

mining whether services are furnished in the "same building."[199] CMS believes that these tests are more flexible, permitting many arrangements to qualify now that previously did not, as well as continuing to allow virtually all arrangements that previously complied with the Phase I test.[200] However, CMS noted that the few arrangements that previously qualified under Phase I, but do not qualify now, must be restructured or unwound before the effective date of Phase II.

The first new test generally describes a building where a physician or group's primary place of practice is located. Under this test, the office must be normally open at least 35 hours per week to patients, and it must be used regularly by the referring physician or by one or more members of his or her group practice to practice medicine and to furnish physician services at least 30 hours per week.[201] Additionally, "some" of the 30 hours of physician services must be unrelated to DHS.

The second test takes a different approach, requiring that the patient receiving the DHS at the site usually receives services from the referring physician or the referring physician's group practice. This test is met if the office is normally open at least eight hours per week for patients, and is used regularly by the referring physician to practice medicine and to furnish physician services at least six hours per week.[202] The six hours per week must consist of "some" physician services unrelated to the furnishing of DHS.

The requirements for the third new test are similar to the second in requiring that the office be open at least eight hours per week, and that it must be used at least six hours per week by the referring physician or by his or her group practice member to furnish services, not all of which may be DHS services.[203] However, this test differs from the second in that, instead of requiring that the patient usually receive services from the referring physician or his or her group member, it requires that the referring physician be present and order the DHS during a patient visit in the office, or the referring physician or a member of his or her group must be present when the DHS is provided on the premises.

All three tests require the office to be open for a specified number of hours each week with the referring physician regularly practicing medicine at the site. CMS noted that it is possible to satisfy these tests even if there are occasional weeks when the offices are open for fewer hours (such as during a vacation), or the offices have open appointments, cancellations, or other occasional gaps in the furnishing of services.[204] Despite certain objections, CMS retained, as the closest thing to a bright-line rule, the post office street address test to determine whether DHS is being provided in the same building.

---

[199] 42 C.F.R. §411.351 (definition of same building); §411.355(b)(1) & (b)(2).

[200] 69 Fed. Reg. at 16,072.

[201] 42 C.F.R. §411.355(b)(2)(i)(A).

[202] *Id.* §411.355(b)(2)(i)(B).

[203] *Id.* §411.355(b)(2)(i)(C).

[204] 69 Fed. Reg. at 16,073.

CMS also declined to set a particular threshold for the requirement that "some" of the physician services must be unrelated to the furnishing or ordering of DHS. Rather, CMS stated that it will interpret "some" according to its "common sense meaning."[205] However, in interpreting the meaning of "physician services unrelated to the furnishing of DHS," CMS retained its Phase I interpretation, requiring that the services be neither federal nor private pay DHS. Commenters pointed out the difficulty in satisfying this requirement for radiology and oncology practices, and CMS suggested that these specialty practices should be able to meet the lower threshold of "some unrelated to DHS services."

There are special rules for physicians who primarily treat patients in their private homes to allow these physicians, who do not actually practice in a building, to meet the exception's building requirement. Under the Final Rules, services are generally designated to be "furnished" under the exception in the location where the service is actually performed on the patient or when an item is dispensed to a patient in a manner that is sufficient to meet Medicare billing and coverage rules.[206] To accommodate this special situation, these physicians can meet the same building test if the DHS are provided in a private home contemporaneously with a physician service that is not DHS. The rule does not apply to services provided in a nursing, long term care, or other facility or institution, but does apply to services provided in a private home within an independent living or assisted living facility. CMS explained that such a residence qualifies as a private home if the patient owns or leases the residence and has the right to exclude others from the premises. However, to fall within the special rule, these assisted living facilities may not share a common examination room.[207]

Finally, CMS clarified that loading docks that are not part of the building do not fall under the definition of "same building" to ensure that mobile vans are not permitted under this exception.[208] However, where the mobile services do not qualify under the exception, physicians and group practices may still purchase and bill for the technical components of mobile services under the purchased diagnostic testing rules.

3. Direct Supervision

To qualify under the exception, DHS must be provided personally by the referring physician, a physician who is a member of the same group practice as the referring physician, or an individual supervised

---

[205] *Id.*

[206] 42 C.F.R. §411.355(b)(5).

[207] 69 Fed. Reg. at 16,074.

[208] 42 C.F.R. §411.351 (definition of "same building").

by the referring physician or another physician in the referring physician's group practice.[209] The supervision requirement is met by complying with the supervision requirements applicable under Medicare and Medicaid payment and coverage rules for the specific services at issue. The supervision requirement does not require the referring physician to be part of a group practice. In addition, a solo practitioner can provide DHS through a shared facility if the exception's other requirements concerning supervision, location, and billing are met. (This means, among other things, that the shared facility may not bill for the services.)

In the Phase II Final Rule, CMS responded to requests for clarification about the level of supervision required for physical therapists working in a physician office, stating that all services that are billed "incident to" will require that level of supervision that is applicable under the Medicare and Medicaid payment and coverage rules governing "incident to" services.[210]

4. Billing Requirements

The Stark law's billing standard for in-office ancillary services requires that the DHS be billed by one of the following:

- the physician performing or supervising the service;
- the group practice in which such physician is a member;
- with respect to services performed or supervised by the supervising physician, the group practice if such physician is a physician in the group practice; or
- an entity that is wholly owned by the referring or supervising physician or the referring or supervising physician's group practice.[211]

For purposes of this requirement "wholly owned" does not include joint ventures between group practices and individual group practice physicians or joint ventures that include other providers or investors that do not qualify as wholly owned entities. The billing number used for billing must be "assigned to the group," and groups "may have, and bill under, more than one Medicare billing number, subject to any applicable Medicare program restrictions."[212] Finally, specific rules are provided for groups using third-party billing companies.

In the Phase II Final Rule, CMS made no substantive changes to the exception's billing requirements. In response to one comment, CMS clarified that compliance with this billing requirement is only a threshold condition for meeting the exception's requirements, and that all other applicable payment and coverage rules therefore still

---

[209] *Id.* §411.355(a).
[210] 69 Fed. Reg. at 16,071–72.
[211] 42 C.F.R. §411.355(b)(3).
[212] *Id.* §411.355(b)(3)(v).

apply. Finally, CMS clarified that physical therapists employed by a physician practice cannot bill using the physical therapist's provider number, but must instead bill through the performing or supervising physician, an entity wholly owned by the performing or supervising physician, or through the group practice using a number assigned to the group. Alternatively, the billing requirement would be met if the physical therapist reassigned his right to payment to the group and the group billed for the services using its provider number.

C. Exception for Physician Services

The Stark law allows an exception for physician services[213] provided personally by, or under the personal supervision of, another physician in the same group practice as the referring physician.[214] This exception is of "limited application."[215] The exception covers services provided by physicians only, not services performed by non-physicians, even when furnished under physician supervision, such as ancillary services that are "incident to" a physician service.

IX. MANAGED CARE PREPAID PLANS AND RISK-SHARING EXCEPTIONS

The Stark law also provides an exception for services furnished to enrollees of certain types of prepaid health plans,[216] and CMS has created a parallel risk-sharing exception.[217]

In its analysis of the statutory prepaid health plan ownership and compensation exception in the Phase I Final Rule, CMS was faced with two principal problems in trying to avoid the unintended disruption of many physician arrangements with health maintenance organizations (HMOs) or managed care organizations (MCOs). First, CMS wanted to ensure that it generally permitted physician ownership of network-type HMOs or MCOs, provider-sponsored organizations (PSOs), and independent practice associations (IPAs).[218] Secondly, the statutory prepaid health plan exception does not protect physician arrangements involving commercial or employer-provided group plans—typically the so-called commercial product paralleling the Medicare MCO product—that include some Medicare retiree members.[219] CMS resolved the first major problem by more clearly defining the party that is furnishing DHS. CMS resolved the second major problem by creating a compensation risk-sharing exception.

---

[213] The term "physicians' services" means professional services performed by physicians, including surgery, consultation, and home, office, and institutional calls. 42 U.S.C. §1395x(q); 42 C.F.R. §411.355(a).

[214] *See* 42 U.S.C. §1395nn(b)(1); *see also* 42 C.F.R. §411.355(a).

[215] 66 Fed. Reg. at 879.

[216] 42 U.S.C. §1395nn(b)(3).

[217] 42 C.F.R. §411.355(c).

[218] 66 Fed. Reg. at 912.

[219] *Id.* at 913.

A. The Prepaid Plan Exception

The prepaid health plan exception protects ownership and compensation arrangements for "services furnished by an organization (or its contractors or subcontractors) to enrollees of one of the [designated] prepaid health plans (not including services provided to enrollees in any other plan or line of business offered or administered by the same organization)."[220] The protected health plans include certain Medicare+ Choice (now Medicare Advantage) plans, health care prepayment plans, demonstration project MCOs, Medicaid managed care plans, and Public Health Service Act–qualifying HMOs.

In defining the term "entity," the Final Rules provide that the entity that will be deemed to be furnishing DHS, as a general matter, is *not* the HMO, MCO, PSO, IPA, or similar entity under contract with other entities directly furnishing DHS. Rather, a person or entity is considered to be furnishing DHS if it is the person or entity to which Medicare payment is made for the DHS, directly or upon assignment on the patient's behalf.[221] Thus, a prepaid health plan, or an MCO, PSO, or IPA with which the health plan contracts directly or indirectly for services to plan enrollees, will be considered to be furnishing DHS only when the services are provided directly through an employee or otherwise, so that Medicare payment is made to the plan for DHS directly, upon assignment on the patient's behalf, or pursuant to a valid reassignment under Medicare reassignment rules; or when services are provided by a supplier employed by the plan or the plan operates a facility able to accept reassignment from the supplier under Medicare reassignment rules.[222] CMS stated that this change makes it possible for physicians to hold ownership interests in most types of network IPAs and MCOs, as most do not provide DHS directly, but rather contract with others for the delivery of services to enrollees.[223] However, in limited situations in which the prepaid health plan will be deemed to be the DHS provider, CMS noted that physicians with an ownership interest in the prepaid health plan would be prohibited from referring patients to that entity for DHS absent an applicable exception.

The Final Rules provide that this exception protects providers, suppliers, and other entities—the "downstream providers"—that provide, either under direct or indirect contract, DHS to enrollees of protected Medicare prepaid health plans.[224] Thus, a physician may refer a patient for DHS covered by the protected Medicare prepaid health plans to an MCO that has a Medicare managed care contract or to any entity, provider, or supplier furnishing the services under a contract or subcontract with the MCO. As noted above, this exception and the

---

[220]*Id.* at 960; 42 C.F.R. §411.355(c).

[221]42 C.F.R. §411.351.

[222]*Id.* §411.351 (definition of "entity"—see subsections (1)(ii) & (2)).

[223]66 Fed. Reg. at 913.

[224]42 C.F.R. §411.351(c).

explicit language of the final rules only protect services furnished to enrollees of one of the protected prepaid health plans. It does not, however, protect "pull through" patients, i.e., other Medicare beneficiaries served by that prepaid health plan or provider pursuant to a commercial product.

B. Regulation-Created Exception for Risk-Sharing Compensation Arrangements

Because there are so many commercial or employer-provided MCO arrangements that serve Medicare beneficiaries, CMS determined that additional protection was needed for managed care incentive compensation (for example, withholds, bonuses, and risk pools not protected by either the employment or personal services exceptions).[225] Therefore, the Final Rules create a risk-sharing compensation exception for compensation pursuant to a risk-sharing arrangement (including, but not limited to, withholds, bonuses, and risk pools) between an MCO or an IPA and a physician (either directly or indirectly through a subcontractor) for services provided to enrollees of a health plan.[226]

Although CMS defined the term "health plan" in the same manner as the federal anti-kickback statute safe harbor, the Final Rules do not define the term "risk sharing," and the preamble of the Phase I Final Rule made clear that this term was specifically intended to be broader than the same term used in the federal anti-kickback statute risk-sharing safe harbors.[227] The arrangement, however, may not violate the federal anti-kickback statute or any law or regulation governing billing or the submission of claims, and, as with the prepaid health plan exception, the "pull through" of non-enrollees (i.e., traditional Medicare fee-for-service patients) is not protected.

In the Phase II Final Rule, CMS clarified that this exception is intended to cover all risk-sharing compensation paid to physicians by any downstream entity, provided that the terms of the exception are met.[228] CMS declined to define the term "managed care organization" to maintain maximum flexibility and to expand the exception to include referrals to entities owned by a managed care organization even if the patients are not enrollees.[229]

X. EXCEPTION FOR ACADEMIC MEDICAL CENTERS

CMS's Phase I AMC exception specified requirements for the various components of an AMC and its relationship with faculty physicians and other referring physicians, all of which will be discussed in

---

[225] 66 Fed. Reg. at 912–13.
[226] 42 C.F.R. §411.357(n).
[227] 66 Fed. Reg. at 914.
[228] 69 Fed. Reg. 16,114.
[229] *Id.*

this section.[230] The AMC exception also contains requirements for the compensation paid to the referring physician, which are discussed separately in Section X.B., below.

CMS created an AMC exception whose principal benefit is that it protects all payments from within a qualifying AMC to a referring physician who is a bona fide employee of one component of the AMC as long as the standards of the exception are met. CMS appears to have recognized that academic physicians often receive compensation from various sources within the organization, such as from the faculty practice plan; the teaching hospital for administrative, supervision and teaching (AS&T) services; the medical school; and perhaps an affiliated research organization. Under the AMC exception an analysis is only required of the aggregate compensation, for example, to make sure it is set at fair market value and is not related to referrals.

Although AMCs will likely find this exception to be of significant benefit, depending on the facts of a particular situation, it may be worth considering whether the requirements of other exceptions, such as for employees or indirect compensation, are easier to meet.

A. Teaching Hospital

The AMC exception permits an academic organization to qualify as an AMC without having an affiliated medical school.[231] The teaching hospital component of the AMC can qualify as an "accredited academic hospital" if (1) it sponsors four or more approved medical education programs (either alone or in conjunction with other parts of the AMC), (2) a majority of its medical staff are faculty members, and (3) a majority the hospital's admissions are made by faculty members.[232]

In the Phase II Final Rule, although CMS did not change the requirements that a majority of the hospital's medical staff must be faculty physicians and that a majority of the admissions must come from faculty physicians, it made the following accommodations to facilitate compliance with these two 50 percent rules:

- The faculty physician may be on the faculty of the medical school or one or more of the educational programs of the accredited academic hospital (AAH).[233] This means that both the faculty of the medical school and the AAH may be counted.

- Any faculty member may be counted, whether or not the physician is an employee, meaning that courtesy or volunteer faculty can be included in the count.

- Residents and non-physician professionals should not be counted.[234]

---

[230] 42 C.F.R. §411.355(e).
[231] *Id.* §411.355(e)(2).
[232] *Id.*
[233] *Id.* §411.355(e)(2)(iii).
[234] *Id.*

B. Referring Physician

The AMC exception covers payments to referring physicians who meet the requirements of the exception. While the referring physician must be a faculty member, as discussed above, he or she must *also* be a bona fide employee (at least on a substantial part-time basis) of a component of the AMC.[235] Thus, although volunteer faculty will be counted for the purposes of determining whether the hospital qualifies as a component of the AMC, payments to such physicians are not permitted under this exception, but must qualify under another exception. The exception allows the parties, in determining whether the referring physician provides *substantial* academic services or clinical teaching, to use any "reasonable and consistent" method for calculating these services. In the Phase II Final Rule, CMS also created a deeming standard for compliance with this AMC service requirement: 20 hours per week or at least 20 percent of the physician's professional time. CMS made clear that this standard was not a formal requirement, and that failure to meet either of these standards did not preclude the parties from showing in other ways that the referring physician provided substantial academic services or clinical teaching services.[236]

Importantly, whereas many compensation exceptions require the arrangement with the physician to be in writing, this is not required by the AMC exception, which therefore permits various informal, unwritten arrangements that typically exist in academic settings.

CMS does require that the compensation be "set in advance." While this requires the compensation to be objectively verifiable, it should be noted that the prohibition on mid-year adjustments to the compensation formula only applies when the adjustment takes into account referrals or business generated.[237] This raises the larger question of why CMS has retained the "set in advance" requirement. As one commenter noted in a publication of the American Health Lawyers Association:

> Notwithstanding the relative ease of complying with the set-in-advance requirement, the question must be raised again as to what abuse CMS believes it is cutting out by imposing this requirement on AMCs. The statutory context for this requirement is found in the personal services exception, yet a requirement of the AMC exception is that the referring physician be an employee of a component of the AMC. Therefore, the academic physician's employment salary could be protected under the employment exception or in many cases under the even broader group practice requirements if the physician is an employee of a faculty practice plan qualifying as a group practice. Importantly, both of these exceptions do not require that the physician's salary to be set in advance. Because the AMC exception covers all compensation from any component of the AMC, the only plausible abusive flow of money that the set-in-advance requirement would serve to snare is the other non-employee-related compensation of the academic physician, such as for AS&T services paid by the

---

[235] 42 C.F.R. §411.355(e)(1)(i).
[236] 69 Fed. Reg. at 16,110.
[237] 42 C.F.R. §411.354(d)(1).

teaching hospital. The problem for CMS's reasoning in imposing this set-in-advance requirement is that these rules only appear to be related to salary-type compensation, such as restricting certain percent of revenue formula. Consequently, given the requirement the referring physician be an employee of the ASC, no abusive compensation is likely to be controlled by requiring that the non-employee compensation be set in advance.[238]

C. Faculty Practice Plans

In addition to a teaching hospital, an AMC must have one or more faculty practice plans. In the Phase II Final Rule, CMS eliminated the requirement that the faculty practice plan must be tax exempt.[239]

D. Other Components and Requirements of an AMC

CMS clarified that the supporting documentation necessary to show the affiliation between components of the AMC need not be in a written agreement, but may be in a series of documents. The preamble to the Phase II Final Rule states that the evidence of an affiliation may be "a clearly established course of conduct that is appropriately documented."[240] An AMC may consist of a single legal entity, in which case the documentation may be financial reports documenting the transfer of funds. Finally, a nonprofit support organization may be included as a component of an AMC, thereby protecting the transfers of funds from that entity so long as the primary purpose of the support organization is supporting the teaching mission of the AMC.[241]

XI. OTHER EXCEPTIONS RELATED TO BOTH OWNERSHIP AND COMPENSATION

In addition to the ownership and compensation exceptions discussed above,[242] the Final Rules also include five additional exceptions.[243] These exceptions created by regulation are for (1) ambulatory surgery center (ASC) implants; (2) EPO and other dialysis-related drugs; (3) preventive screening tests, vaccinations, and immunizations; (4) eyeglasses or contacts following cataract surgery; and (5) intra-family rural referrals. The so-called "composite rate" exception found in the Phase I Final Rule was deleted in the Phase II Final Rule.[244]

---

[238]Thomas S. Crane, *Letter to the Editor: Stark II, Phase II,* 8 HEALTH LAW. NEWS, 2, 2–4 (No. 8) (Aug. 2004).

[239]69 Fed. Reg. at 16,109.

[240]*Id.* at 16,110.

[241]42 C.F.R. §411.355(e)(1)(i).

[242]The statutory exceptions for physician services, in-office ancillary services, and managed care are discussed in Sections VIII. and IX.; the regulation-created exception for AMCs is discussed in Section X.

[243]*See generally* 69 Fed. Reg. at 16,071–81.

[244]69 Fed. Reg. at 16,111.

A. Implants Furnished in Ambulatory Surgery Centers

The Final Rules create an exception to permit referring physicians or members of the referring physician's group practice to implant certain prosthetic devices in Medicare-certified ASCs. The exception applies to implants, including, but not limited to, cochlear implants, intraocular lenses, and other implanted prosthetics, implanted prosthetic devices, and implanted DME that meet the following conditions:

- The implant is furnished by the referring physician or a member of the referring physician's group practice in a Medicare-certified ASC with which the referring physician has a financial relationship.
- The implant is implanted in the patient during a surgical procedure performed in the same ASC where the implant is furnished.
- The arrangement for the furnishing of the implant does not violate the federal anti-kickback statute.
- Billing and claims submission for the implants complies with all federal and state laws and regulations.

This exception does not apply to any financial relationships between the referring physician and any entity other than the ASC in which the implant is furnished to and implanted in the patient.[245]

CMS created this exception to protect surgeons who refer patients needing implantable devices to an ASC in which the surgeon has an ownership interest. In the absence of a special rule, no other existing exception applies in this situation because many of these devices are billed outside of the bundled ASC rate. CMS believed that the exclusion of these implants would not increase the risk of overutilization beyond what was already presented by the surgeon's Part B physician fee. CMS also noted that, as a practical matter, the absence of an applicable exception allowing implantation of these items at ASCs would result in these procedures moving to more costly hospital settings.[246]

This exception is limited to its explicit terms; it does not protect items implanted in other settings. As to implants provided in other settings or those that otherwise do not meet the conditions of this exception, other exceptions may still apply.

B. EPO and Other Dialysis-Related Outpatient Prescription Drugs

CMS created this exception for EPO and other dialysis-related outpatient prescription drugs based on its determination that these end-stage renal disease (ESRD) services are less vulnerable to abuse than other financial arrangements for two reasons: (1) they are performed

---

[245] 42 C.F.R. §411.355(f).
[246] 66 Fed. Reg. at 934.

in conjunction with other services paid for by Medicare under a composite rate; and (2) the composite services are, in turn, subject to strict utilization and coverage criteria.[247] Of note, only ESRD facilities can qualify under this exception.

The Phase I Final Rule established a list of dialysis-related treatments, identified by CPT and HCPCS codes, that qualify for an exception. The Phase II Final Rule expands this list to include certain other drugs, including certain outpatient drugs furnished by the ESRD facility that do not dialyze, but that promote the efficacy of the dialysis treatment, such as thrombolytics for de-clotting catheters.[248] CMS declined commenters' requests to add other drugs to the list where it determined the drug was already included in the Medicare composite rate for their accompanying procedures, and therefore do not constitute DHS.

C. Preventative Screening Tests, Vaccinations, and Immunizations

The Final Rules include an exception for certain legislatively mandated preventive screening and immunization services that are subject to CMS-imposed frequency limits; however, the fee schedule requirement for reimbursement found in the Phase I Final Rule was deleted in the Phase II Final Rule. Preventive screening tests, immunizations, and vaccines that are covered by Medicare and identified by CPT and HCPCS codes meet this exception if the following conditions are satisfied:

- The preventive screening tests, immunizations, and vaccines are subject to CMS-mandated frequency limits (however, the fee schedule requirement for reimbursement has been deleted at Phase II).

- The arrangement for the provision of the preventive screening tests, immunizations, and vaccines does not violate the federal anti-kickback statute.

- Billing and claims submission for such tests, immunizations, and vaccines complies with all federal and state laws and regulations.

- The preventive screening tests, immunizations, and vaccines must be covered by Medicare and must be listed on the CMS Web site and in annual updates.[249]

D. Eyeglasses and Contact Lenses Following Cataract Surgery

The Final Rules create an exception for eyeglasses and contact lenses that are prescribed after cataract surgery. The exception applies when the following conditions are met:

---

[247] 69 Fed. Reg. at 16,117–18; 42 C.F.R. §411.455(g).
[248] 69 Fed. Reg. at 16,117–18; 42 C.F.R. §411.455(g).
[249] 42 C.F.R. §411.355(h).

- The glasses or contact lenses are provided in accordance with Medicare coverage and payment provisions set forth in 42 C.F.R. Sections 410.36(a)(2)(ii) and 414.228.
- The arrangement for the furnishing of the glasses or contact lenses does not violate the federal anti-kickback statute.
- Billing and claim submission for the eyeglasses or contact lenses complies with all federal and state laws and regulations.[250]

CMS created this exception in response to comments urging the exclusion of eyeglasses and contact lenses from the definition of prosthetic devices. CMS noted in the Phase I Final Rule that Medicare coverage of eyeglasses and contact lenses is unique in that it is limited to one pair of either item after each cataract surgery and is available to any patient who has had this surgery. In addition, the Medicare-approved amount of payment does not vary based on the cost of a particular pair of glasses or contact lenses.[251] Accordingly, CMS created this exception because it sees little opportunity or incentive for a physician either to underutilize or overutilize these items in the Medicare program.

E. Intra-Family Referrals in Rural Areas

The Phase II Final Rule contains a new regulatory exception under which a physician can refer a patient living in a rural area to an entity in which his or her immediate family member has either an ownership or compensation interest.[252] This exception is similar to the ownership exception for rural providers (see Section XII.B.2., below), but contains certain differences, most importantly that this exception protects compensation arrangements. This exception applies only if there is no other entity within 25 miles of the patient's home, or otherwise available to furnish DHS in a timely manner based on the patient's condition.[253]

Theoretically, both the referring physician and the entity could be located in an urban area and still avail themselves of the exception. CMS emphasized that, unlike other location-based exceptions, this exception is based on where the DHS services are provided, rather than the location of either the referring physician or the DHS entity.[254] This provision has the unique effect of excepting some, but not all, of the patients referred to an entity by a particular physician. For example, a physician may have both patients who live within 25 miles of another DHS, and patients who do not, but only the latter can be referred to the DHS connected to the family member. Accordingly, providers who utilize this exception should be aware of which patients

---

[250]*Id.* §411.355(i).
[251]66 Fed. Reg. at 936.
[252]42 C.F.R. §411.355(j).
[253]*Id.* §411.355(j)(1)(ii).
[254]69 Fed. Reg. at 16,084.

qualify for the exception and which do not. Those providers should also track their patients' rural or urban geographical classification, and stay abreast of any changes to urban or rural boundaries as defined by the regulations.[255]

This exception recognizes that neither the referring physician nor the immediate family member has an obligation to inquire as to the availability of persons or entities located farther than 25 miles from the patient's residence.[256] However, the physician must make reasonable inquiries as to the availability of other persons or entities within 25 miles of the patient's residence. Moreover, the preamble to the Phase II Final Rule states that if the physician is aware of another person or DHS entity outside the 25-mile radius that is willing to provide the service, he or she may not refer the patient to a family member.[257] Note that this narrow exception does not allow a physician to consider the quality of services rendered. Rather, the focus is on the timeliness of the DHS, given the patient's condition. Presumably, if the physician is aware of another entity that is outside the 25-mile radius but could not serve the patient in a timely manner appropriate to the patient's condition, the physician may still refer the patient to the family member.

XII. OWNERSHIP AND INVESTMENT INTEREST EXCEPTIONS

The Stark law, at its heart, is a ban on referrals where the physician has an ownership interest. However, Congress at the same time recognized that there are legitimate investments that need to be protected through ownership exceptions. CMS implemented these exceptions in the Phase II Final Rule. The discussion of the definition of an ownership or investment interest and financial holdings excluded from that definition, such as certain stock options, is found at Section IV.C.4., above.

A. Publicly Traded Securities and Mutual Funds

The first of these statutory exceptions is for ownership of publicly traded securities or mutual funds. In identifying whether an ownership interest meets the exception for publicly traded securities, the Final Rules apply the following three-part test.

First, the securities owned by the physician or his or her family member "must be securities that may be purchased on terms generally available to the public."[258] Such investments include shares or bonds, debentures, notes, or other debt instruments. CMS interpreted this provision to mean the ownership interest must be in securities that are

---

[255] At this time, it is unclear whether patients living in so-called "micropolitan" statistical areas would be considered rural area patients for the purposes of this exception. CMS states that this issue will be resolved in a forthcoming regulation not related to the Stark law.

[256] 42 C.F.R. §411.355(j)(2).

[257] 69 Fed. Reg. at 16,084.

[258] 42 C.F.R. §411.356(a).

"generally available to the public *at the time of the DHS referral.*"[259] Under this interpretation, securities acquired by a referring physician or his or her family member prior to a public offering will fit within the exception (assuming other conditions in the exception are satisfied) if, at the time of the DHS referral, the securities are available to the public.

Second, to satisfy the exception, the securities owned by physicians must either be: (1) listed for trading with an exchange whose quotes are published daily, such as NYSE or ASE; or (2) traded under an automated interdealer quotation system operated by the National Association of Securities Dealers.[260]

Third, an investment will not constitute a prohibited financial interest as long as the securities are "in a corporation that had shareholder equity exceeding $75 million at the end of the corporation's most recent fiscal year or on average during the previous three fiscal years."[261] Similarly excepted are investments in mutual funds, as defined in Section 851(a) of the Internal Revenue Code, that have total assets exceeding $75 million at the end of the most recent fiscal year, or on average during the previous three fiscal years.[262]

B. Specific Providers

1. Hospital Ownership in Puerto Rico

The Stark law exempts an ownership or investment interest in a hospital located in Puerto Rico, and the Phase II Final Rule tracks this statutory language.[263]

2. Rural Providers

The Stark law's rural provider exception allows ownership or investment interests in providers that furnish DHS in rural areas.[264] Under the Stark law, as amended by the MMA, such rural providers may not be a specialty hospital (see the discussion in the next section) for the 18-month period beginning December 8, 2003. Further, under the Phase II Final Rule, a "rural provider" is an entity that furnishes at least 75 percent of its total DHS to residents of a rural area and is not within an urban area.[265] A rural area must therefore be a region outside of a Metropolitan Statistical Area.

In addition, the Phase II Final Rule creates a limited exception for referrals by a physician to a DHS entity with which his or her immediate family member has a relationship when the patient lives in a rural area. This exception is referred to as the "intra-family exception" and is discussed in more detail at Section XI.E., above.

---

[259] 69 Fed. Reg. at 16,081 (emphasis added).

[260] 42 C.F.R. §411.356(a)(1)(i) & (ii).

[261] *Id.* §411.356(a)(2).

[262] *Id.* §411.356(b).

[263] *Id.* §411.356(c)(2).

[264] *Id.* §411.356(c)(1).

[265] *Id.*

3. Hospital Ownership

The Stark law, as amended by MMA and implemented in the Phase II Final Rule, protects a physician's ownership interest in an entire hospital so long as (1) the referring physician is authorized to perform services at the hospital; (2) the hospital is not a specialty hospital for the 18-month period beginning December 8, 2003 ("the specialty-hospital moratorium"); and (3) the ownership interest is in the hospital as a whole, not merely a department or subsection.[266]

Specialty hospitals include hospitals primarily or exclusively engaged in the care and treatment of patients with a cardiac or orthopedic condition, or patients receiving a surgical procedure.[267] A physician may still refer to a specialty hospital in which he or she has an ownership interest if that hospital was "under development" as of November 18, 2003, as determined by Section 507 of the MMA, or alternatively, by an advisory opinion from CMS.[268] Such referrals are also permitted to specialty hospitals that were in operation as of November 18, 2003, so long as the hospitals do not subsequently: (1) add more physician investors; (2) furnish additional specialized services; or (3) add more beds, other than to the main campus of the hospital, and if so, not by more than five beds or 50 percent of the number of beds as of November 18, 2003. This specialty hospital moratorium also applies to ownership of such hospitals in rural areas that would otherwise be permitted under the rural exception.[269]

Previously, CMS interpreted the words "provided by the hospital" to mean that the services have been provided by a "hospital" under Medicare's conditions of participation, and not by a hospital-owned entity, such as a skilled nursing facility or home health agency.[270] Additionally, a physician can maintain an ownership or investment interest in a hospital through holding an interest in an organization that owns a chain of hospitals, such as a health system, because the statute does not require that the physician have a direct interest in the hospital.[271]

XIII. STATUTORY COMPENSATION EXCEPTIONS

The Phase II Final Rule addresses the statutory compensation exceptions for the first time. We have already discussed the statutory compensation exceptions for employment and personal services arrangements in Sections VI.H. and VIII.C., above.

---

[266]*Id.* §411.356(c)(3).

[267]*Id.* §411.351 (definition of "specialty hospital").

[268]For full text of the Stark law advisory opinions, see the CMS website at http://www.cms.hhs.gov/medlearn/refphys.asp#Specialty%20Hospital%20Issues and http://www.cms.hhs.gov/physicians/aop/ (as of November 2004).

[269]42 C.F.R. §411.356(c)(1).

[270]69 Fed. Reg. at 16,084.

[271]*Id.*

A. Rental of Office Space and Equipment

Virtually all of the exceptions for lease arrangements for office space and equipment contain the same conditions and therefore will be discussed together. The Stark law and Final Rules require the following for both of these exceptions:

- The agreement must be in writing, signed by the parties, and specify the premises or equipment covered.
- The agreement term must be at least one year.
- The rental charges over the term of the agreement must be set in advance and consistent with fair market value and not be determined in a manner that takes into account the volume or value of referrals or other business generated between the parties.
- The agreement would be commercially reasonable even if no referrals were made between the parties.
- The equipment or space rented or leased does not exceed that which is reasonable and necessary for the legitimate business purpose of the lease or rental and is used exclusively by the lessee when being used by the lessee and is not shared with or used by the lessor or any person or entity related to the lessor.
- A holdover month-to-month rental for up to six months immediately following an agreement of at least one year that met the conditions set out above may fall within these exceptions, provided the holdover rental is on the same terms and conditions as the immediately preceding agreement.[272]

Space and equipment rental arrangements have generated a number of specific issues that CMS has addressed in the final rules.

1. Termination Provisions

Under the one-year-term rule, lease or rental agreements may contain termination provisions with or without cause, provided that the parties do not enter into a new agreement during the original term.[273] CMS determined that there is little risk of abuse for month-to-month holdovers that proceed on the same terms and conditions as the original lease or rental terms, so long as the holdover is for a limited duration.[274] Therefore, holdovers that follow a lease agreement meeting all of the exception's requirements are permitted for up to six months.

2. Subleases

The Final Rules permit subleases as long as the lessor does not share—meaning use concurrently—space or equipment with the

---

[272]42 C.F.R. §411.357(a)(1)–(7).

[273]*Id.* §411.357(a)(2).

[274]69 Fed. Reg. at 16,086.

lessee.[275] In the Phase II Final Rule, CMS revisited its interpretation of "exclusively" and found that Congress did not intend for the exclusive use provisions to prohibit sublease arrangements, but intended only that these restrictions prevent concurrent shared use between the lessor and lessee.[276]

For example, the Preamble explains that "exclusively" means that if a physician practice rents examination rooms to a DHS entity, the physician practice may not then use the rooms while the lessee or a sublessee is using them or renting them.[277] However, as a means of preventing referring physicians or group practices from evading the rule by establishing separate real estate holding companies or subsidiaries to act as the "lessor," the Phase II Final Rule modifies the rule to prohibit the sharing of rented space with the lessor or any person *or entity* related to the lessor. Related entities would include, but not be limited to, group practices, group practice physicians, or other providers owned or operated by the lessor.[278]

With respect to space rental arrangements, the Final Rules permit the sharing of common rooms, but only if a specific formula is used.[279] The cost allocated to the lessee for common areas cannot exceed its pro rata share of these expenses based on the percentage of exclusive space used by the lessee compared to the total exclusive space by all other tenants.

CMS cautions that while the exception now permits sublease arrangements, such arrangements could also create indirect compensation arrangements that would need to fit within the indirect compensation exception to be acceptable.

3. "Per Click" or Per Use Leases

The final rules permit "per click" rental payments, provided that they are fair market value and do not take into account the volume or value of the physician's referrals or other business generated by the referring physician.[280] Alternatively, under certain circumstances, equipment rental leases may fit within the new fair market value exception, as discussed at Section VI.D. However, CMS states that because this fair market value exception is limited to items and services provided by physicians, it would not apply to space leases.[281]

4. Capital Leases

Reversing the Proposed Rule's interpretation that the space and equipment lease exceptions apply to operating leases only, the Phase II

---

[275] 42 C.F.R. §411.357(a)(3); 42 C.F.R. §411.357(b)(2).

[276] 69 Fed. Reg. at 16,086.

[277] *Id.*

[278] *Id.* §411.357(a)(3).

[279] *Id.*

[280] 42 C.F.R. §411.351 (definition of "fair market value"); 42 C.F.R. §411.354(d)(2); 69 Fed. Reg. at 16,085.

[281] 69 Fed. Reg. at 16,086.

Final Rule establishes that the exceptions apply to any kind of bona fide lease arrangement, including capital leases.

B. Physician Recruitment

The physician recruitment exception to the Stark law protects remuneration provided by a hospital to a physician for the purpose of inducing the physician to relocate to the geographic area served by the hospital in order to become a member of the hospital's medical staff, if certain conditions are met.[282] Specifically, the physician may not be required to refer patients to the hospital; and the amount of the remuneration under the arrangement may not be determined in a manner that takes into account, directly or indirectly, the volume or value of any referrals by the referring physician. In addition, CMS is authorized to impose other requirements to protect against program or patient abuse.

This exception is implemented in the Phase II Final Rule along with a new exception created by regulation for retention payments to physicians practicing in certain underserved areas, as described in Section XIV.H., below.

1. Providers Subject to the Rule

Tracking closely the statutory exception, the Final Rules generally only permit recruitment payments made by a hospital directly to the recruited physician. The two exceptions are for Federally Qualified Health Centers (FQHCs) and "seeding arrangements."

Federally Qualified Health Centers (FQHCs) are permitted to make recruitment payments to physicians on the same basis as hospitals, provided that the arrangement does not violate the anti-kickback statute or other federal or state laws or regulations governing billing or claims submission.[283] In addition, as discussed more fully below, CMS permits, under very stringent rules, so-called "seeding arrangements" whereby the recruited physician is placed in an existing practice. CMS otherwise declined to extend the exception to other DHS entities, such as nursing homes and home health agencies, or recruitment payments made by physician practices, due to a perceived risk of abuse in these types of arrangements.

2. Unavailability of Other Exceptions

In the Proposed Rule, CMS had suggested that physician recruitment payments to hospital residents living in the area and indirect payments to a physician practice could fit, as an alternative, within the fair market value exception.[284] In the Phase II Final Rule, CMS determined that recruitment payments cannot fit within the fair market value compensation exception because there is no exchange of

---

[282] *See generally* 42 U.S.C. §1395nn(e)(5).

[283] 42 C.F.R. §411.357(e)(4)(vii).

[284] 69 Fed. Reg. at 16,094.

services.[285] It is partly as a result of this rationale that CMS created specific rules for seeding arrangements.

Notwithstanding CMS's stated position—that because there is no exchange of service and therefore other exceptions do not apply—practitioners may wish to make their own evaluation. In particular, it seems that strong arguments can be made that most physician recruitment arrangements have two components to the remuneration. The first component involves direct recruitment-related expenses, such as recruitment fees, travel expenses for interviews, and moving expenses. The second component involves expenses related to start-up salary and practice expense subsidies for the recruited physician. In some cases, these expenses may involve an income guarantee to an independent contractor physician or an employed physician. Difficult analytic issues may need to be addressed in each situation. But one example is relatively straightforward. It is difficult to understand CMS's position that other exceptions do not apply in the case of a hospital recruiting a physician to become an employee, where it seems that both components of the expenses could be structured to fit within the employment exception.

3. Relocation Requirement

Instead of abandoning the relocation requirement as some commenters had urged, CMS has refined it. CMS explained the necessity of the relocation requirement to prevent against abusive recruitment arrangements, such as cross-town recruiting of an established physician practice by a competitor hospital.[286] Under the Final Rules, satisfying this requirement hinges on the location of the physician's practice, rather than the location of the physician's residence as suggested under the Proposed Rule.[287]

To meet the relocation requirement, the relocated physician must either (1) have relocated the site of his practice by at least 25 miles; or (2) derive at least 75 percent of his or her revenues (including inpatient services revenue) from new patients, meaning that the physician has not seen those patients at his prior medical practice site within the past three years.[288] To meet the 75 percent revenue test, the physician has the choice of being tested at the end of the calendar year, or the fiscal year.[289] Finally, CMS created special rules for the initial start-up year that permits physicians to measure the start-up year revenue according to whether it is reasonable to expect that the physician will meet the 75 percent test.[290]

---

[285] *Id.* at 16,095.
[286] *Id.*
[287] 42 C.F.R. §411.357(e)(2).
[288] *Id.* §411.357(e)(2)(i) & (ii).
[289] *Id.* §411.357(e)(ii).
[290] *Id.* §411.357(e)(2).

Additionally, for the first time, CMS defined the hospital's "geographic area" in which the recruited physician must be placed as the lowest number of contiguous postal zip codes from which the hospital draws at least 75 percent of its inpatients.[291]

CMS also waived the relocation requirement for hospital residents and physicians who have been in practice for less than one year. CMS based this special rule on its view that hospital residents and physicians in practice less than a year do not have an established practice to relocate. The only location requirement for these physicians is that they must establish their practice in the hospital's service area.

4. Referral Considerations

Under the Final Rules, the arrangement may not be conditioned on the recruited physician's referrals to the sponsoring hospital, but the physician is expected to join the medical staff of that hospital.[292] In addition, the physician must be allowed to join the medical staff of, and refer patients to, other hospitals, except where required referrals are permitted under the Final Rules.[293] The Phase II Final Rule indicates, however, that credentialing restrictions on physicians becoming competitors of a hospital would not violate this condition.[294]

5. Seeding Arrangements

Seeding arrangements are the most common form of recruitment arrangements for a variety of practical and strategic reasons. These include the natural desire to make sure the physicians do not practice alone and that the physician is a good fit with the existing group practice. This necessarily means that the existing group needs to be actively involved in the recruitment and committed to the successful start-up of the new practice.

While CMS seems to recognize this reality by creating special rules for such seeding arrangements, on closer examination CMS's rules are very narrow and permit few of the common seeding arrangements. It is in this one critical area that CMS does not hold true to its stated promise to avoid "undue disruption" of common financial arrangements.

CMS's narrow approach to seeding arrangements is first seen in the structure of the rule, which protects only hospital recruitment arrangements "paid directly" to the recruited physician, with additional requirements imposed where the payments are made indirectly through the existing group.[295] These additional requirements apply even where the payments are made directly to the recruited physician if that physician joins a group practice. In other words, these rules

---

[291] *Id.*
[292] 42 C.F.R. §411.351(e)(1)(ii).
[293] *Id.* §411.351(e)(1)(iv).
[294] 69 Fed. Reg. at 16,095.
[295] 42 C.F.R. §411.357(e)(1) & (e)(4).

apply in virtually all cases except in the unlikely event that the physician practices alone. Because of its stated concern about potential abuse, the rules require the following:

- the agreement is signed by the group, the hospital or FQHC, and the recruited physician;
- with the exception of actual costs incurred by the group in recruiting the physician, the remuneration must pass directly through to, and remain with, the recruited physician;
- in determining overhead costs for the new physician as part of an income guarantee, the group may allocate only those "actual additional incremental costs" attributable to the recruited physician;
- records of the actual costs and the costs passed through to the group must be retained for a period of at least five years and made available to CMS upon request;
- the "volume or value" restriction on the remuneration applies also to the volume or value of actual or anticipated referrals of the existing group;
- aside from quality conditions, the group may not impose additional practice restrictions, such as a non-compete, on the recruited physician; and
- the arrangement does not violate the anti-kickback statute and other federal or state laws or regulations governing billing and claims submission.[296]

Although some of these provisions are relatively straightforward, a few require further elaboration.

a. Flow of Funds

This part of the rule permits the group to pay the "actual costs incurred . . . in recruiting the new physician,"[297] but aside from those expenses, the remuneration from the hospital must be passed through directly to the recruited physician or remain with that physician if paid directly to him or her. This language raises a number of issues for practitioners.

First, it appears not to permit the group practice to hold and distribute the funds. Arguably, however, the group would be permitted so long as the remuneration eventually flows to the recruited physician. Second, and more troubling, it is not at all clear what CMS means by the words "actual costs." Does CMS mean merely the recruitment-specific costs, or does it include the practice start-up subsidies? This language could be read not to permit any overhead to be paid to the group for the costs it incurs in supporting the physician's practice. How-

---

[296]*Id.* §411.357(e)(4).
[297]*Id.* §411.3573(e)(4)(ii).

ever, this is an illogical reading, and conflicts with other provisions that appear to permit such overhead payments, at least when made as part of an income guarantee. In any case, as discussed above, if the recruited physician becomes an employee of the group, such overhead would clearly be permitted under the employment exception. Accordingly, it is difficult to understand why this provision would be read to prohibit such start-up subsidy payments.

b. Overhead Payments

For reasons that are not made clear, the literal language of the exception seems to permit overhead payments only in the context of income guarantees. Importantly, because of CMS's desire to curb perceived abuse, the exception permits such overhead costs to be picked up by the hospital only to the extent they do not exceed the "actual additional incremental costs" attributed to the recruited physician.[298] This stringent standard prohibits the common form of overhead calculation whereby the group has an allocation formula that applies to the entire group, and that formula is applied to the recruited physician. These formulae vary among groups, but generally apply certain costs (for example, corporate and billing costs) on a pro rata basis; other costs (such as rent and equipment expenses) on a site-specific basis; and still other costs (such as salary expenses) directly to the physician.

These overhead formulae are typically applied to the recruited physician for a number of reasons, including that the existing physicians in the group have a natural expectation that a new physician will help share the load and that special rules applicable only to newly recruited physicians raise complications and can be difficult to apply. The Final Rules, however, will require the parties to create and agree on a formula as to what constitutes the "actual additional incremental costs."

It is difficult to understand what abuse CMS seeks to curb by prohibiting a group practice from using a pre-existing overhead formula it applies to all existing group practice members. Moreover, there may well be situations where the requirements of this provision of the Final Rules lead to the hospital paying *more* than it would otherwise pay. Take for example a situation where the group practice needs to build out space in order to take in a new physician. Under the group's pre-existing rules, the cost of that new space might be allocated pro-rata to the entire group or to the physician members who practice at that location, but in any case through some type of averaging methodology. In this example, the recruited physician would pick up only the average cost of this new space. However, under CMS's methodology, the entire actual additional incremental cost of this new space would be allocated to the recruited physician, and subject to financial support by the hospital.

CMS has provided guidance, clarifying that while the provisions of the recruitment exception regulation went into effect with other

---

[298]*Id.* §411.357(e)(4)(iii).

parts of the Phase II Final Rule on July 26, 2004, "past payments under an income guarantee need not be recalculated so long as, at the time they were paid, the arrangement complied with a reasonable interpretation of the statute."[299]

c. Practice Restrictions

The Final Rules broadly prohibit the group practice from imposing "additional practice restrictions" that are unrelated to quality.[300] The preamble to the Phase II Final Rule cites a non-competition agreement as one type of impermissible practice restriction.[301] This restriction raises numerous questions, some of which turn on the meaning of the word "additional" in this context.

On the one hand, these words could be read to prohibit even the basic requirement that the physician remain in the service area for a specified number of years after the support payments end. On the other hand, the principal purpose of the payments under the exception is to permit the physician to relocate to a new area. Under this reading, perhaps CMS would view a requirement that the physician remain in the service area as not an "additional" practice restriction, but one designed to implement the fundamental purposes of the exception. It is less clear how to analyze a requirement that the recruited physician accept Medicare and Medicaid patients. Although it is difficult to see how or why CMS would want to prohibit such a provision in recruitment agreements, it is even less clear how a textual reading of the exception would permit such requirements.

This provision is another example of the problems CMS has caused by appearing not to permit the employment exception to apply. Where state law permits non-competition agreements, it would seem permissible under the employment exception for a group practice to include such agreements in their employment contracts.

In any case, as discussed above, CMS appears to prohibit in recruitment agreements common formula and contract provisions that group practices apply to all of their members. It is difficult to see the abuse that CMS seems to think exists and needs to be stopped if all group practice members as well as the recruited physicians live under the same rules.

6. Anti-Kickback Compliance

Implicit in the requirement that all recruitment arrangements comply with the anti-kickback statute is that if there is an intent to unlawfully induce referrals from the physician practice whose recruitment the hospital underwrites, this Stark law compensation exception would not apply. A more detailed discussion of the implications of requiring anti-kickback compliance is found at Section XVI., below.

---

[299] No. 3163 of the Frequently Asked Questions posted on CMS's website on July 14, 2004, *available at* http://www.cms.hhs.gov/faqsearch/faqfull.asp?faq_id=3163.

[300] 42 C.F.R. §411.357(e)(4)(vi).

[301] 69 Fed. Reg. at 16,096–97.

7. Other Issues

The Final Rules are starkly silent[302] in two areas that most practitioners consider important for complying with other laws. The recruitment exception does not require that the recruited physician fill a community need. Such community-need analysis, with appropriate documentation, is required by the IRS under its exempt organization rules for tax-exempt hospitals. Many practitioners also consider such community-need analysis important for compliance with the anti-kickback statute.

Also missing under the Final Rules is any requirement that the recruitment payments meet a fair market value test. Thus, the amount of the payments is irrelevant for Stark law compliance, so long as such payments are not based on the volume or value of referrals. Again, such a fair market value test is required by the IRS, and deemed important for compliance with the anti-kickback statute.

C. Isolated Transactions

Consistent with the statutory exception, the Final Rules permit isolated transactions, such as the one-time sale of a property or medical practice, as long as the transaction is consistent with fair market value, meets the volume or value and other business generated standards, and is commercially reasonable even if no referrals are made.[303] In the Phase II Final Rule, CMS provides additional requirements and several useful interpretations.

First, CMS defines the term isolated "transaction" to include "integrally related installment payments," provided that the total aggregate payment amount is established before the first payment is made and does not take into account referrals or other business generated.[304] To curtail the incentive of assuring payments through continued referrals, the Final Rules also require that the payments be immediately negotiable if any outstanding balance is guaranteed by a third party, secured by a negotiable promissory note, or subject to a similar mechanism that assures payment.

Second, the parties may not conduct any additional transactions within six months following the sale, unless the arrangements fit within one of the other exceptions.[305] CMS declined to substitute a maximum number of such allowable transactions.

Third, the Final Rules permit post-closing adjustments made within six months of the date of sale, so long as they are commercially reasonable even in the absence of other referrals or generated business.[306] CMS clarified in the Phase II Final Rule that the prohibition applies to all transactions, because any type of financial relationship—

---

[302] Pun intended.

[303] 42 C.F.R. §411.357(f).

[304] *Id.* §411.351 (definition of "transaction").

[305] *Id.* §411.357(f)(3).

[306] *Id.* §411.357(f)(2).

not only those involving DHS—can create a prohibited financial relationship between a DHS entity and a referring physician.[307]

D. Remuneration Unrelated to the Provision of Designated Health Services

The Stark law creates an exception for remuneration by a hospital that is unrelated to the provision of DHS.[308] In the Phase II Final Rule, CMS interprets this exception very narrowly.[309] Specifically, the remuneration must be "wholly unrelated" to the provision of DHS. The Phase II Final Rule establishes that remuneration is *not* "wholly unrelated" to the provision of DHS if it: (1) is any item, service, or cost that could be allocated in whole or in part to Medicare or Medicaid under applicable cost-reporting principles; (2) is given directly or indirectly, explicitly or implicitly, in a selective, targeted, preferential, or conditional manner to medical staff or other physicians who are in a position to make or influence referrals; or (3) otherwise takes into account the volume or value of referrals or other business generated.

In the preamble to the Phase II Final Rule, CMS commented that payments for the rental of residential property are the type of unrelated remuneration contemplated by the exception, but that payments for malpractice insurance and medical devices would be construed as related to the provision of DHS.[310] Similarly, CMS warned that it would view a loan from a hospital to a physician to finance the physician's purchase in a limited partnership that owns the hospital as related to DHS. Likewise, a hospital's lease of office space in a nearby medical building to physicians in a position to refer to the hospital would be related to DHS.

Viewing any item, service, or cost that could be allocated to Medicare or Medicaid as related to DHS, CMS withdrew its interpretation in the Proposed Rule that administrative and utilization review services are not related to DHS.[311] Further, the Phase II Final Rule explains that under the "wholly unrelated" test, even if the remuneration is not covered by cost-reporting principles, the remuneration may relate to DHS by being given to medical staff who are in a position to make referrals.

CMS declined to extend the exception to cover remuneration from a hospital to a physician's immediate family member. Further, the Phase II Final Rule states that CMS will apply a presumption that payments above fair market value for services unrelated to the provision of DHS are actually related to such services.[312] Responding to the contention that CMS lacked the authority to impose an additional require-

---

[307] 69 Fed. Reg. at 16,018.
[308] 42 U.S.C. §1395nn(e)(4); 42 C.F.R. §411.357(g).
[309] 42 C.F.R. §411.357(g).
[310] 69 Fed. Reg. at 16,093–94.
[311] *Id.*
[312] *Id.* at 16,094.

ment that the payments be at fair market value, CMS stated that payments exceeding that threshold will be carefully scrutinized. CMS also rejected the suggestion that entities other than hospitals should be able to make unrelated DHS payments and qualify for the exception. Finally, despite recognizing that covenants not to compete are not necessarily equivalent to an obligation to make referrals, the Phase II Final Rule clarified that such agreements clearly relate to DHS and, consequently, need to fall within another exception to be acceptable.

E. Certain Group Practice Arrangements With Hospitals

The Phase II Final Rule adopts, with minimal modification, the Stark law exception for group practice arrangements with hospitals in which the group furnishes DHS and the hospital bills for these services.[313] The statute and Final Rules require that the arrangement with the group must have been in effect without interruption since the date of enactment of Stark I (December 19, 1989), and that certain other prophylactic provisions be in place, including that the agreement be in writing, with the compensation at fair market value and meeting the volume or value, other business generated, and commercially reasonable tests. Finally, the statutory exception requires that, with respect to "under arrangement" agreements, substantially all of the services furnished to patients of the hospital be furnished by the group under arrangement. In the Phase II Final Rule, CMS interprets "substantially all" to mean that at least 75 percent of the DHS covered under the arrangement.[314]

F. Payments Made by a Physician for Items and Services

This statutory exception protects payments by a physician either to a laboratory in exchange for the provision of laboratory services, or alternatively, to an entity as compensation for other items or services, when these are furnished at a price consistent with fair market value.[315] In the Phase II Final Rule, CMS extends the exception to cover payments by a referring physician's immediate family member. In addition, CMS interprets the term "other items or services" to mean any kind of items or services that a physician might purchase, but not including clinical laboratory services. CMS abandoned the controversial requirement in the Proposed Rule that the amount of the discount would have to be passed on in full to patients or their insurers and could not in any way benefit the physician.[316] The Phase II Final Rule explains that further consideration of this discount exception led CMS to conclude that legitimate discounts would fall within the range of values that is "fair market value."[317]

---

[313] 42 U.S.C. §1395nn(e)(7); 42 C.F.R. §411.357(h).

[314] 42 C.F.R. §411.357(h)(3).

[315] *Id.* §411.357(i).

[316] *Id.*

[317] 69 Fed. Reg. at 16,099.

Finally, in an attempt to narrow the apparent breadth of this statutory exception, CMS requires that allowable compensation for other items and services must not be specifically excepted under another exception.[318] In other words, CMS is allowing this exception to be used only where no other exception could apply. Although it is understandable why CMS would want to narrow the availability of this exception, there is little textual support for this interpretation, and it does not appear that Congress gave CMS explicit authority to create other regulatory protections for this exception as it did under other exceptions, such as for physician recruitment, or under its authority to grant new ownership and compensation exceptions where CMS finds no risk of program or patient abuse.

XIV. COMPENSATION EXCEPTIONS CREATED BY REGULATION

A. Introduction

In addition to the regulation-created exceptions related to both ownership and compensation arrangements, the Phase I Final Rule also established six regulatory exceptions specific to compensation arrangements. Three of these, including the fair market value, indirect compensation, and risk-sharing exceptions, are discussed above in Sections VI.D., VII., and IX., above. The remaining three, including nonmonetary compensation or gifts, compliance training, and medical staff incidental benefits, as well as six new compensation exceptions promulgated in the Phase II Final Rules, are discussed below in the order they appear in the Final Rules. To help practitioners locate the relevant preamble previsions, we have noted if the exception appears first in Phase I (in which case the exception was modified in Phase II) or Phase II.

B. Charitable Donations by Physicians (Phase II)

In the Phase II Final Rule, CMS reassured commenters that a charitable contribution from a referring physician to a DHS entity will not violate the Stark law.[319] Although CMS could have simply excluded charitable contributions from the definition of remuneration, it has instead chosen to craft a regulatory exception, based on its reasoning that such a payment would constitute remuneration as defined in the statute.[320] For a contribution to qualify for the exception, the recipient of the contribution must be a tax-exempt organization, and the donation from the physician must not be solicited, nor made in any manner that takes into account the volume or value of referrals or other business generated between the physician and the tax-exempt entity.[321] For

---

[318] 42 C.F.R. §411.357(i)(2).
[319] 69 Fed. Reg. at 16,116.
[320] *Id.*
[321] 42 C.F.R. §411.357(j).

example, the exception permits contributions made to a broad-based fund-raising campaign that reaches physicians and non-physicians alike.

C. Nonmonetary Compensation (Phase I)

The nonmonetary compensation exception applies to gifts or benefits provided by a referral recipient to a physician. To comply with the exception, the gift or benefit (1) must not be in cash or a cash equivalent; (2) must not exceed an aggregate of $300 per year; (3) must not be determined so as to take into account the volume or value of referrals or other business generated by the referring physician; (4) must not be solicited by the physician or the physician's practice; and (5) must not violate the federal anti-kickback statute.[322] In the Phase II Final Rule, CMS revised this exception to add that the $300 limit will be adjusted each calendar year based on inflation.[323]

D. Medical Staff Incidental Benefits (Phase I)

Phase I created an exception for incidental benefits, other than cash or cash equivalents, provided by a hospital to a member of its medical staff.[324] The types of benefits that might fall within this exception include reduced or free parking, free computer/Internet access, and meals. In general, this exception requires that the benefits must be used on the hospital's campus and offered to all medical staff members without regard to the volume or value of referrals. In addition, the benefits must be offered only during the periods when staff members are making rounds or performing other hospital or patient-related duties, and must be reasonably related to the hospital's medical services.

Responding to the Phase I version of this exception, commenters voiced concern that referring physicians are often involved in patient care while physically remote from the DHS entity, and urged CMS to modify the exception to include incidental benefits that facilitate these exchanges.[325] In response to these concerns, in the Phase II Final Rule, CMS maintained the so-called "on campus rule," but modified the rule to accommodate the use of electronic or Internet services from a remote site. Accordingly, a DHS entity may provide a physician with a device such as a two-way pager or Internet connection to be used off-site, so long as the usage relates to services or activities that benefit the hospital or its patients (e.g., communication during urgent patient care situations).[326] The Phase II Final Rule also expanded the scope of the exception beyond hospitals to include any DHS entity that has a bona fide medical staff, and eliminated the requirement that incidental

---

[322] *Id.* §411.357(k)(1).
[323] *Id.* §411.357(k)(2).
[324] *Id.* §411.357(m).
[325] 69 Fed. Reg. at 16,112.
[326] 42 C.F.R. §411.357(m)(3).

benefits be comparable to those offered at hospitals in the same region. The benefits offered must not exceed $25 per occurrence and, similar to the non-monetary compensation exception, this $25 limit will be adjusted each calendar year for inflation. In addition, as with many other exceptions, the compensation arrangement must not violate the federal anti-kickback statute.

The exception does not apply if the physician would already employ the technology for his or her own practice, as when, for instance, the physician already had an Internet connection in his or her own office.[327] The referring physician's use of a DHS entity's health information system is addressed in a separate exception discussed below.

E. Compliance Training (Phase I)

The compliance training exception applies to compliance training provided by an entity to a referring physician who practices in the entity's local community or service area, or to the physician's office staff, and requires that such training be held in the local community or service area.[328] Training held outside the entity's service area does not come within the exception, ostensibly because travel to what could be a vacation resort could confer an additional benefit upon the referring physician.

Such training must either cover the basic elements of a compliance program, specific training regarding the requirements of federal and state health care programs, or training regarding other federal, state or local laws, regulations or rules governing the conduct of the party for whom the training is provided.[329] Thus, a qualifying general training program can focus on training-related policies and procedures, training of staff, or internal monitoring and reporting, while a qualifying specific program should focus, for example, on such requirements as billing, coding, medical necessity, and unlawful referral arrangements.

The exception does not include continuing medical education (CME); however, CME may be covered under the nonmonetary compensation exception, depending on the cost of the program.[330]

F. Referral Services and Obstetrical Malpractice Insurance Subsidies (Phase II)

In the Phase II Final Rule, CMS carved out two new regulatory exceptions for conduct that complies with two safe harbors of the anti-kickback statute. The first of these exceptions includes any arrangement that fits within the safe harbor for referral services and the second applies to arrangements complying with the obstetrical malpractice insurance subsidies safe harbor.[331]

---

[327] *Id.*
[328] 42 C.F.R. §411.357(o).
[329] *Id.*
[330] 69 Fed. Reg. at 16,115.
[331] 42 C.F.R. §411.357(q) & (r).

Unfortunately, because the safe harbor for subsidies for obstetrical malpractice applies only to HPSAs,[332] support arrangements outside of HPSAs will not qualify under this Stark law exception, thereby making it difficult for most such subsidies to continue. See Section XVI., below, for a discussion of the interrelationship of the anti-kickback statute and its safe harbors to the Stark law.

G. Professional Courtesy (Phase II)

The Final Rules also exempt professional courtesies from the compensation prohibition. This common and long-standing practice, whereby the DHS entity furnishes medical services at no cost or at a reduced cost to referring physicians and their family and staff, is permitted where (1) the courtesy is offered without regard to the volume or value of referrals generated between the parties; (2) the items or services are of a type routinely provided by the DHS entity; (3) the DHS entity maintains a professional courtesy policy which is set out in writing and approved by the entity's governing body; and (4) the professional courtesy is not offered to a physician who is a federal health care program beneficiary unless there has been a good faith showing of financial need; and (5) the arrangement does not violate the federal anti-kickback statute.[333] If the professional courtesy involves any whole or partial reduction in any coinsurance obligation, the insurer must be informed in writing of the reduction. As noted above, the professional courtesy policy must be approved by the entity's governing body in order to qualify for this exception.

H. Retention Payments in Underserved Areas (Phase II)

In response to commenters' concerns about physician turnover in underserved areas, the Phase II Final Rule provided a new exception for retention payments from a DHS entity hospital or FQHC to a referring physician, irrespective of the physician's specialty.[334] To qualify for the exception, the physician must currently practice within an HPSA, or, as explained below, obtain an advisory opinion from the Secretary confirming that there is a demonstrated need for the physician in the area. The physician must also have a bona fide written recruitment offer, including salary, from another hospital or FQHC. Except as explained below, the offer must require the physician to relocate his or her practice at least 25 miles *and* outside of the current hospital's service area. Further, CMS requires the usual prophylactic rules, for example, that the arrangement must be set out in writing and signed by the parties, cannot be conditioned on the physician's referral of patients to the hospital, must allow the physician to establish staff

---

[332]*Id.* §1001.952(o).

[333]*Id.* §411.357(s).

[334]*Id.* §411.357(t).

privileges at any other hospital except as restricted under an allowable separate employment or services contract, and must not violate the anti-kickback statute.

CMS limits the amount of the retention payment to the lesser of: (1) the difference between the physician's current income from physician and related services and the income proposed in the recruitment offer, calculated over no more than a 24-month period using a consistent methodology; or (2) the reasonable costs the hospital or FQHC must expend to recruit a new physician as a replacement.[335] Any retention payment is subject to the same obligations and restrictions, if any, on repayment or forgiveness of indebtedness as the bona fide recruitment offer. A hospital or FQHC may offer retention payments to a particular physician no more frequently than once every five years. Retention payments paid indirectly to the physician through a physician practice are not permissible.

Finally, the regulation gives CMS the authority to determine on a case-by-case basis, through advisory opinions, whether the physician is serving in areas with a demonstrated need that do not qualify as HPSAs. Additionally, the Secretary may waive, through an advisory opinion, the relocation requirement for a physician practicing in an HPSA or other underserved area.[336]

Both of these advisory opinion processes are new in the Phase II Final Rule and mark the first time that CMS is following the OIG process of case-by-case exceptions. Previously, CMS limited its advisory opinions to answering questions about whether a particular arrangement was prohibited by the Stark law. It will be very interesting to follow how many providers avail themselves of this process and how freely CMS creates exceptions. Although CMS indicated in the preamble to the Phase II Final Rule that it will use this authority sparingly to grant health manpower-need exceptions, it may well be faced with the reality that the hospital will lose the physician in question and then pay more money for a new recruit without needing to show a demonstrated need to CMS.

I. Community-Wide Health Information Systems (Phase II)

In addition to the incidental benefits exception described above permitting payments for certain portable technologies, the Phase II Final Rule also added a separate exception for hardware and software that enable a referring physician to access the DHS entity's health information infrastructure.[337] CMS does not consider this to be remuneration, because it confers a benefit upon the DHS entity and facilitates patient care. A community-wide health information system

---

[335]*Id.* §411.357(t)(1)(iv)(A) & (B).
[336]*Id.* §411.357(t)(2).
[337]*Id.* §411.357(u).

meets this exception if it: (1) is available to all practitioners; (2) allows for sharing of electronic health care records; (3) does not replace hardware or software that the physician would purchase for his or her own practice; (4) does not take into account the volume or value of referrals; and (5) does not violate the anti-kickback statute.

XV. REPORTING REQUIREMENTS AND SANCTIONS

Inadvertently, CMS omitted provisions explaining the reporting requirements from the preamble of the Phase II Final Rule. CMS issued a technical correction on April 6, 2004, with these preamble sections.[338]

A. Reporting Requirements

Under the Stark law, all entities that provide items or services payable under Medicare must comply with the reporting requirements. Under the Final Rules, CMS may collect information on UPIN numbers of the referring physician with a financial relationship, and the covered items and services provided by the DHS entity.[339] The reporting requirements are waived for DHS entities providing 20 or fewer Part A or B services during a calendar year or for DHS provided outside the United States. For physicians with a reportable financial relationship as defined in the Final Rules (see discussion below), CMS may collect information on the nature of the financial relationship as evidenced in records that the entity knows or should know about "in the course of prudently conducting business." This information would include, but is not limited to, records that the entity is already required to retain to comply with IRS, Securities Exchange Commission, and Medicare and Medicaid program rules

A reportable financial relationship includes any ownership or investment interest or any compensation arrangement, except ownership arrangements meeting the exceptions for publicly traded entities and mutual funds.[340] This means that DHS entities whose shares or debt instruments are so traded and meet these exceptions need not keep track of whether its referring physicians own an interest in the entity. The Phase II Final Rule clarified that this exemption only applies to shareholder information, and that DHS entities must report other financial relationships with referring physicians who are shareholders, such as personal service arrangements.[341]

The regulatory history of the reporting requirements illustrates the evolving understanding of CMS of the complications of interpreting

---

[338] Medicare Program; Physicians' Referrals to Health Care Entities With Which They Have Financial Relationships (Phase II); Correction, 69 Fed. Reg. 17,933 (Apr. 6, 2004).

[339] 42 C.F.R. §411.361(c).

[340] *Id.* §411.361(d).

[341] 69 Fed. Reg. at 17,934.

and enforcing the Stark law. The Stark I regulation provided that entities must submit the requisite information on a form prescribed by CMS within 30 days of the request, and that all changes to that information must be submitted to CMS within 60 days from the date of the change.[342] Specifically, HCFA Form 96, effective January 1, 1992, and entitled "Clinical Laboratory Financial Relationships with Physicians," is a Medicare carrier survey requiring disclosure of the financial relationships between entities furnishing clinical laboratory services and physicians. Similarly, HCFA Form 97, also effective January 1, 1992, is a Medicare fiscal-intermediary survey requiring disclosure of financial relationships between physicians and hospital and facility-based clinical laboratories. Although both forms contain a box indicating that a form is being used to update previous information, and indeed the instructions to these forms indicate that such updating is required, CMS informally had indicated that it was not requiring providers of clinical laboratory services to update these forms as financial relationships change.

In the Stark II Proposed Rule, CMS acknowledged that it was still in the process of developing the statutorily prescribed reporting process and the necessary forms, and that until it completed this process, physicians and entities were not required to report.[343] CMS proposed to amend the reporting regulations in three ways: (1) by specifying that entities would need only to report changes to the requested information once a year, instead of within 60 days of the date of the change; (2) by specifying that all financial relationships would need to be reported, even if those relationships satisfy an exception to the Stark law; and (3) by developing a streamlined reporting system that would not require entities to retain and submit large quantities of data.[344]

In the Phase II Final Rule, CMS appears to have backed off completely any requirement for the regular submission of such information with updates as financial relationships change. CMS indicated that it does not even intend to issue any reporting forms at all.[345] Although the regulation preserves CMS's right to collect financial information, if CMS decides to create a form, it would need to obtain Office of Management and Budget approval.

B. Sanctions

Violations of the prohibition on physician self-referrals may result in either Medicare's nonpayment of claims for DHS provided as a result of a prohibited referral, an obligation to refund payment amounts, or, for a knowing violation, a civil monetary

---

[342] *Id.* at 17,933; 42 C.F.R. §411.361.

[343] 63 Fed. Reg. at 1703.

[344] *See generally id.* at 1703–04.

[345] 69 Fed. Reg. at 17,934; 42 C.F.R. §411.361(e).

penalty (CMP) of up to $15,000 per violation or $100,000 per arrangement.[346]

Because there is a violation each time an entity submits a claim for DHS resulting from a prohibited referral, the $15,000 per violation CMP, coupled with the denial of payment sanction, can lead to substantial amounts even for limited infractions of the rules. Significantly, in the Phase I Final Rule, CMS made clear that under the Stark law physicians are not liable for payment recoupments for claims submitted in violation of the law, but are liable only for CMPs, and only where the government has shown the physicians acted with knowledge of the violation.

The Phase II Final Rule made no changes to the existing sanction provisions under subsection (g) of the Stark law. These regulations implementing the civil money penalty provisions were issued by the OIG on March 31, 1995.[347]

XVI. Differences Between the Stark Law and the Federal Anti-Kickback Statute

Although the Stark law and the anti-kickback statute are intended to combat the same perceived harms, the two provisions must be analyzed separately. In enacting Stark I congressional conferees stated:

> The conferees wish to clarify that any prohibition, exemption, or exception authorized under this provision in no way alters (or reflects on) the scope and application of the anti-kickback provisions in section 1128B of the Social Security Act. The conferees do not intend that this provision should be construed as affecting, or in any way interfering with, the efforts of the Inspector General to enforce current law, such as cases described in the recent Fraud Alert issued by the Inspector General. In particular, entities, which would be eligible for a specific exemption, would be subject to all of the provisions of current law.[348]

Two of the most significant differences between the two laws are the differences in the required proof of intent and the need to comply with exceptions or safe harbors. First, a violation of the Stark law occurs without proof of illegal intent, and thus it is a strict liability offense.[349] In other words, if there is a financial relationship between an entity and a physician, and the physician refers Medicare or Medicaid patients to the entity for designated services, then the arrangement *must* fall within one of the exceptions to avoid violating the self-referral prohibition. By contrast, the anti-kickback statute is a criminal statute requiring proof of criminal intent to induce referrals. Violations are punishable by fines, imprisonment, or both.

---

[346]42 U.S.C. §1395nn(g).

[347]Civil Money Penalties for Referrals to Entities and for Prohibited Arrangements and Schemes, 60 Fed. Reg. 16,580 (Mar. 31, 1995), *codified at* 42 C.F.R. §1003.102(a)(5) (2004).

[348]H.R. Conf. Rep. No. 386, at 856 (1989).

[349]As discussed in Section XV.B., above, regarding sanctions, civil monetary penalties are assessed under the Stark law only on proof of a knowing violation.

Second, the exceptions and safe harbors operate very differently under each statute. One of the confusions between the Stark law and anti-kickback statute is that many of the Stark law exceptions were modeled after the anti-kickback statute's safe harbors. In both cases, the fundamental objective is the same: to create a set of prophylactic rules that dissipate any potential influence of money on referral decisions. However, the anti-kickback statute's regulatory safe harbors are made for certain business conduct the government has determined is innocuous or beneficial even if there is a possible taint of money and referrals. If a provider meets all of the standards of a particular safe harbor, the conduct is immune from prosecution. Failure to comply fully with a safe harbor, however, has no legal effect; rather if the government objects to the arrangement it must still prove illegal intent to induce referrals. By implication, if an arrangement substantially—but not fully—complies with a safe harbor, there is no penalty; it merely means that the parties will not be fully protected by that safe harbor. In contrast, the failure to comply *fully and completely* with a Stark law exception means that the entire financial arrangement is not in compliance with the statute.

Other significant differences are set forth below:

- The Stark law applies only to prohibited referrals under the Medicare and Medicaid programs, whereas the anti-kickback statute applies to all federally funded health care programs.[350]
- The Stark law regulates conduct within a physician's own practice, whereas the anti-kickback statute has never been interpreted by a court to apply to a referral to oneself.
- The Stark law regulates physician compensation, whereas the anti-kickback statute generally does not, with the exception that the safe harbors specify that compensation must be at fair market value.
- The Stark law prohibits paying bona fide employees for referrals unless the directed referrals exception is met, whereas the anti-kickback statute does not.
- The Stark law applies only to relationships between physicians and entities, whereas any two parties may violate the anti-kickback statute.
- The Stark law prohibits only referrals, whereas the anti-kickback statute prohibits wider forms of misconduct, including, inter alia, arranging for and/or recommending the purchase of items or services.
- The principal remedy under the Stark law is denial of payment, whereas the anti-kickback statute is principally a criminal felony prohibition.

---

[350] 42 U.S.C. §1320a-7b(b).

- The principal remedy of denial of payment under the Stark law applies only to the provider billing for the service rendered pursuant to a prohibited referral under the Stark law, whereas both parties to an illegal kickback arrangement are equally vulnerable.

Clearly, in some of these cases the ambit of the Stark law is broader than that of the anti-kickback statute, and in other cases it is narrower. Because of these significant differences, it is imperative that practitioners conduct a separate analysis of the applicability of both statutes to a financial relationship.

CMS confuses the supposed distinction between the two statutes in two ways. First, there are several Stark law exceptions (such as physician recruitment, fair market value, and indirect compensation arrangements) that are conditioned on compliance with the anti-kickback statute as defined in the Final Rules.[351] Second, in response to Phase I comments, CMS promulgated two exceptions in Phase II for arrangements that comply with the safe harbors for referral services and obstetrical malpractice insurance subsidies. Each of these exceptions is discussed in detail in Section XIV.F., above.

We find troubling CMS's continued reliance on anti-kickback statute compliance as a condition for qualifying under certain Stark law exceptions. This approach introduces intent as an element of the Stark law analysis, which is inconsistent with CMS's goal of providing clear, bright-line rules. We are also not satisfied with CMS's explanation that this approach is required by the statute's dictate that any exceptions created by regulation must pose "no risk of abuse." The OIG has had close to 15 years of drafting safe harbors, and has sufficient experience in developing prophylactic rules that minimize abuse, without resorting to an analysis of whether there is unlawful intent to induce referrals as a condition of complying with the Stark law.

While conceptually there is merit in certain circumstances to tie safe harbor compliance with compliance with Stark exceptions, the exception for malpractice subsidies demonstrates the pitfalls. The narrowness of the parallel safe harbor for malpractice subsidies combined with the incorporation of that safe harbor into the Stark law renders it difficult for most such subsidies to continue.

We believe, however, that there is an important need to harmonize the compliance provisions of both statutes. We disagree with CMS's position that full compliance with a Stark law exception is irrelevant to compliance with the anti-kickback statute. Rather, the guiding principle should be: (i) as long as an arrangement is covered by the Stark law, (ii) there is no agreement or condition for referrals that does not comply with the final rules' directed referrals exception, and (iii) the arrangement complies with a Stark law exception, the OIG should grant it safe harbor protection as well.

---

[351] 42 C.F.R. §411.351 (definition of "does not violate the anti-kickback statute").

XVII. STARK LAW ADVISORY OPINION FINAL RULE

In 1989, the House of Representatives voted as part of its consideration of Stark I to authorize an advisory opinion process that would permit case-by-case review of arrangements where providers can demonstrate that the services would otherwise be unavailable, more convenient based on reduced travel time, and provided at a lower unit charge and lower overall cost to the Medicare program than comparable services.[352] This approach was rejected by the conferees and lay dormant until 1996—despite commentary urging action[353]—when Congress authorized advisory opinions under the anti-kickback statute.[354] The OIG's implementing regulation in 1997 adopted just such a case-by-case approach.[355]

The BBA extended the advisory opinion process to the Stark law in response to the health care industry's justifiable confusion concerning the parameters of the self-referral prohibition. The advisory opinion final rule established a process for seeking guidance as to whether existing or proposed arrangements violate the Stark law.[356] At the same time, CMS also imposed what could be very difficult criteria for the requests, certain risks, and somewhat onerous burdens on the parties seeking advisory opinions.

In general, based on the congressional directive in the BBA, CMS has patterned the advisory opinion final rule after the OIG anti-kickback advisory opinion regulations, including similar limitations, timing, and procedural rules.[357] The most significant difference between the two advisory opinion processes is that in the anti-kickback advisory opinion process the OIG has adopted a case-specific approach whereby it is free to waive certain safe harbor standards or impose additional requirements on a particular transaction. In contrast, with the exception of the advisory opinions authorized for physician retention payments (see discussion at Section XIV.H., above), the advisory opinions to be issued under the Stark law will analyze merely whether a transaction falls within the statute and, if so, whether it also satisfies the criteria for one of the exceptions. Thus, the advisory opinions under the Stark law are likely to be much narrower and have less utility than those issued under the anti-kickback statute. Given the clear congressional mandate to follow the OIG's process, CMS's rigid

---

[352] H.R. CONF. REP. NO. 386, at 847–48.

[353] *See, e.g.,* Thomas S. Crane, *The Problem of Physician Self Referral Under the Anti-Kickback Statute: The* Hanlester Network *Case and the Safe Harbor Regulation,* 268 JAMA, 85, 90 (1992).

[354] 42 U.S.C. §1320a-7d(b).

[355] 42 C.F.R. pt. 1008.

[356] *See generally* 63 Fed. Reg. at 1646. *See also* Medicare Program; Physicians' Referrals to Entities With Which They Have Financial Relationships (Phase II), Correcting Amendment, 69 Fed. Reg. 57,226 (Sept. 24, 2004), *codified at* 42 C.F.R. §§411.370–.389.

[357] *See generally id.* For regulations on the Stark law advisory opinion process, see Appendix B-3 at the end of this volume. For full text of the advisory opinions, see the CMS website at http://www.cms.hhs.gov/medlearn/refphys.asp#Specialty%20Hospital%20Issues and http://www. cms.hhs.gov/physicians/aop/ (as of November 2004).

approach in the advisory opinion final rule appears to fall well short of fulfilling its statutory mandate.

A Stark law advisory opinion is available only for existing or soon-to-be consummated arrangements. A party submitting a request must certify that all of the information provided is true and correct, and that it intends in good faith to enter into the arrangement if it does not already exist.[358] CMS will not provide an opinion regarding hypothetical or generalized arrangements. Once the advisory opinion is issued, it is binding upon the Secretary and the requesting party. Although the Secretary retains the authority to revoke an opinion after its issuance, the requesting party does not have any recourse if it is not satisfied with the result. In addition, there is a risk of sanctions following any adverse advisory opinion. CMS has indicated that it will use the information disclosed in the process against the requesting party and others in subsequent civil, criminal, or administrative actions.

Despite a lack of explicit statutory authority, the advisory opinion final rule specifies that CMS will charge a fee equal to the costs incurred in responding to the request, and CMS is not obligated to estimate these costs in advance.[359] CMS estimated that the cost will be approximately $75 per hour, and that the total cost of an opinion will depend on the complexity of the arrangement and the quality of the submission.[360] The advisory opinion final rule provides that CMS will generally issue an opinion within 90 days after the request has been formally accepted, unless the request involves complex legal issues or highly complicated fact patterns; in that case, CMS will respond to the request "within a reasonable time period."[361] By contrast, the anti-kickback advisory opinion authority requires the OIG to issue an opinion not later than 60 days after receiving a request.[362]

Once a Stark law advisory opinion has been issued, it will be made available promptly for public inspection, but will be legally binding only on the HHS and the requesting party, and only with respect to the specific conduct of the requesting party.[363] CMS will not be bound with respect to the conduct of any third party, even if the conduct of that party appears similar to the conduct that is the subject of the opinion.

XVIII. CONCLUSION

The Stark law is the natural child of the budget reconciliation process of the 1980s, where Congress saw excesses in the health care business environment and an executive branch it believed needed to be micromanaged. The result was a sweeping per se prohibition of

---

[358] 42 C.F.R. §411.370(a); 42 C.F.R. §411.373(a).

[359] 42 C.F.R. §411.375(b).

[360] 63 Fed. Reg. at 1652.

[361] 42 C.F.R. §411.380(c)(1).

[362] 42 U.S.C. §1320a-7d(b)(5)(B).

[363] 42 C.F.R. §411.384(b); 42 C.F.R. §411.387.

most then-existing forms of self-referral based on ownership interests, coupled with the regulation of physician compensation relationships with outside referral sources, referrals within physicians'
practices, and physician compensation in virtually any setting. All of
this was set in motion in Stark I and II with little discretion granted
to the executive branch to modify by regulation onerous requirements
or requirements rendered meaningless by the sweeping changes in
the health care system since the statute's enactment. Although the
Final Rules attempt to inject common sense into the Stark law in
many areas (with the notable exception of the highly restrictive rules
for physician recruitment), the outcome of self-referral enforcement
is a long way from being final, and Congressman Stark's promise of
"clear bright-line rules" remains elusive.

3

The False Claims Act in Health Care Prosecutions: Application of the Substantive, *Qui Tam,* and Voluntary Disclosure Provisions*

---

*Robert Salcido, Akin, Gump Strauss, Hauer & Feld, L.L.P., Washington, D.C.

II. CONSTRUCTION OF THE "FALSE" AND "KNOWING" ELEMENTS OF THE FALSE CLAIMS ACT

As noted in the Main Volume, several courts had split regarding whether local governmental entities can be sued under the False Claims Act (FCA).[1] Recently the Supreme Court, in *Cook County v. United States* ex rel. *Chandler,*[2] ruled that local governments are "persons" under the FCA and hence are potentially subject to liability under the statute.

A. Defining "Falsity" Under the FCA

1. Cases Establishing Falsity

b. Falsity by Omission or Implicit Certification

As noted in the Main Volume, various courts have struggled to define when a specific claim can be "false or fraudulent" under the FCA when the representations on the claims are accurate. Since publication of the Main Volume, the Second Circuit has considered this issue at length in *United States* ex rel. *Mikes v. Straus.*[3] This case is important because, in the health care context, it limits the circumstances under which a court will find an implicit false certification to those instances where the rule or regulation the defendant breaches expressly conditions payment on compliance. The basis for the court's narrow construction of the FCA is to ensure that the federal government and whistleblowers do not invoke the FCA in quality of care cases to second-guess medical judgment and to use the FCA to supplant the role of state, local, and private medical agencies, boards, and societies in monitoring quality of care issues.

In *Straus,* the relator, a pulmonologist, alleged that the defendants submitted false reimbursement requests to the federal government for spirometry services.[4] Spirometry is an "easy-to-perform pulmonary function test used by doctors to detect both obstructive (such as asthma and emphysema) and restrictive (such as pulmonary fibrosis) lung diseases."[5] The defendants' spirometers measure "the pressure change when a patient blows into a mouthpiece, thereby providing the doctor with on-the-spot analysis of the volume and speed by which patients can exhale."[6]

The relator alleged that the defendants submitted false Medicare reimbursement claims for spirometry procedures because these procedures were not performed in accordance with the relevant standard of care.[7] Specifically, the relator alleged that American Thoracic Society (ATS) guidelines recommend daily calibration of spirometers by

---

[1] 31 U.S.C. §3729 et seq. See Main Volume Chapter 3, Section II.B.3, at 140–41, note 90 (citing cases).

[2] 538 U.S. 119 (2003).

[3] 274 F.3d 687 (2d Cir. 2001).

[4] *Id.* at 693.

[5] *Id.* at 694.

[6] *Id.*

[7] *Id.* at 696.

use of a three-liter calibration syringe, the performance of three successive trials during test administration, and the appropriate training of spirometer technicians.[8] The relator contended that the defendants' performance of spirometry did not conform to the ATS guidelines and thus would yield inherently unreliable data.

In evaluating whether the defendants submitted false claims to the government, the court pointed out that the statutory term "false or fraudulent" is not defined in the FCA. In giving content to the phrase, the court reasoned:

> A common definition of "fraud" is "an intentional misrepresentation, concealment, or nondisclosure for the purpose of inducing another in reliance upon it to part with some valuable thing belonging to him or to surrender a legal right." *Webster's Third New International Dictionary* 904 (1981). "False" can mean "not true," "deceitful," or "tending to mislead." *Id.* at 819. The juxtaposition of the word "false" with the word "fraudulent," plus the meanings of the words comprising the phrase "false claim," suggest an improper claim is aimed at extracting money the government otherwise would not have paid. *See* Clarence T. Kipps, Jr. *et al., Materiality as an Element of Liability Under the False Claims Act,* A.B.A. Center for Continuing Legal Educ. Nat'l Inst. (1998), WL N98CFCB ABA-LGLED B-37, B-46 ("[A] claim cannot be determined to be true or false without consideration of whether the decisionmaker should pay the claim—that is, a claim is 'false' only if the Government or other customer would not pay the claim if the facts about the misconduct alleged to have occurred were known.").[9]

Relevant to the analysis here, in evaluating whether the defendants' spirometry claims were false, the court found that there are two types of falsity that could trigger liability under the FCA: (1) false express certification, which represents compliance with a federal statute or regulation or a prescribed contractual term; or (2) false implied certification, under which a defendant implicitly represents entitlement to payment notwithstanding the breach of some rule or regulation that is not referenced in the certification. The court found that neither type of falsity was present under the facts and circumstances in the *Straus* action.

First, as to the relator's claim that the defendants tendered a false certification to the United States, the court evaluated the standard form that physicians submit to obtain Medicare reimbursement, the CMS-1500, which contains various certifications to which the physician must attest.[10] In formulating its rule regarding whether the defendants'

---

[8] *Id.* at 694.

[9] *Id.* at 696.

[10] For example, a physician, on the CMS-1500 form, will set forth, among other things, the pertinent CPT Code representing the service supplied to the patient and certify that the services set forth on the form are "medically indicated and necessary for the health of the patient and were personally furnished by [the physician] or were furnished incident to [his or her] professional service by [his or her] employee. . . ." The form also contains the following "NOTICE":

> Any person who knowingly files a statement of claim containing any misrepresentation or any false, incomplete or misleading information may be guilty of a criminal act punishable under law and may be subject to civil penalties.

See CMS-1500, *reprinted in* Medicare & Medicaid Guide (CCH) ¶10,261.

claim for payment for the spirometry on the CMS-1500 breached the FCA because the defendants tendered a false certification, the court held that it would "join the Fourth, Fifth, Ninth, and District of Columbia Circuits in ruling that a claim under the Act is legally false only where a party certifies compliance with a statute or regulation as a condition to governmental payment."[11] Under this test, two separate elements must be satisfied: (1) the party must certify compliance with a specific statute or regulation, and (2) the party's certification and compliance with the statute or regulation must be a precondition of governmental payment.

In *Straus,* the court found that the second element was clearly satisfied. Both the CMS-1500, which provides that "[n]o Part B Medicare benefits may be paid unless this form is received as required by existing law and regulations,"[12] and the Medicare Regulations[13] state that certification is a precondition to Medicare reimbursement. However, the court found that the first element was not satisfied because the CMS-1500 did not contain any express certification regarding the quality of the spirometry services.

Specifically, as the court pointed out, a person certifies on the CMS-1500 that "the services shown on this form were *medically* indicated and *necessary* for the health of the patient and were *personally furnished* by [the person] or were furnished incident to [the person's] professional service by [the person's] employee under [the person's] immediate personal supervision."[14] The court ruled that the relator could neither establish that the services lacked medical necessity nor that the physician did not personally furnish the service.

As an initial matter, the court found that the relator's objections to the defendants' spirometry tests did not implicate the standard set out in the CMS-1500 form that the procedure was dictated by "medical necessity" because the medical necessity standard relates to the level of service provided, not its quality.[15] Specifically, the court reasoned:

> The term "medical necessity" does not impart a qualitative element mandating a particular standard of medical care, and [the relator] does not point to any legal authority requiring us to read such a mandate into the form. Medical necessity ordinarily indicates the level—not the quality— of the service. For example, the requisite level of medical necessity may

---

[11] 274 F.3d at 697 (citing United States *ex rel.* Siewick v. Jamieson Sci. & Eng'g, Inc., 214 F.3d 1372, 1376 (D.C. Cir. 2000); Harrison v. Westinghouse Savannah River Co., 176 F.3d 776, 786–87, 793 (4th Cir. 1999); United States *ex rel.* Thompson v. Columbia/HCA Healthcare Corp., 125 F.3d 899, 902 (5th Cir. 1997); United States *ex rel.* Hopper v. Anton, 91 F.3d 1261, 1266–67 (9th Cir. 1996)). According to the court, its holding "is distinct from a requirement imposed by some courts that a false statement or claim must be material to the government's funding decision." *Id.* (citation omitted). It reasoned that a "materiality requirement holds that only a subset of admittedly false claims is subject to False Claims Act liability" and "that not all instances of regulatory noncompliance will cause a claim to become false." *Id.* (citation omitted). Consequently, the court declined to "address whether the Act contains a separate materiality requirement." *Id.*

[12] *See* CMS-1500, *reprinted in* Medicare & Medicaid Guide (CCH) ¶10,261.

[13] *See* 42 C.F.R. §424.32.

[14] 274 F.3d at 698 (emphasis added).

[15] *Id.*

not be met where a party contends that a particular procedure was deleterious or performed solely for profit, *see United States ex rel. Kneepkins
v. Gambro Healthcare, Inc.,* 115 F. Supp. 2d 35, 41–42 (D. Mass. 2000)
(procedures chosen solely for defendants' economic gain are not "medically necessary" as required by claim submission form), or where a party
seeks reimbursement for a procedure that is not traditionally covered,
see Rush v. Parham, 625 F.2d 1150, 1156 (5th Cir. 1980) (upholding
state's exclusion of experimental medical treatment from definition of
"medically necessary" services under Medicaid).

 This approach to the phrase "medically necessary"—as applying
to ex ante coverage decisions but not ex post critiques of how providers
executed a procedure—would also conform to our understanding of the
phrase "reasonable and necessary" as used in the Medicare statute, 42
U.S.C. § 1395y(a)(1)(A) (1994) (disallowing payment for items or services not reasonable and necessary for diagnosis or treatment). *See New
York ex rel. Bodnar v. Sec'y of Health & Human Servs.,* 903 F.2d 122,
125 (2d Cir. 1990) (acknowledging Secretary's authority, in determining
whether procedure is "reasonable and necessary," to consider type of service provided and whether service was provided in appropriate, cost-
effective setting); *Goodman v. Sullivan,* 891 F.2d 449, 450–51 (2d Cir.
1989) (per curiam) (affirming exclusion of experimental procedures from
Medicare coverage pursuant to requirement that procedures be "reasonable and necessary"); *see also Friedrich v. Sec'y of Health & Human
Servs.,* 894 F.2d 829, 831 (6th Cir. 1990) (noting that the Health Care
Financing Administration, when determining whether a procedure is
"reasonable and necessary," considers the procedure's safety, effectiveness, and acceptance by medical community).[16]

The court concluded that, "[i]nasmuch as [the relator] challenges only
the quality of defendants' spirometry tests and not the decisions to
order this procedure for patients, she fails to support her contention
that the tests were not medically necessary."[17]

 Finally, as to the defendants' representation on the certification
that services are "rendered under the physician's immediate personal
supervision by his/her employee," which the court noted covers the medical assistants' performance of spirometry at the defendants' direction,
the court ruled that the relator did not tender "evidence to support an
allegation that the defendants did not 'personally furnish' the spirometry tests as required by the [CMS]-1500 form."[18] Hence, the court held
that the "plaintiff's cause of action insofar as it is founded on express
false certification is without merit."[19]

 As to the second type of falsity alleged by the relator, the court
turned to the relator's contention that the defendants, in submitting the CMS-1500, made an implied false certification. The court
pointed out that under some case law authority a certification can be
implicitly false based on the notion that "the act of submitting a

---

[16] *Id.* at 698–99.
[17] *Id.* at 699.
[18] *Id.*
[19] *Id.*

claim for reimbursement itself implies compliance with governing federal rules that are a precondition to payment."[20]

However, the court specifically declined to expand this doctrine into the health care context because such an expansion would cause the FCA to conflict with local or private regulation of medical issues concerning the standard of care:

> [T]he False Claims Act was not designed for use as a blunt instrument to enforce compliance with all medical regulations—but rather only those regulations that are a precondition to payment—and to construe the impliedly false certification theory in an expansive fashion would improperly broaden the Act's reach. Moreover, a limited application of implied certification in the health care field reconciles, on the one hand, the need to enforce the Medicare statute with, on the other hand, the active role actors outside the federal government play in assuring that appropriate standards of medical care are met. Interests of federalism counsel that the regulation of health and safety matters is primarily, and historically, a matter of local concern.
>
> Moreover, permitting *qui tam* plaintiffs to assert that defendants' quality of care failed to meet medical standards would promote federalization of medical malpractice, as the federal government or the *qui tam* relator would replace the aggrieved patient as plaintiff. *See* Patrick A. Scheiderer, Note, *Medical Malpractice as a Basis for a False Claims Action?*, 33 Ind. L. Rev. 1077, 1098–99 (2000). Beyond that, we observe that the courts are not the best forum to resolve medical issues concerning levels of care. State, local or private medical agencies, boards and societies are better suited to monitor quality of care issues.[21]

Because of the poor fit of the FCA implied certification theory in the health care quality of care context, the court ruled that the "implied false certification is appropriately applied only when the underlying statute or regulation upon which the plaintiff relies expressly states the provider must comply in order to be paid."[22] Accordingly, "[l]iability

---

[20] *Id.* (citation omitted). Specifically, the court cited to Ab-Tech Constr. Inc. v. United States, 31 Fed. Cl. 429 (Fed. Cl. 1994), *aff'd*, 57 F.3d 1084 (Fed. Cir. 1995) (unpublished table decision).

[21] 274 F.3d at 699–700 (citations and internal quotations omitted).

[22] *Id.* at 700 (citation omitted). *Accord In re* Genesis Health Ventures, Inc., 272 B.R. 558, 570 (Bankr. D. Del. Jan. 24, 2002) ("The notion of implied false certification is appropriately applied only when the underlying statute or regulation upon which the plaintiff relies expressly states that the provider must comply in order to be paid. . . . No specificity regarding the provision of credits for returned drugs to Medicaid as a condition of payment to a provider [exists]. Therefore, the claimant's cause fails under the 'legally false certification' theory") (citation omitted). Similarly, at a more general level, courts have continued to rule that if the government or relator cannot demonstrate any breach of a governmental rule or regulation in the first instance, there is no violation of the FCA as a matter of law. *See, e.g.,* United States v. Southland Mgmt. Corp., No. 00-60267, 2003 U.S. App. LEXIS 6275, at *12 (5th Cir. Apr. 1, 2003) (en banc) ("[W]hether a claim is valid depends on the contract, regulations, or statute that supposedly warrants it. It is only those claims for money or property to which a defendant is not entitled that are 'false' for purposes of the False Claims Act") (citation omitted); United States *ex rel.* Bondy v. Consumer Health Found., No. 00-2520, 2001 U.S. App. LEXIS 24238, at *13–15 (4th Cir. Nov. 9, 2001) (relator could not establish falsity because relator did not demonstrate that "HCFA disapproved of [the apportionment statistic] method [the defendant used on its cost report] or that the method chosen was not in accordance with HCFA's established procedures"); United States v. Medica-Rents Co., 285 F. Supp. 2d 742, 770–71 (N.D. Tex. 2003) (noting that "Medicare regulations are among the most completely impenetrable texts within human experience," and finding that the defendants' use of a Healthcare Common Procedure Coding System Code was not false or fraudulent when they were instructed by the regional carrier to bill under that code)

under the Act may properly be found therefore when a defendant submits a claim for reimbursement while knowing—as that term is defined by the Act (*see* 31 U.S.C. § 3729(b))—that payment expressly is precluded because of some noncompliance by the defendant."[23]

Under this interpretation of an implicit false certification, the court found that the relator's claim could not survive. The relator had asserted that compliance with Sections 1395y(a)(1)(A) and 1320c-5(a) of the Medicare statute is a precondition to a request for federal funds and that submission of a CMS-1500 form attests by implication to the providers' compliance with both of those provisions.[24] Section 1395y(a)(1)(A) of the Medicare statute states that "*no payment may be made* under [the Medicare statute] for any expenses incurred for items or services which . . . are not *reasonable and necessary* for the diagnosis or treatment of illness or injury or to improve the functioning of a malformed body member."[25] Because this section contains an express condition of payment—that is, "no payment may be made"—it explicitly links each Medicare payment to the requirement that the particular item or service be "reasonable and necessary."

The court rejected the relator's theory because the "reasonable and necessary" test did not address the quality of a service that was

---

(citations and internal quotation omitted); United States *ex rel.* Perales v. St. Margaret's Hosp., 243 F. Supp. 2d 843, 855 (C.D. Ill. 2003) (rejecting relator's claim because he could not show any falsity based on an alleged breach of the Stark law because "there is nothing illegal per se about a hospital acquiring a physician's practice, the existence of a non-compete agreement, or entering into a subsequent employment contract with that hospital; something more is required to make this conduct illegal, and it is evidence of this something more that is absent here"); United States *ex rel.* Obert-Hong v. Advocate Health Care, 211 F. Supp. 2d 1045 (N.D. Ill. 2002) (because the relator could not establish that defendants' practices breached the Stark law or anti-kickback statute, the relator could not establish a violation of the FCA); United States *ex rel.* Goodstein v. McLaren Reg'l Med. Ctr., 202 F. Supp. 2d 671 (E.D. Mich. 2002) (no violation of FCA because government could not establish violation of Stark law). This same principle has been applied in criminal cases alleging false statements. *See* United States v. Whiteside, 285 F.3d 1345, 1352, 1353 (11th Cir. 2002) (reversing defendants' convictions because "[n]either the regulations nor administrative authority clearly answer the dilemma the defendants faced here. As the FI [fiscal intermediary] testified, under current law, reasonable people could differ as to whether the debt interest was capital-related. The testimony indicates that the experts disagreed as to the validity of the theory of capital reimbursement suggested by the government. This contradictory evidence lends credence to defendants' argument that their interpretation was not unreasonable. Here, competing interpretations of the applicable law [are] far too reasonable to justify these convictions. . . . As such, the government failed to meet its burden of proving the *actus reus* of the offense—actual falsity as a matter of law") (citation and internal quotation omitted). However, when a court finds that a defendant's practices did not conform to rules and regulations governing the government's program or that the defendant's interpretation of the rule or regulation is irrational, the plaintiff may prove falsity. *See* United States *ex rel.* Humphrey v. Franklin-Williamson Human Servs., 189 F. Supp. 2d 862, 873 (S.D. Ill. 2002) (rejecting defendant's FED. R. CIV. P. 12(b)(6) motion because "it appears that [the defendant's] billing practices did not comply with Medicaid statutes and regulations [regarding a person's spend down obligation]," and therefore the relator "may be able to prove that [the defendant] 'knew' that its billing practices were improper and that the statements they [sic] prepared and claims they [sic] made were false or fraudulent").

[23] 274 F.3d at 700. *Accord In re* Cardiac Devices Qui Tam Litig, 221 F.R.D. 318, 345–46 (D. Conn. 2004) (finding CMS UB-92 Form, and its predecessor, UB-82, to be false claims because the defendant implicitly certified that its services were medically necessary and indicated when instead those services were for noncovered investigational devices). The underlying medical necessity issue in In re *Cardiac Devices* was distinguishable from *Straus* in that In re *Cardiac Devices* concerned whether the underlying services were covered or noncovered and did not concern the quality of an indisputably covered service, as was the case in *Straus*.

[24] 274 F.3d at 700.

[25] 42 U.S.C. §1395y(a)(1)(A) (emphasis added).

provided. Specifically, the court reasoned, consistent with its analysis of the relator's express certification claim, that:

> the requirement that a service be reasonable and necessary generally pertains to the selection of the particular procedure and not to its performance. . . . While such factors as the effectiveness and medical acceptance of a given procedure might determine whether it is reasonable and necessary, the failure of the procedure to conform to a particular standard of care ordinarily will not.[26]

Accordingly, because the relator had only contended that the "defendants' performance of spirometry was qualitatively deficient, her allegations that defendants falsely certified compliance with § 1395y(a) (1)(A) may not succeed."[27]

Similarly, the court rejected the relator's claim of an implicit false certification regarding Section 1320c-5(a) of the Medicare Act. That section provides:

> It shall be the obligation of any health care practitioner . . . who provides health care services for which payment may be made . . . to assure, to the extent of his authority that services or items ordered or provided by such practitioner . . .
>
> (1) will be provided economically and only when, and to the extent, medically necessary;
>
> (2) will be of a quality which meets *professionally recognized standards of health care;* and
>
> (3) will be supported by evidence of medical necessity and quality . . . as may reasonably be required by a reviewing peer review organization in the exercise of its duties and responsibilities.[28]

The relator had contended that the ATS guidelines constitute a "professionally recognized standard of health care" for spirometry and that the defendants had implicitly certified compliance with that standard when they submitted CMS-1500 forms for spirometry tests. However, the court concluded that the relator's "allegations cannot establish liability under the False Claims Act because—unlike § 1395y(a)(1)(A)— the Medicare statute does not explicitly condition payment upon compliance with § 1320c-5(a)."[29] Specifically, the court found that this statutory provision simply authorizes the peer review organization to recommend sanctions after reasonable notice and the opportunity for corrective action by the provider. Furthermore, if HHS agrees that sanctions should be imposed and further finds the provider unwilling or unable substantially to comply with its obligations, HHS may exclude the provider from the Medicare program or mandate the repayment of the cost of the noncompliant service to the United States "as a condition to the continued eligibility" of the health care

---

[26] 274 F.3d at 701 (citations omitted).

[27] *Id.*

[28] 42 U.S.C. §1320c-5(a) (emphasis added).

[29] 274 F.3d at 701.

provider in the Medicare program.[30] Accordingly, the court ruled that because Section "1320c-5(a) does not expressly condition payment on compliance with its terms, defendants' certifications on the [CMS]-1500 forms are not legally false. Consequently, defendants did not submit impliedly false claims by requesting reimbursement for spirometry tests that allegedly were not performed according to the recognized standards of health care."[31]

Finally, on policy grounds, the court concluded that its interpretation of what constitutes an implicitly false claim conformed the FCA to the Medicare Act. Specifically, the court reasoned:

> Our holding—that in submitting a Medicare reimbursement form, a defendant implicitly certifies compliance with § 1395y(a)(1)(A), but not § 1320c-5(a)—comports with Congress' purpose. . . . Section 1395y(a)(1)(A) mandates that a provider's choice of procedures be "reasonable and necessary"; it does not obligate federal courts to step outside their primary area of competence and apply a qualitative standard measuring the efficacy of those procedures. The quality of care standard of § 1320c-5(a) is best enforced by those professionals most versed in the nuances of providing adequate health care.[32]

Although the Second Circuit did not reject altogether the view that FCA claims can somehow be "implicitly" false, the court struck an appropriate balance by restricting such assertions to only those occasions in which the defendants knew that the submission of the claim would breach a rule or regulation that would result in denial of the claim. By striking this balance in a quality of care case, the court has appropriately prevented the FCA from becoming a federal malpractice statute and federal courts from becoming specialized medical panels that evaluate whether the care provided could have somehow been better, while appropriately penalizing those who knowingly seek to obtain payment for funds that they are prohibited from receiving.

B. The FCA "Knowing" Standard

3. Defenses Demonstrating Lack of Knowledge

a. Merely Negligent Conduct Does Not Result in Liability Under the FCA

In *United States* ex rel. *Mikes v. Straus,*[33] the Second Circuit considered the issue of whether the defendants' submission of "worthless" spirometry services could constitute a violation of the FCA. As an initial matter, the court concurred with the relator that if the defendants' spirometry was so deficient as to be "worthless," the defendants' claims would be false. However, the court found no liability because the relator "makes no showing that defendants knowingly—as the Act defines

---

[30]*Id.* at 702.

[31]*Id.*

[32]*Id.*

[33]274 F.3d 687 (2d Cir. 2001).

that term—submitted a claim for the reimbursement of worthless services" and "adopted the Ninth Circuit's standard that the 'requisite intent is the knowing presentation of what is known to be false' as opposed to negligence or innocent mistake."[34]

Specifically, the court noted that "[t]he notion of presenting a claim known to be false does not mean the claim is incorrect as a matter of proper accounting, but rather means it is a lie."[35] The court concluded that the relator could not satisfy that test because the defendants tendered evidence of their "genuine belief that their use of spirometry had medical value," such as the fact that a spirometers' instruction manual, which—contrary to the ATS guidelines—indicated that daily calibration is not required and that individual spirometers had been sent out for periodic servicing. Because of this "good faith belief that their spirometry tests were of medical value," the court concluded that the relator's "unsupported allegations to the contrary [did] not raise a triable issue of fact sufficient to bar summary judgment."[36]

b. The Government Cannot Predicate an FCA Action on Ambiguous Regulatory Guidance

Similarly, since publication of the Main Volume, courts have continued to hold that when the government rules and regulations are

---

[34] *Id.* at 703 (citing Hagood v. Sonoma County Water Agency, 81 F.3d 1465, 1478 (9th Cir. 1996)).

[35] *Id.* (citation omitted).

[36] *Id.* at 704 (citation omitted). *See also* United States *ex rel.* Perales v. St. Margaret's Hosp., 243 F. Supp. 2d 843, 866 (C.D. Ill. 2003) (defendant hospital did not bury "its head in the sand and willfully ignore[ ] the law" when "there is evidence that [it] received and considered relevant publications in this area of the law, established a corporate compliance committee, and routinely consulted counsel in drafting the contracts and agreements, which is suggestive of an intent to abide by the law"); United States *ex rel.* Watson v. Connecticut Gen. Life Ins. Co., No. 98-6698, 2003 U.S. Dist. LEXIS 2054, at *55 (E.D. Pa. Feb. 11, 2003) (rejecting the relator's contention that the defendant submitted false claims when 98.6% of the claims were correctly processed because the "high rate of accuracy undermines any contention that [the defendant] knowingly engaged in a pattern of failing" to adhere to the governing standard regarding claims submission), *aff'd,* 87 Fed. Appx. 257 (3d Cir. Jan. 16, 2004). However, a court may find that a defendant was more than negligent or did not act in good faith if the defendant receives notice that a practice is potentially improper and, notwithstanding that notice, fails to act. *See, e.g.,* United States v. NHC Health Care Corp., 163 F. Supp. 2d 1051, 1058 (W.D. Mo. 2001) (ruling that based "upon complaints from staff, residents, surveyors and family members the Defendants knew or should have known that they had a staffing shortage that impinged upon their ability to properly care for their patients. Defendants also knew or should have known that if they did not have sufficient staff to properly care for their residents, then they should not have submitted bills to Medicare and Medicaid which represented that they provided such care") (footnote omitted). Significantly, the court seemingly imposed an affirmative duty on the defendants, once they received complaints, to investigate those complaints or otherwise to be charged with knowingly submitting false claims. *See id.* ("If Defendants had knowledge that they had severe staffing shortages at their facility, then they had a duty to investigate to see whether all their residents, including Residents 1 and 2, were getting the minimum standard of care to which they were entitled. A reasonable jury could conclude from the record before this Court that Defendants knew that the claims for reimbursement which they submitted were false because [the defendant long term care facility] acted in reckless indifference as to whether Residents 1 and 2 were receiving all the care they were entitled to under Medicare and Medicaid. Finally, the Court holds that an entity who is charging the Government for a minimum amount of care provided to its residents should question whether understaffing might lead to undercare. The knowledge of the answer to that question is charged to the Defendants when they submitted their Medicare and Medicaid claim forms"). *See also* United States *ex rel.* Hays v. Hoffman, 325 F.3d 982, 990–91 (8th Cir. 2003). In *Hays,* the Eighth Circuit, while acknowledging that the "knowing violation in this case is very close," found, when viewing the evidence most favorable to the jury's verdict, that the following evidence constituted recklessness:

ambiguous, the government has a heightened burden to demonstrate that the defendant "knowingly" submitted the false claim.[37]

c. Government Knowledge May Provide a Defense

Recently, the Tenth Circuit, in *United States* ex rel. *Stone v. Rockwell,*[38] considered the government knowledge defense in the context of the defendant's challenge to the district court's jury instruction. Specifically, after informing the jury that in order for the defendant to be liable for an FCA violation, the plaintiffs must establish that "Rockwell knew that the statements it made or used or caused to be made or used were false," the judge instructed the jury that:

> Defendant claims that the government, through various employees of the Department of Energy, had prior knowledge of facts relating to the false statements that defendant allegedly made . . . at [its facility]. The government denies the existence of such prior knowledge. In considering whether Rockwell knowingly made any false statements, you must consider all direct and circumstantial evidence, if any, concerning whether one or more government employees with authority to act under the Rockwell contracts with DOE knew the relevant facts . . . , and the costs incurred relating to those activities.
>
> Government knowledge may negate the intent by defendant required to establish a violation of the False Claims Act. If you find that government employees with authority to act under the contracts knew the relevant facts, then you may consider it in determining whether Rockwell knowingly presented a false statement to those facts.[39]

The defendant claimed that the instruction was faulty because it seemingly only applied to knowledge of those who had "authority to act" and thus precluded the jury from considering any knowledge obtained

---

(i) [the defendants'] internal accountants knew employee gifts were not reimbursable under the applicable Medicaid rules; (ii) gift apple invoices for a number of years were entered on [defendants'] general ledger accounts as "resident food"; and (iii) [the relator] and at least one other employee asked whether these purchases should instead be entered as employee gifts and were told by [the chief executive officer ("CEO")] to continue entering them as food. Defendants countered this showing with evidence that employees who prepared the Medicaid cost reports . . . were expected to exclude any non-reimbursable items entered in multi-purpose general ledger accounts such as the food account. But there was also evidence this was a haphazard, unsupervised process, permitting the jury to infer that, when [the CEO] told employees to enter gift apples in the general ledger as resident food, he knew this would result in Medicaid cost reports that improperly included this item as a reimbursable food expense.

[37]*See, e.g., In re* Genesis Health Ventures, Inc., 272 B.R. 558, 570 (Bankr. D. Del. 2002) ("In this murky area in which no specificity exists in the statutory, regulatory or contractual scheme regarding the provision of credits, with no request by either the state or federal government for unpaid credit, either by way of the filing of proofs of claim or otherwise, there is insufficient basis to charge the debtors with the requisite scienter required to establish a factually false certification"). In asserting the FCA defense of legal ambiguity, the defendants initially have the burden to establish that the pertinent legal standards are ambiguous. If established, then the burden switches to the government (or the relator) to demonstrate that the defendant knew that the statement was false notwithstanding the ambiguity. *See, e.g.,* United States *ex rel.* Minnesota Ass'n of Nurse Anesthetists v. Allina Health Sys., 276 F.3d 1032, 1053 (8th Cir. 2002) ("If a statement alleged to be false is ambiguous, the government (or here, the relator) must establish the defendant's knowledge of the falsity of the statement, which it can do by introducing evidence of how the statement would have been understood in context. . . . If the [relator] shows the defendants certified compliance with the regulation knowing that the HCFA interpreted the regulations in a certain way and that their actions did not satisfy the requirements of the regulations as the HCFA interpreted it, any possible ambiguity of the regulations is water under the bridge") (citations omitted).

[38]282 F.3d 787 (10th Cir. 2002).

[39]*Id.* at 811–12 n.10.

by mid- and lower-level government employees.[40] The district court disagreed with the defendant's contention, ruling that "there is nothing in the instructions indicating that the jury was under the impression that they were prohibited from considering [the defendant's] evidence that mid and lower-level [government] employees knew of the environmental, health and safety violations at [the defendant's facility.]"[41]

---

[40] *Id.*

[41] *Id.* at 812. *See generally* United States *ex rel.* Costner v. URS Consultants, 317 F.3d 883, 888 (8th Cir. 2003) ("The record shows that the EPA discussed these problems with the defendants and referred the matter to OSHA for investigation and possible sanctions. Although the record indicates that the defendants' performance under the contract was not perfect, the extent of the government's knowledge through its on-site personnel and other sources shows that . . . the government knew what it wanted, and it got what it paid for. . . . Thus, the district court did not err in finding that the defendants' openness with the EPA about their problems and their close working relationship in solving the problems negated the required scienter regarding these issues") (citation and internal quotation omitted); United States *ex rel.* Becker v. Westinghouse Savannah River, 305 F.3d 284, 289 (4th Cir. 2002) ("we join with our sister circuits and hold that the government's knowledge of the facts underlying an allegedly false record or statement can negate the scienter required for an FCA violation" and hence the government's "full knowledge of the material facts underlying any representations implicit in [the defendant's] conduct negates any knowledge that [the defendant] had regarding the truth or falsity of those representations"); United States *ex rel.* Grynberg v. Praxair, Inc., 207 F. Supp. 2d 1163, 1181 (D. Colo. 2001) (the relator's "allegations all relate to conduct or concerns that the government has known about and approved. [Governmental payment] based on these disclosed and approved practices cannot reasonably be treated as 'knowingly false' statements meant to reduce [payment] obligations to the government"). *See also* United States v. Medica-Rents Co., 285 F. Supp. 2d 742 (N.D. Tex. 2003). In *Medica-Rents,* the district court concluded that in light of the defendants' inquiries of governmental agents and willingness to follow the government's instructions, there was no issue of material fact regarding whether the defendants knowingly submitted false claims to the government:

> Having concluded that the defendants did not have actual knowledge that they could not bill for the ROHO Mattress Overlay under code E0277, the next issue is whether the defendants acted in deliberate ignorance that the ROHO Mattress Overlay could not be billed under code E0277. The plaintiffs claim that suppliers have a duty to familiarize themselves with the legal requirements for Medicare reimbursement, and to clarify any ambiguous or doubtful guidance they receive from Medicare carrier representatives. The plaintiffs further state that a supplier that fails to inform itself of the reimbursement requirements acts in reckless disregard of the truth of its claims. The plaintiffs claim that the evidence shows that Medica-Rents and Walsh knew that code E0277 did not apply to the ROHO Mattress Overlay and that E1399 was the correct code. By not clarifying the ambiguous or doubtful guidance they received from Medicare carrier representatives to bill under code E0277, the plaintiffs assert that the defendants were acting with deliberate ignorance or reckless disregard.
>
> As stated before, the evidence indicates that there was considerable confusion over what products could be billed under code E0277. Furthermore, the evidence clearly establishes that the defendants repeatedly sought advice on how to code the ROHO Mattress Overlay, and that they always followed the most current advice that they received. In addition, the evidence shows that the defendants, on many occasions, did seek clarification and did double-check coding advice that they received. The Court does not see what more can be expected of the defendants, except that they should be allowed to rely on advice they received from the government officials. There is no evidence that the defendants intentionally withheld information from the plaintiffs or purposely turned a blind eye to certain information in an attempt to file a false or fraudulent claim. Consequently, the Court concludes that there is no genuine issue of material fact as to whether the defendants acted with deliberate indifference or reckless disregard of the truth. They did not.

Id. at 775 (footnote omitted). Moreover, the court pointed out that "[a]lthough there is evidence that the defendants may not have explained the whole convoluted history relating to which carriers had allowed them to bill for the ROHO Mattress Overlay under which code, this evidence, without more, does not indicate that the defendants knowingly submitted, caused to be submitted, or conspired to submit false or fraudulent claims. It merely indicates that the defendants were actively trying to obtain permission to bill under a code that allowed them to make the most profit, which is not illegal." *Id.* at 773 n.67.

d. The Defendants' Reliance on Sound Legal Theory Negates an Inference of Fraud

A person does not act in deliberate ignorance or reckless disregard merely by failing to ask the government for its opinion or seeking advice of counsel when the practice is standard in the industry and the defendant has no basis to suspect wrongdoing.[42] In *United States ex rel. Quirk v. Madonna Towers, Inc.,*[43] the defendant, which operated a combined residential and skilled nursing facility, entered into agreements with residents under which in exchange for the residents paying an up-front fee and monthly rent for the residential apartment, the residents, if they were subsequently transferred to the skilled nursing facility, would only be required to pay the residential fee for the first 90 days of occupancy, instead of the higher skilled-nursing facility fee.[44] Because the defendant would submit Medicare claims during the relevant 90-day period, the relator contended that the defendant's practice breached 42 U.S.C. Section 1395y(a)(2)'s mandate that no payment may be made for services provided if the person receiving the services "has no legal obligation to pay."[45] Further, the relator contended that the defendant "knowingly" submitted false claims because the defendant's administrators testified that they did not seek legal advice or an opinion from Medicare regarding the practice of billing Medicare for the first 90 days of a patient's stay in a skilled nursing facility and that this failure to seek guidance demonstrated the defendant's deliberate ignorance of the truth or falsity of the claims it submitted to the government.[46]

The Eighth Circuit rejected the relator's contention, holding that "failing to secure a legal opinion, without more, is not the type of deliberate ignorance that can form the basis for a FCA lawsuit."[47] The court concluded that the administrators refrained from obtaining guidance regarding the questioned practice because they considered the billing practice to be an "acceptable standard procedure."[48] Accordingly, because the relator did not produce any evidence "suggesting anyone was lying to the government" or "suspected something wrong," the court affirmed the district court's dismissal of the action.[49]

---

[42]*See* United States *ex rel.* Quirk v. Madonna Towers, Inc., 278 F.3d 765 (8th Cir. 2002).
[43]*Id.*
[44]*Id.* at 766.
[45]*Id.* at 767.
[46]*Id.* at 768.
[47]*Id.*
[48]*Id.*
[49]*Id.* at 768–69.

III. Defending Against *Qui Tam* Actions

C. Case Law Construing the Public Disclosure Jurisdictional Bar

4. "Based Upon" a Public Disclosure

Recently, the Eighth Circuit, in *United States* ex rel. *Minnesota Ass'n of Nurse Anesthetists v. Allina Health System,*[50] joined the fray by construing what it means for a *qui tam* action to be "based upon" a public disclosure. Specifically, the court held that an action can be "based upon" a public disclosure even if the relator did not rely on the public information in filing the action.

In *Allina,* the relator, the Minnesota Association of Nurse Anesthetists (MANA), filed a *qui tam* action on December 28, 1994, alleging that the defendant hospitals and anesthesiologists had knowingly made false claims on the United States by mischaracterizing services they had provided to Medicare patients.[51] Specifically, the relator claimed that the defendant anesthesiologists and hospitals made the following types of misrepresentations: billing on a reasonable charge basis when the services the anesthesiologists provided did not meet the criteria for reasonable charge reimbursement; billing services as personally performed by the anesthesiologist when the services did not meet the criteria for personal performance; billing as if the anesthesiologist involved were directing fewer concurrent cases than he or she actually did direct; and certifying that it was medically necessary for both an anesthesiologist and anesthetist to personally perform cases that in fact an anesthetist alone personally performed.[52] The relator asserted that the defendants violated the FCA by overcharging the government for their services, and that they had conspired among each other to do so. The United States declined to intervene.[53]

Significantly, however, for purposes of the FCA's public disclosure bar, on November 8, 1994, approximately seven weeks *before* filing its *qui tam* case, the relator and several individual anesthetists sued many of the same defendants, alleging various federal antitrust and state law violations, again in connection with their anesthesia billing practices.[54] The antitrust complaint alleged:

> The defendant anesthesiology groups and their co-conspirators have engaged in a wide-spread practice of fraudulent billing of anesthesia services in violation of . . . Federal statutes, including § 1128(a)(1)(A). Such violations include, but are not limited to, billing for operations at which they were not present and inaccurately designating operations as one-on-one for Medicare purposes.[55]

---

[50] 276 F.3d 1032 (8th Cir. 2002).
[51] *Id.* at 1036.
[52] *Id.* at 1037.
[53] *Id.* at 1040.
[54] *Id.*
[55] *Id.*

These allegations in MANA's antitrust case were immediately reported in the local newspapers in St. Paul and St. Cloud on November 10 and 11.[56] MANA also provided a copy of the antitrust case to the U.S. government.[57] Only after this publicity did MANA file its *qui tam* action, in which it republished these same allegations.[58]

As a result of these public disclosures, the defendants moved to dismiss the relator's action under the FCA's public disclosure bar. One central issue the court had to consider was whether the relator's *qui tam* action was "based upon" the relator's previously filed antitrust action even though the relator had knowledge of the underlying facts independent of the public disclosure. As noted in the Main Volume, the vast majority of circuits have ruled that a relator's allegations are "based upon" public information if they are substantially similar to that information.[59] Conversely, a minority of circuits have ruled that the relator's action must actually be derived from the public information in order to be based upon that information.[60]

Before *Allina,* the Eighth Circuit had not expressly addressed this issue. In evaluating both the majority and the minority views, the court noted that there were two strong arguments in support of the minority view. First, the court opined that the minority view was consistent with the statutory language and that the majority view distorted "the plain meaning of the words 'based upon the public disclosure,' since if the qui tam allegations are not derived from the public disclosure itself, they are not based upon the *public disclosure,* but rather on the *facts* which have been publicly disclosed."[61] Second, the court asserted that an important policy supported the minority interpretation. Specifically, the "second objection to the majority view is that the policy justification sometimes given by courts in the majority, if taken to its logical conclusion, would return us to the rule of [*United States ex rel. Wisconsin v.*

---

[56] *Id.*

[57] *Id.*

[58] *Id.*

[59] *See, e.g.,* United States *ex rel.* Jones v. Horizon Healthcare Corp., 160 F.3d 326, 335 (6th Cir. 1998) (adopting broad interpretation of "based upon" and holding that the relator's lawsuit was based upon an earlier state court action, although the basis for her *qui tam* lawsuit was her personal knowledge, because all that is required to trigger the bar is that the allegations or transactions in a complaint mirror the information in the public domain and not that the relator actually derive her information from the public information); United States *ex rel.* Mistick PBT v. Housing Auth., 186 F.3d 376, 385–88 (3d Cir. 1999), *cert. denied,* 529 U.S. 1018 (2000); United States v. Stanford Univ. Bd. of Trs., 161 F.3d 533 (9th Cir. 1998), *cert. denied,* 526 U.S. 1066 (1999); United States *ex rel.* McKenzie v. BellSouth Telecomms., Inc., 123 F.3d 935, 940 (6th Cir. 1997), *cert. denied,* 522 U.S. 1077 (1998); United States *ex rel.* Findley v. FPC-Boron Employees' Club, 105 F.3d 675 (D.C. Cir. 1997), *cert. denied,* 522 U.S. 865 (1997). *Cf.* United States *ex rel.* Feingold v. Adminastar Fed., Inc., 324 F.3d 492, 497 (7th Cir. 2003) ("a lawsuit is based upon public disclosures when it both depends essentially upon publicly disclosed information and is actually derived from such information") (internal quotation and citation omitted).

[60] United States *ex rel.* Siller v. Becton Dickinson & Co., 21 F.3d 1339 (4th Cir. 1994) (adopting narrow interpretation of "based upon" and holding that the relator's action would not be based upon allegations of fraud in the public domain if the relator could prove that he learned of the allegations independent of the public disclosure); *cf.* United States v. Bank of Farmington, 166 F.3d 853, 863 (7th Cir. 1999) (noting in dicta that the "Fourth Circuit's interpretation of 'based upon' is the better on the grounds of plain meaning and public policy").

[61] 276 F.3d 1032, 1045–46 (8th Cir. 2002).

Dean, 729 F.2d 1100 (7th Cir. 1984)], which Congress was specifically attempting to overrule by means of the 1986 Amendments Act" because Congress sought "to treat relators fairly, which would be frustrated by kicking relators out of court when their claim was not parasitical, but was merely disclosed before the relator had filed suit."[62]

However, the *Allina* court ultimately adopted the majority position and thus held that an action is based upon a public disclosure whenever the allegations in the suit and in the publicly disclosed material are substantially the same regardless of where the relator obtained its information. In reaching this conclusion, the court believed that it had struck the appropriate balance between utility and fairness that underlies the jurisdictional bar and addressed the policy concern identified by the minority position that nonparasitic relators would be barred if the court adhered to the majority position. Specifically, the court reasoned:

> In our view, . . . these policy objections [raised by the minority viewpoint] disappear if one considers the overall design of the public disclosure provision. Congress's fairness concern is not effectuated by each part of the statute read in isolation, but rather by the statute as a whole. The "based upon" clause serves the concern of utility, that is of paying only for useful information, and the "original source" exception serves the concern of fairness, that is of not biting the hand that fed the government the information. If the "based upon" clause threatens to kick relators out of court because the government does not need them, the "original source" exception reopens the courthouse door for certain deserving relators. Therefore, the majority view reaches the correct result, not because Congress cared nothing for fairness and everything for utility, but because it used two different provisions to strike a balance between these concerns.[63]

5. The Original Source Provisions

a. Timing of the Relator's Knowledge and Disclosure of Information

As when it construed the "based upon" standard in the FCA public disclosure jurisdictional bar, the Eighth Circuit, in *United States* ex rel. *Minnesota Ass'n of Nurse Anesthetists v. Allina Health Sys-*

---

[62]*Id.* at 1046, 1047. In *United States* ex rel. *Wisconsin v. Dean,* the State of Wisconsin had investigated Medicaid fraud and, consistent with its duty under the Social Security Act to report various fraud and abuse information to the government, disclosed its findings to the Department of Health and Human Services. *See* 729 F.2d 1100, 1106 (7th Cir. 1984). Notwithstanding the reporting of this information, the Seventh Circuit determined that the relator's action was barred because the suit was based on information in the government's possession, which triggered the pre-1986 FCA jurisdictional bar.

[63]*Id.* at 1047. *See also* United States *ex rel.* Bledsoe v. Community Health Sys., Inc., 342 F.3d 634, 646 (6th Cir. 2003) (where previously filed state court action had alleged some discrete acts of fraud in hospital's psychiatric unit and relator's complaint had alleged those and additional acts of alleged fraud in the psychiatric unit, relator's action was "based upon" the state court action even though relator's "complaint contains more detailed allegations about the fraudulent billing practices in [the hospital's] psychiatric unit" because the state court action "already effectively alerted the public to the fraud occurring therein"). Further, courts have adopted this broad interpretation of the meaning of "based upon" even when the relator was the source of the information that is publicly disclosed. *See* United States *ex rel.* Laird v. Lockheed Martin Eng'g, 336 F.3d 346, 352 n.2 (5th Cir. 2003) (relator "does generally argue that the jurisdictional bar is inapplicable here because he is the one who made the public disclosure in the first place. . . . To the extent [the relator] . . . argues that relators involved in the initial public disclosure of information are not subject to the 'public disclosure' bar, we reject that argument).

tem,[64] returned to the Seventh Circuit's decision in *United States* ex rel. *Wisconsin v. Dean*[65] for guidance regarding the scope of the original source provision. Specifically, the *Allina* court pointed out that, "[s]ince we know from the history of the False Claims Act that the original source provision was added in 1986 to permit claims like the one in *Dean,* in which a claimant investigated the fraud and then revealed it to the government before filing suit, we would expect that the effect of the original source provision is to protect from the public disclosure bar those who first bring a claim to light."[66]

With that thought in mind, the Eighth Circuit turned to the issue of whether the relator must provide the information underlying its lawsuit to the government prior to the time in which the information is publicly disclosed to satisfy the statutory test that the relator must be "an original source of the information" and have "voluntarily provided the information to the Government before filing an action under this section which is based on the information."[67] The defendants contended that the relator could not satisfy this standard because it disclosed the antitrust complaint to the United States only *after* it had

---

[64] 276 F.3d 1032 (8th Cir. 2002).

[65] 729 F.2d 1100 (7th Cir. 1984).

[66] 276 F.3d at 1047–48.

[67] 31 U.S.C. §3730(e)(4). The court had found that the relator had direct knowledge of the information on which the allegations are based because the members of the relator, which was an association of nurse anesthetists, "often did see the [defendant] anesthesiologist filling out forms used for billing with misleading information." 276 F.3d at 1050. Courts continued to find, as a general matter, that nonemployee, noninsider relators lack sufficient knowledge to qualify as original sources. *See, e.g.,* United States *ex rel.* Eitel v. Reagan, No. 99-35099, 2000 WL 1529237, at *1 (9th Cir. Oct. 16, 2000) (relator "was never employed by any of the contractors. Although he did a considerable amount of investigative work, his information about misuse of the [government] program came either from public sources" or from others. "Here . . . the relator's knowledge was not direct and independent because he did not discover firsthand the information underlying his allegation of fraud but rather derived it secondhand from others"); United States *ex rel.* Woods v. Empire Blue Cross & Blue Shield, No. 99-Civ. 4968, 2002 U.S. Dist. LEXIS 15251 (S.D.N.Y. Aug. 19, 2002) (the relator, a former ambulance company owner, did not qualify as an original source when he had no knowledge of the defendant Medicare carrier's method of reporting claims and his assertion that he was "a knowledgeable individual from the industry, one who obviously knows where to look, how to theorize and formulate, and knows where the bones are buried" was insufficient to qualify the relator as an original source); United States *ex rel.* Kinney v. Stoltz, 2002 WL 523869, at *7 (D. Minn. Apr. 5, 2002) (the relator, a county paramedic, could not establish direct knowledge when he learned of the information underlying his action from depositions in a previous *qui tam* action he had filed because "[a]s such, he was a recipient of information and not a direct source"), *aff'd,* 327 F.3d 671 (8th Cir. 2003); United States *ex rel.* Alcohol Found., Inc. v. Kalmanowitz Charitable Found., 186 F. Supp. 2d 458, 463–65 (S.D.N.Y. 2002) (relator claimed that it had direct and independent knowledge because it had compiled information from reports that showed there was an inconsistency between defendants' advertising slogans and reality that resulted in overconsumption of alcohol and adverse health consequences that would be funded in part by the federal government and that the "average member of the public could neither understand the information available in the news media nor perceive a fraud absent [the relator's] compilation" because to understand the fraud "one must understand concepts of time, statistics, science, politics, and the law"; the court rejected the relator's position, pointing out that "the perspective gained from the foregoing combination of skills is easily distinguished from that of the archetypal whistle-blower who is an insider to corporate wrongdoing because one is merely a perceptive third-party while the other has first-hand knowledge of the wrong and its perpetrators" and that this interpretation accorded with the statutory purpose, which is "to create an incentive for civic-minded whistle-blowers, that is, insiders who put their personal employment or other interests at risk in order to vindicate the pecuniary rights of the United States" and "to bar opportunistic persons from abusing the qui tam procedure for self aggrandizement"), *aff'd,* 53 Fed. Appx. 153 (2d Cir. 2002); United States *ex rel.* Grynberg v. Praxair, Inc., 207 F. Supp. 2d 1163, 1184 (D. Colo. 2001) (the relator, who was not an employee or business associate of the defendants and who did not

publicly filed its antitrust action. Although the court recognized that the District of Columbia and Sixth Circuits had adopted this rule,[68] it found that "[t]his additional requirement has no textual basis in the statute."[69] Moreover, balancing fairness versus utility, the court reasoned that the D.C. and Sixth Circuit court rule should be rejected because it undermined the purpose of the original source provision to extend "fairness" to the relator:

> [T]he courts adopting this requirement have justified it by arguing that after public disclosure, the relator has no utility to the government. [United States *ex rel.* Findley v.] *FPC-Boron Employees' Club,* 105 F.3d [675,] at 691 [(D.C. Cir. 1997)] ("Once the information has been publicly disclosed, however, there is little need for the incentive provided by a qui tam action."). However, as we have seen, through the original source provisions Congress chose to reward persons who discovered and revealed fraud, rather than confiscating their claims. At the same time, Congress limited that beneficence by denying the bounty even to those who uncovered the fraud unless they had revealed it to the government before filing suit. Sec. 3730(e)(4)(B). We would change the balance Congress struck if we were to further restrict the class of those whose discoveries had been

---

witness any fraud or identify "a single element of his 'investigation' that involved anything other than second hand information, speculation, background information or collateral research (*i.e.* conversations with [a defendant's] officers, conversations with various third parties, telephone calls to [another defendant], [Freedom of Information Act] requests, research at [a state agency], photographs from a public road, review of oil and gas publications, and speculation regarding what would have been a fair . . . price)" did not have direct and independent knowledge, nor did his "investigation, general knowledge, education, experience and expertise" render him an original source); *but see* United States *ex rel.* Kennard v. Comstock Res., Inc., 363 F.3d 1039, 1046 (10th Cir. 2004) (where the relators "started with innocuous public information [and] completed the equation [of fraud] with information independent of any preexisting public disclosure," they qualified as original sources). Conversely, courts found that employee relators or those with a very close nexus with the defendant can qualify as having direct knowledge of the information underlying the lawsuit. *See, e.g.,* United States *ex rel.* Stone v. Rockwell, 282 F.3d 787, 800–802 (10th Cir. 2002) (the relator, who was an engineer at the defendant's facility, had direct and independent knowledge of the allegations in the complaint—that is, could prove that he discovered the information on which his allegations were based "through his own efforts and not through the labors of others" and that his "information was not derivative of others"—when he submitted an affidavit "detailing his duties and responsibilities at [the facility] and describing his observations there that underpinned his FCA action" including "plant-wide 'troubleshooting' and reviewing designs and existing operations for safety and cost effectiveness" and when he authored a memo pointing out that the defendant's "design will not work"; the court rejected the defendant's contention that the relator lacked direct and independent knowledge because he could not identify specific false claims that the defendant submitted or the specific individuals who submitted those inaccurate claims, ruling that the "relator need not, as [the defendant] says, have in his possession knowledge of the *actual* fraudulent conduct itself; knowledge 'underlying or supporting' the fraud allegation is sufficient. . . . . Thus, we are persuaded that [the relator's] knowledge that a defective . . . manufacturing process would be employed, gained from his review of [the defendant's] plans, constitutes knowledge of information 'underlying or supporting' his allegation concerning [the defendant's] alleged ultimate fraudulent activity (the submission of claims to the DOE falsely stating that [the facility] was in compliance with environmental, health and safety laws)"); *see also* United States *ex rel.* Atkinson v. Pennsylvania Shipbuilding Co., 255 F. Supp. 2d 351, 379 (E.D. Pa. 2002) (relator may establish direct and independent knowledge based on information he learned from a co-relator that was obtained through a joint investigation and the co-relator's review of files at a county courthouse furnished the relator with direct knowledge because there was no evidence that "the Delaware County filing clerk(s) who prepared the index viewed ever interacted with [the co-relator], much less that they ever informed him of the index's contents").

[68] 276 F.3d at 1049 (citing United States *ex rel.* McKenzie v. BellSouth Telecomms., Inc., 123 F.3d 935, 943 (6th Cir. 1997), *cert. denied,* 522 U.S. 1077 (1998); United States *ex rel.* Findley v. FPC-Boron Employees' Club, 105 F.3d 675, 690–91 (D.C. Cir. 1997), *cert. denied,* 522 U.S. 865 (1997).

[69] 276 F.3d at 1050.

made public but who were nevertheless permitted to proceed as relators. We decline to adopt the proposed additional requirement.[70]

The court's ruling in *Allina* that the relator qualified as an original source can be questioned on the following grounds:

- The court misapplied the *Dean* case.
- The court's balancing between "utility" and "fairness" has no basis in the statutory language or the legislative history.
- The court's interpretation of the scope of the original source provision is inconsistent with the statutory language.
- The court did not address the applicable statements in the legislative history regarding who should qualify as an original source.
- The court's opinion undermines the chief purpose underlying the *qui tam* provisions.[71]

First, in construing the public disclosure bar, the court believed that it was critical that it construe the original source provision in a manner consistent with the *Dean* decision. Specifically, as noted, it pointed out that because "we know from the history of the False Claims Act that the original source provision was added in 1986 to permit

---

[70] 276 F.3d at 1050–51. Even under this formulation of the rule, the relator would not be permitted to proceed if it did not voluntarily provide the material evidence underlying the lawsuit to the government prior to filing the action. *See, e.g.,* United States *ex rel.* King v. Hillcrest Health Ctr., 264 F.3d 1271, 1280 (10th Cir. 2001) ("To avoid the jurisdictional bar . . . , a relator must have direct and independent knowledge of the information on which the *qui tam* allegations are based and must have provided the same information to the government *prior* to filing the *qui tam* action.") (emphasis added); United States *ex rel.* Lissack v. Sakura Global Capital Mkts., Inc., No. 95 Civ. 1363, 2003 U.S. Dist. LEXIS 14600, at *46 (S.D.N.Y. Aug. 21, 2003) (relator did not satisfy the "voluntary disclosure" prong when he failed to furnish the government "any specific details" regarding his allegation); United States *ex rel.* Kinney v. Stoltz, 2002 WL 523869, at *7 (D. Minn. Apr. 5, 2002) (even though the relator had previously filed a related *qui tam* action, the relator did not satisfy the "voluntarily provide" prong of the statute when he did not disclose to the government prior to filing his subsequent *qui tam* action information relating to the acts the defendants allegedly committed in the subsequent *qui tam* action); United States *ex rel.* Grynberg v. Praxair, Inc., 207 F. Supp. 2d 1163, 1185–86 (D. Colo. 2001) ("On January 9, 1998, *after* filing his Complaint, [the relator] provided the Department of Justice . . . with notice of his FCA action by letters to the Honorable Janet Reno and to the Colorado U.S. Attorney"; accordingly, the relator "has not met his burden to establish that he made the jurisdictionally required pre-filing disclosures.") (footnote omitted). Further, the Tenth Circuit recently ruled that even if an attorney makes a pre-suit disclosure to the United States, the disclosure will be deemed inadequate to satisfy the original source mandate that information be provided to the government prior to suit if the relator's attorney withheld the identity of the relator and the purported defendants. *See Hillcrest Health Center,* 264 F.3d at 1281 ("The narrow question raised on appeal is whether a relator qualifies as a 'source' if in making his pre-filing disclosure he withholds his identity and the identities of the potential defendants. The identities of the accuser and the accused are information, *i.e.* essential elements of the fraud transaction, on which the *qui tam* allegations are based. As for the information about the fraudulent schemes that was disclosed, there is little question that the government's ability to analyze and assess it was hampered, if not blocked, by this omission of identities. To withhold the identities of the relator and perpetrator deprives the government of key facts necessary in its efforts to confirm, substantiate or evaluate the fraud allegations. Without the identities, the information behind the allegations essentially remains in the relator's possession and undisclosed to the government, and what has been disclosed could be said to be little more than a hypothetical account given by an attorney.").

[71] For a more detailed critique of the Eighth Circuit's decision, see Robert Salcido, *The Public Disclosure Bar of the False Claims Act,* HEALTH CARE FRAUD LITIG. REP. (Andrews) (Apr. 2002).

claims like the one in *Dean,* in which a claimant investigated the fraud and then revealed it to the government before filing suit, we would expect that the effect of the original source provision is to protect from the public disclosure bar those who first bring a claim to light."[72]

However, if the court had compared the facts in *Dean* to those in *Allina,* it would have found that an application of the *Dean* rule would result in the dismissal of the relator in *Allina.* In *Dean,* the following events occurred: the relator investigated the fraud, the relator reported the fraud to the United States, and then the allegations of the fraud were publicly disclosed (in the form of criminal proceedings and news media accounts).[73] Under any interpretation of the public disclosure bar, the relator under the facts in *Dean* should have been protected: the relator broke the conspiracy of silence and divulged critical information to the government so that the government could conduct its own investigation before the same material was publicly disseminated.

That, however, is not what occurred in the *Allina* case. There the sequence was quite different. In *Allina,* the relator apparently investigated the alleged misconduct; the relator publicly disclosed the misconduct (in the form of a civil complaint and newspaper accounts); and only then did the relator disclose the allegations to the government. Hence, in making its disclosure to the government, the relator did not break any conspiracy of silence, but merely handed over to the government public material.

If the *Allina* court had literally adhered to the teaching of the *Dean* case and the language of the public disclosure bar, it would have dismissed the relator. By publicizing the allegations before making any disclosure to the federal government, the relator in *Allina* deprived the government of the very important opportunity to control and conduct its investigation in secrecy without prematurely tipping off the target of the investigation. In *Dean,* conversely, the government was afforded this opportunity. Because the original source provision is intended to benefit relators like the relator in *Dean* who disclosed the information before it became public knowledge, and not relators like the relator in *Allina* that divulge information to the government that has already been publicized, the relator in *Allina* should have been dismissed.

---

[72]276 F.3d at 1047–48.

[73]Although in *Dean* neither the appellate nor the district court set forth the precise dates of the disclosures to the government and the subsequent dates of the publicly disclosed criminal proceedings and news accounts, it seems clear from the state's statutory duty to report misconduct regarding federal grant funds and the court's factual rendition of the disclosures that the state made disclosures to the federal government before any public disclosure of the defendant's misconduct. *See* United States *ex rel.* Wisconsin v. Dean, 729 F.2d 1100, 1106 (7th Cir. 1984) ("Under Title XIX of the Social Security Act, 42 U.S.C. §§ 1396–1396p, states that receive grants from the federal government under the Act must report various fraud and abuse information to the Health Care Financing Administration of the Department of Health and Human Services. 42 C.F.R. § 455.17 (1980)."); *see also* 729 F.2d at 1104 ("First, the Wisconsin Medicaid Fraud Control Unit provided the United States Department of Health and Human Services with many reports about the allegedly fraudulent Medicaid claims during the State's investigation and prosecution of the appellant on state criminal grounds. . . . Second, the state criminal proceedings were reported extensively in two Milwaukee newspapers.").

Second, as noted earlier, another guiding principle in *Allina* concerned its notion that Congress sought to balance utility and fairness in constructing the public disclosure bar. In the context of discussing utility and fairness, the court, in its opinion, did not point to any specific language in the statute or the legislative history to support its construction. None exists. Moreover, from the structure of the statutory language, it appears that Congress' predominant concern was with utility. For example, it prohibited a relator, under Sections 3730(b)(5) and (e)(3), from bringing an action even if there had been no public disclosure and even if the relator otherwise qualified as an original source, because such actions served no utility to the government. There is no basis to believe that it made a different policy choice in the public disclosure bar.

Moreover, the court's conception of "fairness" is elusive and subjective. When the relator does not break the conspiracy of silence by reporting misdeeds to the government before the information is publicized, is it "fair" that the whistleblower obtain up to 30 percent of the government's recovery for republishing public information? Or, under these circumstances, is it fairer that the federal government (and ultimately taxpayers) should receive the full 100 percent? Most courts have ruled that the *qui tam* provisions are a mechanism to supply the government with information to prosecute fraud and not merely a mechanism to enrich relators and their counsel.[74] Under this construction of the public disclosure bar, it would be more fair to have dismissed the relator from the action.[75]

Third, in *Allina,* the court stated that a construction of the public disclosure bar that would require a relator to disclose the allegations to the United States *before* the public disclosure "has no textual basis in the statute."[76] However, a literal construction of the public disclosure bar requires that the relator be the government's informant in order to qualify as an original source.[77]

Fourth, in *Allina,* the court never cited the pertinent legislative history that contradicts its holding that the relator need not disclose its information to the government prior to the publication of the

---

[74] *See, e.g.,* United States v. Health Possibilities, P.S.C., 207 F.3d 335, 340 (6th Cir. 2000) ("The FCA is not designed to serve the parochial interests of relators, but to vindicate civic interests in avoiding fraud against public monies.") (citations omitted); United States v. Northrop Corp., 59 F.3d 953, 968 (9th Cir. 1995) ("The private right of recovery created by the provisions of the FCA exists not to compensate the *qui tam* relator, but the United States. The relator's right to recovery exists solely as a mechanism for deterring fraud and returning funds to the federal treasury.").

[75] The court in *Allina* had stated that the fairness point that Congress had sought to address in the original source provision was that of the government "not biting the hand that fed the government the information." 276 F.3d at 1047. However, when the relator only discloses the information *after* the public disclosure, this is simply not a concern. In *Allina,* for example, the United States could have obtained the same information by simply reading the newspaper. Under these circumstances the relator's information is not necessary, and permitting the relator to proceed only diminishes the government's ultimate potential recovery in the lawsuit.

[76] 276 F.3d at 1050.

[77] For a detailed discussion of the statutory language, see Main Volume Chapter 3, Section III.C.5.a., at 177–79.

information to qualify as an original source. In fact, the legislative history is consistent with the statutory language mandating that the original source be the person that supplies the pertinent information to the government before its public disclosure.[78]

Fifth, the court in *Allina* ignores the primary purpose of the provision. Both the legislative history and several cases make clear that the purpose of the *qui tam* provisions is to ensure that the federal government learns of misconduct at the earliest possible time.[79] Indeed, it is illogical on the one hand to believe that Congress required that lawsuits be placed under seal, as it did, so that the United States' interest could be protected by not prematurely disclosing an investigation to defendants[80] but, on the other hand, that Congress, in the original source provision, would reward relators who publicly disclosed the allegations underlying the lawsuit before informing the government of that conduct. Once the government learns of the information, it may take remedial action and minimize its potential losses. Contrary to this purpose, the court's ruling in *Allina* will encourage potential whistleblowers to wait in the hope that damages will mount and their bounty will increase.

In short, *qui tam* actions should benefit the United States. When there is no public disclosure of the underlying allegations, *qui tam* suits potentially benefit the United States because the Department of Justice (DOJ) presumably receives nonpublic facts that it can then investigate and discharge the Executive's constitutional duty to enforce the law. Alternatively, when the allegations have been publicly disclosed, no *qui tam* action is needed because the appropriate government officials will take action or be held politically accountable for their inaction. Congress, however, even after a public disclosure, would permit a narrow category of individuals to proceed with an action if they had been informants to the United States before the disclosure because these individuals assist the United States by providing it with nonpublic information that it can then investigate.

The Eighth Circuit's decision in *Allina* undermines the language and purpose of the public disclosure jurisdictional bar by permitting non-whistleblowers to proceed with *qui tam* actions that do not benefit the United States. The action does not benefit the United States because the relator tips the defendants off regarding the alleged misconduct before the United States has had an opportunity to investigate and because if the government now determines to proceed with the public allegations it will have to split a substantial portion of the proceeds with relators who did not provide the United States with nonpublic information. Other circuits considering this issue should therefore elect

---

[78] For a description of the pertinent legislative history, see Main Volume Chapter 3, Section III.C.5.a., at 179–80.

[79] See Main Volume Chapter 3, Section III.B., at 153–54 n.123 (citing cases).

[80] *See* 31 U.S.C. §3730(b)(3).

to follow the D.C. Circuit's ruling in *Findley*[81] and the Sixth Circuit's ruling in *McKenzie*[82] and reject the Eighth Circuit's ruling in *Allina*.

IV. PREEMPTING FCA ACTIONS: THE OFFICE OF INSPECTOR GENERAL'S VOLUNTARY DISCLOSURE PROGRAM

B. Benefits and Risks of Submitting a Voluntary Disclosure

1. *Risks of Disclosure*

As noted in the Main Volume, one risk of making a disclosure to the government is that the disclosing party may potentially waive the attorney-client privilege or work product protection associated with the disclosed material. The Sixth Circuit's recent opinion in In re *Columbia/HCA Healthcare Corp. Billing Practices Litigation*[83] illustrates precisely how a disclosure to the government of privileged information may later undermine a company's interest because the confidential information must later be produced to private parties in related litigation.

In *Columbia/HCA Healthcare Corp.*, the Sixth Circuit had to consider whether HCA had waived the attorney-client privilege and work product immunity when it had disclosed the results of an internal investigation to the government. Specifically, beginning in the mid-1990s, HCA, either in response to a government investigation or in anticipation of it, conducted several internal audits of its Medicare patient records.[84] The audits examined the various billing codes HCA assigned to the patients in order to receive reimbursement from the Medicare program and any potential miscoding of the Medicare patients. When the DOJ attempted to obtain the audits, HCA rebuffed the request based on attorney-client privilege and the work product doctrine.[85]

Subsequently, HCA determined to engage in negotiations with the DOJ to settle the fraud investigation.[86] In coordination with this effort, HCA agreed to produce some of the coding audits and related documents to the government. In exchange for this cooperation, the DOJ consented to certain stringent confidentiality provisions governing the disclosure of the documents. Specifically, HCA's agreement with the DOJ provided that

> [t]he disclosure of any report, document, or information by one party to the other does not constitute a waiver of any applicable privilege or

---

[81] United States *ex rel.* Findley v. FPC-Boron Employees' Club, 105 F.3d 675 (D.C. Cir. 1997), *cert. denied*, 522 U.S. 865 (1997).

[82] United States *ex rel.* McKenzie v. BellSouth Telecomms., Inc., 123 F.3d 935, 940 (6th Cir. 1997), *cert. denied*, 522 U.S. 1077 (1998).

[83] 293 F.3d 289 (6th Cir. 2002).

[84] *Id.* at 291–92.

[85] *Id.*

[86] *Id.*

claim under the work product doctrine. Both parties to the agreement reserve the right to contest the assertion of any privilege by the other party to the agreement, but will not argue that the disclosing party, by virtue of the disclosures it makes pursuant to this agreement, has waived any applicable privilege or work product doctrine claim.[87]

As a result of the parties' negotiations, they ultimately reached a settlement, resulting in HCA paying an $840 million fine to the government.[88] Once the results of the DOJ's investigation were publicized, private insurance companies and private individuals undertook to evaluate the billing they received from HCA. This review culminated in the filing of numerous lawsuits around the country in which various plaintiffs contended that HCA overbilled them for various services, as it had the government.[89] Significantly, in these lawsuits, the private plaintiffs alleged that, notwithstanding whatever privilege HCA's coding audits may have held, HCA waived the protections of those privileges by disclosing the materials to the government.[90]

As it had initially with the DOJ, HCA refused to produce the coding audits based on the work product doctrine and attorney-client privilege. Furthermore, HCA pointed out that in disclosing the information to the government, it had expressly reserved the right to assert the attorney-client privilege and the work product doctrine pursuant to the confidentiality agreement it had negotiated with the DOJ.[91]

Notwithstanding that agreement, the district court granted the plaintiffs' motion to compel the production of the coding audit.[92] Specifically, it found that the "voluntary disclosure of privileged materials to the government constitutes a waiver of the attorney-client privilege to all other adversaries."[93] Further, the court found that by disclosing the documents to the DOJ, HCA waived any protections afforded under the work product doctrine as well.[94]

The Sixth Circuit affirmed the district court's ruling. In evaluating the district court's opinion, the Sixth Circuit noted that the general rule is that the "attorney-client privilege is waived by voluntary disclosure of private communications by an individual or corporation to third parties."[95] Notwithstanding the general rule, the court pointed out that various courts have adopted one of three separate positions regarding whether "selective waiver" is possible: (1) some have held that selective waiver is possible; (2) others have found that selective

---

[87] *Id.*

[88] *Id.*

[89] *Id.*

[90] *Id.* at 293.

[91] *Id.*

[92] *See In re* Columbia/HCA Healthcare Corp. Billing Practices Litig., 192 F.R.D. 575 (M.D. Tenn. 2000).

[93] *Id.* at 579.

[94] *Id.* at 579–80.

[95] *In re* Columbia/HCA Healthcare Corp. Billing Practices Litig., 293 F.3d 289, 294 (6th Cir. 2002) (internal quotation and citation omitted).

waiver is not permissible under any circumstances; and (3) some have ruled that selective waiver is possible when the government agrees to a confidentiality order.[96]

As the court noted, the leading case espousing the view that selective waiver is possible is the Eighth Circuit's opinion in *Diversified Industries v. Meredith.*[97] In *Diversified,* an independent audit committee retained outside counsel to review allegations that the company had paid bribes to purchasing agents of other companies to obtain business.[98] Counsel prepared an internal report that was circulated to the company's board of directors and later to the Securities and Exchange Commission (SEC) pursuant to a subpoena.[99] Another company then filed an antitrust action against Diversified and sought the internal report on the grounds that Diversified had waived the privilege by voluntarily surrendering it to the SEC pursuant to its subpoena. The Eighth Circuit rejected the company's request for the document, holding that because "Diversified disclosed these documents in a separate and nonpublic SEC investigation, . . . only a limited waiver of the privilege occurred" and to "hold otherwise may have the effect of thwarting the developing procedure of corporations to employ independent outside counsel to investigate and advise them in order to protect stockholders, potential stockholders and customers."[100]

The Sixth Circuit further noted that several courts have rejected the *Diversified* court's "selective waiver" theory and instead have ruled that any waiver of the privilege to some parties necessarily waives the privilege to all parties.[101] The rationale underlying this viewpoint is that the client should not "be permitted to pick and choose among his opponents, waiving the privilege as to some and resurrecting the claim of confidentiality to obstruct others, or to invoke the privilege as to communications whose confidentiality he has already compromised for his own benefit"[102] because such a selective waiver does nothing to "serve the purpose of encouraging full disclosure to one's attorney in order to obtain informed legal assistance,"[103] which is the purpose underlying the attorney-client privilege.

Finally, the Sixth Circuit pointed out that some courts have held that a disclosure to the government would constitute a waiver unless the right to assert the privilege in subsequent proceedings is specifically

---

[96] *Id.* at 295.

[97] 572 F.2d 596 (8th Cir. 1978) (en banc).

[98] *Id.* at 607.

[99] *Id.* at 611.

[100] *Id.* (citations omitted).

[101] *See, e.g., In re* Columbia/HCA Healthcare Corp. Billing Practices Litig., 293 F.3d 289, 295–98 (6th Cir. 2002).

[102] *Id.* at 296 (quoting Permian Corp. v. United States, 665 F.2d 1214, 1221 (D.C. Cir. 1979)) (footnote omitted).

[103] *Id.* at 297 (quoting Westinghouse Elec. Corp. v. Republic of Philippines, 951 F.2d 1414, 1425 (3d Cir. 1991)).

reserved at the time the disclosure is made.[104] By asserting this right, the party makes clear that it "had made some effort to preserve the privacy of the privileged communication, rather than having engaged in abuse of the privilege by first making a knowing decision to waive the rule's protection and then seeking to retract that decision in subsequent litigation."[105]

Ultimately, the Sixth Circuit adopted the most stringent test, ruling that although the selective waiver approach of *Diversified* had "considerable appeal," policy considerations militated against adopting that rule:

> There is considerable appeal, and justification, for permitting selective waiver when the initial disclosure is to an investigating arm of the Government. Undoubtedly, by waiving privilege as to the Government, a client furthers the "truth-finding process." *Permian* [Corp. v. United States, 665 F.2d 1214,] 1221 [(D.C. Cir. 1981)]. Considerable savings are realized to the Government, and through it to the public, in time and fiscal expenditure related to the investigation of crimes and civil fraud. Such a policy might also . . . increase the likelihood that corporations would engage in the type of self-policing represented by [HCA's] Coding Audits. Without a doubt, disclosure of information to the Government in a cooperative manner encourages settlement of disputes and by encouraging cooperative exchange of information, selective waiver would improve the ability of the Government and private parties to settle certain actions.
>
> However, this argument has several flaws. As noted by the First Circuit, it "has no logical terminus." [United States v. Massachusetts Inst. of Tech., 129 F.3d 681, 686 (1st Cir. 1997)]. Insofar as the "truth-finding process" is concerned, a private litigant stands in nearly the same stead as the Government. This argument holds considerable weight in the numerous circumstances whereby litigants act as private attorneys general, and through their actions vindicate the public interest. A plaintiff in a shareholder derivative action or a qui tam action who exposes accounting and tax fraud provides as much service to the "truth finding process" as an SEC investigator. Recognizing this, a difficult and fretful linedrawing process begins, consuming immeasurable private and judicial resources in a vain attempt to distinguish one private litigant from the next.[106]

---

[104] *See, e.g., id.* at 299–303.

[105] *Id.* at 300 (quoting Teachers Ins. & Annuity Ass'n of Am. v. Shamrock Broadcasting Co., 521 F. Supp. 638, 646 (S.D.N.Y. 1981)).

[106] 293 F.3d at 303. However, as Judge Boggs noted in his dissenting opinion, the majority's view appears to be mistaken. Specifically, as he pointed out, government representatives' interest (the public good) is vastly different from that of private litigants (private financial gain):

> The government's investigations are generally more important. Government officials, with finite litigative resources and no individual monetary stake in the outcome of litigation, generally are more selective regarding the matters they choose to pursue than are private parties. Because of these incentives, government investigations are more likely to be in the public interest. Private litigants, often encouraged by large potential liability, on balance will have a greater incentive to press the legal envelope and to pursue legal actions less certainly within the public interest.

293 F.3d at 312. Indeed, in FCA *qui tam* actions, which the Sixth Circuit panel referenced, relators file actions alleging that a defendant submitted a false or fraudulent claim to the United States and, if their action is successful, obtain a substantial bounty. The Supreme Court has underscored the vastly different footing on which relators stand as opposed to governmental offi-

The Sixth Circuit went on to state that

> [a] countervailing policy concern, heretofore not discussed, is whether the Government should assist in obfuscating the "truth-finding process" by entering into such confidentiality agreements at all. The investigatory agencies of the Government should act to bring to light illegal activities, not to assist wrongdoers in concealing the information from the public domain. Governmental agencies "have means to secure the information they need" other than through voluntary cooperation achieved via selective waiver (albeit at a higher cost in time and money). *MIT,* 129 F.3d at 685. It is not necessary for the courts to create a new method, one which effectively prevents further litigants from obtaining the same information, when other means (means which will not result in the information being concealed from the public) are available to the Government.[107]

Finally, the Sixth Circuit determined that it would not grant work product protection to the requested documents:

> Other than the fact that the initial waiver must be to an "adversary," there is no compelling reason for differentiating waiver of work product

---

cials. Specifically, the court noted that "as a class of plaintiffs, qui tam relators are different in kind than the Government. They are motivated primarily by prospects of monetary reward rather than the public good." Hughes Aircraft Co. v. United States *ex rel.* Schumer, 520 U.S. 939, 949 (1997); *see also* United States *ex rel.* Foulds v. Texas Tech. Univ., 171 F.3d 279, 293 (5th Cir. 1999). Further, the Court pointed out that just because "a qui tam suit is brought by a private party 'on behalf of the United States' . . . does not alter the fact that a relator's interests and the Government's do not necessarily coincide." 520 U.S. at 949 n.5 (citation omitted).

   [107] 293 F.3d at 303. *See also In re* Lupron Mktg. & Sales Practices Litig., 313 F. Supp. 2d 8, 14 (D. Mass. 2004). However, as Judge Boggs pointed out in his dissenting opinion in *Columbia/HCA Healthcare Corp. Billing Practices Litig.,* the majority's view is based on a flawed premise that there is an equal nonprivileged analogue to privileged material that the government is able to obtain, albeit at a higher cost. Specifically, he noted:

> Contrary to the court's argument, increased access to privileged information increases the absolute efficacy of government investigations, regardless of increased investigatory costs to the government. There is some evidence provided by privileged information for which there is no non-privileged substitute or to which there is no path without privileged evidence. The court . . . argues that the government has "other means" to secure the information that they need, while conceding that those other means may consume more government time and money. . . . Presumably, the court is referring to search warrants or civil discovery. It should be emphasized, however, that the government has no other means to secure otherwise privileged information. That the documents or other evidence sought is privileged permits the target of an investigation to refuse production through civil discovery, to quash any subpoena *duces tecum,* or to prevent the admission of the privileged information even by the government. The only way that the government can obtain privileged information is for the holder of the privilege voluntarily to disclose it. The court's argument about the adequacy of other means, suggesting that the only difference between them and voluntary disclosure is cost, requires the premise that all privileged information has a non-privileged analogue that is discoverable with enough effort. That premise, however, does not hold.

Id. at 311. *Cf.* United States v. Bergonzi, 216 F.R.D. 487 (N.D. Cal. 2003). In *Bergonzi,* a company sought to protect a disclosure report and back-up material, such as interview memoranda, that it supplied to the Securities and Exchange Commission (SEC) when it conducted an internal review into whether there was a violation of law. *Id.* at 490–91. Early in the investigation, the company's lawyers met with SEC investigators to inform the SEC regarding the internal review and that the company would disclose its report to the SEC once it was completed. *Id.* The company also entered into a confidentiality agreement to protect against the disclosure of the report to third parties. *Id.* Specifically, the agreement provided that the company did not "waive work product or applicable attorney-client privilege, and the SEC agreed that it would not argue that the voluntary submission of the information would constitute a waiver of the privilege." *Id.* at 491. Under these facts, the court refused to apply the attorney-client privilege because the company created the communication with the intent of disclosing it to the government and hence it never intended the communication to remain confidential, which is a prerequisite to applying the privilege in the first instance. *Id.* at 493–94.

from waiver of attorney-client privilege. Many of the reasons for disallowing selective waiver in the attorney-client privilege context also apply to the work product doctrine. The ability to prepare one's case in confidence, which is the chief reason articulated in *Hickman* [v. Taylor, 329 U.S. 495 (1947)], for the work product protections, has little to do with talking to the Government. Even more than attorney-client privilege waiver, waiver of the protections afforded by the work product doctrine is a tactical litigation decision. Attorney and client both know the material in question was prepared in anticipation of litigation; the subsequent decision on whether or not to "show your hand" is quintessential litigation strategy. Like attorney-client privilege, there is no reason to transform the work product into another "brush on the attorney's palette," used as a sword rather than a shield. [*In re* Steinhardt Partners, L.P., 9 F.3d 230, 235 (2d Cir. 1993).][108]

The teaching of the Sixth Circuit's opinion is that "[r]elatively narrow cooperation with the government in the form of a disclosure of privileged information can expose an individual or firm to massive liability and reveal privileged documents far afield from the disclosure itself."[109] However, one issue not fully addressed in the *Columbia/HCA Healthcare Corp.* opinion is the precise scope of the waiver when a party submits a disclosure to the government. That is, for example, if a company submits a disclosure report to the government, is any privilege that is waived limited to the report itself? Does it include all attorney-client communications and attorney work product related to preparing the report, such as notes of interviews and client correspondence? Or does it include the attorney-client communications and work product regarding the facts discussed in the report, but not attorney opinion work product? Discussed below are the general rules regarding waiver and some tips for making a report to the government that potentially limits the scope of any waiver.[110]

The "attorney-client privilege is waived if the holder of the privilege voluntarily discloses or consents to disclosure of any significant part of the matter of communication."[111] A waiver may further be subcategorized into various types. For example, cases under "the 'waiver' heading include situations as divergent as an express and voluntary surrender of a privilege, partial disclosure of a privileged document, selective disclosure to some outsiders but not all, and inadvertent overhearings or disclosures."[112] A waiver may include both the entirety of communications that a party has disclosed only in part and all other

---

[108] 293 F.3d at 306–07 (footnote omitted).

[109] *Id.* at 311 (Boggs, J., dissenting).

[110] For a more detailed discussion of the application of the attorney-client privilege when submitting disclosures to the government, see David Orbuch & Robert Salcido, *Preserving and Protecting Attorney-Client Information When Operating a Compliance Department*, AM. HEALTH LAW. (Sept. 2002).

[111] *In re* Kidder Peabody Secs. Litig., 168 F.R.D. 459, 468 (S.D.N.Y. 1996) (internal quotation and citations omitted).

[112] United States v. Massachusetts Inst. of Tech., 129 F.3d 681, 684 (1st Cir. 1997).

privileged communications insofar as they touch on subjects voluntarily disclosed by the privilege holder.[113]

Especially relevant to FCA voluntary disclosures are "partial" and "selective" disclosures or waivers. A partial waiver occurs when a party reveals only segments of privileged communication.[114] This situation may occur, for example, when a company submits a disclosure report to the government but does not produce the underlying attorney-client correspondence regarding the scope of the investigation to be conducted and the notes underlying witness interviews. A selective waiver occurs when a party discloses privileged communications to one party but not another.[115] This situation occurs, for example, when, as in the *Columbia/HCA Healthcare Corp.* case,[116] a company takes the position that although it divulged confidential information to the United States, it need not disclose the material to any other third party in related litigation.

A court's treatment of waiver may vary depending on whether it is a partial or selective waiver. In the case of a partial waiver, a court will apply the "fairness doctrine," which aims to prevent prejudice to a party and distortion of the judicial process that may be caused by the privilege holder's partial disclosure to an adversary.[117] Hence, in In re *Kidder Peabody Securities Litigation,*[118] in which a company that was under investigation submitted a report to the SEC to obtain favorable treatment, the court found that the company had waived the privilege both for the report and the underlying documents, such as witness interviews, that would be needed to evaluate the reliability and accuracy of the report.[119] The court reasoned that it would be unfair to find

---

[113]*Kidder Peabody,* 168 F.R.D. at 469.

[114]Harding v. Dana Transp., Inc., 914 F. Supp. 1084, 1092 (D.N.J. 1996).

[115]*Id.; see also* Westinghouse Elec. Corp. v. Republic of Philippines, 951 F.2d 1414, 1423 n.7 (3d Cir. 1991) ("Selective waiver permits the client who has disclosed privileged communications to one party to continue asserting the privilege against other parties. Partial waiver permits a client who has disclosed a portion of privileged communications to continue asserting the privilege as to the remaining portions of the same communications.").

[116]*In re* Columbia/HCA Healthcare Corp. Billing Practices Litig., 293 F.3d 289 (6th Cir. 2002).

[117]*See Westinghouse,* 951 F.2d at 1426 n.12 ("When a party discloses a portion of otherwise privileged materials while withholding the rest, the privilege is waived only as to those communications actually disclosed, unless a partial waiver would be unfair to the party's adversary. . . . If partial waiver does disadvantage the disclosing party's adversary by, for example, allowing the disclosing party to present a one-sided story to the court, the privilege will be waived as to all communications on the same subject."); *Kidder Peabody,* 168 F.R.D. at 469. *See generally In re* Grand Jury Proceedings, 219 F.3d 175 (2d Cir. 2000) ("as the animating principle behind waiver is fairness to the parties, if the court finds that the privilege was waived, then the waiver should be tailored to remedy the prejudice to the [adverse party]").

[118]168 F.R.D. 459, 468 (S.D.N.Y. 1996).

[119]*Id.* at 472; *see also* Harding v. Dana Transp., Inc., 914 F. Supp. 1084, 1093, 1096 (D.N.J. 1996) (when attorney investigated allegations that defendant company had engaged in sexual discrimination and the company represented in its defense in an administrative proceeding that it had "fully investigated the complaints raised in the Verified Complaint and has found that there is no supporting evidence that the same occurred," the company had waived the privilege as to the full scope of the lawyer's investigation (such as interview notes of witnesses, billing sheets or records that reflect the amount of time expended on the investigation, and correspondence between the company and lawyer regarding scope of investigation to be conducted) because "[c]onsistent with the doctrine of fairness, the plaintiffs must be permitted to probe the substance of [the company's] alleged investigation to determine its sufficiency").

that no waiver occurred, because then the company would be able to use the privilege as a sword (by using partial disclosure to obtain lenient treatment from the SEC) and as a shield (by refusing to produce less flattering findings to a private party).[120]

In the case of selective waiver, a court may decline to apply the fairness doctrine and simply rule that a waiver encompassing the entire subject matter exists.[121] The reason for this approach is the view that when there is a disclosure to one adverse party, there is no unfairness to any other adverse party and hence there is no concern of proportionality that exists in cases of partial disclosure.[122] Hence, in In re *Martin Marietta Corp.,*[123] the Fourth Circuit ruled that a position paper the company submitted to the government, which asserted that all consulted by the company would testify that they had no concerns regarding fraudulent conduct, was sufficient to waive the privilege regarding the position paper and underlying details such as witness statements when the company received a subpoena from a former employee.[124]

Finally, consistent with the approach the Sixth Circuit adopted in the *Columbia/HCA Healthcare Corp.* case, most courts have taken a similarly strict view regarding waiver of attorney work product when a company tenders a disclosure to the government.[125] The basis for this viewpoint is that the work product doctrine serves to protect the attorney work product from adversaries, and if an attorney waives the protection as to one party, he or she must be willing to waive it as to all others.[126] However, a court may limit the waiver to non-opinion work

---

[120]*Kidder Peabody,* 168 F.R.D. at 472–73.

[121]*See Westinghouse,* 951 F.2d at 1426 ("Generally, the 'fairness doctrine' is invoked in partial (as opposed to selective) disclosure cases") (footnote omitted); *Harding,* 914 F. Supp. at 1092 ("While the Third Circuit does not apply the fairness doctrine to situations of selective waiver, it has recognized the validity of the District of Columbia Circuit's fairness rationale in partial disclosure cases."); *but see* Dellwood Farms, Inc. v. Cargill, Inc., 128 F.3d 1122, 1127–28 (7th Cir. 1997) (in selective waiver case, refusing to find waiver because the party making the disclosure—the government—was not "using coy disclosure to gain litigation leverage" over other parties).

[122]*See Westinghouse,* 951 F.2d at 1426 n.13; *see also id.* at 1430 ("We decline to extend the fairness doctrine to cases involving selective disclosures because . . . we do not see how disclosing protected materials to one adversary disadvantages another.").

[123]856 F.2d 619 (4th Cir. 1988).

[124]*Id.* at 623. *Cf.* Picard Chem. Inc. Profit Sharing v. Perrigo Co., 951 F. Supp. 679, 688–89 (W.D. Mich. 1996) (no waiver when company did not reveal a significant part of its report and did not summarize evidence found in the report in its motion to dismiss).

[125]*See, e.g.,* United States v. Massachusetts Inst. of Tech., 129 F.3d 681, 687 (1st Cir. 1997); *In re* Steinhardt Partners, L.P., 9 F.3d 230, 235 (2d Cir. 1993); *Martin Marietta,* 856 F.2d at 625 ("The disclosure [report] of [the company] was made broad by its express assurance of completeness of its disclosure to the United States Attorney, so that the subject matter of the disclosure and the waiver is comprehensive, and includes all of the company's non-opinion work product relating to the investigation that it conducted"); United States v. Bergonzi, 216 F.R.D. 487, 498 (N.D. Calif. 2003).

[126]*See, e.g., Steinhardt Partners,* 9 F.3d at 235 (refusing to apply work product doctrine to memorandum attorney furnished to the SEC when the same document was later requested in class action lawsuit, pointing out that "[o]nce a party allows an adversary to share the otherwise privileged thought processes of counsel, the need for the privilege disappears. Courts therefore accept the waiver doctrine as a limitation on work product protection. The waiver doctrine provides that voluntary disclosure of work product to an adversary waives the privilege as to other parties.") (citations omitted).

product.[127] Hence, for example, attorney notes regarding the credibility of certain witnesses or employees or the strength of particular legal theories may remain protected.[128]

The most important lesson in this area is to be immersed in the case law of the applicable circuit when contemplating any disclosure to the government. Unfortunately, however, because a company can typically be sued under the FCA in more than one circuit, a party should be aware of the law of other circuits as well.[129] Moreover, besides knowledge of the case law, some of the following guidelines may be used to reduce the risk of needless waiver of the attorney-client privilege or work product protection:

- *Obtain a Confidentiality Agreement.* Only two circuits have ruled that obtaining another party's consent is irrelevant to determining whether the party sought to waive either the attorney-client privilege or work product protection.[130] Several courts have implied that obtaining such an agreement may

---

[127] *See, e.g., Martin Marietta,* 856 F.2d at 626 ("We think that when there is subject matter waiver, it should not extend to opinion work product for two reasons. First . . . opinion work product is to be accorded great protection by the courts. . . . Secondly, the underlying rationale for the doctrine of subject matter waiver has little application in the context of a pure expression of legal theory or legal opinion. . . . There is relatively little danger that a litigant will attempt to use a pure mental impression or legal theory as a sword and as a shield in the trial of a case so as to distort the fact finding process. Thus, the protection of lawyers from the broad repercussions of subject matter waiver in this context strengthens the adversary process, and, unlike the selective disclosure of evidence, may ultimately and ideally further the search for the truth."); *see also Kidder Peabody,* 168 F.R.D. at 473 ("in the exercise of our discretion, . . . we limit the piercing of the privilege to purely factual summaries of witness statements, and thus avoid any danger that the waiver might encompass core attorney mental processes, for which we are required to demonstrate particular solicitude") (citations omitted).

[128] *See, e.g., Martin Marietta,* 856 F.2d at 626 n.2 ("in the instant case, [the company] having quoted from some audit interviews, the transcript of these interviews has been waived under the broad doctrine of subject matter waiver. Similarly, work product protection has been waived as to most of the internal notes and memoranda on these interviews which, by way of summarizing in substance and format the interview results, [the company] used as the basis of its disclosure to the government on its audit results. These are evidentiary materials from which [the third party former employee] hopes to adduce evidence supporting his scapegoat theory. However, in disclosing such results, [the company] apparently would not disclose nor would intend to disclose, hypothetically, marginal notations on such documents such as: 'This person does not appear credible; let's not call him as a witness if we have to go to trial on this one.' Such an expression of legal opinion, thus detached from the data which [the company] did disclose, would not be subject to subject matter waiver.").

[129] *See, e.g.,* 31 U.S.C. §3732(a) ("Any action under section 3730 may be brought in any judicial district in which the defendant or, in the case of multiple defendants, any one defendant can be found, resides, transacts business, or in which any act proscribed by section 3729 occurred.").

[130] *See In re* Columbia/HCA Healthcare Corp. Billing Practices Litig., 293 F.3d 289, 303 (6th Cir. 2002) (although confidentiality agreement protects "the expectations of the parties," it "does little to serve the 'public ends' of adequate legal representation that the attorney-client privilege is designed to protect") (citation omitted); Westinghouse Elec. Corp. v. Republic of Philippines, 951 F.2d 1414, 1427, 1430 (3d Cir. 1991) (ruling, as to the attorney-client privilege, that "[e]ven though the DOJ apparently agreed not to disclose the information, under traditional waiver doctrine a voluntary disclosure to a third party waives the attorney-client privilege even if the third party agrees not to disclose the communications to anyone else" and, as to the work product doctrine, rejecting the company's "argument that it did not waive the work-product protection because it reasonably expected the agencies to keep the documents it disclosed to them confidential") (citations omitted).

result in a court ruling that there was no waiver.[131] Hence, such an agreement should be requested before any disclosure to the United States of potentially damaging admissions.

- *Carefully Document the Basis for the Waiver of the Privilege.* For example, if the basis for the waiver is to cooperate with government officials, state that plainly in the document. Courts are more likely to find waiver when it appears that the waiver was purely self-interested rather than for the public good.

- *Limit the Scope of the Privileged Material That Is Disclosed.* If the government requests additional privileged material, resist its request to the greatest possible extent and document the basis for assertion of the privilege. A corporation that so documents and raises its concern for privilege establishes a reliance on a continued existence of confidentiality even after disclosure.

- *Avoid Testimonial Use of the Results of the Investigation.* Broad statements vouching for the credibility of corporate employees or the completeness of the review are open invitations to subsequent litigants to state that they have a right to probe into whether such broad representations have merit.[132] Instead, in drafting a disclosure to the government, attempt to address the pertinent issues at a more general level without quoting or paraphrasing (for example, specific witness statements or referencing specific communications with the client).

- *Develop a Disclosure Strategy.* At the start of the investigation, develop a strategy for determining what information needs to be protected under the privilege and what information, because of an eventual release to the government, should not be protected.

Notwithstanding these general guidelines, however, an entity should be aware that any disclosure is fraught with risk and that by submitting a disclosure to the government, a party at some point in the future may have to produce not only the disclosed documents but all related documents underlying the disclosure as well.

---

[131]*See, e.g., In re* Steinhardt Partners, L.P., 9 F.3d 230 (2d Cir. 1993) (refusing to adopt a per se rule that all voluntary disclosures to the government waive the work product rule because establishing "a rigid rule would fail to anticipate situations in which the disclosing party and the government may share a common interest in developing legal theories and analyzing information, or situations in which the SEC and the disclosing party have entered into an explicit agreement that the SEC will maintain the confidentiality to the disclosed materials"); *cf.* United States v. Bergonzi, 216 F.R.D. 487, 496–97 (N.D. Calif. 2003) ("Although [the company] entered into what it fashions to be confidentiality agreements with the Government entities involved, the agreement made by the Government to keep the documents was not unconditional. As such, the Court finds [the company] failed to demonstrate the common interest exception to the waiver of the work product privilege applies. Accordingly, the production of the Report and Back-up Materials to the Government and the SEC constituted waiver of the privilege") (footnote omitted); *Kidder Peabody,* 168 F.R.D. at 471–72 (disclosure of draft report to SEC would waive privilege "unless [the company] has assurances from the [SEC] that no further inquiry will be made" regarding the disclosed documents).

[132]*Compare* Picard Chem. Inc. Profit Sharing Plan v. Perrigo Co., 951 F. Supp. 679, 688–89 (W.D. Mich. 1996) (no waiver because report did not summarize evidence), *with Martin Marietta,* 856 F.2d at 623 (waiver found when company reported what it had learned from those interviewed).

4

Practical Considerations for Defending Health Care Fraud and Abuse Cases*

---

*Patric Hooper, Stacy Rummel Bratcher, Hooper, Lundy & Bookman, Inc., Los Angeles, California.

IV. Enforcement Weapons

E. Federal Administrative Agency Remedies

2. *Suspension of Payments*

A Medicare fiscal intermediary or Medicare carrier does not have
the authority to delay the administrative hearing process during the
pendency of a criminal or civil investigation. Thus, for example, if a
Medicare carrier has temporarily suspended a supplier's Medicare payments due to suspicion of fraud or abuse, the carrier must nevertheless
continue to proceed through the administrative process, including issuing an overpayment determination, which should trigger administrative appeal rights for the affected supplier.[1] Nowhere do the Medicare
statutes or regulations authorize the Secretary of the Department of
Health and Human Services (HHS) to postpone an overpayment
determination pending the outcome of judicial inquiry into the presence of fraud.

---

[1]*See* United States *ex rel.* Rahman v. Oncology Assocs., P.C., 198 F.3d 502, 514 (4th Cir. 1999).

F. State Administrative Agency Remedies

In *Doctor's Medical Laboratory, Inc. v. Connell*,[2] the California state controller was prohibited from unilaterally withholding Medicaid payments from a provider and from auditing the Medicaid payments of the provider because the court held that only the single state Medicaid agency, the State Department of Health Services, had such authority under the controlling federal Medicaid laws and regulations. However, in a subsequent decision, the same court of appeal concluded that a state Medicaid plan approved by HHS and authorizing the state controller to conduct Medicaid audits constituted an interpretation of the federal Medicaid regulations, which allowed the single state Medicaid agency to delegate audit authority to another state agency—here, the state controller's office—so long as the single state agency retained final authority to review the audit results.[3]

Because the controlling federal Medicaid regulation prohibiting the delegation of discretionary authority from the single state Medicaid agency to another state agency[4] did not change between the two California Court of Appeal decisions, it is difficult to reconcile the decisions. However, from a practical standpoint, it is quite obvious that the federal government's approval of a state plan amendment, which expressly permitted the delegation of audit authority from the single state Medicaid agency to the state controller, was considered to be the equivalent of a change in the governing provisions of the Medicaid regulations by the court.

The reasoning of the California Court of Appeal in *RCJ Medical Services*[5] was cited with approval by the U.S. Court of Appeals for the Ninth Circuit in *San Lazaro Ass'n v. Connell*.[6] In reversing the district court decision, which had prohibited the delegation of authority from the single state Medicaid agency to the state controller, the Ninth Circuit concluded that Medicaid providers could not maintain a right of action under the controlling federal Medicaid statute or Medicaid regulation regarding the single state agency provision.

VIII. IMPACT OF INVESTIGATIONS

E. Suing Government Officials for Reckless Investigations and Related Actions [New Topic]

As pointed out in the Main Volume, government fraud and abuse investigations can severely disrupt the operations of a health care provider. Such investigations can result in adverse publicity, which can

---

[2] 81 Cal. Rptr. 2d 829, 69 Cal. App. 4th 891 (1999).

[3] *See* RCJ Medical Servs. v. Bonta, 111 Cal. Rptr. 2d 223, 91 Cal. App. 4th 986 (2001), *cert. denied,* 535 U.S. 1096, 122 S. Ct. 2292 (2002).

[4] 42 C.F.R. §431.10(e).

[5] *See* 111 Cal. Rptr. 2d 223.

[6] 286 F.3d 1088 (9th Cir. 2002), *cert. denied,* 537 U.S. 878, 123 S. Ct. 78 (2002).

destroy a provider's business and reputation. Competitors who learn of the investigation may use the information to attempt to gain a competitive advantage. Moreover, during the course of an investigation, government agencies may withhold or suspend payments to the providers.

When government officials ignore the law and act unreasonably in connection with such actions, providers may have the right to pursue equitable and legal remedies against those officials. Under Section 1983 of the Civil Rights Act,[7] when a person acting under color of state law deprives someone of a constitutional or federal right, the aggrieved person may pursue an action for injunctive relief and damages. Recently, such actions have been successful in compelling state officials to lift Medicaid sanctions. For example, in *Labotest, Inc. v. Bonta*,[8] two providers successfully brought an action to compel the director of the California Department of Health Services to lift certain Medi-Cal sanctions, which, in turn, entitled them to an award of attorneys' fees. Providers may also pursue actions under Section 1983 of the Civil Rights Act for damages against state officials and employees.[9]

These civil rights actions, in which state officials and employees are being sued in their individual capacities, might not only result in providers being compensated for damages caused by constitutional torts, but might also serve to restrain overzealous government enforcement agencies.

X. Litigation Defense Strategies

A. Importance of the Fundamentals

2. *Necessity of Wrongful Intent*

In March 2002, the U.S. Court of Appeals for the Eleventh Circuit issued a very important decision regarding the intent (and act) necessary to sustain a false statement conviction under the criminal false statement laws.[10] In *United States v. Whiteside*,[11] a jury had convicted the defendants of knowingly and willfully filing false statements in certain Medicare and Medicaid cost reports concerning reimbursement for certain capital-related costs claimed in the reports.

The court pointed out that in a criminal case where the truth or falsity of a statement centers on an interpretative question of law, the government bears the burden of proving beyond a reasonable doubt that the defendants' statement is not true under a reasonable interpretation of the law. The court reversed the conviction of the defendants, concluding that as a matter of law the government could not

---

[7] 42 U.S.C. §1983.

[8] 297 F.3d 892 (9th Cir. 2002).

[9] Azer v. Connell, 306 F.3d 930 (9th Cir. 2002), *dismissed on subsequent appeal,* 87 Fed. Appx. 684, 2004 WL 291187 (9th Cir. Feb. 13, 2004) (unpublished).

[10] Although the court spoke in terms of actus reus, the reasoning is probably most useful in a discussion of mens rea, i.e., intent.

[11] 285 F.3d 1345 (11th Cir. 2002).

meet its burden of proof in the case because no Medicare regulation, administrative ruling, or judicial decision existed that clearly required interest expense to be reported in accordance with the position advocated by the government. Because the experts in the case disagreed at trial as to the validity of the theory of reimbursement of the capital-related costs adjusted by the government, the court concluded that the defendants' interpretation was not unreasonable. As a result, "the government failed to meet its burden of proving the actus reus of the offense—actual falsity as a matter of law."[12]

XI. Current Enforcement Priorities

The Office of Inspector General's (OIG's) Fiscal Year 2003 Work Plan for the Centers for Medicare and Medicaid Services[13] contains 49 pages of issues that the OIG is examining. The Work Plan is an excellent source for determining current enforcement priorities.

XII. Enforcement Actions
Involving Pharmaceuticals [New Topic]

A. Introduction [New Topic]

In recent years, state and federal law enforcement agencies have focused resources on eradicating fraud related to the pricing, marketing, and prescribing of pharmaceuticals. Starting in the mid-1990s, the OIG placed prescription drug pricing at the top of its watch list.[14] And since that time, nearly every state has participated in litigation against pharmaceutical manufacturers.

Enforcement actions typically involve four common areas: false claims actions based on manufacturers' pricing methodology or the Medicaid Drug Rebate Program, violations of the federal anti-kickback statute in connection with manufacturers' marketing to physicians and discounting practices, and common-law fraud based on illegal sales of counterfeit drugs or improper internet sales. Typically, enforcement actions allege a combination of violations of multiple anti-fraud provisions (e.g., the federal False Claims Act (FCA) and anti-kickback statute) in connection with certain allegedly illegal activities (e.g., inflated pricing and improper marketing schemes). Although pharmaceutical pricing cases eventually may become obsolete under the Medicare Prescription Drug, Improvement, and Modernization Act of 2003 (MMA), there is no indication that regulators

---

[12]*Id.* at 1352.

[13]Office of Inspector Gen., U.S. Dep't of Health & Human Servs., OIG Work Plan, Fiscal Year 2003, *available at* http://oig.hhs.gov/publications/workplan.html [hereinafter OIG Work Plan FY 2003].

[14]*See* Office of Inspector Gen., U.S. Dep't of Health & Human Servs., OIG Work Plan, Fiscal Year 1999, *available at* http://oig.hhs.gov/reading/workplan/1999/99hcfawp.pdf [hereinafter OIG Work Plan FY 1999].

are slowing their enforcement efforts against the pharmaceutical industry at this time.

Two recent cases against manufacturers yielded landmark settlements that have fueled the enforcement community. In October of 2001, TAP Pharmaceutical Products, Inc., (TAP) paid $875 million to resolve massive claims arising out of sales and marketing practices involving its prostate cancer drug, Lupron.[15] In 2003, AstraZeneca paid $355 million to settle similar claims involving its competing drug, Zoladex.[16] In the TAP and AstraZeneca cases, the government alleged a myriad of fraud allegations in connection with the sale, marketing, and pricing of pharmaceuticals. Specifically, in both cases, initiated by the same *qui tam* relator, the complaint alleged that the companies illegally manipulated the average wholesale price (AWP) of certain drugs, violated the anti-kickback statute in marketing products to physicians, violated the Prescription Drug Marketing Act by encouraging physicians to bill for free samples, and improperly failed to include certain discounts in the Medicaid Best Price calculation. Given these record settlements, powerful enforcement tools, and the new Medicare drug benefit program, this area will certainly prove to be a hotbed of enforcement activity for years to come.

B. Enforcement Actions Involving Pricing Methodologies [New Topic]

1. Price Inflation Through Average Wholesale Price Data [New Topic]

In the mid-1990s, the government began aggressively pursuing pharmaceutical companies in connection with pricing policies.[17] Over the years, state and federal regulators have argued that manufacturers intentionally overstated the AWP of prescription drugs, which resulted in artificially inflated pricing of drugs provided to Medicare and Medicaid beneficiaries. Until enactment of the MMA, payment for prescription drugs under Part B of the Medicare Act was made at the lower of billed charges or 95 percent of the AWP as reported by pharmaceutical manufacturers to information clearinghouses, such as the Red Book or Medspan.[18] Likewise, many states rely on AWP data to set payment rates for prescription drugs reimbursed by the Medicaid program.

According to the OIG, manufacturers could be subject to FCA liability for reporting inaccurate AWP data to information clearinghouses. Specifically, in guidance to manufacturers published in May of 2003, the

---

[15] Press Release, U.S. Dep't of Justice, *TAP Pharmaceutical Products, Inc. and Seven Others Charged with Health Care Crimes; Company Agrees to Pay $875 Million to Settle Charges* (Oct. 3, 2001), *available at* www.usdoj.gov/opa/pr/2001/October/513civ.htm.

[16] Press Release, U.S. Dep't of Justice, *AstraZeneca Pharmaceuticals LP Pleads Guilty to Healthcare Crime; Company Agrees to Pay $355 Million to Settle Charges* (June 20, 2003), *available at* http://www.usdoj.gov/opa/pr/2003/June/03_civ_371.htm

[17] Press Release, U.S. Dep't of Justice, *Bayer Agrees to Settle Allegations That It Caused Providers to Submit Fraudulent Claims to 47 State Medicaid Programs* (Sept. 19, 2000), *available at* www.usdoj.gov/opa/pr/2000/September/551civ.htm; *Bayer to Pay $14 Million in FCA Lawsuit Alleging Fraudulent Medicaid Claims*, 5 HEALTH CARE FRAUD REP. (BNA) 125 (Feb. 7, 2001).

[18] 42 U.S.C. §1395u(o); 42 C.F.R. §405.517; Program Memorandum AB-99-63.

OIG stated that manufacturers may run afoul of the FCA if "reimbursement of the product depends, in whole or in part, on information generated or reported by the manufacturer, directly or indirectly, and the manufacturer has knowingly . . . failed to generate or report such information completely and accurately."[19] The government has argued that manufacturers know that the AWP data they report in wholesalers' catalogs bears little to no resemblance to the actual wholesale prices of the drugs available to health care providers. By intentionally providing inaccurate information about the costs of their products that will form the basis of government reimbursement, enforcement agencies contend that manufacturers have *caused* the submission of false claims.[20]

In 2000, Bayer Corporation settled the first widely reported AWP FCA case with the government for $14 million.[21] The government alleged that Bayer caused providers to submit fraudulently inflated reimbursement claims to the Medicaid programs of 47 states. Specifically, the government alleged that Bayer falsely inflated reported AWP of certain hemophilia drugs and illegally marketed the "spread" between the AWP and actual price to prescribers as an inducement to prescribe the Bayer drugs over competing products. The case started as *qui tam* litigation initiated by Florida-based independent pharmacy Ven-A-Care. As part of the settlement, Bayer signed a five-year corporate integrity agreement obligating the company to provide the government with the average sale prices of the drugs at issue. The government has used this information to bolster its case against the AWP.

Following the Bayer settlement, AWP cases have exploded throughout the country and have yielded record settlements for prosecutors. The record $875 million TAP settlement in 2001 and the $355 million settlement with AstraZeneca in 2003 both concerned allegations that the companies violated the FCA in connection with setting the AWP of their respective cancer drugs in addition to other allegations. Based on the perceived success of these settlements, states have also brought claims against drug manufacturers based on AWP data in addition to claims arising under the Medicaid Drug Rebate Program.[22] As discussed below, AWP claims may eventually evaporate in light of the new pricing structure established by the MMA.

---

[19] OIG Compliance Program Guidelines for Pharmaceutical Manufacturers, 68 Fed. Reg. 23,731, 23,733 (May 5, 2003).

[20] In addition to risking FCA liability in connection with reporting inaccurate AWP data, the OIG has declared that manufacturers risk violating the anti-kickback statute if they knowingly establish or "inappropriately maintain a particular AWP if one purpose is to manipulate the 'spread' to induce customers to purchase its product." *Id.* at 23,737.

[21] Press Release, U.S. Dep't of Justice, *Bayer Agrees to Settle Allegations That It Caused Providers to Submit Fraudulent Claims to 47 State Medicaid Programs* (Sept. 19, 2000), *available at* www.usdoj.gov/opa/pr/2000/September/551civ.htm; *Bayer to Pay $14 Million in FCA Lawsuit Alleging Fraudulent Medicaid Claims,* 5 HEALTH CARE FRAUD REP. (BNA) 125 (No. 3) (Feb. 7, 2001). The government also alleged that Bayer violated the "best price" regulations in agreements with states in connection with the Medicaid Drug Rebate Program.

[22] *See, e.g.,* Connecticut v. Aventis Pharms. Inc., [docket number unavailable] (Conn. Sup. Ct. Mar. 14, 2003); Montana v. Abbott Labs., Inc., Case No. 02-12084-PBS (D. Mass. June 11, 2003); Minnesota v. Pharmacia Corp., Case No. 03-10069-PBS (D. Mass. Jan. 10, 2003); Nevada v. American Home Prods. Corp., Case No. 02-12086-PBS (D. Mass. Oct. 24, 2002).

2. *Medicaid Drug Rebate Program [New Topic]*

Under the federal Medicaid law, state Medicaid agencies must pay the lowest price possible for prescription drugs.[23] Accordingly, manufacturers that participate in the Medicaid program enter into agreements with states that include a provision that requires manufacturers to report to the Centers for Medicare and Medicaid Services the best price they offer to any commercial, for-profit customer and pay a quarterly rebate to Medicaid based upon the best price for each drug sold.[24] Recent OIG guidance suggests that manufacturers must report all "discounts" in the "best price" calculation, including price reductions, cash discounts, free goods, rebates, coupons, grants, and other price concessions.[25] The OIG has opined that the Medicaid Drug Rebate Program encourages manufacturers to conceal discounts because "manufacturers have a strong financial incentive to hide de facto pricing concessions to other purchasers to avoid passing on the same discounts to the states."[26] The government has aggressively prosecuted fraud claims against manufacturers for violation of the Medicaid "best price" regulations. Furthermore, since the 1990s, nearly every state has participated in "best price" litigation based on discounts, rebates, or other financial incentives offered by manufacturers.[27]

For example, in 2002, Pfizer paid $49 million to settle allegations that it failed to include discounts and rebates provided to physicians in its "best price" for the cholesterol drug Lipitor.[28] Parke-Davis Labs, then a subsidiary of Warner-Lambert, which was subsequently acquired by Pfizer in 2000, allegedly overstated the Lipitor best price in the first and second quarters of 1999 by concealing $250,000 of discounts as "educational grants" that were given to a large managed care organization in Louisiana in exchange for favorable status on the organization's drug formulary. The government alleged that Parke-Davis/Warner-Lambert improperly retained over $20 million in Medicaid rebates owed to the Medicaid program in connection with the discounts.

Similarly, in 2003, the Bayer Corporation made headlines again with a settlement involving allegations that the company improperly

---

[23] 42 U.S.C. §1396r-8.

[24] "Best price" is defined as "the lowest price available from the manufacturer during the rebate period to any wholesaler, retailer, provider, health maintenance organization, nonprofit entity, or governmental entity within the United States." 42 U.S.C. §1396r-8(c)(1)(C)(i). "Best price" calculations include discounts and are "without regard to special packaging, labeling, or identifiers on the dosage form or product or package." 42 U.S.C. §1396r-8(c)(1)(C)(ii)(I) and (II). The lower the best price on the drugs, the higher the rebate payment to the states.

[25] OIG Compliance Program Guidance for Pharmaceutical Manufacturers, 68 Fed. Reg. 23,731, 23,733–34 (May 5, 2003), reprinted as Appendix I-3.1 at the end of this Supplement.

[26] 68 Fed. Reg. at 23,735.

[27] *See, e.g.,* Connecticut v. Aventis Pharms. Inc., [docket number unavailable] (Conn. Sup. Ct. Mar. 14, 2003); Montana v. Abbott Labs., Inc., Case No. 02-12084-PBS (D. Mass. June 11, 2003); Minnesota v. Pharmacia Corp., Case No. 03-10069-PBS (D. Mass. Jan. 10, 2003); Nevada v. American Home Prods. Corp., Case No. 02-12086-PBS (D. Mass. Oct. 24, 2002); California *ex rel.* Ven-A-Care v. Abbott Labs., Inc., Case No. BC 287198A (Cal. Super. Ct. Jan. 7, 2003).

[28] Press Release, U.S. Dep't of Justice, *Drug Giant and Two Subsidiaries to Pay $49 Million for Defrauding Medicaid Drug Rebate Program* (Oct. 28, 2002), *available at* http://www.usdoj.gov/opa/pr/2002/October/02_civ_622.htm.

concealed the "best price" of certain drugs through "private labeling" of sales to Kaiser Permanente (Kaiser). This time, Bayer agreed to pay $257 million to settle allegations that Bayer (and its subsidiary Glaxo-SmithKline) gave Kaiser a 40 percent discount on the antibiotic Cipro but reported only a 15 percent discount to the government.[29] Bayer allegedly concealed the true discount by changing labels on products delivered to Kaiser by including Kaiser's National Drug Code (NDC) on the label instead of its own. By so doing, the government alleged that the companies circumvented the reporting requirement, thereby lowering rebates to the Medicaid program.

C. Illegal Marketing [New Topic]

1. Kickbacks [New Topic]

Many of the headline-making cases against pharmaceutical manufacturers allege that the companies' marketing programs include illegal kickbacks to physicians in exchange for prescriptions.[30] Under the federal anti-kickback law, payments, gifts, or other remuneration by manufacturers to physicians or other health care providers made with the intention to generate referrals constitute improper kickbacks.[31] In cases involving pharmaceutical fraud, the government has alleged that companies disguise illegal kickbacks to physicians and others in the form of discounts, educational grants, consultation fees, entertainment, and free goods. The OIG has also opined that a manufacturer's "manipulation" of AWP data to purposely increase a customer's profits by increasing federal reimbursement also implicates the anti-kickback statute.[32]

The OIG first targeted marketing programs in a 1994 fraud alert that detailed several marketing programs that were potentially violative of the anti-kickback law.[33] The suspect scenarios included cash awards to pharmacies for drug switching, frequent flier miles provided to physicians for completing questionnaires after prescribing a company's drug to a new patient, and "research grants" where physicians were paid for de minimis record keeping. In the 1994 fraud alert, the OIG stated that these incentives would violate the anti-kickback

---

[29] The 2001 suit also alleged that Bayer failed to report discounts provided to physicians and home health agencies in its "best price."

[30] *See, e.g.,* Press Release, U.S. Dep't of Justice, *TAP Pharmaceutical Products, Inc. and Seven Others Charged with Health Care Crimes; Company Agrees to Pay $875 Million to Settle Charges* (Oct. 3, 2001), *available at* www.usdoj.gov/opa/pr/2001/October/513civ.htm; United States *ex rel.* Durand v. AstraZeneca Pharms. LP, Case No. 03-122-JJF (D. Del. 2003); Press Release, U.S. Dep't of Justice, *AstraZeneca Pharmaceuticals LP Pleads Guilty to Healthcare Crime; Company Agrees to Pay $355 Million to Settle Charges* (June 20, 2003), *available at* http://www.usdoj.gov/opa/pr/2003/June/03_civ_371.htm; United States *ex rel.* Franklin v. Parke-Davis, Div. of Warner-Lambert Co., Case No. 96-11651-PBS (D. Mass. Aug. 13, 1996).

[31] 42 U.S.C. §1320a-7b(b).

[32] The OIG states that "it is illegal for a manufacturer knowingly to establish or inappropriately maintain a particular AWP if one purpose is to manipulate the 'spread' to induce customers to purchase its product." OIG Compliance Program Guidance for Pharmaceutical Manufacturers, 68 Fed. Reg. 23,731, 23,737 (May 5, 2003).

[33] Special Fraud Alert: Prescription Drug Marketing Schemes, 59 Fed. Reg. 65,376 (Dec. 19, 1994).

statute if even one purpose was to induce the physician to prescribe a drug item reimbursable by Medicaid.[34] The OIG further stated that such conduct would not benefit from safe harbor protection. Since the issuance of this fraud alert, the government, and *qui tam* relators, have aggressively attacked manufacturers' marketing tactics under the anti-kickback statute.

For example, in both the TAP and AstraZeneca cases discussed above, the government and *qui tam* relators alleged that the companies paid physicians and others improper kickbacks in the form of "educational" grants to encourage use of their products. In *TAP,* the *qui tam* relator, an HMO-employed urologist, alleged that the company offered him educational grants if he reversed the HMO's decision to include a competing drug on the formulary.[35] Seven TAP employees were indicted for allegedly paying kickbacks and bribes including free consulting services, trips to golf and ski resorts, and funding office Christmas parties and bar tabs, in addition to the improper "educational grants."[36] And in January of 2004, Joanne Richardson, a TAP regional account manager, was found guilty of perjury in connection with statements she made to a federal grand jury. Federal prosecutors presented evidence that Richardson and others at TAP offered to give a clinic off-contract hidden price reductions in the form of free samples and education and research grants to prescribe Lupron over a competing drug.[37] Similar allegations were made against AstraZeneca.

Similarly, in the recently settled Pfizer [Parke-Davis] case, the *qui tam* relator, a former "medical liaison" for Parke-Davis, alleged that the company violated the anti-kickback statute by paying physicians for inconsequential drug studies, minimal participation in speakers' bureaus, and cash payments for small record-keeping tasks in addition to direct "gifts" of travel and tickets to the Olympics in exchange for prescribing the anti-seizure drug Neurontin.[38]

On the heels of the swell of AWP litigation, the OIG has targeted manufacturers' marketing programs that "actively" market the "spread" to customers. Specifically, in the 2003 Pharmaceutical Compliance Guidance, the OIG stated that active marketing of the spread includes statements by sales representatives "promoting the spread as a reason to purchase the product or guaranteeing a certain profit or spread in exchange for the purchase of a product."[39] Such promotions, according

---

[34] *Id.*

[35] Press Release, U.S. Dep't of Justice, *TAP Pharmaceutical Products, Inc. and Seven Others Charged with Health Care Crimes; Company Agrees to Pay $875 Million to Settle Charges* (Oct. 3, 2001), *available at* www.usdoj.gov/opa/pr/2001/October/513civ.htm.

[36] *Id.* On July 14, 2004, a jury acquitted the TAP employees of charges that they provided illegal incentives to physicians, including free samples, in exchange for prescriptions. *Drug Company Employees Acquitted in Kickback Trial,* USA Today http://www.usatoday.com/money/industries/health/2004-07-14-pharmaceutical-freebies_x.htm.

[37] *Former TAP Pharma Account Manager Found Guilty of Lying to Grand Jury, Health Care Fraud Report,* 8 HEALTH CARE FRAUD REP. (BNA) 109–10 (Feb. 4, 2004).

[38] United States *ex rel.* Franklin v. Parke-Davis, 147 F. Supp. 39, 54 (D. Mass. 2001).

[39] OIG Compliance Program Guidance for Pharmaceutical Manufacturers, 68 Fed. Reg. 23,731, 23,737 (May 5, 2003).

to the OIG, may violate the anti-kickback statute, i.e., "[t]he conjunction of manipulation of the AWP to induce customers to purchase a product with active marketing of the spread is strong evidence of the unlawful intent necessary to trigger the anti-kickback statute."[40] The AstraZeneca case provides a poignant example of government claims of marketing the spread.

In the AstraZeneca case, documents from the company's marketing department revealed that AstraZeneca engaged in a full-scale marketing campaign to physicians detailing the profitability of the "spread" between AWP and the cost to physicians.[41] The program, called a "Return-to-Practice," consisted of inflating the AWP of the cancer drug Zoladex, heavily discounting the price paid by physicians, and marketing the spread between the AWP and the discounted price as an additional profit to be "returned" to the physician's practice.[42] The government used this powerful evidence to elicit a hefty settlement.

2. *Drug Switching [New Topic]*

In the December 19, 1994, fraud alert, the OIG identified a trend of suspicious activity it then termed "product conversion."[43] Product conversion, or drug switching, as it is now known, occurs when a manufacturer or pharmacy benefit manager (PBM) offers cash awards or other incentives to physicians or pharmacies to prescribe its product over a competing product without regard to medical efficacy.[44] The OIG has stated that while switching arrangements between manufacturers and physicians or pharmacies "clearly" trigger the anti-kickback statute, drug switching "may be permissible in certain managed care arrangements."[45] Recently, states have taken an increased interest in drug switching cases arguing that the practice violates the Medicaid Drug Rebate Program as well as state anticompetition laws.

In March of 2004, the State of Louisiana intervened in a *qui tam* case brought by a physician against Merck & Co. (Merck), the manufacturer of Pepcid.[46] The state's complaint alleges that the company paid hospitals and physicians to prescribe Pepcid over its competitor Zantac without regard to the medical efficacy and failed to appreciate side effects associated with the switched drug. The complaint further alleges that Merck offered hospitals significant discounts that were not provided to the state. Specifically, Merck allegedly charged hospitals $0.10 per tablet, while charging the state's Medicaid program

---

[40]*Id.*

[41]Press Release, U.S. Dep't of Justice, *AstraZeneca Pharmaceuticals LP Pleads Guilty to Healthcare Crime; Company Agrees to Pay $355 Million to Settle Charges* (June 20, 2003), *available at* www.usdoj.gov/opa/pr/2003/June/03_civ_371.htm.

[42]*Id.*

[43]Special Fraud Alert: Prescription Drug Marketing Schemes, 59 Fed. Reg. 65,376 (Dec. 19, 1994).

[44]OIG Compliance Program Guidance for Pharmaceutical Manufacturers, 68 Fed. Reg. 23,731, 23,737 (May 5, 2003).

[45]*Id.* at 23,738.

[46]United States *ex rel.* St. John LaCorte v. Merck & Co., No. 99-3807 (E.D. La. Mar. 24, 2004).

$1.65 per tablet.[47] The state argues that by paying incentives for drug switching, the company failed to comply with the "best price" regulations. Furthermore, the state alleged that Merck's actions violated state anticompetition laws.

Similarly, in April 2004, 20 states settled cases against Medco Health Solutions, Inc. (Medco), the world's largest PBM, resolving claims that the company violated state unfair trade practices laws.[48] The states argued that Medco encouraged prescribers to switch patients to prescription drugs based on rebates paid to the company by pharmaceutical manufacturers but failed to pass on savings to patients or health plans. The states further alleged that Medco failed to inform the prescribers and patients of additional rebates that were paid by pharmaceutical manufacturers for using the drugs. Medco paid more than $29 million to states to resolve the case and agreed to make certain disclosures about its pricing policies to physicians and patients, including information about any financial incentives the company receives in connection with prescription drugs.[49]

3. Marketing of Off-Label Uses [New Topic]

The federal Food, Drug, and Cosmetic Act (FDCA) prohibits manufacturers and retailers from promoting any use of a drug that the FDA has not approved.[50] Once the FDA approves a drug for a particular use, the FDCA does not prevent physicians from *prescribing* the drug for another purpose (an "off-label use"); however, the FDCA prohibits manufacturers from *marketing* or *promoting* a drug for that unapproved use.[51] The government often prosecutes off-label marketing cases under the FCA where the government-sponsored health care program at issue limits reimbursement to only those FDA-approved drugs/uses.[52]

In May of 2004, Pfizer agreed to pay $430 million to settle allegations brought against the recently acquired Parke-Davis company that Parke-Davis marketed off-label uses of certain drugs to physicians, who then submitted claims for reimbursement to state Medicaid programs.[53] Although Pfizer settled the *Parke-Davis* case, many of the company's arguments were well received by the court.

---

[47] *Id.*

[48] *See* Press Release, National Ass'n of Attorneys General, *Settlement: 20 Attorneys General Settle Unfair Practices Claims Against Medco Health Solutions* (Apr. 26, 2004), *available at* www.naag.org/issues/20040426-settlement-medco.php.

[49] *Id.*

[50] 21 U.S.C. §331 (2000).

[51] *See* 21 U.S.C. §331(a) and (d), which prohibit distribution of drugs for nonapproved uses and "misbranded" drugs.

[52] *See, e.g.,* definition of "covered outpatient drugs," which does not include drugs that are used for a medical indication which is not a medically accepted indication. 42 U.S.C. §1396r-8(k)(3). The Medicaid Act defines "medically accepted indication" as a use "which is approved under the Federal Food Drug and Cosmetic Act" or which is included in specified drug compendia. 42 U.S.C. §1396r-8(k)(6).

[53] Press Release, U.S. Dep't of Justice, *Warner-Lambert to Pay $430 Million to Resolve Criminal & Civil Health Care Liability Relating to Off-Label Promotion* (May 13, 2004), *available at* www.usdoj.gov/opa/pr/2004/May/04_civ_322.htm.

For example, in August of 2003, the court denied the company's motion for summary judgment based on the existence of factual disputes, but entertained an argument that no false claims were submitted in states where off-label uses are permitted based on a federal law that allows states to reimburse off-label uses, and where such uses were permitted in at least 42 states.[54] The court requested amicus briefs from government officials regarding the legislative intent behind the Medicaid statute and off-label prescription prohibitions, stating, "[i]f the Medicaid statute gives states the discretion to cover off-label, non-compendium prescriptions, and a state exercised its discretion to cover such prescriptions, then an off-label Neurontin prescription in that state would not be a false claim."[55] Earlier in the year, the court partially granted the company's motion to dismiss, forcing the relator to drop certain anti-kickback claims.[56]

4. Free Samples [New Topic]

Some of the most publicized claims in the TAP and AstraZeneca cases were allegations that the companies improperly encouraged prescribers to bill Medicare and Medicaid for free samples provided by the manufacturer in violation of the Prescription Drug Marketing Act (PDMA). The PDMA regulates the distribution and receipt of drug samples, as well as record keeping of manufacturers and distributors.[57] The PDMA prohibits resale of samples and requires recipients to request samples in writing and provide manufacturers and distributors with a written receipt. Violators may be subject to criminal penalties, including up to ten years' imprisonment.[58]

In the criminal prosecution of one of the individual physicians in the TAP case in connection with the illegal sale of Lupron samples, the physician defendant moved to dismiss the case on the grounds that the samples provided by the company were not illegally dispensed under the PDMA.[59] Specifically, Dr. Romano argued that since the Lupron samples were given directly by TAP to him and were then injected by him into the patient, there was no "prescription" for them and therefore, the drugs were not dispensed in violation of the PDMA.[60]

---

[54]The company cited 42 U.S.C. §1396r-8(d)(1)(B), which states in pertinent part: "[a] state *may exclude* or otherwise restrict coverage of a covered outpatient drug if—(i) the prescribed use is not for a medically accepted indication" (emphasis added). United States *ex rel.* Franklin v. Parke-Davis, Div. of Warner-Lambert Co., Case No. 96-11651-PBS, at 5–6 (D. Mass. Aug. 22, 2003).

[55]*Id.* at 7.

[56]United States *ex rel.* Franklin v. Parke-Davis, Div. of Warner-Lambert Co., 147 F. Supp. 2d 39 (D. Mass. 2001).

[57]21 U.S.C. §353 et seq.

[58]21 U.S.C. §353(b)(1).

[59]United States v. MacKenzie, Case No. 01-CR-10350-DPW (D. Mass. June 13, 2003).

[60]Romano argued that the PDMA, 21 U.S.C. §353 et seq., applies to drug samples that are part of a unit of a drug subject to §353(b). Section 353(b) states that it applies to drugs that are dispensed by prescription or refill. Based on this rationale, Dr. Romano argued that the drugs provided by TAP were not "samples" because they were not provided by prescription.

D. Defense Strategies [New Topic]

1. *Federal False Claims Act [New Topic]*

The FCA imposes liability on any person who "(1) knowingly presents, or causes to be presented, to an officer or employee of the United States Government . . . a false or fraudulent claim for payment or approval; [or] (2) knowingly makes, uses, or causes to be made or used, a false record or statement to get a false or fraudulent claim paid or approved by the Government. . . ."[61] In order to assert a valid claim under the FCA, the government must prove three key elements: (1) that the defendant presented or caused another person to present a claim for payment to the government; (2) that the claim was false or fraudulent; and (3) that the defendant knew the claim was false or fraudulent. Defendants in FCA cases such as those discussed above have attacked these elements with varying degrees of success.

a. *Government Knowledge of Pricing Scheme [New Topic]*

In FCA cases based on AWP data, defendants often challenge the action on the ground that the government knows that the AWP does not represent the actual price of drugs, thus negating the requirement that a claim be "false." This strategy has had a mixed track record, with results hinging on the extent of the government's knowledge. Furthermore, the weight given to the government's knowledge is determined by the courts on a case-by-case basis,[62] but the government's knowledge that AWP may not accurately reflect the actual drug price has not been an automatic bar to an FCA claim.

Boisjoly v. Morton Thiokol, Inc., is the seminal case that applied the government knowledge defense to rebut FCA claims.[63] In *Boisjoly,* a *qui tam* relator claimed that the defendant, a manufacturer of space shuttle rocket motors, submitted false claims because it knew that the rocket motor seals and joints were defective and did not meet specifications. The court dismissed the complaint on the grounds that the responsible government officials were aware of the alleged defects in the products when the claims for payment were made. The *Boisjoly* court held that "if the complaint itself alleges that the government knew of those very facts or characteristics which allegedly make the claim false, no claim has been stated."[64]

Similarly, in *Woodbury v. United States,* the court rejected the government's FCA allegations regarding a construction contract for Naval housing.[65] Specifically, the government alleged that the contractor had concealed an additional subcontract regarding appliances provided in connection with pre-fabricated housing packages. The court found that

---

[61] 31 U.S.C. §3729(a).
[62] United States *ex rel.* Durcholz v. FKW Inc., 997 F. Supp. 1159, 1157 (S.D. Ind. 1998).
[63] 706 F. Supp. 795 (D. Utah 1988).
[64] *Id.* at 810.
[65] 232 F. Supp. 49 (D. Or. 1964), *aff'd in part,* 359 F.2d 370 (9th Cir. 1966).

there was no FCA liability because the government knew of the additional contract prior to payment of any claims. The *Woodbury* court explained, "[w]hen a person has knowledge . . . and no effort is made to prevent that person from making a full, adequate and complete inquiry into the exact terms of the transaction, such person will not be heard to say that he has been deceived to his injury by the misrepresentation of the person originally furnished the knowledge."[66]

In the case of pharmaceutical pricing, there are numerous reports detailing the government's knowledge of the character of the AWP data.[67] But the weight of government knowledge has not carried the day in other courts.[68] In *United States v. Southland Management Corp.*, the court rejected the defendant's argument that the government's knowledge of certain housing conditions negated the falsity of the claim for payment.[69] The *Southland* court stated pointedly, "we find it difficult to comprehend how the government's awareness that a claimant's submission was false would in any way affect the truth or falsity of the claim. A lie does not become the truth simply because the person hearing it knows that it is a lie."[70]

Relatedly, in a recent civil Racketeer-Influenced and Corrupt Organizations Act (RICO) suit by cancer patients and health care plans against manufacturers, a federal court dismissed the manufacturers' argument that Congress understood that the AWP would be inflated. The court wrote, "[a]s defendants portray the Congressional purpose in setting the reimbursement rate at 95% of AWP, Congress meant to turn a blind eye to the inflated AWPs as a means of enticing physicians to treat Medicare patients. In other words, Congress deliberately invited the very fraud of which defendants are accused. . . . The suggestion that Congress would deliberately condone a bribery scheme using public funds to enrich drug manufacturers and physicians is, to say the least, unusual."[71]

b. *Challenging Scienter [New Topic]*

The existence of government knowledge is also used to defeat the FCA's scienter requirement with varying degrees of success. To show violation of the FCA, the government must prove that the party making the claim for payment knew at the time the claim was submitted that it was false or fraudulent.[72] "Knowingly," as defined under the FCA, means that the person (1) has actual knowledge of the information; (2) acts in deliberate ignorance of the truth or falsity of the information; or (3) acts

---

[66]*Id.* at 55.

[67]For example, in the FY 1999 Work Plan, the OIG acknowledged that the average wholesale price is "generally inflated over actual acquisition costs." *See* http://www.oig.hhs.gov/reading/workplan/1999/99hcfawp.pdf.

[68]*See* United States *ex rel.* Lamers v. City of Green Bay, 998 F. Supp. 971 (E.D. Wis. 1998).

[69]288 F.3d 665 (5th Cir. 2002), *rev'd on other grounds en banc,* 326 F.3d 669 (5th Cir. 2003).

[70]288 F.3d at 681.

[71]*In re* Lupron, 295 F. Supp. 2d 148, 163 (D. Mass. 2003).

[72]31 U.S.C. §3729(a).

in reckless disregard of the truth or falsity of the information, and no proof of specific intent to defraud is required.[73] Dispelling accusations that a defendant acted "knowingly" is often an effective means of quashing a False Claims Act case.

In *United States* ex rel. *Durcholz v. FKW, Inc.,* the court found that a contractor did not intentionally submit false claims by submitting certain documents related to a contract to clear sedimentation from ponds where the government knew of the methods to be used by the contractor although the documents submitted by the contractor listed a different removal method.[74] In granting summary judgment in favor of the defendants, the *Durcholz* court emphasized the relative value of government knowledge in negating scienter: "[t]he extent and nature of government knowledge may show that the defendant did not 'knowingly' submit a false claim. . . . Conversely, the government's knowledge may be too incomplete or come too late in the process to defeat the 'knowingly' requirement."[75] This position has not been widely adopted.

For example, in *United States* ex rel. *Hagood v. Sonoma County Water Agency,* the Ninth Circuit rejected the government-knowledge defense.[76] In *Hagood,* the court explained that while government knowledge may show that the defendant had no intent to deceive, "the requisite intent [under the FCA] is the knowing presentation of what is known to be false. That the relevant government officials know of the falsity is not in itself a defense."[77] Accordingly, the *Hagood* court left open the viability of the government-knowledge defense for factual situations where the defendant is not acting on what it knows is false information.[78]

Similarly, in *Shaw v. AAA Engineering & Drafting, Inc.,* the court stated that "government knowledge of a contractor's wrongdoing is no longer an automatic defense to an FCA action."[79] The *Shaw* court found that the government's knowledge was not extensive enough to overcome FCA liability because the *qui tam* relator, and not the defendant, provided the information in question to the government, and also because it was shown that the defendant had evaded inquiries from the government regarding the practices that were the basis of the false claims. But the court did not foreclose the government-knowledge defense; rather, the *Shaw* court explained that, "there may still be occasions when the government's knowledge of or cooperation with a contractor's actions is so extensive that the contractor could not as a matter of law possess the requisite state of mind to be liable under the FCA."[80]

---

[73] 31 U.S.C. §3729(b).

[74] 997 F. Supp. 1159, 1171 (S.D. Ind. 1998).

[75] 997 F. Supp. at 1167.

[76] 929 F.2d 1416, 1421 (9th Cir. 1991).

[77] *Id.*

[78] *Id.*

[79] 213 F.3d 519 (10th Cir. 2000).

[80] 213 F.3d at 534, *citing* United States *ex rel.* Butler v. Hughes Helicopters, Inc., 71 F.3d 321, 327 (9th Cir. 1995), *and* Wang *ex rel.* United States v. FMC Corp., 975 F.2d 1412, 1421 (9th Cir. 1992).

And, in *United States v. Southland Management Corp.,* the court rejected the argument that the government's knowledge negated the defendant's intent.[81] In *Southland Management,* the government alleged that owners of a federally subsidized low income apartment complex violated the FCA in submitting claims for housing assistance where the apartments were in deplorable condition. In order to qualify for payments, the property owner was required to submit an application to the Department of Housing and Urban Development certifying that the property is in a "decent, safe, and sanitary condition." Although the *Southland Management* court rejected the government-knowledge defense, the court stated that the defense would remain viable in government-initiated FCA cases, "in the rare situation where the falsity of the claim is unclear and the evidence suggests that the defendant actually believed his claim was not false because the government approved and paid the claim with full knowledge of the relevant facts."[82]

The dissenting opinion disagreed with the majority's attempt to "cabin" the government-knowledge defense. Specifically, the dissent argued that only two scenarios would justify FCA liability in the face of government knowledge: "either the person making the statement did not know that the government knew it was false, or the person making the statement was colluding with a government employee who also knew the claim was false."[83] Apart from these situations, according to the dissent, the government's knowledge of the particulars of a claim and acceptance of what would otherwise have been fraudulent, "effectively negates the fraud or falsity required by the FCA."[84] Thus, the divided court in *Southland Management* emphasizes the sharp discord about the weight of the government-knowledge defense among the circuits.

c. Challenging Causation [New Topic]

To make a claim under the FCA, the government is required to prove that the defendant *caused* a false claim to be presented.[85] Some pharmaceutical manufacturers have challenged the causation element on the ground that they themselves do not submit any claim for payment and merely make their products available to prescribers. This strategy has not been well received by the courts.

As discussed above in Section XII.C.3., in the off-label case filed against Parke-Davis, the relator had alleged that the company marketed off-label uses of certain drugs to physicians, who then submitted claims for reimbursement to state Medicaid programs.[86] In a motion to

---

[81] 288 F.3d 665, 686 (5th Cir. 2002).

[82] *Id.*

[83] *Id.* at 698.

[84] *Id.*

[85] 31 U.S.C. §3729(a).

[86] United States *ex rel.* Franklin v. Parke-Davis, Div. of Warner-Lambert Co., 147 F. Supp. 2d 39 (D. Mass. 2001).

dismiss, Parke-Davis argued that the relator failed to state a claim in part because the acts of the prescribing physicians who wrote the off-label prescriptions, and the pharmacies who sought reimbursement, were the intervening causes of the false claim. The court rejected this argument, stating that "the participation of doctors and pharmacists in the submission of false Medicaid claims was not only foreseeable, it was an intended consequence of the alleged scheme of fraud." The court further explained that the FCA reaches beyond claims made directly by the defendants, "to all fraudulent attempts to cause the Government to pay out sums of money."[87] Although acknowledging that the relator's claims were in "territory that is not well charted by the existing decisional law," the court found that the claims fit squarely within the FCA's remedial purpose.[88]

2. Anti-Kickback Statute [New Topic]

To make a prima facie case of liability under the anti-kickback statute, the government must show that a defendant (1) knowingly and willfully (2) offered or paid remuneration to another person (3) to induce that person to purchase, order, or arrange for the ordering of any good or item for which payment may be made by a federal health care program.[89] As discussed above, numerous cases have included allegations that manufacturers' marketing and discounting practices violate the anti-kickback statute. Alternatively, and in addition, government enforcement agencies and *qui tam* relators have argued that violations of the anti-kickback statute trigger FCA liability in connection with the sale of pharmaceuticals.

a. Kickbacks as False Claims: Lack of Certification [New Topic]

In most circuits, regulatory violations render a claim legally false under the FCA only where compliance with the regulation at issue is a condition of payment. In the case of discounts or other financial incentives provided to physicians by manufacturers, who do not make any certification to the government in connection with receiving a payment, manufacturers have argued that the FCA does not apply. The *Parke-Davis* court agreed and dismissed the relator's claim that the company violated the FCA in allegedly paying kickbacks to physicians.[90] The court held that violation of the anti-kickback statute was not a per se violation of the FCA.[91] The court further held that the relator failed to

---

[87]*Id.* at 53, *citing* United States v. Neifert-White Co., 390 U.S. 228, 233, 88 S. Ct. 959 (1968).

[88]*Id.* Although the *Parke-Davis* court upheld the relator's allegations regarding the company's marketing of off-label uses, the court dismissed claims (with leave to amend) that the company's payment of alleged kickbacks violated the FCA where there was no evidence that the government's payment was conditioned upon any certification of compliance with the anti-kickback statute. *Id.* at 54.

[89]42 U.S.C. §1320a-7b(b).

[90]147 F. Supp. 2d 39 (D. Mass. 2001).

[91]*Id.* at 54–55.

plead any facts showing that the company ever caused or induced a false certification of compliance with the anti-kickback statute.[92]

b. Statutory Exception and Safe Harbor Protection: Discounts and Educational Grants [New Topic]

By its terms, the anti-kickback statute excepts from improper remuneration "a discount or other reduction in price obtained by a provider of services or other entity under a Federal health care program if the reduction in price is properly disclosed and appropriately reflected in the costs claimed or charges made by the provider or entity under a Federal health care program."[93]

Similarly, discounts provided to prescribers may be eligible for safe harbor protection, but such protection requires strict compliance with all applicable conditions set out in the applicable safe harbor. Various different discount safe harbor criteria apply to buyers, offerors, and sellers. Generally speaking, however, under the discount safe harbor, a discount does not violate the anti-kickback statute if: (1) the discount is in the form of a reduction in the price of the good or services based on an arms'-length transaction; (2) the discount is given at the time of sale; and (3) the manufacturer informs the customer of the discount and the customer's reporting obligations with respect to the discount.[94] Therefore, practices that fit the discount exception and/or safe harbor would not violate the anti-kickback statute and thus could not form the basis for an FCA claim.[95]

The OIG has also issued guidance on appropriate educational grants provided to health care providers.[96] The OIG acknowledges that funding of educational activities can provide valuable information to the health care community, but that these activities can run afoul of the anti-kickback law if not provided appropriately. Specifically, the OIG has stated that funding that is in any way contingent on the purchase of the product implicates the statute, even if the educational or research purpose is legitimate.[97] The OIG further cautions that educational activities may be used as inappropriate marketing purposes if the manufacturer has any influence over the substance of the program or presenter.[98] To remove the specter of suspicion, the OIG recommends that manufacturers separate grant-making functions from sales and marketing. Accordingly, strict compliance with the regulatory safe harbor

---

[92] *Id.*

[93] 42 U.S.C. §1320a-7b(b)(3)(A).

[94] 42 C.F.R. §1001.952(h).

[95] Note, however, that the OIG has taken the position that the discount exception and discount safe harbor protect identical conduct although at least one court has disagreed.

[96] OIG Compliance Program Guidance for Pharmaceutical Manufacturers, 68 Fed. Reg. 23,731, 23,735 (May 5, 2003).

[97] *Id.*

[98] *Id.*

and OIG guidance may help sanitize discounts or educational grants from classification as illegal kickbacks.[99]

E. Class Action Lawsuits on Behalf of Private Payors and Patients [New Topic]

Following the avalanche of government and *qui tam* litigation against pharmaceutical companies, citizen groups and private payors have initiated broad-scale litigation against manufacturers on a variety of legal theories.

For example, a group of cancer patients and health care plans brought a class action lawsuit against three major pharmaceutical manufacturers, including TAP, alleging that the companies conspired to artificially inflate the price of Lupron in violation of the civil provisions of RICO.[100] The suit also alleged that the companies violated state anti-competition laws for conduct similar to that targeted in the government's case against TAP. The court dismissed some of the RICO claims on the grounds that the plaintiffs were unable to establish the existence of an "enterprise" among the manufacturer defendants.[101]

Similarly, in December of 2001, a class of consumer groups and senior citizens brought antitrust and civil RICO claims against Abbott Laboratories and more than 20 other manufacturers, challenging the companies' AWP data, alleging illegal discounts that were not passed on to consumers and alleging that the companies improperly encouraged providers to bill for free samples.[102]

F. Counterfeit Drugs, Illegal Wholesaling, and Internet Pharmacies [New Topic]

In addition to the sophisticated enforcement landscape governing drug pricing and marketing, the enforcement community is taking an active role in prosecuting various types of fraudulent prescription schemes. At the federal level, there is increased interest in developing new strategies to monitor web-based pharmacies. Specifically, the White House has established a work group including members of the FDA, the Drug Enforcement Administration (DEA), the White House Office of Drug Control Policy, and various states to develop policies aimed at eradicating fraud by Internet pharmacies. Likewise, a subcommittee of the House Committee on Energy and Commerce recently issued document requests to physicians and drug manufacturers seeking information regarding efforts taken to curb illegal prescriptions.

---

[99] Compliance with informal agency guidance does not afford the same protections as compliance with statutory or regulatory exceptions.

[100] *In re* Lupron Marketing & Sales Practices Litig., MDL No. 1430, Master File No. 01-CV-10861-RGS (D. Mass. May 28, 2001).

[101] *In re* Lupron, 295 F. Supp. 2d 148, 163 (D. Mass. 2003).

[102] Citizens for Consumer Justice v. Abbott Labs., Inc., Case No. 01-12257-PBS (D. Mass. Dec. 19, 2001).

G. New Laws Empowering Enforcement Agencies [New Topic]

Since the late 1990s, the OIG has expanded its presence in the pharmaceutical industry. Most recently, the Medicare Prescription Drug, Improvement, and Modernization Act of 2003 (MMA) vested the OIG with explicit oversight of pharmaceutical pricing.[103] The MMA scraps the AWP pricing methodology for a new system that relies on average sales price (ASP).[104] Under the new system, manufacturers will have to report their ASPs to the Centers for Medicare and Medicaid Services on a quarterly basis beginning in 2004.

Specifically, the MMA requires a senior officer of a pharmaceutical company to certify to the truth, completeness, and accuracy of pricing data reported by the company, which will be subject to audits by the OIG. This requirement could pave the way for new litigation against manufacturers. The MMA further authorizes the OIG to conduct periodic studies to determine the widely available market price (WAMP). If the WAMP is lower than the reported ASP, then the Secretary of Health and Human Services (HHS) may disregard the reported ASP and substitute the lesser of the WAMP or 103 percent of the average manufacturers' price.[105] And through the MMA, which authorizes civil monetary penalties of up to $10,000 for each price misrepresentation in reporting ASP, Congress affirmed the OIG's position that liability may result from inaccurate reporting of pharmaceutical pricing data.[106]

States have also stepped up enforcement capabilities. For example, Florida recently enacted a new law targeting Medicaid prescription drug fraud.[107] Specifically, the proposal creates criminal penalties for buying, selling, or trafficking Medicaid prescriptions and authorizes the state attorney general's Office of Statewide Prosecution to investigate and prosecute Medicaid prescription fraud. Florida also recently enacted a new law requiring manufacturers to post the AWP for the 200 most frequently prescribed drugs for the elderly on a government-sponsored website.[108] The legislation further provides that seniors shall not pay more than a stated percentage of AWP for certain drugs. Similarly, in March 2004, New Mexico enacted a Medicaid False Claims Act that mirrors the federal False Claims Act and that will be used to address Medicaid prescription drug fraud.[109] And in California, the attorney general has backed legislation forcing drug manu-

---

[103] Medicare Prescription Drug, Improvement, and Modernization Act of 2003 (MMA), Pub. L. No. 108-173, 117 Stat. 2066 (codified as amended in scattered sections of 42 U.S.C.).

[104] Pub. L. No. 108-173, §303, *adding* §1874A *and amending* §§1842(o) and 1927(a) of the Social Security Act; the AWP system will remain in force until December 31, 2004.

[105] Medicare Prescription Drug, Improvement, and Modernization Act of 2003 (MMA), §303(c)(1) (codified at 42 U.S.C. §1395w-3).

[106] H.R. CONF. REP. No. 108-391, at 392 (2003).

[107] FLA. STAT. ch. 2004-344 (2004).

[108] FLA. STAT. ch. 409.9066 (2003).

[109] 2004 N.M. Adv. Legis. Serv. 49.

facturers to report accurate pricing data to "end what is arguably the largest, single-source of Medi-Cal fraud and abuse."[110]

H. Conclusion [New Topic]

Based on the fury of massive settlements, enactment of the MMA, and broad reach of the FCA and other anti-fraud provisions, litigation against manufacturers and others in connection with prescription drugs will likely continue to be on the radar screens of *qui tam* relators, government regulators, and private plaintiffs.

XIII. THE INTERSECTION OF THE STARK LAW AND THE FALSE CLAIMS ACT [NEW TOPIC]

A. Introduction [New Topic]

In recent years, the government has expanded its enforcement efforts by trying to use the FCA to prosecute violations of the Stark law.[111] The Stark law prohibits physician "self-referral," which generally means referring Medicare and/or Medicaid patients for certain health care services to entities in which the physician or an immediate family member has a financial relationship.[112] The statute creates exceptions that permit physician compensation or ownership under certain circumstances.[113]

Unlike the anti-kickback statute, the Stark law is a "strict liability" civil statute that has no specific intent requirement. In other words, the government is not required to show that an organization acted "knowingly or willfully" to prove a violation of the prohibition. Furthermore, there was relatively little litigation in the past because the interpretative regulations were not finalized until recently and the full scope of the law had not been defined. With the publication of the Stark II/Phase II final regulations, enforcement efforts relating to Stark/FCA violations are expected to increase.[114]

B. Basis for Liability [New Topic]

In FCA cases involving allegations of regulatory noncompliance, the government typically alleges that the organization made false

---

[110] S.B. 1170 (Cal. 2003); Press Release, Office of Attorney Gen., California Dep't of Justice, *Attorney General Lockyer and Legislators Unveil Bi-Partisan, 10-Point Plan to Fight Medi-Cal Fraud* (Apr. 21, 2004), *available at* http://www.caag.state.ca.us/newsalerts/2004/04-047.htm.

[111] *See, e.g.,* United States *ex rel.* Thompson v. Columbia/HCA Healthcare Corp., 20 F. Supp. 2d 1017 (S.D. Tex. 1998); United States *ex rel.* Barbera v. Tenet, No. 97-CV-6590 (S.D. Fla. May 13, 1997), *notice of election to intervene in part and to decline to intervene in part* (Feb. 16, 2001); United States *ex rel.* Pogue v. Diabetes Treatment Ctrs. of Am., Inc., 238 F. Supp. 2d 258 (D.D.C. 2002).

[112] 42 U.S.C. §1395nn.

[113] 42 U.S.C. §1395nn(b)–(e).

[114] For detailed discussion of the Stark law and the Stark II/Phase II regulations, see Supplement Chapter 2, Federal Physician Self-Referral Restrictions (Crane).

statements to obtain payment through signed certification statements accompanying a cost report, CMS Form 1500, or other claim form.[115] The certifications on these forms often state that the person signing certifies that he or she has complied with all applicable laws and regulations.[116] These certifications form the basis for an "implied certification" theory, under which FCA liability may lie "where the government pays funds to a party, and would not have paid those funds had it known of a violation of a law or regulation, [thus,] the claim submitted for those funds contained an implied certification of compliance with the law or regulation and was fraudulent."[117]

According to certain courts, liability under the implied certification theory requires analysis of whether the government actually conditions payment upon compliance with the statute or regulation at issue.[118] Thus, under this analysis, certification of compliance with the statute or regulation must be so material to the claim for payment that the government would not have honored the claim if it were aware of the violation.[119] Some courts have held that noncompliance with the Stark law is "material" in this way.[120]

C. Recent Litigation Involving the Stark Law and the FCA [New Topic]

The government has achieved some successful settlements using the Stark law and the FCA in tandem. Most recently, in March of 2004, Tenet Health Systems paid a record $22.5 million to resolve allegations that a Florida hospital owned by the chain billed Medicare for referrals by physicians with whom it had prohibited financial arrangements.[121] The government intervened in a *qui tam* action alleging that Tenet violated the FCA by submitting claims for reimbursement to

---

[115] *See, e.g.,* Gublo v. Novacare, Inc., 62 F. Supp. 2d 347 (D. Mass. 1999); *Pogue,* 238 F. Supp. 2d 258.

[116] For example, the certification statement in the Medicare Health Care Provider/Supplier Application provides in pertinent part: "I understand that payment of a claim by Medicare or other federal health care programs is conditioned on the claim and the underlying transaction complying with such laws, regulations and program instructions." OMB Approval No. 0938-0685. See also CMS Form 2552 (cost report) that is certified as follows: "I further certify that I am familiar with the laws and regulations regarding the provision of health care services and that the services identified in this cost report were provided in compliance with such laws and regulations."

[117] *Pogue,* 238 F. Supp. 2d at 264, *citing* Ab-Tech Constr., Inc. v. United States, 31 Fed. Cl. 429, 434 (1994).

[118] *Id.* at 265–66. *See also* Mikes v. Straus, 274 F.3d 687, 699 (2d Cir. 2001) (although the *Mikes* court stated in dicta that the implied certification theory did not apply in the health care context, "because the False Claims Act was not designed for use as a blunt instrument to enforce compliance with all medical regulations—but rather only those regulations that are a precondition to payment . . ."). *Id.*

[119] *Pogue,* 238 F. Supp. 2d at 264.

[120] *See, e.g.,* United States *ex rel.* Thompson v. Columbia/HCA Healthcare Corp., 20 F. Supp. 2d 1017, 1047 (S.D. Tex. 1998); *Pogue,* 238 F. Supp.2d 258 (citing 42 U.S.C. §1395nn(a)(1)(B), which provides "the entity may not present or cause to be presented a claim under this subchapter or bill to any individual, third party payor, or other entity for designated health services furnished pursuant to a referral prohibited under subparagraph (A)").

[121] Press Release, U.S. Dep't of Justice, *Tenet Healthcare to Pay $22.5 Million for Improperly Billing Medicare* (Mar. 24, 2004), *available at* http://www.usdoj.gov/usao/fls/Tenet.html.

the Medicare program for designated health services provided in violation of the Stark law based on Tenet's purchase of certain physician practices.[122] The government claimed that Tenet paid physicians amounts that exceeded payments to virtually all similarly situated health care professionals across the country.[123]

In December 2003, a Michigan hospital paid $6.25 million to settle allegations that the hospital violated the FCA. The government alleged that the hospital violated the Stark law by paying compensation to certain vascular surgeons, which the government contended exceeded fair market value. In that case, the government alleged that the hospital leased office space to two primary care physicians below fair market value and at terms that were not commercially reasonable.[124]

Also in December 2003, a hospital in Rapid City, South Dakota, paid $6.5 million to resolve allegations that it had improperly billed Medicare for referrals from a group of oncologists with which the hospital had a prohibited financial relationship.[125]

D. Defense Strategies [New Topic]

Courts have been reluctant to uphold defense challenges to the Stark/FCA enforcement scheme, concluding that compliance with the Stark law is material for Medicare payment purposes.[126] But defendants have been successful in disputing the underlying allegations of noncompliance with the Stark law. Specifically, several health care providers have successfully defended Stark/FCA cases by presenting evidence that the suspect transactions complied with the Stark law or its exceptions.[127]

For example, in 2003, a federal district court in Illinois dismissed allegations that a hospital violated the Stark law in connection with purchases of physician practices.[128] The court found that the government failed to present evidence demonstrating that the hospital's purchases were above fair market value.[129] The case was initiated by a physician whistleblower who was previously in a contractual relationship with the defendant hospital. In the *Perales* case, the court found a lack of con-

---

[122]United States *ex rel.* Barbera v. Tenet, No. 97-CV-6590 (S.D. Fla. May 13, 1997), *notice of election to intervene in part and to decline to intervene in part* (Feb. 16, 2001).

[123]*Id.*

[124]Press Release, U.S. Dep't of Justice, *Grand Rapids' Metropolitan Hospital & Related Entities to Pay U.S. $6.25 Million to Resolve False Claims Allegations* (Dec. 10, 2003), *available at* http://www.usdoj.gov/opa/pr/2003/December/03_civ_679.htm.

[125]United States *ex rel.* Johnson-Porchardt v. Rapid City Reg'l Hosp., 01-CV-0519-KES (D.S.D. Jan. 21, 2003); Press Release, U.S. Dep't of Justice, *Justice Department Announces Settlements With South Dakota Hospital and Physicians for $6,525,000* (Dec. 20, 2002), *available at* http://www.usdoj.gov/opa/pr/2002/December/02_civ_739.htm.

[126]United States *ex rel.* Thompson v. Columbia/HCA Healthcare Corp., 20 F. Supp. 2d 1017, 1047 (S.D. Tex. 1998); *Pogue*, 238 F. Supp. 2d 258.

[127]*See, e.g.,* United States *ex rel.* Obert-Hong v. Advocate Health Care, 211 F. Supp. 2d 1045 (N.D. Ill. 2002); United States *ex rel.* Goodstein v. McLaren Reg'l Medical Ctr., 202 F. Supp. 2d 671 (E.D. Mich. 2002); United States *ex rel.* Perales v. Saint Margaret's Hosp., 243 F. Supp. 2d 843 (C.D. Ill. 2003).

[128]*Perales,* 243 F. Supp. 2d 843.

[129]*Id.*

sensus among the circuits over whether a *qui tam* relator could use the FCA as a vehicle for pursuing violations of the Stark and anti-kickback laws but dismissed the case on summary judgment based on evidence that the suspect transactions did not violate the Stark law.[130]

In 2002, a federal district court in Illinois dismissed allegations that Advocate Health Care violated the Stark law in connection with the purchase of physician practices and certain employment agreements.[131] The court found that the relator had presented no evidence that the transaction did not fall within the Stark law's "isolated transactions" exception.[132] The court also held that a percentage compensation arrangement between the hospital and its physician employees did not run afoul of the Stark law, because the compensation depended on the work performed by the physician and not the value of any referrals.[133]

Also in 2002, a Michigan hospital defeated allegations that it violated the Stark law and the FCA in connection with medical office building leases entered into with referring physicians.[134] Following trial on the issue of whether the leases were at fair market value, the court held that the hospital did not violate the Stark law. The court wrote, "the Government has failed to present any evidence to establish that because of potential patient referrals, McLaren [the hospital] paid a higher rental rate than it otherwise would have paid, or that FOR [realty company] and the Defendant physicians received a higher rental rate than they would have otherwise received because of any patient referrals that McLaren might receive from the FOA [medical group] physicians."[135]

E. Conclusion [New Topic]

Given the courts' expanded view of the applicability of the FCA and the issuance of the final Stark II regulations, health care organizations can expect increased enforcement efforts aimed at their relationships with physicians. As demonstrated by the recent settlements and court decisions, health care organizations are best advised to structure such relationships in strict compliance with the Stark law.

XIV. EMERGING ISSUES: SARBANES-OXLEY AND THE NEW ERA OF CORPORATE RESPONSIBILITY [NEW TOPIC]

A. Relevant Provisions of the Sarbanes-Oxley Act [New Topic]

The Sarbanes-Oxley Act[136] was enacted in 2002 following the highly publicized demise of the Enron, Global Crossing, and WorldCom

---

[130] *Id.*

[131] *Obert-Hong,* 211 F. Supp. 2d 1045.

[132] *Id.* at 1050.

[133] *Id.* at 1050–51.

[134] United States *ex rel.* Goodstein v. McLaren Reg'l Medical Ctr., 202 F. Supp. 2d 671 (E.D. Mich. 2002).

[135] *Id.* at 686.

[136] Sarbanes-Oxley Act, Pub. L. No. 107-204, 116 Stat. 745 (2002).

corporations. The accounting scandals plaguing these companies resulted in an erosion of public confidence in corporate integrity. Thus, Congress set out to create a regulatory scheme that would infuse a new era of responsibility among publicly traded corporations and their executives.

The three main areas of new regulation under Sarbanes-Oxley include increased responsibility for corporate executives and boards of directors, increased corporate disclosure requirements, and independence of auditors. Sarbanes-Oxley also created new criminal penalties for corporate finance-related crimes.[137] Specifically, the Act requires certain officers to certify that the company's financial statements contain no misstatements and that the financial information provided fairly represents the financial condition of the company. Corporate officers who knowingly sign false financial statements can face fines up to $5 million and up to 20 years in prison.[138]

While there are relatively few publicly traded health care corporations that fall directly within the reach of Sarbanes-Oxley, several of Sarbanes-Oxley's provisions may extend to nonprofits. For example, the Act imposes criminal penalties on anyone who destroys documents "for use in an official proceeding."[139] Additionally, Sarbanes-Oxley creates new protections for whistleblowers and criminalizes whistleblower retaliation that applies in both for-profit and nonprofit settings alike.[140] Furthermore, commentators expect that states will amend existing nonprofit corporate laws to more closely mirror Sarbanes-Oxley.[141]

---

[137] Based on mandates in Sarbanes-Oxley, the United States Sentencing Commission (the Commission) made permanent emergency amendments to the white-collar fraud provisions of the federal sentencing guidelines to include increased penalties. Press Release, U.S. Sentencing Commission, *Sentencing Commission Toughens Penalties for White Collar Fraudsters* (Apr. 18, 2003), *available at* http://www.ussc.gov/PRESS/rel0403.htm. For example, an officer of a publicly traded corporation who defrauds more than 250 employees or investors of more than $1 million will receive a sentence of more than 10 years in prison (121–51 months) under the emergency amendment, almost double the term of imprisonment previously provided by the guidelines. The amendment also increases penalties significantly for offenders who obstruct justice by destroying documents or records. Defendants who substantially interfere with the administration of justice by shredding a substantial number of documents or especially probative documents will receive a guideline sentencing range of approximately three years' imprisonment (30–37 months). Likewise, in April of 2004, the Commission adopted more stringent requirements for corporate compliance programs under the guidelines. Press Release, U.S. Sentencing Comm'n, *Sentencing Commission Toughens Requirements for Corporate Compliance and Ethics Programs* (Apr. 13, 2004), *available at* http://www.ussc.gov/PRESS/rel0404.htm.

[138] Pub. L. No. 107-204, §906 (codified at 18 U.S.C. §1350(c)).

[139] *Id.* §1102 (codified at 18 U.S.C. §1512(c)).

[140] *Id.* §1107 (codified at 18 U.S.C. §1513(e)).

[141] *See* Cynthia Reeves, *Corporate Responsibility Issues for Board Members and Senior Executives of Nonprofit Corporations in a post-Sarbanes-Oxley Act Environment,* CCH Healthcare Compliance Letter (Jan. 12, 2004); BoardSource, *The Sarbanes-Oxley Act and Implications for Nonprofit Organizations* (2003). California recently passed the "Nonprofit Integrity Act" (NIA), which takes effect January 1, 2005. Under the NIA, nonprofit organizations with gross revenues over $2 million must comply with certain auditing and disclosure requirements. S.B. 1262 (Cal. 2004). For further discussion of the Sarbanes-Oxley Act, see Supplement Chapter 1, at I.B., and Supplement Chapter 8, at II.C. and V.

B. Recent Litigation [New Topic]

In 2003, executives of the giant rehabilitation company, Health-South Corporation, faced criminal charges in connection with allegedly filing false financial statements with the Securities and Exchange Commission (SEC).[142] Thereafter, the SEC launched an investigation of HealthSouth and its executives alleging accounting fraud against the company and two of its executives.[143]

The SEC complaint filed against HealthSouth CEO Richard Scrushy alleged that Scrushy caused the company to overstate its earnings by at least $1.4 billion.[144] The SEC alleged that Scrushy directed HealthSouth's accountants to artificially inflate the company's earnings to match earnings projected by Wall Street analysts. The complaint further alleges that by the third quarter of 2002, the company's assets were overstated by at least $800 million, or approximately 10 percent of total assets. Scrushy certified the company's annual financial statements submitted to the SEC, the Form 10-K, stating that the statements contained "no untrue statement of a material fact."

And, in a recent settlement of a shareholder derivative suit with HCA, Inc., the New York State Comptroller touted provisions of the agreement that forced the company to implement new corporate governance standards that were perceived as "tougher" than Sarbanes-Oxley.[145] In 1997, the comptroller sued HCA in his capacity as sole trustee of the state's public pension fund, valued at about $100 billion, alleging that the fund was damaged by health care fraud at HCA. Under the terms of the settlement, HCA is required to assemble an independent board of directors under a stringent definition of "independence."[146] Additionally, the board's audit committee, comprised solely of independent directors, will have more power than under the pre-Sarbanes-Oxley law, and the board is mandated to maintain an ethics and compliance committee to monitor corporate ethics and oversee compliance with applicable standards.[147]

At this time, private or nonprofit health care organizations appear to be shielded from the reach of Sarbanes-Oxley. In the future, however, it is likely that both the courts and states will use Sarbanes-Oxley as a guideline for examining corporate governance in these organizations.

XV. CONCLUSION [RENUMBERED: FORMERLY XII.]

---

[142] *See, e.g.,* United States v. Harris, No. CR-03-3-0157-S (N.D. Ala. Mar. 31, 2003) (charging Emory Harris, Vice President of Finance and Assistant Controller of HealthSouth, with conspiracy to commit wire fraud and securities fraud and falsifying financial information filed with the SEC).

[143] SEC v. HealthSouth Corp., No. CV-03-J-06150S (N.D. Ala. Mar. 19, 2003), *available at* http://www.sec.gov/litigation/complaints/comphealths.htm.

[144] *Id.*

[145] Press Release, New York State Comptroller, *Precedent-Setting Corporate Governance Plan Established in Settlement of HCA Shareholder Suit* (Feb. 4, 2003), *available at* http://www.osc.state.ny.us/press/releases/feb03/20403.htm.

[146] *Id.*

[147] *Id.*

5

Legal Issues Surrounding Hospital and Physician Relationships*

---

*Dennis M. Barry, Vinson & Elkins L.L.P., Washington, D.C.

I. Background on the Nature of Relationships Between Hospitals and Physicians and the Factors Affecting Those Relationships

The Joint Commission on Accreditation of Healthcare Organizations (JCAHO) Hospital Accreditation Standards sections cited in footnote 2 in the Main Volume are now located at Sections LD.2.2, MS.1.10, and MS.2.10.[1]

II. Legal Issues

A. Issuance of the Stark II/Phase II Rule [New Topic]

On March 26, 2004, the Centers for Medicare and Medicaid Services (CMS) issued the anxiously awaited interim final rule on Phase II of the Stark II regulations; correcting amendments were published on

---

[1] Joint Commission on Accreditation of Healthcare Organizations, Hospital Accreditation Standards, LD.2.2, MS.1.10, and MS.2.10 (2004).

September 24, 2004.[2] These regulations became effective on July 26, 2004. The Stark II/Phase II rule creates more Stark law exceptions and provides clarification of certain existing Stark law exceptions. Based on the completion of Stark II rulemaking, it is likely that government enforcement of the Stark laws and regulations in hospital-physician relationships will significantly increase. It is quite important for hospitals and physicians to monitor their relationships and ensure that they are Stark compliant because if a physician in a financial relationship with an entity refers patients for certain "designated health services" (DHS) to that entity, and does not fully satisfy the criteria of an appropriate Stark law exception, it can be very costly. The penalty for failing to comply with an exception when the Stark law is implicated, even if there is no improper intent, is the denial of payment to the entity for almost all DHS[3] furnished to Medicare and Medicaid beneficiaries which were provided pursuant to referrals made by the physician who had the financial relationship with the entity (or whose family member did). Further, if the entity knew or should have known that the referrals were prohibited, the entity could be subject to a civil monetary penalty of up to $15,000 per occurrence.[4] Both unwitting and knowing violations of the Stark law and regulations could result in many thousands, if not millions, of dollars in losses to affected entities.[5]

III. RELATIONSHIPS WITH PHYSICIANS WHO ARE VOLUNTARY MEMBERS OF THE MEDICAL STAFF

A. Medical Staff Membership

1. Open Staff

The JCAHO Hospital Accreditation Standards sections cited in footnote 8 in the Main Volume are now located in Sections MS.1.10, MS.1.20, and MS.1.30.[6]

2. Open Staff and Exclusive Contracts

With the increase in hospital use of economic credentialing criteria in approving members of their medical staff, there has been a rise in legal conflicts between hospitals and physicians who challenge their exclusions from admission to the medical staff. Courts will not usually substitute their own judgment for that of the hospital in conflicts related to medical staff privileges. Indeed, two courts have recently found that the exclusion of a physician from practicing in a private

---

[2]69 Fed. Reg. 16,054 (Mar. 26, 2004); 69 Fed. Reg. 57,226 (Sept. 24, 2004 (correcting amendment).

[3]DHS are defined at 42 U.S.C. §1395nn(h)(6) and include inpatient and outpatient hospital services. The scope of these services are further defined in regulations at 42 C.F.R. §411.351.

[4]42 U.S.C. §1395nn(g)(3).

[5]The Stark law and Phase II regulations are discussed in detail in Chapter 2 of this volume.

[6]JOINT COMMISSION ON ACCREDITATION OF HEALTHCARE ORGANIZATIONS, HOSPITAL ACCREDITATION STANDARDS, MS.1.10, MS.1.20, and MS.1.30 (2004).

hospital is a discretionary matter to be decided by hospital management.[7] When a credentialing decision is based solely on economic interests, however, it is unclear as to whether courts will be as willing to acquiesce to the judgment of the hospital. Recently, one court has acknowledged that hospital implementation of an economic credentialing policy is an appropriate method through which to protect a hospital's financial viability; the court found that health care is a competitive market and physicians who have employment or contractual arrangements with competing health systems can draw significant business away from the credentialing hospital or medical center.[8]

The Office of Inspector General (OIG) recently issued a proposed draft Supplement to its Hospital Compliance Program Guidance,[9] which addresses the issue of economic credentialing for medical staff.[10] The proposed guidelines state that staff privileges based on a particular number of referrals or requiring the performance of a particular number of procedures beyond volumes necessary to demonstrate clinical proficiency implicate the federal anti-kickback statute.[11] At the same time, the OIG indicates a willingness to permit credentialing policies that categorically refuse privileges to physicians with significant conflicts of interest.[12] The OIG has also solicited comments regarding economic credentialing to better understand the potential for fraud and abuse in this setting through a separate notice issued in 2002.[13]

State licensing statutes are also implicated in economic credentialing conflicts. Some states permit more leeway to hospitals in their credentialing policies than others. For example, a Texas licensing statute states: "A hospital, by contract or otherwise, may not refuse or fail to grant or renew staff privileges, or condition staff privileges, based in whole or in part on the fact that the physician, or a partner, associate, or employee of the physician is providing medical or health care services at a different hospital or health system."[14] Conversely, Idaho "recognizes the general rule that hospitals have the authority 'to make such rules, standards or qualifications for medical staff members as they in their discretion, may deem necessary or advisable.' "[15]

---

[7]Madsen v. Audrain Health Care, Inc., 297 F.3d 697 (8th Cir. 2002); Sadler v. Dimensions Healthcare Corp., 836 A.2d 655, 663 (Md. 2003).

[8]Walborn v. UHHS/CSAHS-Cuyahoga, Inc., No. CV-02-479572 (Cuyahoga Cty. Ct. of Common Pleas, June 16, 2003) (unpublished opinion).

[9]69 Fed. Reg. 32,012 (June 8, 2004).

[10]69 Fed. Reg. at 32,023.

[11]*Id.*

[12]*Id.*

[13]67 Fed. Reg. 72,895 (Dec. 9, 2002).

[14]Tex. Health & Safety Code §241.1015(b).

[15]Miller v. St. Alphonsus Reg. Med. Ctr., Inc., 87 P.3d 934, 943 (Idaho 2004) (quoting Idaho Code §39-1395).

B. Credential Review and Corrective Action

1. *Verification of Credentials and Checking Available Databases*

In fiscal year 2003, approximately 3,275 persons, or an average of almost 9 people per day, were excluded from participation in federal health care programs.[16] Hence, screening and detection of excluded individuals are as important as ever to hospitals in ensuring their reimbursement under Medicare and other federal health care programs. Unfortunately, difficulties with the two principal resources for providers—the Office of Inspector General List of Excluded Individuals/Entities (OIG LEIE) and the General Services Administration Excluded Parties List System (GSA EPLS)—have caused problems for users. In a 2001 survey of practitioners operating under a corporate integrity agreement, the OIG found many discrepancies and inaccuracies in the information provided through these websites, as well as difficulty in accessing them, a lack of identifiers for common names, and incomplete data.[17] Despite problems arising because of incomplete information, most providers feel that they can, after inquiry, assure that no members of their medical staffs are on either list of excluded persons. Although CMS has implemented one new screening database (the Provider Enrollment, Chain, and Ownership System (PECOS))[18] and plans to implement another (the Medicare Exclusion Database (MED)),[19] neither database will be available to providers to meet their own screening needs.

3. *Hospital Duty to Deal With Problem Practitioners*

Recently, the Fifth Circuit found that a hospital peer review committee did not conspire to monopolize a cardiology market by suspending the privileges of one of its competitors. The court noted that it was inevitable in any peer review process that a physician's competitors would be involved in the process. However, in this case, the hospital obtained an outside evaluation to confirm the findings of the internal reviewers, which further refuted any idea of conspiring against a competitor. Indeed, the court was impressed by the hospital's effort in

---

[16]OFFICE OF INSPECTOR GEN., U.S. DEP'T OF HEALTH & HUMAN SERVS., SEMIANNUAL REPORT, SPRING AND FALL 2003, at 6, *available at* http://oig.hhs.gov/publications/docs/semiannual/2003/03springsemi.pdf; http://oig.hhs.gov/publications/docs/semiannual/2003/03fallsemi.pdf.

[17]OFFICE OF INSPECTOR GEN., U.S. DEP'T OF HEALTH & HUMAN SERVS., RESULTS OF CORPORATE INTEGRITY AGREEMENT SURVEY (Aug. 2001), *available at* http://oig.hhs.gov/fraud/docs/complianceguidance/ciasurvey.pdf.

[18]PECOS was implemented in the spring of 2002 to assist CMS in determining whether a provider applicant will be permitted to enroll in federal health care plans as well as to combat fraud and abuse. *See* Notice of New System Records, Provider Enrollment, Chain and Ownership System, 66 Fed. Reg. 51,961 (Oct. 11, 2001).

[19]The MED system will be used to aid CMS and contractors in ensuring that no Medicare payments are made to any excluded entity or person that has provided any item or service that was not an emergency item or service. *See* Medicare and Medicaid System of Records; Medicare Exclusion Database, 67 Fed. Reg. 8810 (Feb. 26, 2002).

getting an outside assessment to obtain a different perspective and avoid bias before it made its final decision. Thus, independent review participation in addressing a perceived practitioner problem offers some protection from claims that practitioners involved in the review improperly recommended exclusion of another practitioner for competitive reasons.

C. Corrective Action Under the Medical Staff Bylaws

The OIG has provided guidance on how, in unusual circumstances, an excluded individual may still be employed by a health care entity without subjecting the entity to administrative sanctions. In OIG Advisory Opinion No. 01-16,[20] a health plan requested advice on whether it could employ a physician who had been excluded from participation in federal health care programs. In its analysis of the situation, the OIG explained that

> [a] provider or entity that receives Federal health care program funding may only employ an excluded individual in limited situations. Those situations would include instances where the provider pays the individual's salary, expenses, and benefits exclusively from private funds or from other non-Federal funding sources, and where the services furnished by the excluded individual relate solely to non-Federal programs or patients.[21]

The OIG also notes in the advisory opinion that an excluded employee's work responsibilities must not relate to any medical or administrative skills. The duties of an excluded individual need to be far removed from the provision of items and services to program beneficiaries and should also be unassociated with any federal funding or regulatory mandates in order to avoid administrative sanctions. Although there may be good reasons for a hospital to want to employ an excluded individual, the measures that it would have to take in order to avoid Medicare liability in separating the excluded person from any Medicare-related activity may be so arduous as not to be worth the expense and administrative complications.

The JCAHO Hospital Accreditation Standards section cited in footnote 22 in the Main Volume is now located Section MS.4.50.[22]

D. Physician Attestation of Accuracy of Medicare Diagnoses

In many situations, it is quite difficult for a physician to evaluate whether a patient needs inpatient services or outpatient observation services at the time the services are ordered. Thus, it may be necessary for the physician to reevaluate medical diagnoses and change or modify the original orders he or she has given. Unfortunately, there is very

---

[20] OIG Advisory Op. No. 01-16 (Sept. 28, 2001), *available at* http://oig.hhs.gov/fraud/docs/advisoryopinions/2001/ao01-16.pdf.

[21] *Id.*

[22] JOINT COMMISSION ON ACCREDITATION OF HEALTHCARE ORGANIZATIONS, HOSPITAL ACCREDITATION STANDARDS, MS.4.50 (2004).

little guidance from CMS on what changes may be made and how they can be made. In February 2004, CMS announced a new billing code for form CMS-1450. This new code permits hospitals to bill, as an outpatient service, an inpatient service ordered by a physician.[23] It is expected that CMS will issue instructions on when it is appropriate to use this code in the near future.

E. Physician Coverage of the Emergency Room

Reimbursement for on-call physicians at critical access hospitals was addressed in the August 1, 2001, *Federal Register*.[24] Effective October 1, 2001, reasonable costs of outpatient services for critical access hospitals can include compensation and related costs for a physician who is on call, but who is not present on the premises of the critical access hospital, as long as the on-call physician is not otherwise furnishing physician services, and is not on call at any other provider or facility. In addition, physicians who qualify for on-call status must actually come to the facility when summoned in order to be reimbursable. Further, CMS only reimburses for costs when the requirement to come to the facility when summoned during on-call hours is included in the written contract with physicians.

1. *Emergency Room Physicians' Interpretations of Diagnostic Images [New Topic]*

Medicare policy does not resolve who should interpret images and issue reports that become part of a patient's medical record. However, Medicare does have rules[25] that address whether and to whom Medicare will pay for an interpretation of X rays and electrocardiograms (EKGs). Emergency room physicians can bill for interpretations of X rays and EKGs that they read as long as they create a written narrative report of the interpretation that becomes a part of the patient's medical record. A hospital can insist that all images be interpreted by a radiologist when it has an exclusive contract with a radiology group. However, if this interpretation does not occur contemporaneously with treatment, then there is an issue as to whether the radiologists can properly bill Medicare. It seems, however, that the real policy goal of the "contemporaneous"[26] requirement for reimbursement is to ensure that no double billing occurs when both the emergency room physician and the radiologist interpret an X ray. If CMS receives two claims for the same diagnostic interpretation, it will determine which interpretation contributed to the treatment of the patient-beneficiary and reimburse that one. To the extent that a non-contemporaneous

---

[23] MEDICARE CLAIMS PROCESSING MANUAL, Pub. No. 100-04, Transmittal No. 81 (Feb. 6, 2004) (including condition code 44 where inpatient admission changed to outpatient).

[24] 66 Fed. Reg. 39,828 (Aug. 1, 2001).

[25] 60 Fed. Reg. 63,124, 63,132 (Dec. 8, 1995).

[26] 60 Fed. Reg. at 63,130–31. Although CMS would seem to require that the interpretation occur "contemporaneously" with treatment, the preamble language would indicate that an interpretation by a radiologist would be reimbursed as long as there is no bill from another physician.

interpretation by a radiologist does not affect the patient's treatment, Medicare will deem it to be a quality control measure provided by the hospital, and thus will deny reimbursement for the radiologist's claim.

F. Perquisites for Members of the Medical Staff

The recently released Stark II/Phase II rule ("Phase II rule" or "Phase II")[27] modifies and clarifies the nonmonetary compensation exception of up to $300 per year and the medical staff incidental benefits exceptions, both of which were added by the Stark II/Phase I rule.[28] Additionally, the Phase II rule creates a new regulatory exception for the provision of information technology items and services (including both hardware and software) by an entity to a physician to enable the physician to participate in a communitywide health information system designed to enhance the overall health of the community.[29]

Concerning the nonmonetary compensation exception and the medical staff incidental benefits exception, the Phase II rule provides a mechanism to increase the cost limits in these exceptions to account for inflation.[30] Both the $300 limit in the nonmonetary annual compensation exception and the $25 limit under the incidental benefits exception will be updated annually for inflation based on the Consumer Price Index update, and the updates for these exceptions will be displayed on the CMS self-referral website as soon as possible after September 30 of each year.[31]

Additionally, the Phase II rule clarifies that the exception for medical staff incidental benefits can cover the provision of pagers, two-way radios, electronic, and/or Internet services to physicians, if such items and services are used during times when medical staff members are engaged in hospital or patient activities. For example, it is permissible under the exception to provide pagers and two-way radios to physicians to ensure that they can be contacted in an emergency and other urgent patient-care situations when the physicians are away from the hospital campus.[32] According to the Phase II preamble, the incidental benefits exception also covers including a listing for a physician or practice on a hospital website (however, inclusion of any advertising or promotion for a physician or practice on a hospital

---

[27] 69 Fed. Reg. 16,054 (Mar. 26, 2004); 69 Fed. Reg. 57,226 (Oct. 24, 2004) (correcting amendment).

[28] 42 C.F.R. §411.357(k) and (m).

[29] 69 Fed. Reg. at 16,113; 42 C.F.R. §411.357(u).

[30] 69 Fed Reg. at 16,112.

[31] 42 C.F.R. §411.357(k)(2) and (m)(5).

[32] 69 Fed. Reg. at 16,112–13. The provision of two-way radios and pagers is compliant with 42 C.F.R. §411.357(m) even through these are not incidental benefits provided "on campus." The "on campus" requirement was intended to apply to benefits such as parking, cafeteria meals, etc., which are incidental to services being provided by physicians at the hospital. This way, the provision of tangential, off-site benefits such as restaurant dinners and theater tickets must comply with the exception for nonmonetary compensation up to $300.

website would have to qualify under another Stark II exception such as the $300 nonmonetary compensation exception).[33]

The community-wide health information system exception allows a hospital to provide physicians with use of technology that is dedicated to the service of the hospital and the provision of health care for hospital patients.[34] Under this exception, the hospital or health care system providing the technology must provide access to the technology to all community providers and practitioners who desire to participate and share electronic health care records.[35] Also, this exception only allows hospitals or health systems to provide information technology items that are necessary to enable a physician to participate in the entity's health information system. Thus, if a physician already owns a computer, a hospital could not provide the physician with a new computer.[36] However, the hospital could provide the physician with software or other materials required to allow a physician's existing computer to interface with the hospital's health information system.[37] Among other criteria, this exception required that any community-wide health system arrangement not be provided to a physician in any manner that takes into account the volume or value of referrals or other business generated by the physician, and the arrangement cannot violate the federal anti-kickback statute or any other federal or state law or regulation governing claims submission or billing.[38]

1. Professional Courtesy

The Phase II rule also provides a new exception for professional courtesy.[39] Professional courtesy may be extended to a physician, a physician's immediate family member, or a member of the physician's office staff as long as the following conditions are met:

(1) The professional courtesy is offered to all physicians on the entity's bona fide medical staff or in the entity's local community or service area without regard to the volume or value of referrals or other business generated between the parties;

(2) The health care items and services provided are of a type routinely provided by the entity;

(3) The entity's professional courtesy policy is set out in writing and approved in advance by the entity's governing body;

(4) The professional courtesy is not offered to a physician (or immediate family member) who is a Federal health care program beneficiary, unless there has been a good faith showing of financial need;

---

[33] *Id.*

[34] 69 Fed. Reg. at 16,113.

[35] *Id.;* 42 C.F.R. §411.357(u)(2).

[36] 69 Fed. Reg. at 16,113.

[37] *Id.*

[38] 42 C.F.R. §411.357(u)(1)–(3).

[39] 69 Fed. Reg. at 16,115, 42 C.F.R. §411.357(s). Phase II defines professional courtesy as "the provision of free or discounted health care items or services to a physician or his or her immediate family members or office staff." 69 Fed. Reg. at 16,116.

(5) If the professional courtesy involves any whole or partial reduction of any coinsurance obligation, the insurer is informed in writing of the reduction; and

(6) The arrangement does not violate the anti-kickback statute[40]. . . . , or any Federal or State law or regulation governing billing or claims submission.[41]

In the Phase II rule, CMS strongly cautioned that many professional courtesy arrangements may violate the federal anti-kickback statute[42] or may violate the civil monetary penalties law prohibition against giving inducements to Medicare and Medicaid beneficiaries.[43] Also, CMS noted that many private insurers may have concerns about the use of coinsurance waivers as a form of professional courtesy.[44]

G. Physician-Hospital Organizations

2. Antitrust Issues

The extent to which physician-hospital organizations (PHOs) can negotiate on behalf of their independent physician members has always been an important aspect of health care antitrust enforcement. Both the Federal Trade Commission (FTC) and the Department of Justice (DOJ) have made it clear that a hospital cannot become a vehicle to encourage, facilitate, and thus conspire with otherwise independent physician competitors in what will amount to per se illegal price-fixing, boycott of payor, or unlawful division of markets. Such actions may expose a hospital to potential liability as a consequence of federal antitrust agency enforcement, private party litigation brought by aggrieved payors or patients, or even litigation initiated by state antitrust enforcement officials. Therefore, hospitals must ensure that they do not act as facilitators of per se unlawful conduct by physician competitors in the network.

PHOs cannot establish or negotiate fees for physicians who have not integrated their practices or do not share financial risk. How PHOs are structured and the way that they operate, in practice are therefore very significant questions. The issue of the extent to which PHOs or physician organizations can negotiate on behalf of their independent physician members has recently come to the forefront in FTC consent decrees. For example, the FTC complaint for In the Matter of South Georgia Health Partners[45] described an arrangement where four PHOs consisting of 15 hospitals and 500 physicians (the physicians compris-

---

[40] 42 U.S.C. §1320a-7(b).

[41] 42 C.F.R. §411.357(s)(1)–(6).

[42] See also Office of Inspector Gen., U.S. Dep't of Health & Human Servs., Draft Supplemental Compliance Program Guidance for Hospitals, 69 Fed. Reg. 32,012 (June 8, 2004), which discusses professional courtesy in the context of hospital compliance with the federal anti-kickback statute, the civil monetary penalty law, and the Stark law. 69 Fed. Reg. 32,027–28.

[43] 69 Fed. Reg. at 16,116.

[44] *Id.*

[45] In the Matter of South Georgia Health Partners, L.L.C. (F.T.C. Sept. 9, 2003), *available at* http://www.ftc.gov/os/2003/09/sgeorgiado.pdf.

ing 90 percent of all physicians practicing in the region) joined together to form one large PHO, South Georgia Health Partners "SGHP." The FTC alleged that the PHO, hospital and physician members of SGHP canceled current contracts with payors, and from that point, all physicians and hospitals would only deal with the payors through SGHP. It was also alleged that payors had to accept the SGHP fixed fee schedule and could obtain a fixed discount of no more than 10 percent. The prices demanded by SGHP were found to be higher than the physicians and hospitals would have obtained by negotiating unilaterally. In order to remedy the alleged problematic behavior and artificially increased costs, the consent decree prohibited SGHP from becoming involved in any way with physician negotiations with payors.

In a separate case, the FTC found that a PHO in North Carolina was engaging in price fixing and anticompetitive behavior. Piedmont Health Alliance (PHA) and 10 individual physicians allegedly fixed prices for the services of PHA physician members. Frye Regional Medical Center (Frye) and its parent company, Tenet Healthcare Corporation (Tenet), were involved in the activities of PHA,[46] and this is the first case where the FTC has named a hospital as a participant in an alleged price fixing conspiracy. PHA used a "modified messenger model" to enter into payor contracts. The FTC alleged that instead of correctly using the messenger model to facilitate individual contract negotiations with physicians, PHA coordinated physician responses and set fee schedules on predetermined price levels. Additionally, it was alleged that Frye funds were used in developing PHA and that Frye's chief operating officer initially directed the PHO. Frye and Tenet settled with the FTC and agreed to refrain from interaction with payors in any way on behalf of any physician. Frye and Tenet were also required to cease receiving any payments from fee schedules set under the alleged unlawful fee schedules.

PHOs composed of substantial numbers of physicians in a particular geographic area that act in an exclusive or de facto exclusive capacity can clearly open themselves up to claims of monopolization or attempted monopolization of physician services. Therefore, it is important to take away from both these cases that the safest structure for either a physician-only or hospital-physician organization is one where the group functions solely as a messenger between the physicians and any managed care payor and the physicians negotiate individually with all payors.

H. Including Physicians Who Are Voluntary Members of the Medical Staff in a Wide-Area Computer Network Tied to the Hospital

The community-wide health information system exception created by Stark II Phase II addresses concerns about what equipment

---

[46]Tenet Healthcare Corporation and Frye Regional Medical Center Consent Decree, *available at* http://www.ftc.gov/opa/2003/12/piedmont.htm.

and services a hospital is permitted to furnish to a physician to give the physician access to the hospital's wide-area computer network. This exception is discussed in III.F., above (Perquisites for Members of the Medical Staff).

Additionally, the two OIG advisory opinions on the provision of telemedicine equipment (discussed in the Main Volume and cited in footnote 51) can now be found at new locations on the Web.[47]

I. Medicare Prohibition on Unbundling

The Stark II Phase II final rule clarifies and modifies the different exceptions that may apply where a physician provides services to the hospital that may not be unbundled. The modifications to these exceptions, including the revised definitions of "fair market value" and "set in advance," are addressed below in IV.B., C., D., and I.

IV. CONTRACTUAL RELATIONSHIPS WITH PHYSICIANS

B. Hospitals Often Lease Space to Physicians

The Phase II rule supplements the existing Stark II exception for rental of office space. The six specific criteria set out in the space-lease exception have been modified by the Phase II rule to expand the applicability of the exception.[48] For example, the revised space-lease exception requirements now provide that leases or rental agreements may be terminated with or without cause prior to the end of the first year of the agreement—as long as no further agreement is entered into within the first year of the original lease term and any new lease fits, on its own terms, in an exception. CMS determined that without-cause terminations do not pose a high risk of anti-kickback abuse and, in fact, allow parties to get out of an agreement without the expense of litigation that may arise from leases that can be terminated "for cause" only.[49]

Additionally, the "exclusive use" criterion has been eased to allow subleases. The "exclusive use" test will be considered to be met as long as the lessee or sublessee does not share the rental space with the lessor or any entity related to the lessor[50] during the time it is rented or used by the lessee or sublessee.[51] It is important to note, however, that certain subleases may create indirect compensation arrangements that would have to fit in the indirect compensation arrangement exception.[52]

The Phase II rule also clarifies that month-to-month holdover leases are permissible under the space-lease exception for up to six months if they meet the general lease criteria set forth in the lease-of-

---

[47]For OIG Advisory Op. No. 98-18 (Nov. 25, 1998), see www.oig.hhs.gov/fraud/docs/advisory-opinions/1998/ao98-18.htm (last visited June 1, 2004). For OIG Advisory Op. No. 99-14 (Dec. 28, 1999), see www.oig.hhs.gov/fraud/advisoryopinions/1999/ao99-14.htm (last visited June 1, 2004).

[48]42 C.F.R. §411.357(a)(1)–(6).

[49]69 Fed. Reg. 16,054, 16,086 (Mar. 26, 2004).

[50]*Id.*

[51]42 C.F.R. §411.357(a)(3).

[52]42 C.F.R. §411.357(p).

space exception, and the holdover rental is on the same terms and conditions as the immediately preceding agreement.[53]

Also, as mentioned in the Main Volume, for the purposes of Medicare cost reporting, the costs of hospital space leased to physicians are only significant to cost-reimbursed hospitals. Even fewer hospitals are cost reimbursed than indicated in the Main Volume (see footnote 79 in the Main Volume). Rehabilitation hospitals are now paid under the prospective payment system,[54] and the PPS system for psychiatric hospitals will be implemented soon.[55]

1. Clarification of "Fair Rental Value" [New Topic]

Issued in February 2002, *United States v. McLaren Regional Medical Center*[56] dealt with how to determine fair market value in a space lease.[57] In that case, a *qui tam* relator alleged that McLaren Medical Center (McLaren) induced referrals of Medicare patients to its facility by providing remuneration to physician-owned Family Orthopedic Realty (FOR) by leasing space from FOR. The crux of this case, in determining whether McLaren's payment was meant to induce referrals, was whether the payment made by McLaren to referring FOR physicians for the leased space was at or above fair market value evaluated under the Stark II statute and the Anti-Kickback statute.[58] The court found that the lease agreement was an arm's-length transaction and the agreed-upon rental amount was fair market value.

Much of the court's determination hinged on the fact that the defendant's witnesses engaged in an in-depth, thorough review of types of leases and lease costs for the relevant geographic area in proving that McLaren paid fair market value for its space lease.[59] Additionally, the lengthy negotiations engaged in by the parties and the terms of the lease demonstrated that their transaction was indeed set at fair market value. For example, McLaren and the FOR physicians negotiated for nine months before reaching an agreement on the terms of the lease.[60] Also, McLaren leased space based on measurements from the interior walls rather than the exterior (which would have included a great deal of unusable space), and McLaren did not pay for use of common areas.[61] Thus, McLaren was indeed only paying to lease the space that it was actually using. Further, McLaren did not pay rent while its space was being renovated, it had the option of paying the $35,000 security deposit via promissory note, and was permitted to self-insure.[62] The

---

[53] 42 C.F.R. §411.357(a)(7).
[54] 66 Fed. Reg. 41,316 (Aug. 7, 2001).
[55] 68 Fed. Reg. 66,920 (Nov. 28, 2003).
[56] 202 F. Supp. 2d 671 (E.D. Mich. 2002).
[57] *Id.*
[58] *Id.* at 674–5.
[59] *Id.* at 685.
[60] *Id.* at 676.
[61] *Id.*
[62] *Id.*

analysis of the aforementioned factors can go a long way in determining whether the terms of a space lease are indeed at fair market value.

C. Leases of Equipment

Phase II clarifications concerning the space-lease exception generally also apply to the equipment-lease exception.[63] For example, the Phase II rule permits equipment and space leases to be structured such that lease payments are based on a per-use amount (a "click" fee). This type of arrangement is now permitted because CMS revised the definition of "set in advance,"[64] which is incorporated in the equipment-lease exception[65] and the space-lease exception.[66] The new definition states that compensation will be considered set in advance if

> the aggregate compensation, a time-based or per unit of service based (whether per use or per service) amount, or a specific formula for calculating the compensation is set in an agreement between the parties before the furnishing of the items or services for which the compensation is to be paid. The formula for determining the compensation to be paid must be set forth in sufficient detail so that it can be objectively verified, and the formula may not be changed or modified during the course of the agreement in any manner that reflects the volume or value of referrals or other business generated by the referring physician.[67]

The revised definition of "set in advance" specifically permits payments to be structured as time-based and per unit of service. Furthermore, subsections (d)(2) and (d)(3) of 42 C.F.R. Section 411.354 explain that unit-based—including time-based—compensation will be deemed not to take into account the "volume or value of referrals" or "other business generated between the parties" if the compensation is fair market value for services or items actually provided, and the compensation formula does not vary during the course of the agreement in any manner that takes into account referrals of designated health services or referrals or other business generated by the referring physician—including private-pay health care business. As noted in the Main Volume, equipment leases may also fit under the fair market value exception,[68] whereas space leases are not eligible for this exception.

D. Medical Director Agreements

The Stark exception most applicable to medical director agreements is the exception for personal services arrangements. The original requirements for this exception are set out in the Main Volume. The Phase II rule modifies the original exception to make clear that independent contractor physicians can receive compensation that takes into

---

[63] 42 C.F.R. §411.357(b).
[64] 42 C.F.R. §411.354(d)(1).
[65] 42 C.F.R. §411.357(b)(4).
[66] 42 C.F.R. §411.357(a)(4).
[67] 42 C.F.R. §411.354(d)(1).
[68] 42 C.F.R. §411.357(*l*).

account the volume or value of personally performed services and can be compensated using a percentage-based methodology that is set in advance as defined under the Stark II regulations.[69]

The Phase II rule establishes two new safe harbors for assuring that compensation will be deemed to meet the Stark law's fair market value requirement. These safe harbors are set forth in the fair market value definition,[70] and are for hourly payments to physicians for personal services. These safe harbors are not limited to medical director services, but may be used for any hourly physician compensation for personal services furnished to any designated health services (DHS) entity.[71]

The first safe harbor requires that the hourly rate be equal to or less than the average hourly rate for emergency room physician services in the relevant physician market provided that there are at least three hospitals providing emergency room services in the market.[72] The second safe harbor requires averaging the fiftieth percentile salary for the physician's specialty of four national salary surveys and dividing the resulting figure by 2,000 hours to establish an hourly rate.[73] This option in the safe harbor provides a choice of six nationally recognized surveys from which to obtain salary data.[74]

Another clarification in Phase II regarding the personal services arrangement exception concerns the requirement that the parties' written arrangement specify all of the services to be furnished by the physician (or an immediate family member) to the entity.[75] CMS has clarified that this requirement can be met by cross-referencing all the agreements between the parties or by cross-referencing a master list of agreements that is updated centrally.[76] This master list must be made available to the Secretary upon request.[77]

The Phase II rule also revised the personal services arrangement exception such that an agreement may be terminated with or without cause during the first year of the agreement as long as no new agreement is formed within that year.[78]

E. Employing and Contracting With Physicians for the Provision of Patient Care Services

1. Federal Compliance Issues

In 2003, the OIG issued an advisory opinion on payment to physicians at a county-owned women's health clinic where it allowed the

---

[69] 69 Fed. Reg. 16,054, 16,090 (Mar. 26, 2004).

[70] 42 C.F.R. §411.351.

[71] 69 Fed. Reg. at 16,092.

[72] 42 C.F.R. §411.351.

[73] *Id.*

[74] *Id.*

[75] 69 Fed. Reg. at 16,091.

[76] 69 Fed. Reg. at 16,091; 42 C.F.R. §411.357(d)(1)(ii).

[77] 42 C.F.R. §411.357(d)(1)(ii).

[78] 42 C.F.R. §411.357(d)(1)(iv).

provision of physician services at below fair market value fees.[79] In that opinion, a medical center was seeking to provide physician services to the clinic and to provide inpatient hospital services, including inpatient services at no charge for the county's primarily indigent and low-income self-paying patients. While the arrangement raised potential issues under the federal anti-kickback statute, the OIG concluded that it would not impose sanctions on the arrangement because the requisite intent to induce or reward referrals of federal health care business was not present.

The OIG specifically stated that the annual fee for physician services, while less than fair market value, was not unreasonable because it covered the medical center's additional costs and it gave the medical center an opportunity to strengthen its residency program by allowing its residents to explore a broader range of medical conditions. Also, any benefit of deriving referrals for federal health care programs for inpatient care was offset by the medical center's commitment to provide free care to county clinic patients who were unable to pay for the services, and the arrangement was unlikely to result in overutilization or increased costs to federal health programs since the primary inpatient business generated by the clinic is labor and delivery services. Those admissions would be reimbursed on a prospective fixed fee basis. Additionally, since it was a county clinic, the public derived the benefits of getting the best possible price for the clinic's physician services.

There also may be antitrust concerns when a hospital employs or contracts with physicians for the provision of patient care. Physician practices can be accused of collusion when they negotiate for payment with a hospital. In 2003, two San Diego anesthesiologist groups settled with the FTC based on the allegation that they jointly agreed on certain fees and other relevant competitive terms that they demanded from a San Diego hospital in order to provide on-call services.[80] These two groups made up three-quarters of the anesthesiologists with medical staff privileges at a San Diego hospital and worked on approximately 70 percent of the hospital's cases requiring anesthesiology services. Usually, anesthesiologists are reimbursed for their services by health insurance companies and other third-party payors. In addition to these payments, the anesthesiology groups attempted to obtain stipends from the hospital as payment for obstetric calls and for rendering services to uninsured emergency room patients. The hospital had never paid its anesthesiologists a stipend for taking calls. The FTC viewed the conduct of these two groups in attempting to obtain stipend payments as collusive and anticompetitive. The groups entered consent decrees with the FTC whereby they will refrain from engaging in future anticompetitive practices.

---

[79] OIG Advisory Op. No. 03-06 (Mar. 26, 2003), *available at* http://oig.hhs.gov/fraud/docs/advisoryopinions/2003/ao0306.pdf.

[80] In the Matter of Grossmont Anesthesia Services Medical Group Inc., and In the Matter of Anesthesia Service Medical Group Inc., *at* http://www.ftc.gov/opa/2003/05/asmg.htm.

2. State Corporate Practice of Medicine Prohibitions

Texas has repealed Article 4495b, Section 5.01(a), of the Texas Civil Statutes. However, the exception to the corporate practice of medicine prohibition, which is discussed in the Main Volume, still exists in Texas but has been moved within the Texas Occupations Code.[81] These excepted organizations are no longer called "5.01(a)" organizations.

3. Medicare and Medicaid Prohibitions on the Reassignment of Revenue

The Medicare Prescription Drug, Improvement, and Modernization Act of 2003 (MMA)[82] remedied certain problems related to the furnishing of physician emergency room coverage. Prior to January 1, 2004, hospitals experienced difficulties in obtaining physician coverage of emergency rooms because they were not able to use certain staffing methods. Many hospitals hoped to obtain physician coverage through outside contractors; however, most commercial contractors would require their physicians to assign their revenue from emergency room services to the contractor. Such assignments did not fit within any then-existing Medicare exception to the "prohibition against reassignment." Congress remedied this problem in Section 952 of the MMA by expanding the exception for reassignment of revenue to allow payment to be made to an entity enrolled in the Medicare program that submits a claim for services provided by a physician or other person under a contractual arrangement with that entity, regardless of where the service was furnished. Now, a carrier may make payment to an entity enrolled in the Medicare program that submits a claim for services provided by a physician under a contractual arrangement (such as where the services are furnished in an emergency room) as long as: (1) joint and several liability is shared between the entity submitting the claim and the person actually furnishing the service for any Medicare overpayment relating to such claim, and (2) the person furnishing the service has unrestricted access to claims submitted by the entity for the services provided by that person.[83]

The information on reassignment of revenue cited in the Main Volume in footnotes 101, 102, and 103, is no longer in the *Medicare Carriers Manual.* This information has been relocated to the new CMS Internet-Only Manuals. The information cited in footnote 101 in the Main Volume can be found at *Medicare Claims Processing Manual,* CMS Pub. 100-4, Chapter 1, Sections 30.2 and 30.2.2. The information formerly cited at footnote 102 can now be found at *Medicare Claims Processing Manual,* CMS Pub. 100-4, Chapter 1, Section 30.21. Finally, the information formerly at footnote 103 can be found in *Medicare Claims Processing Manual,* CMS Pub. 100-4, Chapter 1, Section 30.2.15 A and C.

---

[81] TEX. OCC. CODE ANN. §162.001 (exception to the corporate practice of medicine prohibition).

[82] Pub. L. No. 108-173, 117 Stat. 2066 (2003).

[83] Medicare Claims Processing Manual, CMS Pub. 100-4, Chapter 1, §30.2.7.

F. Hospital-Based Physicians

1. *Exclusivity*

The JCAHO Hospital Accreditation Standards sections cited in footnote 106 in the Main Volume are now located at Sections MS.2.10 and MS.2.20.[84]

2. *Kickbacks*

The information cited at footnote 108—the OIG report entitled *Financial Arrangements Between Hospitals and Hospital-Based Physicians*—has been relocated on the Web.[85]

G. Discounts on Reference Laboratory Services

The information cited at footnote 112 in the Main Volume—the letter from Kevin G. McAnaney on charges "Substantially in Excess" and OIG Advisory Opinion Nos. 99-2 and 98-8—have been relocated on the Web.[86] In addition, the OIG has issued a proposed rule on payment "substantially in excess." This proposed rule provides definitions of "substantially in excess" and "usual charges" and would clarify the "good cause" exception for payments in excess.[87]

I. Academic Medical Centers

The Phase II rule makes it easier for entities to qualify for the academic medical center exception.[88] The exception has been expanded to permit an accredited academic hospital to qualify for the exception regardless of whether it is affiliated with an accredited medical school.[89] In order to be deemed an academic medical center, an entity must consist of the following:

1. an accredited medical school or an accredited academic hospital;
2. one or more faculty practice plans that are affiliated with the medical school or academic hospital; and
3. one or more affiliated hospitals in which a majority of the physicians on the medical staff are faculty members, and a majority

---

[84] JOINT COMMISSION ON ACCREDITATION OF HEALTHCARE ORGANIZATIONS, HOSPITAL ACCREDITATION STANDARDS, MS.2.10 and MS.2.20 (2004).

[85] Office of Inspector Gen., U.S. Dep't of Health & Human Servs., *Financial Arrangements Between Hospitals and Hospital-Based Physicians,* OEI-09-89-00330 (Oct. 1991), *available at* http://oig.hhs.gov/oei/reports/oei-09-89-00330.pdf (last visited June 1, 2004).

[86] Letter From Kevin G. McAnaney, Chief, Industry Guidance Branch, Office of Inspector Gen. (Apr. 26, 2000), *available at* oig.hhs.gov/fraud/docs/safeharborregulations/lab.htm (last visited June 1, 2004); OIG Advisory Op. No. 99-2 (Mar. 4, 1999), *available at* oig.hhs.gov/fraud/docs/advisoryopinions/1999/ao99_2.htm (last visited June 1, 2004); and OIG Advisory Op. No. 98-8 (July 6, 1998), *available at* www.oig.hhs.gov/fraud/docs/advisoryopinions/1998/ao98_8.htm (last visited June 1, 2004).

[87] 68 Fed. Reg. 53,939 (Sept. 15, 2003).

[88] 69 Fed. Reg. 16,054, 16,108 (Mar. 26, 2004); 42 C.F.R. §411.355(e).

[89] 42 C.F.R. §411.355(e)(2)(i).

of admissions to the hospital are made by physicians who are faculty members.[90]

In order to be considered an accredited academic hospital, the hospital or health system must sponsor four or more approved medical education programs.[91] Also, the accredited academic hospital and the affiliated hospital may be the same entity.[92] Hospitals may aggregate multiple faculty practice plans to satisfy the requirement in 42 C.F.R. Section 411.355(e)(iii) (listed in item (3), above) that the majority of the medical staff be on the faculty and that the majority of admissions to the hospital are made by faculty members.[93] However, primary care physicians without substantial academic or clinical teaching responsibilities do not qualify for protection under this exception.[94]

To be covered under the academic medical center exception, the referring physician need not be an employee of the medical school. The referring physician must, however, be a bona fide employee of a component of the academic medical center.[95] Also, the referring physician must be engaged in substantial academic services or clinical teaching services.[96]

The revised exception adds a safe harbor for what constitutes substantial academic services or clinical teaching services.[97] Any referring physician who spends at least 20 percent of his or her professional time or eight hours per week providing academic services or clinical teaching services (or a combination of both) will fulfill the requirement.[98] Because this is a safe harbor and not an absolute requirement, there may be referring physicians who do not satisfy this safe harbor but who still provide sufficient academic services or clinical teaching services, depending on the individual physician's circumstances.[99]

Due to the revision of the "set in advance" standard in Phase II, the revised exception now permits a physician's compensation for academic services or clinical teaching services to be calculated using a percentage-based methodology.

The Phase II rule has also clarified the requirement for a written agreement, specifying that all relationships between the different components of the academic medical center may be met through one agreement or multiple agreements.[100] Additionally, where all components of

---

[90] 42 C.F.R. §411.355(e)(2).

[91] 42 C.F.R. §411.355(e)(3).

[92] 42 C.F.R. §411.355(e)(2)(iii).

[93] 69 Fed. Reg. at 16,109.

[94] *Id.*

[95] *Id.*

[96] *Id.*

[97] 42 C.F.R. §411.355(e)(1)(i)(D).

[98] *Id.*

[99] 69 Fed. Reg. at 16,110.

[100] 69 Fed. Reg. at 16,110.

an academic medical center are owned by a single legal entity, the financial reports of the entity which document the transfer of funds between the components, including the medical center, may be sufficient evidence to verify an academic medical center's compliance with the written agreement requirement.[101]

J. Gainsharing

1. Civil Monetary Penalties for Improper Incentive Plans

The OIG has published a Draft Supplemental Compliance Program Guidance for Hospitals.[102] According to the OIG, the final version of the document will supplement the compliance program guidance for hospitals that was issued in 1998.[103]

The information cited at footnotes 118, 120, and 123 in the Main Volume has been relocated on the Web. Footnote 127 cites the Gainsharing Arrangements and CMPs for Hospital Payments to Physicians to Reduce or Limit Services to Beneficiaries.[104] Footnote 129 cites the Lewis Morris letter relating to Social Security Act Sections 1128A(b)(1) and hospital-physician incentive plans for Medicare and Medicaid Beneficiaries.[105] Footnote 132 cites OIG Advisory Opinion No. 01-1 (Jan. 11, 2001), which can now be found elsewhere on the OIG's website.[106]

5. Tax-Exemption Issues for Gainsharing Arrangements

The Internal Revenue Service (IRS) has issued further information on gainsharing programs since the January 1999 unreleased private letter ruling, discussed in the Main Volume. The private letter ruling provides informal guidance to a Medicare demonstration program for certain cardiovascular and orthopedic services.[107] This program provides incentive-based compensation for doctors when they assist the hospital in achieving the goal of improving efficiency in inpatient care for Medicare beneficiaries while maintaining a certain quality of care standard. In addressing the program, the information letter explained that there is no per se rule that would prevent health care organizations from making incentive payments to physicians. Rather, certain incentive compensation factors should be analyzed to determine whether the utilization of an incentive compensation arrangement results in private inurement or impermissible private benefit. The list below is a noninclusive set of factors that, according to the information letter, the IRS will consider in analyzing a gainsharing arrangement for private inurement or impermissible private benefit:

---

[101] *Id.*

[102] *See* 69 Fed. Reg. 32,012, 32,024 (June 8, 2004).

[103] *See* 63 Fed. Reg. 8987 (Feb. 23, 1998), *available at* http://oig.hhs.gov/authorities/docs/cpghosp.pdf.

[104] *See* www.oig.hhs.gov/fraud/docs/alertsandbulleting/gainsh.htm (last visited June 1, 2004).

[105] *See* http://www.oig.hhs.gov.fraud/docs/alertsandbulletins/ssletter.htm (last visited June 1, 2004).

[106] *See* www.oig.hhs.gov/docs/advisoryopinions/2001/ao1_01.pdf (last visited June 1, 2004).

[107] IRS Info. Ltr. No. 2002-0021 (Jan. 9, 2002), *available at* http://www.irs.gov/pub/irs-wd/02-0021.pdf (last visited Oct. 30, 2002).

○ Was the compensation arrangement established by an independent board of directors or by an independent compensation committee? Was the board of directors/compensation committee subject to a conflicts-of-interest policy?

○ Does the compensation arrangement result in total compensation that is reasonable?

○ Is there an arm's-length relationship between the health care organization and the physician?

○ Is there a ceiling or maximum on the amount of the incentive?

○ Does the compensation arrangement have the potential for reducing charitable services or benefits that the organization would otherwise provide?

○ Does the compensation arrangement take into account quality of care and patient satisfaction data?

○ When the compensation arrangement depends on net revenues, does the arrangement accomplish the organization's charitable purposes?

○ Does the compensation arrangement transform the principal activity of the organization into a joint venture between it and a group of physicians?

○ Is the compensation arrangement merely a device to distribute all or a portion of the health care organization's profits to persons in control of the organization?

○ Does the compensation arrangement serve a real and discernible business purpose of the exempt organization?

○ Does the compensation result in any abuse or unwarranted benefits?

○ Does the compensation arrangement reward the services that the physician actually performs?

Although this letter offers helpful guideposts for structuring a gainsharing arrangement so as to mitigate tax-exemption risks, it is important to remember that these are not the only factors that may be analyzed by the IRS and that this is only a nonbinding, nonprecedential information letter.[108]

K. Physician Recruitment

1. Tax Exemption Issues

The database maintained by the Bureau of Health Professions, Health Resources, and Services Administration that is used to determine whether a particular geographic area is a designated

---

[108] Potential risks remain in connection with gainsharing arrangements. The IRS standards do not necessarily satisfy the OIG's anti-kickback standards. For additional discussion, see Supplement Chapter 1 (Baumann, An Introduction to Health Care Fraud and Abuse), at II.D.4.

health professional shortage area (HPSA) (cited in footnote 150 in the Main Volume) has been relocated on the Web.[109]

2. *Anti-Kickback Issues*

OIG's proposed supplement to its hospital compliance guidance outlines factors that a hospital should consider when attempting to recruit physicians.[110] Specifically, hospitals should look at the size and value of the recruitment benefit and whether it is reasonably necessary to attract a qualified physician to the community.[111] Another factor to examine is the duration of the payout of the recruitment benefit.[112] The OIG notes in the proposed guidance that a benefits period extending more than three years would trigger heightened scrutiny of the arrangement.[113] Furthermore, the hospital should look at the existing practice of the physician and whether the physician is a new physician with few or no patients, a physician who has an established practice with potential for referrals, or a physician who will be relocating the practice from a substantial distance so that current patients will be unlikely to follow the physician or to be an established patient base for the relocated practice.[114] Lastly, the draft supplement encourages hospitals to analyze whether there is a need for the recruitment and whether the recruited physician's specialty is necessary to provide adequate care to patients in the community.[115]

OIG Advisory Opinion No. 01-04[116] presents an example of the type of physician recruitment the OIG does not believe should be subject to penalties, even though it does not fit in the safe harbor for physician recruitment.[117] The proposed relationship at issue involved a tax-exempt hospital in a rural, medically underserved area (MUA) and its proposed recruiting arrangement with a medical school resident who was training in otolaryngology—an underrepresented specialty in the hospital's service area. This relationship did not fit in the safe harbor because the hospital was not located in an HPSA and the term of the relationship would exceed the three-year limit imposed in the safe harbor. HPSA determinations are only made when a geographic location is lacking in seven types of health professionals: primary medical care, dental care, mental health care, vision care, podiatric care, pharmacy services, and veterinary services. Thus, an area lacking in otolaryngologists would not be considered an HPSA.

---

[109]*See* http://bphc.hrsa.gov/dsd (last visited June 1, 2004).

[110]69 Fed. Reg. 32,012, 32,022 (June 8, 2004).

[111]*Id.*

[112]*Id.*

[113]*Id.*

[114]*Id.*

[115]*Id.*

[116]OIG Advisory Op. No. 01-04 (May 3, 2001), *available at* http://oig.hhs.gov/fraud/docs/advisoryopinions/2001/ao01-04.pdf.

[117]42 C.F.R. §1001.952(n).

When the OIG evaluates recruitment arrangements that do not fit within the safe harbor, it typically focuses on whether:

1. there is documented objective evidence of a need for the practitioner's services;

2. the practitioner has an existing stream of referrals within the recruiting entity's service area;

3. the benefit is narrowly tailored so that it does not exceed that which is reasonably necessary to recruit a practitioner; and

4. the remuneration directly or indirectly benefits other referral sources.

In the opinion, the OIG elaborated on these factors for analysis. For example, when a physician in one of the seven HPSA-designated specialties listed above is recruited in an HPSA for that specialty, the OIG considers that recruitment prima facie evidence of the need for the physician. However, the OIG will require more evidence for any alleged need for a non-HPSA specialist. Also, the OIG will look more favorably on the recruitment of a practitioner who does not have an established referral base, because there would be less likelihood on the part of both the hospital and the practitioner to have suspect incentives and loyalties. Additionally, the OIG will look at whether an incentive or benefit lasts longer than three years or is broader than the scope of the recruitment.

In *United States v. LaHue / United States v. Anderson,*[118] practitioners and hospital administrators alike were sent a clear message about the types of physician compensation practices that will constitute criminal illegal remuneration under the anti-kickback statute. Indeed, this was the first case where a hospital executive was convicted on criminal charges for violations of the federal anti-kickback statute. The alleged conduct at issue was the type that had been identified as suspect under the 1994 Special Fraud Alert relating to hospital incentives to referring physicians[119]—payment for services that require few, if any, substantive duties by the physician, or payment for services in excess of the fair market value of services rendered.

This case involved a transaction between Baptist Hospital, arranged by Dan Anderson, the chief executive officer (CEO), and Drs. Ronald and Robert LaHue. The contract made the LaHues "Co-directors of Gerontology Services" for Baptist Hospital. As compensation for their roles as co-directors, the LaHues each received $75,000 annually, as well as additional compensation that, when combined, totaled more than $1.8 million between 1985 and 1995. After the payments began, Blue Valley, the LaHues' own medical practice and clinic, began

---

[118] 261 F.3d 993 (10th Cir. 2001).

[119] Office of Inspector Gen., U.S. Dep't of Health & Human Servs., Special Fraud Alerts, 59 Fed. Reg. 65,372 (Dec. 19, 1994), *available at* http://oig.hhs.gov/fraud/docs/alertsandbulletins/121994.html.

to refer many patients who were Medicare beneficiaries to Baptist Hospital. As a result, Blue Valley patients constituted 8 to 10 percent of Baptist hospital admissions and over 90 percent of Baptist's volume in its outpatient clinic.[120] Overall, Baptist received over $39 million in Medicare payments for patients referred to the hospital by the LaHues. The government convinced the jury that neither LaHue ever really operated the gerontology services program at Baptist and that they were only receiving their medical director fees to refer patients from Blue Valley to the hospital. In addition, the jury found that Anderson knew that the hospital's payments to the LaHues were more than fair market value for their actual services. All three defendants were convicted. Anderson was sentenced to 51 months in prison and was fined $75,000; Robert LaHue was sentenced to 70 months in prison and was fined $75,000; and Ronald LaHue was sentenced to 37 months in prison and was fined $25,000.[121]

On appeal to the Tenth Circuit, the defendants argued that the convictions should be overturned because the court instructed jurors to find a defendant guilty if "one purpose" of the payments was to induce referrals, and that conviction is appropriate only when the motivation to solicit or receive remuneration is the person's primary purpose. The Tenth Circuit joined numerous other circuits in rejecting the primary purpose test,[122] stating that, "as a practical matter, if we held otherwise, we could illogically be faced with a case in which the offeror/payor is deemed to violate the statute, but the offeree/payee is not."[123]

The OIG Special Fraud Alert discussed in the Main Volume and cited at footnote 153 has been relocated on the Web.[124]

3. Stark Issues

The Phase II rule significantly revises the Stark law recruitment exception.[125] The newly amended exception focuses on the relocation of a physician's practice rather than the relocation of a physician's residence.[126] Under the revised exception, a recruited physician may either move his or her practice at least 25 miles to relocate to the hospital's geographic area, or establish a new practice where at least 75 percent of the revenues from the new practice are derived from new patients (i.e. patients who have not been seen by the physician for at least three years).[127] A hospital's geographic area is defined as the lowest number

---

[120] 261 F.3d at 998.

[121] *Id.* at 1001–02.

[122] See United States v. Greber, 760 F.2d 68 (3d Cir. 1985); United States v. Kats, 871 F.2d 105, 108 (9th Cir. 1989). *See contra* United States v. Bay State Ambulance & Hosp. Rental Serv., 874 F.2d 20 (1st Cir. 1989). See also Main Volume Chapter 1 (Baumann, An Introduction to Health Care Fraud and Abuse), at Section II.A.1., for further discussion of this issue.

[123] 261 F.3d at 1004.

[124] *See* http://www.oig.hhs.gov/fraud/docs/alertsandbulletins/121994.html (last visited June 1, 2004).

[125] 42 C.F.R. §411.357(e).

[126] 69 Fed. Reg. 16,054, 16,094–95 (Mar. 26, 2004).

[127] 42 C.F.R. §411.357(e)(2) and (3).

of contiguous zip codes from which the hospital draws 75 percent of its patients.[128] Residents and physicians who have been in practice for less than one year may be recruited without meeting either the relocation or "new practice" requirement because they are deemed not to have established a practice in their limited career experience.[129]

In a significant new development, the recruitment exception has also been expanded to allow a hospital to make payments to an existing group practice in order to recruit a new physician to join the group. However, recruitment arrangements involving a group or other physicians in addition to the recruited physician (collectively referred to as "the group") must meet all the following requirements:

- The arrangement between the hospital and the group is set out in writing and signed by the parties.

- Except for actual costs incurred by the group in recruiting the new physician, the remuneration is passed directly through to or remains with the recruited physician. Records of the actual costs and the passed-through amounts must be maintained for a period of at least 5 years and made available to the Secretary of HHS upon request.

- In the case of an income guarantee made by the hospital to a physician who joins a local physician practice, costs allocated by the group to the recruited physician may not exceed the actual additional incremental costs to the group attributable to the recruited physician.

- The new physician must establish a group in the hospital's geographic service area and join the hospital's medical staff.

- The group's arrangement with the recruited physician is set out in writing and signed by the parties.

- The new physician is not required to refer patients to the hospital and is allowed to establish staff privileges at any other hospital(s) and to refer business to other entities (except insofar as required referrals are permitted under [Section] 411.354(d)(4)).

- The remuneration from the hospital under the arrangement is not determined in any manner that takes into account (directly or indirectly) the volume or value of any referrals (actual or anticipated) by the recruited physician or by the group receiving the direct payments from the hospital (or any physician affiliated with that group).

- The group receiving the hospital payments may not impose additional practice restrictions on the recruited physician (for example, a noncompete agreement), but may impose conditions related solely to quality considerations.[130]

L. Physician Retention [New Topic]

1. Stark Exception [New Topic]

The Phase II rule also adds a new retention exception for physicians to assist hospitals in rural and underserved areas in preventing

---

[128] 42 C.F.R. §411.357(e)(2).

[129] 69 Fed. Reg. at 16,094.

[130] 69 Fed. Reg. at 16,096–97; 42 C.F.R. §411.357(e)(1) and (4).

physicians from moving to other locations.[131] The only hospitals eligible
for this exception are those located in an HPSA or those deemed to be
in need of the physician's practice as supported by a Stark advisory
opinion. In order for the hospital to make such a retention payment, the
physician must have a firm, written recruitment offer from an unrelated hospital or federally qualified health center (FQHC) that specifies the remuneration being offered, and the offer must require the
physician to move his or her practice at least 25 miles and have been
located outside the geographic area served by the hospital.[132]

Any retention payment to the physician cannot exceed the lower of
(a) any amount obtained by subtracting the physician's current income
from physician and related services from the income the physician
would receive from performing comparable services under the recruitment offer (for no more than 24 months) or (b) the reasonable costs of
the hospital recruiting a new physician to the geographic area served
by the hospital to replace the physician they would like to retain.[133] The
parties must use a reasonable methodology (and the same methodology) to determine the physician's income from both his or her current
job and the anticipated income from the recruitment offer.[134] The physician may not enter into a retention agreement with a hospital more
than once every five years, and the terms of the agreement may not be
altered during the lifetime of the arrangement to take into account the
volume or value of referrals or other business generated by the physician.[135] It is also important to note that the retention exception does not
protect payments made indirectly to a retained physician via another
person or entity, including a physician group practice. Alternatively, a
retention arrangement may be structured to fit within the employee
exception.[136]

2. Provision of Malpractice Insurance Assistance [New Topic]

With the rising costs of malpractice insurance for physicians, there
is an increased possibility that physicians will curtail or cease practicing in order to avoid these expenses. Many hospitals are looking into
the option of assisting physicians with their malpractice insurance
costs in order to keep them from terminating their practice. Although
CMS and the OIG have not issued clear guidance on this issue, they
have been concerned with the potential fraud and abuse implications
of malpractice subsidies to potential referral sources, including hospital medical staff. There is a limited malpractice premium subsidy
safe harbor under the anti-kickback statute for physicians providing
obstetrical care in primary health care shortage areas.[137] Additionally,

---

[131] 42 C.F.R. §411.357(t).
[132] 69 Fed. Reg. at 16,097; 42 C.F.R. §411.357(t)(1)(iii).
[133] 42 C.F.R. §411.357(t)(1)(iv).
[134] *Id.*
[135] 42 C.F.R. §411.357(t)(1)(vi).
[136] 42 C.F.R. §411.357(c).
[137] 42 C.F.R. §1001.952(o).

the OIG acknowledged that it is possible that malpractice premium subsidies may fit into the employee or physician recruitment safe harbors for the federal anti-kickback statute.[138]

Indeed, in a letter addressing malpractice insurance assistance, Chief Counsel to the Inspector General, Lewis Morris, observed that one proposed malpractice insurance subsidy arrangement contained a number of safeguards.[139] While this letter was unable to offer an opinion on the viability of the proposed arrangement because it was not submitted in accordance with the advisory opinion process set forth at 42 C.F.R. Part 1008, the letter does offer some insight into what policies and procedures may help protect a malpractice insurance subsidy from violating the anti-kickback statute. Additionally, the safeguards cited in this letter have been included in the OIG's recently issued proposed supplement to its hospital compliance guidance.[140] Some of the relevant factors include:

- whether the subsidy is being provided on an interim basis for a fixed period;
- in states where assistance is offered, whether it is only offered to current active medical staff or physicians joining the staff who are new to the locality or have been in practice for less than a year;
- whether the receipt of the subsidy is related to the volume or value of referrals or other business generated;
- whether each physician should pay as much as he or she currently pays now for medical malpractice insurance;
- whether participating physicians are required to perform services for the subsidizing hospital and give up certain litigation rights;
- whether the value of such services and litigation rights is equal to the fair market value of the malpractice insurance assistance; and
- whether the insurance is available regardless of the locations at which the physician provides services, including, but not limited to, other hospitals.[141]

The OIG explained in the draft guidance that no one of these factors is determinative of whether a hospital has a valid malpractice insurance subsidy program, and the list of considerations is not exhaustive. The OIG further noted that the provision of a subsidy implicates the Stark law.[142]

---

[138] *See* Letter From Lewis Morris, Chief Counsel to the Inspector General, on Malpractice Insurance Assistance, *available at* http://oig.hhs.gov/fraud/docs/alertsandbulletins/Malpractice-Program.pdf.

[139] *Id.*

[140] 69 Fed. Reg. 32,012, 32,023 (June 8, 2004).

[141] *Id.*

[142] 69 Fed. Reg. at 32,023–32,024.

6

Managed Care Fraud and Abuse: Risk Areas for Government Program Participants*

*Robert L. Roth, Crowell & Moring, LLP, Washington, D.C., and Alicia J. Palmer, Coventry Health Care, Inc., Bethesda, Maryland. The authors gratefully acknowledge the assistance of Stephen D. Martin, an associate at Crowell & Moring, LLP, in preparing this update.

II. Managed Care Fraud and Abuse Enforcement Efforts

A. Health Care Financing Administration/ Centers for Medicare and Medicaid Services

1. Comprehensive Plan for Program Integrity

On August 7, 2000, the Medicaid Alliance for Program Safeguards (the National Medicaid Fraud and Abuse Initiative) issued *Guidelines for Addressing Fraud and Abuse in Medicaid Managed Care* (the Guidelines).[1] The purpose of the Guidelines is to "assist the Health Care Financing Administration [now the Centers for Medicare and Medicaid Services (CMS)], State Medicaid Agents, Medicaid Fraud Control Units (MFCUs), and managed care organizations in preventing, identifying, investigating, reporting and prosecuting fraud and abuse in a Medicaid Managed Care Environment, and to better equip States with new measures and initiatives to protect against fraud and abuse in Medicaid managed care programs."[2] The 72-page document first defines and identifies types of fraud that can occur in a Medicaid managed care environment. It then goes on to describe (1) the various roles the state Medicaid agencies, CMS, MFCUs, the Office of Inspector General (OIG), and managed care organizations (MCOs) have with respect to preventing, detecting, investigating, reporting, and prosecuting fraud and abuse; (2) the type of, and method for acquiring, reliable data that is necessary to prevent, detect, investigate, report, and prosecute Medicaid managed care fraud; and (3) key components in an effective Medicaid managed care fraud program. Finally, the Guidelines provide suggestions to states as well as items required by federal law

---

[1] Medicaid Alliance for Program Safeguards, Centers for Medicare & Medicaid Servs., U.S. Dep't of Health & Human Servs., Guidelines for Addressing Fraud and Abuse in Medicaid Managed Care (Oct. 2000), *available at* http://www.cms.hhs.gov/states/letters/fraudgd.pdf.

[2] *Id.* at 6.

with respect to the states' contracts with MCOs and the states' Medicaid fraud and abuse detection programs.[3]

2. Enforcement Actions Against Managed Care Organizations

CMS continues to take enforcement actions against MCOs. On July 25, 2003, CMS ordered CarePlus Health Plans, Inc., of South Florida to pay $75,000 for marketing violations by two of its Medicare+Choice Plans. The violations, in part, arose from a misstatement made by a sales representative on a radio talk show.[4] Earlier that same month, on July 18, 2003, CMS ordered another Florida HMO, Vista Healthplan, Inc., to stop marketing of and enrolling members in its Medicare+Choice HMO. The order was to be lifted once CMS approved a corrective action plan for the HMO's marketing plan.[5]

B. The Office of Inspector General

The OIG's FY 2003 and 2004 Work Plans,[6] although containing several additional areas identified for audit, appear to indicate that the OIG is focusing its reviews on the following categories, identified in past work plans, for Medicare+Choice organizations:

- enhanced payments,
- additional benefits,
- adjusted community rate proposals, and
- cost-based MCOs.

2. Enhanced Payments
b. Institutionalized Beneficiaries
The OIG continues to issue reports on this topic.[7]

---

[3] For example, the Guidelines set forth general requirements for states' and MCOs' fraud and abuse plans; suggest Medicaid agency fraud prevention activities; and suggest efforts states should undertake to coordinate fraud and abuse issues.

[4] *CMS Fines South Florida Health Plan for Medicare+Choice Marketing Violations,* 9 HEALTH PLAN & PROVIDER REP. (BNA) 832 (Aug. 6, 2003).

[5] *CMS Orders Florida Health Plan to Halt Marketing, Enrolling Medicare Members,* 9 HEALTH PLAN & PROVIDER REP. (BNA) 808 (July 30, 2003).

[6] OFFICE OF INSPECTOR GEN., U.S. DEP'T OF HEALTH & HUMAN SERVS., WORK PLAN, FISCAL YEAR 2003 (2002), *available at* http://www.oig.hhs.gov/publications/docs/workplan/2004/Work%20Plan%202004.pdf [hereinafter OIG WORK PLAN FY 2003], and OFFICE OF INSPECTOR GEN., U.S. DEP'T OF HEALTH & HUMAN SERVS., WORK PLAN, FISCAL YEAR 2004 (2003), *available at* http://www.oig.hhs.gov/reading/workplan/2004/Work%20Plan%202004.pdf [hereinafter OIG WORK PLAN FY 2004].

[7] *See, e.g.,* OFFICE OF INSPECTOR GEN., U.S. DEP'T OF HEALTH & HUMAN SERVS., REPORT NOS. A-05-02-00078, REVIEW OF MEDICARE PAYMENTS FOR BENEFICIARIES WITH INSTITUTIONAL STATUS (Feb. 24, 2004); A-07-03-00151, REVIEW OF MEDICARE PAYMENTS FOR BENEFICIARIES WITH INSTITUTIONAL STATUS AT THE INDEPENDENT HEALTH ASSOCIATION (June 26, 2003); A-07-02-00150, REVIEW OF MEDICARE PAYMENTS FOR BENEFICIARIES WITH INSTITUTIONAL STATUS AT HEALTHAMERICA PENNSYLVANIA, INC. (June 25, 2003); A-07-02-00148, REVIEW OF MEDICARE PAYMENTS FOR BENEFICIARIES WITH INSTITUTIONAL STATUS AT COVENTRY HEALTH CARE OF KANSAS, INC. ASSOCIATION (Apr. 11, 2003); A-05-01-00094, REVIEW OF MEDICARE PAYMENTS FOR BENEFICIARIES WITH INSTITUTIONAL STATUS—KAISER FOUND. HEALTH PLAN, INC., OAKLAND, CALIF. (Oct. 17, 2002); A05-01-00091, REVIEW OF MEDICARE PAYMENTS FOR BENEFICIARIES WITH INSTITUTIONAL STATUS, UNITED HEALTHCARE OF FLORIDA, SUNRISE, FLA. (Sept. 5, 2002); and A-09-01-00094, REVIEW OF MEDICARE PAYMENTS FOR BENEFICIARIES WITH INSTITUTIONAL STATUS, AETNA U.S. HEALTHCARE, KING OF PRUSSIA, PA. (July 23, 2002).

c. Dually Eligible Beneficiaries

The OIG issued one report in 2002 on this topic.[8]

3. Physician Incentive Plans in Managed Care Contracts

In April 2002, the OIG Office of Evaluations and Inspections issued a report concluding that the data collected under the current physician incentive plan (PIP) reporting system is incomplete, inaccurate, and inconsistent. Furthermore, the process is burdensome on providers and Medicare+Choice MCOs.[9] As a result of this report, CMS has delayed the MCO PIP disclosures described later in this chapter.[10]

4. Additional Benefits

The OIG has issued several reports analyzing the cost of additional benefits.[11]

21. Medicaid Managed Care

The FY 2002[12] and 2003 OIG Work Plans contained only one topic related to reviewing Medicaid managed care plans. The Balanced Budget Act of 1997 (BBA) allowed states, without obtaining a waiver from the Secretary of the Department of Health and Human Services, to establish mandatory enrollment in Medicaid managed care programs. There are many restrictions on these programs, especially with respect to how MCOs may market and enroll Medicaid beneficiaries in the mandatory programs. The OIG will review MCOs' marketing and enrollment practices to determine whether they comply with the BBA requirements.

Several new categories were added under the Medicare Managed Care portion of the FY 2003 and 2004 Work Plan; they are discussed in the following subsections.

---

[8]*See* OFFICE OF INSPECTOR GEN., U.S. DEP'T OF HEALTH & HUMAN SERVS., REPORT NO. A-05-00-00015, REVIEW OF MANAGED CARE PAYMENTS FOR DUAL ELIGIBLE BENEFICIARIES WITH INSTITUTIONAL STATUS (July 16, 2002).

[9]OFFICE OF INSPECTOR GEN., U.S. DEP'T OF HEALTH & HUMAN SERVS., REPORT NO. OEI-05-00-00010, PHYSICIAN INCENTIVE PLAN REPORTING FOR MEDICARE+CHOICE ORGANIZATIONS (Apr. 2002).

[10]Memorandum From Thomas Scully, Administrator, U.S. Dep't of Health & Human Servs., Centers for Medicare & Medicaid Servs., to Janet Rehnquist, Inspector General, U.S. Dep't of Health & Human Servs. (Mar. 14, 2002). See *infra* Section V.G.

[11]*See* OFFICE OF INSPECTOR GEN., U.S. DEP'T OF HEALTH & HUMAN SERVS., REPORT NOS. A-09-02-00077, REVIEW OF THE PRESCRIPTION DRUG ADDITIONAL BENEFIT OFFERED BY KAISER FOUNDATION HEALTH PLAN, SOUTHERN CALIFORNIA IN THE CALENDAR YEAR 2000 ADJUSTED COMMUNITY RATE PROPOSAL (Dec. 23, 2002); A-05-01-00089, ADDITIONAL BENEFITS OFFERED MEDICARE ENROLLEES FOR THE PERIOD JANUARY 1 THROUGH DECEMBER 31, 2000–M-CARE ANN ARBOR, MICHIGAN (Oct. 29, 2002); A-06-01-00048, REVIEW OF MANAGED CARE ADDITIONAL BENEFITS AT OCHSNER HEALTH PLAN OF LA. FOR CONTRACT YEAR 2000 (Oct. 21, 2002); A06-01-00064, REVIEW OF ADDITIONAL BENEFITS REPORTED BY PACIFICARE OF TEX. IN THE CALENDAR YEAR 2000 ADJUSTED COMMUNITY RATE PROPOSAL FOR ITS SAN ANTONIO, TEX. PLAN (May 31, 2002); and A-06-00-00073, REVIEW OF MANAGED CARE ADDITIONAL BENEFITS AT NYLCARE HEALTH PLANS OF SOUTHWEST, INC. FOR CALENDAR YEAR 2000 (Mar. 7, 2002).

[12]OFFICE OF INSPECTOR GEN., U.S. DEP'T OF HEALTH & HUMAN SERVS., WORK PLAN, FISCAL YEAR 2002 (2001), *available at* http://oig.hhs.gov/reading/workplan.html [hereinafter OIG WORK PLAN FY 2002].

22. *Follow-up on Adjusted Community Rate Proposals:*
    FY 2003 and 2004 Work Plans [New Topic]

The purpose of this review is to determine if CMS's actions taken in response to earlier OIG adjusted community rate (ACR) audit reports sufficiently corrected the problems noted in those prior reports.

23. *Intraorganization Transfers: FY 2003 Work Plan Only [New Topic]*

In this review, the OIG plans to look at the allocation of administrative costs included in MCOs' ACRs. Specifically, the OIG plans to look at the allocation of costs charged by corporate or parent companies to Medicare+Choice entities.

24. *Marketing Practices by Managed Care Organizations:*
    FY 2003 and 2004 Work Plans [New Topic]

The BBA, implementing regulations, and CMS directives contain many limitations and restrictions on how an MCO may market its Medicare+Choice product.[13] The OIG intends to examine MCOs' marketing practices to ensure that they are not discriminatory or do not otherwise violate the BBA's or CMS's requirements with respect to marketing Medicare+Choice plans.

25. *Managed Care Encounter Data: FY 2003 and*
    2004 Work Plans [New Topic]

As described in more detail elsewhere,[14] encounter data is used to determine, in part, MCO payment rates. In this review, the OIG intends to evaluate the accuracy of Part A encounter data submitted by MCOs.

26. *Prompt Payment: FY 2004 Work Plan [New Topic]*

As described in more detail elsewhere,[15] MCOs must pay 95 percent of "clean" claims submitted by noncontract providers within 30 days after receipt. The OIG will determine whether MCOs have adhered to the prompt payment requirements applicable to noncontract providers and will examine CMS's oversight of MCOs' compliance with the prompt payment requirement.

E. Federal Employees Health Benefits Program

2. *Enforcement Actions Against Managed Care Organizations*
   in the Federal Employees Health Benefits Program

The U.S. Attorney for the Eastern District of Pennsylvania filed an amended complaint against Merck-Medco Managed Care, LLC, on December 9, 2003. The complaint alleges that Medco Health Solutions, Inc. violated the False Claims Act, the Fraud Injunction statute, and

---

[13] See Main Volume Chapter 6, at Section VIII.
[14] See Main Volume Chapter 6, at Section V.F.3.
[15] See Main Volume Chapter 6, at Section V.F.3.

the Anti-Kickback Act.[16] Medco Health provides mail-order prescription drug benefits for federal health programs, including the Federal Employees Health Benefits Program (FEHBP), the Civilian Health and Medical Program of the Uniformed Services (CHAMPUS), and TRICARE. The complaint alleges that Medco Health, as a pharmacy benefits manager (PBM), caused its employees to falsify prescription orders to appear to meet contractual performance guarantees under the FEHBP contract, as well as allegedly make false records of contacts with physicians about drug risks and interactions. The complaint alleges that Medco Health improperly delivered fewer pills than reported and charged patients, and then created false records about the quantity of drugs that were delivered and dispensed. The complaint also alleged that Medco Health violated the Anti-Kickback laws by paying a federal health plan more than $87 million allegedly to influence the awarding of a PBM subcontract to Medco Health.[17]

In its *Semiannual Report to Congress, April 1, 2003–September 30, 2003,*[18] the OIG and the Office of Personnel Management (OPM) reported on a case prosecuted by the State of Texas Attorney General's Medicaid fraud control unit.[19] A physician, his office administrator, and the walk-in clinic the physician owned in Midland, Texas, were prosecuted for billing fraud. The investigation showed that the office manager falsified medical records and forged prescription information to support false claims. The physician, who became a fugitive from justice, was tried and convicted in absentia, of 46 counts of mail fraud, 1 count of health care fraud, 1 count of conspiracy to commit health care fraud, and 1 count of aiding and abetting health care fraud. The government also proved that the physician received payments of more than $8 million for false claims, of which FEHBP was defrauded of $849,223.

Also in this *Semiannual Report,* the OIG and OPM reported their involvement in an "upcoding" fraud case in Northern Virginia.[20] In September 2003, a federal grand jury indicted a neurologist, as owner/head of the clinic, and his wife as office manager with one count of conspiracy to commit health care fraud and 61 counts of health care fraud. The government alleged that the neurologist was submitting claims that falsely indicated that he had performed comprehensive office visits and procedures when patients had actually come

---

[16]The Amended Complaint is available on the website of the U.S. Attorney for the Eastern District of Pennsylvania at http://www.usdoj.gov/usao/pae/News/Pr/2003/dec/Medcoamended-complaint.pdf.

[17]*See* Amended Complaint, United States v. Merck-Medco Managed Care, LLC, and Medco Health Solutions, Inc., No. 00-CV-737 (E.D. Pa. filed Dec. 9, 2003).

[18]OFFICE OF INSPECTOR GEN., U.S. OFFICE OF PERSONNEL MGMT., SEMIANNUAL REPORT TO CONGRESS, APR. 1, 2003–SEPT. 30, 2003 (Oct. 2003) [hereinafter APR. 1, 2003–SEPT. 30, 2003 SEMIANNUAL REPORT]. The semiannual reports are available on the OIG's website at http://oig.hhs.gov/publications/semiannual.html#1.

[19]*Id.* at 39.

[20]*Id.* at 39–40.

in for routine office visits. The government further alleged that the neurologist's billings indicated that he had performed tests that were not actually performed or for which numbers were inflated, all to increase the level of reimbursement. This case was also referred to OPM's debarment official, who determines whether a health care provider should be debarred or suspended from participating in FEHBP.

In its *Semiannual Report to Congress, April 1, 2001–September 30, 2001,*[21] the OIG and the OPM alleged that Kaiser Foundation Health Plan, Inc., owed the federal government more than $7 million in lost investment income through December 31, 2000, in addition to more than $23 million in overcharges that arose from supposedly improper rate development involving FEHBP.[22] The report also discussed the decision in *Qualmed Plans for Health of New Mexico, Inc. v. United States,*[23] which enabled OPM to collect more than $28 million in interest owed by Qualmed and other plans.[24] The court found that Qualmed had selected inappropriate subscriber groups in determining if the FEHBP rates were reasonable and that this resulted in defective pricing and overcharges to the FEHBP.

In its *Semiannual Report to Congress, October 1, 2001–March 31, 2002,*[25] the OIG-OPM alleged that BlueCross BlueShield of Alabama owed the federal government more than $1.5 million for coordination of benefit payment errors involving nearly 1,500 claim payments where Medicare allegedly was the proper primary insurer, but FEHBP was charged.[26]

In April 2002, after a former employee brought a *qui tam* action, PacifiCare Health Systems agreed to pay $87 million to settle alleged False Claims Act violations.[27] The government had alleged that many PacifiCare-owned health maintenance organizations (HMOs) had overcharged for health benefits under FEHBP contracts by failing to follow applicable OPM rules regarding premium rates. Specifically, PacifiCare allegedly "submitted inflated claims for insurance payments based on rates that were not developed in accordance with OPM regulations and rating instructions."[28]

---

[21] OFFICE OF INSPECTOR GEN., U.S. OFFICE OF PERSONNEL MGMT., SEMIANNUAL REPORT TO CONGRESS, APR. 1, 2001–SEPT. 30, 2001 (Oct. 2001) [hereinafter APR. 1, 2001–SEPT. 30, 2001 SEMIANNUAL REPORT].

[22] *Id.* at 7–9.

[23] 267 F.3d 1319 (Fed. Cir. 2001).

[24] APR. 1, 2001–SEPT. 30, 2001 SEMIANNUAL REPORT, *supra* note 21, at i–ii.

[25] OFFICE OF INSPECTOR GEN., U.S. OFFICE OF PERSONNEL MGMT., SEMIANNUAL REPORT TO CONGRESS, OCT. 1, 2001–MAR. 31, 2002 (Apr. 2002).

[26] *Id.* at 13–15.

[27] *See* Press Release, U.S. Dep't of Justice, PacifiCare Health Systems to Pay U.S. More Than $87 Million to Resolve False Claims Act Allegations (Apr. 12, 2002), *available at* http://www.usdoj.gov/opa/pr/2002/April/02_civ_217.htm.

[28] *Id.*

V. POTENTIAL FALSE CLAIMS ACT AND FALSE STATEMENT LIABILITY UNDER MEDICARE+CHOICE CONTRACTS

G. Compliance Exposure Relating to Physician Risk and Incentive Plan Issues: The Federal Physician Incentive Plan Rule

As noted earlier,[29] CMS has delayed the MCO PIP disclosures required by the Federal Physician Incentive Plan Rule and will be revising the requirements related to PIPs.

12. *Private Class Action Litigation*

In *In re Managed Care Litigation,*[30] Judge Moreno certified a global class of nearly 700,000 physicians in their lawsuit challenging the payment practices of HMOs. The Eleventh Circuit upheld Judge Moreno's certification of this global class to pursue federal claims, but reversed his certification of a national class to pursue state law claims on September 1, 2004.[31] Meanwhile, Judge Moreno granted final approval of a $470 million agreement between Aetna, Inc., and the physician class on October 24, 2003,[32] and granted final approval of a settlement totaling over $1 billion between CIGNA HealthCare and the physician class on February 2, 2004.[33] On December 8, 2003, Judge Moreno ruled that the Racketeer Influenced and Corrupt Organizations Act (RICO) claims brought by the physician class against the insurers could proceed to trial, and allowed six medical associations to join with the physician class in pursuing these claims.[34]

---

[29] See *supra* Section II.B.3.

[30] *See In re* Managed Care Litig., Master File 00-1334-MD-Moreno (S.D. Fla. 2003). Judge Moreno's decision on certification of the class can be found at 209 F.R.D. 678 (S.D. Fla. Sept. 26, 2002).

[31] 2004 U.S. App. LEXIS 18494 (11th Cir. Sept. 1, 2004). This opinion is also available on the Eleventh Circuit's website at http://www.call.uscourts.gov/opinions/ops/200216333.pdf.

[32] *In re* Managed Care Litig., No. 00-1334-MD-Moreno (S.D. Fla. Oct. 24, 2003) (settlement between Aetna Health and physician class approved). *See Judge Approves Aetna-Physician Pact to End Prompt-Pay Class Action Suit,* 8 HEALTH CARE DAILY REP. (BNA) 208 (Oct. 28, 2003).

[33] *In re* Managed Care Litig., No. 00-1334-MD-Moreno (S.D. Fla. Feb. 2, 2004) (settlement between CIGNA Health and physician class approved). *See Court Gives Final Approval to Agreement Ending Doctors' Lawsuit Against CIGNA,* 9 HEALTH CARE DAILY REP. (BNA) 22 (Feb. 4, 2004).

[34] *In re* Managed Care Litig., No. 00-1334-MD-Moreno (S.D. Fla. Dec. 8, 2003) (physician class may proceed on RICO claims against managed care companies). *See Managed Care Litigation Judge Again Rebuffs Attempts to Dismiss Physicians' RICO Claims,* 8 HEALTH CARE DAILY REP. (BNA) 238 (Dec. 11, 2003).

VII. MANAGED CARE COMPLIANCE ISSUES [AMENDED TOPIC HEADING (FORMERLY "PROMPT PAYMENT AND DENIAL OF CARE COMPLIANCE ISSUES")]

A. Prompt Payment

States continue to assess penalties against MCOs for violations of state prompt payment laws.[35]

B. Denial of Care

The State of California has also levied large penalties against health plans for their alleged denials of care.[36]

C. Medicare Secondary Payer Provisions [New Topic]

During the first 15 years of the program, Medicare was primary payer for all services to Medicare beneficiaries, with the sole exception of services covered under workers' compensation. Beginning in 1980, Congress enacted a series of amendments to 42 U.S.C. Section 1395y(b) requiring automobile, liability, no-fault insurance, and, finally, employer-group health plans (EGHPs) to pay primary to Medicare. These are known as the "Medicare secondary payer" (MSP) provisions.

Under the MSP provisions, the primary payment responsibility of EGHPs hinges on the number of employees who work for the employer. On February 11, 2003, the Department of Justice announced that it had partially intervened in an FCA action alleging that Highmark, Inc., in its capacity as insurer for EGHPs, had intentionally underpaid claims presented to it for Medicare beneficiaries entitled to primary coverage under Highmark-insured EGHPs based on the size of the employer.[37]

---

[35] *See, e.g., Health Plans Fined by Regulators For Prompt Payment Law Violations,* 10 HEALTH PLAN & PROVIDER REP. (BNA) 475 (May 5, 2004); *Thirty New York Health Plans Fined for Violating Prompt Pay Law,* 10 HEALTH PLAN & PROVIDER REP. (BNA) 138 (Feb. 4, 2004); *CIGNA Will Pay More than $2 Million to Settle Claims Handling Allegations,* 9 HEALTH PLAN & PROVIDER REP. (BNA) 1288 (Dec. 17, 2003); *Insurance Department Fines Horizon $200,000 for Claims-Handling Violations,* 9 HEALTH PLAN & PROVIDER REP. (BNA) 1076 (Oct. 15, 2003); *Anthem Health Plan Agrees to Pay $1.75 Million for Late, Underpaid Claims,* 9 HEALTH PLAN & PROVIDER REP. (BNA) 882 (Aug. 20, 2003); *Attorney General Announces Settlement of Prompt-Pay Case Against PacifiCare,* 9 HEALTH PLAN & PROVIDER REP. (BNA) 355 (April 2, 2003); *New Jersey Fines CIGNA Under Prompt-Pay Law,* 10 HEALTH CARE POL'Y REP. (BNA) 1520 (Nov. 18, 2002); *Pacific Life Fined for Prompt Pay Violations,* 8 HEALTH PLAN & PROVIDER REP. (BNA) 777 (July 3, 2002); *Oxendine Fines Humana $400,000 for Prompt Pay Law Violations,* ATLANTA BUS. CHRON., Jan. 24, 2002.

[36] *See Kaiser Plan Will Pay $100,000 Fine for Failing to Provide Home Health Care,* 8 HEALTH PLAN & PROVIDER REP. (BNA) 1015 (Sept. 11, 2002); *Kaiser Health Plan To Pay $1,000,000 to Settle Case Involving Patient Death,* 8 HEALTH PLAN & PROVIDER REP. (BNA) 1297 (Nov. 20, 2002).

[37] *See* United States *ex rel.* Drescher v. Highmark Inc., Nos. 00-CV-3513, 03-CV-4883, 2004 U.S. Dist. LEXIS 2752 (E.D. Pa. Feb. 20, 2004) (defendant's motion to dismiss denied).

7

Corporate Compliance Programs*

II. BENEFITS OF A CORPORATE COMPLIANCE PROGRAM

A. Federal Sentencing Guidelines

2. Reduced Fines

The November 2001 revised Sentencing Guidelines consolidated Section 2F1.1[1] into Section 2B1.1.[2] Under Section 2B1.1, the base offense level for false claims of $1.8 million is 6, plus 16 increased lev-

---

*Nancy S. Jones, Bass Berry & Sims PLC, Nashville, Tennessee, Nora L. Liggett and Jennifer L. Weaver, Waller Lansden Dortch & Davis, Nashville, Tennessee.

[1] U.S.S.G. §2F1.1 (fraud and deceit; forgery offenses involving altered or counterfeit instruments other than counterfeit bearer obligations of the United States).

[2] *See* U.S.S.G. §2B1.1 (larceny, embezzlement, and other forms of theft; offenses involving stolen property; property damage or destruction; fraud and deceit; forgery; offenses involving altered or counterfeit instruments other than counterfeit bearer obligations of the United States), U.S. SENTENCING COMM'N GUIDELINES MANUAL (Nov. 2001).

els for the amount of the loss.[3] The resulting total offense level is 22, which sets the base fine at $1.2 million.[4]

Without an effective corporate compliance program, the culpability score is 7,[5] with resulting minimum and maximum multipliers of 1.40 and 2.80, respectively.[6] With an effective compliance program, the culpability score is 4,[7] minimum and maximum multipliers are .80 and 1.60, respectively.[8] The calculation of the fine range under these alternative scenarios would be as follows:

	Base fine	Minimum multiplier/fine	Maximum multiplier/fine
Without a compliance program	$1.2 million	1.40/$1.68 million	2.80/$3.36 million
With a compliance program	$1.2 million	.80/$960,000	1.60/$1.92 million

As these calculations indicate, if the organization in the above situation has an effective corporate compliance program, it would realize a savings of $720,000 if sentenced to a fine at the low end of the range and $1.44 million if sentenced to a fine at the top end.

3. Amendments to the Organizational Sentencing Guidelines [New Topic]

On December 30, 2003, the United States Sentencing Commission issued proposed amendments to the organizational sentencing guidelines, currently contained in Chapter 8 of the Federal Sentencing Guidelines Manual.[9] After the notice and review period, the final amendments (the Amendments) were formally submitted to Congress on May 19, 2004.[10] The Amendments will take effect on November 1, 2004, unless modified by Congress during its 180-day review period.[11] Under the current guidelines, the existence of an effective compliance program is a mitigating factor that reduces an organization's culpability score.[12] The current guidelines define an "effective program" in the commentary to Guideline Section 8A1.2.[13] The Amendments

---

[3] U.S.S.G. §2B1.1(a).

[4] U.S.S.G. §8C2.4(d).

[5] Pursuant to U.S.S.G. §8C2.5(a), the base culpability score is 5. This hypothetical assumes the hospital has more than 50 employees and that the offense involved an individual with substantial authority (as defined in U.S.S.G. §8A1.2), resulting in a two-point increase pursuant to U.S.S.G. §8C2.5(b)(4).

[6] U.S.S.G. §8C2.6.

[7] *See* U.S.S.G. §8C2.5(f). Note that if an individual within high-level personnel or certain other categories participated in the offense, no point decrease is available for the compliance program; further, if an individual with substantial authority participated, there is a rebuttable presumption that the program was not effective (and therefore not subject to a credit for the culpability score). *Id.*

[8] U.S.S.G. §8C2.6.

[9] 68 Fed. Reg. 75,340 (Dec. 30, 2003).

[10] 69 Fed. Reg. 28,994 (May 19, 2004).

[11] 28 U.S.C. §994(p).

[12] U.S.S.G. §8C2.5(f).

[13] U.S.S.G. §8A1.2, App. Note 3(k).

expand and codify the requirements of an effective compliance program in a new guideline to Chapter 8 at Section 8B2.1, and delete the previous criteria set forth in the commentary to Section 8A1.2.[14]

To achieve effective compliance, proposed new Guideline Section 8B2.1(a) provides that organizations must: "(1) Exercise due diligence to prevent and detect criminal conduct;" and "(2) Otherwise promote an organizational culture that encourages ethical conduct and a commitment to compliance with the law."[15] The Amendments depart from the existing guidelines by emphasizing not only disincentives for unethical and/or illegal behavior, but also incentives for ethical behavior and compliance with the law.[16] However, the final Amendments submitted to Congress on May 19, 2004, are less onerous than those originally proposed by the Commission on December 30, 2003. For example, to qualify for a sentencing reduction, the original Amendments required organizations to have compliance programs designed to prevent and detect "violations of law," which were defined as "violations of any law whether criminal or noncriminal (including a regulation) for which the organization is or would be liable."[17] Incorporating the views of commentators from the defense bar, the final Amendments limit their scope to "criminal conduct."[18]

Subsection (b) to new Guideline Section 8B2.1 sets forth the following minimum requirements for an effective compliance program:[19]

1. *Standards and Procedures.* First, the Amendments provide that "[t]he organization shall establish standards and procedures to prevent and detect criminal conduct."[20] The Amendments define such standards and procedures as "standards of conduct and internal controls that are reasonably capable of reducing the likelihood of criminal conduct."[21] Thus, the Amendments clarify that organizations cannot achieve effective compliance by relying on the existence of compliance policy, without taking steps to implement that policy through a system of internal controls.

2. *Responsibility of High-Level Personnel.*[22] Second, the Amendments require that the organization's governing authority "be knowledgeable about the content and operation of the compliance and ethics program."[23] The organization's governing

---

[14] 69 Fed. Reg. 28,994, 29,019 (May 19, 2004).

[15] *Id.*

[16] *Id.*

[17] 68 Fed. Reg. 75,340, 75,357 (Dec. 30, 2003).

[18] 69 Fed. Reg. 28,994, 29,019 (May 19, 2004).

[19] The Sarbanes-Oxley Act of 2002 included a number of criminal sanctions, see e.g., 18 U.S.C. §§1513(e), 1519, and 1520. The incorporation of these provisions in Title 18 makes them equally applicable to both private and public companies.

[20] *Id.*

[21] 69 Fed. Reg. 28,994, 29020 (May 19, 2004).

[22] Regulations adopted pursuant to §406 of the Sarbanes-Oxley Act of 2002 require public companies to disclose whether they have adopted a code of ethics for senior officers.

[23] 69 Fed. Reg. 28,994, 29,019 (May 19, 2004).

authority must also "exercise reasonable oversight with respect to the implementation and effectiveness of the compliance and ethics program."[24] The Amendments define "governing authority" as "(A) the Board of Directors; or (B) if the organization does not have a Board of Directors, the highest-level governing body of the organization."[25] In addition, the Amendments require the organization to assign high-level personnel with "overall responsibility for the compliance and ethics program," as well as specific individual(s) with "day-to-day operational responsibility for the compliance and ethics program."[26] "To carry out such operational responsibility, such individual(s) shall be given adequate resources, appropriate authority, and direct access to the governing authority or an appropriate subgroup of the governing authority."[27]

3. *Screening of High-Level Personnel.* Third, the Amendments require organizations to "use reasonable efforts not to include within the substantial authority personnel of the organization any individual whom the organization knew, or should have known through the exercise of due diligence, has engaged in illegal activities or other conduct inconsistent with an effective compliance and ethics program."[28] Application Note 5 to the Amendments advises that in screening high-level personnel, "an organization shall consider the relatedness of the individual's illegal activities and other misconduct (*i.e,* other conduct inconsistent with an effective compliance and ethics program) to the specific responsibilities the individual is anticipated to be assigned and other factors such as: (i) The recency of the individual's illegal activities and other misconduct; and (ii) whether the individual has engaged in other such illegal activities and other such misconduct."[29]

4. *Training and Communication.* The Amendments require that the organization "take reasonable steps to communicate periodically and in a practical manner its standards and procedures, and other aspects of the compliance and ethics program . . . by conducting effective training programs and otherwise disseminating information appropriate to such individual's respective roles and responsibilities."[30] Under the Amendments, the organization must not only train employees, but must also provide

---

[24] *Id.*

[25] 69 Fed. Reg. at 29,020.

[26] *Id.* at 29,019.

[27] *Id.*

[28] *Id.* (this includes persons whose offenses were not sufficient to warrant exclusion).

[29] *Id.* at 29,020.

[30] *Id.*

compliance training and information to high-level personnel and its governing authority, as well as to its agents.[31]

5. *Auditing and Monitoring.* The fifth factor in achieving an effective program is the requirement that organizations use monitoring and auditing systems to detect criminal conduct and to "evaluate periodically the effectiveness of the organization's compliance and ethics program."[32] Further, the organization must provide and publicize internal reporting systems free from the risk of retaliation, which may include confidential or anonymous reporting mechanisms.[33]

6. *Performance Incentives and Discipline.* The Amendments require the organization to promote and enforce its compliance program through "(A) appropriate incentives to perform in accordance with the compliance and ethics program; and (B) appropriate disciplinary measures for engaging in criminal conduct and for failing to take reasonable steps to prevent or detect criminal conduct."[34]

7. *Remedial Action.* Under the Amendments, if criminal conduct has been detected, the organization must take appropriate remedial action to respond to the criminal conduct and prevent further similar violations.[35] Such remedial action may include "making any necessary modifications to the organization's compliance and ethics program."[36]

In implementing these seven requirements for an effective compliance program, subsection (c) to new Guideline Section 8B2.1 requires that the organization conduct periodic risk assessments.[37] Under the Amendments, the organization must continually evaluate the adequacy of its compliance and ethics program in light of its own history, practices, and legal issues. In addition to the seven requirements for an effective compliance program, the commentary to new Guideline Section 8B2.1 emphasizes the need for the organization's compliance program to incorporate any standards required by applicable government regulations.[38] Failure to incorporate such standards weighs against any finding that the organization's compliance program was effective.

The Amendments also replace the existing Guideline Section 8C2.5(f) with a new provision allowing for a three-point reduction in

---

[31] *Id.*

[32] *Id.*

[33] *Id.*

[34] *Id.*

[35] 69 Fed. Reg. 28,994, 29,019–20 (May 19, 2004).

[36] *Id.* at 29,020.

[37] *Id.*

[38] *Id.*

an organization's culpability score if the organization had an effective compliance and ethics program as defined in new Guideline Section 8B2.1.[39] However, an organization is not eligible for the three-point reduction if "the organization unreasonably delayed in reporting the offense to appropriate governmental authorities."[40] If substantial authority or high-level personnel in the organization participated in, condoned, or were willfully ignorant of the offense, the Amendments create a rebuttable presumption that the organization did not have an effective compliance program.[41] Finally, the Amendments insert new language into existing Guideline Section 8C4.10 providing for an upward departure from the organization's base offense level if the organization was required by law to have an effective compliance and ethics program but did not have such a program.[42]

III. Elements of an Effective Compliance Program

B. Model Corporate Compliance Programs

In addition to the nine industry segments that were addressed in the Main Volume, the government has published compliance program guidance[43] for ambulance suppliers[44] and pharmaceutical manufacturers.[45] Additionally, the Office of the Inspector General (OIG) has issued draft supplemental compliance program guidance for hospitals.[46] The OIG also recently issued a notice for solicitation of information and recommendations regarding the development of compliance program guidance for recipients of research grants from the National Institutes of Health (NIH).[47]

1. Compliance Program Guidance for Hospitals

On June 16, 2002, the OIG published a request for recommendations for revising the compliance program guidance for hospitals.[48] The notice indicated that the OIG is considering revising the guidance in light of the significant changes in payment mechanisms for hospitals (notably, the implementation of the hospital outpatient prospective payment system) and additional insight into hospital compliance activities gained since the initial guidance was promulgated.[49]

---

[39] 69 Fed. Reg. 28,994, 29,021 (May 19, 2004).

[40] *Id.*

[41] *Id.*

[42] *Id.*

[43] All of the OIG compliance program guidance documents are available at http://oig.hhs.gov/fraud/complianceguidance.html.

[44] *See* 67 Fed. Reg. 39,015 (June 6, 2002), *finalized at* 68 Fed. Reg. 14,245 (Mar. 24, 2003).

[45] *See* 67 Fed. Reg. 62,057 (Oct. 3, 2002), *finalized at* 68 Fed. Reg. 23,731 (May 5, 2003) (see Appendix I-3.1 in this Supplement for full text of the final compliance program guidance).

[46] 69 Fed. Reg. 32,012 (June 8, 2004).

[47] 68 Fed. Reg. 52,783 (Sept. 30, 2003).

[48] 67 Fed. Reg. 41,433 (June 18, 2002).

[49] *Id.*

The OIG issued its Draft Supplemental Compliance Program Guidance for Hospitals (CPG) on June 8, 2004.[50] The CPG identifies new fraud and abuse risk areas that are relevant to the hospital industry, offers specific recommendations for assessing and improving existing compliance programs to better address the identified risk areas and ensure that their compliance program is effective, and sets forth actions hospitals should take to self-report possible violations.[51] The identified risk areas are as follows:

- *Submission of Accurate Claims and Information.* The CPG reiterates the general rule that claims for reimbursement "must be complete and accurate and must reflect reasonable and necessary services ordered by an appropriately licensed medical professional who is a participating provider in the health care program from which the individual or entity is seeking reimbursement."[52] Rather than discuss familiar risk areas such as upcoding, duplicate billing, and unbundling of services, the CPG focuses on risk areas the OIG considers "under-appreciated by the industry."[53] These "underappreciated" risk areas include Outpatient Procedure Coding, Admissions and Discharges, Supplemental Payment Considerations, and Use of Information Technology.[54]

- *The Physician Self-Referral Law (Stark Law) and Federal Anti-Kickback Statute.* The CPG places great emphasis on compliance with the Stark law and the anti-kickback statute. First, the CPG warns that "hospitals face significant financial exposure unless their financial relationships with referring physicians fit squarely in statutory or regulatory exceptions to the [Stark law]" and accordingly, "hospitals must diligently review all financial relationships with referring physicians for compliance with the Stark law."[55] To analyze Stark compliance, the CPG suggests the following three questions:

  1. Is there a referral from a physician for a designated health service? If so, the next question is:

  2. Does the physician (or an immediate family member) have a financial relationship with the entity furnishing the designated health service? If so, the next question is:

  3. Does the financial relationship fit in an exception? If not, the Stark law has been violated.[56]

---

[50] 69 Fed. Reg. 32,012 (June 8, 2004).
[51] 69 Fed. Reg. at 32,014.
[52] *Id.*
[53] *Id.*
[54] 69 Fed. Reg. at 32,015–17.
[55] *Id.* at 32,017.
[56] *Id.*

To ensure Stark compliance, the CPG recommends that hospitals undertake "frequent and thorough review of their contracting and leasing processes" and "have appropriate processes for making and documenting reasonable, consistent, and objective determinations of fair market value and for ensuring that needed items and services are furnished or rendered."[57]

The CPG also emphasizes the need for compliance programs to address compliance with the anti-kickback statute, using the following two questions:

1. Does the hospital have any remunerative relationship between itself (or its affiliates or representatives) and persons or entities in a position to generate federal health care program business for the hospital (or its affiliates) directly or indirectly?

2. With respect to any remunerative relationship so identified, could one purpose of the remuneration be to induce or reward the referral or recommendation of business payable in whole or in part by a federal health care program?[58]

The CPG suggests that hospitals focus on arrangements and practices that run the greatest risk of violating the anti-kickback statute, such as arrangements or practices that have the potential to interfere with clinical decision-making, increase costs to federal health care programs, increase risks of overutilization or inappropriate utilization, or that raise patient safety/quality-of-care issues.[59] In particular, the CPG recommends that hospitals closely scrutinize their relationships with joint ventures, compensation arrangements with physicians, relationships with other health care entities, recruitment arrangements, discounts, medical staff credentialing, and malpractice insurance subsidies.[60]

- *Gainsharing Arrangements.* The CPG defines "gainsharing arrangements" as arrangements "in which a hospital gives physicians a percentage share of any reduction in the hospital's cost for patient care attributable in part to the physicians' efforts."[61] The CPG warns that gainsharing arrangements may violate the Civil Monetary Penalty (CMP) statute, the anti-kickback statute, and the Stark law.[62]

- *Emergency Medical Treatment and Active Labor Act (EMTALA).* The CPG recommends that hospitals review their obligations under EMTALA and ensure that all staff understand those

---

[57] *Id.* at 32,018.
[58] *Id.*
[59] 69 Fed. Reg. at 32,019.
[60] *Id.*
[61] 69 Fed. Reg. at 32,024.
[62] *Id.*

obligations.[63] In particular, hospitals need to educate on-call physicians as to their responsibilities to emergency patients and periodically train and remind all emergency room staff regarding the hospital's EMTALA obligations.

- *Substandard Care.* The CPG places strong emphasis on compliance with quality-of-care standards. Compliance programs should be designed to continually measure quality of care against comprehensive standards.[64] "In addition, hospitals should develop their own quality-of-care protocols and implement mechanisms for evaluating compliance with those protocols."[65] Finally, the CPG recommends that "hospitals take an active part in monitoring the quality of medical services provided at the hospital by appropriately overseeing the credentialing and peer review of their medical staff."[66]

- *Relationships with Federal Health Care Beneficiaries.* The CPG identifies as a risk area gifts and gratuities, cost-sharing waivers, and free transportation to federal health care program beneficiaries.[67] These practices should be addressed by compliance programs to avoid potential violations of the CMP statute.[68]

- *Health Insurance Portability and Accountability Act (HIPAA).* The CPG identifies HIPAA privacy and security rules as potential risk areas that should be addressed by a hospital's compliance program.[69]

- *Billing Medicare/Medicaid Substantially in Excess of Usual Charges.* The CPG identifies as a risk area the practice of billing Medicare/Medicaid substantially in excess of the usual charge or cost to other payors.[70]

- *Ensuring Compliance Program Effectiveness.* After identifying these "underappreciated" risk areas, the CPG discusses ways for hospitals to achieve compliance program effectiveness.[71] Reflecting the amendments to the Federal Sentencing Guidelines for Organizations, the CPG emphasizes the importance of "an organizational culture that values compliance."[72] According to

---

[63] *Id.*

[64] *Id.* at 32,025.

[65] *Id.*

[66] *Id.*

[67] 69 Fed. Reg. 32,012, 32,025–32,026 (June 8, 2004).

[68] *Id.*

[69] *Id.* at 32,026.

[70] *Id.* Regulations implementing §1128(b)(6)(A) of the Social Security Act provide that the OIG may exclude from federal health care programs an individual or entity that has "[s]ubmitted, or caused to be submitted, bills or requests for payments under Medicare or any of the State health care programs containing charges or costs for items or services furnished that are substantially in excess of such individual's or entity's usual charges or costs for such items or services." 42 C.F.R. §1001.701(a)(1).

[71] 69 Fed. Reg. at 32,028.

[72] *Id.*

the CPG, this organizational culture should be fostered by the hospital's leadership, particularly the hospital's board of directors, officers, and senior management.[73] The CPG advises that "hospitals' leadership and management should ensure that policies and procedures, including, for example, compensation structures, do not create undue pressure to pursue profit over compliance."[74] The CPG further reemphasizes that hospitals "develop a general organizational statement of ethical and compliance principles [or code of conduct] that will guide the entity's operations."[75]

The CPG suggests that hospitals conduct a regular review of compliance program effectiveness.[76] This review should focus not only on outcome indicators, such as billing and coding error rates, identified overpayments and audit results, but also on the underlying structure and processes of each compliance element.[77] The CPG identifies the following factors to consider in determining a compliance program's effectiveness:

- *Designation of a Compliance Officer and Compliance Committee.* The CPG recommends that a compliance program should be led by a compliance officer who is a member of senior management and is supported by a compliance committee.[78] The compliance officer should regularly report to the hospital's board of directors and senior management.[79]

- *Development of Compliance Policies and Procedures.* The CPG recommends that compliance policies and procedures should be "bright-line rules that help employees carry out their job functions in a manner that ensures compliance with Federal health care program requirements and furthers the mission and objectives of the hospital itself."[80]

- *Development of Open Lines of Communication.* The CPG provides that "open communication is a product of organizational culture and internal mechanisms for reporting instances of potential fraud and abuse."[81] The CPG recommends use of an anonymous hotline or similar mechanism that is well publicized and utilized by employees.[82]

---

[73] *Id.*

[74] *Id.*

[75] *Id.*

[76] *Id.*

[77] *Id.*

[78] *Id.*

[79] 69 Fed. Reg. at 32,029.

[80] *Id.*

[81] *Id.*

[82] *Id.*

- *Appropriate Training and Education.* The CPG advises that "[t]he purpose of conducting a training and education program is to ensure that each employee, contractor, or any other individual that functions on behalf of the hospital is fully capable of executing his or her role in compliance with rules, regulations, and other standards."[83] The CPG suggests that members of the hospital's governing body should also receive compliance training and education.[84]

- *Internal Auditing and Monitoring.* According to the CPG, "[h]ospitals should develop detailed annual audit plans designed to minimize the risks associated with improper claims and billing practices."[85]

- *Response to Detected Deficiencies.* The CPG suggests that hospitals should consistently and quickly respond to detected deficiencies, by utilizing response teams, developing corrective action plans, and promptly reporting overpayments or other probable violations to fiscal intermediaries or other law enforcement agencies.[86]

- *Enforcement of Compliance Standards.* The CPG provides that "[b]y enforcing disciplinary standards, hospitals help create an organizational culture that emphasizes ethical behavior."[87] The CPG recommends that disciplinary standards be well publicized and enforced consistently.[88]

- *Self-Reporting of Violations.* Finally, the CPG addresses the importance of self-reporting incidents of misconduct to the appropriate federal and state authorities.[89] The CPG states that hospitals should promptly self-report "within a reasonable period, but not more than 60 days after determining that there is credible evidence of a violation."[90] According to the CPG, "[p]rompt voluntary reporting will demonstrate the hospital's good faith and willingness to work with governmental authorities to correct and remedy the problem" and "will be considered a mitigating factor by the OIG in determining administrative sanctions (e.g., penalties, assessments, and exclusion), if the reporting hospital becomes the subject of an OIG investigation."[91] The OIG continues to encourage hospitals to use the Provider Self-Disclosure Protocol to aid in the process of self-reporting.[92]

---

[83] *Id.*
[84] *Id.*
[85] 69 Fed. Reg. at 32,030.
[86] *Id.*
[87] *Id.*
[88] *Id.*
[89] *Id.*
[90] *Id.*
[91] *Id.*
[92] *See* 63 Fed. Reg. 58,399 (Oct. 30, 1998).

2. Compliance Program Guidance for Clinical Laboratories

The following additional information relates to discipline and enforcement, one of the seven essential elements of an effective corporate compliance program identified by the Department of Health and Human Services (HHS) Office of Inspector General (OIG) and set forth in the Main Volume.

> 6. *Discipline and enforcement.* The OIG's database of excluded providers is accessible on the Internet; however, the Internet address has changed recently.[93]

10. Draft Compliance Program Guidance for Ambulance Suppliers [New Topic]

The draft compliance program guidance for ambulance suppliers[94] acknowledges that the ambulance industry has experienced several cases of fraud and abuse and has received guidance from the OIG in the form of several advisory opinions[95] and a safe harbor for certain ambulance restocking programs.[96] Additionally, the OIG notes that CMS has adopted a fee schedule for ambulance services.[97] The OIG indicates that it may update or supplement the guidance to address new risk areas after fee-schedule implementation. The current draft guidance suggests implementation of the seven basic elements largely common to all compliance programs, as follows:

> 1. *Compliance policies and procedures.* According to the draft guidance, ambulance suppliers, like all other providers and suppliers, should develop written policies and procedures and written standards of conduct. Suppliers should review the policies periodically and should ensure that the policies represent actual practices. The guidance describes the following risk areas associated with Medicare coverage and reimbursement requirements for ambulance suppliers:
>
>> • *Medical necessity.* Medically unnecessary transport and charging for a higher level of service than was provided (upcoding) have been a focus of prosecution. Nonemergency transports are subject to significant precoverage requirements because of the potential for abuse in such transports.
>>
>> • *Documentation, billing, and reporting.* Faulty documentation is a key risk area. Ambulance suppliers should code only to the highest level of certainty, without making

---

[93] *See* http://oig.hhs.gov/fraud/exclusions.html.

[94] *See* 67 Fed. Reg. 39,015 (June 6, 2002), *finalized at* 68 Fed. Reg. 14,245 (Mar. 24, 2003).

[95] *See, e.g.,* OIG Advisory Op. Nos. 02-2 and 02-3 (Apr. 4, 2002), 02-8 (June 19, 2002), 02-15 (Oct. 7, 2002), 03-09 (Apr. 25, 2003), 03-11 (May 28, 2003), 04-06 (June 14, 2004), and 04-10 (Aug. 11, 2004), *available at* http://oig.hhs.gov/fraud/advisoryopinions/opinions.html.

[96] *See* 66 Fed. Reg. 62,979 (Dec. 4, 2001).

[97] *See* 67 Fed. Reg. 9100 (Feb. 27, 2002).

assumptions.[98] Because payment is based on the distance a patient is transported, origin/destination data must be carefully documented.[99] Suppliers should also take care to determine which payors are primarily and secondarily liable.

- *Medicare Part A payment for services "under arrangements."* Ambulance suppliers should not bill Medicare when a facility is responsible for payment.

- *Medicaid requirements.* Medicaid covers many transportation services not covered by Medicare. Suppliers should be careful to comply with Medicaid requirements for service provided to Medicaid beneficiaries.

- *Arrangements with patients and other providers.* Ambulance suppliers should not offer remuneration to cities or counties in order to secure emergency medical services (EMS) contracts. Similarly, the provision of EMS should not be conditioned on referrals of non-EMS services. Ambulance suppliers are prohibited from making inflated payments to first responders to generate business.[100] Arrangements with hospitals and nursing homes are subject to particular scrutiny because such facilities are key sources of nonemergency business. Additionally, giving patients items of value or waiving co-payments to induce them to select a particular supplier are generally prohibited under both the anti-kickback statute[101] and the CMP statute.[102]

- *Additional risk areas.* In Appendix A to the draft guidance, the OIG identified four additional areas of concern: "no transport" calls and pronouncement of death; multiple-patient transports; multiple ambulances responding to and assisting with a single transport; and billing Medicare substantially in excess of usual charges.

2. *Designating a compliance officer or contact person.* According to the draft guidance, ambulance suppliers should designate a compliance officer to operate and monitor the compliance program.

3. *Training and education.* The draft guidance recommends that ambulance suppliers offer both compliance program training and job-specific training. The OIG further indicates that live, interactive training is preferable but that other training methods may be cost effective.

---

[98] 67 Fed. Reg. 39,022 (June 6, 2002).

[99] *Id.*

[100] 67 Fed. Reg. at 39,024. This prohibition is contained in the anti-kickback statute, 42 U.S.C. §1320a-7b(b).

[101] *See* 42 U.S.C. §1320a-7b(b).

[102] *See* 42 U.S.C. §1320a-7a(a)(5).

4. *Internal monitoring and reviews.* Suppliers should use monitoring methods to detect and identify problems. The draft guidance suggests that particular attention should be given to the following risk areas:

- *The claims submission process.* Ambulance suppliers should conduct pre-billing review of claims, paid claims, and claims denials. Suppliers should consider using the results of benchmarking audits along with external information to set benchmarks for measuring future performance.

- *System reviews and safeguards.* Coding and billing systems should be periodically reviewed for system weaknesses.

- *Sanctioned individuals and entities.* Ambulance suppliers should periodically (not less than annually) check the OIG[103] and General Services Administration (GSA)[104] lists of sanctioned individuals and entities to avoid contracting with excluded persons.

5. *Responding to detected misconduct.* Although responses will vary based on the circumstance, each response should be appropriate to resolve and correct the situation in a timely manner.

6. *Developing open lines of communication.* The draft guidance indicates that ambulance suppliers should maintain a hotline or other reporting system to receive complaints. Policies should allow those making a report to remain anonymous and be protected from retaliation.

7. *Enforcing standards through well-publicized guidelines.* Disciplinary standards should be appropriately and consistently applied.

11. *Compliance Program Guidance for Pharmaceutical Manufacturers [New Topic]*

On May 5, 2003, the OIG issued its final compliance program guidance for pharmaceutical manufacturers[105] (Pharma Guidance). The Pharma Guidance acknowledges the diversity within the industry, noting that some manufacturers are small with limited resources to devote to compliance measures, whereas others are large, multinational corporations with widely dispersed work forces.[106] Accordingly, the Pharma Guidance recommends that manufacturers[107] tailor their compliance programs to address the "areas of potential problems, com-

---

[103]*See* http://oig.hhs.gov/fraud/exclusions.html.

[104]*See* http://epls.arnet.gov.

[105]68 Fed. Reg. 23,731 (May 5, 2003).

[106]*Id.* at 23,732.

[107]Although the OIG's original solicitation of comments indicated that the guidance would address the pharmaceutical industry as a whole, specifically including retail pharmacies (67 Fed. Reg. 62,057 (Oct. 3, 2002)), the final Pharma Guidance addresses only pharmaceutical manufacturers. 68 Fed. Reg. 23,731 (May 5, 2003).

mon concern, or high risk that apply to their own companies."[108] The Pharma Guidance also strongly suggests, as a minimum, voluntary industry compliance with guidance promulgated by the Executive Committee of the Pharmaceutical Research and Manufacturers of America, known as the PhRMA Code on Interactions with Healthcare Professionals (PhRMA Code).[109]

The Pharma Guidance adopts many criteria that are similar to the OIG's Compliance Program Guidances' previous positions, e.g., suggesting that a compliance plan include the seven traditional elements as follows:

1. *Written policies and procedures.*[110] According to the Pharma Guidance, the pharmaceutical manufacturer should develop written policies and procedures and provide copies of those policies and procedures to all persons who might be affected, including agents and independent contractors. The guidance additionally recommends that pharmaceutical manufacturers develop a general "code of conduct." Although specific policies and procedures should be developed under the direction of the compliance officer, compliance committee, and operational managers, the board of directors, chief executive officer (CEO), senior management, and other personnel from various levels should participate in drafting the code of conduct.

2. *Designation of a compliance officer and compliance committee.*[111] According to the Pharma Guidance, every pharmaceutical manufacturer should designate a compliance officer to oversee compliance activities. The individual may have other responsibilities, provided that the manufacturer ensures that the compliance officer devotes adequate time and substantive attention to compliance. The compliance officer should report regularly to the board of directors, compliance committee, and CEO or president. The Pharma Guidance recommends establishing a compliance committee to assist in implementation of the compliance program and advise the compliance officer. If a small manufacturer chooses not to establish a full compliance committee, it should create a task force to address particular compliance issues when they arise.[112]

3. *Conducting effective training and education.*[113] The Pharma Guidance recommends that participation in training programs should be a condition of continued employment and adherence to compliance requirements should be a factor in employee evaluations.

---

[108] 68 Fed. Reg. at 23,732.

[109] *Id.* at 23,738. For the full text of the July 2002 PhRMA Code, see Appendix I-3.2 in this Supplement. For additional information, see PhRMA's website: http://www.phrma.org.

[110] 68 Fed. Reg. 23,733.

[111] *Id.* at 23,739.

[112] *Id.* at 23,740.

[113] *Id.*

4. *Developing effective lines of communication.*[114] Employees must have access to supervisors and the compliance officer in order to ask questions and report problems. Confidentiality and nonretaliation policies should be implemented. The OIG also encourages the use of hotlines and other forms of communication, including exit interview programs. Such mechanisms should be available to all employees and independent contractors.

5. *Auditing and monitoring.*[115] The Pharma Guidance suggests having internal or external evaluators perform regular compliance reviews that focus on areas having substantive involvement with or impact on federal health care programs and on identified risk areas.

6. *Enforcing standards through well-publicized disciplinary guidance.*[116] Appropriate disciplinary actions should be consistently applied.

7. *Responding to detected problems and developing corrective action initiatives.*[117] Prompt voluntary reporting of credible evidence of misconduct is viewed as a demonstration of the pharmaceutical manufacturer's good faith and is considered a mitigating factor by the OIG in determining sanctions.

Compliance programs should pay particular attention to the following three "major potential risk areas" for all pharmaceutical manufacturers identified in the Pharma Guidance:

1. *Integrity of data used by state and federal governments to establish payment.*[118] The pricing of pharmaceuticals has been the focus of numerous government investigations. Manufacturers are cautioned that they may be liable under the False Claims Act[119] for providing incorrect data (or failing to provide necessary data) when government reimbursement is based on data supplied by the manufacturer. The Pharma Guidance suggests that: (a) discounts, price concessions and other benefits offered on purchases of multiple products should be fairly apportioned among products; (b) assumptions underlying price and sales data should be reasoned, consistent and well-documented; and (c) manufacturers should retain all relevant records reflecting reported prices and efforts to comply with federal health care program requirements.

2. *Kickbacks and other illegal remuneration.*[120] Pharmaceutical manufacturers have several areas of risk under the anti-

---

[114]*Id.* at 23,741.
[115]*Id.*
[116]*Id.* at 23,741–42.
[117]*Id.* at 23,742.
[118]*Id.* at 23,733.
[119]31 U.S.C. §3729 et seq.
[120]68 Fed. Reg. 23,734.

kickback statute,[121] and the Pharma Guidance recommends structuring arrangements to satisfy an applicable safe harbor[122] whenever possible. Anti-kickback risks described in the Pharma Guidance include relationships with: (a) purchasers of pharmaceuticals and biologicals (discounts, other terms of sale, and average wholesale price reporting); (b) physicians and other health care professionals (switching arrangements, consulting/advisory payments, and other remuneration); and (c) sales agents (compensation and training). The Pharma Guidance indicates that the PhRMA Code should be viewed as a starting point for developing compliance policies that govern interaction with providers, and that failure to comply with the PhRMA Code's minimum standards could subject an arrangement to increased government scrutiny.

In addition, the Pharma Guidance identifies a two-step process for determining whether an arrangement presents a significant risk of federal health care program abuse. First, the manufacturer should identify any remunerative relationship between itself (and its employees, agents and contractors) and persons or entities in a position to generate federal health care program business, such as pharmacy benefit managers, formulary committee members, and pharmacists. Second, the manufacturer should consider whether one purpose of the remuneration is intended to induce or reward the referral or recommendation of business payable in whole or in part by a federal health care program.

3. *Compliance with laws regulating drug samples.*[123] Manufacturers can minimize the risk of liability by closely following the Prescription Drug Marketing Act (PDMA)[124] requirements and (a) training the sales force to inform sample recipients that samples may not be sold or billed, (b) conspicuously labeling individual samples as not for sale, and (c) including on packaging a notice that the sample is subject to the PDMA and is not for sale. The Pharma Guidance warns that manufacturers who offer free samples without complying with the PDMA may subject themselves to liability under False Claims Act and the anti-kickback statute.

12. *Proposed Compliance Program Guidance for NIH Grant Recipients [New Topic]*

On September 5, 2003, the OIG issued a notice seeking information and recommendations regarding proposed compliance program

---

[121] 42 U.S.C. §1320a-7b(b).

[122] *See* 42 C.F.R. §1001.952.

[123] 68 Fed. Reg. at 23,739.

[124] Prescription Drug Marketing Act of 1987, Pub. L. No. 100-293, 102 Stat. 95 (Apr. 22, 1998).

guidance for recipients of NIH research grants.[125] The OIG proposed the traditional seven elements for comprehensive compliance programs for NIH recipients:

1. implementing written policies and procedures that foster institutional stewardship and compliance;

2. designating a compliance officer and a compliance committee;

3. conducting effective training and education;

4. developing effective lines of communication;

5. conducting internal monitoring and auditing;

6. enforcing compliance standards through well-publicized disciplinary guidelines;

7. responding promptly to detected problems, undertaking corrective action, and reporting to the appropriate federal agency.[126]

The OIG is also considering a novel eighth element—"defining roles and responsibilities, and assigning oversight responsibility."[127] In seeking information and recommendations for this guidance, the OIG identified three risk areas of particular interest: (1) proper allocation of charges to grant projects; (2) "time and effort" reporting, including accurate reporting of the commitment of effort by researchers; and (3) use of program income.[128] Since issuing the solicitation, the OIG has taken no further action on the proposed compliance program guidance for NIH grant recipients.

IV. Practical Issues in Developing and Implementing a Compliance Program

G. Auditing and Monitoring

5. Disclosure Obligations and Repayments

The Joint Commission on the Accreditation of Healthcare Organizations (JCAHO) revised its Sentinel Events policy in July 2002.[129] The Sentinel Events policy encourages self-disclosure of unexpected occurrences involving death or serious injury (or significant risk thereof) to patients. Hospitals experiencing certain reviewable sentinel events are required to perform a root-cause analysis and provide that analysis and an action plan to JCAHO within 45 days of the event. If 45 days have elapsed since the event occurred before the event is determined to be

---

[125] 68 Fed. Reg. 52,783 (Sept. 5, 2003).
[126] *Id.*
[127] *Id.*
[128] *Id.*
[129] *See* www.jcaho.org.

reviewable, the hospital has 15 days to provide the required response. Failure to respond within required time frames places the hospital at risk for being placed on JCAHO's "Accreditation Watch."

The JCAHO has a Sentinel Event Alert Advisory Group that reviews sentinel event reports and identifies annual National Patient Safety Goals, or "NPSGs." The 2004 NPSGs include increasing the use of patient identifiers, decreasing the use of abbreviations in medical records, and reducing the risk of infections.

8

Potential Liabilities for Directors and Officers of Health Care Organizations*

*Linda A. Baumann, Reed Smith LLP, Washington, D.C., and George E. McDavid, Reed Smith LLP, Princeton, New Jersey. The authors thank Arlie R. Nogay, Paul P. Taylor and Joel P. Dennison, Reed Smith LLP, Pittsburgh, Pennsylvania, for their assistance with this chapter.

I. INTRODUCTION

According to the U.S. Department of Justice (DOJ) and Department of Health and Human Services (HHS), in 2002

- federal prosecutors filed 361 criminal indictments in health care fraud cases;

- 480 defendants were convicted of health care fraud–related crimes, with 1,529 civil matters pending and 221 new civil cases filed;

- the federal government won or negotiated more than $1.8 billion in judgments, settlements, and administrative penalties in health care fraud cases and proceedings;

- HHS excluded 3,448 persons and entities from participation in federal health care programs; and

- HHS's Office of Inspector General participated in 753 prosecutions or settlements.[1]

II. RESPONSIBILITIES OF DIRECTORS AND OFFICERS

A. Criminal Liability

2. *Responsible-Corporate-Officer Doctrine*

In a recent decision, a federal district court held that the potential criminal liability of corporate officers under the federal Food, Drug, and Cosmetic Act may justify the imposition of civil liability on these corporate agents as well.[2]

---

[1]U.S. DEP'T OF HEALTH & HUMAN SERVS. & U.S. DEP'T OF JUSTICE, HHS/DOJ HEALTH CARE FRAUD & ABUSE CONTROL PROGRAM ANNUAL REPORT FOR FISCAL YEAR 2002 (Sept. 2003), *available at* http://www.oig.hhs.gov/publications/hcfac.html [REPORT FOR FY 2002].

[2]United States v. Undetermined Quantities of Articles of Drug, 145 F. Supp. 2d 692, 705 (S.D. Md. 2001) (holding that the FDCA rationale for imposing criminal liability on corporate officers was even more persuasive for holding a corporate officer responsible for acts of the corporation where only civil liability was involved).

Various law review articles provide a general discussion of corporate officer liability in the environmental context.[3]

B. Civil Liability

2. *Limitations on the Liability of Directors and Officers*

a. *Business Judgment Rule*

Courts continue to follow the business judgment rule[4] as set forth in *Aronson v. Lewis*,[5] and continue to rely on the *Aronson* standard of gross negligence to determine whether a director has exercised due care.[6] Courts also have maintained that "bad faith" will be inferred only in those rare circumstances where the decision under attack is far beyond the bounds of reasonable judgment.[7]

C. The Sarbanes-Oxley Act and Related Developments [New Topic]

On July 30, 2002, President George W. Bush signed into law the Sarbanes-Oxley Act of 2002,[8] which was, in large part, a response to public outrage over the corporate scandals at Enron and WorldCom. The Sarbanes-Oxley Act mandated numerous corporate governance changes for publicly traded companies, increased the type and frequency of disclosure required for such companies, and dramatically revised the oversight of the public accounting industry.

The Sarbanes-Oxley Act applies generally to each "issuer" (as defined in Section 3 of the Securities Exchange Act of 1934),[9] the securities of which are registered under Section 12 of that Act[10] or that is required to file reports under Section 15(d),[11] or "that files or has filed a registration statement that has not yet become effective under the Securities Act of 1933,"[12] "and that it has not withdrawn."[13] The Sarbanes-Oxley Act directed the Securities and Exchange Commission (SEC) to direct, by rule, the national securities exchanges and national securities associations to prohibit the listing of any security of an issuer that is

---

[3] Noel Wise, *Personal Liability Promotes Responsible Conduct: Extending the Responsible Corporate Officer Doctrine to Federal Civil Environmental Enforcement Cases,* 21 STAN. ENVTL. L.J. 283 (June 2002); Jonathan Snyder, Comment, *Back to Reality: What "Knowingly" Really Means and the Inherently Subjective Nature of the Mental State Requirement in Environmental Criminal Law,* 8 MO. ENVTL. L. & POL'Y REV. 1 (2002).

[4] *See, e.g.,* Emerald Partners v. Berlin, 787 A.2d 85, 90 (Del. 2001); Telxon Corp. v. Meyerson, 802 A.2d 257, 264 (Del. 2002).

[5] 473 A.2d 805 (Del. 1984), *overruled on other grounds by* Brehm v. Eisner, 746 A.2d 244 (Del. 2000).

[6] *See, e.g.,* McCall v. Scott, 250 F.3d 997, 999 (6th Cir. 2001); Roselink Investors, L.L.C. v. Shenkman, No. 01 Civ. 7176 (S.D.N.Y. May 19, 2004).

[7] Orman v. Cullman, 794 A.2d 5, 20 (Del. Ch. 2002); McMichael v. United States Filter Corp., 2001 U.S. Dist. LEXIS 3918, at *31 (C.D. Cal. Feb. 22, 2001).

[8] Pub. L. No. 107-204, 116 Stat. 745 (2002) [hereinafter Sarbanes-Oxley Act].

[9] 15 U.S.C. §78c.

[10] 15 U.S.C. §78e.

[11] 15 U.S.C. §78d.

[12] 15 U.S.C. §§77a et seq.

[13] Sarbanes-Oxley Act §2(a)(7) (codified at 15 U.S.C. §7201).

not in compliance with several enumerated standards regarding issuer audit committees.[14] In April 2003, as required by the Sarbanes-Oxley Act, the SEC adopted Rule 10A-3.[15]

In response to Rule 10A-3, the New York Stock Exchange (NYSE), the National Association of Securities Dealers, Inc. (NASD), and the American Stock Exchange (Amex) have each adopted changes to their self-regulatory organization (SRO) listing standards—i.e., alterations to their respective corporate governance rules—and these changes have been approved by the SEC.[16] In general, registered companies must be in compliance with the SRO rules changes by the earlier of their first annual meeting of shareholders after January 15, 2004, or by October 31, 2004.[17]

A detailed discussion of the Sarbanes-Oxley Act and the SRO rules changes is beyond the scope of this Supplement, but the following discussion outlines some of the more significant provisions. Neither the Sarbanes-Oxley Act nor the SRO rules changes alter a director's duties of care and loyalty under state corporate law. Rather, the corporate governance changes mandated by Sarbanes-Oxley and the SRO rules are largely process-oriented and increase the influence and involvement of a registered company's independent directors by, among other things, mandating that certain decisions be delegated to the independent directors, including decisions relating to the company's audit, the compensation of its executive officers, the nomination of individuals to the company's board of directors, and the overarching governance principles of each registered company.[18]

More specifically, under the Sarbanes-Oxley Act and the SRO rules changes:

- a majority of the board of directors of each registered company must be independent;[19]

- a registered company's outside auditor must report to the audit committee of the board of directors (which must consist solely of independent directors);[20]

---

[14] Sarbanes-Oxley Act §301.

[15] Standards Relating to Listed Company Audit Committees, 68 Fed. Reg. 18,788 (Apr. 16, 2003) (final rule codified at 17 C.F.R. pts. 228, 229, 240, 249, and 274).

[16] NYSE Corporate Governance Rules, as approved by the SEC November 4, 2003, are contained in Section 303A of the NYSE's Listed Company Manual (the NYSE Rules), *available at* http://www.nyse.com; NASDAQ Corporate Governance Rules, as approved by the SEC on November 4, 2003, are contained in NASDAQ Rules, Rule 4000 Series (the NASDAQ Rules), *available at* http://www.nasdaqnews.com; and Amex Corporate Governance Rules, as approved by the SEC on December 1, 2003, are contained in Amex Company Guide Part 1 and Part 8 (the Amex Company Guide), *available at* http://www.amex.com.

[17] 68 Fed. Reg. 18,788 (Apr. 16, 2003).

[18] Sarbanes-Oxley Act §§202, 204, 301; NYSE Rules ¶¶303A.04, 303A.05, 303A.07, and 303A.09; NASDAQ Rules 4350(c) and 4350(d); and Amex Company Guide Part 8 §§804(a) and ¶807.

[19] NYSE Rules ¶303A.01; NASDAQ Rules 4350(c)(1); and Amex Company Guide Part 1 ¶121(A).

[20] Sarbanes-Oxley Act §301.

- the audit committee has the mandate to hire, fire, and perform oversight of the outside auditor,[21] and must pre-approve non-audit services provided by the outside auditor;[22]

- a board committee consisting solely of independent directors (or a majority of all independent directors) must make certain determinations relating to executive compensation;[23]

- a board committee consisting solely of independent directors (or a majority of all independent directors) must make certain determinations relating to board nominations and corporate governance;[24]

- the non-management directors (i.e., those directors not employed by the company) must meet regularly without the executive officers of the company;[25] and

- the definition of "independence" has been tightened.[26]

Under the SRO rules changes, registered companies are required to maintain a code of business conduct and ethics applicable to all employees and directors covering matters such as compliance with laws and avoidance of conflicts of interest.[27] Moreover, the Sarbanes-Oxley Act mandates that each registered company have a code of ethics applicable to the chief executive officer (CEO) and senior financial officer that is reasonably designed to deter wrongdoing and promote, among other things, full, fair, accurate, timely, and understandable disclosure in the reports and documents the company files with the SEC and prompt internal reporting to an appropriate person in the event of a violation of the code.[28]

The disclosure obligations under the Securities Exchange Act of 1934, as amended, and the Securities Act of 1933, as amended, were also revised under the Sarbanes-Oxley Act to require more rapid disclosure of material adverse changes and more detailed disclosure of off-balance-sheet transactions and pro forma financial disclosure.[29] The

---

[21] *Id.*

[22] Sarbanes-Oxley Act §201.

[23] NYSE Rules ¶303A.05; NASDAQ Rules 4350(c)(3); and Amex Company Guide Part 8 ¶805.

[24] NYSE Rules ¶303A.04; NASDAQ Rules 4350(c)(4); and Amex Company Guide Part 8 ¶804.

[25] NYSE Rules ¶303A.03; NASDAQ Rules 4350(c)(2); and Amex Company Guide Part 8 ¶802 (b).

[26] NYSE Rules ¶303A.02; NASDAQ Rules 4200; and Amex Company Guide Part 1 ¶121A.

[27] NYSE Rules ¶303A.010; NASDAQ Rules 4350 (n); and Amex Company Guide Part 8 ¶807A.

[28] Sarbanes-Oxley Act §406; Disclosure Required by §§404, 406, and 407 of the Sarbanes-Oxley Act of 2002, 67 Fed. Reg. 66,208 (SEC Release Nos. 33-8138; 34-46701; IC-25775: File No. S7-40-02) (proposed Oct. 30, 2002).

[29] Sarbanes-Oxley Act §§401, 409.

SEC has issued detailed final rules implementing these additional disclosure requirements.[30]

Two frequently discussed provisions of the Sarbanes-Oxley Act, Sections 302 and 906, place CEOs and chief financial officers (CFOs) of registered companies under the public magnifying glass by requiring personal certifications to the effect that, in pertinent part, the information filed with the SEC complies with all legal requirements and does not omit any fact necessary to make the information not misleadingly incomplete. In addition, the Section 302 certification requires the CEO and CFO to certify, among other things, that the financial statements in the report fairly present in all material respects the financial condition, results of operations, and cash flows of the company, that the company has disclosure controls and procedures and internal controls over financial reporting, and that the CEO and CFO have evaluated the effectiveness of these controls as of the end of the period covered by the report. The Section 906 certification exposes a CEO and a CFO to criminal penalties and fines of up to $5 million, imprisonment of up to 20 years, or both. The Section 302 certification and the annual internal control report mandated under Section 404 of the Sarbanes-Oxley Act require each CEO and CFO of a registered company to accept responsibility for, and periodically assess the effectiveness of, the company's internal disclosure controls and procedures, and internal controls over financial reporting.

In addition, Section 304 of the Sarbanes-Oxley Act mandates the forfeiture by the CEO and the CFO of certain bonuses and other compensation and profits from the sale of certain company securities if a registered company is required to prepare an accounting restatement due to the company's material noncompliance with any financial reporting requirement under the securities laws, due to misconduct (the misconduct that triggers the forfeiture does not have to be the misconduct of the CEO or CFO).

Section 303 of the Sarbanes-Oxley Act makes it unlawful for a director or officer (or person acting under their direction) to fraudulently influence, coerce, manipulate, or mislead a registered company's auditor for purposes of rendering financial statements materially misleading. Conduct that could violate Section 303 includes offering bribes or financial incentives, threatening to cancel the auditor's engagement, and attempting to have the audit partner removed from the engagement. Section 806 of the Sarbanes-Oxley Act strengthens protections intended to protect "whistleblowers" and witnesses from discrimination and retaliation, including fines or imprisonment for knowing violations against witnesses.

---

[30]Additional Form 8-K Disclosure Requirements and Acceleration of Filing Date, 69 Fed. Reg. 15,594 (SEC Release Nos. 33-8400; 34-49562; File No. S7-22-02) (Mar. 16, 2004); Disclosure in Management's Discussion and Analysis About Off-Balance Sheet Arrangements and Aggregate Contractual Obligations (SEC Release Nos. 33-8182; 34-47264; File No. S7-42-02) (Jan. 28, 2003); Conditions for Use of Non-GAAP Financial Measures (SEC Release Nos. 33-8176; 34-47226, File No. S7-43-02) (Jan. 22, 2003).

Although the duties of care and loyalty are not directly altered by the Sarbanes-Oxley Act and the SRO rules changes, it is likely that, in the future, the courts will more closely scrutinize the decision-making process employed by corporate boards. In other words, although the business judgment rule will continue to be respected by courts, appropriate "business judgment" will likely reflect Sarbanes-Oxley standards, e.g., boards may be required to exercise a heightened level of diligence prior to relying on reports of outside experts or officers of the company. Further, many of the disclosure requirements imposed on registered companies may be used by the securities plaintiffs' bar as additional bases for attack and litigation. In addition, although these standards are only legally binding on publicly traded companies, it is likely that attempts will be made to use them against all other companies as well.

III. LITIGATION AGAINST OFFICERS AND DIRECTORS

A. Shareholder Derivative Actions

2. Presuit Demand Requirements

Various courts continue to uphold the *Aronson* rule to determine whether to excuse a plaintiff's failure to make a demand on the board.[31]

B. Class Actions

1. Class Action Requirements

When plaintiffs' counsel are involved in multiple lawsuits against the same defendant, conflicts of interest—or the appearance of conflict—may arise that render counsel inadequate. In *Krim v. pcOrder.Com, Inc.*,[32] the U.S. District Court for the Western District of Texas found that the plaintiffs failed to show the adequacy of counsel. In this case, lead counsel were involved in multiple lawsuits against pcOrder.com, in which counsel sought to represent different classes of pcOrder.com shareholders.[33] Lead counsel had failed to timely disclose to their clients their participation in multiple class representations against the same defendant.[34] According to the court, the multiple representation raised actual and potential conflicts between different classes. This risk of conflict intensified when class counsel participated in negotiations with the defendant for settlement of all the class action cases because the various classes' interests might well not coincide.[35]

---

[31]*See, e.g.,* White v. Panic, 783 A.2d 543, 551 (Del. 2001); Werbowsky v. Collomb, 766 A.2d 123, 138–44 (Md. 2001) (also contains an extended discussion of the demand futility rule); Salsitz v. Nasser, 208 F.R.D. 589, 591 (E.D. Mich. 2002); *In re* Walt Disney Co. Derivative Litig., 825 A.2d 275 (Del. Ch. 2003).

[32]210 F.R.D. 581 (W.D. Tex. Oct. 21, 2002).

[33]*Id.* at 589.

[34]*Id.* at 590.

[35]*Id.*

Courts continue to apply the *Amchem Products, Inc. v. Windsor*[36] approach to determine the appropriateness of settlement in class action matters.[37]

3. *The Private Securities Litigation Reform Act and the Securities Litigation Uniform Standards Act [New Topic]*

Intending to provide national, uniform standards for the securities market and nationally marketed securities,[38] Congress enacted the Private Securities Litigation Reform Act of 1995 (PSLRA).[39] In order to eliminate frivolous securities litigation,[40] the PSLRA heightens the pleading requirements in private securities fraud litigation by requiring that both falsity and scienter be pleaded with particularity.[41] To allege securities fraud, a complaint must now specify:

- each statement alleged to have been misleading;
- the reason or reasons why the statement is misleading; and
- if an allegation regarding the statement or omission is made on information and belief, all facts on which that belief is formed.[42]

The PSLRA also provides guidelines for the appointment of the lead plaintiff in class actions, specifying that the lead plaintiff should be the plaintiff "most capable of adequately representing the interests of class members (. . . the 'most adequate plaintiff')."[43] The PSLRA creates a rebuttable presumption that the plaintiff who (1) has filed the complaint or made a motion to serve as lead plaintiff; (2) has the largest financial interest sought by the class; and (3) otherwise satisfies the requirements of Rule 23 of the Federal Rules of Civil Procedure is the "most adequate plaintiff."[44] After court approval of the lead plaintiff, the lead plaintiff then selects counsel to represent the class.[45] The selection of class counsel is also subject to court approval.[46]

To avoid the PSLRA's strictures, plaintiffs began filing securities fraud litigation actions in state courts under state statutory or common law theories. Congress responded by passing the Securities Litigation Uniform Standards Act of 1998 (SLUSA).[47] This Act establishes a defendant's right to remove "covered securities" litigation actions to

---

[36] 521 U.S. 591 (1997). For further discussion of *Amchem Products,* see Main Volume Chapter 8, at Section III.B.1.

[37] Uhl v. Thoroughbred Tech. & Telecomms., Inc., 309 F.3d 978 (7th Cir. 2002).

[38] *See* Patenaude v. Equitable Assurance Soc'y of U.S., 290 F.3d 1020, 1026 (9th Cir. 2002).

[39] Pub. L. No. 104-67, 109 Stat. 737 (1995) (codified in scattered sections of U.S.C. Title 15).

[40] *See* Falkowski v. Imation Corp., 309 F.3d 1123 (9th Cir. 2002), *reprinted as amended* 320 F.3d 905 (9th Cir. 2003).

[41] *Id.*

[42] 15 U.S.C. §78u-4(b)(1).

[43] 15 U.S.C. §78u-4(a)(3)(B)(i).

[44] 15 U.S.C. §78u-4(a)(3)(B)(iii).

[45] *See* 15 U.S.C. §77z-1(a)(3)(B)(v).

[46] *Id.*

[47] Pub. L. No. 105-353, 112 Stat. 3227 (1998) (codified in scattered sections of U.S.C. Title 15).

federal court.[48] A party seeking to establish that an action falls within the SLUSA's preemptive scope must show that (1) the action is a covered class action under the SLUSA; (2) the action purports to be based on state law; (3) the defendant is alleged to have misrepresented or omitted a material fact (or to have used or employed any manipulative or deceptive device or contrivance); and (4) the defendant is alleged to have engaged in conduct described by criterion (3) in connection with the purchase or sale of a covered security.[49] Generally, a covered security is a security listed on a national stock exchange such as the NYSE or an exchange with equivalent listing standards.[50] Notwithstanding the SLUSA's broad restriction on state securities class actions, it contains a savings clause that permits a narrow range of class actions to remain in state court.[51]

C. The *Caremark* Decision

2. *The Court's Decision*

a. *Board's Duty of Care Responsibilities*

Some other courts have reiterated the proposition in *Caremark*,[52] that in determining whether a director is liable (under the second prong of *Aronson*) a court may not consider "the content of the board decision that leads to corporate loss, apart from consideration of the good faith or rationality of the process employed."[53] However, a few cases have begun considering whether an arrangement can be so egregious on its face that board approval cannot meet the business judgment test.[54]

D. The Columbia/HCA Litigation

1. *Columbia / HCA Operations and Government Investigations*

On May 20, 2002, the Sixth Circuit Court of Appeals vacated the court's order dismissing the complaint in *Morse v. McWhorter*[55] and remanded the case.[56]

2. *Shareholders' Allegations in* McCall v. Scott

The district court's order dismissing the complaint in *Morse v. McWhorter*[57] was vacated by the Sixth Circuit on May 20, 2002, and the case was remanded.[58]

---

[48] 15 U.S.C. §77p(c).

[49] Green v. Ameritrade, Inc., 279 F.3d 590, 597 (8th Cir. 2001). *See* 15 U.S.C. §78bb(f)(1)–(2).

[50] *Green,* 279 F.3d at 596. *See* 15 U.S.C. §78bb(f)(1)–(2). *See also* 15 U.S.C. §78bb(f)(5)(E).

[51] 15 U.S.C. §78bb(f)(3).

[52] *In re* Caremark Int'l Derivative Litig., 698 A.2d 959 (Del. Ch. 1996) [hereinafter *Caremark*].

[53] Salsitz v. Nasser, 208 F.R.D. 589, 591 (E.D. Mich. 2002) (citing *Caremark,* 698 A.2d at 967); *see also* United Artists Theater Co. v. Walton, 315 F.3d 217, 232 (3d Cir. 2003).

[54] *See, e.g.,* In re Abbott Laboratories Derivative Shareholders Litig., 325 F.3d 795 (7th Cir. 2003) [hereinafter *Abbott Laboratories*]. This case is discussed in more detail in Section III.D.

[55] Morse v. McWhorter, 200 F. Supp. 2d 853 (M.D. Tenn. 2000), *vacated by* 290 F.3d 795 (6th Cir. 2002).

[56] *Morse,* 290 F.3d 795 (6th Cir. 2002).

[57] Morse v. McWhorter, 200 F. Supp. 2d 853 (M.D. Tenn. 2000).

[58] *Morse,* 290 F.3d 795.

5. The Appellate Court Decisions

a. The Legal Standards Used

The Delaware Supreme Court vacated the prior decision in *Emerald Partners v. Berlin*[59] on November 28, 2001, and remanded the case to the Delaware Court of Chancery.[60] The lower court had rendered judgment in favor of the corporation's directors, ruling that a provision in the defendant corporation's certificate of incorporation, enacted pursuant to Section 102(b)(7) of Title 8 of the Delaware Code, exculpated the corporation's directors from personal liability for payment of monetary damages.[61] The high court held that the business judgment rule did not apply in the *Emerald Partners* case.[62] Therefore, the chancery court had to evaluate the board members' actions in light of the "entire fairness" standard of review, and the application of Section 102(b)(7) was premature because the lower court was first required to make a finding of "unfairness" and determine the basis of liability for monetary damages before examining the exculpatory nature of the Section 102(b)(7) provision.[63] On remand, the chancery court found the actions in question were in fact fair, and the shareholder appealed. The Delaware Supreme Court held that the finding of fairness was valid despite serious questions as to the independent directors' good faith.[64] In particular, the Supreme Court noted that "many process flaws in this case raise serious questions as to the independent directors' good faith," particularly the directors' "we don't care" attitude about risks to the corporation. However, the Supreme Court upheld the chancery court's finding that the price ultimately paid was fair. As a result, even if the exculpatory clause in the company's certificate of incorporation would not have protected the directors because of their bad faith, they would not be liable for any monetary damages. Thus, the Delaware Supreme Court's decision in *Emerald Partners* implicitly confirms the conclusion in *McCall v. Scott*[65] that the two cases are distinguishable, although for different reasons.

c. McCall v. Scott *and the* Abbott Laboratories *Case*

The district court's decision in In re *Abbott Laboratories Derivative Shareholder Litigation*[66] was reversed and remanded by the Seventh Circuit Court of Appeals after some unusual proceedings.[67] The 2003

---

[59]No. 9700, 2001 Del. Ch. LEXIS 20 (Del. Ch. Feb. 7, 2001), *vacated by* 787 A.2d 85 (Del. 2001).

[60]*Emerald Partners,* 787 A.2d 85 (Del. 2001).

[61]*Id.* at 88.

[62]*Id.* at 97.

[63]*Id.*

[64]*See* 840 A.2d 641 (Del. Dec. 23, 2003) (unpublished opinion).

[65]250 F.3d 997, 1001 (6th Cir. 2001).

[66]*In re* Abbott Labs. Derivative Shareholder Litig., 141 F. Supp. 2d 946 (N.D. Ill. 2001).

[67]The case was initially reversed by the Seventh Circuit in an opinion at 293 F.3d 378 (7th Cir. 2002), which was subsequently withdrawn without explanation at 299 F.3d 898 (7th Cir. 2002). A new opinion by the Seventh Circuit, reversing and remanding the district court decision (and superseding 293 F.3d 378), was issued at 325 F.3d 795 (7th Cir. 2003).

decision in *Abbott Laboratories* (*Abbott Laboratories-2003*) found that under applicable Delaware law, the more stringent *Rales* test,[68] which is generally used rather than the *Aronson*[69] test when board omissions or inaction are alleged, did not apply in this case. Looking back to *Caremark,* the Seventh Circuit found that director liability for breach of the duty to monitor corporate actions could result from an ill-advised or negligent board decision or from "an unconsidered failure of the board to act" in circumstances where due attention might have prevented loss.[70] The Seventh Circuit distinguished the situation in *Caremark* where the directors were "blamelessly unaware of the conduct leading to corporate liability"[71] with no grounds for suspicion, from the *Abbott Laboratories* case where directors were made aware of potential liability in several ways, including: (i) numerous FDA warning letters (some of which were sent or copied directly to board members); (ii) board members annually signed SEC disclosure forms acknowledging noncompliance with certain government requirements; and (iii) several articles were published in the national press discussing the FDA findings that regulatory violations had occurred. While the Seventh Circuit did not cite definitive evidence demonstrating that all board members were aware of these facts, the court found that "where there is a corporate governance structure in place, we must then assume the corporate governance procedures were followed and that the board knew of the problems and decided no action was required."[72] Accordingly, the *Abbott Laboratories-2003* court says the facts are clearly distinguishable from the "unconsidered inaction" in *Caremark,* and the more stringent *Rales* test for demand futility does not apply.[73]

Using the second standard in the *Aronson* test indicating that demand futility may be established if there is reasonable doubt that the challenged transaction resulted from a valid exercise of the directors' business judgment, the Seventh Circuit cites a 1989 case[74] as requiring it to examine both the substance of the transaction, as well as the procedures used by the directors.[75] Then, citing *Emerald Partners*[76] for the proposition that Delaware law imposes three fiduciary duties on directors, i.e., care, loyalty, and good faith, the Seventh Circuit holds the *Abbott Laboratories* allegations support a finding that the directors

---

[68] Rales v. Blasband, 634 A.2d 927 (Del. 1993).

[69] Aronson v. Lewis, 473 A.2d 805 (Del. 1984), *overruled on other grounds by* Brehm v. Eisner, 746 A.2d 244 (Del. 2000).

[70] *In re* Abbott Labs. Derivative Shareholder Litig., 325 F.3d 795, 805 (7th Cir. 2003), *citing Caremark,* 698 A.2d 959, 967 (Del. Ch. 1996).

[71] 325 F.3d at 805, *citing* 698 A.2d at 969.

[72] 325 F.3d at 806. Thus board members may be at risk even if the appropriate compliance structure and procedures are in place, if they do not actively implement and take advantage of them.

[73] *Id.*

[74] Starrels v. First Nat'l Bank of Chicago, 870 F.2d 1168, 1171 (7th Cir. 1989) (citing Grobow v. Perot, 539 A.2d 180, 189 (Del. 1988), *overruled on other grounds by* Brehm v. Eisner, 746 A.2d 244 (Del. 2000)).

[75] *Abbott Laboratories,* 325 F.3d at 807–08.

[76] Emerald Partners v. Berlin, 787 A.2d 85 (Del. 2001).

breached their duty of good faith, thereby taking their conduct outside the protection of the business judgment rule.

While implicitly acknowledging that the lower court had come to the opposite conclusion based on the same set of facts, the appellate court cites six years of noncompliance, FDA inspections and Warning Letters, articles in the press, the largest civil fine ever imposed by the FDA, and the destruction and suspension of products worth approximately $250 million in corporate assets as evidence that the directors' decision to not act was not made in good faith. The appellate court refutes the lower court's finding that the facts in *McCall v. Scott* involved more serious board misconduct, acknowledging that there may have been more specific allegations against certain individual directors in *McCall,* but that the magnitude and duration of the FDA violations by Abbott, which led to the highest fine ever imposed by the FDA, were of an equally serious magnitude and duration to justify a finding of lack of good faith. The Seventh Circuit further emphasizes that the violations in *Abbott Laboratories* continued over a six-year period, while the Columbia Board's failure to act occurred only during a more limited two-year period.[77] The Seventh Circuit also relies heavily on the Sixth Circuit's opinion in *McCall* to find that the Section 102(b)(7) waiver provision similarly would not protect the *Abbott Laboratories* directors if the plaintiffs were able to prove "omissions not in good faith." Further, to the extent the directors' conduct constituted reckless disregard of a known risk, this could well be found to be the "bad faith" that would not be protected by a Section 102(b)(7) waiver provision.[78]

6. *Implications of the* Columbia/HCA *and* Abbott Laboratories-2003 *Decisions*

a. *The Sixth Circuit Decision in* McCall

The standards required for director and officer oversight of corporate affairs continue to evolve. In *Dellastatious v. Williams,*[79] the Fourth Circuit did not cite the district court's decision in *Abbott Laboratories.* However, both courts seemed to accept the premise that "outside" directors should not be held to as high a standard as inside directors and could reasonably rely on legal counsel, accountants, and other experts (unless the outside director had knowledge that such reliance was unwarranted).[80] Stating that "service as director of a corporation should not be a journey through liability land mines,"[81] the *Dellastatious* court cited *Caremark* to support the proposition that directors can avoid liability for insufficiently supervising corporate

---

[77] 325 F.3d at 808–09.
[78] *Id.* at 810.
[79] 242 F.3d 191 (4th Cir. 2001).
[80] *Id.* at 196.
[81] *Id.*

affairs by showing that they attempted, in good faith, to ensure that an adequate information-gathering and reporting system was in place.[82]

Subsequently, the district court's decision in *Abbott Laboratories* was reversed and remanded by the Seventh Circuit Court of Appeals in an opinion, described in more detail above, which brought the standards used by Sixth and Seventh Circuits in evaluating demand futility and Section 102(b)(7) claims into much closer alignment.[83] Nevertheless, the federal district court in Delaware, in a 2004 opinion, indirectly disputed part of the holding in the *Abbott Laboratories-2003* opinion. In *Stanziale v. Nachtomi,*[84] the court referred to the "theoretical exception" to the business judgment rule that some decisions may be so egregious that liability may be imposed even without proof of conflict of interest or improper motivation. Nevertheless, the *Stanziale* court did use the "egregious" standard as part of its analysis of the board's actions in that case. In addition, another federal district court, in *Roselink Investors, LLC v. Shenkman,*[85] specifically refuted the plaintiff's contention that Delaware law recognizes an independent duty of good faith. Nevertheless, the court conceded that such an obligation was subsumed within the duty of loyalty. In both cases, these doctrinal distinctions do not appear to have had a significant practical effect and there appears to be a trend toward increased director accountability.

b. *Other Developments Relating to Presuit Demand*

The *Oxford Health Plans*[86] presuit demand rule was recently followed in *Dollens v. Zionts.*[87]

E. *Spitzer v. Abdelhak*

2. *The Court's Decision*

Litigation between the plaintiffs' class and the directors and officers of Allegheny Health Education and Research Foundation (AHERF) continued following the district court's denial of the defendants' motion to dismiss the RICO claims.[88] The parties reached a settlement, and the case was dismissed on May 6, 2002.[89] The court order

---

[82]*Id.* (citing *Caremark,* 698 A.2d at 969–70). Both *McCall* and the *Abbott Laboratories* district court cases were distinguished by a federal district court in Michigan, in *Salsitz v. Nasser,* 208 F.R.D. 589 (E.D. Mich. 2002), which found that *Salsitz,* unlike the other two cases, did not involve clear violations of federal law or allegations of criminal or civil investigations that would have put the board on notice of illegal behavior. *Salsitz* at 598–99.

[83]*See In re* Abbott Labs., 325 F.3d 795 (7th Cir. 2003).

[84]2004 WL 878469 (D.Del. Apr. 20, 2004).

[85]2004 WL 875262 (S.D.N.Y. May 19, 2004).

[86]*In re* Oxford Health Plans, Inc. Secs. Litig., 192 F.R.D. 111 (S.D.N.Y. 2000).

[87]No. 01 C 2826, 2002 U.S. Dist. LEXIS 13511, 19–20 (N.D. Ill. July 22, 2002) (excusing presuit demand because plaintiffs adequately pleaded that five of eight directors faced a substantial likelihood of personal liability that would prevent them from exercising impartiality in considering a shareholder demand).

[88]Civil Docket at entries 68–111, Spitzer v. Abdelhak, No. 98-6475, 1999 U.S. Dist. LEXIS 19110 (E.D. Pa. Dec. 15, 1999).

[89]*Id.* at entry 111.

approving the settlement awarded over $1.4 million in attorneys' fees to plaintiffs' counsel,[90] but details concerning the size of the settlement fund and the nonmonetary obligations of AHERF officers and directors were not made public.

Chief Financial Officer David McConnell settled a criminal charge that he had misused AHERF funds for allegedly obtaining $25,000 and keeping the balance for personal use after using $7,300 to renovate a box at Pittsburgh's Three Rivers Stadium. He was sentenced to 12 months of probation, and was required to perform 150 hours of community service and to pay $16,700 in restitution. Charges against AHERF's general counsel, including theft, conspiracy, and misapplication of entrusted property, were dropped in May 2001. The court found no evidence that the general counsel knew about the chief executive officer's policy of using AHERF endowment funds for general operating purposes.[91] Finally, Sherif Abdelhak, the AHERF CEO, was sentenced by a Pennsylvania state court for his role in raiding AHERF's charitable endowments in 1998 to postpone its financial collapse, despite the reported finding that the money was used to prop up the failing health care system rather than for personal gain.[92] Abdelhak pleaded no contest to one count of misapplication of entrusted property and was sentenced to a prison term of 11½ to 23 months.[93]

IV. CORPORATE COMPLIANCE

Corporate compliance programs also may form the basis for registered (publicly traded) companies to fulfill certain requirements of the Sarbanes-Oxley Act and the SRO rules changes, such as the required code of ethics.[94]

A. U.S. Sentencing Guidelines

2. Compliance Programs Must Be "Effective"

The U.S. Sentencing Commission established an Advisory Group on Organizational Guidelines to review the general effectiveness of Chapter 8 of the U.S. Sentencing Guidelines. The Advisory Group focused on the application of the criteria for an effective compliance program and requested public comment on a variety of issues, including;

- whether the Sentencing Guidelines should articulate the responsibilities of the CEO, CFO, and/or others responsible for high-level oversight of compliance programs;

---

[90] *Id.*

[91] *Former Nonprofit Health System Executive Sentenced for Misusing Charitable Funds,* 7 HEALTH CARE DAILY REP. (BNA) (Sept. 6, 2002).

[92] *Id.*

[93] *Id.*

[94] See *supra* Section II.C.

- to what extent the responsibilities of boards of directors, board committees, or comparable governance bodies in overseeing compliance programs should be described in the Sentencing Guidelines;
- whether the Sentencing Guidelines should be more specific with regard to required compliance training methodologies;
- whether the Sentencing Guidelines comments should more specifically encourage whistleblowing protections, a privilege for good faith self-assessment and corrective action, or other means to encourage reporting without fear of retribution;
- whether auditing and monitoring activities should be given greater emphasis and importance in the Sentencing Guidelines;
- whether the Sentencing Guidelines should give organizations credit for evaluating employee performance using compliance criteria and increase an organization's culpability score for failure to implement a compliance program;
- whether different considerations apply when implementing and enforcing effective compliance programs depending on the size of the organization; and
- what incentives would encourage greater self-reporting—for example, whether the Sentencing Guidelines should state that the waiver of existing legal privileges will not be required to qualify for a reduction in culpability score.[95]

In addition, Section 1104 of the Sarbanes-Oxley Act called for the U.S. Sentencing Commission to issue new or amended guidelines to enhance penalties for officers or directors of publicly traded corporations who commit fraud and related offenses.[96] The Sarbanes-Oxley Act specifies numerous factors to be considered in carrying out this mandate, including the requirement that guideline offense levels and enhancements for an obstruction of justice offense are adequate when documents or other physical evidence are destroyed or fabricated.

In April 2004, the Sentencing Commission voted to adopt many of the recommendations of the Advisory Group and amended the Organizational Sentencing Guidelines (the amended Sentencing Guidelines) to make the criteria for effective compliance programs more stringent and to place greater responsibility on directors and officers for oversight and management of corporate compliance programs. The amended

---

[95] Advisory Group on Organizational Guidelines to the U.S. Sentencing Comm'n, Request for Additional Public Comment Regarding the U.S. Sentencing Guidelines for Organizations (Aug. 21, 2002), *available at* http://www.ussc.gov/corp/pubcom8_02.pdf.

[96] Sarbanes-Oxley Act §1104. Several other sections in the Sarbanes-Oxley Act also call for various other changes to the Sentencing Guidelines. *See, e.g., id.* §§805, 905.

Sentencing Guidelines were submitted to Congress on May 1, 2004, and became effective November 1, 2004.[97] However, a recently decided U.S. Supreme Court case,[98] and another consolidated case that has been argued before the Supreme Court but not yet decided at the time this Supplement went to press,[99] could result in all or part of the Sentencing Guidelines being struck down as unconstitutional.[100]

Due to the significant possibility that all or part of the proposed Sentencing Guidelines will be invalidated by the Supreme Court as described above, this Supplement will briefly summarize some of the more notable changes in the amended Sentencing Guidelines related to the "Sentencing of Organizations," since this section also addresses certain director and officer obligations. Most of these provisions are not the focus of current controversy. Therefore, even if the Sentencing Guidelines themselves are invalidated in whole or in part, the government may well continue to view these standards related to effective compliance programs as appropriate, and exercise its prosecutorial discretion accordingly. As a result, it would probably be advantageous to follow the criteria in the amended Sentencing Guidelines, to the extent possible, in any event.

The amended Sentencing Guidelines indicate that corporate compliance programs should be focused on detecting and preventing criminal conduct (which is somewhat narrower than the current reference to criminal and civil violations of law). However, in most respects the amended Sentencing Guidelines raise the bar for an "effective" compliance program in various ways. For example, the requirement for "compliance standards and procedures" is defined to include internal controls, thereby imposing an additional requirement for compliance program implementation through auditing and monitoring. In addition, under the amended Sentencing Guidelines, compliance programs should meet the following standards to be considered "effective":[101]

---

[97]The full text of the amended Sentencing Guidelines is available at http://www.ussc.gov/2004guid/tabcon04.htm.

[98]Blakely v. Washington, 124 S. Ct. 2531 (2004).

[99]United States v. Booker, 375 F. 3d 508 (7th Cir. 2004), *cert. granted,* 73 U.S.L.W. 3073 (U.S. Aug. 2, 2004) (No. 04-104).

[100]In *Blakely v. Washington,* the U.S. Supreme Court invalidated a portion of a criminal sentence imposed on a defendant by a judge that was based upon facts that were not admitted by the defendant nor found by a jury. The Supreme Court stated that the additional sentence imposed by the judge constituted a violation of the defendant's Sixth Amendment right to trial by jury. As a direct result of *Blakely,* on October 4, 2004, the Supreme Court heard arguments on the issue whether the Sixth Amendment is violated by the imposition of an enhanced sentence under the Sentencing Guidelines based on the sentencing judge's determination of a fact that was not found by the jury or admitted by the defendant.

[101]These amendments are generally found in §8B2.1 of the amended Sentencing Guidelines (which would replace the current commentary to §8A1.2 which would be largely deleted).

- High-level personnel of the organization[102] must ensure the organization has an effective compliance program with overall responsibility for the program assigned to specified high-level individuals;

- Specified individual(s) within the organization must have daily operational responsibility for the compliance program and periodically report to high-level personnel or the board (or a subgroup of the board). These individuals should have adequate resources, authority and direct access to the governing authority (or an appropriate subgroup);

- The organization should use reasonable efforts and due diligence not to include any individual within its "substantial authority personnel"[103] whom the organization knew/should have known has a history of engaging in violations of law or other conduct inconsistent with an effective compliance program;

- Compliance training should be provided to board members, upper level management, employees and agents, as appropriate;

- Auditing and monitoring systems designed to detect violations of law (that are periodically evaluated), and anonymous reporting systems should be in place;

- Compliance incentives, as well as penalties for compliance violations, should be used to encourage compliance; and

- The organization's governing authority[104] must be knowledgeable about the content and operation of the compliance program and exercise reasonable oversight of its implementation and effectiveness.

In terms of the organization's culpability score, the amended Sentencing Guidelines would allow a three-point deduction for an effective compliance and ethics program. However, the deduction would not be available if the organization unreasonably delayed reporting

---

[102]This term is defined as individuals who have substantial control over the organization or who have a substantial rule in the making of policy within the organization. The term includes: a director; an executive officer; an individual in charge of a major business or functional unit of the organization, such as sales, administration, or finance; and an individual with a substantial ownership interest. Application Note 3(b) to §8A1.2 of the Sentencing Guidelines.

[103]This term includes individuals who within the scope of their authority exercise a substantial measure of discretion in acting on behalf of an organization. The term includes high-level personnel of the organization, individuals who exercise substantial supervisory authority (e.g., a plant manager, a sales manager), and any other individuals who, although not a part of an organization's management, nevertheless exercise substantial discretion when acting within the scope of their authority (e.g., an individual with authority to negotiate or set price levels or to negotiate or approve significant contracts). Application Note 3(c) to §8A1.2 of the amended Sentencing Guidelines.

[104]This term is defined as the Board of Directors, or if the organization does not have a Board of Directors, the highest-level governing body of the organization. Application Note 1 to §8B2.1 of the amended Sentencing Guidelines.

to the appropriate authorities after becoming aware of an offense.[105] The deduction also would not apply if certain high-level personnel participated in, condoned, or were willfully ignorant of the offense.[106] Further, an organization that implemented its compliance program in response to a court or administrative order may lose all or part of the deduction.[107]

However, one of the more controversial provisions in the amended Sentencing Guidelines relates to Section 8C2.5(g) which authorizes a reduction in an organization's culpability score if it fully cooperated in the investigation of its wrongdoing. To mitigate some of the concerns that this provision would increase the pressure on organizations to waive their rights to the protection of attorney-client privilege and/or work product doctrine, the amended Sentencing Guidelines indicate that such waivers are not a prerequisite to a culpability score reduction under Section 8C2.5(g) "unless such waiver is necessary in order to provide timely and thorough disclosure of all pertinent information known to the organization."[108] As a result, under the amended Sentencing Guidelines, the government still will have leverage to press for waiver of attorney-client privilege and work product doctrine. Typically, the privilege belongs to the organization which, therefore, is the only entity entitled to waive it. However, directors and officers may be affected by such a waiver and may need to consult their own legal counsel in connection with any proposed waiver (and before taking any steps to approve or disapprove such waiver since there could be a potential conflict between the interests of the director and the organization).

The amended Sentencing Guidelines contain certain slightly modified criteria for small organizations.[109] Further, in a commentary provision that has not drawn much attention, large organizations are directed to encourage small organizations, especially those that want to do business with them, to implement an effective compliance program.[110] In addition, the commentary indicates that an organization's failure to incorporate and follow applicable industry standards weighs against a finding that the compliance program was effective.[111] This provision makes it particularly important that organizations monitor and

---

[105] Amended Sentencing Guidelines §8C2.5(f). However the commentary to this section indicates that organizations will be allowed a reasonable period to conduct an internal investigation and no report is required if, based on the information available at that time, the organization reasonably concludes that no offense was committed.

[106] There is a further presumption that an organization did not have an effective compliance program if certain specified personnel participated, condoned, or were willfully ignorant of the offense. *Id.*

[107] Amended Sentencing Guidelines §8C4.10.

[108] Application Note 12 to §8C2.5 of the amended Sentencing Guidelines.

[109] For example, the commentary suggests that the Board of a small organization discharge its responsibility for oversight by directly managing the organization's compliance efforts. Application Note 2(C)(iii) to §8B2.1 of the amended Sentencing Guidelines.

[110] Application Note 2(C)(iii) to §8B2.1 of the amended Sentencing Guidelines.

[111] *Id.* at Application Note 2(B) of the amended Sentencing Guidelines.

participate in the development of applicable industry standards to avoid the imposition of a standard that is potentially more stringent than that required by the applicable law and regulations.[112] The amended Sentencing Guidelines further indicate that the board should also receive information on the implementation and effectiveness of the compliance program at least once a year. Further, hiring and promotion decisions, particularly with regard to "high level" and "substantial authority" personnel, should reflect and promote a culture of compliance. In addition, an organization is directed to periodically assess the risk that criminal conduct will occur in light of the organization's business and prior history,[113] and prioritize and modify its actions accordingly in order to reduce the risk.

The Sentencing Guidelines do not contain absolute legal requirements. Nevertheless, in addition to their impact on the sentence ultimately received, they may also affect a court's initial assessment of liability. For example, to the extent they are seen as creating a standard of care and affirmative compliance obligations for an organization and its board, courts may be more willing to adopt the line of reasoning used in the *McCall* and *Abbott Laboratories-2003* cases. However, even cases that succeed on the issue of demand futility will not necessarily prevail on the merits.

B. The Office of Inspector General Compliance Program Guidance

The Office of Inspector General (OIG) also has published a Compliance Program Guidance for Ambulance Suppliers[114] and a Compliance Program Guidance for Pharmaceutical Manufacturers.[115] In addition, the OIG has published a draft document revising the previously issued Compliance Program Guidance for the Hospital Industry, which is notable in part because of the guidelines provided on how to evaluate a compliance program's effectiveness.[116]

---

[112]The PhRMA Code on Interactions with Healthcare Professionals is one recent example of this phenomena (i.e., in the Compliance Program Guidance for Pharmaceutical Manufacturers, the OIG largely adopted the stringent PhRMA Code standards as the baseline criteria required. *See* 68 Fed. Reg. 23,737. Although the OIG Compliance Guidance documents are not legally binding, the ramifications of failure to comply with criteria in the Sentencing Guidelines could have a direct and significant impact on the sentence imposed.

[113]An organization that employs sales personnel who are given the authority to set prices is given as a specific example of a business where there is a greater likelihood that criminal conduct may occur.

[114]Compliance Program Guidance for Ambulance Suppliers, 68 Fed. Reg. 14,245 (Mar. 24, 2003).

[115]Compliance Program Guidance for Pharmaceutical Manufacturers, 68 Fed. Reg. 23,731 (May 5, 2003) (for the text of the final guidance, see Appendix I-3.1 at the end of this Supplement).

[116]Draft Supplemental Compliance Program Guidance for Hospitals, 69 Fed. Reg. 32,012 (June 8, 2004). Also, see the discussion in Supplement Chapter 7, Corporate Compliance Programs (Jones at al.), at Section III.B.1., on this topic.

V. RECOMMENDATIONS TO REDUCE EXPOSURE

In light of recent developments, including the scandals relating to Enron, WorldCom, ImClone, and various other corporations, directors and officers should recognize that their actions are likely to be much more carefully examined by government regulators and the public (some of whom may be potential whistleblowers or plaintiffs in class action and shareholder derivative lawsuits). New restrictive laws and regulations relating to directors and officers of public companies, such as the Sarbanes-Oxley Act and SRO rules changes, have already been promulgated, with additional implementing regulations likely to be issued for some time to come. However, although privately held companies may not be legally obligated to comply, government officials and plaintiffs may well attempt to hold all companies to the criteria set forth in the Sarbanes-Oxley Act, perhaps by describing these criteria as the "industry standard." Some of the Sarbanes-Oxley types of standards will likely be made indirectly applicable to private companies under the application of the Sentencing Guidelines. Moreover, the heightened scrutiny, which is the Enron legacy, will likely be applied to all actions of all directors and officers, not just those actions related to federal health care program reimbursement.[117] Directors should also be aware that the nature and extent of their fiduciary duties can change depending on whether the corporation is solvent.[118]

Various organizations have begun developing "best practice" guidelines to assist non-profit organizations and their boards reduce the risk of liability.[119] Among various suggestions for non-profit governance, these guidelines often emphasize:

- The importance of independent directors, particularly on the audit committee;
- Providing financial "literacy" training for those directors who need it;
- Developing (and enforcing) a strong conflict of interest policy;
- Changing auditors every five years and not having these same firms provide non-audit services;

---

[117] For example, companies that are not "public" and therefore not subject to the Sarbanes-Oxley Act, particularly those that are operated as not-for-profits, are often subject to other specialized legal requirements, such as the IRS rules relating to board member conflict of interest statements and so-called excess benefit transactions, and state laws that regulate the use of charitable assets. Failure to strictly comply with any such legal requirements can create a risk of exposure for the directors and officers of these companies.

[118] *See* Richard Epling et al., *Selected Bankruptcy Problems for Non-Profit Entities,* Hospital Workouts & Restructurings Summit Materials (Dec. 2000) (noting that in light of the growing number of bankruptcies in the health care industry, change in director duties may be increasingly important).

[119] *See, e.g.,* BoardSource, *The Sarbanes-Oxley Act and Implications for Nonprofit Organizations* (BoardSource and Independent Sector 2003); AMERICAN HEALTH LAWYERS ASS'N, LESSONS FOR HEALTHCARE FROM ENRON: A BEST PRACTICES HANDBOOK, *available at* www.healthlawyers.org. Also see ABA SECTION ON BUSINESS LAW, CORPORATE DIRECTOR'S GUIDEBOOK (4th Ed. 2004), *available at* http://www.abanet.org/buslaw/catalog/pubindex.html.

- Having the board, CEO and CFO review and approve Forms 990 and/or 990-PF, and ensure timely filing;

- Prohibiting the provision of private loans to company directors or executives;[120]

- Implementing formal procedures to address compliance complaints and prevent retaliation. Any decision not to take further action should be justified and documented; and

- Adopting a mandatory document retention (and periodic destruction) policy that includes guidelines for electronic files and voicemail, back-up procedures, and prevents any document destruction if an investigation is underway or suspected.[121]

In addition, New York State Attorney General Eliot Spitzer has proposed corporate accountability legislation that has been introduced in the New York State Assembly.[122] If enacted, this legislation could affect operations of both public and private corporations. The Internal Revenue Service (IRS) also has launched a new enforcement effort to identify and halt abuses by tax-exempt organizations that pay excessive compensation and benefits to their officers and other insiders, called the Tax Exempt Compensation Enforcement Project.[123]

The OIG and the American Health Lawyers Association (AHLA) have jointly developed two documents, one entitled "Corporate Responsibility and Corporate Compliance: A Resource for Health Care Boards of Directors" and, more recently, "An Integrated Approach to Corporate Compliance: A Resource for Health Care Boards of Directors."[124] These resources are designed to help health care organization directors ask informed questions related to health care corporate compliance, and help them affirmatively demonstrate that they have followed a reasonable compliance oversight process.

The American Bar Association (ABA) has also adopted a list of recommended corporate governance practices that the ABA recommends for both public and private companies.[125]

---

[120] If such loans are to be provided, they should be formally approved by the board pursuant to a documented process, including disclosure of the value and terms of the loan.

[121] *See* BoardSource, *The Sarbanes-Oxley Act and Implications for Nonprofit Organizations*, at 2–10.

[122] *See* Press Release, Attorney General Spitzer's Proposed Reforms to State Corporate Accountability Laws (Mar. 12, 2003), *available at* http://www.oag.state.ny.us/press/2003/mar/mar12a_03.html.

[123] *See* Press Release, IRS Initiative Will Scrutinize EO Compensation Practices (Aug. 10, 2004), *available at* http://www.irs.gov/newsroom/article/0,,id=128328,00.html.

[124] *Available at* http://oig.hhs.gov/fraud/complianceguidance.html#2. This document elaborates on the OIG's position that the compliance function should be separate from, and not subordinate to, an entity's legal department. This discussion responds to the ABA's position, as set forth in a 2003 Resolution which endorsed giving the general counsel of a public corporation primary responsibility for assuring implementation of an effective compliance program under the Board's oversight. *See* ABA House of Delegates Resolution of August 11–12, 2003, *available at* http://www.abanet.org/leadership/2003/journal/119c.pdf.

[125] *Available at* http://www.abanet.org/leadership/2003/journal/119c.pdf. The ABA has also recommended changes to the Model Rules of Professional Conduct regarding a lawyer's duties with respect to corporate representation and corporate malfeasance of which the lawyer is aware. *See* http://www.abanet.org/buslaw/corporateresponsibility/home.html. A joint publication on corporate governance by the OIG and the ABA may also be issued in the near future.

Therefore, in addition to the other measures described in the Main Volume to reduce the risk of liability, directors and officers of all organizations should be sure they are actively involved in oversight of the corporation, develop a working knowledge of accounting and financial reporting rules, and work closely with the Audit Committee. Toward this end, board members should consider using the following checklist as a guide:

Figure 8-1. Checklist: Recommendations Following Sarbanes-Oxley

☐ Stay abreast of current legal requirements and new developments in the corporate governance area.[126]

☐ Ensure that a corporate information and reporting system exists that is adequate to assure that compliance information will come to the Board's attention in a timely manner as a matter of ordinary operations, and at least annually.

☐ As a part of the corporate information and reporting system, develop a compliance program that proactively promotes compliance.

☐ Ensure that the compliance program is monitored so that if any information that arouses suspicion comes to the company's attention (and, in particular, to the attention of a Board member), it is acted upon and not ignored.

☐ Supplement the existing compliance program code of ethics as necessary to satisfy other applicable legal requirements, including those contained in the Sarbanes-Oxley Act.[127]

☐ Closely monitor the organization's financial situation including investment management and off-balance-sheet arrangements.

☐ Assess "independence" of directors under the new SRO rules and ensure that all members of the Audit Committee and other applicable committees are independent.[128]

☐ Require complete, accurate, and timely disclosure of financial information from the CFO and other corporate managers and employees, for example:

   ☐ Require reports and statements to be based on detailed, documented representations about the substance of the transaction as well as the reporting methodology used; and

   ☐ Focus on high-risk issues, such as arrangements between affiliated organizations, off-balance-sheet transactions, and any public disclosure requirements.

---

[126] For example, directors and officers should monitor the regulations implementing the Sarbanes-Oxley Act, some of which have not yet been finalized.

[127] In some cases, it may be possible to expand the existing code of ethics. However, some organizations may decide to develop a separate code of ethics specific to the CEO and management members, as applicable, to satisfy the Sarbanes-Oxley standards.

[128] *See* Sarbanes-Oxley Act §301; see *supra* Section II.C.

☐ Ask questions about the way arrangements have been structured and reported. For example:

☐ Which accounting policies were used and why?

☐ Are any transactions (or the way they were reported) open to question or likely to create a significant degree of risk?

☐ Did audits identify any irregularities, and if so, what is the explanation for them?

☐ Were auditors subjected to pressure from management?

☐ What, if any, corrective action has been taken?

☐ Bring in outside experts when necessary, such as independent auditors and lawyers, and make sure they have appropriate expertise— for example, experts in health care, tax, or corporate law.

☐ Scrutinize the contractual and other arrangements between the corporation and its auditors.

☐ Ensure that all reports and the judgments they contain are supported by reliable documentation.

☐ Develop a working familiarity, through director education programs or other means, with the major substantive legal requirements relevant to the company's operations, including:

☐ health care laws, particularly Medicare requirements;

☐ IRS regulations;

☐ SEC requirements; and

☐ other applicable federal and state laws.

☐ Review, update if necessary, and implement conflict of interest policies applicable to the Board and management, including policies relating to required pre-approval of "related party" transactions (e.g., contracts between the company and directors or officers (or entities they control)).

☐ Examine executive compensation to be sure it is reasonable in amount, appropriately structured,[129] documented, and approved, as required under applicable law.

☐ Ensure a direct line of communication to the compliance officer.

☐ Ask questions, and be sure to follow up promptly and thoroughly when issues arise. Be alert to news stories as well as allegedly "routine" government investigations. In this environment, Board members ignore "red flags" at their peril.

---

[129] Compensation should avoid incentives that encourage management to adopt a short-term focus or emphasize a particular aspect of the organization's business.

9

The Disclosure Dilemma: How, When, and What to Tell Stockholders and Stakeholders About Your *Qui Tam* Suit or Investigation* [New Chapter]

---

*William W. Horton, Haskell Slaughter Young & Rediker, LLC, Birmingham, Alabama, and Monty G. Humble, Vinson & Elkins L.L.P., Dallas, Texas.

I. INTRODUCTION

A. A Brief Vignette

Mary Jones, general counsel of Megalithic Healthcare, Inc. (NYSE: BIG), completed Megalithic's annual report on Form 10-K, which would be filed with the Securities and Exchange Commission (SEC) the next day. As soon as the filing was confirmed, Megalithic would go effective with the registration statement for its latest public offering: 10 million shares of common stock being sold by the company, and a million being sold by her CEO as he finalized his vacation plans. By Friday, Mary would be finished with her comments on Megalithic's new bank credit agreement, under which a syndicate of financial institutions led by First Second Bank, N.A., would provide the company with a billion-dollar line of credit. When she left her law firm partnership to become Megalithic's general counsel, she had never dreamed how fast the company would grow and how quickly she would be working with the biggest players in the capital markets.

Before leaving the office, she reviewed the day's mail. At the bottom of the pile was an envelope bearing the return address of the U.S. Attorney for the Southern District of North Dakota. Upon opening the letter, she read with growing disbelief:

Dear Ms. Jones:

The United States Attorney's Office for the Southern District of North Dakota, together with the Department of Justice in Washington, D.C., is conducting an investigation to determine whether to intervene in a lawsuit filed under the *qui tam* provisions of the civil False Claims Act, 31 U.S.C. §§3729–3732. This lawsuit has been filed under seal. However, we have obtained a partial lifting of the seal from the Court for the purpose of informing you of our investigation.

While we are not able to provide you with a copy of the complaint at this time, under the partial lifting of the seal we are able to advise you that our investigation concerns the possibility that a large number of Megalithic hospitals have routinely overbilled the Medicare program and have entered into contracts with physicians that violate the Anti-Kickback Statute, 42 U.S.C. §1320a-7b(b). Please call me to arrange a meeting to discuss these matters and certain information that we will be requesting that your company provide us.

You are reminded that this matter is under seal. While we have obtained a partial lifting of the seal for the purposes described in this letter, you are not to disclose the existence of this matter without further order of the Court.

Very truly yours,

Dudley D. Wright
United States Attorney

By M. Gruff Crimedog
Assistant United States Attorney

The following questions quickly came to Mary's mind:—What do I do? My 10-K doesn't say there's any problem.—Do I have to talk about this in my prospectus?—What do I tell my banks?—How do I say anything when the case is under seal?—How can I even figure out what's going on when they won't even tell me who filed the complaint or what the specific claims are?—Will the SEC send me to jail if I don't say something?—Will the judge send me to jail if I break the seal?—What will my CEO do if I make some announcement and our stock price tanks?

B. The Problem

Health care providers, like other business organizations, face numerous circumstances where legal or contractual obligations require them to make various disclosures about their business operations and the material risks, events, and uncertainties that affect them. For a publicly traded health care company, those obligations arise whenever the company seeks to sell its securities in the market and whenever it files the periodic reports required under the securities laws. For a tax-exempt provider, those obligations arise when it seeks to raise capital in the bond markets and may arise when it has existing bonds outstanding. For any provider, those obligations may arise by way of contractual representations when it is obtaining bank loans, seeking funding from venture capitalists, or entering into acquisition or merger agreements with other companies.

Where a business organization operates in a heavily regulated environment, such as health care, a key issue for disclosure recipients—in any context—is understanding the exposure that the organization may have to civil or criminal regulatory sanctions. Thus, if the organization has publicly traded securities, investors, research analysts, prospective underwriters, and other market participants will ask questions and seek information concerning the organization's compliance status and its exposure to regulatory litigation. Similarly, with regard to all providers, lenders, potential merger partners, and others entering into contractual relationships with the organization may well seek representations and warranties concerning these issues.

The disclosure of regulatory problems or enforcement litigation can have a severe impact in any setting. In the world of publicly traded securities, expansive disclosure concerning such matters can cause a company's stock price to plummet and make it impossible to complete transactions, while untimely or inadequate disclosure will likely lead to stockholder suits and investigations by the SEC. For tax-exempt issuers, some types of violations may call into question the validity of the issuer's exempt status and may make its bonds taxable, as well as triggering bondholder suits and SEC investigations. Bad news may also kill a merger or put a credit facility into default.

The current regulatory and enforcement environment in health care (coupled with the intense interest in corporate disclosure, in the post-Enron environment), however, can make it particularly difficult to respond effectively and appropriately to the various disclosure imperatives an organization may face. There are several reasons for this:

- Health care providers are subject to a complex web of state and
  federal laws and regulations, with key statutes often being subjective, ambiguous, or incompletely implemented by regulation.
  Not uncommonly, this body of law is interpreted by hindsight,
  with stricter current standards being applied to the review of
  past events.

- Even purely technical violations of health care regulations can,
  at least theoretically, lead to punitive per-claim penalties,
  exclusion from participation in Medicare and other federal and
  state reimbursement programs, loss of tax-exempt status, and
  other extreme sanctions.[1]

- Increasingly, health care violations can involve a sort of "cross
  default" impact. For example, acts that allegedly violate the federal anti-kickback statute,[2] which carries its own penalties, may
  also expose a provider to sanctions under numerous other health
  care statutes and under the tax laws.[3] Further, a provider that
  incurs sanctions under federal health care programs may find
  that those sanctions raise problems under managed care contracts, credit agreements, and other private arrangements. Thus,
  quantifying the potential risk of a regulatory violation may
  require applying a multiplier effect to the exposure from the
  basic violation.

- The range of penalties theoretically available for regulatory violations may substantially exceed the amounts actually likely to
  be obtained through litigation or settlement. Thus, quantifying
  the materiality of alleged violations may be difficult. Further,
  disclosure of the organization's best estimate of the exposure
  may compromise its ability to defend against the claims.

---

[1] For illustrative lists of relevant statutes and regulations and their associated sanctions,
see Main Volume and Supplement Chapter 1 (Baumann, An Introduction to Health Care Fraud
and Abuse); Thomas C. Fox, Carol Colborn Loepere, & Joseph W. Metro, Health Care Financial Transactions Manual §§7.2–7.9 (West rev. ed. 2003); American Health Lawyers Ass'n,
Health Law Practice Guide §§24:2–24:12; 24:34–24:49 (West rev. ed. 2003) [hereinafter Practice Guide]. As to the interaction with the tax exemption statutes, see Practice Guide §31:10.

[2] 42 U.S.C. §1320a-7b(b).

[3] Claimed violations of the anti-kickback statute may, for example, be alleged, in certain circumstances, to give rise to sanctions under the criminal False Claims Act, 42 U.S.C. §1320a-
7b(a); the civil False Claims Act, 31 U.S.C. §§3729–3733; the Program Fraud Civil Remedies
Act, 31 U.S.C. §§3801–3812; the Health Insurance Portability and Accountability Act (HIPAA)
health care fraud criminal statute, 18 U.S.C. §1347; the Civil Monetary Penalties provisions, 42
U.S.C. §1320a-7a; and the exclusion law, 42 U.S.C. §1320a-7, among others. As a practical matter it is unlikely that the government would seek (or obtain) duplicative relief under *all* these
statutes, but there is nothing on the face of the statutes that prevents cumulating sanctions. In
addition, payments or transactions that violate the anti-kickback statute may also constitute
private inurement, potentially jeopardizing the tax-exempt status of a tax-exempt violator. *See,
e.g.,* Rev. Rul. 97-21, 1997-1 C.B. 121.

- Perhaps most significantly, the government has increasingly relied on *qui tam* cases filed under the civil False Claims Act (FCA)[4] as its chief vehicle for enforcement.[5] The government and the *qui tam* bar have become very aggressive in asserting that alleged violations of the anti-kickback statute, the Stark law,[6] the Medicare conditions of participation, and even quality-of-care standards give rise to false claims.[7] In a scenario that has become quite familiar, a private relator files a sealed complaint under the FCA, and the government utilizes the period allowed for its intervention decision to obtain substantial and far-reaching unilateral discovery while the case is under seal—even where the underlying complaint makes only vague and general allegations that would not survive a motion to dismiss. In that circumstance, the putative defendant frequently lacks adequate information to assess the strength of the potential case and the materiality of the potential exposure, and must weigh its legal and contractual disclosure obligations against the FCA's sealing provisions. In some cases, the government may use its broad investigatory powers to obtain information from the provider without even disclosing the nature or scope of its investigation or the fact that a sealed *qui tam* suit is pending, further clouding the provider's ability to accurately assess the situation.

In this environment, providers face the challenge of reconciling conflicting obligations and prohibitions concerning disclosure, often without the quality and quantity of data that they may be accustomed to using to evaluate loss contingencies. Not infrequently, the advice of securities or corporate counsel and the advice of regulatory or defense counsel on the disclosure issues may conflict. The risk of an erroneous judgment may have enormous consequences, both for the defense of the underlying claims and for the ongoing business interests of the organization. This chapter attempts to provide a brief overview of the substantive law affecting these types of disclosure decisions, combined with practical suggestions as to how to analyze and respond to the issues, with a particular focus on securities law issues affecting publicly traded and tax-exempt provider organizations.

---

[4] 31 U.S.C. §§3729–3733. The Civil False Claims Act is discussed in more detail in Chapter 3 (Salcido, The False Claims Act in Health Care Prosecutions: Application of the Substantive, *Qui Tam,* and Voluntary Disclosure Provisions).

[5] For a succinct discussion of why this is so, see Timothy S. Jost & Sharon L. Davies, *The Empire Strikes Back: A Critique of the Backlash Against Fraud and Abuse Enforcement,* 51 ALA. L. REV. 239, 247–48 (1999).

[6] The Ethics in Patient Referrals Act, 42 U.S.C. §1395nn. The Stark law is described in more detail in Chapter 2 (Crane, Federal Physician Self-Referral Restrictions).

[7] *See, e.g.,* Pamela H. Bucy, *Growing Pains: Using the False Claims Act to Combat Health Care Fraud,* 51 ALA. L. REV. 57, 77–86 (1999); Robert Fabrikant & Glenn E. Solomon, *Application of the Federal False Claims Act to Regulatory Compliance Issues in the Health Care Industry,* 41 ALA. L. REV. 105, 124–56 (1999).

II. SOURCES OF DISCLOSURE OBLIGATIONS UNDER THE FEDERAL SECURITIES LAWS

A. Publicly Traded Issuers[8]

Health care organizations seeking to sell stock to the public, or which have already done so, are subject to myriad affirmative disclosure duties under the Securities Act of 1933[9] and the Securities Exchange Act of 1934.[10] The 1933 Act and the regulations thereunder prescribe the disclosures that must be made in connection with the offer or sale of securities, while the 1934 Act and its regulations establish the duties of issuers to provide ongoing disclosure to the market. In addition, case law, administrative interpretations, and established practice in the securities industry impose additional disclosure standards on publicly traded issuers, both with regard to the disclosures mandated under the 1933 and 1934 Acts and the more informal disclosures issuers may make to current and prospective investors, securities analysts, and others.[11]

In reviewing the particular disclosure obligations imposed by the federal securities laws, as amplified through regulation and interpreted through case law and administrative pronouncements, issuers must always bear in mind the polestar of Section 10(b) of the 1934 Act and Rule 10b-5 thereunder.[12] Rule 10b-5 provides that it is

---

[8]For simplicity, the discussion of securities law issues in this section assumes that the issuer is, or is seeking to become, publicly traded. However, the offer or sale of securities in "private placement" transactions not registered under the federal securities laws is still subject to many of the same disclosure obligations as are public offerings, either directly through the requirements of the registration exemption being relied on or through the application of the antifraud provisions of the securities laws. For additional simplicity, the discussion assumes that the issuer in question is of a size that makes it ineligible to use the "small business issuer" (SB) registration statement forms and periodic reporting forms. There are some differences in the specific requirements for SB issuers, but the substantive principles discussed in this chapter remain the same with respect to them.

[9]15 U.S.C. §§77a–77aa.

[10]15 U.S.C. §§78a–78mm. Disclosure obligations may also arise under state securities laws, or "blue sky" laws, particularly with respect to the offering and sale of securities in private placement transactions and initial public offerings (IPOs). To the extent those obligations differ from the federal statutes, however, they are not addressed in this chapter.

[11]Note that, in addition to legally mandated disclosures, the rules of the stock exchanges and the NASDAQ Stock Market impose disclosure obligations on issuers that, read literally, may be broader in some circumstances than those imposed by the securities laws. Discussion of these obligations is pretermitted in this chapter, in part for considerations of brevity, and in part because, as a practical matter, it is unlikely that those entities will impose disciplinary action in circumstances where there is no associated liability under the securities laws and it is generally held that there is no private right of action under general stock exchange disclosure rules. *See, e.g.,* State Teachers Retirement Bd. v. Fluor Corp., 654 F. 2d 843, 851–53 (2d Cir. 1981). However, in litigation or other proceedings relating to an issuer's alleged wrongful failure to disclose material information, any violation of exchange or NASDAQ standards may well be asserted as additional evidence of the issuer's breach of its disclosure duties.

[12]15 U.S.C. §78j(b) and 17 C.F.R. §240.10b-5, respectively. *See also* §11(a) of the 1933 Act, 15 U.S.C. §77k(a) (liability of persons for material misrepresentations or omissions in registration statement); §12(a)(2) of the 1933 Act, 15 U.S.C. §77l(a)(2) (liability of persons for material misrepresentations or omissions in prospectus or oral communication relating to offers or sales of securities); §15 of the 1933 Act, 15 U.S.C. §77o (liability of "control persons" for violations of §§11 and 12); §17(a) of the 1933 Act, 15 U.S.C. §77q(a) (liability of persons who obtain money or property in connection with the offer or sale of securities by means of material misrepresentations or omissions or otherwise through fraud or deceit); and the respective regulations promulgated thereunder.

unlawful, in connection with the purchase or sale of securities, to make an untrue statement of a material fact or to fail to state a material fact necessary to make the statements made not misleading. This regulation provides the principal private right of action against an issuer or its affiliates for fraud in connection with the purchase or sale of securities.

The next few sections of this chapter outline some of the statutory, regulatory, and case law requirements with which health care issuers must grapple in determining how to handle disclosure issues regarding government investigations and related litigation.[13] Later sections will discuss the particular application of those requirements in the health care industry and suggest practical approaches for responding to those requirements.

1. The 1934 Act

Although disclosure issues may have the greatest immediacy in the context of a pending offering of securities, they are perhaps most easily understood in the context of the ongoing integrated disclosure system established under the 1934 Act, which sets forth detailed requirements for periodic and current reports for issuers with a class of securities registered under the federal securities laws. Under the 1934 Act, an issuer is required to file reports designed to ensure that the market has detailed current information concerning the issuer and its business and financial condition on which investors can rely when buying or selling its securities in everyday trading. These reports comprise the annual report on Form 10-K, which (for most issuers) must be filed within 75 days (soon to be decreased to 60 days) after the end of the issuer's fiscal year; quarterly reports on Form 10-Q, which must be filed within 40 days (soon to be decreased to 30 days) after the end of each fiscal quarter; and current reports on Form 8-K, which must be filed on a relatively immediate basis when certain specified events occur and which may also be filed when the issuer elects to report information not otherwise required to be disclosed in an 8-K but that it "deems of importance to security holders."[14]

---

[13]For a broad, if somewhat dated, overview of securities disclosure requirements and practice as applied to the health care industry, see William W. Horton & F. Hampton McFadden, Jr., *Disclosure Obligations of the Newly Public Healthcare Company: Practical Strategies for the Company and Its Counsel*, 32 J. HEALTH L. 1 (1999) [hereinafter *Disclosure Obligations*]. For a more specific discussion of the federal securities disclosure regime as applied to disclosure of unpleasant corporate events, including government investigations, see Linda C. Quinn & Ottilie L. Jarmel, *Disclosing Bad News: An Overview for Securities Counsel*, in COUNSELING CLIENTS IN TURBULENT MARKETS & UNCERTAIN TIMES: DISCLOSURE & FINANCING ISSUES 7 (Practising Law Institute 2001).

[14]See generally *Disclosure Obligations, supra* note 13, at 4–13. In 2004, the SEC added various new disclosure requirements to Form 8-K, as well as modifying the time periods within which an 8-K must be filed. See Final Rule: Additional Form 8-K Disclosure Requirements and Acceleration of Filing Date, Securities Act Release No. 33-8400 (Mar. 16, 2004), *available at* www.sec.gov/rules/final/33-8400.htm.

a. The 10-K and General Principles of 1934 Act Disclosure

The 10-K is intended to provide a comprehensive overview of the issuer's business, its financial condition, and its results of operations. The 10-K requires disclosure under enumerated "Items," which in turn refer to information required under the SEC's Regulation S-K[15] (covering information other than financial statements) and Regulation S-X[16] (covering the form and content of financial statements). Three specific items under Regulation S-K may, depending on the circumstances, require disclosure of potential civil or criminal exposure relating to violation of health care laws and regulations:[17]

- Item 103 of Regulation S-K requires disclosure regarding "any material pending legal proceedings, other than ordinary routine litigation" to which the issuer is a party. Item 103 also requires similar disclosure regarding "any such proceedings *known to be contemplated* by governmental authorities."[18]

- Item 303 of Regulation S-K requires various disclosures concerning the issuer's financial condition, changes in its financial condition, and its results of operations. Such disclosures are required in the 10-K under Item 7, "Management's Discussion and Analysis of Financial Condition and Results of Operations," commonly referred to as "MD&A." Included in the MD&A requirements are requirements that the issuer "[i]dentify any known demands, commitments, events or uncertainties that will result in or that are reasonably likely to result in [its] liquidity increasing or decreasing in any material way";[19] "[d]escribe any known trends or uncertainties that have had or that [the issuer] reasonably expects will have a material favorable or unfavorable impact on net sales or revenues or income from continuing operations";[20] and focus its discussion and analysis "on material events and uncertainties known to management that would cause reported financial information not to be

---

[15] 17 C.F.R. Subparts 229.1–229.900.

[16] 17 C.F.R. §§210.1-01 through 210.12-29.

[17] In addition, note that Item 101(c)(1) of Regulation S-K requires the issuer to discuss, "[t]o the extent material to an understanding of the [issuer's] business as a whole," the "dependence of [a business segment of the issuer] upon a single customer, or a few customers, the loss of any one or more of which would have a material adverse effect on the [issuer]" and to provide a "description of any material portion of the business that may be subject to renegotiation of profits or termination of contracts or subcontracts at the election of the Government. . . ." Does, for example, the risk of exclusion from federal reimbursement programs fit within those types of disclosure requirements? Note also that Item 101(c)(1)(xii) specifically requires "[a]ppropriate disclosure as to the material effects that compliance with Federal, State and local" environmental protection laws "may have upon the capital expenditures, earnings and competitive position" of the issuer.

[18] 17 C.F.R. Subparts 229.1–229.900 (emphasis added).

[19] Item 303(a)(1).

[20] Item 303(a)(3)(ii).

necessarily indicative of future operating results or of future financial condition."[21]

- Finally, Item 401(f)(2) requires certain disclosure relating to a director, nominee for director, or executive officer of the issuer if, during the previous 5 years, "[s]uch person was convicted in a criminal proceeding or is a named subject of a pending criminal proceeding" if the information is "material to an evaluation of the ability or integrity of such person."[22]

The requirements of Item 103 and Item 401(f) are, with some wrinkles imposed by the case law, relatively straightforward.[23] Aside from the threshold question of materiality, which is discussed later,[24] the first issue in the application of each of these provisions is whether there is a "proceeding." In the context of Item 103, it has been said that,

> [w]hile there is little guidance, either in the Commission's regulations or elsewhere, as to what constitutes a "proceeding" for purposes of Item 103, the plain meaning of the term "proceeding" as stated in Item 103 suggests that it refers to administrative or adjudicatory proceedings rather than law enforcement investigations.[25]

Assuming that to be the case, Item 103 still requires disclosure of material proceedings "known to be contemplated" by government authorities, even if they are not yet pending. However, as a former director of the SEC's Division of Enforcement has pointed out, it is frequently difficult to determine exactly when an issuer *knows* that a proceeding is contemplated, given the protracted investigatory

---

[21] Item 303(a), Instruction 3.

[22] Item 401(f)(2). Item 401(g) imposes the same requirements with respect to "promoters" and "control persons" for certain types of issuers. In addition, note that Item 401(f)(3)(ii) requires disclosure if any of the foregoing persons has been the subject of any order, judgment, or decree "enjoining him from, or otherwise limiting . . . [e]ngaging in any type of business practice." That language is sandwiched between two subsections that relate solely to securities, banking, and other financial and insurance activities; however, the "business practice" language stands curiously distinct and nonlimited between those subsections, suggesting that it could have broader application. Note that Item 401(f)(2) requires disclosure only with respect to a person who is a "named subject" of a pending criminal proceeding, while Item 401(f)(3) speaks only of someone who is a "subject" of the types of orders, judgments or decrees enumerated therein. At least one court has read this distinction to mean that Item 401(f)(3) imposes a duty of disclosure under that item where a director, nominee for director, or executive officer knows himself or herself to be the subject of such an order, even if such person is not expressly named therein. *See* United States v. Yeaman, 987 F. Supp. 373, 381–82 (E.D. Pa. 1997).

[23] Note that most cases discussing Item 401 arise in claims alleging fraud in proxy solicitations governed by Section 14(a) of the 1934 Act and the regulations thereunder. Item 401 disclosure is required in proxy statements relating to the election of directors, and, indeed, many issuers satisfy the Item 401 10-K disclosure requirements by incorporating information by reference to their proxy statements, as permitted under rules of the Securities and Exchange Commission (SEC). Because, however, Item 401 information must be disclosed in the 10-K, either at length or through incorporation by reference, Item 401 issues are discussed here in the 10-K context.

[24] *See infra* Section II.A.4.

[25] Karl A. Groskaufmanis, Matt T. Morley, & Michael J. Rivera, *To Tell or Not to Tell: Reassessing Disclosure of Uncharged Misconduct*, 1 33RD ANNUAL INSTITUTE ON SECURITIES REGULATION 457, 459 (internal page 3) (Practising Law Institute 2001) (republished from INSIGHTS, June 1999).

process that government agencies tend to engage in before filing civil, criminal, or administrative proceedings and the multiple layers of authority that often must approve the decision to institute formal proceedings.[26] Item 401(f) does not require disclosure with respect to contemplated proceedings, but only with respect to past convictions or proceedings that are actually pending (and note that Item 401(f) only applies where the proceedings involve the individual in question, and not where they only involve the issuer as an entity or other persons related to the issuer who are not directors, director nominees, or executive officers).

Although the cases are not uniform, a number of them affirmatively hold that neither Item 103 nor Item 401(f) requires disclosure of uncharged criminal conduct, at least in the context of actions alleging that such nondisclosure itself constituted a criminal violation of the federal securities laws.[27] In the leading case of *United States v. Matthews*,[28] which involved a claim of an alleged criminal violation of the proxy rules under the 1934 Act, the Second Circuit held that Item 401(f) (as applied in that case to proxy statements under Section 14(a) of the 1934 Act) did not require the disclosure of uncharged criminal conduct[29] and that, in the absence of a lawfully promulgated regulation requiring such disclosure, "nondisclosure of such conduct cannot be the basis of a criminal prosecution."[30]

Matthews was extensively analyzed, approved, and expanded by the U.S. District Court for the District of Columbia in *United States v.*

---

[26] *See* Gary G. Lynch & Eric F. Grossman, *Disclosure of Corporate Wrongdoing,* in RESPONDING TO BAD NEWS: HOW TO DEAL WITH THE BOARD OF DIRECTORS, STOCKHOLDERS, THE PRESS, ANALYSTS, REGULATORS AND THE PLAINTIFFS' BAR 207, 220–21 (internal pages 10–11) (Practising Law Institute 1999) (questioning whether such things as subpoenas for documents, employee subpoenas, requests for "Wells submissions," and receipt of "target" and "subject" letters from prosecutors give rise to knowledge of a threatened proceeding, where the ultimate decision to initiate a proceeding must still be approved at higher levels).

[27] For useful surveys and discussion of the case law, see Groskaufmanis, Morley & Rivera, *supra* note 25, at 458–63 (internal pages 2–5), and Lynch & Grossman, *supra* note 26, at 217–29 (internal pages 7–19).

[28] 787 F.2d 38 (2d Cir. 1986). The facts in *Matthews* are, in themselves, quite interesting. Matthews, who had begun his career as an SEC staff attorney, was the general counsel of the issuer. He was approached about being nominated for the board of directors. At the time of the nomination, he and the issuer were aware that he was one of the "subjects" of a grand jury investigation involving an alleged conspiracy to bribe certain state tax officials for the benefit of the issuer. After consulting counsel, Matthews and the issuer determined not to disclose this fact in the proxy statement relating to the election of directors. Two years later, the issuer and two individuals were indicted for conspiracy to commit bribery and tax fraud. One year after that, Matthews was indicted as a co-conspirator and was also indicted for an alleged criminal violation of the 1934 Act for failure to disclose, in the proxy statement relating to his original election as a director, his knowledge that he was a subject of the grand jury investigation. The U.S. Attorney's Office prosecuted the indictment without involvement by the SEC, and both SEC Regional Director Ira Sorkin and former SEC General Counsel Harvey Pitt (who later served as chairman of the SEC) publicly questioned the validity of the securities fraud prosecution. At trial, Matthews was acquitted on the conspiracy count but was convicted on the securities fraud count—that is, he was convicted for concealing an uncharged criminal offense of which he was subsequently acquitted, and the conviction, remarkably, occurred in the same trial as the acquittal. The Second Circuit reversed the conviction and remanded the case with instructions to dismiss the indictment.

[29] *See id.* at 46–48.

[30] *Id.* at 49.

Crop Growers Corp.[31] In *Crop Growers* (a case brought by the independent counsel investigating former U.S. Secretary of Agriculture Mike Espy), the defendants, including both the issuer and individual officers of the issuer, were accused of criminally violating the securities laws by failing to disclose alleged violations of the Federal Election Campaign Act in the issuer's SEC filings, which violations were first charged in the same indictment as the securities fraud counts.[32] The defendants relied on *Matthews* for the proposition that there was no duty to disclose uncharged criminal conduct. After reviewing *Matthews* and cases interpreting it in both the civil and criminal contexts, the court concluded that there was no duty to disclose uncharged criminal conduct under Items 103, 303, and 401, at least in the context of a criminal prosecution for such nondisclosure.[33] In reaching that conclusion, the court noted that

> [t]he specific forms at issue [both 1933 Act and 1934 Act forms] do not specify that criminal liability can be imposed if the forms are not completed in compliance with law. Further, the terms of the regulations do not set forth required disclosures in precise terms. Qualitative terms such as "risk," "trend," and "uncertainty" do not provide sufficient notice that a particular disclosure is required to allow criminal liability to attach for alleged non-disclosure. . . . Such terms are, quite simply, too vague and amorphous to give fair notice, required by the Due Process clause, of what disclosure is required. . . . Thus, neither regulation [i.e., items 303 and 503 of Regulation S-K], even when read in conjunction with [Rule 12b-20 under the 1934 Act], will support criminal liability for failing to disclose uncharged, uninvestigated criminal conduct.[34]

Although there appears to be some consensus, if not necessarily a universal one, that the securities laws should not be read to impose criminal liability for failure to disclose uncharged criminal conduct, the case law arising from civil proceedings is more mixed. For example, in *Roeder v. Alpha Industries,*[35] a class action suit seeking damages and declaratory relief, the First Circuit found that information concerning alleged bribery by officers of the issuer in order to obtain defense subcontracts could be "material information" under the 1934 Act, even at a time before the indictment of one of the officers.[36] In its analysis, the court distinguished *Matthews* on the basis that *Matthews*

---

[31] 954 F. Supp. 335 (D.D.C. 1997).

[32] *See id.* at 339–40.

[33] *See id.* at 345–48. The court also held that disclosure was not required under Item 503 of Regulation S-K, which relates to the disclosure of material risk factors in a 1933 Act registration statement.

[34] *Id.* at 348. Rule 12b-20, 17 C.F.R. §240.12b-20, requires that, "[i]n addition to the information expressly required to be included in a statement or report, there shall be added such further material information, if any, as may be necessary to make the required statements, in light of the circumstances under which they are made[,] not misleading."

[35] 814 F.2d 22 (1st Cir. 1987).

[36] *See id.* at 24–26.

was an appeal from a criminal conviction involving Fifth Amendment issues.[37] However, the court affirmed the district court's dismissal of the class action, finding that there was no liability under Rule 10b-5 for failure to disclose material information absent an affirmative duty to disclose it:

> [The plaintiff] claims that a corporation has an affirmative duty to disclose all material information even if there is no insider trading, no statute or regulation requiring disclosure, and no inaccurate, incomplete, or misleading prior disclosures. The prevailing view, however, is that there is no such affirmative duty of disclosure.[38]

In *Ballan v. Wilfred American Educational Corp.,*[39] the plaintiff claimed that the defendants had violated Rule 10b-5 by failing to disclose in the issuer's 1934 Act filings (1) that they had failed to comply with certain government regulations (for which indictments subsequently issued) and (2) "the potential consequences of government investigations into that failure."[40] The court noted that the issuer had no obligation "to disclose information of which it had no knowledge or about which it could only speculate" and that "it would be misleading for it to do so."[41] However, the court went on to suggest that disclosure of facts relating to specific acts and specific practices could be material, even if those acts might be alleged to be crimes: "Such acts or practices are not speculations or confessions but 'facts' relevant to a person's decision to invest in [the issuer]."[42] Without analyzing the existence of any duty to disclose such facts, the court denied the defendants' motion to dismiss the securities fraud claims.

Further, in *In re Par Pharmaceutical, Inc. Securities Litigation,*[43] the court reaffirmed the principle that, in order for liability to attach under Rule 10b-5, the defendant must have failed to disclose material information in the face of a duty to disclose it.[44] The court also held that the issuer "was not obligated to speculate as to the myriad of consequences, ranging from minor setbacks to complete ruin, that might have befallen the company if the [scheme to bribe Food and Drug Administration (FDA) officials to obtain expedited drug manufactur-

---

[37] *Id.* at 26.

[38] *Id.* at 26–27. *See also* Gallagher v. Abbott Labs., 269 F.3d 806, 808 (7th Cir. 2001) ("Much of plaintiffs' argument [relating to defendants' "deferred" disclosure of $100 million FDA fine] reads as if firms have an absolute duty to disclose all information material to stock prices as soon as news comes into their possession. Yet that is not the way the securities laws work. We do not have a system of continuous disclosure. Instead firms are entitled to keep silent (about good news as well as bad news) unless positive law creates a duty to disclose"). However, see *infra* n. 191 for observations concerning the expanding requirements of "positive law."

[39] 720 F. Supp. 241 (E.D.N.Y. 1989).

[40] *Id.* at 243.

[41] *Id.* at 248.

[42] *Id.* at 249.

[43] 733 F. Supp. 668 (S.D.N.Y. 1990).

[44] *See id.* at 674.

ing approvals] was discovered, disclosed or terminated."[45] However, the court denied the defendants' motion to dismiss with respect to claims that the failure to disclose the bribery scheme (for which the issuer and some of the individual defendants entered guilty pleas) rendered statements made by the issuer in its 1934 Act filings and press releases, which concerned the issuer's success and expertise in obtaining FDA approvals, misleading.[46]

Carried through to a logical conclusion, these cases arising in the civil context suggest that, for purposes of the 10-K, the most important consideration may not be the relatively narrowly defined disclosure required by Items 103 and 401. Instead, the greater potential exposure under the securities laws may arise from the more intrinsically subjective requirements for MD&A disclosure contained in Item 303. As noted earlier, Item 303 requires the disclosure of known trends, events, and uncertainties that could materially affect the issuer's future financial position, liquidity, or results of operations or cause future results to differ materially from historic results.[47] In interpreting those requirements in the context of governmental investigations and litigation, it is instructive to review the SEC's 1988 interpretive release relating to a nationwide investigation into misconduct in defense contract procurement, also known as the Defense Contractors Release.[48]

In the Defense Contractors Release, the SEC advised defense companies to "review on an ongoing basis the need for appropriate disclosure" in the context of a national investigation into "illegal or unethical activity in the procurement of defense contracts," while

---

[45] *Id.* at 678.

[46] *See id.* at 675–79. In contrast to *Matthews,* where the facts were almost unreasonably favorable to the defendant, the *Par Pharmaceutical* case presents a particularly unappealing case for the defense. Based on the facts alleged, throughout the period that the bribery scheme was in effect, the issuer went out of its way to tout its success in obtaining rapid FDA approvals in its SEC filings and press releases. Even after publicly disclosing the existence of a congressional investigation into FDA generic drug approvals and after disclosing that it was a target of the investigation, the issuer continued to affirmatively disclaim any knowledge of wrongdoing or any reason to think there would be a material impact on its business. *See id.* at 672–74, 675–77. Consider whether the result would have been different if the issuer's disclosures had been more subdued and temperate.

[47] For general discussion of the SEC's view of MD&A requirements, see Management's Discussion and Analysis of Financial Conditions and Results of Operations; Certain Investment Company Disclosures, Securities Act Release No. 6835, Fed. Sec. L. Rep. (CCH) ¶72,436 (May 18, 1989); *In re* Caterpillar, Inc., Exchange Act Release No. 30,532, Fed. Sec. L. Rep. (CCH) ¶73,830 (Mar. 31, 1992); Securities & Exchange Comm'n v. Sony Corp., Exchange Act Release No. 40,305, 1998 SEC LEXIS 1650 (Aug. 5, 1998). Note that in *Gallagher,* the court assumed the correctness of the plaintiffs' claim that Item 303 required disclosure of a letter to the issuer from the FDA threatening "severe consequences" for noncompliance with regulatory requirements and subsequent negotiating demands from the FDA, but held that the issuer did not have a duty to disclose the information at the specific time in question. *See* Gallagher v. Abbott Labs., 269 F.3d 806, 810 (7th Cir. 2001).

[48] Statement of the Commission Regarding Disclosure Obligations of Companies Affected by the Government's Defense Contract Procurement Inquiry and Related Issues, Securities Act Release No. 6791, 1988 SEC LEXIS 1580 (Aug. 3, 1988).

acknowledging that "the exact subjects and scope" of the investigation were "still unknown."[49] The SEC noted that the considerations suggested in the release

> equally apply to companies that are subject to the inquiry and to companies that, although not targeted in the investigation, otherwise may be materially affected by the investigation as a result of additional expenditures incurred or policies and practices altered in connection with defense contract procurement. For example, disclosure of a change in practice may be required where a company, through its consultants, agents or otherwise, has been engaged in questionable conduct and thereafter alters its policies for obtaining defense contracts, or if general industry procedures change as a result of issues highlighted by the inquiry.[50]

The Defense Contractors Release noted that Items 103, 401(f), and 303 were potentially implicated by the government's investigation, and went on to suggest that disclosure should be provided "when, *in light of the uncertainty regarding the government's inquiry,* reported financial information would not necessarily be indicative of the company's future operating results or financial condition"[51]—a somewhat unusual suggestion in light of the admitted lack of clarity as to the scope of the investigation, and one that would seem to carry the concept of known trends or uncertainties to its extreme. The release focused on the need to disclose "additional material information, beyond information specifically required to be disclosed, that is necessary to make the required statements not misleading,"[52] and indicated that issuers must consider the financial and business impact of various possible events, such as the likelihood that, as a result of illegal acts, their rights to receive payment under government contracts might be suspended, their government contracts might be terminated, they might have to alter business practices, or their competitive position might be harmed. The Defense Contractors Release is somewhat unique in suggesting that disclosure might be required not only if the issuer itself were under investigation, indicted, or convicted, but also if it were likely to be affected by the general industry impact of the investigation.

The Defense Contractors Release suggests a very expansive view of disclosure obligations, particularly as it construes the already broad MD&A requirements concerning disclosure of known trends, events, and uncertainties. Although, as described earlier, there is significant case law authority questioning and contradicting the notion that issuers must disclose uncharged criminal conduct involving

---

[49] *Id.*, 1988 SEC LEXIS 1580, at *1–2.
[50] *Id.* at *2–3.
[51] *Id.* at *6 (emphasis added).
[52] *Id.* at *7.

themselves and their officers and directors,[53] the Defense Contractors Release seems to indicate that an issuer might be required to disclose facts and potential facts that could have the effect of implicating it in criminal activity, even where the issuer has no notice that it (or any of its officers, directors or agents) is the specific subject or target of an investigation.

The approach suggested by the Defense Contractors Release takes on renewed force in light of recent pronouncements by the SEC's Division of Enforcement. The Division's Director has announced that the Division intends to pursue "investigations where, at the outset, it is not clear that a securities violation has occurred . . . to probe industries or practices about which [the Division has] concerns or suspicions, but no clear roadmap to wrongdoing."[54] This practice, known to the Division staff as "wildcatting," has already been reflected in a number of wide-ranging investigations, and it has been suggested that issuers in a targeted industry should consider the need to make public disclosure of industry-wide investigations, at least in some circumstances.[55] While issuers will want to be cautious about premature disclosures where it does not appear that they themselves are particular targets of an investigation, if it becomes publicly known that practices of a type engaged in by an issuer are the focus of such a general investigation, that issuer should consider whether the principles enunciated in the Defense Contractors Release might apply.

b. Quarterly Reports on Form 10-Q

In addition to the 10-K, the 1934 Act requires most issuers to file quarterly reports on Form 10-Q within 40 days after the end of each fiscal quarter (soon to be reduced to 30 days). The 10-Q is primarily a financial document, and the bulk of the typical 10-Q consists of comparative financial statements for the quarter then ended and the fiscal year to date. However, while there is no requirement for a detailed business description, Part I, Item 2 of Form 10-Q requires the issuer to include an MD&A section covering the interim periods and meeting the relevant requirements of Item 303, and Part II, Item 1 requires disclosure under Item 103 of legal proceedings in the quarter in which they first become reportable and in subsequent quarters in which there are material developments. Thus, the considerations discussed earlier with respect to Items 103 and 303 remain

---

[53] For additional discussion of director and officer liability generally, see Main Volume and Supplement Chapter 8 (Baumann & McDavid, Potential Liabilities for Directors and Officers of Health Care Organizations).

[54] *See* Speech by SEC Staff: *Remarks Before the District of Columbia Bar Ass'n* (Feb. 11, 2004), *available at* www.sec.gov/news/speech/spch021104smc.htm (remarks of Stephen M. Cutler, Director, Division of Enforcement).

[55] *See generally* Latham & Watkins Client Alert No. 380, " 'Wildcatting' for Fraud: A New Investigative Approach by SEC Enforcement?" (Apr. 12, 2004), *available at* www.lw.com/resource/Publications/_pdf/pub970_1.pdf.

relevant, as applicable in particular quarters, to the issuer's 10-Q disclosure obligations.[56]

c. *Current Reports on Form 8-K*

In general, the provisions of Form 8-K that require a report to be filed in a specific time frame would not pick up alleged criminal conduct, charged or uncharged, or regulatory violations. However, Item 8.01 (formerly Item 5) provides for discretionary disclosure of events that the issuer deems material, and an issuer that has determined that disclosure is appropriate or necessary may elect to file an Item 8.01 Form 8-K as a means of disseminating that information.[57] Current reports on Form 8-K are not subject to the specific requirements of Regulation S-K, but the disclosures, once made, would be subject to the same 10b-5 standards as those described earlier. In addition, an issuer may use an 8-K to satisfy its obligations under Regulation FD, as discussed later.[58]

2. *The 1933 Act*

While the 1934 Act regulates the disclosures that must be made by an issuer with a class of securities registered under the federal securities laws, the 1933 Act regulates the disclosures that must be made by an issuer seeking to sell securities in a registered public offering. Under the 1933 Act, an issuer seeking to offer securities to the public must file with the SEC a registration statement that must include a prospectus

---

[56] In Securities & Exchange Comm'n v. Fehn, 97 F.2d 1276 (9th Cir. 1996), the court upheld a permanent injunction obtained by the SEC against an outside securities lawyer for his role in aiding and abetting an issuer's 10b-5 violations in its 10-Qs. In that case, the issuer had committed various 1933 Act violations (as well as violations of state blue sky laws) in connection with its IPO and had failed, in its IPO registration statement, to disclose that the FDA had banned sales of its primary product. The issuer had also failed to file required 10-Qs. Fehn, the lawyer, advised the issuer that it must file the 10-Qs and disclose in them the adverse FDA action. He also advised the issuer that it was unnecessary to disclose in the 10-Qs the apparent 1933 Act violations. The issuer disclosed the FDA action in the 10-Qs but did not correct the other misstatements in its registration statement or disclose the potential civil liability associated with the 1933 Act and blue sky violations. Fehn assisted the issuer in preparing and filing the 10-Qs, although the extent of that assistance was disputed. *See id.* at 1279–81. In determining whether there was a primary violation of Section 10(b) and Rule 10b-5 that would support the aiding and abetting charge, the court held that disclosure of the potential exposure arising from the earlier violations of the securities laws was required in order to make the disclosures contained within the 10-Qs "not misleading," even where such disclosure was not expressly required by Form 10-Q. The court stated that, even though the potential liabilities faced by the issuer were "not inevitable, but . . . contingent, [disclosure was required because] they represented a potentially large financial loss to [the issuer]." *See id.* at 1289–91. The court, in particular, focused on the presence in the 10-Qs of misleading affirmative disclosure concerning the facts underlying the 1933 Act violations. *See id.* at 1290 n.12. *Cf.* Gallagher v. Abbott Labs., 269 F.3d 806, 809 (7th Cir. 2001) (10-Q only requires disclosure as to items specified therein; no duty to update 10-K disclosure in 10-Q unless a specific 10-Q item so requires).

[57] In addition, new Item 2.04 requires the disclosure of a "triggering event" that accelerates or increases a direct (or indirect) financial obligation of an issuer. *See* Final Rule: Additional Form 8-K Disclosure Requirements and Acceleration of Filing Date, Securities Act Release No. 33-8400 (Mar. 16, 2004), *available at* www.sec.gov/rules/final/33-8400.htm. If, for example, a government investigation or FCA suit were an event of default giving rise to acceleration of indebtedness under a credit facility, the issuer might be required to disclose the event under Item 2.04 whether or not the issuer had otherwise determined that it had a disclosure obligation.

[58] See *infra* Section II.A.3.

containing (or, where permitted, incorporating by reference from the issuer's 1934 Act filings) extensive information concerning the issuer's business and financial condition.

The disclosures described earlier under Items 101, 103, 303, and 401 of Regulation S-K must be included or incorporated by reference in a 1933 Act registration statement. In addition, Item 503(c) of Regulation S-K requires that a 1933 Act prospectus include a "Risk Factors" section that "[discusses] the most significant factors that make the offering speculative or risky," as specifically relevant to the particular issuer and offering.[59] Many health care issuers include general descriptions of the regulatory and enforcement environment in their risk factors. Where an issuer knows that it is the subject of an investigation, an FCA suit, or other enforcement action, the issuer must consider whether the potential impact of such an investigation or proceeding must, because of its materiality, be identified as a risk that investors in the offering should take into account.

Note that, although an issuer that treads carefully may avoid encountering a duty to disclose information until its next relevant 1934 Act report, even where that information is material and adverse, the circumstance is different when the issuer is engaged in a securities offering. It is a well-settled principle that "[a]n issuer has a duty to disclose material information prior to trading in its own securities."[60] Thus, an issuer engaged in a 1933 Act registration undertakes a heightened duty to evaluate the need for early disclosure of investigations and similar events.[61] It has been held that "[t]he failure of an offering document to disclose a company's violations of law provides a valid basis for asserting claims under the [1933] Act if the violations were material."[62] Where an issuer's knowledge of a pending investigation puts it on notice that it may have committed such violations, it

---

[59]Although risk factor disclosure, as such, is not required in a 10-K or in other 1934 Act filings, many issuers now include a "Risk Factors" section in their 10-K disclosure, and some even include such a section in their 10-Qs. This facilitates incorporation of risk factor information by reference in other documents and in disclosures seeking to take advantage of the safe harbor for forward-looking statements provided under the Private Securities Litigation Reform Act of 1995, 15 U.S.C. §77z-2.

[60]Meredith B. Cross, Denise Manning-Cabrol, & Deborah M. Wiggin, *Overview of Disclosure Obligations of Public Companies: Mandatory Disclosure, Voluntary Disclosure and Duties of Officers and Directors,* in THE ART OF COUNSELING DIRECTORS, OFFICERS & INSIDERS: HOW, WHEN & WHAT TO DISCLOSE 7, 16 (internal page 8) (Practising Law Institute 1998) (citing LOUIS LOSS & JOEL SELIGMAN, FUNDAMENTALS OF SECURITIES REGULATION 789–90 (1995)).

[61]Note also that corporate insiders proposing to trade for their own account in the issuer's securities also have a duty to disclose material information in their possession or abstain from trading. *See, e.g.,* Chiarella v. United States, 445 U.S. 222, 228–29 (1980). *See also* Securities & Exchange Comm'n v. Brenner, Civil Action No. 1:97-CV-0607-GET (N.D. Ga.), Litigation Release No. 15301, 1997 SEC LEXIS 626 (Mar. 19, 1997) (Medaphis general counsel advised her mother and a co-defendant that FBI had executed two search warrants on Medaphis offices before issuer's public announcement of the investigation; mother, co-defendant, and co-defendant's father and brother sold stock before announcement; general counsel forced to pay disgorgement and civil penalties and was permanently enjoined from further violations). In some situations, then, the trading desires of a corporate insider may conflict with the issuer's own perceived disclosure obligations, to the potential detriment of all concerned.

[62]*In re* MobileMedia Sec. Litig., 28 F. Supp. 2d 901, 932 (D.N.J. 1998).

may be alleged that the issuer has a responsibility to make appropriate disclosure in a 1933 Act registration statement.[63]

3. Informal Disclosures: Analysts, Investor Relations, the Press, and Regulation FD

Although the 1934 Act and the 1933 Act prescribe standards for formal, required disclosures in statutorily mandated contexts, issuers must be aware that in many ways the market's perception of them is shaped more, and more immediately, by informal, frequently unstructured disclosures: discussions with securities analysts who "follow" the issuer's securities for brokerage firms;[64] presentations at investor conferences; conference calls with investors and analysts; press releases and interviews; and the daily interaction between the issuer's investor relations personnel and securityholders, whether institutional money managers or "widow and orphan" retail investors.[65]

There are no substantive regulatory requirements as to what an issuer communicates through these avenues, as there are required disclosures in 1933 Act and 1934 Act forms, but an issuer is no less subject to liability under the antifraud provisions for false or misleading disclosures made through informal channels such as these.[66] Thus, if an issuer undertakes a duty to disclose information in such contexts—for example, by voluntarily choosing to comment on particular matters that it otherwise has no duty to talk about—the issuer will be deemed to have undertaken a duty to disclose such information as is necessary to make the voluntary disclosures not false or misleading.[67]

---

[63] *See id.* at 932–33. *See also* Greenfield v. Professional Care, Inc., 677 F. Supp. 110 (E.D.N.Y. 1987) (failure to disclose a pending criminal investigation in both 1934 Act filings and a 1933 Act registration statement; discussed *infra* text accompanying notes 88–91). *But see* United States v. Crop Growers Corp., 954 F. Supp. 335, 348 (D.D.C. 1997) (passage quoted *supra* text accompanying note 34). In addition, where an issuer has filed a registration statement relating to a current offering or distribution, the issuer has a duty to amend or supplement it to disclose material changes that have occurred since the original filing of the registration statement, so long as the registration statement remains "live." *See, e.g.,* Gallagher v. Abbott Labs., 269 F.3d 806, 810–11 (7th Cir. 2001).

[64] The term "analysts" can be used to refer both to "sell-side" analysts, who are employed by brokerage firms to provide research and analysis to customers of the brokerage, generally through reports that are widely available in the market, and to "buy-side" analysts, who work for money managers and institutional investors and who perform research solely for their employers or clients. Communications with buy-side analysts are, thus, equivalent to communications to specific securityholders, and not to the market in general. As used in this chapter, the term is intended to refer to sell-side analysts.

[65] For an overview of certain general considerations in these types of informal disclosures, see *Disclosure Obligations, supra* note 13, at 16–25.

[66] *See, e.g.,* Basic, Inc. v. Levinson, 485 U.S. 224, 227 n.4 (1988) (describing allegedly misleading statements in interview and press release); *In re* Par Pharm., Inc. Sec. Litig., 733 F. Supp. 668, 673 (S.D.N.Y. 1990) (describing press release with misleading information); Simon v. American Power Conversion Corp., 945 F. Supp. 416, 430 (D.R.I. 1996) (issuer could be responsible for misrepresentations in analyst reports if it provided false or misleading information to the analyst). In the municipal securities market, there may also be a blurry line dividing information that "speaks to the markets," which must conform to the requirements of Rule 10b-5, and "political speech," which is permitted to be less than candid. See *infra* Section II.B.

[67] *See, e.g., In re* Presstek, Inc., Exchange Act Release No. 39,472, 1997 SEC LEXIS 2645 (Dec. 22, 1997) (issuer found liable where it edited some projections in draft of analyst's report, but failed to correct other projections that were misleading).

This duty was made more complex and compelling on October 23, 2000, the effective date of the SEC's controversial Regulation FD,[68] which is designed to eliminate the practice of "selective disclosure." Regulation FD requires that, when an issuer or a person acting on behalf of an issuer selectively discloses any material, nonpublic information regarding the issuer or its securities to, essentially, any investment professional (a broker, an analyst, a money manager, a mutual fund or hedge fund, etc.) or to any securityholder of the issuer, in circumstances where it is reasonably foreseeable that the securityholder will purchase or sell the issuer's securities on the basis of the information, the issuer must simultaneously make public disclosure of that information (if the selective disclosure was intentional) or promptly make public disclosure of that information (if the selective disclosure was unintentional; "promptly" means within 24 hours or before the opening of the market on the next trading day, whichever is later).[69] Such public disclosure must be made through an 8-K filing[70] or through a broadly disseminated press release or similar method designed to get the information out broadly to the market as a whole.[71]

The Regulation FD Adopting Release identifies a number of specific types of information that could be considered material under Regulation FD.[72] Nothing in this illustrative, nonexclusive list specifically addresses government investigations or uncharged criminal conduct. However, it is clear that Regulation FD can pose particular challenges for the issuer and its investor relations personnel in that context. First, in an industry such as health care where such investigations are ever more common (and rumors of investigations even more so), it is likely that analysts and institutional investors may from time to time question the issuer about whether it is the subject of an investigation or *qui tam* suit, based on

---

[68] Final Rule: Selective Disclosure and Insider Trading, Securities Act Release No. 33-7881, 65 Fed. Reg. 51,716 (Aug. 24, 2000), *available at* http://www.sec.gov/rules/final/33-7881.htm [hereinafter FD Adopting Release].

[69] *See id.* §II.B.

[70] Regulation FD added a new Item 9 to Form 8-K (renumbered as Item 7.01 in 2004), pursuant to which an issuer may "furnish" information that it wishes to disclose in compliance with Regulation FD, but that information will not be deemed "filed" (and thus automatically incorporated by reference into those 1933 Act registration statements that require 8-Ks to be so incorporated and subject to liability under §11 of the 1933 Act and §18 of the 1934 Act). *See id.* §II.B.4.a.

[71] *See id.* §II.B.4.b. There has been much discussion and writing about Regulation FD, both before and after its adoption. For general overviews and commentary, see, e.g., John J. Huber & Thomas J. Kim, *The SEC's Regulation FD—Fair Disclosure,* in COUNSELING CLIENTS IN TURBULENT MARKETS & UNCERTAIN TIMES: DISCLOSURE & FINANCING ISSUES 113 (Practising Law Institute 2001) [hereinafter HUBER & KIM—REGULATION FD]; Karl A. Groskaufmanis & Daniel H. Anixt, *The Twilight Zone of Disclosure: A Perspective on the SEC's Selective Disclosure Rules,* in 1 33d ANNUAL INSTITUTE ON SECURITIES REGULATION 435 (Practising Law Institute 2001) (reprinted from INSIGHTS); *see also* NATIONAL INVESTOR RELATIONS INST., STANDARDS OF PRACTICE FOR INVESTOR RELATIONS, App. B (2d ed. Jan. 2001); NATIONAL INVESTOR RELATIONS INST., NIRI SYMPOSIUM: REGULATION FAIR DISCLOSURE (May 8, 2001), *available at* http://www.niri.org/attach/ Symposium2001.pdf; Letter From the Committee on Federal Regulation of Securities, Business Law Section, American Bar Association, to Jonathan G. Katz, Secretary, Securities & Exchange Comm'n, Selective Disclosure (May 8, 2000) (File No. S7-31-99), *available at* http://www.sec.gov/ rules/proposed/s73199/keller2.htm [hereinafter ABA FD COMMENT LETTER] (commenting on originally proposed form of Regulation FD).

[72] *See* FD Adopting Release at text accompanying n.47.

publicly disclosed investigations of similar issuers, issuer-specific rumors, or blind poking around based on the industry environment. Assuming that the issuer wishes to retain some discretion over how and when it makes such disclosures, it is critical that the issuer maintain a consistent policy over how it is going to answer such questions— whether that answer is something general and noncommittal, or simply "no comment." An issuer that, on nine occasions, says "We don't have any problems" and, on the tenth occasion, says "We can't comment on that" has probably effectively disclosed a problem.[73] This analysis holds true even in the absence of Regulation FD, but the new rule puts even more pressure on an issuer and its investor relations personnel to handle such issues with great care and consistency.

Further, although the practice may have been questionable in the pre-FD era, Regulation FD essentially eliminates the ability of an issuer to filter bad news out to the market through analysts before making a formal public disclosure. Under the conventions prevailing before Regulation FD, an issuer that communicated information simultaneously to all analysts who regularly followed its stock was ordinarily not regarded as engaging in selective disclosure, but was instead utilizing a means generally accepted as providing broad disclosure to the market, even if that means was not expressly sanctioned by the law.[74] Thus, an issuer who felt that it was necessary or desirable to disclose the existence of a government investigation, an actual or pending indictment, or a similar event might, before putting out a press release or filing an 8-K, disclose the matter to its analyst group in a way that allowed the issuer to put its desired spin on the matter before a sophisticated, industry-familiar audience. The issuer would, presumably, hope and expect that at least some of the analysts would interpret and report on the disclosure in a manner relatively favorable to the issuer, thus ameliorating some of the potential adverse market reaction.

Under Regulation FD, however, this type of practice is expressly proscribed. If the information to be communicated is material, the issuer must communicate it in a way that provides broad dissemination to the public. Further, if the issuer inadvertently communicates the information, as when an investor relations officer is caught off-guard by an unexpected question, the issuer must promptly correct that error through broad dissemination. The split-second nature of the materiality decisions that must be made in the world of Regulation FD puts

---

[73] *Cf.* Basic, Inc. v. Levinson, 485 U.S. 224, 239 n.17 (1988) ("It has been suggested that given current market practices, a 'no comment' statement [in response to questions about a possible merger] is tantamount to an admission that merger discussions are underway.... That may well hold true to the extent that issuers adopt a policy of truthfully denying merger rumors when no discussions are underway, and of issuing 'no comment' statements when they are in the midst of negotiations.").

[74] *See generally Disclosure Obligations, supra* note 13, at 19. Thus, issuers would commonly discuss material developments in conference calls that were open to all analysts following their stock, but were closed to the general public and the press. On the other hand, communications to one analyst (or a few favored analysts), without general simultaneous disclosure to all analysts following the issuer's stock, have always been regarded as troublesome.

a great premium on having a management and investor relations team that pays attention to every question and every answer and has a plan in place for dealing with questions about investigations and regulatory litigation at all times.

4. The Elusive Concept of "Materiality"

Although almost all disclosure requirements in the federal securities laws—including those under Regulation FD[75]—are predicated on the threshold standard that the information must be "material" in order for disclosure to be required, the concept of materiality is not defined in the 1933 or 1934 Act or the regulations thereunder. Instead, the concept has historically been developed and articulated through case law and through the evolution of accepted practices among securities professionals. However, recent interpretive guidance from the SEC adds new dimensions to materiality analysis.

a. Common Law and Lore

The seminal case in defining materiality is the U.S. Supreme Court's decision in *TSC Industries, Inc. v. Northway, Inc.,*[76] which held that, in the context of a proxy solicitation, "an omitted fact is material if there is a substantial likelihood that a reasonable shareholder would consider it important in deciding how to vote."[77] The *TSC Industries* Court went on to state that in order for an omitted fact to be material, "there must be a substantial likelihood that [its] disclosure . . . would have been viewed by the reasonable investor as having significantly altered the 'total mix' of information made available."[78] In *Basic, Inc. v. Levinson,*[79] the Supreme Court "expressly adopt[ed]" the standard of materiality in *TSC Industries* for application in the Section 10(b)/Rule 10b-5 context.[80] The *Basic* Court went on to state:

> Where the impact of [a] corporate development is certain and clear, the *TSC Industries* materiality definition admits straightforward application. Where, on the other hand, the event is contingent or speculative in nature, it is difficult to ascertain whether the "reasonable investor" would have considered the omitted information significant at the time.[81]

---

[75] Indeed, one of the concerns expressed by the securities bar and others when Regulation FD was proposed was that, if an issuer expressly disclosed information pursuant to Regulation FD, the issuer might be deemed to have conceded that such information was "material" and would thus be estopped from arguing that point. *See* ABA FD COMMENT LETTER, *supra* note 71, at 10. As finally adopted, Regulation FD provided that filing or furnishing information on Form 8-K would not, in and of itself, constitute an admission of materiality. *See* FD Adopting Release, *supra* text accompanying notes 68–72; Form 8-K, General Instruction B.6.

[76] 426 U.S. 438 (1976).

[77] *Id.* at 449.

[78] *Id.*

[79] 485 U.S. 224 (1988).

[80] *Id.* at 232. The SEC incorporated this standard in the definitional provisions of Rule 12b-2 under the 1934 Act and Rule 405 under the 1933 Act.

[81] *Basic,* 485 U.S. at 232.

The Disclosure Dilemma

In discussing the evaluation of materiality in the context of "contingent or speculative" developments, the Court quoted with approval an earlier Second Circuit decision: "Under such circumstances, materiality 'will depend at any given time upon a balancing of both the indicated probability that the event will occur and the anticipated magnitude of the event in light of the totality of the company activity.' "[82]

Numerous cases involving the disclosure of uncharged criminal conduct have considered the application of this standard in that context, with varying results. In *United States v. Matthews,*[83] the court implicitly concluded that the lack of a specific requirement in SEC proxy regulations to disclose such conduct amounted to a determination by the SEC that such disclosure was not material in that setting, at least in the context of a criminal prosecution for nondisclosure.[84] In contrast, in *Roeder v. Alpha Industries,*[85] the court "[did] not think it is necessarily true that information about bribery is not material until it becomes the subject of an indictment" and noted that "otherwise material information does not become any less material because someone may be indicted if it is discovered by the authorities."[86] In language that has some resonance in the health care arena, the *Roeder* court said:

> Illegal payments that are so small as to be relatively insignificant to the corporation's bottom line can still have vast economic implications. See *SEC v. Jos. Schlitz Brewing Co.,* 452 F. Supp. 824, 830 (E.D. Wis. 1978) (it may be material that brewery risked losing its license to sell beer by engaging in illegal practices). Even small illegal payments can seriously endanger a corporation's business, especially when it relies heavily on government contracts, because such activity can result in the corporation being barred from obtaining future government contracts or subcontracts. . . . Such a bar would be devastating to Alpha [the issuer]; it relied on defense-related contracts for sixty to sixty-five percent of its sales.[87]

In a case directly involving health care fraud, *Greenfield v. Professional Care, Inc.,*[88] the court articulated a distinction between "qualitative" information concerning alleged misconduct and information that directly related to the financial condition and results of the issuer. In that case, the issuer, two of its officers, and another employee had been indicted for various offenses relating to Medicaid fraud. The plaintiff brought a class action complaint, alleging that numerous 10-Ks and 10-Qs and a 1933 Act registration statement

---

[82]*Id.* at 238 (quoting Securities & Exchange Comm'n v. Texas Gulf Sulphur Co., 401 F.2d 833, 849 (2d Cir. 1968)).

[83]787 F.2d 38 (2d Cir. 1986) (discussed *supra* text accompanying notes 28–30).

[84]*Id.* at 46–49.

[85]814 F.2d 22 (1st Cir. 1987) (discussed *supra* text accompanying notes 35–38).

[86]*Id.* at 25.

[87]*Id.* at 26.

[88]677 F. Supp. 110 (E.D.N.Y. 1987).

filed by the issuer before the indictment were "materially misleading for failing to disclose that certain portions of [the issuer's] earnings reflected payments that were illegally obtained and subject to forfeiture," as well as for failing to disclose that the issuer had engaged in various practices that could (and eventually did) result in its being excluded from Medicaid participation. The plaintiff also alleged that some of the filings were misleading for failing to disclose a pending state investigation into the alleged fraud.[89]

In denying the defendants' motion to dismiss, the court distinguished *Matthews* and various cases discussed therein on the basis that they related to the question of whether disclosure of " 'qualitative' information relating to management ability and integrity" was required.[90] In contrast, the court stated that

> the [*Greenfield*] complaint alleges that defendants made misstatements and omissions that directly related to [the issuer's] earnings. Information going directly to the financial condition of the company falls squarely within the range of information for which there is a "substantial likelihood that a reasonable shareholder would consider . . . important in deciding [whether to invest]." Thus, unlike the purely "qualitative" information cases, the omitted information here is material, . . . and, if true, ought to have been disclosed in order to render [the issuer's] public statements concerning its financial condition not misleading.[91]

The court did not distinguish between the failure to disclose the alleged facts that, if true, would have made the issuer's financial information materially misleading and the failure to disclose the issuer's alleged knowledge of the pre-indictment investigation.

What is apparent from these and other precedents is that the question of materiality is highly fact- and context-specific[92] and, in the context of alleged disclosure violations relating to government investigations and uncharged criminal conduct, the courts appear to be greatly influenced by (1) whether the issue arises in the context of a charge of criminal securities fraud or in a private stockholder suit and (2) whether the underlying investigation resulted in indictments or convictions. Further, it is apparent that it is critical to the analysis to remember that the question of materiality is distinct from the question of whether there is, in the particular situation, a duty to disclose,

---

[89]*Id.* at 111–12.

[90]*Id.*

[91]*Id.* at 113 (quoting TSC Indus. v. Northway, Inc., 426 U.S. 438, 449 (1976)) (citations omitted).

[92]*See In re* MobileMedia Sec. Litig., 28 F. Supp. 2d 901, 932 (D.N.J. 1998) ("The issue of materiality is a mixed question of law and fact which ordinarily is decided by the trier of fact. . . . If the alleged misrepresentations and omissions, however, are so obviously unimportant to an investor that reasonable minds cannot differ on the question of materiality, the allegations are not actionable as a matter of law. . . . When assessing materiality, not only the statement or omission itself but, as well, the context in which it occurs must be considered.") (citations omitted).

and the defendant in such a case must strive to ensure that the court undertakes those inquiries as separate analyses.[93]

b. *SAB 99*

Although, as noted earlier, neither the 1933 nor the 1934 Act, nor the regulations thereunder, establish a definition of materiality, the SEC staff undertook to articulate a more specific analytical approach to materiality in the context of financial statements in Staff Accounting Bulletin (SAB) 99, released on August 12, 1999.[94] While this chapter does not attempt to address the accounting issues associated with contingencies relating to regulatory violations and investigations relating thereto, it is useful to look at some of the staff's analytical approach to materiality issues in the financial statement context.

In SAB 99, the staff cautioned issuers and their auditors about using numerical "rules of thumb" to conclude that an item is not material.[95] The staff stressed that the issuer and its auditor must take into account "*all* the relevant circumstances," including "[q]ualitative factors [that] may cause misstatements of quantitatively small amounts to be material."[96] Included in a list of qualitative factors to be considered in assessing the materiality of misstatements in financial information is "whether the misstatement involves concealment of an unlawful transaction."[97] SAB 99 also suggested that the issuer and its auditors should take into account any expectation of "a significant positive or negative market reaction" resulting from a "known misstatement."[98]

Although SAB 99 purports to relate only to materiality in the context of financial information, it has been suggested that its "qualita-

---

[93] *See* Basic, Inc. v. Levinson, 485 U.S. 224, 239 n.17 (1988) ("Silence, absent a duty to disclose, is not misleading under Rule 10b-5."). Note, however, that silence is easily distinguishable from false, incomplete, or otherwise misleading affirmative statements, which then give rise to an obligation to make disclosure sufficient to correct the statements or make them not misleading. See *infra* notes 191–97.

[94] SEC Staff Accounting Bulletin No. 99—Materiality (Aug. 12, 1999), *available at* http://www.sec.gov/interps/account/sab99.htm [hereinafter SAB 99]. For an extensive critical discussion of SAB 99 in the context of historical materiality analysis, see John J. Huber & Thomas J. Kim, *SAB 99: Materiality as We Know It or Brave New World for Securities Law*, in COUNSELING CLIENTS IN TURBULENT MARKETS & UNCERTAIN TIMES: DISCLOSURE & FINANCING ISSUES 213 (Practising Law Institute 2001) [hereinafter HUBER & KIM—SAB 99].

[95] In particular, the staff criticized "exclusive reliance" on a particular rule of thumb that "suggests that the misstatement or omission [in an issuer's financial statements] of an item that falls under a 5% threshold is not material in the absence of particularly egregious circumstances, such as self-dealing or misappropriation by senior management." *See* SAB 99, text accompanying n.2.

[96] SAB 99, text preceding n.13 (emphasis in original).

[97] *Id.*, text preceding n.15.

[98] *Id.*, text accompanying n.17. This suggestion is sharply criticized in HUBER & KIM—SAB 99, *supra* note 94, at 225–26 (internal pages 11–12) ("Following SAB 99 would mean that any potential impact, real or believed, has to be included in the materiality analysis, but the absence of any market impact does not alone provide a basis for a conclusion that the fact or event is not material."). *But see* Helwig v. Vencor, Inc., 251 F.3d 540, 563 (6th Cir. 2001) (en banc) ("Materiality is about marketplace effects, not just mathematics.").

tive factors" analysis may well be extended to other contexts.[99] Thus, the analytical framework of SAB 99 should, as a matter of prudence, be reviewed in considering the materiality of potential disclosures concerning regulatory violations and related investigations, particularly where (as in the *Greenfield* case), those violations may have a direct effect on reported financial information.

B. Tax-Exempt Issuers

Unlike corporate issuers, not-for-profit providers do not issue equity securities, and their debt securities are usually issued by special purpose units of government created to permit tax-exempt financing to be available for not-for-profit borrowers. As a result, such tax-exempt securities are exempt from registration under the 1933 Act[100] and from the periodic reporting requirements under the 1934 Act.[101] However, such exemptions do not apply to the antifraud provisions of Sections 12 and 17 of the 1933 Act or Section 10(b) of the 1934 Act and Rule 10b-5 thereunder.[102] This means that, although there is no regulatory scheme that dictates disclosure on a line-item basis for a tax-exempt issuer, the issuer must decide what to disclose and when to disclose it based on common sense and the antifraud provisions.

The general absence of a periodic disclosure regime provides the tax-exempt issuer with substantial luxury to determine the time and manner of disclosure, because there is no general obligation to disclose material events either in the corporate world or the not-for-profit world.[103] Silence is almost always an option, although certain circumstances may force disclosure. For example, a proposed primary offering of municipal securities generally requires thorough disclosure;[104] annual reports filed in response to an undertaking under Rule 15c2-12 under the 1934 Act[105] must contain annual financial statements, so that any information material to the financial position of the issuer is likely to be required to be disclosed; discovery of a misstatement that was erro-

---

[99]*See* HUBER & KIM—SAB 99, *supra* note 94, at 233–35 (internal pages 19–21) (predicting expansive application of SAB 99 and quoting news reports suggesting that SEC officials expect SAB 99 to influence the materiality analysis in nonfinancial statement contexts). *See also* THE BUSINESS ROUNDTABLE—SEC SAB 99 CONFERENCE CALL TRANSCRIPT (Oct. 13, 1999), at 2 (then-SEC General Counsel Harvey Goldschmid (who became an SEC commissioner in July 2002): "[SAB 99's] focus is on financial statements, but we understand that it has implications for other areas. Materiality is a unified concept. The basic law is controlled by the Supreme Court. What happens in one area will have implications in another.") and 4 ("Our focus in drafting the SAB was on financial statements. But [there are] clear implications through other areas. [There] have to be. We used the same words, we used the same concept."), *available at* http://www.brtable.org/document.cfm/344 (links to PDF file); HUBER & KIM—REGULATION FD, *supra* note 71, at 128 (internal page 14) (noting that the FD Adopting Release "approvingly references" SAB 99 and suggesting that the SEC "intends by Regulation FD to extend the scope of SAB 99's application beyond materiality in financial statements to all communications").

[100]*See* Securities Act of 1933 §3(a)(2), 15 U.S.C. §77c(a)(2).

[101]*See* Securities Exchange Act of 1934 §3(a)(12)(A)(ii), 15 U.S.C. §78c(a)(12)(A)(ii).

[102]See *supra* note 12 and accompanying text.

[103]*See* Basic, Inc. v. Levinson, 485 U.S. 224 n.17 (1988).

[104]See *supra* note 60 and accompanying text.

[105]17 C.F.R. §240.15c2-12.

neous when made in a document that remains "live" probably must be corrected; and voluntary statements by the issuer that are expected to reach the market must be accurate and complete, even if the statements are not compelled in the first instance.[106]

The considerations related to primary offering disclosure in the tax-exempt offering context are similar to those in the corporate context, although there is no registration statement and no specific list of items that must be disclosed. Instead, there is a general understanding of the types of information expected to be disclosed, including financial information, information about the issuer, a description of the securities, relevant risk factors, and so on. There has also long been an understanding that Rule 10b-5 applies to a primary offering of municipal securities by an issuer.[107] Accordingly, as in the corporate context, information that a reasonable investor would consider as altering the "total mix" of available information in assessing whether to purchase the offered securities must be disclosed.[108] In general, the analysis of what is material does not change substantially from the analysis of what is material for a corporate issuer.[109] A bond default or risk of nonpayment is not a prerequisite to an SEC enforcement proceeding, so the standards of materiality for municipal investors are likely to be similar to those applicable to corporate equity investors.[110]

Until July 1995, there was no requirement for a municipal issuer to provide any information to bondholders following the primary offering of the securities. Thus, fixed-rate securities could remain in the market for 30 years without any additional or updated information regarding the issuer being disclosed. In July 1995, however, amendments to Rule 15c2-12 under the 1934 Act became effective, and, with limited exceptions, broker-dealers were barred from entering into underwriting agreements with a municipal issuer unless they had determined that the issuer had entered into a binding agreement to provide, on an annual basis, statistical and financial information of the type provided in the bond offering document.[111] There was some initial uncertainty about the sanctions for supplying inaccurate or

---

[106] See *infra* notes 191–97 and accompanying text.

[107] *See, e.g.*, Securities & Exchange Comm'n v. Whatcom County Water Dist. #13, Case No. C77-103 (W.D. Wash.), Litigation Release No. 7912, 12 SEC Docket 417, 1977 WL 175582 (May 10, 1977) (final settled order); Securities & Exchange Comm'n v. San Antonio Mun. Util. Dist. No. 1, Civil Action No. H-77-1868 (S.D. Tex.), Litigation Release No. 8195, 13 SEC Docket 920, 1977 WL 173871 (Nov. 18, 1977) (final settled order); Municipal Securities Disclosure, Exchange Act Release No. 26,985, 1989 WL 281659 (July 10, 1989), at n.84.

[108] See *supra* notes 76–93 and accompanying text.

[109] *See* Statement of the Commission Regarding Disclosure Obligations of Municipal Securities Issuers and Others, Securities Act Release No. 7049, 1994 WL 73628 (Mar. 9, 1994) [hereinafter 1994 Interpretive Release], at nn. 46–59 and accompanying text.

[110] *See, e.g., In re* Maricopa County, Ariz., Sec. Act Release No. 7345 (Sept. 30, 1996), *available at* http://www.sec.gov/litigation/admin/337345.txt (alleging that municipal issuer violated antifraud provisions by providing misleading or erroneous information in offering documents concerning worsening financial condition and actual use of bond proceeds and by failing to revise or supplement offering documents).

[111] *See* Municipal Securities Disclosure, Exchange Act Release No. 34961, 1994 WL 640013 (Nov. 10, 1994).

misleading information in reports filed pursuant to undertakings under the rule, but that uncertainty was dispelled by the SEC enforcement proceedings brought against the City of Miami[112] and against certain individuals associated with the Allegheny Health, Education and Research Foundation.[113] It is now clear that, despite the "warm and fuzzy" noises coming from the staff of the SEC at the time the 1995 Rule 15c2-12 amendments were being considered ("Just file the material that you have always prepared for internal use"), filings under the rule must meet the same standards of accuracy and completeness that other filings that include full financial statements must meet.

The 1994 Interpretive Release made clear that, even in the absence of continuous reporting obligations under the 1934 Act, when an issuer

> releases information to the public that is reasonably expected to reach investors and the trading markets, those disclosures are subject to the antifraud provisions. The fact that they are not published for purposes of informing the securities markets does not alter the mandate that they not violate antifraud proscriptions. Those statements are a principal source of significant, current information about the issuer of the security, and thus reasonably can be expected to reach investors and the trading market.[114]

As a result, there is a need for tax-exempt issuers to carefully vet other public statements that may be misleading where they have determined not to disclose a threatened investigation.

C. Disclosure as a Matter of Prudence

The foregoing sections discuss some of the specific statutory and regulatory requirements for disclosure of government investigations and related litigation, as well as some of the judicial interpretations of those requirements. It should not be overlooked, however, that the question of whether, how, and when to disclose problems of this nature may be more than simply a question of what the law requires. For any number of reasons, an issuer may elect to disclose the existence of an investigation even when it has a defensible position that disclosure was not, or at least not yet, required.[115] An issuer may, for example, be pummeled by rumors in the market about the potential existence of an investigation and may wish to bring those rumors down to earth by dis-

---

[112]*In re* City of Miami, Fla., Cesar Odio and Manohar Surana, Initial Decision Release No. 185 (June 22, 2001), *available at* http://www.sec.gov/litigation/aljdec/id185bpm.htm.

[113]*In re* Albert Adamczak, C.P.A., Exchange Act Release No. 42743 ((May 2, 2000), *available at* http://www.sec.gov/litigation/admin/34-42743.htm. *See also* In the Matter of Allegheny Health, Education and Research Foundation, Exchange Act Release No. 42992, 72 SEC Docket 1978, 2000 WL 868604 (June 30, 2000).

[114]1994 Interpretive Release, *supra* note 109, text accompanying nn.88–90.

[115]For example, in *Ballan v. Wilfred American Educational Corp.,* 720 F. Supp. 241 (E.D.N.Y. 1989), the issuer disclosed the existence of investigations against the issuer and certain employees before any indictments issued, although the issuer apparently did not argue that no disclosure was necessary at that time. 720 F. Supp. at 244–45, 248.

closing the specific situation it faces. Likewise, an issuer may believe that its future plans (for example, a merger or a significant financing transaction) make disclosure inevitable and may wish to get the news out in the open before it is under time pressure to do so. The nature of the investigation itself and the associated likelihood of information leaks may make early disclosure seem the wisest course; if, for example, armed FBI agents (or postal inspectors, or what have you) stage a daylight raid on 10 of the issuer's facilities and seize all the computers, the issuer must recognize that there is a good chance that the story will get out, even if no misconduct has yet been charged.

Later portions of this chapter suggest some possible approaches to making these sorts of timing decisions on disclosure.[116] For present purposes, however, two critical points should be noted: (1) the question of when disclosure *is required* does not always answer the question of when disclosure *should be made,* and (2) regardless of whether disclosure is required or voluntary at the time it is made, an issuer that begins disclosure of an investigation or similar problem must be prepared to disclose all material facts necessary to make the disclosure not misleading.[117]

III. THE PROBLEM, RESTATED AND AMPLIFIED

After the foregoing overview of the general securities law issues surrounding the disclosure of government investigations, uncharged criminal conduct, and the like, it is probably appropriate to revisit the peculiar nature of the current regulatory and enforcement environment in the health care industry and to attempt to place it in context in light of the securities law principles described earlier.

A. The Nature of Health Care Investigations and Prosecutions in General

As alluded to in the introduction to this chapter, health care investigations, prosecutions, and civil and administrative proceedings have a somewhat unique nature, and one that may present particular problems in the disclosure context.

1. Complexity of the Regulatory Environment

Health care providers are, of course, subject to a plethora of complex laws and regulations arising under federal and state law, relating to facility licensure, clinician licensure, certification for participation in reimbursement programs, business arrangements among providers, sources of patient or business referrals, and so on. The scope and complexity of this regulatory structure, absent any other considerations,

---

[116] See *infra* Section IV.
[117] See *infra* notes 191–97 and accompanying text.

would make it difficult for providers to ensure that they are operating in compliance with all material laws and regulations affecting their business and that they do not have material exposure to enforcement actions for noncompliance. In addition, many health care statutes take years to be interpreted and clarified by regulation, during which time providers may have difficulty determining whether they are complying with vague and general statutory provisions.[118]

This situation is, moreover, exacerbated by the fact that the anti-kickback statute and the Stark law, among others, impose liability for business arrangements that, in settings not covered by those statutes, might be regarded as simply good business.[119] Further, liability under some of those statutes requires a (frequently subjective) determination of the intent of the parties, which means that a transaction that may be innocuous if undertaken with a pure heart may result in civil or criminal liability if, with the benefit of hindsight, it is determined to have an improper purpose.[120] Thus, it may be difficult in some circumstances to assess whether a particular set of facts may, at some point, give rise to material exposure or whether it will be possible to raise effective defenses to any claim of liability.

2. *The Wide Range of Remedial Statutes*

Under federal law alone, the enforcement agencies have available to them a multitude of potentially duplicative remedies for violations of health care laws. Some of these statutes, such as the anti-kickback statute, both substantively regulate conduct and provide penalties for violations, while others, such as the Civil Monetary Penalties law,[121] simply establish penalties and sanctions generally available for violations of other statutes. Some of them relate specifically to health care programs and claims, while others relate more broadly to fraud or misconduct in connection with government programs generally. Many of these statutes impose civil or criminal penalties on a "per claim" or "per item" basis, which, in the health care context, can lead to staggering numbers, because the government may assert that each bill, each line item on a bill, or each service encounter constitutes a separate claim

---

[118] For example, the original version of the Stark law was passed in 1989. It was amended and expanded in 1992. Proposed regulations under the initial version were promulgated in 1992, but were not issued in final form until 1995. Proposed regulations under the amended version were not issued until January 1998. Partial final regulations under the amended version were then issued in January 2001 (and amended in November 2001), and the remaining final regulations (which may modify parts of the first phase of the final regulations) have not, as of this writing, been published.

[119] In many businesses (for example, the legal profession), providing expensive gifts, lavish trips, and so forth to those persons who provide business is regarded as good marketing and "relationship building." In health care, it can mean 5 years in prison. *See generally* Daniel R. Roach & Cori MacDonneil, *The Compliance Conundrum*, 32 J. HEALTH L. 565, 577–78 (Fall 1999).

[120] *See, e.g.,* United States v. Greber, 760 F.2d 68 (3d Cir.), *cert. denied,* 474 U.S. 988 (1985) (business arrangement may violate the anti-kickback statute if even one purpose of the arrangement is to induce Medicare referrals).

[121] See the discussion in Main Volume Chapter 1, at Section II.D.

or item. Thus, a provider that makes the same error in 1,000 Medicare claims can be subject to 1,000 times the maximum civil penalty or criminal fine applicable under each relevant statute, in addition to being liable for actual damages (which may be doubled or trebled under some statutes). These civil penalties may, in many cases, exceed the available penalties under applicable criminal statutes and lack the procedural protections provided for defendants under criminal statutes. Further, many of these civil statutes provide for enforcement through administrative, rather than judicial, processes, meaning that the first time the provider is able to make a case before a truly independent judge is when the provider is seeking to overturn an administrative sanction that has already been imposed.[122]

In addition to the specific penalties provided for in these statutes, the government also has the hammer of exclusion to hold over a provider's head. Section 1128 of the Social Security Act[123] mandates that individuals convicted of program-related crimes, federal or state crimes relating to patient abuse or neglect, federal or state health care fraud felonies, or federal or state controlled substance–related felonies be excluded from participation in any federal health care program for not less than five years. The statute also gives permissive (i.e., discretionary) exclusion authority to the Secretary of Health and Human Services with respect to persons or entities who have taken (or failed to take) any of a laundry list of specified actions, including violating the anti-kickback statute and other "substantive behavior" statutes.[124] The statute also provides that state Medicaid agencies may impose their own exclusions, the length of which may exceed the federal exclusions.[125] Exclusion may be imposed in administrative proceedings, without the necessity of filing a lawsuit.[126]

3. The Overarching Impact of the False Claims Act[127]

Increasingly more significant than this veritable smorgasbord of available remedies is the role played by the civil FCA.[128] Originally adopted during the Civil War to combat profiteering by Union Army contractors, the FCA now imposes civil penalties ranging from $5,500

---

[122] It is beyond the scope of this chapter to enumerate and discuss the specifics of the remedial statutes, but they are extensively described in the sources listed *supra* note 1.

[123] 42 U.S.C. §1320a-7.

[124] See the discussion in Main Volume Chapter 1, at Section II.E.

[125] *See* 42 U.S.C. §1320a-7(d).

[126] Note that the practical effects of exclusion may exceed those specified in the statute. For example, many managed care agreements require that providers be participating or eligible providers under Medicare, and an exclusion may have the effect of foreclosing a provider from such private contracts as well as from federal reimbursement programs.

[127] Portions of this section are adapted from William W. Horton, *An Overview of Key Medicare Compliance Statutes, or Through the Looking Glass and What the Inspector General Found There,* in Medicare and Medicaid Fraud and Abuse Update in Alabama (Lorman Education Services 2001).

[128] See Chapter 3 (Salcido, The False Claims Act in Health Care Prosecutions), for additional detailed discussion of this topic.

to $11,000 per claim, plus treble damages, on persons or entities who knowingly present, or cause to be presented, to the federal government any false or fraudulent claim for payment. The statute defines "knowingly" to mean that the defendant acted with actual knowledge that information was false or in deliberate ignorance or reckless disregard of the truth or falsity of information, expressly disclaiming any necessity for proof of a specific intent to defraud. Although the government may directly initiate actions under the statute, the FCA also authorizes *qui tam* suits brought by private individuals in the name and on behalf of the government. As described earlier, such suits are initially filed under seal, and the government is given an opportunity to "intervene" and take over prosecution of the action. If the government declines to do so, the *qui tam* plaintiff—the relator—may proceed with the action, subject to certain rights of the government. A relator is entitled to receive 15 to 25 percent of the ultimate recovery (whether by judgment or settlement) if the government intervenes, or 25 to 30 percent if the government declines to intervene, plus reasonable attorneys' fees and expenses incurred.[129]

The FCA has become the vehicle of overwhelming choice for health care fraud investigations, for three major reasons:

- The "per claim" sanctions under the statute quickly aggregate to enormous levels with respect to ordinary health care billing practices, because the typical bill or claim consists of numerous individual items or services, and providers typically are engaged in rendering services or providing items to numerous patients for relatively small amounts (in contrast to, for example, defense contract fraud, which may involve a handful of large claims over a long period). These per-claim penalties, plus treble damages, are mandatory if the defendant litigates the case and loses at trial or on appeal.[130]

- These penalties are potentially hugely punitive, but by proceeding under the FCA the government can avoid the higher burden of proof and other restraints on prosecutors imposed in criminal actions.

- The *qui tam* provisions of the statute, in effect, deputize as bounty hunters disgruntled employees and ex-employees, disappointed business partners, unfaithful consultants, total strangers, and even the occasional "patriot" referred to by government prosecutors. *Qui tam* relators, even those who

---

[129] *See generally* Fox, Loepere, & Metro, *supra* note 1, at §7.8; PRACTICE GUIDE, *supra* note 1, at §24.12; Jack E. Meyer & Stephanie E. Anthony, REDUCING HEALTH CARE FRAUD: AN ASSESSMENT OF THE IMPACT OF THE FALSE CLAIMS ACT 26–31 (New Directions for Policy for Taxpayers Against Fraud, Sept. 2001).

[130] As to the effect of per-claim penalties, see, for example, United States v. Krizek, 111 F.3d 934 (D.C. Cir. 1997), in which the court characterized the $81 million in damages sought by the government on $245,392 in actual damages as "extraordinary" and "astronomical." *Id.* at 936, 940.

file flimsy and unsustainable complaints, both bring potential prosecutions to the government's attention and, by virtue of the sealing and intervention provisions of the statute, provide a basis for the government to begin unilateral discovery before the defendant is even served with the action.[131]

Further, because the statute does not describe in detail what makes a claim "false," both the government and the relators' bar have sought to use almost any violation of a substantive health care statute or standard of practice as a basis for alleging that a claim for payment is a false claim, even where there is no question that services were rendered or that they were medically necessary. Thus, alleged violations of the anti-kickback statute and the Stark law have been used to support allegations that claims resulting from associated patient referrals were false claims, without regard to whether the services were necessary, whether they were actually rendered, or whether the amounts billed for them were otherwise appropriate.[132] Other cases have sought to impose liability where the quality of services rendered allegedly fell so far below applicable standards as to render fraudulent the claims for payment with respect to those services.[133]

As of the fiscal year ended September 30, 2000, government recoveries in civil fraud cases since 1986, primarily arising under the FCA, totaled nearly $7 billion, with $2.85 billion of that coming from health care–related cases. Some $4 billion of that was generated from *qui tam* cases, with $2.3 billion of that coming from health care–related cases.[134] In fiscal year 2001, the government "won or negotiated more than $1.7 billion in judgments, settlements, and administrative proceedings in health care fraud cases and proceedings" and collected over $1.3 billion in health care fraud cases (including some amounts relating to previous years).[135] As these figures make clear, the government's focus on health care fraud continues to intensify, and the dollar amounts involved continue to grow. Much of that focus appears from the statistics to be directed at matters originally arising as *qui tam* cases under the FCA.

---

[131] *See* Jost & Davies, *supra* note 5, at 247–48.

[132] *See, e.g.,* United States *ex rel.* Thompson v. Columbia/HCA Healthcare Corp., 938 F. Supp. 399 (S.D. Tex. 1996), *aff'd in part, vacated in part and remanded in part,* 125 F.3d 899 (5th Cir. 1997), *on remand,* 20 F. Supp. 2d 1017 (S.D. Tex. 1998); United States *ex rel.* Pogue v. American Healthcorp, Inc., 914 F. Supp. 1507 (M.D. Tenn. 1996). *See also* John T. Boese & Beth C. McClain, *Why* Thompson *Is Wrong: Misuse of the False Claims Act to Enforce the Anti-Kickback Act,* 51 ALA. L. REV. 1 (1999). As to the Stark law in the FCA context, see Robert Salcido, *The Government Unleashes the Stark Law to Enforce the False Claims Act: The Implications of the Government's Theory for the Future of False Claims Act Enforcement,* 13 HEALTH LAW. 1 (Aug. 2001).

[133] For cases illustrating these and other theories, see Bucy, *supra* note 7, at 77–86; Fabrikant & Solomon, *supra* note 7, at 124–56. See also Chapter 3, at Section II.A.1.b.

[134] *See* Meyer & Anthony, *supra* note 129, at 32–35.

[135] U.S. DEP'T OF HEALTH & HUMAN SERVS. & U.S. DEP'T OF JUSTICE, HEALTH CARE FRAUD & ABUSE CONTROL PROGRAM ANNUAL REPORT FOR FY 2001, *available at* http://www.usdoj.gov/ dag/pubdoc/hipaa01fe19.htm (Apr. 2002) [hereinafter 2001 FRAUD CONTROL REPORT]. The figures cited are not limited to FCA recoveries, but include criminal fines, civil money penalties under other statutes, etc., as well.

4. *The Curious Nature of Prosecutorial Discretion in Health Care Cases*

Even before the substantial influx of new resources devoted to rooting out and punishing health care fraud that began in the late 1990s as a result of the Health Insurance Portability and Accountability Act of 1996 (HIPAA),[136] one commentator memorably summarized the peculiar environment created by the current health care enforcement scheme:

> The modern American medical center has the legal status of a speakeasy because lawless conduct is being ignored. Though illegal, conduct deemed harmless by enforcement authorities is being countenanced. Enforcement authorities refuse to provide legal safeguards because of their perception that such safeguards would insulate abusive as well as appropriate conduct. Prosecutorial discretion—trust us—has replaced the rule of law. Thus, innovative participants in the marketplace can follow the law and be condemned by the realities of the market, or they can participate in the health care speakeasy and hope for the best—a prospect made more risky by the potential availability of private-party (*qui tam*) actions under the [False Claims Act].[137]

Prosecutors in any field enjoy a certain level of discretion, of course. In general, government agencies, as do others with prosecutorial authority, have significant flexibility to determine whether or not to pursue potential violations of law based on their assessment of the seriousness of the offense, the presence or absence of any necessary level of scienter or criminal intent, the quality of the evidence that may be offered, and any countervailing public policy considerations, among other things.[138]

However, the enforcement scheme that has evolved with respect to federal health care offenses has arguably taken prosecutorial discretion to new heights (or depths, depending on one's perspective):

- First, as noted earlier, any given violation of federal health care laws likely involves potential remedies under numerous

---

[136]Pub. L. No. 104-191, 110 Stat. 1936. HIPAA, among many other things, provided voluminous multi-year appropriations for health care fraud enforcement initiatives, as well as creating a new federal criminal offense of "health care fraud" (§242 of HIPAA, now codified as 18 U.S.C. §1347).

[137]James F. Blumstein, The Fraud and Abuse Statute in an Evolving Health Care Marketplace: Life in the Health Care Speakeasy, 22 AM. J.L. & MED. 205, 224–25 (1996).

[138]Indeed, it may be argued that there is an evolving institutionalization of prosecutorial consideration of countervailing public policy considerations in the health care enforcement arena. Under 42 U.S.C. §1320a-7d(b), the Office of Inspector General (OIG) of the Department of Health and Human Services (HHS) must respond to written requests for advisory opinions interpreting the anti-kickback statute in connection with particular fact situations. The OIG has posted a list of recommended preliminary questions and supplementary information to be included in such requests at http://oig.hhs.gov/fraud/docs/advisoryopinions/prequestions.htm. Included in the suggested topics to be covered are various considerations relating to whether the arrangement in question may result in increased access to health care services, increased quality of services, increased patient freedom of choice among providers, increased competition among providers, increased services to medically underserved areas or populations, and decreased cost to federal health care programs. Although it is not apparent from the statute why these considerations should make an otherwise impermissible remuneration arrangement—indeed, one that violates a criminal prohibition—legal, the OIG has frequently looked at these and other factors in indicating that it would not prosecute an arrangement that, despite potentially violating the anti-kickback statute, was deemed by the OIG not to have a significant potential for program abuse.

statutes—ranging from civil money penalties to criminal fines, to program exclusion, to imprisonment—as well as the potential for double or treble damages.

* As also noted, many of the remedies may be obtained through administrative proceedings, without the necessity of filing a lawsuit in court.

* The civil penalties available for many violations exceed, in financial terms, the criminal penalties available, thus allowing the government to obtain punitive financial relief without dealing with the "beyond a reasonable doubt" standard of proof required for a criminal conviction.

* The threat of voluminous per-claim penalties, multiple damages, and program exclusion makes it an enormous gamble for a provider to risk going to trial even on questionable theories of prosecution.

As the government's emphasis on use of the FCA as the dominant vehicle for enforcing all manner of health care regulations has grown, there have been many allegations and much concern over the abuse of prosecutorial discretion and authority under the statute. In July 1998, the U.S. General Accounting Office (GAO) issued a report criticizing some prosecution practices under the statute and acknowledging legitimate concerns raised by providers, who, the GAO noted, were "surprised" by the "relatively recent" "widespread application [of the False Claims Act] to the health care field."[139] The July 1998 GAO report described in some detail the much-criticized "72-Hour Window Project," in which Department of Justice (DOJ) officials sent demand letters to over 3,000 hospitals, indicating that the government had determined that it was likely that the hospitals had filed false claims and that it would pursue lawsuits, fines, and even program exclusion if the hospitals did not promptly enter into a settlement for a specified amount—an approach undertaken even though the government would have ordinarily had the fiscal intermediary seek repayment of improperly billed amounts.[140] The GAO report also described the similarly criticized "Lab Unbundling Project," in which providers complained that the government's "overly aggressive" demand letters ignored conflicting guidance from intermediaries and were often unsupported by accurate data.[141] The GAO report stressed that it was important that DOJ officials test the data underlying FCA allegations before threatening action, and "give providers a realistic opportunity to review and analyze the data in

---

[139] U.S. GOVERNMENT ACCOUNTING OFFICE, MEDICARE—APPLICATION OF THE FALSE CLAIMS ACT TO HOSPITAL BILLING PRACTICES, GAO/HEHS-98-195 (July 1998), at 18 [hereinafter GAO JULY 1998 REPORT].

[140] See GAO JULY 1998 REPORT at 6–10. *See also* Roach & MacDonneil, *supra* note 119, at 570–72, 580–81.

[141] *See* GAO JULY 1998 REPORT, *supra* note 139, at 10–15. *See also* Roach & MacDonneil, *supra* note 119, at 574–75.

question before legal action against providers is either threatened or undertaken."[142]

Even before this report, some DOJ officials had apparently recognized the validity of some of the issues raised. In June 1998, Deputy Attorney General Eric Holder had advised all U.S. Attorneys and a range of other DOJ personnel on a series of steps that must be undertaken and factors that must be considered before proceeding with an FCA action, including giving providers "(i) an adequate opportunity to discuss the matter before a demand for settlement is made, and (ii) an adequate time to respond."[143] However, an August 1999 GAO report concluded that the DOJ's "process for assessing the U.S. Attorneys' Offices' compliance [with the June 1998 guidance] may be superficial."[144] This report described several circumstances in which U.S. Attorneys' offices had alleged FCA violations against hospitals based on insufficient, unverified, or incomplete data and had failed to share necessary data with the hospitals, all in violation of the June 1998 guidance. In one case, the allegations were made without evidence of false claims, but primarily on the basis that the subject hospitals were the largest Medicare billers in the state.[145] Other anecdotal reports abound of government attorneys pursuing heavy-handed threats against providers and failing to give providers information necessary to evaluate and defend the claims.[146]

Government attorneys, perhaps unsurprisingly, protest that they use the discretion and flexibility provided to them firmly but wisely.[147]

---

[142]*See* GAO July 1998 Report, *supra* note 139, at 18.

[143]Memorandum from Eric H. Holder, Jr., Deputy Attorney General, to All United States Attorneys, Guidance on the Use of the False Claims Act in Civil Health Care Matters (June 3, 1998), *available at* http://www.ffhsj.com/quitam/chcm.htm.

[144]U.S. Government Accounting Office, Medicare Fraud and Abuse—DOJ's Implementation of False Claims Act Guidance in National Initiatives Varies, GAO/HEHS-99-170 (Aug. 1999), at 4 [hereinafter GAO August 1999 Report].

[145]*See id.* at 11–13.

[146]For examples, *see generally* Roach & MacDonneil, *supra* note 119, *passim*. *See also* Siddiqi v. United States, 98 F.3d 1427, 1440 (2d Cir. 1996) (in non-FCA health care fraud case, court was "firmly convinced . . . that the conviction would not have occurred but for the government's shifting of theories that impaired both [the defense of the case and the court's consideration on the first appeal]"). In fairness, however, the GAO more recently concluded that the DOJ "seems to have made substantive progress in ensuring compliance with the False Claims Act guidance." U.S. Government Accounting Office, Medicare Fraud and Abuse—DOJ Has Improved Oversight of False Claims Act Guidance, GAO-01-506 (Mar. 2001), at 11. In its fifth and final required report on the DOJ's compliance with the FCA guidance, the GAO found that the "DOJ has instituted sufficient monitoring of U.S. Attorneys' Offices participating in the national initiatives and other civil health care fraud matters to help ensure that offices use the [False Claims Act] in a fair and even-handed manner." U.S. Government Accounting Office, Medicare Fraud and Abuse—DOJ Continues to Promote Compliance with False Claims Act Guidance, GAO-02-546 (Apr. 2002), at 13.

[147]*See generally, e.g.,* D. McCarty Thornton, *"Sentinel Effect" Shows Fraud Control Effort Works,* 32 J. Health Law. 493 (Fall 1999). *See also* GAO July 1998 Report, *supra* note 139, at 14 (DOJ officials and a U.S. Attorney in Texas "indicated [to the GAO] that the harsher aspects of the [lab unbundling] demand letters do not reflect the reality of the process. For example, they stated that hospitals in Texas have always been granted additional time to analyze their situation if they requested it, *and the threat of legal action if hospitals failed to respond within 14 days has never been carried out.*") (emphasis added). The quality of mercy, it appears, remains unstrained.

It would be wrong to suggest that government investigators or attorneys have improper motives in pursuing health care fraud, or to question that, in most cases, they proceed with professionalism and diligence. Even so, it seems indisputable that the growing use of the FCA—with its per-claim penalties and treble damages—to combat financial and nonfinancial health care fraud far beyond what most observers would have thought the statute contemplated, combined with the vast range of other remedies available to investigators and prosecutors, gives a significant advantage to the government and makes the evaluation of exposure difficult for the provider.

The provider who is notified of a government investigation or a *qui tam* suit must try to judge its potential liability and evaluate the prospects for a successful defense in light of the many statutes under which the government may elect to proceed, with their potentially voluminous penalties.[148] Further, the provider is seldom allowed to forget that the government may have available to it the option of proceeding under criminal statutes as well as pursuing civil and administrative remedies.[149] Oftentimes, the provider will not have a complete understanding of the theories under which the government is proceeding, and it may not be given access to the data on which the government is relying in determining the probable existence of a violation. In addition, where the seal of the FCA is in place, the government will likely seek to obtain, voluntarily or otherwise, extensive information from the provider while not being itself subject to discovery requests from the provider.[150] This further disadvantages the provider, which

---

[148] *See, e.g.*, Ohio Hosp. Ass'n v. Shalala, 978 F. Supp. 735 (N.D. Ohio 1997), *aff'd in part and rev'd in part,* 201 F.3d 418 (6th Cir. 1999). The district court noted the plaintiffs' argument that "even though they would not be found guilty under the False Claims Act, they cannot risk rejecting the [Secretary of Health and Human Services'] invitation to settle, because the damages available under the False Claims Act are so overwhelming," and stated that, despite the "heavy handed" actions of the Secretary, "the practical barriers of challenging the Secretary leave the hospitals with little choice and no bargaining room. . . ." 978 F. Supp. at 738, 742.

[149] *See, e.g., Ohio Hosp. Ass'n,* 201 F.3d at 421 ("Some of the hospitals were first apprised of the investigation [part of the Lab Unbundling Project mentioned earlier] when agents of the Federal Bureau of Investigation appeared on their premises, unannounced, and began interviewing hospital staffers. The FBI agents said that they were conducting an investigation that might lead to the imposition of civil or criminal sanctions, including imprisonment."). Anecdotally, it is common practice in some U.S. Attorneys' Offices for criminal prosecutors to sit in on meetings involving civil health care fraud claims, and it appears to be the routine practice for the government, in settling civil fraud litigation, to decline to expressly release claims under criminal statutes.

[150] *Cf.* United States *ex rel.* Costa v. Baker & Taylor, Inc., 955 F. Supp. 1188 (N.D. Cal. 1997). In ordering a non-health-care-related *qui tam* FCA case unsealed after 18 months, the court noted that "the government appears to be fully engaged in its discovery, without giving the defendants the opportunity even to answer the complaint," and further found that "[t]his practice of conducting one-sided discovery for months or years while the case is under seal was not contemplated by Congress and is not authorized by the statute." *Id.* at 1190, 1191. The *Costa* court also implicitly criticized the government's apparent use of the seal to exploit an information disequilibrium in settlement negotiations: "[The defendants] are apparently discussing the settlement of a case without knowing with certainty the allegations leveled against them. . . . [O]ne cannot help wondering whether the fact that the defendants must guess about the case filed against them is not the more significant settlement advantage [i.e., more significant than the benefit of keeping the charges confidential if the case is settled] currently enjoyed by the government." *Id.* at 1190–91.

may be forced to devote significant time and resources to responding to these information requests (or demands) without even being served with a complaint, much less having the opportunity to challenge its legal sufficiency.[151]

The provider's analysis and evaluation can be further complicated by the element of nonprosecutorial discretion vested in private relators under the FCA. As described earlier, the financial data indicate that a growing majority of health care fraud recoveries arise as a result of *qui tam* suits. The dissenting opinion in *Riley v. St. Luke's Episcopal Hospital*[152] eloquently describes the role of the *qui tam* relator:

> The decision to initiate the lawsuit is made by the relator, without input from the Executive [branch of the government]. The Executive has absolutely no control of the relator and therefore no way to ensure that he "takes care that the laws be faithfully executed." The relator does not have to follow [DOJ] policies, has no agency relationship with the government, has no fiduciary or other duties to it, and has no obligation whatsoever to pursue the best interests of the United States. Instead, the relator can negotiate a settlement in his own interest rather than in the public interest. While the government must be consulted in all such settlements, there is no guarantee that it will take an active interest in these cases or that the settlements reached by a relator and approved by the DOJ will be of the same sort that the government would reach on its own for the benefit of the public.
>
> Nor may the Executive [branch] freely dismiss a qui tam action. If the relator objects to the decision to dismiss, the government must notify him of the filing of the motion to dismiss, and the court must grant him a hearing before deciding whether to permit dismissal. Moreover, the Executive may not freely settle a qui tam action. If the relator objects to the government's attempt to settle, the government must obtain court approval, and the court may approve only after it holds a hearing and finds that the settlement is "fair, adequate, and reasonable under all the circumstances.

---

[151] A recent example of this is found in the investigation of Apria Healthcare Group, Inc. According to Apria, it began to receive subpoenas and document requests from various U.S. Attorneys' Offices and HHS that sought various documents relating to its billing practices. In January 2001, one U.S. Attorney's Office informed Apria that the investigation conducted by that office related to its determination whether to intervene in pending *qui tam* litigation. As of July 16, 2001, Apria reportedly had not been informed of the "identity of the court or courts where the proceedings are pending, the date or dates instituted, the identity of the [relator] plaintiffs or the factual bases alleged to underlie the proceedings"; however, it was advised by government representatives and relator's counsel that Apria's potential exposure, giving effect to per-claim penalties and treble damages, could (based on an extrapolation from a 300-patient sample to Apria's total billings under government programs) range from $4.8 billion to over $9 billion. *See* Apria Healthcare Group, Inc.'s Form S-3/A, Amendment No. 1 to Form S-3 Registration Statement (Registration No. 333-62556) (filed July 16, 2001), at 31–32; *see also* Press Release, Apria Healthcare Comments on SEC Filing (July 16, 2001), *available at* http://www.apria.com/about_apria/0,2746,77-80,00.html. The range of liability described, it should be noted, represented a multiple of several times Apria's then-current market capitalization, and an even larger multiple of its then-current stockholders' equity. As of Apria's Annual Report on Form 10-K for the fiscal year ended December 31, 2003, the matter remained unresolved.

[152] 252 F.3d 749 (5th Cir. 2001).

The Executive may not freely restrict the relator's position in the qui tam action. . . . Nor can the Executive control the breadth of the matter litigated by the relator. . . . Finally, the Executive has no power to remove the relator from the litigation under any circumstances."[153]

As is apparent from this description, even in a case where the government intervenes, a recalcitrant relator can potentially delay the resolution of a *qui tam* case and affect the amount required to settle it. Further, available data overwhelmingly suggest that the ultimate value of a case is greatly affected by the government's intervention decision. One study notes that, "while the government has intervened in only about 22 percent of *qui tam* cases to date, recoveries in these cases represent about 95 percent of the total recoveries [in *qui tam* cases from 1986 through September 2000]."[154] In addition to the analytical problems for the provider described earlier, this suggests yet another set of highly subjective judgments that the provider must make in evaluating exposure that arises through a *qui tam* case:

- How much is the case worth if the government intervenes?
- How likely is it that the relator will, because of particular knowledge or sheer persistence, be able to drive that amount up?
- How likely is it that the government will intervene, how likely is it that the relator will proceed if the government declines, and how much is the case worth if the relator must go it alone?

Obviously, the provider's opinion with regard to these matters, as well as the others discussed earlier, will not be a constant but will evolve as the investigation progresses, stalls, or shifts direction. Frequently, the provider will not know who the relator is until fairly far along in the process, and the provider may or may not be given the actual *qui tam* complaint to review as part of its early negotiations with the government.[155] Further, the provider's first sign that an investigation is going on may not put it on notice of a pending *qui tam* suit at all. Instead, the government's investigation may take the initial form of letters from DOJ or agency lawyers requesting particular information, the appearance of agency or intermediary auditors, a

---

[153]*Id.* at 761–63 (Smith, J., dissenting) (citations and footnotes omitted).

[154]Meyer & Anthony, *supra* note 129, at 36. The data include both health care and other FCA cases and include the apparently anomalous year of 1999, in which $149.5 million was recovered in *qui tam* cases in which intervention was declined. *See* TAXPAYERS AGAINST FRAUD, *QUI TAM* Statistics, *available at* http://www.taf.org/statistics.html; *see also Riley,* 252 F.3d at 767 n.37 (Smith, J., dissenting).

[155]The government may suggest that this is necessary to ensure that the relator is not the subject of retaliation, that key documents are not destroyed or altered, and the like, all of which may be true in particular cases. However, a review of unsealed *qui tam* complaints, particularly those in which the government has declined intervention, may suggest a further concern—that it is not desirable for the putative defendant to see how vulnerable the original complaint is to attack for failure to meet applicable pleading standards relating to knowledge, particularity, and so forth.

suspension of payments from the intermediary, or some other more indirect approach that may not give the provider any meaningful basis to assess the potential problem or its associated exposure.

B. Special Problems for Tax-Exempt Providers[156]

The November 1991 issuance of General Counsel Memorandum (GCM) 39,862[157] by the Internal Revenue Service (IRS), announcing that a provider's failure to comply with governmental health care program regulatory requirements—in that case, the anti-kickback statute—would be viewed as a basis for attacking the provider's tax-exempt status, marked the emergence of a new set of problems for tax-exempt providers. Now, the stakes for regulatory violations not only included potential civil and monetary penalties and exclusion from participation in governmental health care programs, but also the loss of tax-exempt status, potentially resulting in a whole cascade of additional horrors, including loss of tax-exempt status for interest paid on bonds issued to provide capital for the provider;[158] income tax liabilities; loss of tax deductions for donors; and, frequently, loss of state sales, income, franchise, and ad valorem tax exemptions that are commonly conditioned on or linked to federal tax exemption under Section 501(c)(3) of the Internal Revenue Code.

The analysis offered by the GCM was as follows:

> We believe that engaging in conduct or arrangements that violate the anti-kickback statute is inconsistent with continued exemption as a charitable hospital. No matter how economically rewarding, such activities cannot be viewed as furthering exempt purposes. . . . [A] section 501(c)(3) hospital is a charitable trust. All charitable trusts (and, by implication, all charitable organizations, regardless of their form) are subject to the requirement that their purposes or activities may not be illegal or contrary to public policy. See Restatement (Second) of Trusts, section 377, comment c. (1959) (a charitable trust cannot be created for a purpose which is illegal or contrary to public policy); IVA A. Scott, The Law of Trusts, section 377 (4th ed. 1989) (where a policy is articulated in a statute making certain conduct a criminal offense, a trust is illegal if its performance involves such criminal conduct or tends to encourage such conduct). . . .

---

[156] Although states enjoy immunity from FCA liability (*see* Vermont Agency of Natural Resources v. United States *ex rel.* Stevens, 529 U.S. 765 (2000)), cities and counties are subject to such liability. Cook County v. United States *ex rel.* Chandler, 538 U.S. 119 (2003). Nonprofit corporation providers are subject to the FCA.

[157] General Counsel Memorandum No. 39,862, 1991 WL 776308 (Nov. 22, 1991). The holding of GCM 39,862 was reaffirmed in Rev. Rul 97-21, 1997-1 C.B. 121.

[158] The stakes would be further raised and personalized by the proposed amendments to Circular 230, 68 Fed. Reg. 75,186 (2003) (to be codified at 31 C.F.R. pt. 10) (proposed Dec. 30, 2003), which would bring the issuance of opinions related to tax-exempt bonds within the scope of opinions subject to potential sanctions by the Office of Professional Responsibility in the Internal Revenue Service. One of the facts that counsel would undoubtedly be required to establish if the proposed amendments to Circular 230 became effective in their current form would be the tax-exempt status of the borrower. Failure to do so could result in the lawyer's disbarment from practice before the IRS.

In GCM 36153, I-4036 (Jan. 21, 1975) (considering Rev. Rul. 75-384), this Office stated that "As a matter of general trust law, one of the main sources of the law of charity, it may be said that planned activities that violate laws cannot be in furtherance of a charitable purpose.["] Of particular relevance to the issue at hand is the finding in Rev. Rul. 75-384 that the generation of illegal acts increases the burdens of government, which is directly inconsistent with charitable ends. If, in the instant cases, the net revenue stream purchase [associated with certain joint ventures between physicians and hospitals] results in illegal remunerations, the arrangements could increase the burdens of government by creating incentives for unnecessary utilization of hospital services at government expense. See also GCM 34631, I-4111 (Oct. 4, 1971) (stating that illegal acts that make up a substantial portion of an organization's activities will disqualify it from exemption and that violations of law are not in furtherance of exempt purposes even where, for example, illegally obtained funds are used to finance a charity.)[159]

The GCM indicated that the illegal activity must be "substantial" and, in noting that "the relative amount required to be considered substantial will vary according to the character and non-exempt quality of the activity," suggested that the following might indicate that the activity engaged in by the exempt hospitals was substantial:

> [T]he arrangements at issue were (1) likely authorized by the directors and most senior managers of the hospitals involved with knowledge of the risk that they might violate the anti-kickback law, (2) central to the activities through which the hospitals accomplish their exempt purposes, and (3) potentially harmful to the charitable class the hospitals were established to serve.[160]

The IRS will not generally get into an analysis of the health care law aspects of a particular arrangement, but any activity by the DOJ related to alleged false claims or violations of the anti-kickback statute has the potential to trigger an IRS audit, and if a settlement of liability for health care law violations is undertaken, a closing agreement—an agreement between a taxpayer and the IRS that resolves a tax dispute—is usually a prudent companion. Likewise, for the not-for-profit provider, any disclosure of potential perils associated with the investigation must take into account the potential loss of tax-exempt status, even though there are no known cases of loss of tax-exempt status for bonds issued to finance a hospital.[161]

Loss of exempt status may not have direct economic implications for the provider, because most not-for-profit hospitals have relatively small margins and would owe little if any income tax. The more severe problems arise in connection with the corollaries to loss of tax-exempt status: the hospital's tax-exempt bonds will be treated as

---

[159] GCM 39,862, at text accompanying nn.14–16 (footnotes omitted).

[160] *Id.* at n.16.

[161] Mark Scott, Director, Tax Exempt Bonds, Internal Revenue Service, personal communication (Jan. 28, 2002) (quoted with permission).

taxable industrial development bonds, and the hospital is likely to become subject to state taxes such as sales and ad valorem taxes that are imposed without regard to net income—all in all an ugly picture.

C. The Problem Summarized

As shown by the foregoing, the provider that must meet its obligations under the securities laws in the face of a government health care investigation, particularly one stemming from a sealed *qui tam* suit, is likely to feel that it is between a very large rock and a place that is not only quite hard, but rather thorny as well. The securities laws contemplate that an issuer must, in meeting whatever disclosure duties are applicable, make judgments about materiality. In any sort of litigation, particularly that involving government regulators, that judgment may have high stakes associated with it.

However, in the garden-variety circumstance, an issuer facing a litigation-related disclosure decision will have been served with a complaint (or, in more gloomy circumstances, an indictment) informing the issuer of the essential claims against it and providing at least an outline of the basis of such claims, and an issuer will have available to it a forum to challenge the sufficiency of such claims at an early stage. Further, ordinary litigation complaints are publicly available documents, and the issuer (1) will be aware that information about the complaint will be available to those interested enough to look for it or will be disclosed in the media if it is sufficiently sensational, and (2) will ordinarily not be subject to potential sanctions for discussing it.

In the health care setting, in contrast, the issuer may well not be aware that a complaint is pending for some time; may not see the contents of the complaint—much less be served with it—for even longer; may be subject to broad investigational and informational demands without specific explanation; and may be told that, notwithstanding the lack of service (and thus technical lack of jurisdiction over the issuer), a court has ordered that the issuer not disclose or discuss the action and may impose sanctions on the issuer for doing so.

Further, because the extensive remedial arsenal available to the government potentially involves financial penalties greatly in excess of actual overpayments or other damages, the issuer is hard-pressed to make a quantitative calculation of its likely potential exposure. Does it assess materiality based on what it can discern of the actual potential damages involved, or must it take into account the many and duplicative penalties that may be imposed on top of those damages? Going still further, where it appears that the case involves innovative and speculative theories of liability—for example, categorizing claims as "false" because they allegedly relate in some way to violations of "behavioral" statutes (such as the anti-kickback statute) or issues of quality, even where the claims relate to necessary services actually rendered—should the issuer assume the validity of those theories or discount them?

The issuer must consider whether the materiality standard is affected by the nature of the proceeding: whether it is civil, criminal, or administrative. Much of the securities case law involves disclosure of criminal proceedings. On the other hand, many health care cases present facts that may be pursued criminally, civilly, or at the administrative agency level, at the discretion of the prosecuting or investigating agency or department. Is a criminal proceeding necessarily more or less material than a civil or administrative proceeding? What about the situation where civil monetary sanctions actually exceed potential criminal fines?

Finally, what about the potential for "death penalty" sanctions, such as program exclusion or loss of exempt status? Does the existence of a statutory vehicle for such sanctions always make the underlying proceedings material, even where it appears unlikely that they would come into play?[162]

All of these considerations make the evaluation of disclosure issues in the health care environment potentially much more complicated than it is in other settings. How, then, can a health care issuer make a reasonable (and defensible) determination of what it can, should, or must do when faced with a *qui tam* suit or other nonpublic investigation?

IV. An Approach to Analyzing and Responding to Disclosure Issues in the Health Care Setting

When facing the question, "Should we make a public disclosure of this potential problem?" the default answer of the securities lawyer is normally, "Yes, and sooner rather than later." From a defensive perspective, there is always some merit to that position, if for no other

---

[162]For example, the threat of program exclusion is potentially implicated in any serious health care violation. However, it appears not to be commonly acted on in cases involving corporate entities (other than those that are effectively alter egos of individuals who themselves become excluded). *See, e.g.,* U.S. Dep't of Health & Human Servs., Office of Inspector Gen., Semiannual Report, October 1, 2000–March 31, 2001, at 20–21, *available at* http://oig.hhs.gov/reading/semiannual/2001/01ssemi.pdf (during the period in question, OIG imposed exclusions on 1,610 individuals and entities, but the five specific examples described involved only individuals, two of whom were apparently program beneficiaries rather than providers); U.S. Dep't of Health & Human Servs., Office of Inspector Gen., Semiannual Report to the Congress, April–September 2001, at 21–22, *available at* http://oig.hhs.gov/reading/semiannual/2001/01fsemi.pdf (2,146 exclusions during period; the five specific examples provided involved only individuals, and only two of those related to program fraud); U.S. Dep't of Health & Human Servs., Office of Inspector Gen., Semiannual Report to the Congress, October 2001–March 2002, at 15–16, *available at* http://oig.hhs.gov/reading/semiannual/2002/Spring%20SemiAnnual%202002.pdf (1,366 exclusions during period; only two specific examples given, both of which involved individuals). *But see* 2001 Fraud Control Report, *supra* note 135 (noting that "[e]xclusions in [federal fiscal year] 2001 were at a record high. A total of 3,756 individuals and entities were excluded from participation in Federal programs . . . [representing] a 12.1 percent increase from 3,350 exclusions in 2000."). In recent years, the government has entered into many seven-, eight- and nine-figure settlements with entities without excluding those entities. Although those cases are, of course, settlements and not judgments, so that lack of exclusion is part of the negotiation, (1) most large health care fraud cases do settle, (2) the likelihood of a settlement involving an exclusion of a large entity is, in most cases, remote, because there would be no incentive for the entity to settle, and thus (3) the likelihood of exclusion's actually being an issue is arguably remote as well, except as it affects the dollar value of the settlement.

reason than the fact that the sooner the issuer discloses a potentially adverse contingency, the sooner the issuer cuts off the potential class period for securities fraud claims. Indeed, despite the arguments suggested by the *Matthews* line of cases, many issuers may decide for various reasons to disclose the existence of an investigation well before it is clear, as a legal matter, that such disclosure is required.

However, such a course of action may not always be wise, or even particularly good disclosure practice, even where issues of the statutory seal under the FCA are not involved. In *TSC Industries*,[163] the Supreme Court noted that

> [s]ome information is of such dubious significance that insistence on its disclosure may accomplish more harm than good. The potential liability for a Rule 14a-9 [relating to proxy disclosures] violation can be great indeed, and if the standard of materiality is unnecessarily low, not only may the corporation and its management be subjected to liability for insignificant omissions or misstatements, but also management's fear of exposing itself to substantial liability may cause it simply to bury the shareholders in an avalanche of trivial information—a result that is hardly conducive to informed decisionmaking.[164]

Perhaps it is rare that information concerning a government investigation is fairly characterized as "trivial" for a health care issuer, but there is still reason to be concerned that premature, ill-informed disclosure of such an event is inconsistent with the issuer's duty to its stockholders or bondholders. Any disclosure of a government investigation, particularly one implicating the exorbitant penalties available in the health care context, is likely to cause the issuer's stock price to drop, perhaps precipitously, and may cause rating agency downgrades or other adverse events affecting the issuer's bondholders.[165] Where the issuer lacks sufficient information to adequately assess and disclose the materiality of its potential exposure, disclosing a worst-case scenario (or simply indicating that the results, although potentially awful, cannot be estimated) may not provide meaningful information—conducive to making informed investment decisions—to the market, and may work an extreme, and perhaps unjustified, disservice on those who hold the issuer's stock or bonds at the time the announcement is made.[166]

---

[163] TSC Indus. v. Northway, Inc., 426 U.S. 438 (1976).

[164] *Id.* at 448–49. This statement was quoted with approval by the Supreme Court in *Basic,* which, as already noted, extended the *TSC Industries* materiality standard beyond the proxy context to Section 10(b) and Rule 10b-5. *See* Basic, Inc. v. Levinson, 485 U.S. 224, 231 (1988).

[165] A rating agency downgrade will typically cause the yield demanded by bond purchasers in the secondary market to increase, thereby lowering the trading price of the bonds to the detriment of existing bondholders seeking to sell the bonds (as well as of bondholders such as insurance companies who are relying on the value of the bonds to meet statutory capital requirements, for example). Further, a downgrade may cause bondholders who are subject to limitations on the credit quality of bonds in their portfolios—for example, pension funds subject to "legal investment" limitations or mutual funds whose investment policies limit them to holding bonds with a particular minimum rating—to dump their holdings quickly into the market, thus further increasing the downward pressure on the secondary market price of the bonds in question.

[166] "Unjustified" in the sense that, if the matter were ultimately resolved without liability or with immaterial liability—a result that may be quite likely if, after investigation, the government declines to intervene in a *qui tam* suit, for example—the holders who sold their securities in the aftermath of the announcement may have incurred significant but unnecessary losses.

In the context of a sealed *qui tam* case, of course, the issuer's situation is rendered more complex, not only by its probable lack of specific information about the details and strength of the case against it, or even the particular claims asserted, but also by the asserted requirement that it not make any disclosure while the case remains under seal. It may be questioned whether a court has the power to enforce the seal over an issuer who has not been served with a complaint, but the practical reality of the situation is that an issuer who may one day have to appear before that court to defend against the claims will not lightly make disclosure in the face of the seal. In that situation, even if the issuer believes that prompt disclosure of the matter is required or prudent, the issuer will likely conclude that it must make some effort to get relief from the seal, delaying its disclosure until that effort is resolved.

Further, although it has frequently been noted that the fact that disclosure may cause various kinds of adverse results to the issuer does not obviate the duty to make such disclosure (if such duty exists in the particular circumstance),[167] an issuer must remain sensitive to the degree to which the timing and nature of the disclosure may compromise legitimate corporate interests. An issuer that has concluded that it has a duty to disclose information concerning an investigation or suit will not want to make that disclosure in such a way that its ability to defend the claim or negotiate a settlement limiting its exposure is jeopardized. That concern, perhaps, has even more immediacy in the context of a typical health care investigation, where the issuer may still lack crucial information concerning the facts and allegations of the case at the time it initially makes its disclosure.

With these considerations in mind, then, the following sections suggest an approach to analyzing disclosure duties and structuring disclosure in the health care investigation/*qui tam* litigation context, recognizing that there is no strategy that is either suitable for all situations or perfectly defensible in the cold eye of hindsight.

A. Determining When to Disclose

1. *What Does the Issuer Know About the Existence and Procedural Context of the Investigation or Proceeding (and How Did It Come By That Knowledge)?*

Other than plaintiffs' securities litigators, whose capacity to argue from hindsight is without peer, virtually no one would argue that an issuer has a duty to disclose mere suspicions that a government agency or department is conducting an investigation or considering initiating litigation (or intervening in *qui tam* litigation of which the issuer has

---

[167] *See, e.g.*, Roeder v. Alpha Indus., 814 F.2d 22, 25 (1st Cir. 1987) ("The securities laws do not operate under the assumption that material information need not be disclosed if management has reason to suppress it."); *In re* Par Pharm., Inc. Sec. Litig., 733 F. Supp. 668, 675 (S.D.N.Y. 1990) ("The illegality of corporate behavior is not a justification for withholding information that the corporation is otherwise obligated to disclose."); Ballan v. Wilfred Am. Educ. Corp., 720 F. Supp. 241, 249 (E.D.N.Y. 1989) ("The fact that a defendant's act may be a crime does not justify its concealment.").

not been notified).[168] Health care providers in today's environment are continually subject to requests for information, records reviews, and audits by agency and government contractor personnel. Sometimes these activities are routine, sometimes they relate to investigations of others doing business or having relationships with the provider (such as pharmaceutical or equipment vendors, physicians on the provider's medical staff, and so on), sometimes they relate to generalized investigations of industry practices,[169] and sometimes they relate to inquiries or investigations concerning the provider itself. At an early stage, it may not be easy to discern which of these situations—or even some other circumstance—obtains.[170]

Even if the provider believes that audit or review activities or unusual requests for information relate to an investigation of (or potential action against) itself, in most circumstances, disclosure at this stage would be unwise. In general, the provider is unlikely to have enough information to make such disclosure meaningful, and there are many things at this stage that could still derail or dissipate an investigation. Instead, the provider and its investors are probably best served if the provider reasonably cooperates with the (assumedly) investigatory activities and seeks to obtain further information about the specific matters at issue.

What if the provider receives a more pointed request for information (but not a demand letter, as in the 72-Hour Window Project) from, for example, an Office of Inspector General (OIG) or DOJ attorney (whether from Washington or from a local U.S. Attorney's Office)? This situation clearly requires more thought. Particularly if the request comes from the DOJ, there is a greater likelihood that a *qui tam* case is involved. However, at this stage the provider may still lack enough information to say with confidence what is at issue, much less what its materiality is. These sorts of requests may still relate to investigatory activities that are directed at persons other than the provider,[171] and they may not be focused specifically enough to allow the provider even to make a good guess at what the underlying questions are. For exam-

---

[168] *See, e.g., Ballan,* 720 F. Supp. at 248 ("[The issuer] was not obligated to disclose information of which it had no knowledge or about which it could only speculate. Indeed, it would be misleading for it to do so.") (citation omitted).

[169] In that context, however, a provider/issuer in an industry where such an industry-wide investigation has become public knowledge should evaluate its position in light of the SEC's rather sweeping pronouncements in the Defense Contractors Release and the more recent announcement of its "wildcatting" enforcement initiatives, both of which are discussed *supra* notes 48–55 and accompanying text.

[170] *See* Patric Hooper, *Challenges to Warrantless Searches in the Healthcare Industry,* 13 HEALTH LAW. 8, 11 (Oct. 2000) ("Seemingly, every Medicare and Medicaid reviewer, surveyor or inspector is in the fraud-busting business these days. Thus, when a [California] State Medi-Cal auditor knocks at the door of a provider, the provider cannot be certain whether the result of a 'search' will be an educational audit of the provider's billing practices, or will ultimately be the provider's imprisonment as a member of 'organized crime,' as defined by the State Legislature [under what is essentially a state criminal false claims statute relating to the California Medicaid program].").

[171] For example, the DOJ may be seeking information on industry practices in order to evaluate claims asserted in a *qui tam* suit against another provider.

ple, a simple, unexplained request for patient records may alert the provider that something is going on, but it will not provide much clarity as to what that something may be. In that context, it is difficult to determine what meaningful disclosure would be, much less whether there is a material issue that might require such disclosure. Similarly, the request may relate to a practice or policy that the provider feels comfortable complies with applicable laws and regulations, and the provider may be comfortable that its response will be adequate to defuse whatever the situation is. In that case, the provider may likewise be comfortable that it need not consider disclosure of the inquiry, because it may feel comfortable that its ultimate disposition will not be material.

The situation ratchets up still further if the provider receives a subpoena or civil investigative demand. The government may sometimes use such techniques, rather than voluntary requests for information, to obtain information from the provider with respect to third parties under investigation, but their use tends to suggest that it is more likely that the provider itself is a subject or a target. Although it is not uncommon for a provider/issuer to decide to make some disclosure when it receives such formal process, even a subpoena may not give the provider meaningful notice as to what is at issue or what its exposure might be. At this point, the provider may well decide that it is appropriate to defer disclosure until it takes other steps—negotiating a suspension of enforcement of the subpoena in exchange for more limited voluntary production of information, seeking to obtain more information from the issuing authority as to what its objectives and interests are, or initiating an internal investigation (if it has not already done so) to attempt to determine whether it has problems and the scope of its potential liability. The provider may also, of course, seek to challenge the validity of the subpoena, but that may entail actions that would involve a greater need for early disclosure. Where formal process is received, the provider will want to carefully analyze its particular disclosure situation, and may want to get guidance from independent outside counsel if it has not already done so.

In any of these situations, where the provider has not been notified of or directly threatened with litigation (or an administrative proceeding), the timing of potential disclosure may be significantly affected by external and practical considerations. If, for example, the provider's initial notice of an investigation comes by way of a dawn raid by federal agents on the provider's facilities or business offices, there is a good chance that this will be picked up by the media or other external observers. In such a case, the provider will almost indisputably need to make some sort of disclosure—probably by a press release with an accompanying 8-K filing—even where it has no clear idea of what it is suspected of or what the consequences may be. Less dramatically, if the provider has chosen to cooperate with a request for information or respond to a subpoena and carrying out that plan requires informing many nonmanagement employees, outside vendors, consultants, etc., of the investigation or inquiry, the provider may determine that it is advisable to make a public disclosure in order to avoid the risk of unmanageable leaks, potential insider trading, or similar problems. Thus, even in a "pre-threat" situation, the provider must take into account all relevant factors in determining whether disclosure is advisable, even when it is not necessarily required by law.

The provider's decision (as to both disclosure and timing) becomes more complicated when it is actually threatened with litigation by the government (as in the 72-Hour Window Project demand letter scenario), and perhaps most complicated when it is notified that the government is evaluating intervention in a *qui tam* case that remains under seal. As noted earlier,[172] it may be argued that neither of those things necessarily constitutes a proceeding "known to be contemplated by governmental authorities" required to be disclosed under Item 103 of Regulation S-K or a known event or uncertainty required to be discussed under Item 303, but to the extent those items are applicable (because the actual initiation of litigation or intervention in a *qui tam* case probably still requires certain approvals that may not have been obtained at the time the provider is notified), this argument becomes an increasingly fine one to make and defend. Further, if the matter is under seal, the provider has to determine how it will reconcile the obligation of confidentiality sought to be imposed on it by the seal with any obligation of disclosure that it may conclude the securities laws impose. The decision to disclose at this stage is still not automatic, especially where the seal is in place. However, when faced with a direct threat of this nature, the provider/issuer must probably rely primarily on its evaluation of the materiality of the potential action and its determination whether it has an affirmative duty to disclose information concerning it, rather than simply assuming that it will someday be able to rest on an argument that, at this stage, it had still not been "charged" with misconduct.[173]

2. *What Does the Issuer Know About the Materiality of the Investigation or Proceeding?*

At this point, the provider/issuer will want to review the information available to it to determine what it can, in good faith, conclude about the materiality of the investigation or action. Any unfriendly interest by the government in a provider's business dealings has the potential to be material, but that conclusion is not a foregone one, and

---

[172] See *supra* note 26 and accompanying text.

[173] The questions of materiality and duty, of course, are relevant at any of the earlier points in the process discussed in this section. However, at those earlier points, it will normally be much easier to take and defend the position that the situation is too speculative to require disclosure than it will be when the provider has an actual demand letter or notice of a pending *qui tam* suit in hand.

several factors may influence the position that the provider should ultimately take.

a. What Is the Nature of the Claims at Issue?

Because the scope of health care matters that are now addressed through the adversarial process (as opposed to being addressed through audits, reviews, and refunds, as was once the case) has grown so expansively, even cases superficially characterized as fraud encompass a wide range of scenarios, some of which are intuitively more likely to be seen as material. Where a provider is accused of violating the anti-kickback statute over a long period of time, potentially involving a substantial volume of services rendered as a result of referrals sought to be characterized as illegal, that may clearly be material. On the other hand, where the provider is alleged to have committed a violation in an isolated historical circumstance—improperly accounting for capital costs in a particular cost reporting period, for example—the materiality of that claim may be less clear. More colloquially, if the provider can resolve the claim simply by "paying the ticket" for a specific violation, as opposed to having to defend against a pattern and practice of violations (and, perhaps, substantially change its method of operations going forward), the provider may be able to reach a justified conclusion that the matter is not material, at least if the "ticket" is not too punitive.

More broadly, a case that involves classic fraud—kickbacks, billing for services not rendered, blatant upcoding, and the like—will most likely be viewed as material, even where the dollars involved are relatively small.[174] On the other hand, a case that involves alleged noncompliance with highly technical, frequently ambiguous requirements (such as, for example, the circumstances involved in the Lab Unbundling Project cases) may be less likely to be perceived at an early stage as material, even if the case seeks to describe such noncompliance as fraud.

Further, following the significant consolidation of the health care industry in the early to mid-1990s and the associated boomlet in divestitures beginning in the late 1990s, it has become increasingly common for the alleged violations at issue in a particular case to have occurred under the previous ownership and management of a predecessor or acquired entity, sometimes several transactions removed from the entity from which the government now seeks relief. Ignoring for a moment the potential financial exposure, an acquiror/issuer may determine that such a claim is not material because it is an inherited problem that is neither a reflection of the competence and integrity of

---

[174]*But see* Groskaufmanis, Morley, & Rivera, *supra* note 25, at 469–70 (internal pages 13–14) (suggesting that earlier SEC statements and dicta in *Roeder v. Alpha Indus.,* 814 F.2d 22 (1st Cir. 1987), and other cases involving the "qualitative materiality" concept "lack[] vitality today"). *Cf. Greenfield,* discussed *supra* notes 88–91 and accompanying text.

current management nor related to business practices engaged in by the acquiror today.[175]

b. *Does the Issuer Have Good Defenses (and Will That Be Apparent to the Government at an Early Stage)?*

Perhaps so obvious as to be overlooked, one factor in the materiality analysis is whether the issuer has a strong position that it has no liability. In some cases, the claims are just wrong—they involve an incorrect understanding of the facts, for example, or a failure to understand the applicable regulations and program policies. DOJ attorneys usually depend on information from agency or contractor personnel or on relators for their initial understanding of a case, and sometimes that information is erroneous or incomplete.[176] Where such a circumstance is apparent to the issuer, it may determine that the allegations in the case are not material.

That determination, of course, is dependent on the issuer's belief that it will be able to make the relevant facts and law known to the government early on and persuade the government of its error. The issuer may not itself have enough information to pursue that course of action at an early stage, depending on how clearly the claims have been articulated to it. Further, the issuer may not be able to persuade the government investigators or attorneys to listen to its arguments and explanations in a particularly prompt fashion. Where the issuer believes that it will prevail on the merits but may not be able to do so until the proceeding progresses well down the line, the issuer may not so readily conclude that the fact of the investigation or proceeding is not material. Similarly, if the issuer determines that it really does have a problem, this prong of the materiality analysis does not help it justify delaying or avoiding disclosure. However, the issuer should always consider whether it might, in fact, be innocent of wrongdoing and take that factor into account in determining if, when, and how to make disclosure.

c. *What Is the Potential Financial Exposure?*

Many factors may go into materiality analysis, but the bottom line, in both the literal and figurative senses, is normally the expected financial impact of an investigation, prosecution, or civil or administrative

---

[175] Somewhat paradoxically, however, early disclosure may be more attractive in this sort of situation. The acquiror may want to get the allegations out in the open quickly, to avoid any claim that it failed to meet its disclosure obligations, while making the argument that the problem is irrelevant to the market because it relates to acts or omissions by another entity at another time.

[176] One of the authors has personal knowledge of an investigation that was halted when the government attorney realized that the intermediary personnel who had concluded that a statutory violation had occurred had done so because they read the wrong column on a spreadsheet. *See also* GAO AUGUST 1999 REPORT, *supra* note 144, at 11–13 (outlining various circumstances where U.S. Attorneys' Offices had initiated Lab Unbundling Project investigations based on data later acknowledged to be flawed). It may not happen often, but it does happen.

proceeding on the provider/issuer. If the matter will be resolved with a one-time payment that is relatively insignificant to the issuer's financial position, the issuer's conclusion that the matter was not material will probably not be successfully challenged later. If that payment is large, or if it has an ongoing impact on the issuer's financial position and results (as, for example, where the issuer will have to substantially restructure its business operations or relationships or lose significant government program reimbursement), the matter is more likely to be material.[177]

The touchstone of this analysis, of course, is the probability/magnitude balancing test articulated in *Texas Gulf Sulphur*[178] and adopted by the Supreme Court in *Basic*.[179] However, that balancing test is particularly difficult in the health care setting. The "magnitude" factor is, at least at first blush, greatly enhanced by the punitive remedies available to the government under the FCA and other statutes applicable to health care providers, as described earlier. The "probability" factor is similarly enhanced, because, simply put, health care fraud cases settle; the risk involved in litigation is too great.[180]

In fact, however, the materiality calculus may not be this simplistic. Despite the ominous specter of treble damages, which may be raised early in FCA proceedings, the government still must establish that the provider knowingly submitted a false claim, and many proceedings settle for a simple refund of overpayments.[181] Further, while the huge numbers tossed around in FCA allegations relate in large part to the arithmetic impact of per-claim penalties,[182] it appears that per-claim penalties are of significance primarily in adding pres-

---

[177]*See, e.g.,* Roeder v. Alpha Indus., 814 F.2d 22, 26 (1st Cir. 1987) (passage quoted *supra* text accompanying note 87); Greenfield v. Professional Care, Inc., 677 F. Supp. 110, 113 (E.D.N.Y. 1987) (passage quoted *supra* text accompanying note 91).

[178]Securities & Exchange Comm'n v. Texas Gulf Sulphur Co., 401 F.2d 833 (2d Cir. 1968).

[179]Basic, Inc. v. Levinson, 485 U.S. 224 (1988). See *supra* text accompanying note 82.

[180]*See, e.g.,* American Health Lawyers Ass'n, Fraud and Abuse: Do Current Laws Protect the Public Interest? A Report on the 1999 Public Interest Colloquium Held January 29–30, 1999, Washington, D.C. 33–34 (1999) [hereinafter COLLOQUIUM REPORT] (colloquium participant noted that "[t]he current system [of enforcement through the FCA] almost forces the providers to settle . . . disputes rather than contest the government's demands" and stated that "the providers can't afford to defend themselves when the potential damages are that high").

[181]*See, e.g.,* GAO JULY 1998 REPORT, *supra* note 139, at 9 (of 3,000 hospitals that received demand letters in 72-Hour Window Project by April 1998, 2,400 had settled, of which 1,700 paid no damages but simply refunded overpayments); COLLOQUIUM REPORT, *supra* note 180, at 19 (government panelist stated that the average settlement in 72-Hour Window Project cases was $25,000 and noted that the average FCA case settled for "a very modest amount of money"). *See also* GAO AUGUST 1999 REPORT, *supra* note 144, at 13 (despite U.S. Attorney's Office allegations of false claims against three dozen hospitals in Lab Unbundling Project, office had subsequently concluded that one-fourth of the hospitals should not be pursued for FCA violations; in another U.S. Attorney's Office, over 40% of Lab Unbundling Project settlements involved only recovery of overpayments, despite GAO's conclusion that this office had stronger evidence than others it reviewed).

[182]*See, e.g.,* COLLOQUIUM REPORT, *supra* note 180, at 34 (example demonstrating that a provider who submits 2,000 claims for $50 each can be liable for $20 million in per-claim penalties, although its maximum exposure on treble damages would be only $300,000). Note that the $20 million would be $22 million under current law.

sure to settle and are not significant in the amount of settlements actually obtained.[183]

The conservative disclosure position, obviously, would be to take into account the maximum possible exposure in evaluating the magnitude component of the materiality calculation. However, the probability that the provider will be exposed to the maximum statutory liability will probably be quite small in most cases. Further, the issuer/provider may well be concerned that disclosing a maximum liability figure that, as a practical matter, may bear little relationship to the actual settlement value of the case may itself be misleading to investors, who may lack sufficient knowledge to evaluate what such an exorbitant number actually means. This may make the issuer's balancing test more of a balancing act, but the issuer may be justified, in the course of its materiality analysis, in at least attempting to estimate what its practically probable exposure is—in view of the nature of the claims at issue, the actual damages being asserted, its assessment of its own culpability, and the degree to which it is cooperating with the government—rather than simply considering statutory penalties that may not bear a meaningful relationship to the actual value of the case.

d. Is the Proceeding Civil or Criminal?

Whether a proceeding is civil or criminal in nature would seem to be very relevant in determining the materiality of that proceeding, especially in view of the mandatory program exclusion that accompanies a criminal health care fraud conviction. Intuitively, it would also seem that most observers would likely consider a criminal action to be almost by definition more serious than a civil or administrative proceeding.

However, this distinction may not have much practical significance in many health care cases. As previously described, the statutory enforcement scheme provides a variety of means by which the same alleged offense can be pursued under both criminal and civil statutes, and the financial penalties associated with liability under the civil statutes can be as punitive as, or even more punitive than, fines under the criminal statutes. Further, because the government's burden of proof in civil or administrative proceedings is less demanding than it is in criminal actions (and the procedural protections for defendants are likewise lower in civil or administrative proceedings), the government may well elect to proceed under a civil statute even where it could also

---

[183] *See, e.g.,* GAO July 1998 Report, *supra* note 139, at 10 (of 2,400 hospitals that had then settled 72-Hour Window Project cases, none had been assessed per-claim penalties). *See also* United States v. Krizek, 111 F.3d 934, 938–40 (D.C. Cir. 1997) (extensively analyzing government's position as to what constitutes a "claim" and remanding the case for recalculation of civil penalty from "astronomical" $81 million on actual damages of $245,392). At a recent health law seminar, a leading federal prosecutor, responding to an argument that the FCA needed to be amended to revise or eliminate per-claim penalties for health care claims, suggested that health care cases were never settled on the basis of per-claim penalties. Remarks of James G. Sheehan, 2001 Annual Meeting of the American Health Lawyers Ass'n (June 18–20, 2001) (author's notes of presentation).

pursue criminal charges.[184] It also seems intuitively likely that the government may believe that a provider would be more likely to feel that it had to litigate criminal charges, and would thus believe that both the likelihood of an early settlement and the value of a settlement would be increased in a civil proceeding. Thus, although the civil/criminal distinction should not be ignored in analyzing materiality, it seems unlikely to be determinative in most health care cases.

e. Is the Proceeding a Qui Tam *Suit at the Pre-Intervention Stage?*

Where, as increasingly seems the common case, the investigation relates to a *qui tam* suit in which the government is evaluating its position on intervention, the issuer has still further refinements to add to its materiality analysis. As discussed earlier, the government intervenes in a fairly small proportion of *qui tam* suits, and the ultimate judgment or settlement amount in a suit that the government declines is likely to be much lower than it would have been had the government intervened.[185]

Of course, in many cases where the government has declined intervention, the provider may have no notice of the case until it is unsealed and served, if it is served at all. In cases where the provider does have such notice, however, it may be able to form a judgment about the likelihood of intervention that will help it more appropriately estimate its potential exposure. If the government appears to be aggressively pursuing the investigation—scheduling meetings with the provider, submitting extensive information requests, seeking employee interviews, and so forth—the provider may be well advised to assume that the government is likely to intervene and to evaluate the case accordingly. On the other hand, if the government's inquiries are perfunctory, or if the provider is able to articulate its defenses early on and the government seems responsive to them, the provider may feel that it has a basis to discount the value of the case for materiality purposes.

In any event, the provider may believe that it cannot reasonably evaluate materiality if it has not been given the actual complaint or at least been given the specifics of the claims against it, a common situation at an early stage in a *qui tam*–related investigation. Thus, even without regard to the FCA seal, the provider may determine that it can, in good faith, defer disclosure until it has enough information to make such disclosure in an intelligent and informed manner.[186] The

---

[184] *See, e.g.,* Salcido, *supra* note 132, at 5–6 (suggesting that the government was moving toward a strategy of pursuing FCA cases based on alleged violations of the Stark law, even where the anti-kickback statute would also apply, because the anti-kickback statute is a criminal statute).

[185] See *supra* note 154 and accompanying text.

[186] In *Basic,* the Supreme Court noted that "[w]here . . . [a corporate] event is contingent or speculative in nature, it is difficult to ascertain whether the 'reasonable investor' would have considered the omitted information significant at the time." Basic, Inc. v. Levinson, 485 U.S. 224, 232 (1988). At least at the early stage of the intervention decision, there is an argument to be made that the nature of the action and its potential consequences are contingent and speculative. *See also In re* Par Pharm., Inc. Sec. Litig., 733 F. Supp. 668, 678 (S.D.N.Y. 1990) (issuer "not obligated to speculate as to the myriad of consequences, ranging from minor setbacks to complete ruin, that might have befallen [it]" if bribery scheme were discovered).

seal, of course, adds more difficulty to the issue, a difficulty that is discussed later.[187]

f. Is the Issuer Pursuing a Settlement Strategy or Litigating Aggressively?

As it evaluates its position with regard to an investigation or *qui tam* suit, a provider/issuer must determine whether it intends to seek an expeditious settlement of the matter or to pursue a strategy of noncooperation, vigorous defense, and, possibly, counterattack. While the choice of strategy may not seem to have an impact on the materiality of the matter, it does seem to present at least two relevant considerations.

First, to the extent the issuer is relying on an attempt to quantify "real" financial exposure, as discussed earlier, a strategy that is aimed at an effort to respond cooperatively and settle the case may lower that exposure. As noted earlier, a settlement is unlikely to involve per-claim penalties and may involve lower (or no) damage multipliers, depending on the facts of the case and the degree to which the provider is able to successfully argue its defenses in the settlement negotiations. Further, if the case is a criminal matter, the federal sentencing guidelines provide for lower multipliers in a case where the defendant cooperates with the government and acknowledges culpability at an early stage.[188] If the provider intends to withhold cooperation and aggressively fight the matter until close to trial (or even until trial), it runs a greater risk of increased exposure.

Moreover, although not directly related to the concept of materiality, a provider that does not cooperate with the investigation and is not disposed to engage in meaningful early settlement talks is more likely to reach a procedural posture where nondisclosure is impracticable. If the provider is going to fight, it will eventually have to do so in some judicial or administrative forum, in which the allegations are likely to emerge publicly. At that point, the provider will be subject to retrospective attack for not disclosing the matter at an earlier date. Thus, unless a provider is deeply convinced that it can both fight and win, its decision to pursue an aggressive, confrontational strategy may suggest that it should look for an opportunity to make early disclosure of the allegations.

g. What Is the Likely Market Reaction?

SAB 99[189] includes the issuer's perception of the likely market reaction to a disclosure (in the financial statement context) as one of the factors that may indicate materiality. If, as some predict, SAB 99 principles are expanded beyond the financial statement context, the

---

[187] See *infra* Section IV.B.1.

[188] *See* U.S. Sentencing Comm'n, Guidelines Manual (Nov. 2002) §§3E1.1, 8C2.5(g), *available at* www.ussc.gov/2002guid/2002guid.pdf; see also proposed Amendments to the Sentencing Guidelines, Policy Statements, and Official Commentary (May 1, 2004), *available at* www.ussc.gov/2004guid/2004cong.pdf.

[189] SEC Staff Accounting Bulletin No. 99—Materiality (Aug. 12, 1999), *available at* http://www.sec.gov/interps/account/sab99.htm (discussed *supra* Section II.A.4.b.).

issuer will need to take that into account in nonfinancial disclosures as well.

This is not a particularly helpful standard, however. In today's information-addicted market, where analysts' estimates and stock prices chase each other downward like lemmings on any adverse news, quantitatively predicting the market's reaction to a disclosure can be a highly speculative exercise. Further, the nature of the current health care enforcement environment means that news of an investigation or *qui tam* suit, in and of itself, may be a relative nonevent if the issuer is in a position to disclose enough information about it to satisfy the market that its outcome will not be disastrous. Although it is an unfortunate commentary in various ways, news that a health care provider is *not* under some sort of investigation has developed a "man bites dog" sort of newsworthiness; news that it *is* under investigation now borders on the routine.

The standard is also unlikely to help in the context of a nonprofit organization: Given the linkage between program violations and tax-exempt status, the threat to tax-exempt status of a nonprofit organization's bond debt has to be factored into the analysis, and the tax-exempt market takes no prisoners when the subject of tax exemption comes up. The bonds immediately become "illiquid," and the "bid and ask" spread widens dramatically.

Thus, the "market reaction" analysis is, in reality, probably just a distillation of factors of the type described in the preceding paragraphs. If an issuer believes that those factors can be incorporated into a disclosure, if and when one is made, in such a way as to persuade others that the information was not material (or at least was not susceptible of a materiality determination) at any earlier date, the issuer can probably also reach a defensible conclusion that the anticipated market reaction at such earlier date would not have indicated materiality.

3. Does the Issuer Have a Duty of Disclosure?

It is, as noted previously, important to remember that even where information is material, there can be no liability for failure to disclose the information unless there is a duty to disclose it. An issuer may defer disclosure until such a duty arises even if the information is quite material indeed. Thus, in determining the timing of a disclosure, the issuer should first consider the circumstances that may require disclosure to be made in the particular circumstance (bearing in mind always that the issuer always—subject to the FCA seal, if applicable—retains the option to disclose information at an earlier time than is required if the issuer determines that to be a prudent or advantageous course of action).

a. Is There a Specific Requirement of Disclosure Under the 1933 Act or the 1934 Act?

The requirements for disclosure under various 1933 and 1934 Act forms are discussed at considerable length earlier[190] and are not

---

[190] See *supra* Sections II.A.1.–2.

usefully rehashed at this point. Again, the fundamental question is whether applicable Items of Regulation S-K require disclosure in the 1933 Act registration statement or 1934 Act report at issue, and that question is essentially resolved by the materiality determination made by the issuer under the analysis outlined in the preceding subsections.[191]

b. Is Disclosure Necessary to Ensure That Other Statements by the Issuer Are Not Misleading?

Absent a specific duty to disclose information, the issuer may simply remain silent, no matter how material the information in question may be.[192] However, if the issuer undertakes to speak on an issue, it must provide enough information to cause the statements made not to be misleading in any material respect.[193] Thus, where an issuer that is the subject of an investigation or a *qui tam* suit makes affirmative statements concerning things relevant to the subject matter, the issuer may well be found to have undertaken a duty to disclose the existence of the investigation or the action, or at least to disclose the risk that it may have committed illegal acts.[194] It is even possible that such a duty

---

[191] Note, however, that the concept of required disclosures under the 1934 Act may well broaden in the near future. Partially as a response to the wave of corporate scandals beginning with the collapse of Enron in late 2001 and partially, one assumes, as part of former SEC Chairman Harvey Pitt's oft-stated interest in moving to a "current disclosure" regime from the existing periodic disclosure regime, in June 2002 the SEC proposed regulations that would add numerous new required disclosures to Form 8-K and substantially accelerate the required time for filing. *See Proposed Rule: Additional Form 8-K Disclosure Requirements and Acceleration of Filing Date,* Securities Act Release No. 33-8106, 67 Fed. Reg. 42,914 (June 25, 2002), *available at* www.sec.gov/rules/proposed/33-8106.htm. Some of these proposals were adopted in modified form in 2004. *See Final Rule: Additional Form 8-K Disclosure Requirements and Acceleration of Filing Date,* Securities Act Release No. 33-8400 (Mar. 16, 2004), *available at* www.sec.gov/rules/final/33-8400.htm. Although none of the new items proposed or thus far adopted would directly require disclosure of a governmental investigation or suit, the proposal indicates the increased focus on more timely and expansive disclosure outside of the regularly scheduled periodic reports. In addition, Section 409 of the Sarbanes-Oxley Act of 2002, Pub. L. 107-204, 116 Stat. 745, amends Section 13 of the 1934 Act to require issuers to disclose "on a rapid and current basis such additional information concerning material changes in the financial condition or operations of the issuer . . . as the [SEC] determines, by rule, is necessary or useful for the protection of investors and in the public interest." Although the impact of Section 409 is subject to rulemaking thereunder by the SEC (some of which is reflected in the 2004 8-K revisions), this new statutory provision may signal a trend toward a more generalized duty of disclosure than the one that exists under current law. *See* Michael W. Peregrine, William W. Horton, & John Libby, *The New "Corporate Responsibility" Law: How It Affects Health Care,* 11 HEALTH L. REP. (BNA) 1231, at 1236–37 (Aug. 22, 2002).

[192] *See* Basic, Inc. v. Levinson, 485 U.S. 224, 239 n.17 (1988) (quoted *supra* note 93).

[193] *See, e.g., In re* Par Pharm., Inc. Sec. Litig., 733 F. Supp. 668, 675 (S.D. N.Y. 1990) ("Under [Rule 10b-5], even though no duty to make a statement on a particular matter has arisen, once corporate officers undertake to make statements, they are obligated to speak truthfully and to make such additional disclosures as are necessary to avoid rendering the statements made misleading [citing Securities & Exchange Comm'n v. Texas Gulf Sulphur Co., 401 F.2d 833, 860–62 (2d Cir. 1968)]."); *In re* Cirrus Logic Sec. Litig., 946 F. Supp. 1446, 1467 (N.D. Cal. 1996) ("If a company chooses to speak to the market on a subject, . . . it is obligated to make a full and fair disclosure to ensure that its statements are not materially misleading."); Helwig v. Vencor, Inc., 251 F.3d 540, 561 (6th Cir. 2001) ("With regard to future events, uncertain figures, and other so-called soft information, a company may choose silence or speech elaborated by the factual basis as then known—but it may not choose half-truths.").

[194] *See, e.g., Par Pharmaceutical,* 733 F. Supp. at 675–78 (describing numerous affirmative statements by issuer suggesting that its success in obtaining FDA approvals was due to its special expertise and finding jury question as to whether such statements were misleading because they did not disclose bribery scheme); Ballan v. Wilfred Am. Educ. Corp., 720 F. Supp. 241, 249–50 (E.D.N.Y. 1989) (where issuer "issued reports suggesting that its prosperity would

may be found where the person speaking on behalf of the issuer was not aware of the underlying facts.[195] Thus, in evaluating the duty to disclose, an issuer should take into account earlier affirmative statements concerning its compliance with laws, projections concerning its future financial performance, and so forth. It is not necessary for an issuer "to direct conclusory accusations at itself or to characterize its behavior in a pejorative manner," even if it is aware of alleged violations of law.[196] However, where the possibility of such violations is brought to its attention by an investigation, the issuer must be cautious about affirmative statements that would be made false or misleading if such violations were borne out by the investigation.

It should be noted that a real danger in this area arises if the issuer engages in reviewing and commenting on analysts' reports before their release. That practice has, presumably, diminished somewhat after Regulation FD, but it remains commonplace, and many issuers, particularly smaller ones seeking to obtain and retain analyst coverage, feel that they must engage in some level of review. The practice poses many perils for issuers, and a full description of those perils is beyond the scope of this chapter.[197] However, where an issuer goes beyond correcting inaccurate historical information in draft analysts' reports and comments on those analysts' projections, the issuer's ability to keep silent on matters known to it that may affect those projections—such as the impact of pending government investigations that may affect the issuer's future financial position—can be compromised.[198]

c. What About Rumors?

Given the pattern of health care enforcement activity in recent years, it is common for health care issuers to be the subject of rumors

---

continue . . . [it] was then obliged to reveal any 'facts' suggesting otherwise so as to make the matters disclosed not materially misleading"); *In re* MobileMedia Sec. Litig., 28 F. Supp. 2d 901, 932–33 (D.N.J. 1998) (where prospectus contained "affirmative representations which falsely assured investors [that issuer] was in compliance with applicable law . . . [t]he fact that [issuer] could face serious legal consequences as a result of . . . alleged violations is information a reasonable investor would find important," and thus failure to disclose violations could be a basis for liability). *Cf.* Roeder v. Alpha Indus., 814 F.2d 22, 26–28 (1st Cir. 1987) (upholding dismissal of securities fraud claim where complaint did not allege existence of misleading reports or statements, even though issuer did not disclose material information concerning alleged violations of law); Gallagher v. Abbott Labs., 269 F.3d 806, 810–11 (7th Cir. 2001) (upholding dismissal where plaintiffs could not successfully identify any statements that were untrue or materially misleading when made, even though defendant subsequently settled claim of regulatory violations for $100 million fine).

[195]*See, e.g., In re* Carnation Co., Exchange Act Release No. 22,214, 33 SEC Docket 1025 (July 8, 1985) (Rule 10b-5 violation where corporate spokesman erroneously represented that no merger negotiations were under way, even though spokesman was personally unaware of such negotiations).

[196]*Ballan,* 720 F. Supp. at 249.

[197]A pre-FD overview of some of those dangers may be found at *Disclosure Obligations, supra* note 13, at 20–24.

[198]*See* Elkind v. Liggett & Myers, Inc., 635 F.2d 156, 163–64 (2d Cir. 1980) ("A company which undertakes to correct errors in reports presented to it for review may find itself forced to choose between raising no objection to a statement which, because it is contradicted by internal information, may be misleading and making that statement public at a time when corporate interest would best be served by confidentiality.").

concerning pending investigations, and this presents a delicate situation for an issuer. Unless the rumors are somehow attributable to the issuer, an issuer "has no duty to correct or verify rumors in the marketplace."[199] Thus, an issuer that maintains a strict policy against commenting on rumors can, absent some independent duty of disclosure, stand mute in the face of rumors, including those relating to investigations and enforcement activity. However, an issuer that chooses to speak must provide disclosure that is complete and accurate.[200] Further, an issuer that has—intentionally or unintentionally—made a materially inaccurate statement has a duty to correct such statement for so long as the earlier statement remains "live"—i.e., for so long as it is reasonable for investors to rely on it.[201] Thus, if the issuer goes down a path of commenting on rumors, the issuer must be prepared to make full, nonmisleading disclosure, and an issuer that has adopted a practice of denying unfounded rumors of investigations may, when the rumors arise in the face of actual, known investigations, find that it has undertaken a duty of disclosure that it might not otherwise have.[202]

B. Determining How and What to Disclose

1. How Does the Issuer Deal With a False Claims Act Seal?

Where the problem at hand is an issuer's perceived obligation to disclose a matter that is the subject of a *qui tam* suit that remains under seal, the question the issuer must confront is how to reconcile the disclosure obligation with the obligations of the seal.[203] One option, of course, is to conclude that the securities laws trump the FCA and simply disclose the existence of the suit, notwithstanding the seal. While this may be a defensible position, it is unlikely to be the way to win friends and influence judges in the *qui tam* case.

A more palatable alternative may be to file a motion in the *qui tam* suit to unseal the case. Although this involves delay in making the disclosure, it would seem to demonstrate good faith on the issuer's part, and such delay may not cause harm if the issuer is careful not to make statements or take actions that would arguably require affirmative disclosure while the motion is pending. However, the government may oppose such a motion if it believes that lifting the seal would impair its ability to investigate and prosecute the action, and it is possible that the relator may oppose it as well if the relator is, as relators usually

---

[199] State Teachers Retirement Bd. v. Fluor Corp., 654 F.2d 843, 850 (2d Cir. 1981).

[200] *See, e.g.,* Roeder v. Alpha Indus., 814 F.2d 22, 26 (1st Cir. 1987).

[201] *See* Quinn & Jarmel, *supra* note 13, at 18–19 (internal pages 6–7); Cross, Manning-Cabrol, & Wiggin, *supra* note 60, at 16–17 (internal pages 8–9).

[202] *See* Basic, Inc. v. Levinson, 485 U.S. 224, 239 n.17 (1988) (quoted *supra* note 73).

[203] Note that there is precedent approving, in some contexts, an issuer's failure to make disclosure at a particular time because of a legal or contractual requirement of confidentiality. *See, e.g., Fluor Corp.,* 654 F.2d at 850 (lack of disclosure represented "a good faith effort to comply with the [contractual] publicity embargo"). However, that line of reasoning presumably only applies where the issuer is not making other statements that are misleading in the absence of the omitted disclosure. *See id.* at 853.

are, averse to having his or her identity made public.[204] If this course of action is pursued, it will almost certainly be desirable to give the government advance notice of the motion, in the hope of reaching a negotiated resolution of any conflicts before the court rules on the motion.

Still another alternative is to disclose key facts underlying the investigation, and perhaps even the issuer's belief that an investigation is pending, without disclosing the existence of the specific *qui tam* suit. This is certainly consistent with the many cases discussed in this chapter that hold that, while an issuer may not be required to disclose the fact of a government investigation, the issuer may be required to disclose facts relating to its potential violations of law that are the subject of the investigation. However, making that sort of disclosure meaningful is, to say the least, challenging.

Something along the lines of "We believe that our [contracts with physicians/cost reporting practices/coding practices] comply with applicable law, but we could be wrong, which could expose us to all manner of problems" is good, traditionally defensive securities lawyer language, but will undoubtedly be attacked as vague and inadequate by plaintiffs' lawyers if there is an adverse market impact when and if the case actually becomes public. "Our [contracts with physicians/cost reporting practices/coding practices] violate numerous federal regulations" falls within the category of self-accusatory disclosures characterized as " 'silly' and 'unworkable' " by the court in *Ballan,*[205] at least until such violations have been charged and proved. "We understand that our [contracts with physicians/cost reporting practices/coding practices] are under investigation for possible violations of law, and we expect to vigorously defend against such allegations" requires some context if it is to be meaningful disclosure (for example, what is the potential financial impact of the allegations? What is the scope of the claims?), and providing such context may arguably violate the seal, compromise the ability to defend the claims, or both.

In practice, where there has been no public disclosure of a suit or investigation, most issuers will probably rely on a general description of key regulatory factors applicable to their business, a description of the range of penalties available for violation of those factors, and an identification, where appropriate, of business practices that may involve particular exposure in light of those factors (reliance on joint ventures, for example), at least until they have concluded that they have enough information to make an informed materiality judgment and provide meaningful specifics to investors. Where an issuer has determined that the time is ripe to disclose a specific matter, but it is unable or unwilling to have the case unsealed, the issuer is probably well advised to disclose

---

[204] This latter problem could presumably be mitigated by a partial unsealing of the case, in which the relator's identity remains confidential.

[205] Ballan v. Wilfred Am. Educ. Corp., 720 F. Supp. 241, 249 (E.D.N.Y. 1989) (quoting Amalgamated Clothing & Textile Workers v. J. P. Stevens & Co., 475 F. Supp. 328, 332 (S.D.N.Y. 1979), *vacated as moot,* 638 F.2d 7 (2d Cir. 1980)).

the existence of the investigation and as much as possible about the nature of the claims and exposure, while disclosing as little as practicable about the specifics of the sealed action itself.

2. By What Means Should the Issuer Make Disclosure?

Under Regulation FD, an issuer that determines to disclose material information must do so in a way reasonably calculated to lead to broad public dissemination of the information. If the issuer is a reporting company and circumstances do not require the disclosure of a suit or investigation to be made earlier than the next Form 10-K filing, 10-K disclosure provides an opportunity to put the information in the context of the issuer's total business. From a practical standpoint, while there is no dispute that 10-K disclosure constitutes broad public dissemination, the reality of the matter is that it may take awhile for the information to be picked up by the market (particularly if, like most issuers, the issuer is a calendar-year reporting company and thus files its 10-K at the same time as the rest of the issuer world is also filing 10-Ks). This may give the issuer an opportunity (*after* the information is publicly available in the 10-K) to focus its analysts' attention on the information in a way that helps ensure that the issuer's side of the story is fully understood (always being careful not to provide material information that is not included in the 10-K disclosure, however).

Frequently, however, the luxury of waiting for the 10-K may not be available to the issuer. Where events dictate that disclosure must be made sooner rather than later (including, of course, the circumstance where the issuer has determined that it need not disclose the information until the case is unsealed, which time has now come), the issuer will need to resort to more immediate means of disclosure. This will typically take the form of a press release, which will frequently be accompanied by a simultaneous 8-K filing with the same information.[206] Where an issuer's press releases are not reliably picked up by the national press and wire services, as is frequently the case with small issuers, the issuer must probably file an 8-K to ensure that its obligations under Regulation FD are satisfied.[207]

If the event precipitating disclosure is an offering of securities by the issuer, the issuer will need to make disclosure in its 1933 Act prospectus, either in the text itself or by incorporation by reference from an 8-K or other 1934 Act report. Where the issuer makes disclosure in full in the prospectus, it is probably prudent for it also to put out a press release (or file an 8-K) in order to avoid any risk of a contention that a disclosure in a 1933 Act form (which will presumably be most actively

---

[206] Note that stock exchange and NASDAQ rules typically require that disclosure be made by press release, and after the adoption of Regulation FD, the New York Stock Exchange stated its position that disclosure by other means contemplated by Regulation FD, including the filing of an 8-K, did not satisfy the Exchange's requirements. *See* Quinn & Jarmel, *supra* note 13, at 49–50 (internal pages 37–38).

[207] *See* FD Adopting Release, *supra* note 68, at text accompanying nn.73–74.

perused by prospective purchasers in the offering) does not provide appropriately broad dissemination to the general market.

It has become increasingly common practice for corporate issuers to hold conference calls with analysts to discuss and provide additional flavor on material corporate developments shortly after they are announced through a press release or other public disclosure.[208] Conference calls can provide an issuer with the opportunity to amplify points made in its press release, ensure a uniform response to questions (as opposed to having many spokespersons answering many individual phone calls), and otherwise put a more expansive spin on its disclosure. However, where the disclosure in question relates to a government investigation or suit, an issuer is probably wiser to put as much detail as it believes appropriate in its press release or 8-K and eschew the temptation to have a conference call. The risk that management personnel will convey information that may compromise the defense of the case or employ a tone that will be unhelpful for subsequent settlement discussions in a conference call is just too great. If the issuer does elect to have a call, it should under all circumstances assume that the government's representatives will be on the call, and the issuer's management personnel who are on the call should conduct themselves accordingly.

As usual, the tax-exempt municipal issuer is forced to rely on common sense, tradition, and analogy to the corporate disclosure regime in determining how to proceed with disclosure.[209] Because Regulation FD is based on powers of the SEC under Section 15 of the 1934 Act, the regulation does not apply to municipal issuers, who are exempt from those provisions. Likewise, municipal issuers are not required to file Forms 10-K, 10-Q, and 8-K. As a result, there is no regulation (other than the omnipresent Rule 10b-5) that guides the decision to disclose, the content of the disclosure, or the method of dissemination for municipal issuers. Even so, there are some obvious points for such issuers to bear in mind. First, anything said should be accurate and should not be misleading through the omission of other information. Information that is reasonably expected to reach investors and trading markets is subject to the antifraud provisions, and the antifraud provisions are equally applicable to disclosures in the secondary market for municipal securities.[210]

Second, because the absence of equity trading makes analyst coverage unlikely for not-for-profit issuers, dissemination of information may be a real challenge. Use of the nationally recognized municipal securities information repositories mandated by Rule 15c2-12 for filing

---

[208] Since the adoption of Regulation FD, these conference calls are overwhelmingly open to the public, via publication of a call-in number or, more commonly, via "Webcast."

[209] For a more complete discussion of these issues, see National Ass'n of Bond Lawyers, Providing Information to the Secondary Market Regarding Municipal Securities (Sept. 20, 2000), *available at* http://www.nabl.org/library/comments/pdf/secmktmunisec.pdf.

[210] *See* 1994 Interpretive Release, *supra* note 109, at text accompanying nn.85–90.

of annual reports and information concerning 11 specified "material events" is not likely to produce sufficient dispersion of information, but this method should probably be used because it is a mandated way for broad dissemination of information and can be used as a defense to any claim of selective disclosure.[211] Likewise, even though Regulation FD does not apply to municipal securities, a press release sent to financial wire services and to *The Bond Buyer* (a municipal industry periodical) is a prudent course.

Third, the issuer should probably inform certain key players contemporaneously with the release of information. These include nationally recognized statistical rating organizations that maintain ratings on the issuer's municipal securities, relevant credit and liquidity providers, and remarketing agents and investment banks that are active in the secondary market for the issuer's securities. Rating agencies and credit and liquidity providers can generally be provided information in advance of the actual public release on a confidential basis, but it is difficult to imagine an issuer becoming comfortable with providing such information to remarketing agents or trading desks until it is publicly available.

Finally, given the cross-linkage between health care program violations and tax-exempt status, special consideration should be given to making disclosure to the IRS, taking into account both whether to provide the information and whether to begin the process of seeking a closing agreement. Obviously, seeking a closing agreement presumes that the issuer does not expect the underlying health care claims simply to disappear.

3. What Should the Disclosure Actually Say?

Having made the determination that disclosure is required or advisable and that it is most appropriately made by a particular means, the issuer must, of course, actually write the disclosure. The issuer should consider the text of the disclosure well before the last minute, as the language used may affect both the issuer's defense of the case and the market's perception of the risk to the issuer's fortunes. Indeed, it has been suggested that the issuer prepare a press release very early in the process in order to ensure that it is not caught flatfooted if information concerning the investigation leaks out before the issuer has planned to make disclosure.[212]

Fraud is, as they say, an ugly word. Despite the government's recent predilection to characterize any violation of a health care regulation or standard as a fraudulent or false claim, the issuer does not have to

---

[211]*See* Letter From Investment Company Institute to Martha Mahan Haines, Director, Office of Municipal Securities, U.S. Securities & Exchange Comm'n (Nov. 12, 2001), *available at* http://www.ici.org/statements/cmltr/01_sec_muni_disclose_com.html (noting, among other things, that the repository system is "inefficient and ineffective" and that it "does not meet the needs of municipal securities investors"). *See also* Mary Chris Jaklevic, *Toward full disclosure,* MODERN HEALTHCARE (Feb. 19, 2001), at 50–54.

[212]*See* Groskaufmanis, Morley, & Rivera, *supra* note 25, at 467 (internal page 11).

accept and use that characterization. Many FCA cases, as discussed earlier, are based on alleged violations of highly technical and ambiguous laws, regulations, and policies. The issuer may be well served by pointing this out in its disclosure and by describing the nature of the claims in some detail. Where possible, it may be desirable to describe the specific statutes involved: "The government has alleged that we have committed technical violations of the regulations requiring that [insert specifics], and that, as a result, we have received overpayments from the Medicare program"—assuming that this is an accurate characterization—is certainly less inflammatory than "The government has alleged that we have defrauded the Medicare program." While it is important that the disclosure not be misleading, the issuer should not ignore the "MEGO factor"[213] associated with descriptions of complex and technical regulations.

The issuer should also disclose whatever mitigating facts it can point to without compromising its defense. The issuer should certainly state that it has cooperated and is continuing to cooperate with the government's investigation, if that is the case. If the issuer has conducted an internal investigation that contradicts the allegations, it may wish to say so, or it may wish at least to state that it has an internal investigation in process if that is true. If the allegations relate to acts or omissions by a previous owner or by prior management, the issuer will almost undoubtedly want to point that out. Where the government has declined to intervene in a *qui tam* case that the relator continues to pursue, the issuer will certainly want to make it clear that the government has declined the case. In the circumstance where the investigation relates purely to isolated historical circumstances, to a discontinued line of business, or to any other situation that suggests that the impact on future operations (beyond the expense of the judgment or settlement) will be slight or nonexistent, that is helpful information. Specific quantitative information on the potential exposure is, of course, helpful if it can be provided without harming the issuer's settlement position.

In that regard, if the claims involve the potential for per-claim penalties or multiplied damages, that possibility should be noted. However, it will normally be preferable to try to quantify the alleged single-damage exposure, if that is possible, and then indicate the additional liability that may be imposed if things go badly. This will give the disclosure recipient a more objective basis to assess the probable risk associated with the litigation than simply tossing out exorbitant worst-case scenarios without appropriate context.

Finally, although the principal concern of this chapter is disclosure issues that arise before a case is resolved, the issuer must also be prepared for the disclosure it will make when the case is settled, as it most

---

[213] "MEGO" stands for "my eyes glaze over"—a not uncommon reaction in the lay reader who encounters a description of the rules governing bundled versus unbundled laboratory claims, for example.

likely will be. If the case is of any significance, the government will put out its own press release, which will normally describe the alleged violations in quite pejorative terms. It will be critical for the issuer to get its own side of the story out at the same time as the government's press release, if not earlier. The government will not typically allow the issuer to review its release, but it may be possible to try to negotiate the inclusion of some language regarding cooperation with the investigation and to get the government to agree to provide the issuer with a copy of its release simultaneously with its distribution. The issuer's release should focus on any mitigating factors that are available regarding future impact of the settlement and should attempt to provide as objective a view as possible of the nature of the claims that were settled in order to counteract the more inflammatory descriptions that will likely be in the government's release.

C. Protecting the Disclosure Decision

Pat Dye, at the time head football coach of Auburn University, once noted that "Hindsight is 50/50."[214] As is apparent from the above discussion, the issuer's determination as to if, when, and how to disclose information concerning a government investigation is a matter of subjective judgment, usually based on imperfect and evolving knowledge of the situation, and that determination may be subject to attack by the SEC or the plaintiffs' bar after the fact. The issuer must, accordingly, consider how it can best prepare to defend its decision in the face of such an examination based on hindsight.[215]

First, it is critical that the issuer carefully control who in its organization is permitted to speak to analysts, investors, and the press and ensure that those persons are aware of the issuer's policies concerning disclosure, including when to say "no comment" and how to avoid running afoul of Regulation FD. Given the delicate assessments required in determining when and how to disclose matters relating to government investigations, it is critical that the issuer not be forced into premature disclosure by careless, inadvertent, or ill-informed remarks. Similarly, the issuer's investor relations and press relations personnel should be cautioned to report to those persons responsible for the issuer's securities disclosures any information they receive—such as reports of rumors from analysts, questions from the press about a potential investigation, and so forth—suggesting that information about the investigation is making its way into the public. The issuer

---

[214] *See* Kevin Scarbinsky, *Kickoff's comin' and we're feelin' all right,* Birmingham News, July 28, 2000.

[215] It has been pointed out that such judgments in hindsight may frequently be based on an adverse market reaction after disclosure is ultimately made, without regard to whether that reaction was foreseeable based on information available at the time in question. *See* Groskaufmanis, Morley, & Rivera, *supra* note 25, at 465–67 (internal pages 9–11). Pages 463–70 (internal pages 7–14) of this article contain an excellent summary of practical considerations involved in the disclosure of uncharged misconduct, to which the analysis in this subsection is much indebted.

will need to determine whether this information is a result of leaks originating in some way with the issuer, and it will also want to be prepared to respond in the event that the press or an analyst produces an unexpected report on the matter.

The issuer will also want to ensure that its regular periodic disclosures and other public statements do not contain information that would require disclosure of the investigation (or the facts underlying it) in order to make such disclosures not misleading. Counsel knowledgeable about the investigation should carefully review in advance the issuer's public statements concerning its compliance with laws and any business practices or relationships involved in the investigation in order to avoid the *Par Pharmaceutical*–type situation, where glowing statements about business success directly implicate the alleged violations under investigation.[216]

As described earlier, in many cases an issuer's decision to defer disclosure relating to an investigation will be based on its then-current assessment that the matter is not material, or that it lacks sufficient information to make the materiality determination—in other words, that the possibility of a materially adverse outcome is, at the time, speculative or contingent.[217] That assessment is, by its nature, subject to change as information concerning the progress and direction of the investigation becomes available to the issuer. While remaining sensitive to issues of privilege and the potential for subsequent discoverability, the issuer should also consider establishing a paper trail concerning these assessments, or at least the facts underlying them (such as internal studies concerning the potential exposure, review of the claims at issue, and so forth). Such a paper trail may help demonstrate that, even if the failure to make disclosure at a particular time proves in hindsight to have been a poor decision, the issuer did not have the scienter necessary to support a 10b-5 claim.

In that regard, the issuer should consider periodically consulting with experienced, independent outside counsel, perhaps both securities counsel and (if different) regulatory and defense counsel advising the issuer on the matter.[218] (In that circumstance, it is of course essential that securities counsel be informed of the investigation and any facts the issuer knows that are relevant to it.) This consultation will be

---

[216] *See In re* Par Pharm., Inc. Sec. Litig., 733 F. Supp. 668 (S.D.N.Y. 1990). See *supra* text at notes 43–46.

[217] *See* Basic, Inc. v. Levinson, 485 U.S. 224, 232 (1988).

[218] In that regard, however, the issuer should be cautious about requesting written opinions from counsel, and counsel should be cautious in rendering them. Although counsel, as a matter both of professional responsibility and of enlightened self-interest, will want to give comprehensive advice concerning the legal risks involved in both the investigation or litigation itself and the disclosure issues, the issuer may find itself in an uncomfortable corner if it has received a written opinion from counsel—perhaps based on a premature or incomplete understanding of the facts—directing the issuer toward a course of action that, in the event, it does not pursue. On the other hand, carefully structured dialogues between outside counsel and the issuer's senior management team may help to establish the absence of requisite "scienter" where there is a substantial effort to determine the nature of the information available and whether the information is material.

particularly important if the issuer is undertaking an offering of its securities in the face of an undisclosed investigation, because it will need to determine whether it has a prospectus disclosure obligation that might not otherwise arise until a future periodic report is due. While outside counsel may not be as familiar as internal counsel with either the intricacies of the regulatory structure applicable to the particular issuer or the details of the specifically relevant facts, the judgment of outside counsel with respect to both the disclosure issues and the exposure risk in the underlying matter may be perceived as less likely to be influenced by personal concerns (personal financial impact, status and security within the organization, and so on).

When it becomes aware of the investigation, the issuer will generally need to undertake some sort of internal investigation or review in order to determine both its potential realistic exposure and its defense strategy. Virtually as a matter of course, the issuer will want to have such investigation conducted under the direction of outside counsel and to have communications concerning it channeled through outside counsel, in order to obtain the protection of the attorney-client privilege to the greatest extent possible. Such an investigation will, as it progresses, provide the issuer with a greater ability to assess the materiality of the situation, and those among the issuer's personnel responsible for fulfilling its securities disclosure obligations should stay informed of material developments and findings in the investigation in order to ensure that disclosure decisions are continually reevaluated as appropriate.

Finally, the issuer will want to consider whether it needs to impose additional limitations on trading by its officers and directors. As discussed earlier, a corporate insider trading for his own account may have a disclosure obligation that is separate and distinct, at least as a matter of timing, from the issuer's disclosure obligations. In order to avoid the risk of liability for its insiders and to avoid the risk of being forced into a premature corporate disclosure, the issuer may find it desirable to limit the market activity of those persons who are knowledgeable about the investigation (and, as well, those persons who might be presumed by their positions to be knowledgeable about it).

V. Brief Thoughts on Investigation-Related Disclosure Issues in Other Contexts

The primary concern of this chapter is the analysis and handling of disclosure issues relating to government investigations and FCA suits as they affect providers who have publicly traded securities and are thus subject to ongoing disclosure obligations under the federal securities laws. However, these same issues present themselves in other contexts where disclosure may be legally or contractually required, even though the provider does not have publicly traded securities. A discussion of common-law fraud and other principles that may be applicable in such situations is beyond the scope of this chapter, but it is perhaps worthwhile to briefly outline some of those situations and some thoughts on addressing them.

A. Venture Capital/Private Equity Transactions

After a torrid but ultimately disappointing fling with the Internet, there is some indication that the venture capital community is once again turning a bit toward the familiar but still enticing charms of health care. Venture capital or private equity investments are typically structured as acquisitions of convertible preferred stock by the venture investors pursuant to exemptions from registration under the securities laws. Those investments are commonly made without a formal offering document containing prospectus-like disclosure.[219] Instead, the venture investors will rely on representations and warranties given by the issuer in a stock purchase agreement, including representations and warranties concerning the absence of pending or threatened litigation and the issuer's compliance with applicable laws and regulations.

Notwithstanding the lack of an offering document like those used in 1933 Act registrations or public bond offerings by exempt issuers, a venture capital investment is a securities transaction, and the issuer is subject to potential liability under Section 10(b) and Rule 10b-5, as well as to liability under common-law fraud and breach of contract theories. Thus, a provider issuing securities in a private equity transaction is subject to the same types of exposure that are discussed earlier in this chapter if the provider's disclosures in connection with the transaction are inaccurate or misleading. Thus, the provider/issuer will want to apply the same general type of analysis.

There is, however, an important difference in the venture capital setting. Where an issuer has publicly traded securities in the marketplace, the issuer must be concerned about the potential impact on the market value of its securities of the failure to make a required disclosure and of the making of a disclosure that is inaccurate or misleading. As noted previously, the issuer is potentially exposed to liability if it discloses too little, too late, as well as to liability (or at least to unfairly harsh results for its investors) if its disclosures overestimate the adverse effects of an investigation or suit. For a venture-stage issuer, however, there is no public trading market for its securities, and the issuer will not have a duty to make broad public disclosure, perhaps in the face of time pressure arising from rumors or impending press or analyst reports. Instead, the issuer will have an opportunity to present its side of the story to a presumably sophisticated audience, normally under the protection of a confidentiality agreement from the prospective investors. Thus, subject to any concerns relating to an FCA seal, a venture-stage company will probably be best served by making full and early disclosure to prospective venture investors.

---

[219] In some cases, the venture-stage company may utilize a private placement memorandum similar to a 1933 Act prospectus, but most venture investments are made by sophisticated investors pursuant to exemptions that do not require specific formal disclosure documents.

B. Loan Agreements

Banks and other institutions that lend to health care providers have become increasingly knowledgeable about, and sensitive to, the risks associated with the current health care enforcement environment. Accordingly, it is common for loan agreements with health care providers to contain representations and warranties concerning compliance with government program regulations, absence of pending or threatened litigation, and so forth. Thus, a provider under investigation is confronted with difficult disclosure decisions in that context, as well as in the securities law contexts discussed earlier. However, unlike the securities law context, there are no specific regulations governing the form and context of such disclosure, and the provider may be less worried about the prospect of a lawsuit over nondisclosure than it is about a default under the loan agreement, potentially resulting in the acceleration of indebtedness and an inability to obtain further credit. The problem is exacerbated where the provider/borrower also has publicly traded securities, because it would normally be regarded as undesirable for the issuer's loan documents to disclose material information not also disclosed in a publicly available source.[220]

The first step in managing the risks inherent in this situation is for the borrower to carefully negotiate credit agreement representations, ensuring that appropriate qualifications regarding knowledge and materiality are included. Although the concepts of materiality that have been articulated in the securities law context may or may not be persuasive in the credit agreement context, limiting the required disclosures to material matters should allow the borrower some flexibility to defend against an argument that it has breached its credit agreement representations. Similarly, where possible, the borrower should seek to limit the representations to pending actions or actions in which it has received some sort of formal process, although the lender may not be receptive to this concession.

If the borrower does not have publicly traded securities, it may well want to raise the issue at an early stage (giving due attention to a seal, if one is present). As in the venture capital situation described earlier, the borrower can sit down with its lender and attempt to explain why the problem is not as large as it may appear and why it is still a good credit risk. Even if the lender is not entirely pacified, the borrower may be able to negotiate some leeway, such as a limitation of the lender's ability to declare a default so long as the proceedings are civil in nature or the liability exposure does not exceed a certain dollar threshold or involve an exclusion.

---

[220] Indeed, given the increasingly blurry lines between commercial banks and investment banks with brokerage and money management arms, selective disclosure of material information to a bank could, in the absence of an appropriate confidentiality agreement, involve a violation of Regulation FD.

Where the borrower has some other disclosure obligation, under the securities laws or otherwise, and has not previously disclosed the issue to its lender, it will want to disclose the information to the lender simultaneously with its public disclosure and promptly seek to ameliorate any concerns that the lender has. In that context, it should be remembered that there is an important difference between stockholders and lenders. Stockholders who have allegedly been harmed by an issuer's failure to make appropriate disclosure essentially have nothing to lose by participating in a securities fraud class action. They have already lost their money when the stock price dropped; given that a class action suit allows them a shot at getting some of it back at no additional out-of-pocket expense, most stockholders will be delighted to join in. Lenders, on the other hand, have significant incentives to try to work with the borrower to salvage the situation. No lender is enthusiastic about having a defaulted loan or a bankrupt borrower. Lenders will act aggressively to limit their exposure to a credit that has suddenly turned bad, but they typically realize that their most desirable outcome will result from working out a solution with the borrower that allows for an orderly restructuring of the debt, if that is necessary. Thus, the borrower that is confronted with the need to make an unexpected, unhappy disclosure to its lender will be best served by doing it promptly and fully and by offering realistic assurances to the lender that the present difficulties, although serious, are not disastrous for the borrower (assuming, of course, that this is the case).

C. Merger and Acquisition Transactions

Similarly, a provider that is engaged in a merger or acquisition transaction, whether as acquiror or target, may well be confronted with the need to provide representations and warranties concerning its compliance status and the nature of pending or threatened litigation against it. Such disclosures will almost invariably be required from the target company in such a transaction, and may frequently be requested from the acquiror as well, particularly if the acquiror is offering its securities as consideration or if all or part of the purchase price is deferred.[221]

The considerations in such a circumstance are likely not much different from those the borrower faces in the bank loan situation described earlier. The provider's first focus should be to obtain appropriate materiality qualifications in the representations and warranties, in order to ensure that there is no need to disclose immaterial information. The provider may also want to carefully negotiate any language purporting to define its "knowledge" for purposes of representations

---

[221] In a cash deal, where the entire purchase price is being paid at closing, the acquiror may be able to resist requests for representations and warranties concerning anything other than its due organization and existence and its ability to pay. However, in some circumstances the target may insist on such representations even in a cash deal, and, because it is awkward to protest too much on these types of subjects, the acquiror may have to give in.

and warranties and may seek to have disclosures regarding violations of laws limited to those for which it has received some sort of formal notice, rather than simply requiring it to disclose any known violations of law. The provider's ability to do this will, of course, depend on its relative negotiating leverage and the sophistication of the other party.

Where the acquiror is using its stock or other securities as consideration for the transaction, it must be mindful that Section 10(b) and Rule 10b-5 will apply to the representations it makes in the acquisition agreement. In addition, if the securities are to be issued to the target or its stockholders in a registered transaction, as in a public company merger, the acquiror will file a registration statement with respect to the transaction and will be subject to potential liability under the 1933 Act as well. Accordingly, in such a situation, the acquiror will need to analyze its disclosure duties under the principles described in earlier sections of this chapter.

Finally, as in the loan situation described earlier, where the acquiror or target, as the case may be, can disclose information to the other party without triggering other disclosure obligations, it should in most circumstances ensure that there are appropriate confidentiality protections in place and make the disclosure with appropriate explanations of mitigating factors. Where, on the other hand, disclosure under the acquisition agreement would likely entail an obligation (whether legal or practical) to make broader public disclosure, the entity may decide to make the best case it can that disclosure is not required under the applicable representations and warranties and fight the matter out when and if it becomes necessary.[222]

---

[222] A recent California case presented an interesting, if unusual, juxtaposition of a number of issues in the acquisition area, although none of them precisely fits into the discussion here. In *Franklin Cal. Tax-Free Income Fund v. OrNda Hosp. Corp.*, No. BC247279 (Cal. Super. Ct. filed Mar. 26, 2001), 10 municipal bond funds sued the seller of a hospital and its parent company in a claim arising out of a divestiture of a hospital required in connection with the parent's acquisition of the seller. According to the complaint, the seller failed to disclose to the purchaser "false and fraudulent billing and treatment practices" in a pain management program responsible for over 30% of the hospital's revenues. The purchase of the hospital was financed through the sale of tax-exempt bonds to the plaintiff funds. The complaint alleged that the seller did not disclose the allegedly fraudulent practices, of which it had supposedly been aware for several years, to either the purchaser or the bond funds. After the purchase, the purchaser discontinued the program and self-reported the alleged fraud. The purchaser then defaulted on the interest obligation on the bonds, which then caused a cross-default on other outstanding bonds, all allegedly as a result of the loss of revenues from the discontinued program. The complaint alleged that the seller made inaccurate and misleading representations both in the purchase agreement and the offering document relating to the bonds, and alleges that the seller and its parent should thus be liable as sellers of the bonds, even though they were issued by a municipality and for the benefit of the purchaser. *See Municipal Bond Mutual Funds Sue Tenet In Sale of Bonds Used to Purchase Hospital*, 10 HEALTH L. REP. (BNA) 543–44 (Apr. 5, 2001). Had the case been litigated to a decision, it could have had significant implications in terms of the disclosure obligations of providers involved in acquisition transactions toward those to whom they would not otherwise seem to have a duty of disclosure. Fortunately, perhaps, for the parties, but unfortunately for jurisprudence, the litigation was settled before trial, as reported in Tenet Healthcare Corporation's Quarterly Report on Form 10-Q for the quarterly period ended June 30, 2003.

D. Research Grant Activities

The government-wide effect of an exclusion from governmental health care programs[223] means that a provider facing serious health care enforcement proceedings must also consider the potential effect of such proceedings on its research- and grant-related activities. Among other things, persons who have been debarred or suspended from participation in government programs may not receive payments, even for goods or services actually delivered or performed.[224] Further, persons seeking grants and other arrangements are required to certify, inter alia, that they are not "presently . . . criminally or civilly charged by a governmental entity (Federal, State or local) with commission of any of the offenses" enumerated in the certificate, including fraud, falsification of records or documents, or making false statements.[225] Furthermore, the participant is required to provide immediate notice if it becomes aware that the certification has become erroneous because of changed circumstances.[226] Because the certification is itself a statement made to the government, it can presumably also become the subject of a separate claim if it is false.[227] Failure to be able to certify does not lead to automatic denial of participation, so dialogue is again probably a safer course than concealment.[228]

The exclusion also bars other government contractors from using the provider as a subcontractor. As a result, academic research centers facing suspension or debarment will cause significant hardships for researchers working in their facilities, because it will not be possible for the research center to receive payment for the use of its facilities in connection with government-funded research activities—a highly unlikely outcome, no doubt, but one that may affect the recruitment of star research scientists.

E. Private Philanthropy

The potential loss of tax-exempt status implicit in any governmental program investigation that alleges unlawful conduct may also complicate private fundraising activities for not-for-profit organizations. In addition to seeking to endow various worthy causes, donors are without doubt expecting tax deductions for their beneficence. Except in rare instances, loss of tax-exempt status would also mean loss of the tax deductions for donors. Given the possibility that the donor may make

---

[223]*See* 45 C.F.R. §76.110(d).

[224]*See* 45 C.F.R. §225.

[225]45 C.F.R. Part 76, App. A, Item (1)(c).

[226]45 C.F.R. Part 76, App. A, Instruction 4.

[227]*See, e.g.,* Cook County v. United States *ex rel.* Chandler, 538 U.S. 119 (2003).

[228]45 C.F.R. Part 76, App. A, Instruction 2.

the gift by will, when the decision tends to be exceedingly final, the stakes for deciding to disclose the investigation and the associated risk may be quite high. Because there have been no reported cases of actual loss of exempt status, it may be tempting for the provider to delay disclosure on the assumption that the closing agreement will always protect innocent donors who contributed expecting simply to help the cause and had no hand in whatever bad acts led to the regulatory sanctions. However, if the donor is one who might continue to provide future support, failure to disclose may injure the trust necessary to continue the relationship.

VI. A SIDEBAR: WHAT IF THE ATTORNEY AND THE ISSUER DISAGREE?

While a full exploration of the issue is beyond the scope of this chapter, one question that the attorney for the publicly traded health care organization cannot afford to ignore is what his or her duties are if the attorney's conclusions regarding the issuer's obligations are different from those of the issuer's management. Section 307 of the Sarbanes-Oxley Act required the SEC to adopt a regulation that would require an attorney who "appears and practices" before the SEC in the representation of an issuer to (a) "report evidence of a material violation of securities law or breach of fiduciary duty or similar violation by the [issuer] or any agent thereof, to the chief legal counsel or the chief executive officer of the [issuer]," and (b) if there is not an appropriate response (including appropriate remedial measures or sanctions) forthcoming from such officer(s), to report such evidence to the audit committee of the issuer's board of directors (or to another committee of nonemployee directors, or to the full board).[229] The SEC's initial and continuing response to this statutory requirement holds significant implications for the lawyer advising health care issuers on disclosure requirements.[230]

In November 2002, the SEC proposed rules under Section 307 of Sarbanes-Oxley that not only would have imposed a duty on a lawyer appearing and practicing before the SEC to report such evidence of a material violation "up the ladder" within the issuer, but also would have required the lawyer to withdraw from representing the issuer and disclose such withdrawal to the SEC (and to disaffirm any part of any document filed with or submitted to the SEC that the attorney prepared or assisted in preparing and reasonably believed was or might be materially false or misleading) *if,* in the lawyer's view, the

---

[229] Section 307 of Sarbanes-Oxley is codified at 15 U.S.C. §7245.

[230] For a more comprehensive description of the history, status, and particulars of the SEC's rulemaking under Section 307, see William W. Horton, *Representing the Healthcare Organization in a Post-Sarbanes-Oxley World: New Rules, New Paradigms, New Perils,* forthcoming in J. HEALTH L. (2004) (copy on file with author). For other considerations concerning potential exposure for attorneys representing health care organizations, see Chapter 1 in the Main Volume (Baumann, An Introduction to Health Care Fraud and Abuse), at Section §I.C.

issuer had not made a timely and appropriate response to such a report.[231] After considerable controversy, the SEC adopted a final rule that limited the lawyer's obligations to up-the-ladder reporting and did not require the "noisy withdrawal" contemplated by the initial proposal.[232] However, in an accompanying release the SEC continued to propose the rules originally contained in the initial proposal that would require the lawyer to withdraw and notify the SEC (or, alternatively, to require the issuer to make an 8-K filing disclosing such withdrawal and "the circumstances relating thereto") if the lawyer did not receive what the lawyer determined to be an appropriate and timely response to his or her report of evidence of a material violation.[233] Further, while the final rules did not require the attorney to make a "noisy withdrawal," they did permit the attorney to disclose confidential information to the SEC, without the issuer's consent:

> to the extent the attorney reasonably believes necessary: (i) [t]o prevent the issuer from committing a material violation that is likely to cause substantial injury to the financial interest or property of the issuer or investors; (ii) [t]o prevent the issuer, in [an SEC] investigation or administrative proceeding, from committing perjury . . . ; suborning perjury . . . ; or committing any act proscribed in 18 U.S.C. [Section] 1001 that is likely to perpetrate a fraud upon the [SEC]; or (iii) [t]o rectify the consequences of a material violation by the issuer that caused, or may cause, substantial injury to the financial interest or property of the issuer or investors in the furtherance of which the attorney's services were used.[234]

As discussed above, the determination whether the securities laws require disclosure of an investigation or sealed *qui tam* suit, or of potential underlying wrongdoing that has not been charged, is a complex one, and one as to which reasonable lawyers and reasonable clients may differ. However, the new SEC rules raise the stakes for the lawyer who counsels in favor of disclosure if the client declines to make such disclosure.[235] If the lawyer believes not only that disclosure is the prudent course, but also that a failure to make such disclosure could be reasonably construed by another competent lawyer with knowledge of the same facts to constitute a material violation of the securities laws by the issuer, the lawyer is, at a minimum, required to report the matter up the ladder within the issuer. If the SEC adopts any version of its proposed noisy withdrawal/reporting-out requirements,

---

[231] *See* Proposed Rule: Implementation of Standards of Professional Conduct for Attorneys, Securities Act Release No. 33-8150 (Nov. 21, 2002), *available at* www.sec.gov/rules/proposed/33-8150.htm.

[232] *See* Final Rule: Implementation of Standards of Professional Conduct for Attorneys, Securities Act Release No. 33-8185 (Jan. 29, 2003), *available at* www.sec.gov/rules/final/33-8185.htm.

[233] *See* Proposed Rule: Implementation of Standards of Professional Conduct for Attorneys, Securities Act Release No. 33-8186, *available at* www.sec.gov/rules/proposed/33-8186.htm.

[234] *See* 17 C.F.R. §205.3(d)(2).

[235] In addition to the disclosure issue, of course, the lawyer who is aware of the substantive law violation that gives rise to the disclosure issue has duties relating to reporting evidence of that violation up the ladder within the organization, separate and apart from any violation that nondisclosure may entail, at least if the lawyer is deemed under the rule to be "appearing and practicing" before the SEC.

the lawyer may have further affirmative duties if the issuer persists in nondisclosure contrary to the lawyer's advice. Even under the current permissive reporting-out provisions of the SEC rules, the lawyer who continues to represent the nondisclosing issuer may be exposed to criticism, and perhaps to liability as well, once the issuer has made it clear that it does not intend to make any disclosure that the lawyer believes should be made.[236]

The final scope of the SEC's rulemaking under Sarbanes-Oxley Section 307 remains to be established, as does the ultimate outcome of the public debate over the proper role of lawyers in the post-Enron world.[237] What is immediately clear, however, is that the lawyer advising a health care issuer on disclosure matters must bear in mind not only the impact of a disclosure decision on the issuer, but also the potential impact on the lawyer himself or herself if the lawyer acquiesces in the issuer's decision not to make disclosure contrary to the lawyer's advice and, in hindsight, that decision proves to have been the wrong one. What this dynamic will mean for the professional relationship between the lawyer and the client continues to be a subject of much debate.[238]

---

[236] In that regard, see, e.g., the Independent Examiner's Report Concerning Spiegel, Inc. (Sept. 5, 2003), filed in *Securities & Exch. Comm'n v. Spiegel, Inc.*, Case No. 03-C-1685 (N.D. Ill.), available as Exhibit 99.2 to Spiegel, Inc.'s Current Report on Form 8-K, dated Sept. 12, 2003. In that case, according to the Independent Examiner's filings, Spiegel did not file various 1934 Act reports because doing so would have involved filing audited financial statements containing a "going concern" qualification in the auditor's report. Both internal counsel and external securities counsel advised Spiegel's audit committee and another committee of the board on multiple occasions that the reports were required to be filed and that failure to file them exposed the corporation to various potential consequences, including the possibility of SEC enforcement action. Nonetheless, and apparently relying on advice from another law firm engaged by Spiegel's controlling shareholder to advise the company, Spiegel neither filed the required reports nor disclosed what the Independent Examiner found to be the true reason that it had not filed them. Although the Independent Examiner noted that the new SEC rules had not become effective at any relevant time, and that no version of the reporting-out/noisy withdrawal proposals had yet been adopted in any event, the Independent Examiner was sharply critical of external securities counsel for continuing to represent Spiegel in the face of such nondisclosure. It is clear that, in the Independent Examiner's view, the lawyers at least bore moral culpability for, in effect, deferring to their client's judgment after having made extensive efforts to give appropriate advice to the client and having been overruled by the client, after the client's consultation with other counsel. *See id.* at 80–84, 212.

[237] In that regard, consider also the amendments to Rules 1.6 and 1.13 of the American Bar Association's Model Rules of Professional Conduct, *available at* www.abanet.org/cpr/mrpc/mrpc_toc.html (providing permission for a lawyer to reveal client confidences to prevent (or mitigate or rectify the effects of) a crime or fraud committed by the client or, if the client is an organization, where the lawyer believes that such disclosure is in the best interests of the organization even where no crime or fraud is involved, in each case subject to certain requirements and conditions precedent set forth in the amended Model Rules). *See generally* Horton, *Representing the Healthcare Organization in a Post-Sarbanes-Oxley World, supra* note 230, *passim;* Lawrence A. Hamermesh, *Up the ladder and out the door? Illegal activities, new Model Rules and reporting obligations,* BUS. LAW TODAY (May/June 2004), at 11.

[238] *See, e.g.,* Hearing of the Subcommittee on Capital Markets, Insurance and Government Sponsored Enterprises, Committee on Financial Services, U.S. House of Representatives, on "The Role of Attorneys in Corporate Governance," Feb. 4, 2004 (prepared statements available at http://financialservices.house.gov/hearings.asp?formmode=detail&hearing=274).

VII. CONCLUSION: NOW WE SEE AS THROUGH A GLASS, DARKLY (BUT LATER, THE PLAINTIFF WILL CLEAR THINGS UP FOR US)

In a recent Broadway musical, an exchange along the following lines occurs toward the end of the last act, accompanying the impending doom of all the remaining cast:

Little Sally: What kind of a happy ending is *that?*

Officer Lockstock: I told you, Little Sally, it's not that kind of a musical.[239]

This chapter began with a story, of sorts, and readers of a story may have an expectation that it will have a happy ending. However, the nature of the problems faced by providers evaluating their disclosure obligations amid the vagaries of the current health care enforcement environment makes the likelihood of a happy ending—one in which the provider can feel comfortable that its disclosure decisions are fully insulated from challenge in hindsight—as speculative and contingent as any underlying liabilities themselves may be. The various potential resolutions of an investigation, the uncertain outcome of a pre-intervention *qui tam* suit, the unpredictable reaction of the market, and the many issues that may be raised by other constituencies and stakeholders all make it difficult for a provider to be sure that it is doing the right thing at the right time, and any bad result makes it likely that the provider's decisions will be extensively scrutinized after the fact. Those undertaking that scrutiny will have the benefit of knowledge of facts that are frequently unclear, and sometimes even unsuspected, at the time that the provider must make those decisions.

That being the case, the provider must soldier on with the information at hand, recognizing that it is critical to assess and reassess its disclosure status based on the continually evolving nature and scope of its knowledge and the particular circumstances in which it finds itself. In that ongoing reassessment, the provider must recognize that the lines are not clear, and that the issues of materiality and duty to disclose are inextricably intertwined with the facts involved in the underlying investigation or action and the direction in which that matter seems to be heading. The analysis simply does not admit of black-letter rules, and there is case law to support or rebut almost any position that the provider might take.

In such a treacherous environment, then, the provider must integrate its disclosure analysis with its developing knowledge of the investigation or action and must recognize that its ability to defend

---

[239]Music & Lyrics by Mark Hollman, Book & Lyrics by Greg Kotis, *Urinetown—The Musical.* (This quote, based on memory, is paraphrased.)

against subsequent claims of inadequate, inaccurate, or misleading disclosure will depend largely on its ability to articulate a reasoned process that it followed in making the decision as to if, when, what, and how to disclose. That process must be informed by the case law that is out there, with its many nuances and subtle distinctions, and it must be informed by knowledge of how government investigations proceed and how they are resolved. Further, it must involve close interaction between counsel and the provider's executive management and, as applicable, investor and press relations personnel, because the dangers involved where the team is not on the same page—as to knowledge, as to strategy, and as to legal requirements—are potentially immense.

This chapter attempts to summarize a large body of relevant legal and factual considerations, and to suggest a somewhat disciplined approach to such a process. In the end, the success or failure of a challenge to a provider's decisions as to the timing and content of disclosure may stand or fall as much on the outcome of the investigation or action itself as on the "correctness" of those disclosure decisions. However, the provider that undertakes such an informed process in making those decisions will stand a much better chance of defending them than the provider that simply steps blindly into the situation.

Appendix Table of Contents

[***Editor's Note:*** Readers are cautioned that documents on the Internet and websites generally are subject to change; readers should consult the appropriate website for updates and further information on topics of interest.]

Appendix A

Anti-Kickback Statute Materials

Appendix A-1

Anti-Kickback Statute

Source: 42 U.S.C. Section 1320a-7b(b).

Section 1320a-7b. Criminal penalties for acts involving Federal health care programs

. . .

(b) Illegal remunerations

    (1) Whoever knowingly and willfully solicits or receives any remuneration (including any kickback, bribe, or rebate) directly or indirectly, overtly or covertly, in cash or in kind—

        (A) in return for referring an individual to a person for the furnishing or arranging for the furnishing of any item or service for which payment may be made in whole or in part under a Federal health care program, or

        (B) in return for purchasing, leasing, ordering, or arranging for or recommending purchasing, leasing, or ordering any good, facility, service, or item for which payment may be made in whole or in part under a Federal health care program,

shall be guilty of a felony and upon conviction thereof, shall be fined not more than $25,000 or imprisoned for not more than five years, or both.

(2) Whoever knowingly and willfully offers or pays any remuneration (including any kickback, bribe, or rebate) directly or indirectly, overtly or covertly, in cash or in kind to any person to induce such person

        (A) to refer an individual to a person for the furnishing or arranging for the furnishing of any item or service for which payment may be made in whole or in part under a Federal health care program, or

        (B) to purchase, lease, order, or arrange for or recommend purchasing, leasing, or ordering any good, facility, service, or item for which payment may be made in whole or in part under a Federal health care program,

shall be guilty of a felony and upon conviction thereof, shall be fined not more than $25,000 or imprisoned for not more than five years, or both.

(3) Paragraphs (1) and (2) shall not apply to—

(A) a discount or other reduction in price obtained by a provider of services or other entity under a Federal health care program if the reduction in price is properly disclosed and appropriately reflected in the costs claimed or charges made by the provider or entity under a Federal health care program;

(B) any amount paid by an employer to an employee (who has a bona fide employment relationship with such employer) for employment in the provision of covered items or services;

(C) any amount paid by a vendor of goods or services to a person authorized to act as a purchasing agent for a group of individuals or entities who are furnishing services reimbursed under a Federal health care program if—

(i) the person has a written contract, with each such individual or entity, which specifies the amount to be paid the person, which amount may be a fixed amount or a fixed percentage of the value of the purchases made by each such individual or entity under the contract, and

(ii) in the case of an entity that is a provider of services (as defined in section 1395x(u) of this title or in regulations under section 1395w-103(e)(6) of this title), the person discloses (in such form and manner as the Secretary requires) to the entity and, upon request, to the Secretary the amount received from each such vendor with respect to purchases made by or on behalf of the entity;

(D) a waiver of any coinsurance under part B of subchapter XVIII of this chapter by a Federally qualified health care center with respect to an individual who qualifies for subsidized services under a provision of the Public Health Service Act (42 U.S.C. 201 et seq.);

(E) any payment practice specified by the Secretary in regulations promulgated pursuant to section 14(a) of the Medicare and Medicaid Patient and Program Protection Act of 1987;

(F) any remuneration between an organization and an individual or entity providing items or services, or a combination thereof, pursuant to a written agreement between the organization and the individual or entity if the organization is an eligible organization under section 1395mm of this title or if the written agreement, through a risk-sharing arrangement, places the individual or entity at substantial financial risk for the cost or utilization of the items or services, or a combination thereof, which the individual or entity is obligated to provide;

(G) the waiver or reduction by pharmacies (including pharmacies of the Indian Health Service, Indian tribes, tribal organizations, and urban Indian organizations) of any cost-sharing imposed under part D of subchapter XVIII of this chapter, if the conditions described in clauses (i) through (iii) of section 1320a-7a(i)(6)(A) of this title are met with respect to the waiver or reduction (except that, in the case of such a waiver or reduction on behalf of a subsidy eligible individual (as defined in section 1395w-114(a)(3) of this title), section 1320a-7a(i)(6)(A) of this title shall be applied without regard to clauses (ii) and (iii) of that section); and

(H) any remuneration between a health center entity described under clause (i) or (ii) of section 1396d(l)(2)(B) of this title and any individual or entity providing goods, items, services, donations, loans, or a combination thereof, to such health center entity pursuant to a contract, lease, grant, loan, or other agreement, if such agreement contributes to the ability of the health center entity to maintain or increase the availability, or enhance the quality, of services provided to a medically underserved population served by the health center entity.

Pub. L. No. 108-173, Section 237(d)(3), added a second subparagraph (H), effective on January 1, 2006:

(H) any remuneration between a federally qualified health center (or an entity controlled by such a health center) and an MA organization pursuant to a written agreement described in section 1395w-23(a)(4) of this title.

SOURCE—
(Pub. L. No. 108-173, Title II, §237(d), (e), Dec. 8, 2003, 117 Stat. 2213.)

SOURCE—
(Aug. 14, 1935, ch. 531, title XI, Sec. 1128B, formerly title XVIII, Sec. 1877(d), and title XIX, Sec. 1909, as added and amended Pub. L. 92-603, title II, Sec. 242(c), 278(b)(9), Oct. 30, 1972, 86 Stat. 1419, 1454; Pub. L. 95-142, Sec. 4(a), (b), Oct. 25, 1977, 91 Stat. 1179, 1181; Pub. L. 96-499, title IX, Sec. 917, Dec. 5, 1980, 94 Stat. 2625; Pub. L. 98-369, div. B, title III, Sec. 2306(f)(2), July 18, 1984, 98 Stat. 1073; renumbered title XI, Sec. 1128B, and amended Pub. L. 100-93, Sec. 4(a)-(d), 14(b), Aug. 18, 1987, 101 Stat. 688, 689, 697; Pub. L. 100-203, title IV, Sec. 4039(a), 4211(h)(7), Dec. 22, 1987, 101 Stat. 1330-81, 1330-206; Pub. L. 100-360, title IV, Sec. 411(a)(3)(A), (B)(i), July 1, 1988, 102 Stat. 768; Pub. L. 101-239, title VI, Sec. 6003(g)(3)(D)(ii), Dec. 19, 1989, 103 Stat. 2153; Pub. L. 101-508, title IV, Sec. 4161(a)(4), 4164(b)(2), Nov. 5, 1990, 104 Stat. 1388-94, 1388-102; Pub. L. 103-432, title I, Sec. 133(a)(2), Oct. 31, 1994, 108 Stat. 4421; Pub. L. 104-191, title II, Sec. 204(a), 216(a), 217, Aug. 21, 1996, 110 Stat. 1999, 2007, 2008; Pub. L. 105-33, title IV, Sec. 4201(c)(1), 4704(b), 4734, Aug. 5, 1997, 111 Stat. 373, 498, 522; Pub. L. No. 108-173, title I, Secs. 101(e)(2), (8)(A), title IV, Sec. 431(a), Dec. 8, 2003, 117 Stat. 2150, 2152, 2287.)

REFERENCES IN TEXT
Part B of subchapter XVIII of this chapter, referred to in subsec. (b)(3)(D), is classified to section 1395j et seq. of this title.

The Public Health Service Act, referred to in subsec. (b)(3)(D), is act July 1, 1944, ch. 373, 58 Stat. 682, as amended, which is classified generally to chapter 6A (Sec. 201 et seq.) of this title. For complete classification of this Act to the Code, see Short Title note set out under section 201 of this title and Tables.

Section 14(a) of the Medicare and Medicaid Patient and Program Protection Act of 1987, referred to in subsec. (b)(3)(E), is section 14(a) of Pub. L. 100-93, ...

Appendix A-2

Anti-Kickback Safe Harbor Regulations—Ambulance Restocking Safe Harbor and Sample Written Disclosure

Editor's Note: Section 1001.952(v), the ambulance restocking safe harbor, is reprinted immediately below. Appendix A to Subpart C of Part 1001 follows; Appendix A is a sample written disclosure for purposes of satisfying the requirements of §1001.952(v)(3)(i)(B)(*1*)(*i*).

The complete text of Section 1001.952 as updated through 2002 appears following the text of subsection (v) (the ambulance restocking safe harbor) and Appendix A to Subpart C of Part 1001 (the sample written disclosure).

The text of Section 1001.952 below updates and replaces the text of 42 C.F.R. Section 1001.952 that appears in this Appendix in the Main Volume. Note that the remaining sections in Part 1001 that were updated in 2002 are reprinted in this Supplement in Appendix D-5, below.

Source: 42 C.F.R. Section 1001.952; 66 Fed. Reg. 62,979 (Dec. 4, 2001); 67 Fed. Reg. 11,928 (Mar. 18, 2002)

Section 1001.952(v) Ambulance restocking safe harbor

The following payment practices shall not be treated as a criminal offense under section 1128B of the Act and shall not serve as the basis for an exclusion:

. . .

(v) *Ambulance replenishing.* (1) As used in section 1128B of the Act, "remuneration" does not include any gift or transfer of drugs or medical supplies (including linens) by a hospital or other receiving facility to an ambulance provider for the purpose of replenishing comparable

347

drugs or medical supplies (including linens) used by the ambulance provider (or a first responder) in connection with the transport of a patient by ambulance to the hospital or other receiving facility if all of the standards in paragraph (v)(2) of this section are satisfied *and* all of the applicable standards in *either* paragraph (v)(3)(i), (v)(3)(ii) or (v)(3)(iii) of this section are satisfied. However, to qualify under paragraph (v), the ambulance that is replenished must be used to provide emergency ambulance services an average of three times per week, as measured over a reasonable period of time. Drugs and medical supplies (including linens) initially used by a first responder and replenished at the scene of the illness or injury by the ambulance provider that transports the patient to the hospital or other receiving facility will be deemed to have been used by the ambulance provider.

(2) To qualify under paragraph (v) of this section, the ambulance replenishing arrangement must satisfy *all* of the following four conditions—

(i)(A) Under no circumstances may the ambulance provider (or first responder) and the receiving facility both bill for the same replenished drug or supply. Replenished drugs or supplies may only be billed (including claiming bad debt) to a Federal health care program by either the ambulance provider (or first responder) or the receiving facility.

(B) All billing or claims submission by the receiving facility, ambulance provider or first responder for replenished drugs and medical supplies used in connection with the transport of a Federal health care program beneficiary must comply with all applicable Federal health care program payment and coverage rules and regulations.

(C) Compliance with paragraph (v)(2)(i)(B) of this section will be determined separately for the receiving facility and the ambulance provider (and first responder, if any), so long as the receiving facility, ambulance provider (or first responder) refrains from doing anything that would impede the other party or parties from meeting their obligations under paragraph (v)(2)(i)(B).

(ii)(A) The receiving facility or ambulance provider, or both, must

(1) Maintain records of the replenished drugs and medical supplies and the patient transport to which the replenished drugs and medical supplies related;

(2) Provide a copy of such records to the other party within a reasonable time (unless the other party is separately maintaining records of the replenished drugs and medical supplies); and

(3) Make those records available to the Secretary promptly upon request.

(B) A pre-hospital care report (including, but not limited to, a trip sheet, patient care report or patient encounter report) prepared by the ambulance provider and filed with the receiving facility will meet the requirements of paragraph (v)(2)(ii)(A) of this section, provided that it documents the specific type and amount of medical supplies and drugs used on the patient and subsequently replenished.

(C) For purposes of paragraph (v)(2)(ii) of this section, documentation may be maintained and, if required, filed with the other party in hard copy or electronically. If a replenishing arrangement includes linens, documentation need not be maintained for their exchange. If documentation is not maintained for the exchange of linens, the receiving facility will be presumed to have provided an exchange of comparable clean linens for soiled linens for each ambulance transport of a patient to the receiving facility. Records required under paragraph (v)(2)(ii)(A) of this section must be maintained for 5 years.

(iii) The replenishing arrangement must not take into account the volume or value of any referrals or business otherwise generated between the parties for which payment may be made in whole or in part under any Federal health care program (other than the referral of the particular patient to whom the replenished drugs and medical supplies were furnished).

(iv) The receiving facility and the ambulance provider otherwise comply with all Federal, State, and local laws regulating ambulance services, including, but not limited to, emergency services, and the provision of drugs and medical supplies, including, but not limited to, laws relating to the handling of controlled substances.

(3) To qualify under paragraph (v) of this section, the arrangement must satisfy *all* of the standards in *one* of the following three categories:

(i) *General replenishing.* (A) The receiving facility must replenish medical supplies or drugs on an equal basis for all ambulance providers that bring patients to the receiving facility in any one of the categories described in paragraph (v)(3)(i)(A)(*1*), (*2*), or (*3*) of this section. A receiving facility may offer replenishing to one or more of the categories and may offer different replenishing arrangements to different categories, so long as the replenishing is conducted uniformly within each category. For example, a receiving facility may offer to replenish a broader array of drugs or supplies for ambulance providers that do not charge for their services than for ambulance providers that charge for their services. Within each category, the receiving facility may limit its replenishing arrangements to the replenishing of emergency ambulance transports only. A receiving facility may offer replenishing to one or more of the categories—

(*1*) All ambulance providers that do not bill any patient or insurer (including Federal health care programs) for ambulance services, regardless of the payor or the patient's ability to pay (*i.e.,* ambulance providers, such as volunteer companies, that provide ambulance services without charge to any person or entity);

(*2*) All not-for-profit and State or local government ambulance service providers (including, but not limited to, municipal and volunteer ambulance services providers); or

(*3*) All ambulance service providers.

(B)(*1*) The replenishing arrangement must be conducted in an open and public manner. A replenishing arrangement will be considered to be conducted in an open and public manner if one of the following two conditions are satisfied:

(*i*) A written disclosure of the replenishing program is posted conspicuously in the receiving facility's emergency room or other location where the ambulance providers deliver patients and copies are made available upon request to ambulance providers, Government representatives, and members of the public (subject to reasonable photocopying charges). The written disclosure can take any reasonable form and should include the category of ambulance service providers that qualifies for replenishment; the drugs or medical supplies included in the replenishment program; and the procedures for documenting the replenishment. A sample disclosure form is included in Appendix A to subpart C of this part for illustrative purposes only. No written contracts between the parties are required for purposes of paragraph (v)(3)(i)(B)(*1*)(*i*) of this section; or

(*ii*) The replenishment arrangement operates in accordance with a plan or protocol of general application promulgated by an Emergency Medical Services (EMS) Council or comparable entity, agency or organization, provided a copy of the plan or protocol is available upon request to ambulance providers, Government representatives and members of the public (subject to reasonable photocopying charges). While parties are encouraged to participate in collaborative, comprehensive, community-wide EMS systems to improve the delivery of EMS in their local communities, nothing in this paragraph shall be construed as requiring the involvement of such organizations or the development or implementation of ambulance replenishment plans or protocols by such organizations.

(*2*) Nothing in this paragraph (v)(3)(i) shall be construed as requiring disclosure of confidential proprietary or financial information related to the replenishing arrangement (including, but not limited to, information about cost, pricing or the volume of replenished drugs or supplies) to ambulance providers or members of the general public.

(ii) *Fair market value replenishing.* (A) Except as otherwise provided in paragraph (v)(3)(ii)(B) of this section, the ambulance provider must pay the receiving facility fair market value, based on an arms-length transaction, for replenished medical supplies; and

(B) If payment is not made at the same time as the replenishing of the medical supplies, the receiving facility and the ambulance provider must make commercially reasonable payment arrangements in advance.

(iii) *Government mandated replenishing.* The replenishing arrangement is undertaken in accordance with a State or local statute, ordinance, regulation or binding protocol that requires hospitals or receiving facilities in the area subject to such requirement to replenish ambulances that deliver patients to the hospital with drugs or medical supplies (including linens) that are used during the transport of that patient.

(4) For purposes of paragraph (v) of this section—

(i) A *receiving facility* is a hospital or other facility that provides emergency medical services.

(ii) An *ambulance provider* is a provider or supplier of ambulance transport services that provides emergency ambulance services. The term does not include a provider of ambulance transport services that provides only non-emergency transport services.

(iii) A *first responder* includes, but is not limited to, a fire department, paramedic service or search and rescue squad that responds to an emergency call (through 9-1-1 or other emergency access number) and treats the patient, but does not transport the patient to the hospital or other receiving facility.

(iv) An *emergency ambulance service* is a transport by ambulance initiated as a result of a call through 9-1-1 or other emergency access number or a call from another acute care facility unable to provide the higher level care required by the patient and available at the receiving facility.

(v) *Medical supplies* includes linens, unless otherwise provided.

Appendix A to Subpart C of Part 1001 [Sample written disclosure for satisfying the requirements of §1001.952(v)(3)(i)(B)(*1*)(*i*)]

The following is a sample written disclosure for purposes of satisfying the requirements of §1001.952(v)(3)(i)(B)(1)(i) of this part. This form is for illustrative purposes only; parties may, but are not required to, adapt this sample written disclosure form.

Notice of Ambulance Restocking Program

Hospital X offers the following ambulance restocking program:

1. We will restock all ambulance providers (other than ambulance providers that do not provide emergency services) that bring patients to Hospital X [or to a subpart of Hospital X, such as the emergency room] in the following category or categories: [insert description of category of ambulances to be restocked, i.e., all ambulance providers, all ambulance providers that do not charge patients or insurers for their services, or all nonprofit and Government ambulance providers]. [Optional: We only offer restocking of emergency transports.]

2. The restocking will include the following drugs and medical supplies, and linens, used for patient prior to delivery of the patient to Hospital X: [insert description of drugs and medical supplies, and linens to be restocked].

3. The ambulance providers [will/will not] be required to pay for the restocked drugs and medical supplies, and linens.

4. The restocked drugs and medical supplies, and linens, must be documented as follows: [insert description consistent with the documentation requirements described in §1001.952(v). By way of example only, documentation may be by a patient care report filed with the receiving facility within 24 hours of delivery of the patient that records the name of the patient, the date of the transport, and the relevant drugs and medical supplies.]

5. This restocking program does not apply to the restocking of ambulances that only provide non-emergency services or to the general stocking of an ambulance provider's inventory.

6. To ensure that Hospital X does not bill any Federal health care program for restocked drugs or supplies for which a participating ambulance provider bills or is eligible to bill, all participating ambulance providers must notify Hospital X if they intend to submit claims for restocked drugs or supplies to any Federal health care program. Participating ambulance providers must agree to work with Hospital X to ensure that only one party bills for a particular restocked drug or supply.

7. All participants in this ambulance restocking arrangement that bill Federal health care programs for restocked drugs or supplies must comply with all applicable Federal program billing and claims filing rules and regulations.

8. For further information about our restocking program or to obtain a copy of this notice, please contact [name] at [telephone number].

Dated:_____

/s/:_____
Appropriate officer or official

Section 1001.952 Exceptions.

The following payment practices shall not be treated as a criminal offense under section 1128B of the Act and shall not serve as the basis for an exclusion:

(a) *Investment interests.* As used in section 1128B of the Act, "remuneration" does not include any payment that is a return on an investment interest, such as a dividend or interest income, made to an investor as long as all of the applicable standards are met within one of the following three categories of entities:

(1) If, within the previous fiscal year or previous 12 month period, the entity possesses more than $50,000,000 in undepreciated net tangible assets (based on the net acquisition cost of purchasing such assets from an unrelated entity) related to the furnishing of health care items and services, all of the following five standards must be met—

(i) With respect to an investment interest that is an equity security, the equity security must be registered with the Securities and Exchange Commission under 15 U.S.C. 781 (b) or (g).

(ii) The investment interest of an investor in a position to make or influence referrals to, furnish items or services to, or otherwise generate business for the entity must be obtained on terms (including any direct or indirect transferability restrictions) and at a price equally available to the public when trading on a registered securities exchange, such as the New York Stock Exchange or the American Stock Exchange, or in accordance with the National Association of Securities Dealers Automated Quotation System.

(iii) The entity or any investor must not market or furnish the entity's items or services (or those of another entity as part of a cross referral agreement) to passive investors differently than to non-investors.

(iv) The entity or any investor (or other individual or entity acting on behalf of the entity or any investor in the entity) must not loan funds to or guarantee a loan for an investor who is in a position to make or influence referrals to, furnish items or services to, or otherwise generate business for the entity if the investor uses any part of such loan to obtain the investment interest.

(v) The amount of payment to an investor in return for the investment interest must be directly proportional to the amount of the capital investment of that investor.

(2) If the entity possesses investment interests that are held by either active or passive investors, all of the following eight applicable standards must be met—

(i) No more than 40 percent of the value of the investment interests of each class of investment interests may be held in the previous fiscal year or previous 12 month period by investors who are in a position to make or influence referrals to, furnish items or services to, or otherwise generate business for the entity. (For purposes of paragraph (a)(2)(i) of this section, equivalent classes of equity investments may be combined, and equivalent classes of debt instruments may be combined.)

(ii) The terms on which an investment interest is offered to a passive investor, if any, who is in a position to make or influence referrals to, furnish items or services to, or otherwise generate business for the entity must be no different from the terms offered to other passive investors.

(iii) The terms on which an investment interest is offered to an investor who is in a position to make or influence referrals to, furnish items or services to, or otherwise generate business for the entity must not be related to the previous or expected volume of referrals, items or services furnished, or the amount of business otherwise generated from that investor to the entity.

(iv) There is no requirement that a passive investor, if any, make referrals to, be in a position to make or influence referrals to, furnish items or services to, or otherwise generate business for the entity as a condition for remaining as an investor.

(v) The entity or any investor must not market or furnish the entity's items or services (or those of another entity as part of a cross referral agreement) to passive investors differently than to non-investors.

(vi) No more than 40 percent of the entity's gross revenue related to the furnishing of health care items and services in the previous fiscal year or previous 12-month period may come from referrals or business otherwise generated from investors.

(vii) The entity or any investor (or other individual or entity acting on behalf of the entity or any investor in the entity) must not loan funds to or guarantee a loan for an investor who is in a position to make or influence referrals to, furnish items or services to, or otherwise generate business for the entity if the investor uses any part of such loan to obtain the investment interest.

(viii) The amount of payment to an investor in return for the investment interest must be directly proportional to the amount of the capital investment (including the fair market value of any pre-operational services rendered) of that investor.

(3)(i) If the entity possesses investment interests that are held by either active or passive investors and is located in an underserved area, all of the following eight standards must be met—

(A) No more than 50 percent of the value of the investment interests of each class of investments may be held in the previous fiscal year or previous 12-month period by investors who are in a position to make or influence referrals to, furnish items or services to, or otherwise generate business for, the entity. (For purposes of paragraph (a)(3)(i)(A) of this section, equivalent classes of equity investments may be combined, and equivalent classes of debt instruments may be combined.)

(B) The terms on which an investment interest is offered to a passive investor, if any, who is in a position to make or influence referrals to, furnish items or services to, or otherwise generate business for the entity must be no different from the terms offered to other passive investors.

(C) The terms on which an investment interest is offered to an investor who is in a position to make or influence referrals to, furnish items or services to, or otherwise generate business for the entity must not be related to the previous or expected volume of referrals, items or services furnished, or the amount of business otherwise generated from that investor to the entity.

(D) There is no requirement that a passive investor, if any, make referrals to, be in a position to make or influence referrals to, furnish items or services to, or otherwise generate business for the entity as a condition for remaining as an investor.

(E) The entity or any investor must not market or furnish the entity's items or services (or those of another entity as part of a cross-referral agreement) to passive investors differently than to non-investors.

(F) At least 75 percent of the dollar volume of the entity's business in the previous fiscal year or previous 12-month period must be derived from the service of persons who reside in an underserved area or are members of medically underserved populations.

(G) The entity or any investor (or other individual or entity acting on behalf of the entity or any investor in the entity) must not loan funds to or guarantee a loan for an investor who is in a position to make or influence referrals to, furnish items or services to, or otherwise generate business for the entity if the investor uses any part of such loan to obtain the investment interest.

(H) The amount of payment to an investor in return for the investment interest must be directly proportional to the amount of the capital investment (including the fair market value of any pre-operational services rendered) of that investor.

(ii) If an entity that otherwise meets all of the above standards is located in an area that was an underserved area at the time of the initial investment, but subsequently ceases to be an underserved area, the entity will be deemed to comply with paragraph (a)(3)(i) of this section for a period equal to the lesser of

(A) The current term of the investment remaining after the date upon which the area ceased to be an underserved area or

(B) Three years from the date the area ceased to be an underserved area.

(4) For purposes of paragraph (a) of this section, the following terms apply. *Active investor* means an investor either who is responsible for the day-to-day management of the entity and is a bona fide general partner in a partnership under the Uniform Partnership Act or who agrees in writing to undertake liability for the actions of the entity's agents acting within the scope of their agency. *Investment interest* means a security issued by an entity, and may include the following classes of investments: shares in a corporation, interests or units in a partnership or limited liability company, bonds, debentures, notes, or other debt instruments. *Investor* means an individual or entity either who directly holds an investment interest in an entity, or who holds such investment interest indirectly by, including but not limited to, such means as having a family member hold such investment interest or holding a legal or beneficial interest in another entity (such as a trust or holding company) that holds such investment interest. *Passive investor* means an investor who is not an active investor, such as a limited partner in a partnership under the Uniform Partnership Act, a shareholder in a corporation, or a holder of a debt security. *Underserved area* means any defined geographic area that is designated as a Medically Underserved Area (MUA) in accordance with regulations issued by the Department. *Medically underserved population* means a Medically Underserved Population (MUP) in accordance with regulations issued by the Department.

(b) *Space rental.* As used in section 1128B of the Act, "remuneration" does not include any payment made by a lessee to a lessor for the use of premises, as long as all of the following six standards are met—

(1) The lease agreement is set out in writing and signed by the parties.

(2) The lease covers all of the premises leased between the parties for the term of the lease and specifies the premises covered by the lease.

(3) If the lease is intended to provide the lessee with access to the premises for periodic intervals of time, rather than on a full-time basis for the term of the lease, the lease specifies exactly the schedule of such intervals, their precise length, and the exact rent for such intervals.

(4) The term of the lease is for not less than one year.

(5) The aggregate rental charge is set in advance, is consistent with fair market value in arms-length transactions and is not determined in a manner that takes into account the volume or value of any referrals or business otherwise generated between the parties for which payment may be made in whole or in part under Medicare, Medicaid or other Federal health care programs.

(6) The aggregate space rented does not exceed that which is reasonably necessary to accomplish the commercially reasonable busi-

ness purpose of the rental. Note that for purposes of paragraph (b) of this section, the term *fair market value* means the value of the rental property for general commercial purposes, but shall not be adjusted to reflect the additional value that one party (either the prospective lessee or lessor) would attribute to the property as a result of its proximity or convenience to sources of referrals or business otherwise generated for which payment may be made in whole or in part under Medicare, Medicaid and all other Federal health care programs.

(c) *Equipment rental.* As used in section 1128B of the Act, "remuneration" does not include any payment made by a lessee of equipment to the lessor of the equipment for the use of the equipment, as long as all of the following six standards are met—

(1) The lease agreement is set out in writing and signed by the parties.

(2) The lease covers all of the equipment leased between the parties for the term of the lease and specifies the equipment covered by the lease.

(3) If the lease is intended to provide the lessee with use of the equipment for periodic intervals of time, rather than on a full-time basis for the term of the lease, the lease specifies exactly the schedule of such intervals, their precise length, and the exact rent for such interval.

(4) The term of the lease is for not less than one year.

(5) The aggregate rental charge is set in advance, is consistent with fair market value in arms-length transactions and is not determined in a manner that takes into account the volume or value of any referrals or business otherwise generated between the parties for which payment may be made in whole or in part under Medicare, Medicaid or all other Federal health care programs.

(6) The aggregate equipment rental does not exceed that which is reasonably necessary to accomplish the commercially reasonable business purpose of the rental. Note that for purposes of paragraph (c) of this section, the term *fair market value* means that the value of the equipment when obtained from a manufacturer or professional distributor, but shall not be adjusted to reflect the additional value one party (either the prospective lessee or lessor) would attribute to the equipment as a result of its proximity or convenience to sources of referrals or business otherwise generated for which payment may be made in whole or in part under Medicare, Medicaid or other Federal health care programs.

(d) *Personal services and management contracts.* As used in section 1128B of the Act, "remuneration" does not include any payment made by a principal to an agent as compensation for the services of the agent, as long as all of the following seven standards are met—

(1) The agency agreement is set out in writing and signed by the parties.

(2) The agency agreement covers all of the services the agent provides to the principal for the term of the agreement and specifies the services to be provided by the agent.

(3) If the agency agreement is intended to provide for the services of the agent on a periodic, sporadic or part-time basis, rather than on a full-time basis for the term of the agreement, the agreement specifies exactly the schedule of such intervals, their precise length, and the exact charge for such intervals.

(4) The term of the agreement is for not less than one year.

(5) The aggregate compensation paid to the agent over the term of the agreement is set in advance, is consistent with fair market value in arms-length transactions and is not determined in a manner that takes into account the volume or value of any referrals or business otherwise generated between the parties for which payment may be made in whole or in part under Medicare, Medicaid or other Federal health care programs.

(6) The services performed under the agreement do not involve the counselling or promotion of a business arrangement or other activity that violates any State or Federal law.

(7) The aggregate services contracted for do not exceed those which are reasonably necessary to accomplish the commercially reasonable business purpose of the services.

For purposes of paragraph (d) of this section, an agent of a principal is any person, other than a bona fide employee of the principal, who has an agreement to perform services for, or on behalf of, the principal.

(e) *Sale of practice.* (1) As used in section 1128B of the Act, "remuneration" does not include any payment made to a practitioner by another practitioner where the former practitioner is selling his or her practice to the latter practitioner, as long as both of the following two standards are met—

(i) The period from the date of the first agreement pertaining to the sale to the completion of the sale is not more than one year.

(ii) The practitioner who is selling his or her practice will not be in a professional position to make referrals to, or otherwise generate business for, the purchasing practitioner for which payment may be made in whole or in part under Medicare, Medicaid or other Federal health care programs after 1 year from the date of the first agreement pertaining to the sale.

(2) As used in section 1128B of the Act, "remuneration" does not include any payment made to a practitioner by a hospital or other entity where the practitioner is selling his or her practice to the hospital or other entity, so long as the following four standards are met:

(i) The period from the date of the first agreement pertaining to the sale to the completion date of the sale is not more than three years.

(ii) The practitioner who is selling his or her practice will not be in a professional position after completion of the sale to make or influence referrals to, or otherwise generate business for, the purchasing hospital or entity for which payment may be made under Medicare, Medicaid or other Federal health care programs.

(iii) The practice being acquired must be located in a Health Professional Shortage Area (HPSA), as defined in Departmental regulations, for the practitioner's specialty area.

(iv) Commencing at the time of the first agreement pertaining to the sale, the purchasing hospital or entity must diligently and in good faith engage in commercially reasonable recruitment activities that:

(A) May reasonably be expected to result in the recruitment of a new practitioner to take over the acquired practice within a one year period and

(B) Will satisfy the conditions of the practitioner recruitment safe harbor in accordance with paragraph (n) of this section.

(f) *Referral services.* As used in section 1128B of the Act, "remuneration" does not include any payment or exchange of anything of value between an individual or entity ("participant") and another entity serving as a referral service ("referral service"), as long as all of the following four standards are met—

(1) The referral service does not exclude as a participant in the referral service any individual or entity who meets the qualifications for participation.

(2) Any payment the participant makes to the referral service is assessed equally against and collected equally from all participants, and is only based on the cost of operating the referral service, and not on the volume or value of any referrals to or business otherwise generated by either party for the referral service for which payment may be made in whole or in part under Medicare, Medicaid or other Federal health care programs.

(3) The referral service imposes no requirements on the manner in which the participant provides services to a referred person, except that the referral service may require that the participant charge the person referred at the same rate as it charges other persons not referred by the referral service, or that these services be furnished free of charge or at reduced charge.

(4) The referral service makes the following five disclosures to each person seeking a referral, with each such disclosure maintained by the referral service in a written record certifying such disclosure and signed by either such person seeking a referral or by the individual making the disclosure on behalf of the referral service—

(i) The manner in which it selects the group of participants in the referral service to which it could make a referral;

(ii) Whether the participant has paid a fee to the referral service;

(iii) The manner in which it selects a particular participant from this group for that person;

(iv) The nature of the relationship between the referral service and the group of participants to whom it could make the referral; and

(v) The nature of any restrictions that would exclude such an individual or entity from continuing as a participant.

(g) *Warranties.* As used in section 1128B of the Act, "remuneration" does not include any payment or exchange of anything of value under a warranty provided by a manufacturer or supplier of an item to the buyer (such as a health care provider or beneficiary) of the item, as long as the buyer complies with all of the following standards in paragraphs (g)(1) and (g)(2) of this section and the manufacturer or supplier complies with all of the following standards in paragraphs (g)(3) and (g)(4) of this section—

(1) The buyer must fully and accurately report any price reduction of the item (including a free item), which was obtained as part of the warranty, in the applicable cost reporting mechanism or claim for payment filed with the Department or a State agency.

(2) The buyer must provide, upon request by the Secretary or a State agency, information provided by the manufacturer or supplier as specified in paragraph (g)(3) of this section.

(3) The manufacturer or supplier must comply with either of the following two standards—

(i) The manufacturer or supplier must fully and accurately report the price reduction of the item (including a free item), which was obtained as part of the warranty, on the invoice or statement submitted to the buyer, and inform the buyer of its obligations under paragraphs (a)(1) and (a)(2) of this section.

(ii) Where the amount of the price reduction is not known at the time of sale, the manufacturer or supplier must fully and accurately report the existence of a warranty on the invoice or statement, inform the buyer of its obligations under paragraphs (g)(1) and (g)(2) of this section, and, when the price reduction becomes known, provide the buyer with documentation of the calculation of the price reduction resulting from the warranty.

(4) The manufacturer or supplier must not pay any remuneration to any individual (other than a beneficiary) or entity for any medical, surgical, or hospital expense incurred by a beneficiary other than for the cost of the item itself.

For purposes of paragraph (g) of this section, the term *warranty* means either an agreement made in accordance with the provisions of 15 U.S.C. 2301(6), or a manufacturer's or supplier's agreement to replace another manufacturer's or supplier's defective item (which is covered by an agreement made in accordance with this statutory provision), on terms equal to the agreement that it replaces.

(h) *Discounts.* As used in section 1128B of the Act, "remuneration" does not include a discount, as defined in paragraph (h)(5) of this section, on an item or service for which payment may be made in whole or in part under Medicare, Medicaid or other Federal health care programs for a buyer as long as the buyer complies with the applicable standards of paragraph (h)(1) of this section; a seller as long as the seller complies with the applicable standards of paragraph (h)(2) of this section; and an offeror of a discount who is not a seller under paragraph (h)(2) of this section so long as such offeror complies with the applicable standards of paragraph (h)(3) of this section.

(1) With respect to the following three categories of buyers, the buyer must comply with all of the applicable standards within one of the three following categories—

(i) If the buyer is an entity which is a health maintenance organization (HMO) or a competitive medical plan (CMP) acting in accordance with a risk contract under section 1876(g) or 1903(m) of the Act, or under another State health care program, it need not report the discount except as otherwise may be required under the risk contract.

(ii) If the buyer is an entity which reports its costs on a cost report required by the Department or a State health care program, it must comply with all of the following four standards—

(A) The discount must be earned based on purchases of that same good or service bought within a single fiscal year of the buyer;

(B) The buyer must claim the benefit of the discount in the fiscal year in which the discount is earned or the following year;

(C) The buyer must fully and accurately report the discount in the applicable cost report; and

(D) the buyer must provide, upon request by the Secretary or a State agency, information provided by the seller as specified in paragraph (h)(2)(ii) of this section, or information provided by the offeror as specified in paragraph (h)(3)(ii) of this section.

(iii) If the buyer is an individual or entity in whose name a claim or request for payment is submitted for the discounted item or service and payment may be made, in whole or in part, under Medicare, Medicaid or other Federal health care programs (not including individuals or entities defined as buyers in paragraph (h)(1)(i) or (h)(1)(ii) of this section), the buyer must comply with both of the following standards—

(A) The discount must be made at the time of the sale of the good or service or the terms of the rebate must be fixed and disclosed in writing to the buyer at the time of the initial sale of the good or service; and

(B) the buyer (if submitting the claim) must provide, upon request by the Secretary or a State agency, information provided by the seller as specified in paragraph (h)(2)(iii)(B)

of this section, or information provided by the offeror as specified in paragraph (h)(3)(iii)(A) of this section.

(2) The seller is an individual or entity that supplies an item or service for which payment may be made, in whole or in part, under Medicare, Medicaid or other Federal health care programs to the buyer and who permits a discount to be taken off the buyer's purchase price. The seller must comply with all of the applicable standards within one of the following three categories—

(i) If the buyer is an entity which is an HMO [or] a CMP acting in accordance with a risk contract under section 1876(g) or 1903(m) of the Act, or under another State health care program, the seller need not report the discount to the buyer for purposes of this provision.

(ii) If the buyer is an entity that reports its costs on a cost report required by the Department or a State agency, the seller must comply with either of the following two standards—

(A) Where a discount is required to be reported to Medicare or a State health care program under paragraph (h)(1) of this section, the seller must fully and accurately report such discount on the invoice, coupon or statement submitted to the buyer; inform the buyer in a manner that is reasonably calculated to give notice to the buyer of its obligations to report such discount and to provide information upon request under paragraph (h)(1) of this section; and refrain from doing anything that would impede the buyer from meeting its obligations under this paragraph; or

(B) Where the value of the discount is not known at the time of sale, the seller must fully and accurately report the existence of a discount program on the invoice, coupon or statement submitted to the buyer; inform the buyer in a manner reasonably calculated to give notice to the buyer of its obligations to report such discount and to provide information upon request under paragraph (h)(1) of this section; when the value of the discount becomes known, provide the buyer with documentation of the calculation of the discount identifying the specific goods or services purchased to which the discount will be applied; and refrain from doing anything which would impede the buyer from meeting its obligations under this paragraph.

(iii) If the buyer is an individual or entity not included in paragraph (h)(2)(i) or (h)(2)(ii) of this section, the seller must comply with either of the following two standards—

(A) Where the seller submits a claim or request for payment on behalf of the buyer and the item or service is separately claimed, the seller must provide, upon request by the Secretary or a State agency, information provided by the offeror as specified in paragraph (h)(3)(iii)(A) of this section; or

(B) Where the buyer submits a claim, the seller must fully and accurately report such discount on the invoice, coupon or statement submitted to the buyer; inform the buyer in a manner reasonably calculated to give notice to the buyer of its obligations to report such discount and to provide information upon request under paragraph (h)(1) of this section; and refrain from doing anything that would impede the buyer from meeting its obligations under this paragraph.

(3) The offeror of a discount is an individual or entity who is not a seller under paragraph (h)(2) of this section, but promotes the purchase of an item or service by a buyer under paragraph (h)(1) of this section at a reduced price for which payment may be made, in whole or in part, under Medicare, Medicaid or other Federal health care programs. The offeror must comply with all of the applicable standards within the following three categories—

(i) If the buyer is an entity which is an HMO or a CMP acting in accordance with a risk contract under section 1876(g) or 1903(m) of the Act, or under another State health care program, the offeror need not report the discount to the buyer for purposes of this provision.

(ii) If the buyer is an entity that reports its costs on a cost report required by the Department or a State agency, the offeror must comply with the following two standards—

(A) The offeror must inform the buyer in a manner reasonably calculated to give notice to the buyer of its obligations to report such a discount and to provide information upon request under paragraph (h)(1) of this section; and

(B) The offeror of the discount must refrain from doing anything that would impede the buyer's ability to meet its obligations under this paragraph.

(iii) If the buyer is an individual or entity in whose name a request for payment is submitted for the discounted item or service and payment may be made, in whole or in part, under Medicare, Medicaid or other Federal health care programs (not including individuals or entities defined as buyers in paragraph (h)(1)(i) or (h)(1)(ii) of this section), the offeror must comply with the following two standards—

(A) The offeror must inform the individual or entity submitting the claim or request for payment in a manner reasonably calculated to give notice to the individual or entity of its obligations to report such a discount and to provide information upon request under paragraphs (h)(1) and (h)(2) of this section; and

(B) The offeror of the discount must refrain from doing anything that would impede the buyer's or seller's ability to meet its obligations under this paragraph.

(4) For purposes of this paragraph, a *rebate* is any discount the terms of which are fixed and disclosed in writing to the buyer at

the time of the initial purchase to which the discount applies, but which is not given at the time of sale.

(5) For purposes of this paragraph, the term *discount* means a reduction in the amount a buyer (who buys either directly or through a wholesaler or a group purchasing organization) is charged for an item or service based on an arms-length transaction. The term *discount* does not include—

(i) Cash payment or cash equivalents (except that rebates as defined in paragraph (h)(4) of this section may be in the form of a check);

(ii) Supplying one good or service without charge or at a reduced charge to induce the purchase of a different good or service, unless the goods and services are reimbursed by the same Federal health care program using the same methodology and the reduced charge is fully disclosed to the Federal health care program and accurately reflected where appropriate, and as appropriate, to the reimbursement methodology;

(iii) A reduction in price applicable to one payer but not to Medicare, Medicaid or other Federal health care programs;

(iv) A routine reduction or waiver of any coinsurance or deductible amount owed by a program beneficiary;

(v) Warranties;

(vi) Services provided in accordance with a personal or management services contract; or

(vii) Other remuneration, in cash or in kind, not explicitly described in paragraph (h)(5) of this section.

(i) *Employees.* As used in section 1128B of the Act, "remuneration" does not include any amount paid by an employer to an employee, who has a bona fide employment relationship with the employer, for employment in the furnishing of any item or service for which payment may be made in whole or in part under Medicare, Medicaid or other Federal health care programs. For purposes of paragraph (i) of this section, the term employee has the same meaning as it does for purposes of 26 U.S.C. 3121(d)(2).

(j) *Group purchasing organizations.* As used in section 1128B of the Act, "remuneration" does not include any payment by a vendor of goods or services to a group purchasing organization (GPO), as part of an agreement to furnish such goods or services to an individual or entity as long as both of the following two standards are met—

(1) The GPO must have a written agreement with each individual or entity, for which items or services are furnished, that provides for either of the following—

(i) The agreement states that participating vendors from which the individual or entity will purchase goods or services will pay a fee to the GPO of 3 percent or less of the purchase price of the goods or services provided by that vendor.

(ii) In the event the fee paid to the GPO is not fixed at 3 percent or less of the purchase price of the goods or services, the agreement specifies the amount (or if not known, the maximum amount) the GPO will be paid by each vendor (where such amount may be a fixed sum or a fixed percentage of the value of purchases made from the vendor by the members of the group under the contract between the vendor and the GPO).

(2) Where the entity which receives the goods or service from the vendor is a health care provider of services, the GPO must disclose in writing to the entity at least annually, and to the Secretary upon request, the amount received from each vendor with respect to purchases made by or on behalf of the entity. Note that for purposes of paragraph (j) of this section, the term *group purchasing organization* (GPO) means an entity authorized to act as a purchasing agent for a group of individuals or entities who are furnishing services for which payment may be made in whole or in part under Medicare, Medicaid or other Federal health care programs, and who are neither wholly-owned by the GPO nor subsidiaries of a parent corporation that wholly owns the GPO (either directly or through another wholly-owned entity).

(k) *Waiver of beneficiary coinsurance and deductible amounts.* As used in section 1128B of the Act, "remuneration" does not include any reduction or waiver of a Medicare or a State health care program beneficiary's obligation to pay coinsurance or deductible amounts as long as all of the standards are met within either of the following two categories of health care providers:

(1) If the coinsurance or deductible amounts are owed to a hospital for inpatient hospital services for which Medicare pays under the prospective payment system, the hospital must comply with all of the following three standards—

(i) The hospital must not later claim the amount reduced or waived as a bad debt for payment purposes under Medicare or otherwise shift the burden of the reduction or waiver onto Medicare, a State health care program, other payers, or individuals.

(ii) The hospital must offer to reduce or waive the coinsurance or deductible amounts without regard to the reason for admission, the length of stay of the beneficiary, or the diagnostic related group for which the claim for Medicare reimbursement is filed.

(iii) The hospital's offer to reduce or waive the coinsurance or deductible amounts must not be made as part of a price reduction agreement between a hospital and a third-party payer (including a health plan as defined in paragraph (l)(2) of this section), unless the agreement is part of a contract for the furnishing of items or services to a beneficiary of a Medicare supplemental policy issued under the terms of section 1882(t)(1) of the Act.

(2) If the coinsurance or deductible amounts are owed by an individual who qualifies for subsidized services under a provision of the

Public Health Services Act or under titles V or XIX of the Act to a federally qualified health care center or other health care facility under any Public Health Services Act grant program or under title V of the Act, the health care center or facility may reduce or waive the coinsurance or deductible amounts for items or services for which payment may be made in whole or in part under part B of Medicare or a State health care program.

(*l*) *Increased coverage, reduced cost-sharing amounts, or reduced premium amounts offered by health plans.* (1) As used in section 1128B of the Act, "remuneration" does not include the additional coverage of any item or service offered by a health plan to an enrollee or the reduction of some or all of the enrollee's obligation to pay the health plan or a contract health care provider for cost-sharing amounts (such as coinsurance, deductible, or copayment amounts) or for premium amounts attributable to items or services covered by the health plan, the Medicare program, or a State health care program, as long as the health plan complies with all of the standards within one of the following two categories of health plans:

(i) If the health plan is a risk-based health maintenance organization, competitive medical plan, prepaid health plan, or other health plan under contract with CMS or a State health care program and operating in accordance with section 1876(g) or 1903(m) of the Act, under a Federal statutory demonstration authority, or under other Federal statutory or regulatory authority, it must offer the same increased coverage or reduced cost-sharing or premium amounts to all Medicare or State health care program enrollees covered by the contract unless otherwise approved by CMS or by a State health care program.

(ii) If the health plan is a health maintenance organization, competitive medical plan, health care prepayment plan, prepaid health plan or other health plan that has executed a contract or agreement with CMS or with a State health care program to receive payment for enrollees on a reasonable cost or similar basis, it must comply with both of the following two standards—

(A) The health plan must offer the same increased coverage or reduced cost-sharing or premium amounts to all Medicare or State health care program enrollees covered by the contract or agreement unless otherwise approved by CMS or by a State health care program; and

(B) The health plan must not claim the costs of the increased coverage or the reduced cost-sharing or premium amounts as a bad debt for payment purposes under Medicare or a State health care program or otherwise shift the burden of the increased coverage or reduced cost-sharing or premium amounts to the extent that increased payments are claimed from Medicare or a State health care program.

(2) For purposes of paragraph (l) of this section, the terms—

Contract health care provider means an individual or entity under contract with a health plan to furnish items or services to enrollees who are covered by the health plan, Medicare, or a State health care program.

Enrollee means an individual who has entered into a contractual relationship with a health plan (or on whose behalf an employer, or other private or governmental entity has entered into such a relationship) under which the individual is entitled to receive specified health care items and services, or insurance coverage for such items and services, in return for payment of a premium or a fee.

Health plan means an entity that furnishes or arranges under agreement with contract health care providers for the furnishing of items or services to enrollees, or furnishes insurance coverage for the provision of such items and services, in exchange for a premium or a fee, where such entity:

(i) Operates in accordance with a contract, agreement or statutory demonstration authority approved by CMS or a State health care program;

(ii) Charges a premium and its premium structure is regulated under a State insurance statute or a State enabling statute governing health maintenance organizations or preferred provider organizations;

(iii) Is an employer, if the enrollees of the plan are current or retired employees, or is a union welfare fund, if the enrollees of the plan are union members; or

(iv) Is licensed in the State, is under contract with an employer, union welfare fund, or a company furnishing health insurance coverage as described in conditions (ii) and (iii) of this definition, and is paid a fee for the administration of the plan which reflects the fair market value of those services.

(m) *Price reductions offered to health plans.* (1) As used in section 1128B of the Act, "remuneration" does not include a reduction in price a contract health care provider offers to a health plan in accordance with the terms of a written agreement between the contract health care provider and the health plan for the sole purpose of furnishing to enrollees items or services that are covered by the health plan, Medicare, or a State health care program, as long as both the health plan and contract health care provider comply with all of the applicable standards within one of the following four categories of health plans:

(i) If the health plan is a risk-based health maintenance organization, competitive medical plan, or prepaid health plan under contract with CMS or a State agency and operating in accordance with section 1876(g) or 1903(m) of the Act, under a Federal statutory demonstration authority, or under other Federal statutory or regulatory authority, the contract health care provider must not claim payment in any form from the Department or the State agency for items or services furnished in accordance with the agreement except as approved by CMS or the State health care program, or otherwise shift the burden of such an agreement to the extent that increased payments are claimed from Medicare or a State health care program.

(ii) If the health plan is a health maintenance organization, competitive medical plan, health care prepayment plan, prepaid health plan, or other health plan that has executed a contract or agreement with CMS or a State health care program to receive payment for enrollees on a reasonable cost or similar basis, the health plan and contract health care provider must comply with all of the following four standards—

(A) The term of the agreement between the health plan and the contract health care provider must be for not less than one year;

(B) The agreement between the health plan and the contract health care provider must specify in advance the covered items and services to be furnished to enrollees, and the methodology for computing the payment to the contract health care provider;

(C) The health plan must fully and accurately report, on the applicable cost report or other claim form filed with the Department or the State health care program, the amount it has paid the contract health care provider under the agreement for the covered items and services furnished to enrollees; and

(D) The contract health care provider must not claim payment in any form from the Department or the State health care program for items or services furnished in accordance with the agreement except as approved by CMS or the State health care program, or otherwise shift the burden of such an agreement to the extent that increased payments are claimed from Medicare or a State health care program.

(iii) If the health plan is not described in paragraphs (m)(1)(i) or (m)(1)(ii) of this section and the contract health care provider is not paid on an at-risk, capitated basis, both the health plan and contract health care provider must comply with all of the following six standards—

(A) The term of the agreement between the health plan and the contract health care provider must be for not less than one year;

(B) The agreement between the health plan and the contract health care provider must specify in advance the covered items and services to be furnished to enrollees, which party is to file claims or requests for payment with Medicare or the State health care program for such items and services, and the schedule of fees the contract health care provider will charge for furnishing such items and services to enrollees;

(C) The fee schedule contained in the agreement between the health plan and the contract health care provider must remain in effect throughout the term of the agreement, unless a fee increase results directly from a payment update authorized by Medicare or the State health care program;

(D) The party submitting claims or requests for payment from Medicare or the State health care program for items and services furnished in accordance with the agreement must not claim or request payment for amounts in excess of the fee schedule;

(E) The contract health care provider and the health plan must fully and accurately report on any cost report filed with Medicare or a State health care program the fee schedule amounts charged in accordance with the agreement and, upon request, will report to the Medicare or a State health care program the terms of the agreement and the amounts paid in accordance with the agreement; and

(F) The party to the agreement, which does not have the responsibility under the agreement for filing claims or requests for payment, must not claim or request payment in any form from the Department or the State health care program for items or services furnished in accordance with the agreement, or otherwise shift the burden of such an agreement to the extent that increased payments are claimed from Medicare or a State health care program.

(iv) If the health plan is not described in paragraphs (m)(1)(i) or (m)(1)(ii) of this section, and the contract health care provider is paid on an at-risk, capitated basis, both the health plan and contract health care provider must comply with all of the following five standards—

(A) The term of the agreement between the health plan and the contract health provider must be for not less than one year;

(B) The agreement between the health plan and the contract health provider must specify in advance the covered items and services to be furnished to enrollees and the total amount per enrollee (which may be expressed in a per month or other time period basis) the contract health care provider will be paid by the health plan for furnishing such items and services to enrollees and must set forth any copayments, if any, to be paid by enrollees to the contract health care provider for covered services;

(C) The payment amount contained in the agreement between the health care plan and the contract health care provider must remain in effect throughout the term of the agreement;

(D) The contract health care provider and the health plan must fully and accurately report to the Medicare and State health care program upon request, the terms of the agreement and the amounts paid in accordance with the agreement; and

(E) The contract health care provider must not claim or request payment in any form from the Department, a State health care program or an enrollee (other than copayment amounts described in paragraph (m)(2)(iv)(B) of this section) and the health plan must not pay the contract care provider in excess of the amounts described in paragraph (m)(2)(iv)(B) of this section for items and services covered by the agreement.

(2) For purposes of this paragraph, the terms *contract health care provider, enrollee,* and *health plan* have the same meaning as in paragraph (l)(2) of this section.

(n) *Practitioner recruitment.* As used in section 1128B of the Act, "remuneration" does not include any payment or exchange of anything of value by an entity in order to induce a practitioner who has been practicing within his or her current specialty for less than one year to locate, or to induce any other practitioner to relocate, his or her primary place of practice into a HPSA for his or her specialty area, as defined in Departmental regulations, that is served by the entity, as long as all of the following nine standards are met—

(1) The arrangement is set forth in a written agreement signed by the parties that specifies the benefits provided by the entity, the terms under which the benefits are to be provided, and the obligations of each party.

(2) If a practitioner is leaving an established practice, at least 75 percent of the revenues of the new practice must be generated from new patients not previously seen by the practitioner at his or her former practice.

(3) The benefits are provided by the entity for a period not in excess of 3 years, and the terms of the agreement are not renegotiated during this 3-year period in any substantial aspect; provided, however, that if the HPSA to which the practitioner was recruited ceases to be a HPSA during the term of the written agreement, the payments made under the written agreement will continue to satisfy this paragraph for the duration of the written agreement (not to exceed 3 years).

(4) There is no requirement that the practitioner make referrals to, be in a position to make or influence referrals to, or otherwise generate business for the entity as a condition for receiving the benefits; provided, however, that for purposes of this paragraph, the entity may require as a condition for receiving benefits that the practitioner maintain staff privileges at the entity.

(5) The practitioner is not restricted from establishing staff privileges at, referring any service to, or otherwise generating any business for any other entity of his or her choosing.

(6) The amount or value of the benefits provided by the entity may not vary (or be adjusted or renegotiated) in any manner based on the volume or value of any expected referrals to or business otherwise generated for the entity by the practitioner for which payment may be made in whole or in part under Medicare, Medicaid or any other Federal health care programs.

(7) The practitioner agrees to treat patients receiving medical benefits or assistance under any Federal health care program in a nondiscriminatory manner.

(8) At least 75 percent of the revenues of the new practice must be generated from patients residing in a HPSA or a Medically Underserved Area (MUA) or who are part of a Medically Underserved Population (MUP), all as defined in paragraph (a) of this section.

(9) The payment or exchange of anything of value may not directly or indirectly benefit any person (other than the practitioner being recruited) or entity in a position to make or influence referrals to the entity providing the recruitment payments or benefits of items or services payable by a Federal health care program.

(o) *Obstetrical malpractice insurance subsidies.* As used in section 1128B of the Act, "remuneration" does not include any payment made by a hospital or other entity to another entity that is providing malpractice insurance (including a self-funded entity), where such payment is used to pay for some or all of the costs of malpractice insurance premiums for a practitioner (including a certified nurse-midwife as defined in section 1861(gg) of the Act) who engages in obstetrical practice as a routine part of his or her medical practice in a primary care HPSA, as long as all of the following seven standards are met—

(1) The payment is made in accordance with a written agreement between the entity paying the premiums and the practitioner, which sets out the payments to be made by the entity, and the terms under which the payments are to be provided.

(2)(i) The practitioner must certify that for the initial coverage period (not to exceed one year) the practitioner has a reasonable basis for believing that at least 75 percent of the practitioner's obstetrical patients treated under the coverage of the malpractice insurance will either—

(A) Reside in a HPSA or MUA, as defined in paragraph (a) of this section; or

(B) Be part of a MUP, as defined in paragraph (a) of this section.

(ii) Thereafter, for each additional coverage period (not to exceed one year), at least 75 percent of the practitioner's obstetrical patients treated under the prior coverage period (not to exceed one year) must have—

(A) Resided in a HPSA or MUA, as defined in paragraph (a) of this section; or

(B) Been part of a MUP, as defined in paragraph (a) of this section.

(3) There is no requirement that the practitioner make referrals to, or otherwise generate business for, the entity as a condition for receiving the benefits.

(4) The practitioner is not restricted from establishing staff privileges at, referring any service to, or otherwise generating any business for any other entity of his or her choosing.

(5) The amount of payment may not vary based on the volume or value of any previous or expected referrals to or business otherwise generated for the entity by the practitioner for which payment may be made in whole or in part under Medicare, Medicaid or any other Federal health care programs.

(6) The practitioner must treat obstetrical patients who receive medical benefits or assistance under any Federal health care program in a nondiscriminatory manner.

(7) The insurance is a bona fide malpractice insurance policy or program, and the premium, if any, is calculated based on a bona fide assessment of the liability risk covered under the insurance. For purposes of paragraph (o) of this section, *costs of malpractice insurance premiums* means:

(i) For practitioners who engage in obstetrical practice full-time, any costs attributable to malpractice insurance; or

(ii) For practitioners who engage in obstetrical practice on a part-time or sporadic basis, the costs:

(A) Attributable exclusively to the obstetrical portion of the practitioner's malpractice insurance and

(B) Related exclusively to obstetrical services provided in a primary care HPSA.

(p) *Investments in group practices.* As used in section 1128B of the Act, "remuneration" does not include any payment that is a return on an investment interest, such as a dividend or interest income, made to a solo or group practitioner investing in his or her own practice or group practice if the following four standards are met—

(1) The equity interests in the practice or group must be held by licensed health care professionals who practice in the practice or group.

(2) The equity interests must be in the practice or group itself, and not some subdivision of the practice or group.

(3) In the case of group practices, the practice must:

(i) Meet the definition of "group practice" in section 1877(h)(4) of the Social Security Act and implementing regulations; and

(ii) Be a unified business with centralized decision-making, pooling of expenses and revenues, and a compensation/profit distribution system that is not based on satellite offices operating substantially as if they were separate enterprises or profit centers.

(4) Revenues from ancillary services, if any, must be derived from "in-office ancillary services" that meet the definition of such term in section 1877(b)(2) of the Act and implementing regulations.

(q) *Cooperative hospital service organizations.* As used in section 1128B of the Act, "remuneration" does not include any payment made between a cooperative hospital service organization (CHSO) and its patron-hospital, both of which are described in section 501(e) of the Internal Revenue Code of 1986 and are tax-exempt under section 501(c)(3) of the Internal Revenue Code, where the CHSO is wholly owned by two or more patron-hospitals, as long as the following standards are met—

(1) If the patron-hospital makes a payment to the CHSO, the payment must be for the purpose of paying for the bona fide operating expenses of the CHSO, or

(2) If the CHSO makes a payment to the patron-hospital, the payment must be for the purpose of paying a distribution of net earnings required to be made under section 501(e)(2) of the Internal Revenue Code of 1986.

(r) *Ambulatory surgical centers.* As used in section 1128B of the Act, "remuneration" does not include any payment that is a return on an investment interest, such as a dividend or interest income, made to an investor, as long as the investment entity is a certified ambulatory surgical center (ASC) under part 416 of this title, whose operating and recovery room space is dedicated exclusively to the ASC, patients referred to the investment entity by an investor are fully informed of the investor's investment interest, and all of the applicable standards are met within one of the following four categories—

(1) *Surgeon-owned ASCs*—If all of the investors are general surgeons or surgeons engaged in the same surgical specialty, who are in a position to refer patients directly to the entity and perform surgery on such referred patients; surgical group practices (as defined in this paragraph) composed exclusively of such surgeons; or investors who are not employed by the entity or by any investor, are not in a position to provide items or services to the entity or any of its investors, and are not in a position to make or influence referrals directly or indirectly to the entity or any of its investors, all of the following six standards must be met—

(i) The terms on which an investment interest is offered to an investor must not be related to the previous or expected volume of referrals, services furnished, or the amount of business otherwise generated from that investor to the entity.

(ii) At least one-third of each surgeon investor's medical practice income from all sources for the previous fiscal year or previous 12-month period must be derived from the surgeon's performance of procedures (as defined in this paragraph).

(iii) The entity or any investor (or other individual or entity acting on behalf of the entity or any investor) must not loan funds to or guarantee a loan for an investor if the investor uses any part of such loan to obtain the investment interest.

(iv) The amount of payment to an investor in return for the investment must be directly proportional to the amount of the capital investment (including the fair market value of any pre-operational services rendered) of that investor.

(v) All ancillary services for Federal health care program beneficiaries performed at the entity must be directly and integrally related to primary procedures performed at the entity, and none may be separately billed to Medicare or other Federal health care programs.

(vi) The entity and any surgeon investors must treat patients receiving medical benefits or assistance under any Federal health care program in a nondiscriminatory manner.

(2) *Single-Specialty ASCs*—If all of the investors are physicians engaged in the same medical practice specialty who are in a position to refer patients directly to the entity and perform procedures on such referred patients; group practices (as defined in this paragraph) composed exclusively of such physicians; or investors who are not employed by the entity or by any investor, are not in a position to provide items or services to the entity or any of its investors, and are not in a position to make or influence referrals directly or indirectly to the entity or any of its investors, all of the following six standards must be met—

(i) The terms on which an investment interest is offered to an investor must not be related to the previous or expected volume of referrals, services furnished, or the amount of business otherwise generated from that investor to the entity.

(ii) At least one-third of each physician investor's medical practice income from all sources for the previous fiscal year or previous 12-month period must be derived from the surgeon's performance of procedures (as defined in this paragraph).

(iii) The entity or any investor (or other individual or entity acting on behalf of the entity or any investor) must not loan funds to or guarantee a loan for an investor if the investor uses any part of such loan to obtain the investment interest.

(iv) The amount of payment to an investor in return for the investment must be directly proportional to the amount of the capital investment (including the fair market value of any pre-operational services rendered) of that investor.

(v) All ancillary services for Federal health care program beneficiaries performed at the entity must be directly and integrally related to primary procedures performed at the entity, and none may be separately billed to Medicare or other Federal health care programs.

(vi) The entity and any physician investors must treat patients receiving medical benefits or assistance under any Federal health care program in a nondiscriminatory manner.

(3) *Multi-Specialty ASCs*—If all of the investors are physicians who are in a position to refer patients directly to the entity and perform procedures on such referred patients; group practices, as defined in this paragraph, composed exclusively of such physicians; or investors who are not employed by the entity or by any investor, are not in a position to provide items or services

to the entity or any of its investors, and are not in a position to make or influence referrals directly or indirectly to the entity or any of its investors, all of the following seven standards must be met—

(i) The terms on which an investment interest is offered to an investor must not be related to the previous or expected volume of referrals, services furnished, or the amount of business otherwise generated from that investor to the entity.

(ii) At least one-third of each physician investor's medical practice income from all sources for the previous fiscal year or previous 12-month period must be derived from the physician's performance of procedures (as defined in this paragraph).

(iii) At least one-third of the procedures (as defined in this paragraph) performed by each physician investor for the previous fiscal year or previous 12-month period must be performed at the investment entity.

(iv) The entity or any investor (or other individual or entity acting on behalf of the entity or any investor) must not loan funds to or guarantee a loan for an investor if the investor uses any part of such loan to obtain the investment interest.

(v) The amount of payment to an investor in return for the investment must be directly proportional to the amount of the capital investment (including the fair market value of any pre-operational services rendered) of that investor.

(vi) All ancillary services for Federal health care program beneficiaries performed at the entity must be directly and integrally related to primary procedures performed at the entity, and none may be separately billed to Medicare or other Federal health care programs.

(vii) The entity and any physician investors must treat patients receiving medical benefits or assistance under any Federal health care program in a nondiscriminatory manner.

(4) *Hospital/Physician ASCs*—If at least one investor is a hospital, and all of the remaining investors are physicians who meet the requirements of paragraphs (r)(1), (r)(2) or (r)(3) of this section; group practices (as defined in this paragraph) composed of such physicians; surgical group practices (as defined in this paragraph); or investors who are not employed by the entity or by any investor, are not in a position to provide items or services to the entity or any of its investors, and are not in a position to refer patients directly or indirectly to the entity or any of its investors, all of the following eight standards must be met—

(i) The terms on which an investment interest is offered to an investor must not be related to the previous or expected volume of referrals, services furnished, or the amount of business otherwise generated from that investor to the entity.

(ii) The entity or any investor (or other individual or entity acting on behalf of the entity or any investor) must not loan funds to or guarantee a loan for an investor if the investor uses any part of such loan to obtain the investment interest.

(iii) The amount of payment to an investor in return for the investment must be directly proportional to the amount of the capital investment (including the fair market value of any pre-operational services rendered) of that investor.

(iv) The entity and any hospital or physician investor must treat patients receiving medical benefits or assistance under any Federal health care program in a nondiscriminatory manner.

(v) The entity may not use space, including, but not limited to, operating and recovery room space, located in or owned by any hospital investor, unless such space is leased from the hospital in accordance with a lease that complies with all the standards of the space rental safe harbor set forth in paragraph (b) of this section; nor may it use equipment owned by or services provided by the hospital unless such equipment is leased in accordance with a lease that complies with the equipment rental safe harbor set forth in paragraph (c) of this section, and such services are provided in accordance with a contract that complies with the personal services and management contracts safe harbor set forth in paragraph (d) of this section.

(vi) All ancillary services for Federal health care program beneficiaries performed at the entity must be directly and integrally related to primary procedures performed at the entity, and none may be separately billed to Medicare or other Federal health care programs.

(vii) The hospital may not include on its cost report or any claim for payment from a Federal health care program any costs associated with the ASC (unless such costs are required to be included by a Federal health care program).

(viii) The hospital may not be in a position to make or influence referrals directly or indirectly to any investor or the entity.

(5) For purposes of paragraph (r) of this section, *procedures* means any procedure or procedures on the list of Medicare-covered procedures for ambulatory surgical centers in accordance with regulations issued by the Department and *group practice* means a group practice that meets all of the standards of paragraph (p) of this section. *Surgical group practice* means a group practice that meets all of the standards of paragraph (p) of this section and is composed exclusively of surgeons who meet the requirements of paragraph (r)(1) of this section.

(s) *Referral arrangements for specialty services.* As used in section 1128B of the Act, "remuneration" does not include any exchange of value among individuals and entities where one party agrees to refer a patient to the other party for the provision of a specialty service payable in whole or in part under Medicare, Medicaid or any other Federal health care programs in return for an agreement on the part of the other party to refer that patient back at a mutually agreed upon time or circumstance as long as the following four standards are met—

(1) The mutually agreed upon time or circumstance for referring the patient back to the originating individual or entity is clinically appropriate.

(2) The service for which the referral is made is not within the medical expertise of the referring individual or entity, but is within the special expertise of the other party receiving the referral.

(3) The parties receive no payment from each other for the referral and do not share or split a global fee from any Federal health care program in connection with the referred patient.

(4) Unless both parties belong to the same group practice as defined in paragraph (p) of this section, the only exchange of value between the parties is the remuneration the parties receive directly from third-party payors or the patient compensating the parties for the services they each have furnished to the patient.

(t) *Price reductions offered to eligible managed care organizations.*

(1) As used in section 1128(B) of the Act, "remuneration" does not include any payment between:

(i) An eligible managed care organization and any first tier contractor for providing or arranging for items or services, as long as the following three standards are met—

(A) The eligible managed care organization and the first tier contractor have an agreement that:

(*1*) Is set out in writing and signed by both parties;

(*2*) Specifies the items and services covered by the agreement;

(*3*) Is for a period of at least one year; and

(*4*) Specifies that the first tier contractor cannot claim payment in any form directly or indirectly from a Federal health care program for items or services covered under the agreement, except for:

(*i*) HMOs and competitive medical plans with cost-based contracts under section 1876 of the Act where the agreement with the eligible managed care organization sets out the arrangements in accordance with which the first tier contractor is billing the Federal health care program;

(*ii*) Federally qualified HMOs without a contract under sections 1854 or 1876 of the Act, where the agreement with the eligible managed care organization sets out the arrangements in accordance with which the first tier contractor is billing the Federal health care program; or

(*iii*) First tier contractors that are Federally qualified health centers that claim supplemental payments from a Federal health care program.

(B) In establishing the terms of the agreement, neither party gives or receives remuneration in return for or to induce the provision or acceptance of business (other than business covered by the agreement) for which payment may be made in whole or in part by a Federal health care program on a fee-for-service or cost basis.

(C) Neither party to the agreement shifts the financial burden of the agreement to the extent that increased payments are claimed from a Federal health care program.

(ii) A first tier contractor and a downstream contractor or between two downstream contractors to provide or arrange for items or services, as long as the following four standards are met—

(A) The parties have an agreement that:

(*1*) Is set out in writing and signed by both parties;

(*2*) Specifies the items and services covered by the agreement;

(*3*) Is for a period of at least one year; and

(*4*) Specifies that the party providing the items or services cannot claim payment in any form from a Federal health care program for items or services covered under the agreement.

(B) In establishing the terms of the agreement, neither party gives or receives remuneration in return for or to induce the provision or acceptance of business (other than business covered by the agreement) for which payment may be made in whole or in part by a Federal health care program on a fee-for-service or cost basis.

(C) Neither party shifts the financial burden of the agreement to the extent that increased payments are claimed from a Federal health care program.

(D) The agreement between the eligible managed care organization and first tier contractor covering the items or services that are covered by the agreement between the parties does not involve:

(*1*) A Federally qualified health center receiving supplemental payments;

(*2*) A HMO or CMP with a cost-based contract under section 1876 of the Act; or

(*3*) A Federally qualified HMO, unless the items or services are covered by a risk based contract under sections 1854 or 1876 of the Act.

(2) For purposes of this paragraph, the following terms are defined as follows:

(i) *Downstream contractor* means an individual or entity that has a subcontract directly or indirectly with a first tier contractor for the provision or arrangement of items or services that are covered by an agreement between an eligible managed care organization and the first tier contractor.

(ii) *Eligible managed care organization*[1] means—

(A) A HMO or CMP with a risk or cost based contract in accordance with section 1876 of the Act;

(B) Any Medicare Part C health plan that receives a capitated payment from Medicare and which must have its total Medicare beneficiary cost sharing approved by CMS under section 1854 of the Act;

(C) Medicaid managed care organizations as defined in section 1903(m)(1)(A) that provide or arrange for items or services for Medicaid enrollees under a contract in accordance with section 1903(m) of the Act (except for fee-for-service plans or medical savings accounts);

(D) Any other health plans that provide or arrange for items and services for Medicaid enrollees in accordance with a risk-based contract with a State agency subject to the upper payment limits in Sec. 447.361 of this title or an equivalent payment cap approved by the Secretary;

(E) Programs For All Inclusive Care For The Elderly (PACE) under sections 1894 and 1934 of the Act, except for for-profit demonstrations under sections 4801(h) and 4802(h) of Pub. L. 105-33; or

(F) A Federally qualified HMO.

(iii) *First tier contractor* means an individual or entity that has a contract directly with an eligible managed care organization to provide or arrange for items or services.

(iv) *Items and services* means health care items, devices, supplies or services or those services reasonably related to the provision of health care items, devices, supplies or services including, but not limited to, non-emergency transportation, patient education, attendant services, social services (*e.g.,* case management), utilization review and quality assurance. Marketing and other pre-enrollment activities are not "items or services" for purposes of this section.

(u) *Price reductions offered by contractors with substantial financial risk to managed care organizations.* (1) As used in section 1128(B) of the Act, "remuneration" does not include any payment between:

(i) A qualified managed care plan and a first tier contractor for providing or arranging for items or services, where the following five standards are met—

(A) The agreement between the qualified managed care plan and first tier contractor must:

(*1*) Be in writing and signed by the parties;

(*2*) Specify the items and services covered by the agreement;

---

[1]The eligible managed care organizations in paragraphs (u)(2)(ii)(A)–(F) of this section are only eligible with respect to items or services covered by the contracts specified in those paragraphs.

(*3*) Be for a period of a least one year;

(*4*) Require participation in a quality assurance program that promotes the coordination of care, protects against underutilization and specifies patient goals, including measurable outcomes where appropriate; and

(*5*) Specify a methodology for determining payment that is commercially reasonable and consistent with fair market value established in an arms-length transaction and includes the intervals at which payments will be made and the formula for calculating incentives and penalties, if any.

(B) If a first tier contractor has an investment interest in a qualified managed care plan, the investment interest must meet the criteria of paragraph (a)(1) of this section.

(C) The first tier contractor must have substantial financial risk for the cost or utilization of services it is obligated to provide through one of the following four payment methodologies:

(*1*) A periodic fixed payment per patient that does not take into account the dates services are provided, the frequency of services, or the extent or kind of services provided;

(*2*) Percentage of premium;

(*3*) Inpatient Federal health care program diagnosis-related groups (DRGs) (other than those for psychiatric services);

(*4*) Bonus and withhold arrangements, provided—

(*i*) The target payment for first tier contractors that are individuals or non-institutional providers is at least 20 percent greater than the minimum payment, and for first tier contractors that are institutional providers, *i.e.,* hospitals and nursing homes, is at least 10 percent greater than the minimum payment;

(*ii*) The amount at risk, *i.e.,* the bonus or withhold, is earned by a first tier contractor in direct proportion to the ratio of the contractor's actual utilization to its target utilization;

(*iii*) In calculating the percentage in accordance with paragraph (u)(1)(i)(C)(*4*)(*i*) of this section, both the target payment amount and the minimum payment amount include any performance bonus, *e.g.,* payments for timely submission of paperwork, continuing medical education, meeting attendance, etc., at a level achieved by 75 percent of the first tier contractors who are eligible for such payments;

(*iv*) Payment amounts, including any bonus or withhold amounts, are reasonable given the historical utilization patterns and costs for the same or comparable populations in similar managed care arrangements; and

(*v*) Alternatively, for a first tier contractor that is a physician, the qualified managed care plan has placed the physician at risk for referral services in an amount that exceeds the substantial financial risk threshold set forth in 42 CFR 417.479(f) and the arrangement is in compliance with the stop-loss and beneficiary survey requirements of 42 CFR 417.479(g).

(D) Payments for items and services reimbursable by Federal health care program must comply with the following two standards—

(*1*) The qualified managed care plan (or in the case of a self-funded employer plan that contracts with a qualified managed care plan to provide administrative services, the self-funded employer plan) must submit the claims directly to the Federal health care program, in accordance with a valid reassignment agreement, for items or services reimbursed by the Federal health care program. (Notwithstanding the foregoing, inpatient hospital services, other than psychiatric services, will be deemed to comply if the hospital is reimbursed by a Federal health care program under a DRG methodology.)

(*2*) Payments to first tier contractors and any downstream contractors for providing or arranging for items or services reimbursed by a Federal health care program must be identical to payment arrangements to or between such parties for the same items or services provided to other beneficiaries with similar health status, provided that such payments may be adjusted where the adjustments are related to utilization patterns or costs of providing items or services to the relevant population.

(E) In establishing the terms of an arrangement—

(*1*) Neither party gives or receives remuneration in return for or to induce the provision or acceptance of business (other than business covered by the arrangement) for which payment may be made in whole or in part by a Federal health care program on a fee-for-service or cost basis; and

(*2*) Neither party to the arrangement shifts the financial burden of such arrangement to the extent that increased payments are claimed from a Federal health care program.

(ii) A first tier contractor and a downstream contractor, or between downstream contractors, to provide or arrange for items or services, as long as the following three standards are met—

(A) Both parties are being paid for the provision or arrangement of items or services in accordance with one of the payment methodologies set out in paragraph (u)(1)(i)(C) of this section;

(B) Payment arrangements for items and services reimbursable by a Federal health care program comply with paragraph (u)(1)(i)(D) of this section; and

(C) In establishing the terms of an arrangement—

(*1*) Neither party gives or receives remuneration in return for or to induce the provision or acceptance of business (other than business covered by the arrangement) for which payment may be made in whole or in part by a Federal health care program on a fee-for-service or cost basis; and

(*2*) Neither party to the arrangement shifts the financial burden of the arrangement to the extent that increased payments are claimed from a Federal health care program.

(2) For purposes of this paragraph, the following terms are defined as follows:

(i) *Downstream contractor* means an individual or entity that has a subcontract directly or indirectly with a first tier contractor for the provision or arrangement of items or services that are covered by an agreement between a qualified managed care plan and the first tier contractor.

(ii) *First tier contractor* means an individual or entity that has a contract directly with a qualified managed care plan to provide or arrange for items or services.

(iii) *Is obligated to provide* for a contractor refers to items or services:

(A) Provided directly by an individual or entity and its employees;

(B) For which an individual or entity is financially responsible, but which are provided by downstream contractors;

(C) For which an individual or entity makes referrals or arrangements; or

(D) For which an individual or entity receives financial incentives based on its own, its provider group's, or its qualified managed care plan's performance (or combination thereof).

(iv) *Items and services* means health care items, devices, supplies or services or those services reasonably related to the provision of health care items, devices, supplies or services including, but not limited to, non-emergency transportation, patient education, attendant services, social services (*e.g.,* case management), utilization review and quality assurance. Marketing or other pre-enrollment activities are not "items or services" for purposes of this definition in this paragraph.

(v) *Minimum payment* is the guaranteed amount that a provider is entitled to receive under an agreement with a first tier or downstream contractor or a qualified managed care plan.

(vi) *Qualified managed care plan* means a health plan as defined in paragraph (*l*)(2) of this section that:

(A) Provides a comprehensive range of health services;

(B) Provides or arranges for—

(*1*) Reasonable utilization goals to avoid inappropriate utilization;

(*2*) An operational utilization review program;

(*3*) A quality assurance program that promotes the coordination of care, protects against underutilization, and specifies patient goals, including measurable outcomes where appropriate;

(*4*) Grievance and hearing procedures;

(*5*) Protection of enrollees from incurring financial liability other than copayments and deductibles; and

(*6*) Treatment for Federal health care program beneficiaries that is not different than treatment for other enrollees because of their status as Federal health care program beneficiaries; and

(C) Covers a beneficiary population of which either—

(*1*) No more than 10 percent are Medicare beneficiaries, not including persons for whom a Federal health care program is the secondary payer; or

(*2*) No more than 50 percent are Medicare beneficiaries (not including persons for whom a Federal health care program is the secondary payer), provided that payment of premiums is on a periodic basis that does not take into account the dates services are rendered, the frequency of services, or the extent or kind of services rendered, and provided further that such periodic payments for the non-Federal health care program beneficiaries do not take into account the number of Federal health care program fee-for-service beneficiaries covered by the agreement or the amount of services generated by such beneficiaries.

(vii) *Target payment* means the fair market value payment established through arms length negotiations that will be earned by an individual or entity that:

(A) Is dependent on the individual or entity's meeting a utilization target or range of utilization targets that are set consistent with historical utilization rates for the same or comparable populations in similar managed care arrangements, whether based on its own, its provider group's or the qualified managed care plan's utilization (or a combination thereof); and

(B) Does not include any bonus or fees that the individual or entity may earn from exceeding the utilization target.

(v) *Ambulance replenishing.* (1) As used in section 1128B of the Act, "remuneration" does not include any gift or transfer of drugs or medical supplies (including linens) by a hospital or other receiving facility to an ambulance provider for the purpose of replenishing comparable drugs or medical supplies (including linens) used by the ambulance provider (or a first responder) in connection with the transport of a patient by ambulance to the hospital or other receiving facility if all of the standards in paragraph (v)(2) of this section are satisfied *and* all of the applicable standards in *either* paragraph (v)(3)(i), (v)(3)(ii) or (v)(3)(iii) of this section are satisfied. However, to qualify under paragraph (v), the ambulance that is replenished must be used to provide emergency ambulance services an average of three times per week, as measured over a reasonable period of time. Drugs and medical supplies (including linens) initially used by a first responder and replenished at the scene of the illness or injury by the ambulance provider that transports the patient to the hospital or other receiving facility will be deemed to have been used by the ambulance provider.

(2) To qualify under paragraph (v) of this section, the ambulance replenishing arrangement must satisfy all of the following four conditions—

(i)(A) Under no circumstances may the ambulance provider (or first responder) and the receiving facility both bill for the same replenished drug or supply. Replenished drugs or supplies may only be billed (including claiming bad debt) to a Federal health care program by either the ambulance provider (or first responder) or the receiving facility.

(B) All billing or claims submission by the receiving facility, ambulance provider or first responder for replenished drugs and medical supplies used in connection with the transport of a Federal health care program beneficiary must comply with all applicable Federal health care program payment and coverage rules and regulations.

(C) Compliance with paragraph (v)(2)(i)(B) of this section will be determined separately for the receiving facility and the ambulance provider (and first responder, if any), so long as the receiving facility, ambulance provider (or first responder) refrains from doing anything that would impede the other party or parties from meeting their obligations under paragraph (v)(2)(i)(B).

(ii)(A) The receiving facility or ambulance provider, or both, must

(*1*) Maintain records of the replenished drugs and medical supplies and the patient transport to which the replenished drugs and medical supplies related;

(*2*) Provide a copy of such records to the other party within a reasonable time (unless the other party is separately maintaining records of the replenished drugs and medical supplies); and

(*3*) Make those records available to the Secretary promptly upon request.

(B) A pre-hospital care report (including, but not limited to, a trip sheet, patient care report or patient encounter report) prepared by the ambulance provider and filed with the receiving facility will meet the requirements of paragraph (v)(2)(ii)(A) of this section, provided that it documents the specific type and amount of medical supplies and drugs used on the patient and subsequently replenished.

(C) For purposes of paragraph (v)(2)(ii) of this section, documentation may be maintained and, if required, filed with the other party in hard copy or electronically. If a replenishing arrangement includes linens, documentation need not be maintained for their exchange. If documentation is not maintained for the exchange of linens, the receiving facility will be presumed to have provided an exchange of comparable clean linens for soiled linens for each ambulance transport of a patient to the receiving facility. Records required under paragraph (v)(2)(ii)(A) of this section must be maintained for 5 years.

(iii) The replenishing arrangement must not take into account the volume or value of any referrals or business otherwise generated between the parties for which payment may be made in whole or in part under any Federal health care program (other than the referral of the particular patient to whom the replenished drugs and medical supplies were furnished).

(iv) The receiving facility and the ambulance provider otherwise comply with all Federal, State, and local laws regulating ambulance services, including, but not limited to, emergency services, and the provision of drugs and medical supplies, including, but not limited to, laws relating to the handling of controlled substances.

(3) To qualify under paragraph (v) of this section, the arrangement must satisfy *all* of the standards in *one* of the following three categories:

(i) *General replenishing.* (A) The receiving facility must replenish medical supplies or drugs on an equal basis for all ambulance providers that bring patients to the receiving facility in any one of the categories described in paragraph (v)(3)(i)(A)(*1*), (*2*), or (*3*) of this section. A receiving facility may offer replenishing to one or more of the categories and may offer different replenishing arrangements to different categories, so long as the replenishing is conducted uniformly within each category. For example, a receiving facility may offer to replenish a broader array of drugs or supplies for ambulance providers that do no not charge for their services than for ambulance providers that charge for their services. Within each category, the receiving facility may limit its replenishing arrangements to the replenishing of emergency ambulance transports only. A receiving facility may offer replenishing to one or more of the categories—

(*1*) All ambulance providers that do not bill any patient or insurer (including Federal health care programs) for ambulance services, regardless of the payor or the patient's ability to pay (*i.e.,* ambulance providers, such as volunteer companies, that provide ambulance services without charge to any person or entity);

(*2*) All not-for-profit and State or local government ambulance service providers (including, but not limited to, municipal and volunteer ambulance services providers); or

(*3*) All ambulance service providers.

(B)(*1*) The replenishing arrangement must be conducted in an open and public manner. A replenishing arrangement will be considered to be conducted in an open and public manner if one of the following two conditions are satisfied:

(*i*) A written disclosure of the replenishing program is posted conspicuously in the receiving facility's emergency room or other location where the ambulance providers deliver patients and copies are made available upon request to ambulance providers, Government representatives, and members of the public (subject to reasonable photocopying charges). The written disclosure can take any reasonable form and should include the category of ambulance service providers that qualifies for replenishment; the drugs or medical supplies included in the replenishment program; and the procedures for documenting the replenishment. A sample disclosure form is included in Appendix A to subpart C of this part for illustrative purposes only. No written contracts between the parties are required for purposes of paragraph (v)(3) (i)(B)(*1*)(i) of this section; or

(*ii*) The replenishment arrangement operates in accordance with a plan or protocol of general application promulgated by an Emergency Medical Services (EMS) Council or comparable entity, agency or organization, provided a copy of the plan or protocol is available upon request to ambulance providers, Government representatives and members of the public (subject to reasonable photo-copying charges). While parties are encouraged to participate in collaborative, comprehensive, community-wide EMS systems to improve the delivery of EMS in their local communities, nothing in this paragraph shall be construed as requiring the involvement of such organizations or the development or implementation of ambulance replenishment plans or protocols by such organizations.

(2) Nothing in this paragraph (v)(3)(i) shall be construed as requiring disclosure of confidential proprietary or financial information related to the replenishing arrangement (including, but not limited to, information about cost, pricing or the volume of replenished drugs or supplies) to ambulance providers or members of the general public.

(ii) *Fair market value replenishing.* (A) Except as otherwise provided in paragraph (v)(3)(ii)(B) of this section, the ambulance provider must pay the receiving facility fair market value, based on an arms-length transaction, for replenished medical supplies; and

(B) If payment is not made at the same time as the replenishing of the medical supplies, the receiving facility and the ambulance provider must make commercially reasonable payment arrangements in advance.

(iii) *Government mandated replenishing.* The replenishing arrangement is undertaken in accordance with a State or local statute, ordinance, regulation or binding protocol that requires hospitals or receiving facilities in the area subject to such requirement to replenish ambulances that deliver patients to the hospital with drugs or medical supplies (including linens) that are used during the transport of that patient.

(4) For purposes of paragraph (v) of this section—

(i) A *receiving facility* is a hospital or other facility that provides emergency medical services.

(ii) An *ambulance provider* is a provider or supplier of ambulance transport services that provides emergency ambulance services. The term does not include a provider of ambulance transport services that provides only non-emergency transport services.

(iii) A *first responder* includes, but is not limited to, a fire department, paramedic service or search and rescue squad that responds to an emergency call (through 9-1-1 or other emergency access number) and treats the patient, but does not transport the patient to the hospital or other receiving facility.

(iv) An *emergency ambulance service* is a transport by ambulance initiated as a result of a call through 9-1-1 or other emergency access number or a call from another acute care facility unable to provide the higher level care required by the patient and available at the receiving facility.

(v) *Medical supplies* includes linens, unless otherwise provided.

[SOURCE: 57 Fed. Reg. 3330 (Jan. 29, 1992), *as amended at* 57 Fed. Reg. 52,729 (Nov. 5, 1992); 61 Fed. Reg. 2135 (Jan. 25, 1996); 64 Fed. Reg. 63,513 (Nov. 19, 1999); 64 Fed. Reg. 63,551 (Nov. 19, 1999); 64 Fed. Reg. 71,317 (Dec. 21, 1999); 66 Fed. Reg. 62,989 (Dec. 4, 2001); 66 Fed. Reg. 63,749 (Dec. 10, 2001); 67 Fed. Reg. 11,933 (Mar. 18, 2002).]

Appendix B

Stark Self-Referral Law Materials

Editor's Note: Effective July 26, 2004, the Stark Phase II Final Regulations superseded the Stark I Regulations and the Stark II Phase I Regulations. Refer to Appendix B in the Main Volume for text of the Stark I and Stark II Phase I Regulations.

Appendix B-1

Stark Self-Referral Law

Source: 42 U.S.C. Section 1395nn.

Section 1395nn. Limitation on Certain Physician Referrals

(a) Prohibition of certain referrals

    (1) In general

        Except as provided in subsection (b) of this section, if a physician (or an immediate family member of such physician) has a financial relationship with an entity specified in paragraph (2), then—

        (A) the physician may not make a referral to the entity for the furnishing of designated health services for which payment otherwise may be made under this subchapter, and

        (B) the entity may not present or cause to be presented a claim under this subchapter or bill to any individual, third party payor, or other entity for designated health services furnished pursuant to a referral prohibited under subparagraph (A).

    (2) Financial relationship specified

        For purposes of this section, a financial relationship of a physician (or an immediate family member of such physician) with an entity specified in this paragraph is—

        (A) except as provided in subsections (c) and (d) of this section, an ownership or investment interest in the entity, or

        (B) except as provided in subsection (e) of this section, a compensation arrangement (as defined in subsection (h)(1) of this section) between the physician (or an immediate family member of such physician) and the entity.

        An ownership or investment interest described in subparagraph (A) may be through equity, debt, or other means and includes an interest in an entity that holds an ownership or investment interest in any entity providing the designated health service.

(b) General exceptions to both ownership and compensation arrangement prohibitions

Subsection (a)(1) of this section shall not apply in the following cases:

(1) Physicians' services

In the case of physicians' services (as defined in section 1395x(q) of this title) provided personally by (or under the personal supervision of) another physician in the same group practice (as defined in subsection (h)(4) of this section) as the referring physician.

(2) In-office ancillary services

In the case of services (other than durable medical equipment (excluding infusion pumps) and parenteral and enteral nutrients, equipment, and supplies)—

(A) that are furnished—

(i) personally by the referring physician, personally by a physician who is a member of the same group practice as the referring physician, or personally by individuals who are directly supervised by the physician or by another physician in the group practice, and

(ii)(I) in a building in which the referring physician (or another physician who is a member of the same group practice) furnishes physicians' services unrelated to the furnishing of designated health services, or

(II) in the case of a referring physician who is a member of a group practice, in another building which is used by the group practice—

(aa) for the provision of some or all of the group's clinical laboratory services, or

(bb) for the centralized provision of the group's designated health services (other than clinical laboratory services), unless the Secretary determines other terms and conditions under which the provision of such services does not present a risk of program or patient abuse, and

(B) that are billed by the physician performing or supervising the services, by a group practice of which such physician is a member under a billing number assigned to the group practice, or by an entity that is wholly owned by such physician or such group practice,

if the ownership or investment interest in such services meets such other requirements as the Secretary may impose by regulation as needed to protect against program or patient abuse.

(3) Prepaid plans

In the case of services furnished by an organization—

(A) with a contract under section 1395mm of this title to an individual enrolled with the organization,

(B) described in section 1395l(a)(1)(A) of this title to an individual enrolled with the organization,

(C) receiving payments on a prepaid basis, under a demonstration project under section 1395b-1(a) of this title or under section 222(a) of the Social Security Amendments of 1972, to an individual enrolled with the organization,

(D) that is a qualified health maintenance organization (within the meaning of section 300e-9(d)[1] of this title) to an individual enrolled with the organization, or

(E) that is a Medicare+Choice organization under part C of this subchapter that is offering a coordinated care plan described in section 1395w-21(a)(2)(A) of this title to an individual enrolled with the organization.

(4) Other permissible exceptions

In the case of any other financial relationship which the Secretary determines, and specifies in regulations, does not pose a risk of program or patient abuse.

(5) Electronic prescribing

An exception established by regulation under section 1395w-103(e)(6) of this title.

(c) General exception related only to ownership or investment prohibition for ownership in publicly traded securities and mutual funds

Ownership of the following shall not be considered to be an ownership or investment interest described in subsection (a)(2)(A) of this section:

(1) Ownership of investment securities (including shares or bonds, debentures, notes, or other debt instruments) which may be purchased on terms generally available to the public and which are—

(A)(i) securities listed on the New York Stock Exchange, the American Stock Exchange, or any regional exchange in which quotations are published on a daily basis, or foreign securities listed on a recognized foreign, national, or regional exchange in which quotations are published on a daily basis, or

(ii) traded under an automated interdealer quotation system operated by the National Association of Securities Dealers, and

(B) in a corporation that had, at the end of the corporation's most recent fiscal year, or on average during the previous 3 fiscal years, stockholder equity exceeding $75,000,000.

(2) Ownership of shares in a regulated investment company as defined in section 851(a) of the Internal Revenue Code of 1986, if such company had, at the end of the company's most recent fiscal year, or on average during the previous 3 fiscal years, total assets exceeding $75,000,000.

(d) Additional exceptions related only to ownership or investment prohibition

The following, if not otherwise excepted under subsection (b) of this section, shall not be considered to be an ownership or investment interest described in subsection (a)(2)(A) of this section:

(1) Hospitals in Puerto Rico

In the case of designated health services provided by a hospital located in Puerto Rico.

---

[1] See References in Text note below.

(2) Rural providers

In the case of designated health services furnished in a rural area (as defined in section 1395ww(d)(2)(D) of this title) by an entity, if—

(A) substantially all of the designated health services furnished by the entity are furnished to individuals residing in such a rural area; and

(B) effective for the 18-month period beginning on December 8, 2003, the entity is not a specialty hospital (as defined in subsection (h)(7) of this section).

(3) Hospital ownership

In the case of designated health services provided by a hospital (other than a hospital described in paragraph (1)) if—

(A) the referring physician is authorized to perform services at the hospital, and

(B) effective for the 18-month period beginning on December 8, 2003, the hospital is not a specialty hospital (as defined in subsection (h)(7) of this section); and

(C) the ownership or investment interest is in the hospital itself (and not merely in a subdivision of the hospital).

(e) Exceptions relating to other compensation arrangements

The following shall not be considered to be a compensation arrangement described in subsection (a)(2)(B) of this section:

(1) Rental of office space; rental of equipment

(A) Office space

Payments made by a lessee to a lessor for the use of premises if—

(i) the lease is set out in writing, signed by the parties, and specifies the premises covered by the lease,

(ii) the space rented or leased does not exceed that which is reasonable and necessary for the legitimate business purposes of the lease or rental and is used exclusively by the lessee when being used by the lessee, except that the lessee may make payments for the use of space consisting of common areas if such payments do not exceed the lessee's pro rata share of expenses for such space based upon the ratio of the space used exclusively by the lessee to the total amount of space (other than common areas) occupied by all persons using such common areas,

(iii) the lease provides for a term of rental or lease for at least 1 year,

(iv) the rental charges over the term of the lease are set in advance, are consistent with fair market value, and are not determined in a manner that takes into account the volume or value of any referrals or other business generated between the parties,

(v) the lease would be commercially reasonable even if no referrals were made between the parties, and

(vi) the lease meets such other requirements as the Secretary may impose by regulation as needed to protect against program or patient abuse.

(B) Equipment

Payments made by a lessee of equipment to the lessor of the equipment for the use of the equipment if—

(i) the lease is set out in writing, signed by the parties, and specifies the equipment covered by the lease,

(ii) the equipment rented or leased does not exceed that which is reasonable and necessary for the legitimate business purposes of the lease or rental and is used exclusively by the lessee when being used by the lessee,

(iii) the lease provides for a term of rental or lease of at least 1 year,

(iv) the rental charges over the term of the lease are set in advance, are consistent with fair market value, and are not determined in a manner that takes into account the volume or value of any referrals or other business generated between the parties,

(v) the lease would be commercially reasonable even if no referrals were made between the parties, and

(vi) the lease meets such other requirements as the Secretary may impose by regulation as needed to protect against program or patient abuse.

(2) Bona fide employment relationships

Any amount paid by an employer to a physician (or an immediate family member of such physician) who has a bona fide employment relationship with the employer for the provision of services if—

(A) the employment is for identifiable services,

(B) the amount of the remuneration under the employment—

(i) is consistent with the fair market value of the services, and

(ii) is not determined in a manner that takes into account (directly or indirectly) the volume or value of any referrals by the referring physician,

(C) the remuneration is provided pursuant to an agreement which would be commercially reasonable even if no referrals were made to the employer, and

(D) the employment meets such other requirements as the Secretary may impose by regulation as needed to protect against program or patient abuse.

Subparagraph (B)(ii) shall not prohibit the payment of remuneration in the form of a productivity bonus based on services performed personally by the physician (or an immediate family member of such physician).

(3) Personal service arrangements

(A) In general

Remuneration from an entity under an arrangement (including remuneration for specific physicians' services furnished to a nonprofit blood center) if—

(i) the arrangement is set out in writing, signed by the parties, and specifies the services covered by the arrangement,

(ii) the arrangement covers all of the services to be provided by the physician (or an immediate family member of such physician) to the entity,

(iii) the aggregate services contracted for do not exceed those that are reasonable and necessary for the legitimate business purposes of the arrangement,

(iv) the term of the arrangement is for at least 1 year,

(v) the compensation to be paid over the term of the arrangement is set in advance, does not exceed fair market value, and except in the case of a physician incentive plan described in subparagraph (B), is not determined in a manner that takes into account the volume or value of any referrals or other business generated between the parties,

(vi) the services to be performed under the arrangement do not involve the counseling or promotion or a business arrangement or other activity that violates any State or Federal law, and

(vii) the arrangement meets such other requirements as the Secretary may impose by regulation as needed to protect against program or patient abuse.

(B) Physician incentive plan exception

(i) In general

In the case of a physician incentive plan (as defined in clause (ii)) between a physician and an entity, the compensation may be determined in a manner (through a withhold, capitation, bonus, or otherwise) that takes into account directly or indirectly the volume or value of any referrals or other business generated between the parties, if the plan meets the following requirements:

(I) No specific payment is made directly or indirectly under the plan to a physician or a physician group as an inducement to reduce or limit medically necessary services provided with respect to a specific individual enrolled with the entity.

(II) In the case of a plan that places a physician or a physician group at substantial financial risk as determined by the Secretary pursuant to section 1395mm(i) (8)(A)(ii) of this title, the plan complies with any requirements the Secretary may impose pursuant to such section.

(III) Upon request by the Secretary, the entity provides the Secretary with access to descriptive information regarding the plan, in order to permit the Secretary to determine whether the plan is in compliance with the requirements of this clause.

(ii) "Physician incentive plan" defined

For purposes of this subparagraph, the term "physician incentive plan" means any compensation arrangement between an entity and a physician or physician group that may directly or indirectly have the effect of reducing or limiting services provided with respect to individuals enrolled with the entity.

(4) Remuneration unrelated to the provision of designated health services

In the case of remuneration which is provided by a hospital to a physician if such remuneration does not relate to the provision of designated health services.

(5) Physician recruitment

In the case of remuneration which is provided by a hospital to a physician to induce the physician to relocate to the geographic area served by the hospital in order to be a member of the medical staff of the hospital, if—

(A) the physician is not required to refer patients to the hospital,

(B) the amount of the remuneration under the arrangement is not determined in a manner that takes into account (directly or indirectly) the volume or value of any referrals by the referring physician, and

(C) the arrangement meets such other requirements as the Secretary may impose by regulation as needed to protect against program or patient abuse.

(6) Isolated transactions

In the case of an isolated financial transaction, such as a one-time sale of property or practice, if—

(A) the requirements described in subparagraphs (B) and (C) of paragraph (2) are met with respect to the entity in the same manner as they apply to an employer, and

(B) the transaction meets such other requirements as the Secretary may impose by regulation as needed to protect against program or patient abuse.

(7) Certain group practice arrangements with a hospital

(A)[2] In general

An arrangement between a hospital and a group under which designated health services are provided by the group but are billed by the hospital if—

(i) with respect to services provided to an inpatient of the hospital, the arrangement is pursuant to the provision of

---

[2] So in original. No subpar. (B) has been enacted.

inpatient hospital services under section 1395x(b)(3) of this title.

(ii) the arrangement began before December 19, 1989, and has continued in effect without interruption since such date,

(iii) with respect to the designated health services covered under the arrangement, substantially all of such services furnished to patients of the hospital are furnished by the group under the arrangement,

(iv) the arrangement is pursuant to an agreement that is set out in writing and that specifies the services to be provided by the parties and the compensation for services provided under the agreement,

(v) the compensation paid over the term of the agreement is consistent with fair market value and the compensation per unit of services is fixed in advance and is not determined in a manner that takes into account the volume or value of any referrals or other business generated between the parties,

(vi) the compensation is provided pursuant to an agreement which would be commercially reasonable even if no referrals were made to the entity, and

(vii) the arrangement between the parties meets such other requirements as the Secretary may impose by regulation as needed to protect against program or patient abuse.

(8) Payments by a physician for items and services

Payments made by a physician—

(A) to a laboratory in exchange for the provision of clinical laboratory services, or

(B) to an entity as compensation for other items or services if the items or services are furnished at a price that is consistent with fair market value.

(f) Reporting requirements

Each entity providing covered items or services for which payment may be made under this subchapter shall provide the Secretary with the information concerning the entity's ownership, investment, and compensation arrangements, including—

(1) the covered items and services provided by the entity, and

(2) the names and unique physician identification numbers of all physicians with an ownership or investment interest (as described in subsection (a)(2)(A) of this section), or with a compensation arrangement (as described in subsection (a)(2)(B) of this section), in the entity, or whose immediate relatives have such an ownership or investment interest or who have such a compensation relationship with the entity.

Such information shall be provided in such form, manner, and at such times as the Secretary shall specify. The requirement of this subsection shall not apply to designated health services provided outside the United States or to entities which the Secretary determines provides[3] services for which payment may be made under this subchapter very infrequently.

(g) Sanctions

   (1) Denial of payment

      No payment may be made under this subchapter for a designated health service which is provided in violation of subsection (a)(1) of this section.

   (2) Requiring refunds for certain claims

      If a person collects any amounts that were billed in violation of subsection (a)(1) of this section, the person shall be liable to the individual for, and shall refund on a timely basis to the individual, any amounts so collected.

   (3) Civil money penalty and exclusion for improper claims

      Any person that presents or causes to be presented a bill or a claim for a service that such person knows or should know is for a service for which payment may not be made under paragraph (1) or for which a refund has not been made under paragraph (2) shall be subject to a civil money penalty of not more than $15,000 for each such service. The provisions of section 1320a-7a of this title (other than the first sentence of subsection (a) and other than subsection (b)) shall apply to a civil money penalty under the previous sentence in the same manner as such provisions apply to a penalty or proceeding under section 1320a-7a(a) of this title.

   (4) Civil money penalty and exclusion for circumvention schemes

      Any physician or other entity that enters into an arrangement or scheme (such as a cross-referral arrangement) which the physician or entity knows or should know has a principal purpose of assuring referrals by the physician to a particular entity which, if the physician directly made referrals to such entity, would be in violation of this section, shall be subject to a civil money penalty of not more than $100,000 for each such arrangement or scheme. The provisions of section 1320a-7a of this title (other than the first sentence of subsection (a) and other than subsection (b)) shall apply to a civil money penalty under the previous sentence in the same manner as such provisions apply to a penalty or proceeding under section 1320a-7a(a) of this title.

   (5) Failure to report information

      Any person who is required, but fails, to meet a reporting requirement of subsection (f) of this section is subject to a civil money penalty of not more than $10,000 for each day for which reporting is required to have been made. The provisions of section 1320a-7a of this title (other than the first sentence of subsection (a) and other than subsection (b)) shall apply to a civil money penalty under the previous sentence in the same manner as such provisions apply to a penalty or proceeding under section 1320a-7a(a) of this title.

---

[3] So in original. Probably should be "provide".

(6) Advisory opinions
    (A) In general
        The Secretary shall issue written advisory opinions concerning whether a referral relating to designated health services (other than clinical laboratory services) is prohibited under this section. Each advisory opinion issued by the Secretary shall be binding as to the Secretary and the party or parties requesting the opinion.
    (B) Application of certain rules
        The Secretary shall, to the extent practicable, apply the rules under subsections (b)(3) and (b)(4) of this section and take into account the regulations promulgated under subsection (b)(5) of section 1320a-7d of this title in the issuance of advisory opinions under this paragraph.
    (C) Regulations
        In order to implement this paragraph in a timely manner, the Secretary may promulgate regulations that take effect on an interim basis, after notice and pending opportunity for public comment.
    (D) Applicability
        This paragraph shall apply to requests for advisory opinions made after the date which is 90 days after August 5, 1997, and before the close of the period described in section 1320a-7d(b)(6) of this title.
(h) Definitions and special rules
  For purposes of this section:
  (1) Compensation arrangement; remuneration
    (A) The term "compensation arrangement" means any arrangement involving any remuneration between a physician (or an immediate family member of such physician) and an entity other than an arrangement involving only remuneration described in subparagraph (C).
    (B) The term "remuneration" includes any remuneration, directly or indirectly, overtly or covertly, in cash or in kind.
    (C) Remuneration described in this subparagraph is any remuneration consisting of any of the following:
        (i) The forgiveness of amounts owed for inaccurate tests or procedures, mistakenly performed tests or procedures, or the correction of minor billing errors.
        (ii) The provision of items, devices, or supplies that are used solely to—
            (I) collect, transport, process, or store specimens for the entity providing the item, device, or supply, or
            (II) order or communicate the results of tests or procedures for such entity.
        (iii) A payment made by an insurer or a self-insured plan to a physician to satisfy a claim, submitted on a fee for service basis, for the furnishing of health services by that

physician to an individual who is covered by a policy with the insurer or by the self-insured plan, if—

(I) the health services are not furnished, and the payment is not made, pursuant to a contract or other arrangement between the insurer or the plan and the physician,

(II) the payment is made to the physician on behalf of the covered individual and would otherwise be made directly to such individual,

(III) the amount of the payment is set in advance, does not exceed fair market value, and is not determined in a manner that takes into account directly or indirectly the volume or value of any referrals, and

(IV) the payment meets such other requirements as the Secretary may impose by regulation as needed to protect against program or patient abuse.

(2) Employee

An individual is considered to be "employed by" or an "employee" of an entity if the individual would be considered to be an employee of the entity under the usual common law rules applicable in determining the employer-employee relationship (as applied for purposes of section 3121(d)(2) of the Internal Revenue Code of 1986).

(3) Fair market value

The term "fair market value" means the value in arms length transactions, consistent with the general market value, and, with respect to rentals or leases, the value of rental property for general commercial purposes (not taking into account its intended use) and, in the case of a lease of space, not adjusted to reflect the additional value the prospective lessee or lessor would attribute to the proximity or convenience to the lessor where the lessor is a potential source of patient referrals to the lessee.

(4) Group practice

(A) Definition of group practice

The term "group practice" means a group of 2 or more physicians legally organized as a partnership, professional corporation, foundation, not-for-profit corporation, faculty practice plan, or similar association—

(i) in which each physician who is a member of the group provides substantially the full range of services which the physician routinely provides, including medical care, consultation, diagnosis, or treatment, through the joint use of shared office space, facilities, equipment and personnel,

(ii) for which substantially all of the services of the physicians who are members of the group are provided through the group and are billed under a billing number assigned to the group and amounts so received are treated as receipts of the group,

(iii) in which the overhead expenses of and the income from the practice are distributed in accordance with methods previously determined,

(iv) except as provided in subparagraph (B)(i), in which no physician who is a member of the group directly or indirectly receives compensation based on the volume or value of referrals by the physician,

(v) in which members of the group personally conduct no less than 75 percent of the physician-patient encounters of the group practice, and

(vi) which meets such other standards as the Secretary may impose by regulation.

(B) Special rules

(i) Profits and productivity bonuses

A physician in a group practice may be paid a share of overall profits of the group, or a productivity bonus based on services personally performed or services incident to such personally performed services, so long as the share or bonus is not determined in any manner which is directly related to the volume or value of referrals by such physician.

(ii) Faculty practice plans

In the case of a faculty practice plan associated with a hospital, institution of higher education, or medical school with an approved medical residency training program in which physician members may provide a variety of different specialty services and provide professional services both within and outside the group, as well as perform other tasks such as research, subparagraph (A) shall be applied only with respect to the services provided within the faculty practice plan.

(5) Referral; referring physician

(A) Physicians' services

Except as provided in subparagraph (C), in the case of an item or service for which payment may be made under part B of this subchapter, the request by a physician for the item or service, including the request by a physician for a consultation with another physician (and any test or procedure ordered by, or to be performed by (or under the supervision of) that other physician), constitutes a "referral" by a "referring physician".

(B) Other items

Except as provided in subparagraph (C), the request or establishment of a plan of care by a physician which includes the provision of the designated health service constitutes a "referral" by a "referring physician".

(C) Clarification respecting certain services integral to a consultation by certain specialists.

A request by a pathologist for clinical diagnostic laboratory tests and pathological examination services, a request by a radiologist for diagnostic radiology services, and a request by a radiation oncologist for radiation therapy, if such services are furnished by (or under the supervision of) such pathologist, radiologist, or radiation oncologist pursuant to a consultation requested by another physician does not constitute a "referral" by a "referring physician."

(6) Designated health services

The term "designated health services" means any of the following items or services:

(A) Clinical laboratory services.

(B) Physical therapy services.

(C) Occupational therapy services.

(D) Radiology services, including magnetic resonance imaging, computerized axial tomography scans, and ultrasound services.

(E) Radiation therapy services and supplies.

(F) Durable medical equipment and supplies.

(G) Parenteral and enteral nutrients, equipment, and supplies.

(H) Prosthetics, orthotics, and prosthetic devices and supplies.

(I) Home health services.

(J) Outpatient prescription drugs.

(K) Inpatient and outpatient hospital services.

(7) Specialty hospital

(A) In general

For purposes of this section, except as provided in subparagraph (B), the term "specialty hospital" means a subsection (d) hospital (as defined in section 1395ww(d)(1)(B) of this title) that is primarily or exclusively engaged in the care and treatment of one of the following categories:

(i) Patients with a cardiac condition.

(ii) Patients with an orthopedic condition.

(iii) Patients receiving a surgical procedure.

(iv) Any other specialized category of services that the Secretary designates as inconsistent with the purpose of permitting physician ownership and investment interests in a hospital under this section.

(B) Exception

For purposes of this section, the term "specialty hospital" does not include any hospital—

(i) determined by the Secretary—

(I) to be in operation before November 18, 2003; or

(II) under development as of such date;

(ii) for which the number of physician investors at any time on or after such date is no greater than the number of such investors as of such date;

(iii) for which the type of categories described in subparagraph (A) at any time on or after such date is no different than the type of such categories as of such date;

(iv) for which any increase in the number of beds occurs only in the facilities on the main campus of the hospital and

does not exceed 50 percent of the number of beds in the hospital as of November 18, 2003, or 5 beds, whichever is greater; and
(v) that meets such other requirements as the Secretary may specify.

SOURCE—

(Aug. 14, 1935, ch. 531, title XVIII, Sec. 1877, as added Pub. L. 101-239, title VI, Sec. 6204(a), Dec. 19, 1989, 103 Stat. 2236; amended Pub. L. 101-508, title IV, Sec. 4207(e)(1)-(3), (k)(2), formerly Sec. 4027(e)(1)-(3), (k)(2), Nov. 5, 1990, 104 Stat. 1388-121, 1388-122, 1388-124, renumbered Pub. L. 103-432, title I, Sec. 160(d)(4), Oct. 31, 1994, 108 Stat. 4444; Pub. L. 103-66, title XIII, Sec. 13562(a), Aug. 10, 1993, 107 Stat. 596; Pub. L.103-432, title I, Sec. 152(a), (b), Oct. 31, 1994, 108 Stat. 4436; Pub. L. 105-33, title IV, Sec. 4314, Aug. 5, 1997, 111 Stat. 389; Pub. L. 106-113, div. B, Sec. 1000(a)(6) (title V, Sec. 524(a)), Nov. 29, 1999, 113 Stat. 1536, 1501A-387; Pub. L. No. 108-173, title I, Sec. 101(e)(8)(B), title V, Sec. 507(a), Dec. 8, 2003, 117 Stat. 2152, 2295.)

REFERENCES IN TEXT

Section 222(a) of the Social Security Amendments of 1972, referred to in subsec. (b)(3)(C), is section 222(a) of Pub. L. 92-603, Oct. 30, 1972, 86 Stat. 1329, which is set out as a note under section 1395b-1 of this title.

Section 300e-9(d) of this title, referred to in subsec. (b)(3)(D), was redesignated section 300e-9(c) of this title by Pub. L. 100-517, Sec. 7(b), Oct. 24, 1988, 102 Stat. 2580.

Part C of this subchapter, referred to in subsec. (b)(3)(E), is classified to section 1395w-21 et seq. of this title.

The Internal Revenue Code, referred to in subsecs. (c)(2) and (h)(2), is classified generally to Title 26, Internal Revenue Code.

Part B of this subchapter, referred to in subsec. (h)(5)(A), is classified to section 1395j et seq. of this title.

Appendix B-2

Stark Phase II Final Regulations (effective July 26, 2004) [New]

Source: 69 Fed. Reg. 16,054, 16,126–43 (Mar. 26, 2004), *codified at* 42 C.F.R. §§411.350–.361.

For the reasons set forth in the preamble, CMS amends 42 CFR chapter IV as set forth below:

PART 411—EXCLUSIONS FROM MEDICARE AND LIMITATIONS ON MEDICARE PAYMENT

1. The authority citation for part 411 continues to read as follows:

Authority: Secs. 1102 and 1871 of the Social Security Act (42 U.S.C. 1302 and 1395hh).

**Subpart A—General Exclusions and
Exclusion of Particular Services**

2. In § 411.1, paragraph (a) is republished to read as follows:

§ 411.1 Basis and scope.

(a) *Statutory basis.* Sections 1814(a) and 1835(a) of the Act require
that a physician certify or recertify a patient's need for home health
services but, in general, prohibit a physician from certifying or recertifying the need for services if the services will be furnished by an
HHA in which the physician has a significant ownership interest, or
with which the physician has a significant financial or contractual relationship. Sections 1814(c), 1835(d), and 1862 of the Act exclude from
Medicare payment certain specified services. The Act provides special
rules for payment of services furnished by the following: Federal
providers or agencies (sections 1814(c) and 1835(d)); hospitals and
physicians outside of the U.S. (sections 1814(f) and 1862(a)(4)); and
hospitals and SNFs of the Indian Health Service (section 1880 of the
Act). Section 1877 of the Act sets forth limitations on referrals and
payment for designated health services furnished by entities with
which the referring physician (or an immediate family member of the
referring physician) has a financial relationship.

* * * * *

**Subpart J—Financial Relationships Between Physicians and
Entities Furnishing Designated Health Services**

3. The heading for subpart J is revised as set forth above, and subpart
   J is revised to read as follows:

**Subpart J—Financial Relationships Between Physicians and
Entities Furnishing Designated Health Services**

Subpart J—Financial Relationships Between Physicians and Entities Furnishing Designated Health Services

§ 411.350 Scope of subpart.

(a) This subpart implements section 1877 of the Act, which generally prohibits a physician from making a referral under Medicare for designated health services to an entity with which the physician or a member of the physician's immediate family has a financial relationship.

(b) This subpart does not provide for exceptions or immunity from civil or criminal prosecution or other sanctions applicable under any State laws or under Federal law other than section 1877 of the Act. For example, although a particular arrangement involving a physician's financial relationship with an entity may not prohibit the physician from making referrals to the entity under this subpart, the arrangement may nevertheless violate another provision of the Act or other laws administered by HHS, the Federal Trade Commission, the Securities and Exchange Commission, the Internal Revenue Service, or any other Federal or State agency.

(c) This subpart requires, with some exceptions, that certain entities furnishing covered services under Medicare Part A or Part B report information concerning ownership, investment, or compensation arrangements in the form, in the manner, and at the times specified by CMS.

§ 411.351 Definitions.

As used in this subpart, unless the context indicates otherwise:

Centralized building means all or part of a building, including, for purposes of this subpart only, a mobile vehicle, van, or trailer that is owned or leased on a full-time basis (that is, 24 hours per day, 7 days per week, for a term of not less than 6 months) by a group practice and that is used exclusively by the group practice. Space in a building or a mobile vehicle, van, or trailer that is shared by more than one group practice, by a group practice and one or more solo practitioners, or by a group practice and another provider or supplier (for example, a diagnostic imaging facility) is not a centralized building for purposes of this subpart. This provision does not preclude a group practice from providing services to other providers or suppliers (for example, purchased diagnostic tests) in the group practice's centralized building. A group practice may have more than one centralized building.

Clinical laboratory services means the biological, microbiological, serological, chemical, immunohematological, hematological, biophysical, cytological, pathological, or other examination of materials derived from the human body for the purpose of providing information for the diagnosis, prevention, or treatment of any disease or impairment of, or the assessment of the health of, human beings, including procedures to determine, measure, or otherwise describe the presence or absence of various substances or organisms in the body, as specifically identified by the List of CPT/HCPCS Codes. All services so identified on the List of CPT/HCPCS Codes are clinical laboratory services for purposes of this subpart. Any service not specifically identified as a clinical laboratory service on the List of CPT/HCPCS Codes is not a clinical laboratory service for purposes of this subpart.

Consultation means a professional service furnished to a patient by a physician if the following conditions are satisfied:

(1) The physician's opinion or advice regarding evaluation and/or management of a specific medical problem is requested by another physician.

(2) The request and need for the consultation are documented in the patient's medical record.

(3) After the consultation is provided, the physician prepares a written report of his or her findings, which is provided to the physician who requested the consultation.

(4) With respect to radiation therapy services provided by a radiation oncologist, a course of radiation treatments over a period of time will be considered to be pursuant to a consultation, provided the radiation oncologist communicates with the referring physician on a regular basis about the patient's course of treatment and progress.

Designated health services (DHS) means any of the following services (other than those provided as emergency physician services furnished outside of the U.S.), as they are defined in this section:

(1) Clinical laboratory services.

(2) Physical therapy, occupational therapy, and speech-language pathology services.

(3) Radiology and certain other imaging services.

(4) Radiation therapy services and supplies.

(5) Durable medical equipment and supplies.

(6) Parenteral and enteral nutrients, equipment, and supplies.

(7) Prosthetics, orthotics, and prosthetic devices and supplies.

(8) Home health services.

(9) Outpatient prescription drugs.

(10) Inpatient and outpatient hospital services.

Except as otherwise noted in this subpart, the term "designated health services" or DHS means only DHS payable, in whole or in part, by Medicare. DHS do not include services that are reimbursed by Medicare as part of a composite rate (for example, ambulatory surgical center services or SNF Part A payments), except to the extent the services listed in paragraphs (1) through (10) of this definition are themselves payable through a composite rate (for example, all services provided as home health services or inpatient and outpatient hospital services are DHS).

Does not violate the anti-kickback statute, as used in this subpart only, means that the particular arrangement—

(1) Meets a safe harbor under the anti-kickback statute in § 1001.952 of this title, "Exceptions";

(2) Has been specifically approved by the OIG in a favorable advisory opinion issued to a party to the particular arrangement

(e.g., the entity furnishing DHS) with respect to the particular arrangement (and not a similar arrangement), provided that the arrangement is conducted in accordance with the facts certified by the requesting party and the opinion is otherwise issued in accordance with part 1008 of this title, "Advisory Opinions by the OIG"; or

(3) Does not violate the anti-kickback provisions in section 1128B(b) of the Act.

A favorable advisory opinion for purposes of this definition means an opinion in which the OIG opines that—

(1) The party's specific arrangement does not implicate the anti-kickback statute, does not constitute prohibited remuneration, or fits in a safe harbor under § 1001.952 of this title; or

(2) The party will not be subject to any OIG sanctions arising under the anti-kickback statute (for example, under sections 1128(a)(7) and 1128a(b)(7) of the Act) in connection with the party's specific arrangement.

Durable medical equipment (DME) and supplies has the meaning given in section 1861(n) of the Act and § 414.202 of this chapter.

Employee means any individual who, under the common law rules that apply in determining the employer-employee relationship (as applied for purposes of section 3121(d)(2) of the Internal Revenue Code of 1986), is considered to be employed by, or an employee of, an entity. (Application of these common law rules is discussed in 20 CFR 404.1007 and 26 CFR 31.3121(d)-1(c).)

Entity means—

(1) A physician's sole practice or a practice of multiple physicians or any other person, sole proprietorship, public or private agency or trust, corporation, partnership, limited liability company, foundation, not-for-profit corporation, or unincorporated association that furnishes DHS. An entity does not include the referring physician himself or herself, but does include his or her medical practice. A person or entity is considered to be furnishing DHS if it—

(i) Is the person or entity to which CMS makes payment for the DHS, directly or upon assignment on the patient's behalf; or

(ii) Is the person or entity to which the right to payment for the DHS has been reassigned pursuant to § 424.80(b)(1) (employer), (b)(2) (facility), or (b)(3) (health care delivery system) of this chapter (other than a health care delivery system that is a health plan (as defined in § 1001.952(l) of this title), and other than any managed care organization (MCO), provider-sponsored organization (PSO), or independent practice association (IPA) with which a health plan contracts for services provided to plan enrollees).

(2) A health plan, MCO, PSO, or IPA that employs a supplier or operates a facility that could accept reassignment from a supplier pursuant to § 424.80(b)(1) and (b)(2) of this chapter, with respect to any designated health services provided by that supplier.

(3) For purposes of this subpart, "entity" does not include a physician's practice when it bills Medicare for a diagnostic test in accordance with § 414.50 of this chapter (Physician billing for purchased diagnostic tests) and section 3060.4 of the Medicare Carriers Manual (Purchased diagnostic tests), as amended or replaced from time to time.

Fair market value means the value in arm's-length transactions, consistent with the general market value. "General market value" means the price that an asset would bring as the result of *bona fide* bargaining between well-informed buyers and sellers who are not otherwise in a position to generate business for the other party, or the compensation that would be included in a service agreement as the result of *bona fide* bargaining between well-informed parties to the agreement who are not otherwise in a position to generate business for the other party, on the date of acquisition of the asset or at the time of the service agreement. Usually, the fair market price is the price at which *bona fide* sales have been consummated for assets of like type, quality, and quantity in a particular market at the time of acquisition, or the compensation that has been included in *bona fide* service agreements with comparable terms at the time of the agreement, where the price or compensation has not been determined in any manner that takes into account the volume or value of anticipated or actual referrals. With respect to rentals and leases described in § 411.357(a), (b), and (l) (as to equipment leases only), "fair market value" means the value of rental property for general commercial purposes (not taking into account its intended use). In the case of a lease of space, this value may not be adjusted to reflect the additional value the prospective lessee or lessor would attribute to the proximity or convenience to the lessor when the lessor is a potential source of patient referrals to the lessee. For purposes of this definition, a rental payment does not take into account intended use if it takes into account costs incurred by the lessor in developing or upgrading the property or maintaining the property or its improvements.

An hourly payment for a physician's personal services (that is, services performed by the physician personally and not by employees, contractors, or others) shall be considered to be fair market value if the hourly payment is established using either of the following two methodologies:

(1) The hourly rate is less than or equal to the average hourly rate for emergency room physician services in the relevant physician market, provided there are at least three hospitals providing emergency room services in the market.

(2) The hourly rate is determined by averaging the 50th percentile national compensation level for physicians with the same physician specialty (or, if the specialty is not identified in the survey, for general practice) in at least four of the following surveys and dividing by 2,000 hours. The surveys are:

• Sullivan, Cotter & Associates, Inc.—Physician Compensation and Productivity Survey

- Hay Group—Physicians Compensation Survey
- Hospital and Healthcare Compensation Services—Physician Salary Survey Report
- Medical Group Management Association—Physician Compensation and Productivity Survey
- ECS Watson Wyatt—Hospital and Health Care Management Compensation Report
- William M. Mercer—Integrated Health Networks Compensation Survey

Home health services means the services described in section 1861(m) of the Act and part 409, subpart E of this chapter.

Hospital means any entity that qualifies as a "hospital" under section 1861(e) of the Act, as a "psychiatric hospital" under section 1861(f) of the Act, or as a "critical access hospital" under section 1861(mm)(1) of the Act, and refers to any separate legally organized operating entity plus any subsidiary, related entity, or other entities that perform services for the hospital's patients and for which the hospital bills. However, a "hospital" does not include entities that perform services for hospital patients "under arrangements" with the hospital.

HPSA means, for purposes of this subpart, an area designated as a health professional shortage area under section 332(a)(1)(A) of the Public Health Service Act for primary medical care professionals (in accordance with the criteria specified in part 5 of this title).

Immediate family member or member of a physician's immediate family means husband or wife; birth or adoptive parent, child, or sibling; stepparent, stepchild, stepbrother, or stepsister; father-in-law, mother-in-law, son-in-law, daughter-in-law, brother-in-law, or sister-in-law; grandparent or grandchild; and spouse of a grandparent or grandchild.

"Incident to" services means those services that meet the requirements of section 1861(s)(2)(A) of the Act, 42 CFR § 410.26, and section 2050 of the Medicare Carriers (CMS Pub. 14-3), Part 3—Claims Process, as amended or replaced from time to time.

Inpatient hospital services means those services defined in section 1861(b) of the Act and § 409.10(a) and (b) of this chapter and include inpatient psychiatric hospital services listed in section 1861(c) of the Act and inpatient critical access hospital services, as defined in section 1861(mm)(2) of the Act. "Inpatient hospital services" do not include emergency inpatient services provided by a hospital located outside of the U.S. and covered under the authority in section 1814(f)(2) of the Act and part 424, subpart H of this chapter, or emergency inpatient services provided by a nonparticipating hospital within the U.S., as authorized by section 1814(d) of the Act and described in part 424, subpart G of this chapter. "Inpatient hospital services" also do not include dialysis furnished by a hospital that is not certified to provide end-stage renal dialysis (ESRD) services under subpart U of part 405 of this chapter. "Inpatient hospital services" include services that are furnished either by the hospital directly or under arrangements made by the hospital with others. "Inpatient hospital services" do not include professional services performed by physicians, physician assistants, nurse practitioners, clinical nurse specialists, certified nurse midwives, and certified registered nurse anesthetists and qualified psychologists if Medicare reimburses the services independently and not as part of the inpatient hospital service (even if they are billed by a hospital under an assignment or reassignment).

Laboratory means an entity furnishing biological, microbiological, serological, chemical, immunohematological, hematological, biophysical, cytological, pathological, or other examination of materials derived from the human body for the purpose of providing information for the diagnosis, prevention, or treatment of any disease or impairment of, or the assessment of the health of, human beings. These examinations also include procedures to determine, measure, or otherwise describe the presence or absence of various substances or organisms in the body. Entities only collecting or preparing specimens (or both) or only serving as a mailing service and not performing testing are not considered laboratories.

List of CPT/HCPCS Codes means the list of CPT and HCPCS codes that identifies those items and services that are designated health services under section 1877 of the Act or that may qualify for certain exceptions under section 1877 of the Act. It is updated annually, as published in the **Federal Register,** and is posted on the CMS Web site at http://www.cms.gov/medlearn/refphys.asp.

Locum tenens physician means a physician who substitutes (that is, "stands in the shoes") in exigent circumstances for a physician, in accordance with applicable reassignment rules and regulations, including section 3060.7 of the Medicare Carriers Manual (CMS Pub. 14-3), Part 3—Claims Process, as amended or replaced from time to time.

Member of the group or member of a group practice means, for purposes of this subpart, a direct or indirect physician owner of a group practice (including a physician whose interest is held by his or her individual professional corporation or by another entity), a physician employee of the group practice (including a physician employed by his or her individual professional corporation that has an equity interest in the group practice), a locum tenens physician (as defined in this section), or an on-call physician while the physician is providing on-call services for members of the group practice. A physician is a member of the group during the time he or she furnishes "patient care services" to the group as defined in this section. An independent contractor or a leased employee is not a member of the group (unless the leased employee meets the definition of an "employee" under this § 411.351).

Outpatient hospital services means the therapeutic, diagnostic, and partial hospitalization services listed under sections 1861(s)(2)(B) and (s)(2)(C) of the Act; outpatient services furnished by a psychiatric hospital, as defined in section 1861(f) of the Act; and outpatient critical access hospital services, as defined in section 1861(mm)(3) of the Act.

"Outpatient hospital services" do not include emergency services furnished by nonparticipating hospitals and covered under the conditions described in section 1835(b) of the Act and subpart G of part 424 of this chapter. "Outpatient hospital services" include services that are furnished either by the hospital directly or under arrangements made by the hospital with others. "Outpatient hospital services" do not include professional services performed by physicians, physician assistants, nurse practitioners, clinical nurse specialists, certified nurse midwives, certified registered nurse anesthetists, and qualified psychologists if Medicare reimburses the services independently and not as part of the outpatient hospital service (even if they are billed by a hospital under an assignment or reassignment).

Outpatient prescription drugs means all prescription drugs covered by Medicare Part B.

Parenteral and enteral nutrients, equipment, and supplies means the following services (including all HCPCS level 2 codes for these services):

(1) *Parenteral nutrients, equipment, and supplies,* meaning those items and supplies needed to provide nutriment to a patient with permanent, severe pathology of the alimentary tract that does not allow absorption of sufficient nutrients to maintain strength commensurate with the patient's general condition, as described in section 65-10 of the Medicare Coverage Issues Manual (CMS Pub. 6), as amended or replaced from time to time; and

(2) *Enteral nutrients, equipment, and supplies,* meaning items and supplies needed to provide enteral nutrition to a patient with a functioning gastrointestinal tract who, due to pathology to or nonfunction of the structures that normally permit food to reach the digestive tract, cannot maintain weight and strength commensurate with his or her general condition, as described in section 65-10 of the Medicare Coverage Issues Manual (CMS Pub. 6), as amended or replaced from time to time.

Patient care services means any task(s) performed by a physician in the group practice that address the medical needs of specific patients or patients in general, regardless of whether they involve direct patient encounters or generally benefit a particular practice. Patient care services can include, for example, the services of physicians who do not directly treat patients, such as time spent by a physician consulting with other physicians or reviewing laboratory tests, or time spent training staff members, arranging for equipment, or performing administrative or management tasks.

Physical therapy, occupational therapy, and speech-language pathology services means those particular services so identified on the List of CPT/HCPCS Codes. All services so identified on the List of CPT/HCPCS Codes are physical therapy, occupational therapy, and speech-language pathology services for purposes of this subpart. Any service not specifically identified as physical therapy, occupational therapy or speech-language pathology on the List of CPT/HCPCS Codes is not a physical therapy, occupational therapy, or speech-language pathology service for purposes of this subpart. The list of codes identifying physical therapy, occupational therapy, and speech-language pathology services for purposes of this regulation includes the following:

(1) *Physical therapy services,* meaning those outpatient physical therapy services (including speech-language pathology services) described at section 1861(p) of the Act that are covered under Medicare Part A or Part B, regardless of who provides them, if the services include—

(i) Assessments, function tests and measurements of strength, balance, endurance, range of motion, and activities of daily living;

(ii) Therapeutic exercises, massage, and use of physical medicine modalities, assistive devices, and adaptive equipment;

(iii) Establishment of a maintenance therapy program for an individual whose restoration potential has been reached; however, maintenance therapy itself is not covered as part of these services; or

(iv) Speech-language pathology services that are for the diagnosis and treatment of speech, language, and cognitive disorders that include swallowing and other oral-motor dysfunctions.

(2) *Occupational therapy services,* meaning those services described at section 1861(g) of the Act that are covered under Medicare Part A or Part B, regardless of who provides them, if the services include—

(i) Teaching of compensatory techniques to permit an individual with a physical or cognitive impairment or limitation to engage in daily activities;

(ii) Evaluation of an individual's level of independent functioning;

(iii) Selection and teaching of task-oriented therapeutic activities to restore sensory-integrative function; or

(iv) Assessment of an individual's vocational potential, except when the assessment is related solely to vocational rehabilitation.

Physician means a doctor of medicine or osteopathy, a doctor of dental surgery or dental medicine, a doctor of podiatric medicine, a doctor of optometry, or a chiropractor, as defined in section 1861(r) of the Act.

Physician in the group practice means a member of the group practice, as well as an independent contractor physician during the time the independent contractor is furnishing patient care services (as defined in this section) for the group practice under a contractual arrangement with the group practice to provide services to the group practice's patients in the group practice's facilities. The contract must contain the same restrictions on compensation that apply to members of the group practice under § 411.352(g) (or the contract must fit in the personal services exception in § 411.357(d)), and the independent contractor's arrangement with the group practice must comply with the reassignment rules at § 424.80(b)(3) of this chapter (see also section

3060.3 of the Medicare Carriers Manual (CMS Pub. 14-3), Part 3—
Claims Process, as amended or replaced from time to time). Referrals
from an independent contractor who is a physician in the group practice are subject to the prohibition on referrals in § 411.353(a), and the
group practice is subject to the limitation on billing for those referrals
in § 411.353(b).

Physician incentive plan means any compensation arrangement
between an entity (or downstream subcontractor) and a physician or
physician group that may directly or indirectly have the effect of reducing or limiting services furnished with respect to individuals enrolled with the entity.

Plan of care means the establishment by a physician of a course
of diagnosis or treatment (or both) for a particular patient, including
the ordering of services.

Professional courtesy means the provision of free or discounted
health care items or services to a physician or his or her immediate
family members or office staff.

Prosthetics, Orthotics, and Prosthetic Devices and Supplies means
the following services (including all HCPCS level 2 codes for these
items and services that are covered by Medicare):

(1) *Orthotics,* meaning leg, arm, back, and neck braces, as listed
in section 1861(s)(9) of the Act.

(2) *Prosthetics,* meaning artificial legs, arms, and eyes, as described
in section 1861(s)(9) of the Act.

(3) *Prosthetic devices,* meaning devices (other than a dental device)
listed in section 1861(s)(8) of the Act that replace all or part of an
internal body organ, including colostomy bags, and one pair of con-
ventional eyeglasses or contact lenses furnished subsequent to
each cataract surgery with insertion of an intraocular lens.

(4) *Prosthetic supplies,* meaning supplies that are necessary for
the effective use of a prosthetic device (including supplies directly
related to colostomy care).

Radiation therapy services and supplies means those particular
services and supplies so identified on the List of CPT/HCPCS Codes.
All services and supplies so identified on the List of CPT/HCPCS
Codes are radiation therapy services and supplies for purposes of this
subpart. Any service or supply not specifically identified as radiation
therapy services or supplies on the List of CPT/HCPCS Codes is not a
radiation therapy service or supply for purposes of this subpart. The list
of codes identifying radiation therapy services and supplies is based on
section 1861(s)(4) of the Act and § 410.35 of this chapter, but does not
include nuclear medicine procedures.

Radiology and certain other imaging services means those particular services so identified on the List of CPT/HCPCS Codes. All services so identified on the List of CPT/HCPCS Codes are radiology and
certain other imaging services for purposes of this subpart. Any service not specifically identified as radiology and certain other imaging
services on the List of CPT/HCPCS Codes, is not a radiology or certain

other imaging service for purposes of this subpart. The list of codes identifying radiology and certain other imaging services includes the professional and technical components of any diagnostic test or procedure using x-rays, ultrasound, or other imaging services, computerized axial tomography, or magnetic resonance imaging, as covered under section 1861(s)(3) of the Act and § 410.32 and § 410.34 of this chapter but does not include—

(1) X-ray, fluoroscopy, or ultrasound procedures that require the insertion of a needle, catheter, tube, or probe through the skin or into a body orifice;

(2) Radiology procedures that are integral to the performance of a nonradiological medical procedure and performed—

(i) During the nonradiological medical procedure; or

(ii) Immediately following the nonradiological medical procedure when necessary to confirm placement of an item placed during the nonradiological medical procedure; and

(3) Diagnostic nuclear medicine procedures.

Referral—

(1) Means either of the following:

(i) Except as provided in paragraph (2) of this definition, the request by a physician for, or ordering of, or the certifying or recertifying of the need for, any designated health service for which payment may be made under Medicare Part B, including a request for a consultation with another physician and any test or procedure ordered by or to be performed by (or under the supervision of) that other physician, but not including any designated health service personally performed or provided by the referring physician. A designated health service is not personally performed or provided by the referring physician if it is performed or provided by any other person, including, but not limited to, the referring physician's employees, independent contractors, or group practice members.

(ii) Except as provided in paragraph (2) of this definition, a request by a physician that includes the provision of any designated health service for which payment may be made under Medicare, the establishment of a plan of care by a physician that includes the provision of such a designated health service, or the certifying or recertifying of the need for such a designated health service, but not including any designated health service personally performed or provided by the referring physician. A designated health service is not personally performed or provided by the referring physician if it is performed or provided by any other person including, but not limited to, the referring physician's employees, independent contractors, or group practice members.

(2) Does not include a request by a pathologist for clinical diagnostic laboratory tests and pathological examination services, by a radiologist for diagnostic radiology services, and by a radiation oncologist for radiation therapy, if—

(i) The request results from a consultation initiated by another physician (whether the request for a consultation was made to a particular physician or to an entity with which the physician is affiliated); and

(ii) The tests or services are furnished by or under the supervision of the pathologist, radiologist, or radiation oncologist, or under the supervision of a pathologist, radiologist, or radiation oncologist, respectively, in the same group practice as the pathologist, radiologist, or radiation oncologist.

(3) Can be in any form, including, but not limited to, written, oral, or electronic.

Referring physician means a physician who makes a referral as defined in this section or who directs another person or entity to make a referral or who controls referrals made by another person or entity. A referring physician and the professional corporation of which he or she is a sole owner are the same for purposes of this subpart.

Remuneration means any payment or other benefit made directly or indirectly, overtly or covertly, in cash or in kind, except that the following are not considered remuneration for purposes of this section:

(1) The forgiveness of amounts owed for inaccurate tests or procedures, mistakenly performed tests or procedures, or the correction of minor billing errors.

(2) The furnishing of items, devices, or supplies (not including surgical items, devices, or supplies) that are used solely to collect, transport, process, or store specimens for the entity furnishing the items, devices, or supplies or are used solely to order or communicate the results of tests or procedures for the entity.

(3) A payment made by an insurer or a self-insured plan (or a subcontractor of the insurer or plan) to a physician to satisfy a claim, submitted on a fee-for-service basis, for the furnishing of health services by that physician to an individual who is covered by a policy with the insurer or by the self-insured plan, if—

(i) The health services are not furnished, and the payment is not made, under a contract or other arrangement between the insurer or the plan (or a subcontractor of the insurer or plan) and the physician;

(ii) The payment is made to the physician on behalf of the covered individual and would otherwise be made directly to the individual; and

(iii) The amount of the payment is set in advance, does not exceed fair market value, and is not determined in a manner that takes into account directly or indirectly the volume or value of any referrals.

Same building means a structure with, or combination of structures that share, a single street address as assigned by the U.S. Postal Service, excluding all exterior spaces (for example, lawns, courtyards, driveways, parking lots) and interior loading docks or parking garages.

For purposes of this section, the "same building" does not include a mobile vehicle, van, or trailer.

Specialty hospital means a subsection (d) hospital (as defined in section 1886(d)(1)(B)) that is primarily or exclusively engaged in the care and treatment of one of the following: Patients with a cardiac condition; patients with an orthopedic condition; patients receiving a surgical procedure; or any other specialized category of services that the Secretary designates as inconsistent with the purpose of permitting physician ownership and investment interests in a hospital. A "specialty hospital" does not include any hospital—

(1) Determined by the Secretary to be in operation before or under development as of November 18, 2003;

(2) For which the number of physician investors at any time on or after such date is no greater than the number of such investors as of such date;

(3) For which the type of categories described above is no different at any time on or after such date than the type of such categories as of such date;

(4) For which any increase in the number of beds occurs only in the facilities on the main campus of the hospital and does not exceed 50 percent of the number of beds in the hospital as of November 18, 2003, or 5 beds, whichever is greater; and

(5) that meets such other requirements as the Secretary may specify.

Transaction means an instance or process of two or more persons or entities doing business. An isolated transaction means one involving a single payment between two or more persons or entities or a transaction that involves integrally related installment payments provided that—

(1) The total aggregate payment is fixed before the first payment is made and does not take into account, directly or indirectly, the volume or value of referrals or other business generated by the referring physician; and

(2) The payments are immediately negotiable or are guaranteed by a third party, secured by a negotiable promissory note, or subject to a similar mechanism to assure payment even in the event of default by the purchaser or obligated party.

§ 411.352 Group practice.

For purposes of this subpart, a group practice is a physician practice that meets the following conditions:

(a) *Single legal entity.* The group practice must consist of a single legal entity operating primarily for the purpose of being a physician group practice in any organizational form recognized by the State in which the group practice achieves its legal status, including, but not limited to, a partnership, professional corporation, limited liability company, foundation, not-for-profit corporation, faculty practice plan, or similar association. The single legal entity may be organized by any party or parties, including, but not limited to, physicians, health care facilities, or other persons or entities (including, but not limited to, physicians individually incorporated as professional corporations). The single legal entity may be organized or owned (in whole or in part) by another medical practice, provided that the other medical practice is not an operating physician practice (and regardless of whether the medical practice meets the conditions for a group practice under this section). For purposes of this subpart, a single legal entity does not include informal affiliations of physicians formed substantially to share profits from referrals, or separate group practices under common ownership or control through a physician practice management company, hospital, health system, or other entity or organization. A group practice that is otherwise a single legal entity may itself own subsidiary entities. A group practice operating in more than one State will be considered to be a single legal entity notwithstanding that it is composed of multiple legal entities, provided that—

(1) The States in which the group practice is operating are contiguous (although each State need not be contiguous to every other State);

(2) The legal entities are absolutely identical as to ownership, governance, and operation; and

(3) Organization of the group practice into multiple entities is necessary to comply with jurisdictional licensing laws of the States in which the group practice operates.

(b) *Physicians.* The group practice must have at least two physicians who are members of the group (whether employees or direct or indirect owners), as defined in § 411.351.

(c) *Range of care.* Each physician who is a member of the group, as defined in § 411.351, must furnish substantially the full range of patient care services that the physician routinely furnishes, including medical care, consultation, diagnosis, and treatment, through the joint use of shared office space, facilities, equipment, and personnel.

(d) *Services furnished by group practice members.* (1) Except as otherwise provided in paragraphs (d)(3), (d)(4), (d)(5), and (d)(6) of this section, substantially all of the patient care services of the physicians who are members of the group (that is, at least 75 percent of the total patient care services of the group practice members) must be furnished through the group and billed under a billing number assigned to the group, and the amounts received must be treated as receipts of the group. "Patient care services" must be measured by one of the following:

(i) The total time each member spends on patient care services documented by any reasonable means (including, but not limited to, time cards, appointment schedules, or personal diaries). (For example, if a physician practices 40 hours a week and spends 30 hours a week on patient care services for a group practice, the physician has spent 75 percent of his or her time providing patient care services for the group.)

(ii) Any alternative measure that is reasonable, fixed in advance of the performance of the services being measured, uniformly applied over time, verifiable, and documented.

(2) The data used to calculate compliance with this "substantially all test" and related supportive documentation must be made available to the Secretary upon request.

(3) The "substantially all test" set forth in paragraph (d)(1) of this section does not apply to any group practice that is located solely in an HPSA, as defined in § 411.351.

(4) For a group practice located outside of an HPSA (as defined in § 411.351), any time spent by a group practice member providing services in an HPSA should not be used to calculate whether the group practice has met the "substantially all test," regardless of whether the member's time in the HPSA is spent in a group practice, clinic, or office setting.

(5) During the "start up" period (not to exceed 12 months) that begins on the date of the initial formation of a new group practice, a group practice must make a reasonable, good faith effort to ensure that the group practice complies with the "substantially all" test requirement set forth in paragraph (d)(1) of this section as soon as practicable, but no later than 12 months from the date of the initial formation of the group practice. This paragraph (d)(5) does not apply when an existing group practice admits a new member or reorganizes.

(6)(i) If the addition to an existing group practice of a new member who would be considered to have relocated his or her practice under § 411.457(e)(2) would result in the existing group practice not meeting the "substantially all" test set forth in paragraph (d)(1) of this section, the group practice will have 12 months following the addition of the new member to come back into full compliance, provided that—

(A) For the 12-month period the group practice is fully compliant with the "substantially all" test if the new member is not counted as a member of the group for purposes of § 411.352; and

(B) The new member's employment with, or ownership interest in, the group practice is documented in writing no later than the beginning of his or her new employment, ownership, or investment.

(ii) This paragraph (d)(6) does not apply when an existing group practice reorganizes or admits a new member who is not relocating his or her practice.

(e) *Distribution of expenses and income.* The overhead expenses of, and income from, the practice must be distributed according to methods that are determined before the receipt of payment for the services giving rise to the overhead expense or producing the income. Nothing in this section prevents a group practice from adjusting its compensation methodology prospectively, subject to restrictions on the distribution of revenue from DHS under § 411.352(i).

(f) *Unified business.* (1) The group practice must be a unified business having at least the following features:

(i) Centralized decision-making by a body representative of the group practice that maintains effective control over the group's assets and liabilities (including, but not limited to, budgets, compensation, and salaries); and

(ii) Consolidated billing, accounting, and financial reporting.

(2) Location and specialty-based compensation practices are permitted with respect to revenues derived from services that are not DHS and may be permitted with respect to revenues derived from DHS under § 411.352(i).

(g) *Volume or value of referrals.* No physician who is a member of the group practice directly or indirectly receives compensation based on the volume or value of referrals by the physician, except as provided in § 411.352(i).

(h) *Physician-patient encounters.* Members of the group must personally conduct no less than 75 percent of the physician-patient encounters of the group practice.

(i) *Special rule for productivity bonuses and profit shares.* (1) A physician in a group practice may be paid a share of overall profits of the group, or a productivity bonus based on services that he or she has personally performed (including services "incident to" those personally performed services as defined in § 411.351), provided that the share or bonus is not determined in any manner that is directly related to the volume or value of referrals of DHS by the physician.

(2) Overall profits means the group's entire profits derived from DHS payable by Medicare or Medicaid or the profits derived from DHS payable by Medicare or Medicaid of any component of the group practice that consists of at least five physicians. Overall profits should be divided in a reasonable and verifiable manner that is not directly related to the volume or value of the physician's referrals of DHS. The share of overall profits will be deemed not to relate directly to the volume or value of referrals if one of the following conditions is met:

(i) The group's profits are divided per capita (for example, per member of the group or per physician in the group).

(ii) Revenues derived from DHS are distributed based on the distribution of the group practice's revenues attributed to services that are not DHS payable by any Federal health care program or private payer.

(iii) Revenues derived from DHS constitute less than 5 percent of the group practice's total revenues, and the allocated portion of those revenues to each physician in the group practice constitutes 5 percent or less of his or her total compensation from the group.

(3) A productivity bonus should be calculated in a reasonable and verifiable manner that is not directly related to the volume or value of the physician's referrals of DHS. A productivity bonus will

be deemed not to relate directly to the volume or value of referrals of DHS if one of the following conditions is met:

(i) The bonus is based on the physician's total patient encounters or relative value units (RVUs). (The methodology for establishing RVUs is set forth in § 414.22 of this chapter.)

(ii) The bonus is based on the allocation of the physician's compensation attributable to services that are not DHS payable by any Federal health care program or private payer.

(iii) Revenues derived from DHS are less than 5 percent of the group practice's total revenues, and the allocated portion of those revenues to each physician in the group practice constitutes 5 percent or less of his or her total compensation from the group practice.

(4) Supporting documentation verifying the method used to calculate the profit share or productivity bonus under paragraphs (i)(2) and (i)(3) of this section, and the resulting amount of compensation, must be made available to the Secretary upon request.

§ 411.353 Prohibition on certain referrals by physicians and limitations on billing.

(a) *Prohibition on referrals.* Except as provided in this subpart, a physician who has a direct or indirect financial relationship with an entity, or who has an immediate family member who has a direct or indirect financial relationship with the entity, may not make a referral to that entity for the furnishing of DHS for which payment otherwise may be made under Medicare. A physician's prohibited financial relationship with an entity that furnishes DHS is not imputed to his or her group practice or its members or its staff; however, a referral made by a physician's group practice, its members, or its staff may be imputed to the physician, if the physician directs the group practice, its members, or its staff to make the referral or if the physician controls referrals made by his or her group practice, its members, or its staff.

(b) *Limitations on billing.* An entity that furnishes DHS pursuant to a referral that is prohibited by paragraph (a) of this section may not present or cause to be presented a claim or bill to the Medicare program or to any individual, third party payer, or other entity for the DHS performed pursuant to the prohibited referral.

(c) *Denial of payment.* Except as provided in paragraph (e) of this section, no Medicare payment may be made for a designated health service that is furnished pursuant to a prohibited referral.

(d) *Refunds.* An entity that collects payment for a designated health service that was performed under a prohibited referral must refund all collected amounts on a timely basis, as defined in § 1003.101 of this title.

(e) *Exception for certain entities.* Payment may be made to an entity that submits a claim for a designated health service if—

(1) The entity did not have actual knowledge of, and did not act in reckless disregard or deliberate ignorance of, the identity of the

physician who made the referral of the designated health service to the entity; and

(2) The claim otherwise complies with all applicable Federal and State laws, rules, and regulations.

(f) *Exception for certain arrangements involving temporary noncompliance.* (1) Except as provided in paragraphs (f)(2), (f)(3), and (f)(4) of this section, an entity may submit a claim or bill and payment may be made to an entity that submits a claim or bill for a designated health service if—

> (i) The financial relationship between the entity and the referring physician fully complied with an applicable exception under § 411.355, § 411.356, or § 411.357 for at least 180 consecutive calendar days immediately preceding the date on which the financial relationship became noncompliant with the exception;
>
> (ii) The financial relationship has fallen out of compliance with the exception for reasons beyond the control of the entity, and the entity promptly takes steps to rectify the noncompliance; and
>
> (iii) The financial relationship does not violate the anti-kickback statute (section 1128B(b) of the Act), and the claim or bill otherwise complies with all applicable Federal and State laws, rules, and regulations.

(2) Paragraph (f)(1) of this section applies only to DHS furnished during the period of time it takes the entity to rectify the noncompliance, which must not exceed 90 consecutive calendar days following the date on which the financial relationship became noncompliant with an exception.

(3) This paragraph (f) may only be used by an entity once every 3 years with respect to the same referring physician.

(4) This paragraph (f) does not apply if the exception with which the financial relationship previously complied was § 411.357(k) or (m).

§ 411.354 Financial relationship, compensation, and ownership or investment interest.

(a) *Financial relationships.* (1) *Financial relationship means*—

> (i) A direct or indirect ownership or investment interest (as defined in paragraph (b) of this section) in any entity that furnishes DHS; or
>
> (ii) A direct or indirect compensation arrangement (as defined in paragraph (c) of this section) with an entity that furnishes DHS.

(2) A *direct* financial relationship exists if remuneration passes between the referring physician (or a member of his or her immediate family) and the entity furnishing DHS without any intervening persons or entities. (3) An *indirect* financial relationship exists under the conditions described in paragraphs (b)(5) and (c)(2) of this section.

(b) *Ownership or investment interest.* An ownership or investment interest may be through equity, debt, or other means, and includes an interest in an entity that holds an ownership or investment interest in any entity that furnishes DHS.

(1) An ownership or investment interest includes, but is not limited to, stock, stock options other than those described in § 411.354(b)(3)(ii), partnership shares, limited liability company memberships, as well as loans, bonds, or other financial instruments that are secured with an entity's property or revenue or a portion of that property or revenue.

(2) An ownership or investment interest in a subsidiary company is neither an ownership or investment interest in the parent company, nor in any other subsidiary of the parent, unless the subsidiary company itself has an ownership or investment interest in the parent or such other subsidiaries. It may, however, be part of an indirect financial relationship.

(3) Ownership and investment interests do not include, among other things—

(i) An interest in a retirement plan;

(ii) Stock options and convertible securities received as compensation until the stock options are exercised or the convertible securities are converted to equity (before this time the stock options or convertible securities are compensation arrangements as defined in paragraph (c) of this section);

(iii) An unsecured loan subordinated to a credit facility (which is a compensation arrangement as defined in paragraph (c) of this section); or

(iv) An "under arrangements" contract between a hospital and an entity owned by one or more physicians (or a group of physicians) providing DHS "under arrangements" with the hospital (such a contract is a compensation arrangement as defined in paragraph (c) of this section).

(4) An ownership or investment interest that meets an exception set forth in § 411.355 or § 411.356 need not also meet an exception for compensation arrangements set forth in § 411.357 with respect to profit distributions, dividends, or interest payments on secured obligations.

(5) *Indirect ownership or investment interest.* (i) An indirect ownership or investment interest exists if—

(A) Between the referring physician (or immediate family member) and the entity furnishing DHS there exists an unbroken chain of any number (but no fewer than one) of persons or entities having ownership or investment interests; and

(B) The entity furnishing DHS has actual knowledge of, or acts in reckless disregard or deliberate ignorance of, the fact that the referring physician (or immediate family member) has some ownership or investment interest (through any number of intermediary ownership or investment interests) in the entity furnishing the DHS.

(ii) An indirect ownership or investment interest exists even though the entity furnishing DHS does not know, or act in reckless disregard or deliberate ignorance of, the precise composition of the unbroken chain or the specific terms of the ownership or investment interests that form the links in the chain.

(iii) Notwithstanding anything in this paragraph (b)(5), common ownership or investment in an entity does not, in and of itself, establish an indirect ownership or investment interest by one common owner or investor in another common owner or investor.

(iv) An indirect ownership or investment interest requires an unbroken chain of ownership interests between the referring physician and the entity furnishing DHS such that the referring physician has an indirect ownership or investment interest in the entity furnishing DHS.

(c) *Compensation arrangement.* A compensation arrangement is any arrangement involving remuneration, direct or indirect, between a physician (or a member of a physician's immediate family) and an entity. An "under arrangements" contract between a hospital and an entity providing DHS "under arrangements" to the hospital creates a compensation arrangement for purposes of these regulations.

(1) A compensation arrangement does not include the portion of any business arrangement that consists solely of the remuneration described in section 1877(h)(1)(C) of the Act and in paragraphs (1) through (3) of the definition of the term "remuneration" in § 411.351. (However, any other portion of the arrangement may still constitute a compensation arrangement.)

(2) *Indirect compensation arrangement.* An indirect compensation arrangement exists if—

(i) Between the referring physician (or a member of his or her immediate family) and the entity furnishing DHS there exists an unbroken chain of any number (but not fewer than one) of persons or entities that have financial relationships (as defined in paragraph (a) of this section) between them (that is, each link in the chain has either an ownership or investment interest or a compensation arrangement with the preceding link);

(ii) The referring physician (or immediate family member) receives aggregate compensation from the person or entity in the chain with which the physician (or immediate family member) has a direct financial relationship that varies with, or otherwise reflects, the volume or value of referrals or other business generated by the referring physician for the entity furnishing the DHS, regardless of whether the individual unit of compensation satisfies the special rules on unit-based compensation under § 411.354(d)(2) or (d)(3). If the financial relationship between the physician (or immediate family member) and the person or entity in the chain with which the referring physician (or immediate family member) has a direct financial relationship is an ownership or investment interest, the determination whether the aggregate compensation varies with, or otherwise reflects, the volume or value of referrals or other business generated by the referring physician for the entity furnishing the DHS will be measured by the nonownership or noninvestment interest closest to the referring physician (or immediate family member). (For example, if a referring physician has an ownership interest in company A, which owns company B, which has a compensation arrangement with company C, which has a compensation arrangement with entity D that furnishes DHS, we would look to the aggregate compensation between company B and company C for purposes of this paragraph (c)(2)(ii)); and

(iii) The entity furnishing DHS has actual knowledge of, or acts in reckless disregard or deliberate ignorance of, the fact that the referring physician (or immediate family member) receives aggregate compensation that varies with, or otherwise reflects, the volume or value of referrals or other business generated by the referring physician for the entity furnishing the DHS.

(d) *Special rules on compensation.* The following special rules apply only to compensation under section 1877 of the Act and subpart J of this part.

(1) Compensation will be considered "set in advance" if the aggregate compensation, a time-based or per unit of service based (whether per-use or per-service) amount, or a specific formula for calculating the compensation is set in an agreement between the parties before the furnishing of the items or services for which the compensation is to be paid. The formula for determining the compensation must be set forth in sufficient detail so that it can be objectively verified, and the formula may not be changed or modified during the course of the agreement in any manner that reflects the volume or value of referrals or other business generated by the referring physician.

(2) Unit-based compensation (including time-based or per unit of service based compensation) will be deemed not to take into account "the volume or value of referrals" if the compensation is fair market value for services or items actually provided and does not vary during the course of the compensation agreement in any manner that takes into account referrals of DHS.

(3) Unit-based compensation (including time-based or per unit of service based compensation) will be deemed to not take into account "other business generated between the parties" so long as the compensation is fair market value for items and services actually provided and does not vary during the course of the compensation arrangement in any manner that takes into account referrals or other business generated by the referring physician, including private pay health care business (except for services personally per-

formed by the referring physician, which will not be considered "other business generated" by the referring physician).

(4) A physician's compensation from a *bona fide* employer or under a managed care or other contract may be conditioned on the physician's referrals to a particular provider, practitioner, or supplier, so long as the compensation arrangement—

    (i) Is set in advance for the term of the agreement;

    (ii) Is consistent with fair market value for services performed (that is, the payment does not take into account the volume or value of anticipated or required referrals);

    (iii) Otherwise complies with an applicable exception under § 411.355 or § 411.357;

    (iv) Complies with the following conditions:

        (A) The requirement to make referrals to a particular provider, practitioner, or supplier is set forth in a written agreement signed by the parties;

        (B) The requirement to make referrals to a particular provider, practitioner, or supplier does not apply if the patient expresses a preference for a different provider, practitioner, or supplier; the patient's insurer determines the provider, practitioner, or supplier; or the referral is not in the patient's best medical interests in the physician's judgment; and

    (v) The required referrals relate solely to the physician's services covered by the scope of the employment or the contract and the referral requirement is reasonably necessary to effectuate the legitimate business purposes of the compensation relationship. In no event may the physician be required to make referrals that relate to services that are not provided by the physician under the scope of his or her employment or contract.

§ 411.355 General exceptions to the referral prohibition related to both ownership/investment and compensation.

The prohibition on referrals set forth in § 411.353 does not apply to the following types of services:

(a) *Physician services.* (1) Physician services as defined in § 410.20(a) of this chapter that are furnished—

    (i) Personally by another physician who is a member of the referring physician's group practice or is a physician in the same group practice (as defined in § 411.351) as the referring physician; or

    (ii) Under the supervision of another physician who is a member of the referring physician's group practice or is a physician in the same group practice (as defined at § 411.351) as the referring physician, provided that the supervision complies with all other applicable Medicare payment and coverage rules for the physician services.

(2) For purposes of paragraph (a) of this section, physician services" include only those "incident to" services (as defined in
§ 411.351) that are physician services under § 410.20(a) of this
chapter.

(3) All other "incident to" services (for example, diagnostic tests,
physical therapy) are outside the scope of paragraph (a) of this
section.

(b) *In-office ancillary services.* Services (including certain items of
durable medical equipment (DME), as defined in paragraph (b)(4) of
this section, and infusion pumps that are DME (including external
ambulatory infusion pumps), but excluding all other DME and parenteral and enteral nutrients, equipment, and supplies (such as infusion pumps used for PEN)), that meet the following conditions:

(1) They are furnished personally by one of the following individuals:

(i) The referring physician.

(ii) A physician who is a member of the same group practice
as the referring physician.

(iii) An individual who is supervised by the referring physician or, if the referring physician is in a group practice, by another physician in the group practice, provided the supervision
complies with all other applicable Medicare payment and coverage rules for the services.

(2) They are furnished in one of the following locations:

(i) The same building (as defined in § 411.351), but not necessarily in the same space or part of the building, in which all of
the conditions of paragraph (b)(2)(i)(A), (b)(2)(i)(B), or (b)(2)(i)(C)
of this section are satisfied:

(A)*(1)* The referring physician or his or her group practice
(if any) has an office that is normally open to the physician's
or group's patients for medical services at least 35 hours per
week; *and*

(2) The referring physician or one or more members of
the referring physician's group practice regularly practices medicine and furnishes physician services to patients at least 30 hours per week. The 30 hours must
include some physician services that are unrelated to
the furnishing of DHS payable by Medicare, any other
Federal health care payer, or a private payer, even
though the physician services may lead to the ordering
of DHS; or

(B)*(1)* The patient receiving the DHS usually receives
physician services from the referring physician or members of the referring physician's group practice (if any);

(2) The referring physician or the referring physician's group practice owns or rents an office that is
normally open to the physician's or group's patients
for medical services at least 8 hours per week; and

(3) The referring physician regularly practices medicine and furnishes physician services to patients at least 6 hours per week. The 6 hours must include some physician services that are unrelated to the furnishing of DHS payable by Medicare, any other Federal health care payer, or a private payer, even though the physician services may lead to the ordering of DHS; or

(C)*(1)* The referring physician is present and orders the DHS during a patient visit on the premises as set forth in paragraph (b)(2)(i)(C)*(2)* of this section or the referring physician or a member of the referring physician's group practice (if any) is present while the DHS is furnished during occupancy of the premises as set forth in paragraph (b)(2)(i)(C)*(2)* of this section;

(2) The referring physician or the referring physician's group practice owns or rents an office that is normally open to the physician's or group's patients for medical services at least 8 hours per week; and

(3) The referring physician or one or more members of the referring physician's group practice regularly practices medicine and furnishes physician services to patients at least 6 hours per week. The 6 hours must include some physician services that are unrelated to the furnishing of DHS payable by Medicare, any other Federal health care payer, or a private payer, even though the physician services may lead to the ordering of DHS.

(ii) A centralized building (as defined in § 411.351) that is used by the group practice for the provision of some or all of the group practice's clinical laboratory services.

(iii) A centralized building (as defined in § 411.351) that is used by the group practice for the provision of some or all of the group practice's DHS (other than clinical laboratory services).

(3) They are billed by one of the following:

(i) The physician performing or supervising the service.

(ii) The group practice of which the performing or supervising physician is a member under a billing number assigned to the group practice.

(iii) The group practice if the supervising physician is a "physician in the group practice" (as defined at § 411.351) under a billing number assigned to the group practice.

(iv) An entity that is wholly owned by the performing or supervising physician or by that physician's group practice under the entity's own billing number or under a billing number assigned to the physician or group practice.

(v) An independent third party billing company acting as an agent of the physician, group practice, or entity specified in paragraphs (b)(3)(i) through (b)(3)(iv) of this section under a billing number assigned to the physician, group practice, or entity, provided the billing arrangement meets the requirements of § 424.80(b)(6) of this chapter. For purposes of this paragraph (b)(3), a group practice may have, and bill under, more than one Medicare billing number, subject to any applicable Medicare program restrictions.

(4) For purposes of paragraph (b) of this section, DME covered by the in-office ancillary services exception means canes, crutches, walkers and folding manual wheelchairs, and blood glucose monitors, that meet the following conditions:

(i) The item is one that a patient requires for the purposes of ambulating, uses in order to depart from the physician's office, or is a blood glucose monitor (including one starter set of test strips and lancets, consisting of no more than 100 of each). A blood glucose monitor may be furnished only by a physician or employee of a physician or group practice that also furnishes outpatient diabetes self-management training to the patient.

(ii) The item is furnished in a building that meets the "same building" requirements in the in-office ancillary services exception as part of the treatment for the specific condition for which the patient-physician encounter occurred.

(iii) The item is furnished personally by the physician who ordered the DME, by another physician in the group practice, or by an employee of the physician or the group practice.

(iv) A physician or group practice that furnishes the DME meets all DME supplier standards located in § 424.57(c) of this chapter.

(v) The arrangement does not violate the anti-kickback statute (section 1128B(b) of the Act), or any Federal or State law or regulation governing billing or claims submission.

(vi) All other requirements of the in-office ancillary services exception in paragraph (b) of this section are met.

(5) A designated health service is "furnished" for purposes of paragraph (b) of this section in the location where the service is actually performed upon a patient or where an item is dispensed to a patient in a manner that is sufficient to meet the applicable Medicare payment and coverage rules.

(6) *Special rule for home care physicians.* In the case of a referring physician whose principal medical practice consists of treating patients in their private homes, the "same building" requirements of paragraph (b)(2)(i) of this section are met if the referring physician (or a qualified person accompanying the physician, such as a nurse or technician) provides the DHS contemporaneously with a physician service that is not a designated health service provided by the referring physician to the patient in the patient's private home. For purposes of paragraph (b)(5) of this section only, a private home does not include a nursing, long-

term care, or other facility or institution, except that a patient may have a private home in an assisted living or independent living facility.

(c) *Services furnished by an organization (or its contractors or subcontractors) to enrollees.* Services furnished by an organization (or its contractors or subcontractors) to enrollees of one of the following prepaid health plans (not including services provided to enrollees in any other plan or line of business offered or administered by the same organization):

(1) An HMO or a CMP in accordance with a contract with CMS under section 1876 of the Act and part 417, subparts J through M of this chapter.

(2) A health care prepayment plan in accordance with an agreement with CMS under section 1833(a)(1)(A) of the Act and part 417, subpart U of this chapter.

(3) An organization that is receiving payments on a prepaid basis for Medicare enrollees through a demonstration project under section 402(a) of the Social Security Amendments of 1967 (42 U.S.C. 1395b-1) or under section 222(a) of the Social Security Amendments of 1972 (42 U.S.C. 1395b-1 note).

(4) A qualified HMO (within the meaning of section 1310(d) of the Public Health Service Act).

(5) A coordinated care plan (within the meaning of section 1851(a)(2)(A) of the Act) offered by an organization in accordance with a contract with CMS under section 1857 of the Act and part 422 of this chapter.

(6) A managed care organization (MCO) contracting with a State under section 1903(m) of the Act.

(7) A prepaid inpatient health plan (PIHP) or prepaid ambulance health plan (PAHP) contracting with a State under part 438 of this chapter.

(8) A health insuring organization (HIO) contracting with a State under part 438, subpart D of this chapter.

(9) An entity operating under a demonstration project under sections 1115(a), 1915(a), 1915(b), or 1932(a) of the Act.

(d) [Reserved]

(e) *Academic medical centers.* (1) Services provided by an academic medical center if all of the following conditions are met:

(i) The referring physician—

(A) Is a *bona fide* employee of a component of the academic medical center on a full-time or substantial part-time basis. (A "component" of an academic medical center means an affiliated medical school, faculty practice plan, hospital, teaching facility, institution of higher education, departmental professional corporation, or nonprofit support organization whose primary purpose is supporting the teaching mission of the academic medical center.) The components need not be separate legal entities;

(B) Is licensed to practice medicine in the State(s) in which he or she practices medicine;

(C) Has a *bona fide* faculty appointment at the affiliated medical school or at one or more of the educational programs at the accredited academic hospital; and

(D) Provides either substantial academic services or substantial clinical teaching services (or a combination of academic services and clinical teaching services) for which the faculty member receives compensation as part of his or her employment relationship with the academic medical center. Parties should use a reasonable and consistent method for calculating a physician's academic services and clinical teaching services. A physician will be deemed to meet this requirement if he or she spends at least 20 percent of his or her professional time or 8 hours per week providing academic services or clinical teaching services (or a combination of academic services or clinical teaching services). A physician who does not spend at least 20 percent of his or her professional time or 8 hours per week providing academic services or clinical teaching services (or a combination of academic services or clinical teaching services) is not precluded from qualifying under this paragraph (e)(1)(i)(D).

(ii) The total compensation paid by all academic medical center components to the referring physician is set in advance and, in the aggregate, does not exceed fair market value for the services provided, and is not determined in a manner that takes into account the volume or value of any referrals or other business generated by the referring physician within the academic medical center.

(iii) The academic medical center must meet all of the following conditions:

(A) All transfers of money between components of the academic medical center must directly or indirectly support the missions of teaching, indigent care, research, or community service.

(B) The relationship of the components of the academic medical center must be set forth in written agreement(s) or other written document(s) that have been adopted by the governing body of each component. If the academic medical center is one legal entity, this requirement will be satisfied if transfers of funds between components of the academic medical center are reflected in the routine financial reports covering the components.

(C) All money paid to a referring physician for research must be used solely to support *bona fide* research or teaching and must be consistent with the terms and conditions of the grant.

(iv) The referring physician's compensation arrangement does not violate the anti-kickback statute (section 1128B(b) of the Act), or any Federal or State law or regulation governing billing or claims submission.

(2) The "academic medical center" for purposes of this section consists of—

(i) An accredited medical school (including a university, when appropriate) or an accredited academic hospital (as defined at § 411.355(e)(3));

(ii) One or more faculty practice plans affiliated with the medical school, the affiliated hospital(s), or the accredited academic hospital; and

(iii) One or more affiliated hospital(s) in which a majority of the physicians on the medical staff consists of physicians who are faculty members and a majority of all hospital admissions are made by physicians who are faculty members. The hospital for purposes of this paragraph (e)(2)(iii) may be the same hospital that satisfies the requirement of paragraph (e)(2)(i) of this section. For purposes of this provision, a faculty member is a physician who is either on the faculty of the affiliated medical school or on the faculty of one or more of the educational programs at the accredited academic hospital. In meeting this paragraph (e)(2)(iii), faculty from any affiliated medical school or accredited academic hospital education program may be aggregated, and residents and non-physician professionals need not be counted. Any faculty member may be counted, including courtesy and volunteer faculty.

(3) An accredited academic hospital for purposes of this section means a hospital or a health system that sponsors four or more approved medical education programs.

(f) *Implants furnished by an ASC.* Implants furnished by an ASC, including, but not limited to, cochlear implants, intraocular lenses, and other implanted prosthetics, implanted prosthetic devices, and implanted DME that meet the following conditions:

(1) The implant is implanted by the referring physician or a member of the referring physician's group practice in a Medicare-certified ASC (under part 416 of this chapter) with which the referring physician has a financial relationship.

(2) The implant is implanted in the patient during a surgical procedure paid by Medicare to the ASC as an ASC procedure under § 416.65.

(3) The arrangement for the furnishing of the implant does not violate the anti-kickback statute (section 1128B(b) of the Act).

(4) All billing and claims submission for the implants does not violate any Federal or State law or regulation governing billing or claims submission.

(5) The exception set forth in this paragraph (f) does not apply to any financial relationships between the referring physician and

any entity other than the ASC in which the implant is furnished to, and implanted in, the patient.

(g) *EPO and other dialysis-related drugs furnished in or by an ESRD facility.* EPO and other dialysis-related drugs that meet the following conditions:

(1) The EPO and other dialysis-related drugs are furnished in or by an ESRD facility. For purposes of this paragraph (g): "EPO and other dialysis-related drugs" means certain outpatient prescription drugs that are required for the efficacy of dialysis and identified as eligible for this exception on the List of CPT/HCPCS Codes; and "furnished" means that the EPO or dialysis-related drugs are administered to a patient in the ESRD facility, or, in the case of EPO or Aranesp (or equivalent drug identified on the List of CPT/HCPCS Codes) only, are dispensed by the ESRD facility for use at home.

(2) The arrangement for the furnishing of the EPO and other dialysis-related drugs does not violate the anti-kickback statute (section 1128B(b) of the Act).

(3) All billing and claims submission for the EPO and other dialysis-related drugs does not violate any Federal or State law or regulation governing billing or claims submission.

(4) The exception set forth in this paragraph (g) does not apply to any financial relationship between the referring physician and any entity other than the ESRD facility that furnishes the EPO and other dialysis-related drugs to the patient.

(h) *Preventive screening tests, immunizations, and vaccines.* Preventive screening tests, immunizations, and vaccines that meet the following conditions:

(1) The preventive screening tests, immunizations, and vaccines are subject to CMS-mandated frequency limits.

(2) The arrangement for the provision of the preventive screening tests, immunizations, and vaccines does not violate the anti-kickback statute (section 1128B(b) of the Act).

(3) All billing and claims submission for the preventive screening tests, immunizations, and vaccines does not violate any Federal or State law or regulation governing billing or claims submission.

(4) The preventive screening tests, immunizations, and vaccines must be covered by Medicare and must be listed as eligible for this exception on the List of CPT/HCPCS Codes.

(i) *Eyeglasses and contact lenses following cataract surgery.* Eyeglasses and contact lenses that are covered by Medicare when furnished to patients following cataract surgery that meet the following conditions:

(1) The eyeglasses or contact lenses are provided in accordance with the coverage and payment provisions set forth in § 410.36(a)(2)(ii) and § 414.228 of this chapter, respectively.

(2) The arrangement for the furnishing of the eyeglasses or contact lenses does not violate the anti-kickback statute (section 1128B(b) of the Act).

(3) All billing and claims submission for the eyeglasses or contact lenses does not violate any Federal or State law or regulation governing billing or claims submission.

(j) *Intra-family rural referrals.* (1) Services provided pursuant to a referral from a referring physician to his or her immediate family member or to an entity furnishing DHS with which the immediate family member has a financial relationship, if all of the following conditions are met:

(i) The patient who is referred resides in a rural area as defined in § 411.356(c)(1);

(ii) Except as provided in paragraph (j)(1)(iii) of this section, no other person or entity is available to furnish the services in a timely manner in light of the patient's condition within 25 miles of the patient's residence;

(iii) In the case of services furnished to patients where they reside (for example, home health services or in-home DME), no other person or entity is available to furnish the services in a timely manner in light of the patient's condition; and

(iv) The financial relationship does not violate the anti-kickback statute (section 1128B(b) of the Act), or any Federal or State law or regulation governing billing or claims submission;

(2) The referring physician or the immediate family member must make reasonable inquiries as to the availability of other persons or entities to furnish the DHS. However, neither the referring physician nor the immediate family member has any obligation to inquire as to the availability of persons or entities located farther than 25 miles from the patient's residence.

§ 411.356 Exceptions to the referral prohibition related to ownership or investment interests.

For purposes of § 411.353, the following ownership or investment interests do not constitute a financial relationship:

(a) *Publicly-traded securities.* Ownership of investment securities (including shares or bonds, debentures, notes, or other debt instruments) that at the time the DHS referral was made could be purchased on the open market and that meet the requirements of paragraphs (a)(1) and (a)(2) of this section.

(1) They are either—

(i) Listed for trading on the New York Stock Exchange, the American Stock Exchange, or any regional exchange in which quotations are published on a daily basis, or foreign securities listed on a recognized foreign, national, or regional exchange in which quotations are published on a daily basis; or

(ii) Traded under an automated interdealer quotation system operated by the National Association of Securities Dealers.

(2) They are in a corporation that had stockholder equity exceeding $75 million at the end of the corporation's most recent fiscal year or on average during the previous 3 fiscal years. "Stockholder

equity" is the difference in value between a corporation's total assets and total liabilities.

(b) *Mutual funds.* Ownership of shares in a regulated investment company as defined in section 851(a) of the Internal Revenue Code of 1986, if the company had, at the end of its most recent fiscal year, or on average during the previous 3 fiscal years, total assets exceeding $75 million.

(c) *Specific providers.* Ownership or investment interest in the following entities, for purposes of the services specified:

(1) A rural provider, in the case of DHS furnished in a rural area by the provider. A "rural provider" is an entity that furnishes substantially all (not less than 75 percent) of the DHS that it furnishes to residents of a rural area and, for the 18-month period beginning on December 8, 2003 (or such other period as Congress may specify), is not a specialty hospital. A rural area for purposes of this paragraph (c)(1) is an area that is not an urban area as defined in § 412.62(f)(1)(ii) of this chapter.

(2) A hospital that is located in Puerto Rico, in the case of DHS furnished by such a hospital.

(3) A hospital that is located outside of Puerto Rico, in the case of DHS furnished by such a hospital, if—

(i) the referring physician is authorized to perform services at the hospital;

(ii) effective for the 18-month period beginning on December 8, 2003 (or such other period as Congress may specify), the hospital is not a specialty hospital; and

(iii) the ownership or investment interest is in the entire hospital and not merely in a distinct part or department of the hospital.

§ 411.357 Exceptions to the referral prohibition related to compensation arrangements.

For purposes of § 411.353, the following compensation arrangements do not constitute a financial relationship:

(a) *Rental of office space.* Payments for the use of office space made by a lessee to a lessor if there is a rental or lease agreement that meets the following requirements:

(1) The agreement is set out in writing, is signed by the parties, and specifies the premises it covers.

(2) The term of the agreement is at least 1 year. To meet this requirement, if the agreement is terminated during the term with or without cause, the parties may not enter into a new agreement during the first year of the original term of the agreement.

(3) The space rented or leased does not exceed that which is reasonable and necessary for the legitimate business purposes of the lease or rental and is used exclusively by the lessee when being used by the lessee (and is not shared with or used by the lessor or any person or entity related to the lessor), except that the lessee may make payments for the use of space consisting of common areas if

the payments do not exceed the lessee's pro rata share of expenses for the space based upon the ratio of the space used exclusively by the lessee to the total amount of space (other than common areas) occupied by all persons using the common areas.

(4) The rental charges over the term of the agreement are set in advance and are consistent with fair market value.

(5) The rental charges over the term of the agreement are not determined in a manner that takes into account the volume or value of any referrals or other business generated between the parties.

(6) The agreement would be commercially reasonable even if no referrals were made between the lessee and the lessor.

(7) A holdover month-to-month rental for up to 6 months immediately following an agreement of at least 1 year that met the conditions of this paragraph (a) will satisfy this paragraph (a), provided the holdover rental is on the same terms and conditions as the immediately preceding agreement.

(b) *Rental of equipment.* Payments made by a lessee to a lessor for the use of equipment under the following conditions:

(1) A rental or lease agreement is set out in writing, is signed by the parties, and specifies the equipment it covers.

(2) The equipment rented or leased does not exceed that which is reasonable and necessary for the legitimate business purposes of the lease or rental and is used exclusively by the lessee when being used by the lessee and is not shared with or used by the lessor or any person or entity related to the lessor.

(3) The agreement provides for a term of rental or lease of at least 1 year. To meet this requirement, if the agreement is terminated during the term with or without cause, the parties may not enter into a new agreement during the first year of the original term of the agreement.

(4) The rental charges over the term of the agreement are set in advance, are consistent with fair market value, and are not determined in a manner that takes into account the volume or value of any referrals or other business generated between the parties.

(5) The agreement would be commercially reasonable even if no referrals were made between the parties.

(6) A holdover month-to-month rental for up to 6 months immediately following an agreement of at least 1 year that met the conditions of this paragraph (b) will satisfy this paragraph (b), provided the holdover rental is on the same terms and conditions as the immediately preceding agreement.

(c) *Bona fide employment relationships.* Any amount paid by an employer to a physician (or immediate family member) who has a *bona fide* employment relationship with the employer for the provision of services if the following conditions are met:

(1) The employment is for identifiable services.

(2) The amount of the remuneration under the employment is—

(i) Consistent with the fair market value of the services; and

(ii) Except as provided in paragraph (c)(4) of this section, is not determined in a manner that takes into account (directly or indirectly) the volume or value of any referrals by the referring physician.

(3) The remuneration is provided under an agreement that would be commercially reasonable even if no referrals were made to the employer.

(4) Paragraph (c)(2)(ii) of this section does not prohibit payment of remuneration in the form of a productivity bonus based on services performed personally by the physician (or immediate family member of the physician).

(d) *Personal service arrangements. (1) General*—Remuneration from an entity under an arrangement or multiple arrangements to a physician, an immediate family member of the physician, or to a group practice, including remuneration for specific physician services furnished to a nonprofit blood center, if the following conditions are met:

(i) Each arrangement is set out in writing, is signed by the parties, and specifies the services covered by the arrangement.

(ii) The arrangement(s) covers all of the services to be furnished by the physician (or an immediate family member of the physician) to the entity. This requirement will be met if all separate arrangements between the entity and the physician and the entity and any family members incorporate each other by reference or if they cross-reference a master list of contracts that is maintained and updated centrally and is available for review by the Secretary upon request. The master list should be maintained in a manner that preserves the historical record of contracts. A physician or family member can "furnish" services through employees whom they have hired for the purpose of performing the services; through a wholly owned entity; or through locum tenens physicians (as defined in § 411.351, except that the regular physician need not be a member of a group practice).

(iii) The aggregate services contracted for do not exceed those that are reasonable and necessary for the legitimate business purposes of the arrangement(s).

(iv) The term of each arrangement is for at least 1 year. To meet this requirement, if an arrangement is terminated during the term with or without cause, the parties may not enter into the same or substantially the same arrangement during the first year of the original term of the arrangement.

(v) The compensation to be paid over the term of each arrangement is set in advance, does not exceed fair market value, and, except in the case of a physician incentive plan, is not determined in a manner that takes into account the volume or value of any referrals or other business generated between the parties.

(vi) The services to be furnished under each arrangement do not involve the counseling or promotion of a business arrangement or other activity that violates any State or Federal law.

(2) *Physician incentive plan exception.* In the case of a physician incentive plan (as defined in § 411.351) between a physician and an entity (or downstream subcontractor), the compensation may be determined in a manner (through a withhold, capitation, bonus, or otherwise) that takes into account directly or indirectly the volume or value of any referrals or other business generated between the parties, if the plan meets the following requirements:

(i) No specific payment is made directly or indirectly under the plan to a physician or a physician group as an inducement to reduce or limit medically necessary services furnished with respect to a specific individual enrolled with the entity.

(ii) Upon request of the Secretary, the entity provides the Secretary with access to information regarding the plan (including any downstream subcontractor plans), in order to permit the Secretary to determine whether the plan is in compliance with paragraph (d)(2) of this section.

(iii) In the case of a plan that places a physician or a physician group at substantial financial risk as defined in § 422.208, the entity (and/or any downstream contractor) complies with the requirements concerning physician incentive plans set forth at § 422.208 and § 422.210 of this chapter.

(e) *Physician recruitment.* (1) Remuneration provided by a hospital to recruit a physician that is paid directly to the physician and that is intended to induce the physician to relocate his or her medical practice to the geographic area served by the hospital in order to become a member of the hospital's medical staff, if all of the following conditions are met:

(i) The arrangement is set out in writing and signed by both parties;

(ii) The arrangement is not conditioned on the physician's referral of patients to the hospital;

(iii) The hospital does not determine (directly or indirectly) the amount of the remuneration to the physician based on the volume or value of any actual or anticipated referrals by the physician or other business generated between the parties; and

(iv) The physician is allowed to establish staff privileges at any other hospital(s) and to refer business to any other entities (except as referrals may be restricted under a separate employment or services contract that complies with § 411.354(d)(4)).

(2) The "geographic area served by the hospital" is the area composed of the lowest number of contiguous zip codes from which the hospital draws at least 75 percent of its inpatients. A physician will be considered to have relocated his or her medical practice if—

(i) The physician moves his or her medical practice at least 25 miles; or

(ii) The physician's new medical practice derives at least 75 percent of its revenues from professional services furnished to patients (including hospital inpatients) not seen or treated by the physician at his or her prior medical practice site during the preceding 3 years, measured on an annual basis (fiscal or calendar year). For the initial "start up" year of the recruited physician's practice, the 75 percent test in the preceding sentence will be satisfied if there is a reasonable expectation that the recruited physician's medical practice for the year will derive at least 75 percent of its revenues from professional services furnished to patients not seen or treated by the physician at his or her prior medical practice site during the preceding 3 years.

(3) Residents and physicians who have been in practice 1 year or less will not be subject to the relocation requirement of this paragraph, except that the recruited resident or physician must establish his or her medical practice in the geographic area served by the hospital.

(4) In the case of remuneration provided by a hospital to a physician either indirectly through payments made to another physician or physician practice, or directly to a physician who joins a physician practice, the following additional conditions must be met:

(i) The written agreement in § 411.357(e)(1) is also signed by the party to whom the payments are directly made;

(ii) Except for actual costs incurred by the physician or physician practice in recruiting the new physician, the remuneration is passed directly through to or remains with the recruited physician;

(iii) In the case of an income guarantee made by the hospital to a recruited physician who joins a physician or physician practice, the costs allocated by the physician or physician practice to the recruited physician do not exceed the actual additional incremental costs attributable to the recruited physician;

(iv) Records of the actual costs and the passed through amounts are maintained for a period of at least 5 years and made available to the Secretary upon request;

(v) The remuneration from the hospital under the arrangement is not to be determined in a manner that takes into account (directly or indirectly) the volume or value of any actual or anticipated referrals by the recruited physician or the physician practice (or any physician affiliated with the physician practice) receiving the direct payments from the hospital;

(vi) The physician or physician practice may not impose additional practice restrictions on the recruited physician other than conditions related to quality of care; and

(vii) The arrangement does not violate the anti-kickback statute (section 1128B(b) of the Act), or any Federal or State law or regulation governing billing or claims submission.

(5) This paragraph (e) applies to remuneration provided by a federally qualified health center in the same manner as it applies to remuneration provided by a hospital, so long as the arrangement does not violate the anti-kickback statute (section 1128B(b) of the

Act), or any Federal or State law or regulation governing billing or claims submission.

(f) *Isolated transactions.* Isolated financial transactions, such as a one-time sale of property or a practice, if all of the following conditions are met:

(1) The amount of remuneration under the isolated transaction is—

(i) Consistent with the fair market value of the transaction; and

(ii) Not determined in a manner that takes into account (directly or indirectly) the volume or value of any referrals by the referring physician or other business generated between the parties.

(2) The remuneration is provided under an agreement that would be commercially reasonable even if the physician made no referrals.

(3) There are no additional transactions between the parties for 6 months after the isolated transaction, except for transactions that are specifically excepted under the other provisions in § 411.355 through § 411.357 and except for commercially reasonable post-closing adjustments that do not take into account (directly or indirectly) the volume or value of referrals or other business generated by the referring physician.

(g) *Certain arrangements with hospitals.* Remuneration provided by a hospital to a physician if the remuneration does not relate, directly or indirectly, to the furnishing of DHS. To qualify as "unrelated," remuneration must be wholly unrelated to the furnishing of DHS and must not in any way take into account the volume or value of a physician's referrals. Remuneration relates to the furnishing of DHS if it—

(1) Is an item, service, or cost that could be allocated in whole or in part to Medicare or Medicaid under cost reporting principles;

(2) Is furnished, directly or indirectly, explicitly or implicitly, in a selective, targeted, preferential, or conditioned manner to medical staff or other persons in a position to make or influence referrals; or

(3) Otherwise takes into account the volume or value of referrals or other business generated by the referring physician.

(h) *Group practice arrangements with a hospital.* An arrangement between a hospital and a group practice under which DHS are furnished by the group but are billed by the hospital if the following conditions are met:

(1) With respect to services furnished to an inpatient of the hospital, the arrangement is pursuant to the provision of inpatient hospital services under section 1861(b)(3) of the Act.

(2) The arrangement began before, and has continued in effect without interruption since, December 19, 1989.

(3) With respect to the DHS covered under the arrangement, at least 75 percent of these services furnished to patients of the hospital are furnished by the group under the arrangement.

(4) The arrangement is in accordance with a written agreement that specifies the services to be furnished by the parties and the compensation for services furnished under the agreement.

(5) The compensation paid over the term of the agreement is consistent with fair market value, and the compensation per unit of service is fixed in advance and is not determined in a manner that takes into account the volume or value of any referrals or other business generated between the parties.

(6) The compensation is provided in accordance with an agreement that would be commercially reasonable even if no referrals were made to the entity.

(i) *Payments by a physician.* Payments made by a physician (or his or her immediate family member)—

(1) To a laboratory in exchange for the provision of clinical laboratory services; or

(2) To an entity as compensation for any other items or services that are furnished at a price that is consistent with fair market value, and that are not specifically excepted under another provision in § 411.355 through § 411.357 (including, but not limited to, § 411.357(l)). "Services" in this context means services of any kind (not just those defined as "services" for purposes of the Medicare program in § 400.202).

(j) *Charitable donations by a physician. Bona fide* charitable donations made by a physician (or immediate family member) to an entity if all of the following conditions are satisfied:

(1) The charitable donation is made to an organization exempt from taxation under the Internal Revenue Code (or to a supporting organization);

(2) The donation is neither solicited, nor made, in any manner that takes into account the volume or value of referrals or other business generated between the physician and the entity; and

(3) The donation arrangement does not violate the anti-kickback statute (section 1128B(b) of the Act), or any Federal or State law or regulation governing billing or claims submission.

(k) *Non-monetary compensation up to $300.* (1) Compensation from an entity in the form of items or services (not including cash or cash equivalents) that does not exceed an aggregate of $300 per year, if all of the following conditions are satisfied:

(i) The compensation is not determined in any manner that takes into account the volume or value of referrals or other business generated by the referring physician.

(ii) The compensation may not be solicited by the physician or the physician's practice (including employees and staff members).

(iii) The compensation arrangement does not violate the anti-kickback statute (section 1128B(b) of the Act) or any Federal or State law or regulation governing billing or claims submission.

(2) The $300 limit in this paragraph (k) will be adjusted each calendar year to the nearest whole dollar by the increase in the Consumer Price Index-Urban All Items (CPI-U) for the 12-month period ending the preceding September 30. CMS intends to display as soon as possible after September 30 each year, both the increase

in the CPI-U for the 12-month period and the new non-monetary compensation limit on the physician self-referral Web site: *http://cms.hhs.gov/medlearn/refphys.asp.*

(l) *Fair market value compensation.* Compensation resulting from an arrangement between an entity and a physician (or an immediate family member) or any group of physicians (regardless of whether the group meets the definition of a group practice set forth in § 411.352) for the provision of items or services by the physician (or an immediate family member) or group of physicians to the entity, if the arrangement is set forth in an agreement that meets the following conditions:

(1) The arrangement is in writing, signed by the parties, and covers only identifiable items or services, all of which are specified in the agreement.

(2) The writing specifies the timeframe for the arrangement, which can be for any period of time and contain a termination clause, provided the parties enter into only one arrangement for the same items or services during the course of a year. An arrangement made for less than 1 year may be renewed any number of times if the terms of the arrangement and the compensation for the same items or services do not change.

(3) The writing specifies the compensation that will be provided under the arrangement. The compensation must be set in advance, consistent with fair market value, and not determined in a manner that takes into account the volume or value of referrals or other business generated by the referring physician.

(4) The arrangement would be commercially reasonable (taking into account the nature and scope of the transaction) and furthers the legitimate business purposes of the parties.

(5) It does not violate the anti-kickback statute (section 1128B(b) of the Act), or any Federal or State law or regulation governing billing or claims submission.

(6) The services to be performed under the arrangement do not involve the counseling or promotion of a business arrangement or other activity that violates a State or Federal law.

(m) *Medical staff incidental benefits.* Compensation in the form of items or services (not including cash or cash equivalents) from a hospital to a member of its medical staff when the item or service is used on the hospital's campus, if all of the following conditions are met:

(1) The compensation is provided to all members of the medical staff practicing in the same specialty (but not necessarily accepted by every member to whom it is offered) without regard to the volume or value of referrals or other business generated between the parties.

(2) Except with respect to identification of medical staff on a hospital Web site or in hospital advertising, the compensation is provided only during periods when the medical staff members are making rounds or are engaged in other services or activities that benefit the hospital or its patients.

(3) The compensation is provided by the hospital and used by the medical staff members only on the hospital's campus. Compensation, including, but not limited to, Internet access, pagers, or two-way radios, used away from the campus only to access hospital medical records or information or to access patients or personnel who are on the hospital campus, as well as the identification of the medical staff on a hospital Web site or in hospital advertising, will meet the "on campus" requirement of this paragraph (m).

(4) The compensation is reasonably related to the provision of, or designed to facilitate directly or indirectly the delivery of, medical services at the hospital.

(5) The compensation is of low value (that is, less than $25) with respect to each occurrence of the benefit (for example, each meal given to a physician while he or she is serving patients who are hospitalized must be of low value). The $25 limit in this paragraph (m)(5) will be adjusted each calendar year to the nearest whole dollar by the increase in the Consumer Price Index-Urban All Items (CPI-U) for the 12-month period ending the preceding September 30. CMS intends to display as soon as possible after September 30 each year both the increase in the CPI-U for the 12-month period and the new limits on the physician self-referral Web site: *http:// cms.hhs.gov/medlearn/refphys.asp.*

(6) The compensation is not determined in any manner that takes into account the volume or value of referrals or other business generated between the parties.

(7) The compensation arrangement does not violate the anti-kickback statute, (section 1128B(b) of the Act), or any Federal or State law or regulation governing billing or claims submission.

(8) Other facilities and health care clinics (including, but not limited to, federally qualified health centers) that have *bona fide* medical staffs may provide compensation under this paragraph (m) on the same terms and conditions applied to hospitals under this paragraph (m).

(n) *Risk-sharing arrangements.* Compensation pursuant to a risk-sharing arrangement (including, but not limited to, withholds, bonuses, and risk pools) between a managed care organization or an independent physicians' association and a physician (either directly or indirectly through a subcontractor) for services provided to enrollees of a health plan, provided that the arrangement does not violate the anti-kickback statute (section 1128B(b) of the Act), or any Federal or State law or regulation governing billing or claims submission. For purposes of this paragraph (n), "health plan" and "enrollees" have the meanings ascribed to those terms in § 1001.952(l) of this title.

(o) *Compliance training.* Compliance training provided by an entity to a physician (or to the physician's immediate family member or office staff) who practices in the entity's local community or service area, provided the training is held in the local community or service area. For purposes of this paragraph (o), "compliance training" means training regarding the basic elements of a compliance program (for example, establishing policies and procedures, training of staff, internal monitoring, reporting); specific training regarding the requirements of Federal and State health care programs (for example, billing, coding, reasonable and necessary services, documentation, unlawful referral arrangements); or training regarding other Federal, State, or local laws, regulations, or rules governing the conduct of the party for whom the training is provided (but not including continuing medical education).

(p) *Indirect compensation arrangements.* Indirect compensation arrangements, as defined in § 411.354(c)(2), if all of the following conditions are satisfied:

(1) The compensation received by the referring physician (or immediate family member) described in § 411.354(c)(2)(ii) is fair market value for services and items actually provided and not determined in any manner that takes into account the value or volume of referrals or other business generated by the referring physician for the entity furnishing DHS.

(2) The compensation arrangement described in § 411.354(c)(2)(ii) is set out in writing, signed by the parties, and specifies the services covered by the arrangement, except in the case of a *bona fide* employment relationship between an employer and an employee, in which case the arrangement need not be set out in a written contract, but must be for identifiable services and be commercially reasonable even if no referrals are made to the employer.

(3) The compensation arrangement does not violate the anti-kickback statute (section 1128B(b) of the Act), or any Federal or State law or regulation governing billing or claims submission.

(q) *Referral services.* Remuneration that meets all of the conditions set forth in § 1001.952(f) of this title.

(r) *Obstetrical malpractice insurance subsidies.* Remuneration to the referring physician that meets all of the conditions set forth in § 1001.952(o) of this title.

(s) *Professional courtesy.* Professional courtesy (as defined in § 411.351) offered by an entity to a physician or a physician's immediate family member or office staff if all of the following conditions are met:

(1) The professional courtesy is offered to all physicians on the entity's *bona fide* medical staff or in the entity's local community or service area without regard to the volume or value of referrals or other business generated between the parties;

(2) The health care items and services provided are of a type routinely provided by the entity;

(3) The entity's professional courtesy policy is set out in writing and approved in advance by the entity's governing body;

(4) The professional courtesy is not offered to a physician (or immediate family member) who is a Federal health care program beneficiary, unless there has been a good faith showing of financial need;

(5) If the professional courtesy involves any whole or partial reduction of any coinsurance obligation, the insurer is informed in writ-

ing of the reduction; and (6) The arrangement does not violate the anti-kickback statute (section 1128B(b) of the Act), or any Federal or State law or regulation governing billing or claims submission.

(t) *Retention payments in underserved areas.* (1) Remuneration provided by a hospital or federally qualified health center directly to a physician on the hospital's or federally qualified health center's medical staff to retain the physician's medical practice in the geographic area served by the hospital or federally qualified health center (as defined in paragraph (e)(2) of this section), if all of the following conditions are met:

(i) Paragraphs 411.357(e)(1)(i) through 411.357(e)(1)(iv) are satisfied;

(ii) The geographic area served by the hospital or federally qualified health center is a HPSA (regardless of the physician's specialty) or is an area with demonstrated need for the physician as determined by the Secretary in an advisory opinion issued according to section 1877(g)(6) of the Act;

(iii) The physician has a *bona fide* firm, written recruitment offer from a hospital or federally qualified health center that is not related to the hospital or the federally qualified health center making the payment, and the offer specifies the remuneration being offered and would require the physician to move the location of his or her practice at least 25 miles and outside of the geographic area served by the hospital or federally qualified health center making the retention payment;

(iv) The retention payment is limited to the lower of—

(A) The amount obtained by subtracting (1) the physician's current income from physician and related services from (2) the income the physician would receive from comparable physician and related services in the *bona fide* recruitment offer, provided that the respective incomes are determined using a reasonable and consistent methodology, and that they are calculated uniformly over no more than a 24-month period; or

(B) The reasonable costs the hospital or federally qualified health center would otherwise have to expend to recruit a new physician to the geographic area served by the hospital or federally qualified health center in order to join the medical staff of the hospital or federally qualified health center to replace the retained physician;

(v) Any retention payment is subject to the same obligations and restrictions, if any, on repayment or forgiveness of indebtedness as the *bona fide* recruitment offer;

(vi) The hospital or federally qualified health center does not enter into a retention arrangement with a particular referring physician more frequently than once every 5 years and the amount and terms of the retention payment are not altered during the term of the arrangement in any manner that takes into account the volume or value of referrals or other business generated by the physician;

(vii) The arrangement otherwise complies with all of the conditions of this section; and

(viii) The arrangement does not violate the anti-kickback statute (section 1128B(b) of the Act), or any Federal or State law or regulation governing billing or claims submission.

(2) The Secretary may waive the relocation requirement of paragraph (t)(1) of this section for payments made to physicians practicing in a HPSA or an area with demonstrated need for the physician through an advisory opinion issued according to section 1877(g)(6) of the Act, if the retention payment arrangement otherwise complies with all of the conditions of this paragraph.

(u) *Community-wide health information systems.* Items or services of information technology provided by an entity to a physician that allow access to, and sharing of, electronic health care records and any complementary drug information systems, general health information, medical alerts, and related information for patients served by community providers and practitioners, in order to enhance the community's overall health, provided that—

(1) The items or services are available as necessary to enable the physician to participate in a community-wide health information system, are principally used by the physician as part of the community-wide health information system, and are not provided to the physician in any manner that takes into account the volume or value of referrals or other business generated by the physician;

(2) The community-wide health information systems are available to all providers, practitioners, and residents of the community who desire to participate; and

(3) The arrangement does not violate the anti-kickback statute, (section 1128B(b) of the Act), or any Federal or State law or regulation governing billing or claims submission.

§ 411.361 Reporting requirements.

(a) *Basic rule.* Except as provided in paragraph (b) of this section, all entities furnishing services for which payment may be made under Medicare must submit information to CMS or to the Office of Inspector General (OIG) concerning their reportable financial relationships (as defined in paragraph (d) of this section), in the form, manner, and at the times that CMS or OIG specifies.

(b) *Exception.* The requirements of paragraph (a) of this section do not apply to entities that furnish 20 or fewer Part A and Part B services during a calendar year, or to any Medicare covered services furnished outside the United States.

(c) *Required information.* The information requested by CMS or OIG can include the following:

(1) The name and unique physician identification number (UPIN) of each physician who has a reportable financial relationship with the entity.

(2) The name and UPIN of each physician who has an immediate family member (as defined in § 411.351) who has a reportable financial relationship with the entity.

(3) The covered services furnished by the entity.

(4) With respect to each physician identified under paragraphs (c)(1) and (c)(2) of this section, the nature of the financial relationship (including the extent and/or value of the ownership or investment interest or the compensation arrangement) as evidenced in records that the entity knows or should know about in the course of prudently conducting business, including, but not limited to, records that the entity is already required to retain to comply with the rules of the Internal Revenue Service and the Securities and Exchange Commission and other rules of the Medicare and Medicaid programs.

(d) *Reportable financial relationships.* For purposes of this section, a reportable financial relationship is any ownership or investment interest, as defined in § 411.354(b) or any compensation arrangement, as defined in § 411.354(c), except for ownership or investment interests that satisfy the exceptions set forth in § 411.356(a) or § 411.356(b) regarding publicly-traded securities and mutual funds.

(e) *Form and timing of reports.* Entities that are subject to the requirements of this section must submit the required information, upon request, within the time period specified by the request. Entities are given at least 30 days from the date of the request to provide the information. Entities must retain the information, and documentation sufficient to verify the information, for the length of time specified by the applicable regulatory requirements for the information, and, upon request, must make that information and documentation available to CMS or OIG.

(f) *Consequences of failure to report.* Any person who is required, but fails, to submit information concerning his or her financial relationships in accordance with this section is subject to a civil money penalty of up to $10,000 for each day following the deadline established under paragraph (e) of this section until the information is submitted. Assessment of these penalties will comply with the applicable provisions of part 1003 of this title.

(g) *Public disclosure.* Information furnished to CMS or OIG under this section is subject to public disclosure in accordance with the provisions of part 401 of this chapter.

Appendix B-3

Stark Phase II Final Regulations: Interim Final Rule with Comment Period; Correcting Amendment Pertaining to Advisory Opinion Process (effective July 26, 2004) [New]

Source: 69 Fed. Reg. 57,226 (Sept. 24, 2004), *codified at* 42 C.F.R. §§ 411.370–.389.

Editor's Note: According to CMS, the physician self-referral advisory opinion regulations were inadvertently deleted from Part 411 in the March 26, 2004, interim final rule published at 69 Fed. Reg. 16,054 (Mar. 26, 2004), which was effective July 26, 2004. A correcting amendment published Sept. 24, 2004, reinstated retroactively those advisory opinion regulations.

* * * * *

Accordingly, 42 CFR chapter IV is corrected by making the following correcting amendments:

PART 411—EXCLUSIONS FROM MEDICARE AND LIMITATIONS ON MEDICARE PAYMENT

1. The authority citation for part 411 continues to read as follows:

Authority: Secs. 1102 and 1871 of the Social Security Act (42 U.S.C. 1302 and 1395hh).

Subpart J—Financial Relationships Between Physicians and Entities Furnishing Designated Health Services

2. In Subpart J, Sec. 411.370 is added to read as follows.

§ 411.370 Advisory opinions relating to physician referrals.

(a) *Period during which CMS will accept requests.* The provisions of § 411.370 through § 411.389 apply to requests for advisory opinions that are submitted to CMS after November 3, 1997, and before August 21, 2000, and to any requests submitted during any other time period during which CMS is required by law to issue the advisory opinions described in this subpart.

(b) *Matters that qualify for advisory opinions and who may request one.* Any individual or entity may request a written advisory opinion from CMS concerning whether a physician's referral relating to designated health services (other than clinical laboratory services) is prohibited under section 1877 of the Act. In the advisory opinion, CMS determines whether a business arrangement described by the parties to that arrangement appears to constitute a "financial relationship" (as defined in section 1877(a)(2) of the Act) that could potentially restrict a physician's referrals, and whether the arrangement or the designated health services at issue appear to qualify for any of the exceptions to the referral prohibition described in section 1877 of the Act.

(1) The request must involve an existing arrangement or one into which the requestor, in good faith, specifically plans to enter. The planned arrangement may be contingent upon the party or parties receiving a favorable advisory opinion. CMS does not consider, for purposes of an advisory opinion, requests that present a general question of interpretation, pose a hypothetical situation, or involve the activities of third parties.

(2) The requestor must be a party to the existing or proposed arrangement.

(c) *Matters not subject to advisory opinions.* CMS does not address through the advisory opinion process—

(1) Whether the fair market value was, or will be, paid or received for any goods, services, or property; and

(2) Whether an individual is a *bona fide* employee within the requirements of section 3121(d)(2) of the Internal Revenue Code of 1986.

(d) *Facts subject to advisory opinions.* CMS considers requests for advisory opinions that involve applying specific facts to the subject matter described in paragraph (b) of this section. Requestors must include in the advisory opinion request a complete description of the arrangement that the requestor is undertaking, or plans to undertake, as described in § 411.372.

(e) *Requests that will not be accepted.* CMS does not accept an advisory opinion request or issue an advisory opinion if—

(1) The request is not related to a named individual or entity;

(2) CMS is aware that the same, or substantially the same, course of action is under investigation, or is or has been the subject of a proceeding involving the Department of Health and Human Services or another governmental agency; or

(3) CMS believes that it cannot make an informed opinion or could only make an informed opinion after extensive investigation, clinical study, testing, or collateral inquiry.

(f) *Effects of an advisory opinion on other Governmental authority.* Nothing in this part limits the investigatory or prosecutorial authority of the OIG, the Department of Justice, or any other agency of the Government. In addition, in connection with any request for an advisory opinion, CMS, the OIG, or the Department of Justice may conduct whatever independent investigation it believes appropriate.

3. Sections 411.372 and 411.373 are added to subpart J to read as follows.

§ 411.372 Procedure for submitting a request.

(a) *Format for a request.* A party or parties must submit a request for an advisory opinion to CMS in writing, including an original request and 2 copies. The request must be addressed to: Centers for Medicare & Medicaid Services, Department of Health and Human Services, Office of Financial Management, Division of Premium Billing and Collections, Mail Stop C3-09-27, Attention: Advisory Opinions, 7500 Security Boulevard, Baltimore, MD 21244-1850.

(b) *Information CMS requires with all submissions.* The request must include the following:

(1) The name, address, telephone number, and Taxpayer Identification Number of the requestor.

(2) The names and addresses, to the extent known, of all other actual and potential parties to the arrangement that is the subject of the request.

(3) The name, title, address, and daytime telephone number of a contact person who will be available to discuss the request with CMS on behalf of the requestor.

(4) A complete and specific description of all relevant information bearing on the arrangement, including—

(i) A complete description of the arrangement that the requestor is undertaking, or plans to undertake, including: the purpose of the arrangement; the nature of each party's (including each entity's) contribution to the arrangement; the direct or indirect relationships between the parties, with an emphasis on the relationships between physicians involved in the arrangement (or their immediate family members who are involved) and any entities that provide designated health services; the types of services for which a physician wishes to refer, and whether the referrals will involve Medicare or Medicaid patients;

(ii) Complete copies of all relevant documents or relevant portions of documents that affect or could affect the arrangement, such as personal services or employment contracts, leases, deeds, pension or insurance plans, financial statements, or stock certificates (or, if these relevant documents do not yet exist, a complete description, to the best of the requestor's knowledge, of what these documents are likely to contain);

(iii) Detailed statements of all collateral or oral understandings, if any; and

(iv) Descriptions of any other arrangements or relationships that could affect CMS's analysis.

(5) Complete information on the identity of all entities involved either directly or indirectly in the arrangement, including their names, addresses, legal form, ownership structure, nature of the business (products and services) and, if relevant, their Medicare and Medicaid provider numbers. The requestor must also include a brief description of any other entities that could affect the outcome of the opinion, including those with which the requestor, the other parties, or the immediate family members of involved physicians, have any financial relationships (either direct or indirect, and as defined in section 1877(a)(2) of the Act and § 411.351), or in which any of the parties holds an ownership or control interest as defined in section 1124(a)(3) of the Act.

(6) A discussion of the specific issues or questions the requestor would like CMS to address including, if possible, a description of why the requestor believes the referral prohibition in section 1877 of the Act might or might not be triggered by the arrangement and which, if any, exceptions to the prohibition the requestor believes might apply. The requestor should attempt to designate which facts are relevant to each issue or question raised in the request and should cite the provisions of law under which each issue or question arises.

(7) An indication of whether the parties involved in the request have also asked for or are planning to ask for an advisory opinion on the arrangement in question from the OIG under section 1128D(b) of the Act (42 U.S.C. 1320a-7d(b)) and whether the arrangement is or is not, to the best of the requestor's knowledge, the subject of an investigation.

(8) The certification(s) described in § 411.373. The certification(s) must be signed by—

(i) The requestor, if the requestor is an individual;

(ii) The chief executive officer, or comparable officer, of the requestor, if the requestor is a corporation;

(iii) The managing partner of the requestor, if the requestor is a partnership; or

(iv) A managing member, if the requestor is a limited liability company.

(9) A check or money order payable to CMS in the amount described in § 411.375(a).

(c) *Additional information CMS might require.* If the request does not contain all of the information required by paragraph (b) of this section, or, if either before or after accepting the request, CMS believes it needs more information in order to render an advisory opinion, it may request whatever additional information or documents it deems necessary. Additional information must be provided in writing, signed by the same person who signed the initial request (or by an individual in a comparable position), and be certified as described in § 411.373.

§ 411.373 Certification.

(a) Every request must include the following signed certification: "With knowledge of the penalties for false statements provided by 18 U.S.C. 1001 and with knowledge that this request for an advisory opinion is being submitted to the Department of Health and Human Services, I certify that all of the information provided is true and correct, and constitutes a complete description of the facts regarding which an advisory opinion is sought, to the best of my knowledge and belief."

(b) If the advisory opinion relates to a proposed arrangement, in addition to the certification required by paragraph (a) of this section, the following certification must be included and signed by the requestor: "The arrangement described in this request for an advisory opinion is one into which [the requestor], in good faith, plans to enter." This statement may be made contingent on a favorable advisory opinion, in which case the requestor should add one of the following phrases to the certification:

(1) "if CMS issues a favorable advisory opinion."

(2) "if CMS and the OIG issue favorable advisory opinions."

4. Section 411.375 is added to subpart J to read as follows.

§ 411.375 Fees for the cost of advisory opinions.

(a) *Initial payment.* Parties must include with each request for an advisory opinion submitted through December 31, 1998, a check or money order payable to CMS for $250. For requests submitted after this date, parties must include a check or money order in this amount, unless CMS has revised the amount of the initial fee in a program issuance, in which case, the requestor must include the revised amount. This initial payment is nonrefundable.

(b) *How costs are calculated.* Before issuing the advisory opinion, CMS calculates the costs the Department has incurred in responding to the request. The calculation includes the costs of salaries, benefits, and overhead for analysts, attorneys, and others who have worked on the request, as well as administrative and supervisory support for these individuals.

(c) *Agreement to pay all costs.* (1) By submitting the request for an advisory opinion, the requestor agrees, except as indicated in paragraph (c)(3) of this section, to pay all costs the Department incurs in responding to the request for an advisory opinion.

(2) In its request for an advisory opinion, the requestor may designate a triggering dollar amount. If CMS estimates that the costs of processing the advisory opinion request have reached or are likely to exceed the designated triggering dollar amount, CMS notifies the requestor.

(3) If CMS notifies the requestor that the actual or estimated cost of processing the request has reached or is likely to exceed the triggering dollar amount, CMS stops processing the request until the requestor makes a written request for CMS to continue. If CMS is delayed in processing the request for an advisory opinion because of this procedure, the time within which CMS must issue an advisory opinion is suspended until the requestor asks CMS to continue working on the request.

(4) If the requestor chooses not to pay for CMS to complete an advisory opinion, or withdraws the request, the requestor is still obligated to pay for all costs CMS has identified as costs it incurred in processing the request for an advisory opinion, up to that point.

(5) If the costs CMS has incurred in responding to the request are greater than the amount the requestor has paid, CMS, before issuing the advisory opinion, notifies the requestor of any additional amount that is due. CMS does not issue an advisory opinion until the requestor has paid the full amount that is owed. Once the requestor has paid CMS the total amount due for the costs of processing the request, CMS issues the advisory opinion. The time period CMS has for issuing advisory opinions is suspended from the time CMS notifies the requestor of the amount owed until the time CMS receives full payment.

(d) *Fees for outside experts.* (1) In addition to the fees identified in this section, the requestor also must pay any required fees for expert opinions, if any, from outside sources, as described in § 411.377.

(2) The time period for issuing an advisory opinion is suspended from the time that CMS notifies the requestor that it needs an outside expert opinion until the time CMS receives that opinion.

5. Sections 411.377 through 411.380 are added to subpart J to read as follows.

§ 411.377 Expert opinions from outside sources.

(a) CMS may request expert advice from qualified sources if CMS believes that the advice is necessary to respond to a request for an advisory opinion. For example, CMS may require the use of accountants or business experts to assess the structure of a complex business arrangement or to ascertain a physician's or immediate family member's financial relationship with entities that provide designated health services.

(b) If CMS determines that it needs to obtain expert advice in order to issue a requested advisory opinion, CMS notifies the requestor of that fact and provides the identity of the appropriate expert and an estimate of the costs of the expert advice. As indicated in § 411.375(d), the requestor must pay the estimated cost of the expert advice.

(c) Once CMS has received payment for the estimated cost of the expert advice, CMS arranges for the expert to provide a prompt review of the issue or issues in question. CMS considers any additional expenses for the expert advice, beyond the estimated amount, as part of the costs CMS has incurred in responding to the request, and the responsibility of the requestor, as described in § 411.375(c).

§ 411.378 Withdrawing a request.

The party requesting an advisory opinion may withdraw the request before CMS issues a formal advisory opinion. This party must submit the withdrawal in writing to the same address as the request, as indicated in § 411.372(a). Even if the party withdraws the request, the party must pay the costs the Department has expended in processing the request, as discussed in § 411.375. CMS reserves the right to keep any request for an advisory opinion and any accompanying documents and information, and to use them for any governmental purposes permitted by law.

§ 411.379 When CMS accepts a request.

(a) Upon receiving a request for an advisory opinion, CMS promptly makes an initial determination of whether the request includes all of the information it will need to process the request.

(b) Within 15 working days of receiving the request, CMS—

    (1) Formally accepts the request for an advisory opinion;

    (2) Notifies the requestor about the additional information it needs; or

    (3) Declines to formally accept the request.

(c) If the requestor provides the additional information CMS has requested, or otherwise resubmits the request, CMS processes the resubmission in accordance with paragraphs (a) and (b) of this section as if it were an initial request for an advisory opinion.

(d) Upon accepting the request, CMS notifies the requestor by regular U.S. mail of the date that CMS formally accepted the request.

(e) The 90-day period that CMS has to issue an advisory opinion set forth in § 411.380(c) does not begin until CMS has formally accepted the request for an advisory opinion.

§ 411.380 When CMS issues a formal advisory opinion.

(a) CMS considers an advisory opinion to be issued once it has received payment and once the opinion has been dated, numbered, and signed by an authorized CMS official.

(b) An advisory opinion contains a description of the material facts known to CMS that relate to the arrangement that is the subject of the advisory opinion, and states CMS's opinion about the subject matter of the request based on those facts. If necessary, CMS includes in the advisory opinion material facts that could be considered confidential information or trade secrets within the meaning of 18 U.S.C. 1095.

(c)(1) CMS issues an advisory opinion, in accordance with the provisions of this part, within 90 days after it has formally accepted the request for an advisory opinion, or, for requests that CMS determines, in its discretion, involve complex legal issues or highly complicated fact patterns, within a reasonable time period.

    (2) If the 90th day falls on a Saturday, Sunday, or Federal holiday, the time period ends at the close of the first business day following the weekend or holiday;

    (3) The 90-day period is suspended from the time CMS'

      (i) Notifies the requestor that the costs have reached or are likely to exceed the triggering amount as described in § 411.375 (c)(2) until CMS receives written notice from the requestor to continue processing the request;

      (ii) Requests additional information from the requestor until CMS receives the additional information;

      (iii) Notifies the requestor of the full amount due until CMS receives payment of this amount; and

      (iv) Notifies the requestor of the need for expert advice until CMS receives the expert advice.

(d) After CMS has notified the requestor of the full amount owed and has received full payment of that amount, CMS issues the advisory opinion and promptly mails it to the requestor by regular first class U.S. mail.

6. Section 411.382 is added to subpart J to read as follows.

§ 411.382 CMS's right to rescind advisory opinions.

Any advice CMS gives in an opinion does not prejudice its right to reconsider the questions involved in the opinion and, if it determines that it is in the public interest, to rescind or revoke the opinion. CMS provides notice to the requestor of its decision to rescind or revoke the opinion so that the requestor and the parties involved in the requestor's arrangement may discontinue any course of action they have taken in accordance with the advisory opinion. CMS does not proceed against the requestor with respect to any action the requestor and the involved parties have taken in good faith reliance upon CMS's advice under this part, provided—

(a) The requestor presented to CMS a full, complete and accurate description of all the relevant facts; and

(b) The parties promptly discontinue the action upon receiving notice that CMS had rescinded or revoked its approval, or discontinue the action within a reasonable "wind down" period, as determined by CMS.

7. Section 411.384 is added to subpart J to read as follows.

§ 411.384 Disclosing advisory opinions and supporting information.

(a) Advisory opinions that CMS issues and releases in accordance with the procedures set forth in this subpart are available to the public.

(b) Promptly after CMS issues an advisory opinion and releases it to the requestor, CMS makes available a copy of the advisory opinion for public inspection during its normal hours of operation and on the DHHS/CMS Web site.

(c) Any predecisional document, or part of such predecisional document, that is prepared by CMS, the Department of Justice, or any other Department or agency of the United States in connection with an advisory opinion request under the procedures set forth in this part is exempt from disclosure under 5 U.S.C. 552, and will not be made publicly available.

(d) Documents submitted by the requestor to CMS in connection with a request for an advisory opinion are available to the public to the extent they are required to be made available by 5 U.S.C. 552, through procedures set forth in 45 CFR part 5.

(e) Nothing in this section limits CMS's obligation, under applicable laws, to publicly disclose the identity of the requesting party or parties, and the nature of the action CMS has taken in response to the request.

8. Sections 411.386 through 411.389 are added to subpart J to read as follows.

§ 411.386 CMS's advisory opinions as exclusive.

The procedures described in this subpart constitute the only method by which any individuals or entities can obtain a binding advisory opinion on the subject of a physician's referrals, as described in § 411.370. CMS has not and does not issue a binding advisory opinion on the subject matter in § 411.370, in either oral or written form, except through written opinions it issues in accordance with this subpart.

§ 411.387 Parties affected by advisory opinions.

An advisory opinion issued by CMS does not apply in any way to any individual or entity that does not join in the request for the opinion. Individuals or entities other than the requestor(s) may not rely on an advisory opinion.

§ 411.388 When advisory opinions are not admissible evidence.

The failure of a party to seek or to receive an advisory opinion may not be introduced into evidence to prove that the party either intended or did not intend to violate the provisions of sections 1128, 1128A or 1128B of the Act.

§ 411.389 Range of the advisory opinion.

(a) An advisory opinion states only CMS's opinion regarding the subject matter of the request. If the subject of an advisory opinion is an arrangement that must be approved by or is regulated by any other agency, CMS's advisory opinion cannot be read to indicate CMS's views on the legal or factual issues that may be raised before that agency.

(b) An advisory opinion that CMS issues under this part does not bind or obligate any agency other than the Department. It does not affect the requestor's, or anyone else's, obligations to any other agency, or under any statutory or regulatory provision other than that which is the specific subject matter of the advisory opinion.

Appendix D

Civil Monetary Penalties and Exclusion Materials

Appendix D-3

Exclusion of Entities From Government Health Care Programs Statute

Source: 42 U.S.C. Section 1320a-7

Section 1320a-7. Exclusion of certain individuals and entities from participation in Medicare and State health care programs

(a) Mandatory exclusion

The Secretary shall exclude the following individuals and entities from participation in any Federal health care program (as defined in section 1320a-7b(f) of this title):

(1) Conviction of program-related crimes

Any individual or entity that has been convicted of a criminal offense related to the delivery of an item or service under subchapter XVIII of this chapter or under any State health care program.

(2) Conviction relating to patient abuse

Any individual or entity that has been convicted, under Federal or State law, of a criminal offense relating to neglect or abuse of patients in connection with the delivery of a health care item or service.

(3) Felony conviction relating to health care fraud

Any individual or entity that has been convicted for an offense which occurred after August 21, 1996, under Federal or State law, in connection with the delivery of a health care item or service or with respect to any act or omission in a health care program (other than those specifically described in paragraph (1)) operated by or financed in whole or in part by any Federal, State, or local government agency, of a criminal offense consisting of a felony relating to fraud, theft, embezzlement, breach of fiduciary responsibility, or other financial misconduct.

(4) Felony conviction relating to controlled substance

Any individual or entity that has been convicted for an offense which occurred after August 21, 1996, under Federal or State law, of a criminal offense consisting of a felony relating to the unlawful manufacture, distribution, prescription, or dispensing of a controlled substance.

(b) Permissive exclusion

The Secretary may exclude the following individuals and entities from participation in any Federal health care program (as defined in section 1320a-7b(f) of this title):

(1) Conviction relating to fraud

Any individual or entity that has been convicted for an offense which occurred after August 21, 1996, under Federal or State law—

(A) of a criminal offense consisting of a misdemeanor relating to fraud, theft, embezzlement, breach of fiduciary responsibility, or other financial misconduct—

(i) in connection with the delivery of a health care item or service, or

(ii) with respect to any act or omission in a health care program (other than those specifically described in subsection (a)(1) of this section) operated by or financed in whole or in part by any Federal, State, or local government agency; or

(B) of a criminal offense relating to fraud, theft, embezzlement, breach of fiduciary responsibility, or other financial misconduct with respect to any act or omission in a program (other than a health care program) operated by or financed in whole or in part by any Federal, State, or local government agency.

(2) Conviction relating to obstruction of an investigation

Any individual or entity that has been convicted, under Federal or State law, in connection with the interference with or obstruction of any investigation into any criminal offense described in paragraph (1) or in subsection (a) of this section.

(3) Misdemeanor conviction relating to controlled substance

Any individual or entity that has been convicted, under Federal or State law, of a criminal offense consisting of a misdemeanor relating to the unlawful manufacture, distribution, prescription, or dispensing of a controlled substance.

(4) License revocation or suspension

Any individual or entity—

(A) whose license to provide health care has been revoked or suspended by any State licensing authority, or who otherwise lost such a license or the right to apply for or renew such a license, for reasons bearing on the individual's or entity's professional competence, professional performance, or financial integrity, or

(B) who surrendered such a license while a formal disciplinary proceeding was pending before such an authority and the proceeding concerned the individual's or entity's professional competence, professional performance, or financial integrity.

(5) Exclusion or suspension under Federal or State health care program

Any individual or entity which has been suspended or excluded from participation, or otherwise sanctioned, under—

(A) any Federal program, including programs of the Department of Defense or the Department of Veterans Affairs, involving the provision of health care, or

(B) a State health care program,

for reasons bearing on the individual's or entity's professional competence, professional performance, or financial integrity.

(6) Claims for excessive charges or unnecessary services and failure of certain organizations to furnish medically necessary services

Any individual or entity that the Secretary determines—

(A) has submitted or caused to be submitted bills or requests for payment (where such bills or requests are based on charges or cost) under subchapter XVIII of this chapter or a State health care program containing charges (or, in applicable cases, requests for payment of costs) for items or services furnished substantially in excess of such individual's or entity's usual charges (or, in applicable cases, substantially in excess of such individual's or entity's costs) for such items or services, unless the Secretary finds there is good cause for such bills or requests containing such charges or costs;

(B) has furnished or caused to be furnished items or services to patients (whether or not eligible for benefits under subchapter XVIII of this chapter or under a State health care program) substantially in excess of the needs of such patients or of a quality which fails to meet professionally recognized standards of health care;

(C) is—

(i) a health maintenance organization (as defined in section 1396b(m) of this title) providing items and services under a State plan approved under subchapter XIX of this chapter, or

(ii) an entity furnishing services under a waiver approved under section 1396n(b)(1) of this title,

and has failed substantially to provide medically necessary items and services that are required (under law or the contract with the State under subchapter XIX of this chapter) to be provided to individuals covered under that plan or waiver, if the failure has adversely affected (or has a substantial likelihood of adversely affecting) these individuals; or

(D) is an entity providing items and services as an eligible organization under a risk-sharing contract under section 1395mm of this title and has failed substantially to provide medically necessary items and services that are required (under law or such contract) to be provided to individuals covered under the risk-sharing contract, if the failure has adversely affected (or has a substantial likelihood of adversely affecting) these individuals.

(7) Fraud, kickbacks, and other prohibited activities

Any individual or entity that the Secretary determines has committed an act which is described in section 1320a-7a, 1320a-7b, or 1320a-8 of this title.

(8) Entities controlled by a sanctioned individual

Any entity with respect to which the Secretary determines that a person—

(A)(i) who has a direct or indirect ownership or control interest of 5 percent or more in the entity or with an ownership or control interest (as defined in section 1320a-3(a)(3) of this title) in that entity,

(ii) who is an officer, director, agent, or managing employee (as defined in section 1320a-5(b) of this title) of that entity; or

(iii) who was described in clause (i) but is no longer so described because of a transfer of ownership or control interest, in anticipation of (or following) a conviction, assessment, or exclusion described in subparagraph (B) against the person, to an immediate family member (as defined in subsection (j)(1) of this section) or a member of the household of the person (as defined in subsection (j)(2) of this section) who continues to maintain an interest described in such clause—

is a person—

(B)(i) who has been convicted of any offense described in subsection (a) of this section or in paragraph (1), (2), or (3) of this subsection;

(ii) against whom a civil monetary penalty has been assessed under section 1320a-7a or 1320a-8 of this title; or

(iii) who has been excluded from participation under a program under subchapter XVIII of this chapter or under a State health care program.

(9) Failure to disclose required information

Any entity that did not fully and accurately make any disclosure required by section 1320a-3 of this title, section 1320a-3a of this title, or section 1320a-5 of this title.

(10) Failure to supply requested information on subcontractors and suppliers

Any disclosing entity (as defined in section 1320a-3(a)(2) of this title) that fails to supply (within such period as may be specified by the Secretary in regulations) upon request specifically addressed to the entity by the Secretary or by the State agency administering or supervising the administration of a State health care program—

(A) full and complete information as to the ownership of a subcontractor (as defined by the Secretary in regulations) with whom the entity has had, during the previous 12 months, business transactions in an aggregate amount in excess of $25,000, or

(B) full and complete information as to any significant business transactions (as defined by the Secretary in regulations), occurring during the five-year period ending on the date of such request, between the entity and any wholly owned supplier or between the entity and any subcontractor.

(11) Failure to supply payment information

Any individual or entity furnishing items or services for which payment may be made under subchapter XVIII of this chapter or a State health care program that fails to provide such information as the Secretary or the appropriate State agency finds necessary to determine whether such payments are or were due and the amounts thereof, or has refused to permit such examination of its records by or on behalf of the Secretary or that agency as may be necessary to verify such information.

(12) Failure to grant immediate access

Any individual or entity that fails to grant immediate access, upon reasonable request (as defined by the Secretary in regulations) to any of the following:

(A) To the Secretary, or to the agency used by the Secretary, for the purpose specified in the first sentence of section 1395aa(a) of this title (relating to compliance with conditions of participation or payment).

(B) To the Secretary or the State agency, to perform the reviews and surveys required under State plans under paragraphs (26), (31), and (33) of section 1396a(a) of this title and under section 1396b(g) of this title.

(C) To the Inspector General of the Department of Health and Human Services, for the purpose of reviewing records, documents, and other data necessary to the performance of the statutory functions of the Inspector General.

(D) To a State medicaid fraud control unit (as defined in section 1396b(q) of this title), for the purpose of conducting activities described in that section.

(13) Failure to take corrective action

Any hospital that fails to comply substantially with a corrective action required under section 1395ww(f)(2)(B) of this title.

(14) Default on health education loan or scholarship obligations

Any individual who the Secretary determines is in default on repayments of scholarship obligations or loans in connection with health professions education made or secured, in whole or in part, by the Secretary and with respect to whom the Secretary has taken all reasonable steps available to the Secretary to secure repayment of such obligations or loans, except that (A) the Secretary shall not exclude pursuant to this paragraph a physician who is the sole community physician or sole source of essential specialized services in a community if a State requests that the physician not be excluded, and (B) the Secretary shall take into account, in determining whether to exclude any other physician pursuant to this paragraph, access of beneficiaries to physician services for which payment may be made under subchapter XVIII or XIX of this chapter.

(15) Individuals controlling a sanctioned entity

(A) Any individual—

(i) who has a direct or indirect ownership or control interest in a sanctioned entity and who knows or should know (as defined in section 1320a-7a(i)(6)[1] of this title) of the action constituting the basis for the conviction or exclusion described in subparagraph (B); or

(ii) who is an officer or managing employee (as defined in section 1320a-5(b) of this title) of such an entity.

(B) For purposes of subparagraph (A), the term "sanctioned entity" means an entity—

(i) that has been convicted of any offense described in subsection (a) of this section or in paragraph (1), (2), or (3) of this subsection; or

(ii) that has been excluded from participation under a program under subchapter XVIII of this chapter or under a State health care program.

(c) Notice, effective date, and period of exclusion

(1) An exclusion under this section or under section 1320a-7a of this title shall be effective at such time and upon such reasonable notice to the public and to the individual or entity excluded as may be specified in regulations consistent with paragraph (2).

(2)(A) Except as provided in subparagraph (B), such an exclusion shall be effective with respect to services furnished to an individual on or after the effective date of the exclusion.

(B) Unless the Secretary determines that the health and safety of individuals receiving services warrants the exclusion taking effect earlier, an exclusion shall not apply to payments made under subchapter XVIII of this chapter or under a State health care program for—

(i) inpatient institutional services furnished to an individual who was admitted to such institution before the date of the exclusion, or

(ii) home health services and hospice care furnished to an individual under a plan of care established before the date of the exclusion,

until the passage of 30 days after the effective date of the exclusion.

(3)(A) The Secretary shall specify, in the notice of exclusion under paragraph (1) and the written notice under section 1320a-7a of this title, the minimum period (or, in the case of an exclusion of an individual under subsection (b)(12) of this section or in the case described in subparagraph (G), the period) of the exclusion.

(B) Subject to subparagraph (G), in the case of an exclusion under subsection (a) of this section, the minimum period of exclusion shall be not less than five years, except that, upon the request of the administrator of a Federal health care program (as defined in section 1320-7b(f) of this title) who determines that the exclusion would impose a hardship on individuals entitled to benefits under part A of subchapter XVIII of this chapter or enrolled under part B of subchapter VIII of this chapter, or both, the Secretary may, after consulting with the Inspector General of the Department of Health and Human Services, waive the exclusion under subsection (a)(1), (a)(3), or (a)(4) of this section with respect to that program in the case of an individual or entity that is the sole community physician or sole source of essential specialized services in a community. The Secretary's decision whether to waive the exclusion shall not be reviewable.

(C) In the case of an exclusion of an individual under subsection (b)(12) of this section, the period of the exclusion shall be equal to the sum of—

(i) the length of the period in which the individual failed to grant the immediate access described in that subsection, and

(ii) an additional period, not to exceed 90 days, set by the Secretary.

(D) Subject to subparagraph (G), in the case of an exclusion of an individual or entity under paragraph (1), (2), or (3) of subsection (b) of this section, the period of the exclusion shall be 3 years, unless the Secretary determines in accordance with published regulations that a shorter period is appropriate because of mitigating circumstances or that a longer period is appropriate because of aggravating circumstances.

(E) In the case of an exclusion of an individual or entity under subsection (b)(4) or (b)(5) of this section, the period of the exclusion shall not be less than the period during which the individual's or entity's license to provide health care is revoked, suspended, or surrendered, or the individual or the entity is excluded or suspended from a Federal or State health care program.

(F) In the case of an exclusion of an individual or entity under subsection (b)(6)(B) of this section, the period of the exclusion shall be not less than 1 year.

(G) In the case of an exclusion of an individual under subsection (a) of this section based on a conviction occurring on or after August 5, 1997, if the individual has (before, on, or after August 5, 1997) been convicted—

(i) on one previous occasion of one or more offenses for which an exclusion may be effected under such subsection, the period of the exclusion shall be not less than 10 years, or

(ii) on 2 or more previous occasions of one or more offenses for which an exclusion may be effected under such subsection, the period of the exclusion shall be permanent.

(d) Notice to State agencies and exclusion under State health care programs

(1) Subject to paragraph (3), the Secretary shall exercise the authority under this section and section 1320a-7a of this title in a manner that results in an individual's or entity's exclusion from all the programs under subchapter XVIII of this chapter and all the State health care programs in which the individual or entity may otherwise participate.

(2) The Secretary shall promptly notify each appropriate State agency administering or supervising the administration of each State health care program (and, in the case of an exclusion effected pursuant to subsection (a) of this section and to which section 824(a)(5) of title 21 may apply, the Attorney General)—

(A) of the fact and circumstances of each exclusion effected against an individual or entity under this section or section 1320a-7a of this title, and

(B) of the period (described in paragraph (3)) for which the State agency is directed to exclude the individual or entity from participation in the State health care program.

(3)(A) Except as provided in subparagraph (B), the period of the exclusion under a State health care program under paragraph (2) shall be the same as any period of exclusion under subchapter XVIII of this chapter.

(B)(i) The Secretary may waive an individual's or entity's exclusion under a State health care program under paragraph (2) if the Secretary receives and approves a request for the waiver with respect to the individual or entity from the State agency administering or supervising the administration of the program.

(ii) A State health care program may provide for a period of exclusion which is longer than the period of exclusion under subchapter XVIII of this chapter.

(e) Notice to State licensing agencies

The Secretary shall—

(1) promptly notify the appropriate State or local agency or authority having responsibility for the licensing or certification of an individual or entity excluded (or directed to be excluded) from participation under this section or section 1320a-7a of this title, of the fact and circumstances of the exclusion,

(2) request that appropriate investigations be made and sanctions invoked in accordance with applicable State law and policy, and

(3) request that the State or local agency or authority keep the Secretary and the Inspector General of the Department of Health and Human Services fully and currently informed with respect to any actions taken in response to the request.

(f) Notice, hearing, and judicial review

(1) Subject to paragraph (2), any individual or entity that is excluded (or directed to be excluded) from participation under this section is entitled to reasonable notice and opportunity for a hearing thereon by the Secretary to the same extent as is provided in section 405(b) of this title, and to judicial review of the Secretary's final decision after such hearing as is provided in section 405(g) of this title, except that, in so applying such sections and section 405(l) of this title, any reference therein to the Commissioner of Social Security or the Social Security Administration shall be considered a reference to the Secretary or the Department of Health and Human Services, respectively.

(2) Unless the Secretary determines that the health or safety of individuals receiving services warrants the exclusion taking effect earlier, any individual or entity that is the subject of an adverse determination under subsection (b)(7) of this section shall be entitled to a hearing by an administrative law judge (as provided under section 405(b) of this title) on the determination under subsection (b)(7) of this section before any exclusion based upon the determination takes effect.

(3) The provisions of section 405(h) of this title shall apply with respect to this section and sections 1320a-7a, 1320a-8, and 1320c-5 of this title to the same extent as it is applicable with respect to subchapter II of this chapter, except that, in so applying such section and section 405(l) of this title, any reference therein to the Commissioner of Social Security shall be considered a reference to the Secretary.

(g) Application for termination of exclusion

(1) An individual or entity excluded (or directed to be excluded) from participation under this section or section 1320a-7a of this title may apply to the Secretary, in the manner specified by the Secretary in regulations and at the end of the minimum period of exclusion provided under subsection (c)(3) of this section and at such other times as the Secretary may provide, for termination of the exclusion effected under this section or section 1320a-7a of this title.

(2) The Secretary may terminate the exclusion if the Secretary determines, on the basis of the conduct of the applicant which occurred after the date of the notice of exclusion or which was unknown to the Secretary at the time of the exclusion, that—

(A) there is no basis under subsection (a) or (b) of this section or section 1320a-7a(a) of this title for a continuation of the exclusion, and

(B) there are reasonable assurances that the types of actions which formed the basis for the original exclusion have not recurred and will not recur.

(3) The Secretary shall promptly notify each appropriate State agency administering or supervising the administration of each State health care program (and, in the case of an exclusion effected pursuant to subsection (a) of this section and to which section 824(a)(5) of title 21 may apply, the Attorney General) of the fact and circumstances of each termination of exclusion made under this subsection.

(h) "State health care program" defined

For purposes of this section and sections 1320a-7a and 1320a-7b of this title, the term "State health care program" means—

(1) a State plan approved under subchapter XIX of this chapter,

(2) any program receiving funds under subchapter V of this chapter or from an allotment to a State under such subchapter,

(3) any program receiving funds under subchapter XX of this chapter or from an allotment to a State under such subchapter, or

(4) a State child health plan approved under subchapter XXI of this chapter.

(i) "Convicted" defined

For purposes of subsections (a) and (b) of this section, an individual or entity is considered to have been "convicted" of a criminal offense—

(1) when a judgment of conviction has been entered against the individual or entity by a Federal, State, or local court, regardless of whether there is an appeal pending or whether the judgment of conviction or other record relating to criminal conduct has been expunged;

(2) when there has been a finding of guilt against the individual or entity by a Federal, State, or local court;

(3) when a plea of guilty or nolo contendere by the individual or entity has been accepted by a Federal, State, or local court; or

(4) when the individual or entity has entered into participation in a first offender, deferred adjudication, or other arrangement or program where judgment of conviction has been withheld.

(j) Definition of immediate family member and member of household

For purposes of subsection (b)(8)(A)(iii) of this section:

(1) The term "immediate family member" means, with respect to a person—

(A) the husband or wife of the person;

(B) the natural or adoptive parent, child, or sibling of the person;

(C) the stepparent, stepchild, stepbrother, or stepsister of the person;

(D) the father-, mother-, daughter-, son-, brother-, or sister-in-law of the person;

(E) the grandparent or grandchild of the person; and

(F) the spouse of a grandparent or grandchild of the person.

(2) The term "member of the household" means, with respect to any person, any individual sharing a common abode as part of a single family unit with the person, including domestic employees and others who live together as a family unit, but not including a roomer or boarder.

SOURCE—

(Aug. 14, 1935, ch. 531, title XI, Sec. 1128, as added Pub. L. 96-499, title IX, Sec. 913(a), Dec. 5, 1980, 94 Stat. 2619; amended Pub. L. 97-35, title XXI, Sec. 2105(b), title XXIII, Sec. 2353(k), Aug. 13, 1981, 95 Stat. 791, 873; Pub. L. 98-369, div. B, title III, Sec. 2333(a), (b), July 18, 1984, 98 Stat. 1089; Pub. L. 99-509, title IX, Sec. 9317(c), Oct. 21, 1986, 100 Stat. 2008; Pub. L. 100-93, Sec. 2, Aug. 18, 1987, 101 Stat. 680; Pub. L. 100-203, title IV, Sec. 4118(e)(2)-(5), Dec. 22, 1987, 101 Stat. 1330-155, as amended Pub. L. 100-360, title IV, Sec. 411(k)(10)(D), July 1, 1988, 102 Stat. 795; Pub. L. 100-360, title IV, Sec. 411(k)(10)(C), July 1, 1988, 102 Stat. 795; Pub. L. 101-239, title VI, Sec. 6411(d)(1), Dec. 19, 1989, 103 Stat. 2270; Pub. L. 101-508, title IV, Sec. 4164(b)(3), Nov. 5, 1990, 104 Stat. 1388-102; Pub. L. 102-54, Sec. 13(q)(3)(A)(ii), June 13, 1991, 105 Stat. 279; Pub. L. 103-296, title I, Sec. 108(b)(9), title II, Sec. 206(b)(2), Aug. 15, 1994, 108 Stat. 1483, 1513;

Pub. L. 104-191, title II, Secs. 211-213, Aug. 21, 1996, 110 Stat. 2003-2005; Pub. L. 105-33, title IV, Secs. 4301, 4303(a), 4331(c), 4901(b)(2), Aug. 5, 1997, 111 Stat. 382, 396, 570; Pub. L. No. 108-173, title IX, Sec. 949, Dec. 8, 2003, 117 Stat. 2426.)

SECTION REFERRED TO IN OTHER SECTIONS

This section is referred to in sections 704, 1320a-3a, 1320a-5, 1320a-7a, 1320a-7b, 1320a-7c, 1320a-7d, 1320a-7e, 1320a-8, 1320c-5, 1395a, 1395b-5, 1395l, 1395m, 1395u, 1395w-27, 1395y, 1395cc, 1395mm, 1395ww, 1395aaa, 1396a, 1396b, 1396r-2, 1396r-6, 1397d of this title; title 21 section 824.

Appendix D-4

Civil Monetary Penalties Regulations

Editor's Note: The following regulations were updated in 2004, and the text below updates and replaces the text of 42 C.F.R. Sections 1003.100, 1003.101, 1003.102, and 1003.103 that appear in this Appendix in the Main Volume.

Source: 42 C.F.R. Part 1003

Section 1003.100 Basis and purpose.

(a) *Basis.* This part implements sections 1128(c), 1128A, 1140, 1860D-31(i)(3), 1876(i)(6), 1877(g), 1882(d) and 1903(m)(5) of the Social Security Act; sections 421(c) and 427(b)(2) of Pub. L. 99-660; and section 201(i) of Pub. L. 107-188 (42 U.S.C. 1320-7(c), 1320a-7a, 1320b-10, 1395w-141(i)(3), 1395dd(d)(1), 1395mm, 1395ss(d), 1396b(m), 11131(c), 11137(b)(2) and 262)

(b) *Purpose.* This part—

(1) Provides for the imposition of civil money penalties and, as applicable, assessments against persons who—

(i) Have knowingly submitted certain prohibited claims under Federal health care programs;

(ii) Seek payment in violation of the terms of an agreement or a limitation on charges or payments under the Medicare program, or a requirement not to charge in excess of the amount permitted under the Medicaid program;

(iii) Give false or misleading information that might affect the decision to discharge a Medicare patient from the hospital;

(iv)(A) Fail to report information concerning medical malpractice payments or who improperly disclose, use or permit access to information reported under part B of title IV of Public Law 99-660, and regulations specified in 45 CFR part 60, or

(B) Are health plans and fail to report information concerning sanctions or other adverse actions imposed on providers as required to be reported to the Healthcare Integrity and

Protection Data Bank (HIPDB) in accordance with section 1128E of the Act;

(v) Misuse certain Departmental and Medicare and Medicaid program words, letters symbols or emblems;

(vi) Violate a requirement of section 1867 of the Act or Sec. 489.24 of this title;

(vii) Substantially fail to provide an enrollee with required medically necessary items and services; engage in certain marketing, enrollment, reporting, claims payment, employment or contracting abuses; or do not meet the requirements for physician incentive plans for Medicare specified in Secs. 417.479(d) through (f) of this title;

(viii) Present or cause to be presented a bill or claim for designated health services (as defined in Sec. 411.351 of this title) that they know, or should know, were furnished in accordance with a referral prohibited under Sec. 411.353 of this title;

(ix) Have collected amounts that they know or should know were billed in violation of Sec. 411.353 of this title and have not refunded the amounts collected on a timely basis;

(x) Are physicians or entities that enter into an arrangement or scheme that they know or should know has as a principal purpose the assuring of referrals by the physician to a particular entity which, if made directly, would violate the provisions of Sec. 411.353 of this title;

(xi) Are excluded, and who retain an ownership or control interest of five percent or more in an entity participating in Medicare or a State health care program, or who are officers or managing employees of such an entity (as defined in section 1126(b) of the Act);

(xii) Offer inducements that they know or should know are likely to influence Medicare or State health care program beneficiaries to order or receive particular items or services;

(xiii) Are physicians who knowingly misrepresent that a Medicare beneficiary requires home health services;

(xiv) Have submitted, or caused to be submitted, certain prohibited claims, including claims for services rendered by excluded individuals employed by or otherwise under contract with such person, under one or more Federal health care programs;

(xv) Violate the Federal health care programs' anti-kickback statute as set forth in section 1128B of the Act;

(xvi) Violate the provisions of part 73 of this title, implementing section 351A(b) and (c) of the Public Health Service Act, with respect to the possession and use within the United States, receipt from outside the United States, and transfer within the United States, of select agents and toxins in use, or transfer of listed biological agents and toxins; or

(xvii) Violate the provisions of part 403, subpart H of this title, implementing the Medicare prescription drug discount card and transitional assistance program, by misleading or defrauding program beneficiaries, by overcharging a discount program enrollee, or by misusing transitional assistance funds.

(2) Provides for the exclusion of persons from the Medicare or State health care programs against whom a civil money penalty or assessment has been imposed, and the basis for reinstatement of persons who have been excluded; and

(3) Sets forth the appeal rights of persons subject to a penalty, assessment and exclusion.

[SOURCE: 65 Fed. Reg. 24,414 (Apr. 26, 2000), *as amended at* 67 Fed. Reg. 11,935 (Mar. 18, 2002); 67 Fed. Reg. 76,905 (Dec. 13, 2002); 69 Fed Reg. 28,845 (May 19, 2004).]

Section 1003.101 Definitions.

For purposes of this part:

Act means the Social Security Act.

Adverse effect means medical care has not been provided and the failure to provide such necessary medical care has presented an imminent danger to the health, safety, or well-being of the patient or has placed the patient unnecessarily in a high-risk situation.

ALJ means an Administrative Law Judge.

Assessment means the amount described in Sec. 1003.104, and includes the plural of that term.

Claim means an application for payment for an item or service to a Federal health care program (as defined in section 1128B(f) of the Act).

CMS stands for Centers for Medicare & Medicaid Services, formerly the Health Care Financing Administration (HCFA).

Contracting organization means a public or private entity, including of a health maintenance organization (HMO), competitive medical plan, or health insuring organization (HIO) which meets the requirements of section 1876(b) of the Act or is subject to the requirements in section 1903(m)(2)(A) of the Act and which has contracted with the Department or a State to furnish services to Medicare beneficiaries or Medicaid recipients.

Department means the Department of Health and Human Services.

Enrollee means an individual who is eligible for Medicare or Medicaid and who enters into an agreement to receive services from a contracting organization that contracts with the Department under title XVIII or title XIX of the Act.

Exclusion means the temporary or permanent barring of a person from participation in a Federal health care program (as defined in section 1128B(f) of the Act).

Inspector General means the Inspector General of the Department or his or her designees.

Item or service includes—

(a) any item, device, medical supply or service provided to a patient (i) which is listed in an itemized claim for program payment or a request for payment, or (ii) for which payment is included in other

Federal or State health care reimbursement methods, such as a prospective payment system; and

(b) in the case of a claim based on costs, any entry or omission in a cost report, books of account or other documents supporting the claim.

Maternal and Child Health Services Block Grant program means the program authorized under Title V of the Act.

Medicaid means the program of grants to the States for medical assistance authorized under title XIX of the Act.

Medical malpractice claim or action means a written complaint or claim demanding payment based on a physician's, dentist's or other health care practitioner's provision of, or failure to provide health care services, and includes the filing of a cause of action based on the law of tort brought in any State or Federal court or other adjudicative body.

Medicare means the program of health insurance for the aged and disabled authorized under Title XVIII of the Act.

Participating hospital means (1) a hospital or (2) a rural primary care hospital as defined in section 1861(mm)(1) of the Act that has entered into a Medicare provider agreement under section 1866 of the Act.

Penalty means the amount described in Sec. 1003.103 and includes the plural of that term.

Person means an individual, trust or estate, partnership, corporation, professional association or corporation, or other entity, public or private.

Physician incentive plan means any compensation arrangement between a contracting organization and a physician group that may directly or indirectly have the effect of reducing or limiting services provided with respect to enrollees in the organization.

Preventive care, for purposes of the definition of the term Remuneration as set forth in this section and the preventive care exception to section 231(h) of HIPAA, means any service that—

(1) Is a prenatal service or a post-natal well-baby visit or is a specific clinical service described in the current U.S. Preventive Services Task Force's *Guide to Clinical Preventive Services,* and

(2) Is reimbursable in whole or in part by Medicare or an applicable State health care program.

Remuneration, as set forth in Sec. 1003.102(b)(13) of this part, is consistent with the definition contained in section 1128A(i)(6) of the Act, and includes the waiver of coinsurance and deductible amounts (or any part thereof) and transfers of items or services for free or for other than fair market value. The term "remuneration" does not include—

(1) The waiver of coinsurance and deductible amounts by a person, if the waiver is not offered as part of any advertisement or solicitation; the person does not routinely waive coinsurance or deductible amounts; and the person waives coinsurance and deductible amounts after determining in good faith that the individual is in financial need or failure by the person to collect coinsurance or deductible amounts after making reasonable collection efforts;

(2) Any permissible practice as specified in section 1128B(b)(3) of the Act or in regulations issued by the Secretary;

(3) Differentials in coinsurance and deductible amounts as part of a benefit plan design (as long as the differentials have been disclosed in writing to all beneficiaries, third party payers and providers), to whom claims are presented; or

(4) Incentives given to individuals to promote the delivery of preventive care services where the delivery of such services is not tied (directly or indirectly) to the provision of other services reimbursed in whole or in part by Medicare or an applicable State health care program. Such incentives may include the provision of preventive care, but may not include—

(i) Cash or instruments convertible to cash; or

(ii) An incentive the value of which is disproportionally large in relationship to the value of the preventive care service (i.e., either the value of the service itself or the future health care costs reasonably expected to be avoided as a result of the preventive care).

Request for payment means an application submitted by a person to any person for payment for an item or service.

Respondent means the person upon whom the Department has imposed, or proposes to impose, a penalty, assessment or exclusion.

Responsible physician means a physician who is responsible for the examination, treatment, or transfer of an individual who comes to a participating hospital's emergency department seeking assistance and includes a physician on call for the care of such individual.

Secretary means the Secretary of the Department or his or her designees.

Select agents and toxins means agents and toxins that are listed by the HHS Secretary as having the potential to pose a severe threat to public health and safety, in accordance with section 351A(a)(1) of the Public Health Service Act.

Should know or *should have known* means that a person, with respect to information—

(1) Acts in deliberate ignorance of the truth or falsity of the information; or

(2) Acts in reckless disregard of the truth or falsity of the information. For purposes of this definition, no proof of specific intent to defraud is required.

Social Services Block Grant program means the program authorized under title XX of the Social Security Act.

State includes the District of Columbia, Puerto Rico, the Virgin Islands, Guam, American Samoa, the Northern Mariana Islands, and the Trust Territory of the Pacific Islands.

State health care program means a State plan approved under title XIX of the Act, any program receiving funds under title V of the Act or from an allotment to a State under such title, or any program receiving funds under title XX of the Act or from an allotment to a State under such title.

Timely basis means, in accordance with Sec. 1003.102(b)(9) of this part, the 60-day period from the time the prohibited amounts are collected by the individual or the entity.

Transitional assistance means the subsidy funds that Medicare beneficiaries enrolled in the prescription drug discount card and transitional assistance program may apply toward the cost of covered discount card drugs in the manner described in § 403.808(d) of this title.

[SOURCE: 51 Fed. Reg. 34,777 (Sept. 30, 1986), *as amended at* 56 Fed. Reg. 28,492 (June 21, 1991); 57 Fed. Reg. 3345 (Jan. 29, 1992); 59 Fed. Reg. 32,124 (June 22, 1994); 59 Fed. Reg. 36,086 (July 15, 1994); 60 Fed. Reg. 16,584 (Mar. 31, 1995); 61 Fed. Reg. 13,449 (Mar. 27, 1996); 65 Fed. Reg. 24,415 (Apr. 26, 2000); 65 Fed. Reg. 35,584 (June 5, 2000); 66 Fed. Reg. 39,452 (July 31, 2001); 67 Fed. Reg. 11,935 (Mar. 18, 2002); 67 Fed. Reg. 76,905 (Dec. 13, 2002); 69 Fed. Reg. 28,845 (May 19, 2004).]

Section 1003.102 Basis for civil money penalties and assessments.

(a) The OIG may impose a penalty and assessment against any person whom it determines in accordance with this part has knowingly presented, or caused to be presented, a claim which is for—

(1) An item or service that the person knew, or should have known, was not provided as claimed, including a claim that is part of a pattern or practice of claims based on codes that the person knows or should know will result in greater payment to the person than the code applicable to the item or service actually provided;

(2) An item or service for which the person knew, or should have known, that the claim was false or fraudulent, including a claim for any item or service furnished by an excluded individual employed by or otherwise under contract with that person;

(3) An item or service furnished during a period in which the person was excluded from participation in the Federal health care program to which the claim was made;

(4) A physician's services (or an item or service) for which the person knew, or should have known, that the individual who furnished (or supervised the furnishing of) the service—

(i) Was not licensed as a physician;

(ii) Was licensed as a physician, but such license had been obtained through a misrepresentation of material fact (including cheating on an examination required for licensing); or

(iii) Represented to the patient at the time the service was furnished that the physician was certified in a medical specialty board when he or she was not so certified;

(5) A payment that such person knows, or should know, may not be made under § 411.353 of this title; or

(6) An item or service that a person knows or should know is medically unnecessary, and which is part of a pattern of such claims.

(b) The OIG may impose a penalty, and where authorized, an assessment against any person (including an insurance company in the case of paragraphs (b)(5) and (b)(6) of this section) whom it determines in accordance with this part—

(1) Has knowingly presented or caused to be presented a request for payment in violation of the terms of—

(i) An agreement to accept payments on the basis of an assignment under section 1842(b)(3)(B)(ii) of the Act;

(ii) An agreement with a State agency or other requirement of a State Medicaid plan not to charge a person for an item or service in excess of the amount permitted to be charged;

(iii) An agreement to be a participating physician or supplier under section 1842(h)(1); or

(iv) An agreement in accordance with section 1866(a)(1)(G) of the Act not to charge any person for inpatient hospital services for which payment had been denied or reduced under section 1886(f)(2) of the Act.

(2) [Reserved]

(3) [Reserved]

(4) Has knowingly given or caused to be given to any person, in the case of inpatient hospital services subject to the provisions of section 1886 of the Act, information that he or she knew, or should have known, was false or misleading and that could reasonably have been expected to influence the decision when to discharge such person or another person from the hospital.

(5) Fails to report information concerning—

(i) A payment made under an insurance policy, self-insurance or otherwise, for the benefit of a physician, dentist or other health care practitioner in settlement of, or in satisfaction in whole or in part of, a medical malpractice claim or action or a judgment against such a physician, dentist or other practitioner in accordance with section 421 of Public Law 99-660 (42 U.S.C. 11131) and as required by regulations at 45 CFR part 60; or

(ii) An adverse action required to be reported to the Healthcare Integrity and Protection Data Bank as established by section 221 of Public Law 104-191 and set forth in section 1128E of the Act.

(6) Improperly discloses, uses or permits access to information reported in accordance with part B of title IV of Pub.L. 99-660, in violation of section 427 of Pub.L. 99-660 (42 U.S.C. 11137) or regulations at 45 CFR part 60. (The disclosure of information reported in accordance with part B of title IV in response to a subpoena or a discovery request is considered to be an improper disclosure in violation of section 427 of Pub.L. 99-660. However, disclosure or release by an entity of original documents or underlying records from which the reported information is obtained or derived is not considered to be an improper disclosure in violation of section 427 of Pub.L. 99-660.)

(7) Has made use of the words, letters, symbols or emblems as defined in paragraph (b)(7)(i) of this section in such a manner that

such person knew or should have known would convey, or in a manner which reasonably could be interpreted or construed as conveying, the false impression that an advertisement, solicitation or other item was authorized, approved or endorsed by the Department or CMS, or that such person or organization has some connection with or authorization from the Department or CMS. Civil money penalties—

(i) May be imposed, regardless of the use of a disclaimer of affiliation with the United States Government, the Department or its programs, for misuse of—

(A) The words "Department of Health and Human Services," "Health and Human Services," "Centers for Medicare & Medicaid Services," "Medicare," or "Medicaid," or any other combination or variation of such words;

(B) The letters "DHHS," "HHS," or "CMS," or any other combination or variation of such letters; or

(C) A symbol or emblem of the Department or CMS (including the design of, or a reasonable facsimile of the design of, the Medicare card, the check used for payment of benefits under title II, or envelopes or other stationery used by the Department or CMS) or any other combination or variation of such symbols or emblems; and

(ii) Will not be imposed against any agency or instrumentality of a State, or political subdivision of the State, that makes use of any symbol or emblem, or any words or letters which specifically identifies that agency or instrumentality of the State or political subdivision.

(8) Is a contracting organization that CMS determines has committed an act or failed to comply with the requirements set forth in § 417.500(a) or § 434.67(a) of this title or failed to comply with the requirement set forth in § 434.80(c) of this title.

(9) Has not refunded on a timely basis, as defined in § 1003.101 of this part, amounts collected as the result of billing an individual, third party payer or other entity for a designated health service that was provided in accordance with a prohibited referral as described in § 411.353 of this title.

(10) Is a physician or entity that enters into—

(i) A cross referral arrangement, for example, whereby the physician owners of entity "X" refer to entity "Y," and the physician owners of entity "Y" refer to entity "X" in violation of § 411.353 of this title, or

(ii) Any other arrangement or scheme that the physician or entity knows, or should know, has a principal purpose of circumventing the prohibitions of § 411.353 of this title.

(11) Has violated section 1128B of the Act by unlawfully offering, paying, soliciting or receiving remuneration in return for the referral of business paid for by Medicare, Medicaid or other Federal health care programs.

(12) Who is not an organization, agency or other entity, and who is excluded from participating in Medicare or a State health care program in accordance with sections 1128 or 1128A of the Act, and who—

(i) Knows or should know of the action constituting the basis for the exclusion, and retains a direct or indirect ownership or control interest of five percent or more in an entity that participates in Medicare or a State health care program; or

(ii) Is an officer or managing employee (as defined in section 1126(b) of the Act) of such entity.

(13) Offers or transfers remuneration (as defined in § 1003.101 of this part) to any individual eligible for benefits under Medicare or a State health care program, that such person knows or should know is likely to influence such individual to order or to receive from a particular provider, practitioner or supplier any item or service for which payment may be made, in whole or in part, under Medicare or a State health care program.

(14) Is a physician and who executes a document falsely by certifying that a Medicare beneficiary requires home health services when the physician knows that the beneficiary does not meet the eligibility requirements set forth in sections 1814(a)(2)(C) or 1835(a)(2)(A) of the Act.

(15) Has knowingly and willfully presented, or caused to be presented, a bill or request for payment for items and services furnished to a hospital patient for which payment may be made under the Medicare or another Federal health care program, if that bill or request is inconsistent with an arrangement under section 1866(a)(1)(H) of the Act, or violates the requirements for such an arrangement.

(16) Is involved in the possession or use in the United States, receipt from outside the United States, or transfer within the United States, of select agents and toxins in violation of part 73 of this chapter as determined by the HHS Secretary, in accordance with sections 351A(b) and (c) of the Public Health Service Act.

(17) Is an endorsed sponsor under the Medicare prescription drug discount card program who knowingly misrepresented or falsified information in outreach material or comparable material provided to a program enrollee or other person.

(18) Is an endorsed sponsor under the Medicare prescription drug discount card program who knowingly charged a program enrollee in violation of the terms of the endorsement contract.

(19) Is an endorsed sponsor under the Medicare prescription drug discount card program who knowingly used transitional assistance funds of any program enrollee in any manner that is inconsistent with the purpose of the transitional assistance program.

(c)(1) The Office of the Inspector General (OIG) may impose a penalty for violations of section 1867 of the Act or § 489.24 of this title against—

(i) Any participating hospital with an emergency department that—

(A) Knowingly violates the statute on or after August 1, 1986 or;

(B) Negligently violates the statute on or after May 1, 1991; and

(ii) Any responsible physician who—

(A) Knowingly violates the statute on or after August 1, 1986;

(B) Negligently violates the statute on or after May 1, 1991;

(C) Signs a certification under section 1867(c)(1)(A) of the Act if the physician knew or should have known that the benefits of transfer to another facility did not outweigh the risks of such a transfer; or

(D) Misrepresents an individual's condition or other information, including a hospital's obligations under this section.

(2) For purposes of this section, a responsible physician or hospital "knowingly" violates section 1867 of the Act if the responsible physician or hospital recklessly disregards, or deliberately ignores a material fact.

(d)(1) In any case in which it is determined that more than one person was responsible for presenting or causing to be presented a claim as described in paragraph (a) of this section, each such person may be held liable for the penalty prescribed by this part, and an assessment may be imposed against any one such person or jointly and severally against two or more such persons, but the aggregate amount of the assessments collected may not exceed the amount that could be assessed if only one person was responsible.

(2) In any case in which it is determined that more than one person was responsible for presenting or causing to be presented a request for payment or for giving false or misleading information as described in paragraph (b) of this section, each such person may be held liable for the penalty prescribed by this part.

(3) In any case in which it is determined that more than one person was responsible for failing to report information that is required to be reported on a medical malpractice payment, or for improperly disclosing, using, or permitting access to information, as described in paragraphs (b)(5) and (b)(6) of this section, each such person may be held liable for the penalty prescribed by this part.

(4) In any case in which it is determined that more than one responsible physician violated the provisions of section 1867 of the Act or of § 489.24 of this title, a penalty may be imposed against each responsible physician.

(5) Under this section, a principal is liable for penalties and assessments for the actions of his or her agent acting within the scope of the agency.

(e) For purposes of this section, the term "knowingly" is defined consistent with the definition set forth in the Civil False Claims Act (31 U.S.C. 3729(b)), that is, a person, with respect to information, has actual knowledge of information, acts in deliberate ignorance of the truth or falsity of the information, or acts in reckless disregard of the truth or falsity of the information, and that no proof of specific intent to defraud is required.

[SOURCE: 52 Fed. Reg. 11,652 (Apr. 10, 1987); 56 Fed. Reg. 28,492 (June 21, 1991); 56 Fed. Reg. 42,537 (Aug. 28, 1991); 57 Fed. Reg. 3345 (Jan. 29, 1992); 57 Fed. Reg. 9670 (Mar. 20, 1992); 59 Fed. Reg. 32,124 (June 22, 1994); 59 Fed. Reg. 36,086 (July 15, 1994); 60 Fed. Reg. 16,584 (Mar. 31, 1995); 60 Fed. Reg. 58,241 (Nov. 27, 1995); 64 Fed. Reg. 39,428 (July 22, 1999); 65 Fed. Reg. 18,550 (Apr. 7, 2000); 65 Fed. Reg. 24,415 (Apr. 26, 2000); 65 Fed. Reg. 35,584 (June 5, 2000); 65 Fed. Reg. 40,535 (June 30, 2000); 67 Fed. Reg. 76,905 (Dec. 13, 2002); 69 Fed. Reg. 28,845 (May 19, 2004).]

Section 1003.103 Amount of penalty.

(a) Except as provided in paragraphs (b) and (d) through (k) of this section, the OIG may impose a penalty of not more than $10,000 for each item or service that is subject to a determination under § 1003.102.

(b) The OIG may impose a penalty of not more than $15,000 for each person with respect to whom a determination was made that false or misleading information was given under § 1003.102(b)(4), or for each item and service that is subject to a determination under §1003.102(a)(5) or § 1003.102(b)(9) of this part. The OIG may impose a penalty of not more than $100,000 for each arrangement or scheme that is subject to a determination under § 1003.102(b)(10) of this part.

(c) The OIG may impose a penalty of not more than $11,000[1] for each payment for which there was a failure to report required information in accordance with § 1003.102(b)(5), or for each improper disclosure, use or access to information that is subject to a determination under § 1003.102(b)(6).

(d)(1) The OIG may impose a penalty of not more than $5,000 for each violation resulting from the misuse of Departmental, CMS, Medicare or Medicaid program words, letters, symbols or emblems as described in § 1003.102(b)(7) relating to printed media, and a penalty of not more than $25,000 in the case of such misuse related to a broadcast or telecast, that is related to a determination under § 1003.102(b)(7).

   (2) For purposes of this paragraph, a violation is defined as—

      (i) In the case of a direct mailing solicitation or advertisement, each separate piece of mail which contains one or more words, letters, symbols or emblems related to a determination under § 1003.102(b)(7);

      (ii) In the case of a printed solicitation or advertisement, each reproduction, reprinting or distribution of such item related to a determination under § 1003.102(b)(7); and

---

[1]As adjusted in accordance with the Federal Civil Monetary Penalty Inflation Adjustment Act of 1990 (Pub.L. 101-140), as amended by the Debt Collection Improvement Act of 1996 (Pub.L. 104-134).

(iii) In the case of a broadcast or telecast, each airing of a single commercial or solicitation related to a determination under § 1003.102(b)(7).

(e) For violations of section 1867 of the Act or § 489.24 of this title, the OIG may impose—

(1) Against each participating hospital with an emergency department, a penalty of not more than $50,000 for each negligent violation occurring on or after May 1, 1991, except that if the participating hospital has fewer than 100 State-licensed, Medicare-certified beds on the date the penalty is imposed, the penalty will not exceed $25,000; and

(2) Against each responsible physician, a penalty of not more than $50,000 for each negligent violation occurring on or after May 1, 1991.

(f)(1) The OIG may, in addition to or in lieu of other remedies available under law, impose a penalty of up to $25,000 for each determination by CMS that a contracting organization has—

(i) Failed substantially to provide an enrollee with required medically necessary items and services and the failure adversely affects (or has the likelihood of adversely affecting) the enrollee;

(ii) Imposed premiums on enrollees in excess of amounts permitted under section 1876 or title XIX of the Act;

(iii) Acted to expel or to refuse to re-enroll a Medicare beneficiary in violation of the provisions of section 1876 of the Act and for reasons other than the beneficiary's health status or requirements for health care services;

(iv) Misrepresented or falsified information furnished to an individual or any other entity under section 1876 or section 1903(m) of the Act;

(v) Failed to comply with the requirements of section 1876(g) (6)(A) of the Act, regarding prompt payment of claims; or

(vi) Failed to comply with the requirements of § 417.479(d) through (i) of this title for Medicare, and § 417.479(d) through (g) and (i) of this title for Medicaid, regarding certain prohibited incentive payments to physicians.

(2) The OIG may, in addition to or in lieu of other remedies available under law, impose a penalty of up to $25,000 for each determination by CMS that a contracting organization with a contract under section 1876 of the Act—

(i) Employs or contracts with individuals or entities excluded, under section 1128 or section 1128A of the Act, from participation in Medicare for the provision of health care, utilization review, medical social work, or administrative services; or

(ii) Employs or contracts with any entity for the provision of services (directly or indirectly) through an excluded individual or entity.

(3) The OIG may, in addition to or in lieu of other remedies available under law, impose a penalty of up to $100,000 for each determination that a contracting organization has—

(i) Misrepresented or falsified information to the Secretary under section 1876 of the Act or to the State under section 1903(m) of the Act; or

(ii) Acted to expel or to refuse to re-enroll a Medicaid recipient because of the individual's health status or requirements for health care services, or engaged in any practice that would reasonably be expected to have the effect of denying or discouraging enrollment (except as permitted by section 1876 or section 1903(m) of the Act) with the contracting organization by Medicare beneficiaries and Medicaid recipients whose medical condition or history indicates a need for substantial future medical services.

(4) If enrollees are charged more than the allowable premium, the OIG will impose an additional penalty equal to double the amount of excess premium charged by the contracting organization. The excess premium amount will be deducted from the penalty and returned to the enrollee.

(5) The OIG will impose an additional $15,000 penalty for each individual not enrolled when CMS determines that a contracting organization has committed a violation described in paragraph (f)(3)(ii) of this section.

(6) For purposes of paragraph (f) of this section, a violation is each incident where a person has committed an act listed in § 417.500(a) or § 434.67(a) of this title, or failed to comply with a requirement set forth in § 434.80(c) of this title.

(g) The OIG may impose a penalty of not more than $25,000 against a health plan for failing to report information on an adverse action required to be reported to the Healthcare Integrity and Protection Data Bank in accordance with section 1128E of the Act and § 1003.102(b)(5)(ii).

(h) For each violation of § 1003.102(b)(11), the OIG may impose—

(1) A penalty of not more than $50,000, and

(2) An assessment of up to three times the total amount of remuneration offered, paid, solicited or received, as specified in § 1003.104(b).

(i) For violations of § 1003.102(b)(14) of this part, the OIG may impose a penalty of not more than the greater of—

(1) $5,000, or

(2) Three times the amount of Medicare payments for home health services that are made with regard to the false certification of eligibility by a physician in accordance with sections 1814(a)(2)(C) or 1835(a)(2)(A) of the Act.

(j) The OIG may impose a penalty of not more than $10,000 per day for each day that the prohibited relationship described in § 1001.102(b)(12) of this part occurs.

(k) For violations of section 1862(a)(14) of the Act and § 1003.102(b)(15), the OIG may impose a penalty of not more than $2,000 for each bill or request for payment for items and services furnished to a hospital patient.

(l) For violatons of section 351A(b) or (c) of the Public Health Service Act and 42 CFR part 73, the OIG may impose a penalty of not more than $250,000 in the case of an individual, and not more than $500,000 in the case of any other person.

(m) For violations of section 1860D-31 of the Act and 42 CFR part 403, subpart H, regarding the misleading or defrauding of program beneficiaries, or the misuse of transitional assistance funds, the OIG may impose a penalty of not more than $10,000 for each individual violation.

[SOURCE: 56 Fed. Reg. 28,493 (June 21, 1991); 56 Fed. Reg. 42,537 (Aug. 28, 1991); 57 Fed. Reg. 3346 (Jan. 29, 1992); 59 Fed. Reg. 32,125 (June 22, 1994); 59 Fed. Reg. 36,086 (July 15, 1994); 59 Fed. Reg. 48,566 (Sept. 22, 1994); 60 Fed. Reg. 16,584 (Mar. 31, 1995); 60 Fed. Reg. 58,241 (Nov. 27, 1995); 61 Fed. Reg. 13,449 (Mar. 27, 1996); 61 Fed. Reg. 46,384 (Sept. 3, 1996); 61 Fed. Reg. 52,301 (Oct. 7, 1996); 64 Fed. Reg. 39,429 (July 22, 1999); 65 Fed. Reg. 18,550 (Apr. 7, 2000); 65 Fed. Reg. 24,416 (Apr. 26, 2000); 65 Fed. Reg. 35,584 (June 5, 2000); 65 Fed. Reg. 40,535 (June 30, 2000); 67 Fed. Reg. 75,905 (Dec. 13, 2002); 69 Fed. Reg. 28,845 (May 19, 2004).]

Appendix D-5

Regulations on Exclusion of Entities From Participation in Government Health Care Programs

Editor's Note: The following regulations were updated in 2002, and the text below updates and replaces the text of 42 C.F.R. Sections 1001.101, 1001.102, 1001.201, 1001.951, 1001.1501, 1001.2007, and 1001.3005 that appear in this Appendix in the Main Volume. Note that Section 1001.952 in this Part, which was updated in 2001 and 2002, is reprinted in this Supplement in Appendix A-2, above (see page 353).

Source: 42 C.F.R. Part 1001

Section 1001.101 Basis for liability.

The OIG will exclude any individual or entity that—
(a) Has been convicted of a criminal offense related to the delivery of an item or service under Medicare or a State health care program, including the performance of management or administrative services relating to the delivery of items or services under any such program;
(b) Has been convicted, under Federal or State law, of a criminal offense related to the neglect or abuse of a patient, in connection with the delivery of a health care item or service, including any offense that the OIG concludes entailed, or resulted in, neglect or abuse of patients (the delivery of a health care item or service includes the provision of any item or service to an individual to meet his or her

physical, mental or emotional needs or well-being, whether or not reimbursed under Medicare, Medicaid or any Federal health care program);
(c) Has been convicted, under Federal or State law, of a felony that occurred after August 21, 1996, relating to fraud, theft, embezzlement, breach of fiduciary responsibility, or other financial misconduct—

    (1) In connection with the delivery of a health care item or service, including the performance of management or administrative services relating to the delivery of such items or services, or

    (2) With respect to any act or omission in a health care program (other than Medicare and a State health care program) operated by, or financed in whole or in part, by any Federal, State or local government agency; or

(d) Has been convicted, under Federal or State law, of a felony that occurred after August 21, 1996 relating to the unlawful manufacture, distribution, prescription or dispensing of a controlled substance, as defined under Federal or State law. This applies to any individual or entity that—

    (1) Is, or has ever been, a health care practitioner, provider or supplier;

    (2) Holds, or has held, a direct or indirect ownership or control interest (as defined in section 1124(a)(3) of the Act) in an entity that is a health care provider or supplier, or is, or has ever been, an officer, director, agent or managing employee (as defined in section 1126(b) of the Act) of such an entity; or

    (3) Is, or has ever been, employed in any capacity in the health care industry.

[SOURCE: 63 Fed. Reg. 46,686 (Sept. 2, 1998), *as amended at* 67 Fed. Reg 11,932 (Mar. 18, 2002).]

Section 1001.102 Length of exclusion.

(a) No exclusion imposed in accordance with Sec. 1001.101 will be for less than 5 years.

(b) Any of the following factors may be considered to be aggravating and a basis for lengthening the period of exclusion—

    (1) The acts resulting in the conviction, or similar acts, that caused, or were intended to cause, a financial loss to a Government program or to one or more entities of $5,000 or more. (The entire amount of financial loss to such programs or entities, including any amounts resulting from similar acts not adjudicated, will be considered regardless of whether full or partial restitution has been made);

    (2) The acts that resulted in the conviction, or similar acts, were committed over a period of one year or more;

    (3) The acts that resulted in the conviction, or similar acts, had a significant adverse physical, mental or financial impact on one or more program beneficiaries or other individuals;

    (4) In convictions involving patient abuse or neglect, the action that resulted in the conviction was premeditated, was part of a

continuing pattern of behavior, or consisted of non-consensual sexual acts;

(5) The sentence imposed by the court included incarceration;

(6) The convicted individual or entity has a prior criminal, civil or administrative sanction record;

(7) The individual or entity has at any time been overpaid a total of $1,500 or more by Medicare, Medicaid or any other Federal health care programs as a result of *intentional* improper billings;

(8) The individual or entity has previously been convicted of a criminal offense involving the same or similar circumstances; or

(9) Whether the individual or entity was convicted of other offenses besides those which formed the basis for the exclusion, or has been the subject of any other adverse action by any Federal, State or local government agency or board, if the adverse action is based on the same set of circumstances that serves as the basis for imposition of the exclusion.

(c) Only if any of the aggravating factors set forth in paragraph (b) of this section justifies an exclusion longer than 5 years, may mitigating factors be considered as a basis for reducing the period of exclusion to no less than 5 years. Only the following factors may be considered mitigating—

(1) The individual or entity was convicted of 3 or fewer misdemeanor offenses, and the entire amount of financial loss (both actual loss and intended loss) to Medicare or any other Federal, State or local governmental health care program due to the acts that resulted in the conviction, and similar acts, is less than $1,500;

(2) The record in the criminal proceedings, including sentencing documents, demonstrates that the court determined that the individual had a mental, emotional or physical condition before or during the commission of the offense that reduced the individual's culpability; or

(3) The individual's or entity's cooperation with Federal or State officials resulted in—

    (i) Others being convicted or excluded from Medicare, Medicaid and all other Federal health care programs,

    (ii) Additional cases being investigated or reports being issued by the appropriate law enforcement agency identifying program vulnerabilities or weaknesses, or

    (iii) The imposition against anyone of a civil money penalty or assessment under part 1003 of this chapter.

(d) In the case of an exclusion under this subpart, based on a conviction occurring on or after August 5, 1997, an exclusion will be—

(1) For not less than 10 years if the individual has been convicted on one other occasion of one or more offenses for which an exclusion may be effected under section 1128(a) of the Act (The aggravating and mitigating factors in paragraphs (b) and (c) of this section can be used to impose a period of time in excess of the 10-year mandatory exclusion); or

(2) Permanent if the individual has been convicted on two or more other occasions of one or more offenses for which an exclusion may be effected under section 1128(a) of the Act.

[SOURCE: 57 Fed. Reg. 3330 (Jan. 29, 1992), *as amended at* 63 Fed. Reg. 46,686 (Sept. 2, 1998); 63 Fed. Reg. 57,918 (Oct. 29, 1998); 64 Fed. Reg. 39,426 (July 22, 1999); 67 Fed. Reg. 11,932 (Mar. 18, 2002).]

Section 1001.201 Conviction relating to program or health care fraud.

(a) *Circumstance for exclusion.* The OIG may exclude an individual or entity convicted under Federal or State law of—
    (1) A misdemeanor relating to fraud, theft, embezzlement, breach of fiduciary responsibility, or other financial misconduct—
        (i) In connection with the delivery of any health care item or service, including the performance of management or administrative services relating to the delivery of such items or services, or
        (ii) With respect to any act or omission in a health care program, other than Medicare and a State health care program, operated by, or financed in whole or in part by, any Federal, State or local government agency; or
    (2) Fraud, theft, embezzlement, breach of fiduciary responsibility, or other financial misconduct with respect to any act or omission in a program, other than a health care program, operated by or financed in whole or in part by any Federal, State or local government agency.

(b) *Length of exclusion.* (1) An exclusion imposed in accordance with this section will be for a period of 3 years, unless aggravating or mitigating factors listed in paragraphs (b)(2) and (b)(3) of this section form a basis for lengthening or shortening that period.
    (2) Any of the following factors may be considered to be aggravating and a basis for lengthening the period of exclusion—
        (i) The acts resulting in the conviction, or similar acts that caused, or reasonably could have been expected to cause, a financial loss of $5,000 or more to a Government program or to one or more other entities, or had a significant financial impact on program beneficiaries or other individuals. (The total amount of financial loss will be considered, including any amounts resulting from similar acts not adjudicated, regardless of whether full or partial restitution has been made);
        (ii) The acts that resulted in the conviction, or similar acts, were committed over a period of one year or more;
        (iii) The acts that resulted in the conviction, or similar acts, had a significant adverse physical or mental impact on one or more program beneficiaries or other individuals;
        (iv) The sentence imposed by the court included incarceration;

(v) Whether the individual or entity has a documented history of criminal, civil or administrative wrongdoing; or

(vi) Whether the individual or entity was convicted of other offenses besides those which formed the basis for the exclusion, or has been the subject of any other adverse action by any Federal, State or local government agency or board, if the adverse action is based on the same set of circumstances that serves as the basis for the imposition of the exclusion.

(3) Only the following factors may be considered as mitigating and a basis for reducing the period of exclusion—

(i) The individual or entity was convicted of 3 or fewer offenses, and the entire amount of financial loss (both actual loss and reasonably expected loss) to a Government program or to other individuals or entities due to the acts that resulted in the conviction and similar acts is less than $1,500;

(ii) The record in the criminal proceedings, including sentencing documents, demonstrates that the court determined that the individual had a mental, emotional or physical condition, before or during the commission of the offense, that reduced the individual's culpability;

(iii) The individual's or entity's cooperation with Federal or State officials resulted in—

(A) Others being convicted or excluded from Medicare, Medicaid or any of the other Federal health care programs, or

(B) Additional cases being investigated or reports being issued by the appropriate law enforcement agency identifying program vulnerabilities or weaknesses, or

(C) The imposition of a civil money penalty against others; or

(iv) Alternative sources of the type of health care items or services furnished by the individual or entity are not available.

[SOURCE: 57 Fed. Reg. 3330 (Jan. 29, 1992), *as amended at* 63 Fed. Reg. 46,687 (Sept. 2, 1998); 64 Fed. Reg. 39,426 (July 22, 1999); 67 Fed. Reg. 11,932 (Mar. 18, 2002); 67 Fed. Reg. 21,579 (May 1, 2002).]

Section 1001.951 Fraud and kickbacks and other prohibited activities.

(a) *Circumstance for exclusion.* (1) Except as provided for in paragraph (a)(2)(ii) of this section, the OIG may exclude any individual or entity that it determines has committed an act described in section 1128B(b) of the Act.

(2) With respect to acts described in section 1128B of the Act, the OIG—

(i) May exclude any individual or entity that it determines has knowingly and willfully solicited, received, offered or paid any remuneration in the manner and for the purposes described therein, irrespective of whether the individual or entity may be able to prove that the remuneration was also intended for some other purpose; and

(ii) Will not exclude any individual or entity if that individual or entity can prove that the remuneration that is the subject of the exclusion is exempted from serving as the basis for an exclusion.

(b) *Length of exclusion.* (1) The following factors will be considered in determining the length of exclusion in accordance with this section—

(i) The nature and circumstances of the acts and other similar acts;

(ii) The nature and extent of any adverse physical, mental, financial or other impact the conduct had on program beneficiaries or other individuals or the Medicare, Medicaid and all other Federal health care programs;

(iii) Whether the individual or entity has a documented history of criminal, civil or administrative wrongdoing (The lack of any prior record is to be considered neutral);

(iv) The individual or entity has been the subject of any other adverse action by any Federal, State or local government agency or board, if the adverse action is based on the same set of circumstances that serves as the basis for the imposition of the exclusion; or

(v) Any other facts bearing on the nature and seriousness of the individual's or entity's misconduct.

(2) It will be considered a mitigating factor if—

(i) The individual had a documented mental, emotional, or physical condition before or during the commission of the prohibited act(s) that reduced the individual's culpability for the acts in question;

(ii) The individual's or entity's cooperation with Federal or State officials resulted in the—

(A) Sanctioning of other individuals or entities, or

(B) Imposition of a civil money penalty against others; or

(iii) Alternative sources of the type of health care items or services provided by the individual or entity are not available.

[SOURCE: 57 Fed. Reg. 3330 (Jan. 29, 1992), *as amended at* 63 Fed. Reg. 46,689 (Sept. 2, 1998); 67 Fed. Reg. 11,933 (Mar. 18, 2002).]

Section 1001.952 Exceptions.

[***Editor's Note:*** 42 C.F.R. Section 1001.952 is reprinted in full beginning on page 353 of this Supplement in Appendix A-2 in the Anti-Kickback Statute Materials.]

Section 1001.1501 Default of health education loan or scholarship obligations.

(a) *Circumstance for exclusion.* (1) Except as provided in paragraph (a)(4) of this section, the OIG may exclude any individual that the Public Health Service (PHS) determines is in default on repayments of scholarship obligations or loans in connection with health professions education made or secured in whole or in part by the Secretary.

(2) Before imposing an exclusion in accordance with paragraph (a)(1) of this section, the OIG must determine that PHS has taken all reasonable administrative steps to secure repayment of the loans or obligations. If PHS has offered a Medicare offset arrangement as required by section 1892 of the Act, the OIG will find that all reasonable steps have been taken.

(3) The OIG will take into account access of beneficiaries to physicians' services for which payment may be made under Medicare, Medicaid or other Federal health care programs in determining whether to impose an exclusion.

(4) The OIG will not exclude a physician who is the sole community physician or the sole source of essential specialized services in a community if a State requests that the physician not be excluded.

(b) *Length of exclusion.* The individual will be excluded until such time as PHS notifies the OIG that the default has been cured or that there is no longer an outstanding debt. Upon such notice, the OIG will inform the individual of his or her right to apply for reinstatement.

[SOURCE: 57 Fed. Reg. 3330 (Jan. 29, 1992), *as amended at* 64 Fed. Reg. 39,427 (July 22, 1999); 67 Fed. Reg. 11,935 (Mar. 18, 2002).]

Section 1001.2007 Appeal of exclusions.

(a)(1) Except as provided in Sec. 1001.2003, an individual or entity excluded under this Part may file a request for a hearing before an ALJ only on the issues of whether:

(i) The basis for the imposition of the sanction exists, and

(ii) The length of exclusion is unreasonable.

(2) When the OIG imposes an exclusion under subpart B of this part for a period of 5 years, paragraph (a)(1)(ii) of this section will not apply.

(3) The request for a hearing should contain the information set forth in Sec. 1005.2(d) of this chapter.

(b) The excluded individual or entity has 60 days from the receipt of notice of exclusion provided for in Sec. 1001.2002 to file a request for such a hearing.

(c) The standard of proof at a hearing is preponderance of the evidence.

(d) When the exclusion is based on the existence of a criminal conviction or a civil judgment imposing liability by Federal, State or local court, a determination by another Government agency, or any other prior determination where the facts were adjudicated and a final decision was made, the basis for the underlying conviction, civil judgment or determination is not reviewable and the individual or entity may not collaterally attack it either on substantive or procedural grounds in this appeal.

(e) The procedures in part 1005 of this chapter will apply to the appeal.

[SOURCE: 57 Fed. Reg. 3330 (Jan. 29, 1992), *as amended at* 67 Fed. Reg. 11,935 (Mar. 18, 2002).]

Section 1001.3005 Reversed or vacated decisions.

(a) An individual or entity will be reinstated into Medicare, Medicaid and other Federal health care programs retroactive to the effective date of the exclusion when such exclusion is based on—

    (1) A conviction that is reversed or vacated on appeal;
    (2) An action by another agency, such as a State agency or licensing board, that is reversed or vacated on appeal; or
    (3) An OIG exclusion action that is reversed or vacated at any stage of an individual's or entity's administrative appeal process.

(b) If an individual or entity is reinstated in accordance with paragraph (a) of this section, CMS and other Federal health care programs will make payment for services covered under such program that were furnished or performed during the period of exclusion.

(c) The OIG will give notice of a reinstatement under this section in accordance with Sec. 1001.3003(a).

(d) An action taken by the OIG under this section will not require any other Federal health care program to reinstate the individual or entity if such program has imposed an exclusion under its own authority.

(e) If an action which results in the retroactive reinstatement of an individual or entity is subsequently overturned, the OIG may reimpose the exclusion for the initial period of time, less the period of time that was served prior to the reinstatement of the individual or entity.

[SOURCE: 57 Fed. Reg. 3330 (Jan. 29, 1992), *as amended at* 64 Fed. Reg. 39,428 (July 22, 1999); 67 Fed. Reg. 11,935 (Mar. 18, 2002).]

Appendix F

Special Fraud Alerts and Advisory Bulletins

Editor's Note: New in this print Supplement: Appendix F-18, the OIG Special Advisory Bulletin on Offering Gifts and Other Inducements to Beneficiaries.

All Special Fraud Alerts and Advisory Bulletin materials in **Appendix F** in the Main Volume are on the accompanying disk in the folder **FA_AB**. The Special Fraud Alert documents are in the subfolder **FRDALRT**. The Advisory Bulletin and Management Advisory Report documents are in the subfolder **ADVBULL**.

File names for the individual documents on disk are shown on the right under the column "File Name."

Appendix		*File Name*	*Main Volume*	*Supplement*
F-1	**Special Fraud Alert: Rental of Space in Physician Offices by Persons or Entities to Which Physicians Refer (Feb. 2000)**			
	Folder:			
	FA_AB\FRDALRT .... (*Source:* oig.hhs.gov/fraud/docs/ alertsandbulletins/office%20space.htm)[1]	RENTAL	disk	—
F-2	**Special Fraud Alert: Physician Liability for Certifications in the Provision of Medical Equipment and Supplies and Home Health Services (Jan. 1999)**			
	Folder:			
	FA_AB\FRDALRT .... (*Source:* oig.hhs.gov/fraud/docs/ alertsandbulletins/dme.htm)	PHYSCERT	disk	—

---

[1] Web addresses are subject to change. Readers may wish to check the OIG's website for updates or further information on topics of interest: oig.hhs.gov. For links to fraud alerts and advisory bulletins, readers should check the OIG's website at oig.hhs.gov/fraud/fraudalerts.html.

Appendix	File Name	Main Volume	Supplement
F-3	**Special Fraud Alert: Fraud and Abuse in Nursing Home Arrangements With Hospices (Mar. 1998)**		
	Folder:		
	FA_AB\FRDALRT .... NURSHSPC	disk	—
	(*Source:* oig.hhs.gov/fraud/docs/ alertsandbulletins/hospice.pdf)		
F-4	**Special Fraud Alert: Fraud and Abuse in the Provision of Services in Nursing Facilities (May 1996)**		
	Folder:		
	FA_AB\FRDALRT .... SERVNURS	disk	—
F-5	**Special Fraud Alert: Provision of Medical Supplies to Nursing Facilities (Aug. 1995)**		
	Folder:		
	FA_AB\FRDALRT .... SUPPNURS	disk	—
	(*Source:* oig.hhs.gov/fraud/docs/ alertsandbulletins/081095.html)		
F-6	**Special Fraud Alert: Home Health Fraud (June 1995)**		
	Folder:		
	FA_AB\FRDALRT .... HOMEHLTH	disk	—
	(*Source:* oig.hhs.gov/fraud/docs/ alertsandbulletins/081095.html)		
F-7	**Special Fraud Alert: Arrangements for the Provision of Clinical Laboratory Services (Oct. 1994)**		
	Folder:		
	FA_AB\FRDALRT .... CLIN_LAB	disk	—
	(*Source:* oig.hhs.gov/fraud/docs/ alertsandbulletins/121994.html)		
F-8	**Special Fraud Alert: Prescription Drug Marketing Schemes (Aug. 1994)**		
	Folder:		
	FA_AB\FRDALRT .... PRESDRUG	disk	—
	(*Source:* oig.hhs.gov/fraud/docs/ alertsandbulletins/121994.html)		

Appendix		File Name	Main Volume	Supple- ment

F-9   **Special Fraud Alert: Hospital Incentives to Referring Physicians (May 1992)**

Folder:

FA_AB\FRDALRT...................... HOSP_INC   disk   —
(*Source:* oig.hhs.gov/fraud/docs/
alertsandbulletins/121994.html)

F-10   **Special Fraud Alert: Routine Waiver of Copayments or Deductibles Under Medicare Part B (May 1991)**

Folder:

FA_AB\FRDALRT...................... WAIV_CP   disk   —
(*Source:* oig.hhs.gov/fraud/docs/
alertsandbulletins/121994.html)

F-11   **Special Fraud Alert: Joint Venture Arrangements (Aug. 1989)**

Folder:

FA_AB\FRDALRT...................... JV_ARRNG   disk   —
(*Source:* oig.hhs.gov/fraud/docs/
alertsandbulletins/121994.html)

F-12   **Special Advisory Bulletin: Practices of Business Consultants (June 2001)**

Folder:

FA_AB\ADVBULL...................... BUSCNSLT   disk   —
(*Source:* oig.hhs.gov/fraud/docs/
alertsandbulletins/consultants.pdf)

F-13   **Special Advisory Bulletin: The Patient Anti-Dumping Statute (Nov. 1999)**

Folder:

FA_AB\ADVBULL...................... ANTIDUMP   disk   —
(*Source:* oig.hhs.gov/fraud/docs/
alertsandbulletins/frdump.pdf)

F-14   **Special Advisory Bulletin: The Effect of Exclusion From Participation in Federal Health Care Programs (Sept. 1999)**

Folder:

FA_AB\ADVBULL...................... EXCLUSN   disk   —
(*Source:* oig.hhs.gov/fraud/docs/
alertsandbulletins/effected.htm)

Appendix F-18

OIG Special Advisory Bulletin: Offering Gifts and Other Inducements to Beneficiaries

Source: Office of Inspector General, Department of Health & Human Services, 66 Fed. Reg. 55,855 (Aug. 30, 2002), *available at* http://oig.hhs.gov/fraud/docs/alertsandbulletins/SABGiftsandInducements.pdf

(August 2002)

INTRODUCTION

Under section 1128A(a)(5) of the Social Security Act (the Act), enacted as part of Health Insurance Portability and Accountability Act of 1996 (HIPAA), a person who offers or transfers to a Medicare or Medicaid beneficiary any remuneration that the person knows or should know is likely to influence the beneficiary's selection of a particular provider, practitioner, or supplier of Medicare or Medicaid payable items or services may be liable for civil money penalties (CMPs) of up to $10,000 for each wrongful act. For purposes of section 1128A(a)(5) of the Act, the statute defines "remuneration" to include, without limitation, waivers of copayments and deductible amounts (or any part thereof) and transfers of items or services for free or for other than fair market value. (*See* section 1128A(i)(6) of the Act.) The statute and implementing regulations contain a limited number of exceptions. (*See* section 1128A(i)(6) of the Act; 42 CFR 1003.101.)

Offering valuable gifts to beneficiaries to influence their choice of a Medicare or Medicaid provider[1] raises quality and cost concerns. Providers may have an economic incentive to offset the additional costs attributable to the giveaway by providing unnecessary services or by substituting cheaper or lower quality services. The use of giveaways to attract business also favors large providers with greater financial resources for such activities, disadvantaging smaller providers and businesses.

---

[1]For convenience, in this Special Advisory Bulletin, the term "provider" includes practitioners and suppliers, as defined in 42 CFR 400.202.

499

The Office of Inspector General (OIG) is responsible for enforcing section 1128A(a)(5) through administrative remedies. Given the broad language of the prohibition and the number of marketing practices potentially affected, this Bulletin is intended to alert the health care industry as to the scope of acceptable practices. To that end, this Bulletin provides bright-line guidance that will protect the Medicare and Medicaid programs, encourage compliance, and level the playing field among providers. In particular, the OIG will apply the prohibition according to the following principles:

- *First,* the OIG has interpreted the prohibition to permit Medicare or Medicaid providers to offer beneficiaries inexpensive gifts (other than cash or cash equivalents) or services without violating the statute. For enforcement purposes, inexpensive gifts or services are those that have a retail value of no more than $10 individually, and no more than $50 in the aggregate annually per patient.

- *Second,* providers may offer beneficiaries more expensive items or services that fit within one of the five statutory exceptions: waivers of cost-sharing amounts based on financial need; properly disclosed copayment differentials in health plans; incentives to promote the delivery of certain preventive care services; any practice permitted under the federal anti-kickback statute pursuant to 42 CFR 1001.952; or waivers of hospital outpatient copayments in excess of the minimum copayment amounts.

- *Third,* the OIG is considering several additional regulatory exceptions. The OIG may solicit public comments on additional exceptions for complimentary local transportation and for free goods in connection with participation in certain clinical studies.

- *Fourth,* the OIG will continue to entertain requests for advisory opinions related to the prohibition on inducements to beneficiaries. However, as discussed below, given the difficulty in drawing principled distinctions between categories of beneficiaries or types of inducements, favorable opinions have been, and are expected to be, limited to situations involving conduct that is very close to an existing statutory or regulatory exception.

In sum, unless a provider's practices fit within an exception (as implemented by regulations) or are the subject of a favorable advisory opinion covering a provider's own activity, any gifts or free services to beneficiaries should not exceed the $10 per item and $50 annual limits.[2]

In addition, valuable services or other remuneration can be furnished to financially needy beneficiaries by an independent entity, such as a patient advocacy group, even if the benefits are funded by providers, so long as the independent entity makes an independent determination of need and the beneficiary's receipt of the remuneration does not depend, directly or indirectly, on the beneficiary's use of any particular

---

[2]The OIG will review these limits periodically and may adjust them for inflation if appropriate.

provider. An example of such an arrangement is the American Kidney Fund's program to assist needy patients with end stage renal disease with funds donated by dialysis providers, including paying for their supplemental medical insurance premiums. (*See, e.g.,* OIG Advisory Opinion No. 97-1 and No. 02-1.)

Elements of the Prohibition

Remuneration. Section 1128A(a)(5) of the Act prohibits the offering or transfer of "remuneration". The term "remuneration" has a well-established meaning in the context of various health care fraud and abuse statutes. Generally, it has been interpreted broadly to include "anything of value." The definition of "remuneration" for purposes of section 1128A(a)(5)—which includes waivers of coinsurance and deductible amounts, and transfers of items or services for free or for other than fair market value—affirms this broad reading. (*See* section 1128A(i)(6).) The use of the term "remuneration" implicitly recognizes that virtually any good or service has a monetary value.[3]

The definition of "remuneration" in section 1128A(i)(6) contains five specific exceptions:

- *Non-routine, unadvertised waivers of copayments or deductible amounts based on individualized determinations of financial need or exhaustion of reasonable collection efforts.* Paying the premiums for a beneficiary's Medicare Part B or supplemental insurance is *not* protected by this exception.

- *Properly disclosed differentials in a health insurance plan's copayments or deductibles.* This exception covers incentives that are part of a health plan design, such as lower plan copayments for using preferred providers, mail order pharmacies, or generic drugs. Waivers of Medicare or Medicaid copayments are *not* protected by this exception.

- *Incentives to promote the delivery of preventive care.* Preventive care is defined in 42 CFR 1003.101 to mean items and services that (i) are covered by Medicare or Medicaid and (ii) are either pre-natal or post-natal well-baby services or are services described in the *Guide to Clinical Preventive Services* published by the U.S. Preventive Services Task Force (available online at http://odphp.osphs.dhhs.gov/pubs/guidecps). Such incentives may not be in the form of cash or cash equivalents and may not be disproportionate to the value of the preventive care provided. (*See* 42 CFR 1003.101; 65 FR 24400 and 24409.)

- *Any practice permitted under an anti-kickback statute safe harbor* at 42 CFR 1001.952.[4]

---

[3] Some services, such as companionship provided by volunteers, have psychological, rather than monetary value. (*See, e.g.,* OIG Advisory Opinion No. 00-3.)

[4] For example, anti-kickback statute safe harbors exist for warranties; discounts; employee compensation; waivers of certain beneficiary coinsurance and deductible amounts; and increased coverage, reduced cost-sharing amounts, or reduced premium amounts offered by health plans. *See* 42 CFR 1001.952(g), (h), (i), and (k).

- *Waivers of copayment amounts in excess of the minimum co-payment amounts under the Medicare hospital outpatient fee schedule.*

(*See* section 1128A(i)(6) of the Act; 42 CFR 1003.101.)

In addition, in the Conference Committee report accompanying the enactment of section 1128A(a)(5), Congress expressed its intent that inexpensive gifts of nominal value be permitted. (*See* Joint Explanatory Statement of the Committee of Conference, section 231 of HIPAA, Public Law 104-191.) Accordingly, the OIG interprets the prohibition to exclude offers of inexpensive items or services, and no specific exception for such items or services is required. (*See* 65 FR 24400 and 24410.) The OIG has interpreted inexpensive to mean a retail value of no more than $10 per item or $50 in the aggregate per patient on an annual basis. *Id.* at 24411.

Inducement. Section 1128A(a)(5) of the Act bars the offering of remuneration to Medicare or Medicaid beneficiaries where the person offering the remuneration knows or should know that the remuneration is likely to influence the beneficiary to order or receive items or services from a particular provider. The "should know" standard is met if a provider acts with deliberate ignorance or reckless disregard. No proof of specific intent is required. (*See* 42 CFR 1003.101.)

The "inducement" element of the offense is met by any offer of valuable (*i.e.,* not inexpensive) goods and services as part of a marketing or promotional activity, regardless of whether the marketing or promotional activity is active or passive. For example, even if a provider does not directly advertise or promote the availability of a benefit to beneficiaries, there may be indirect marketing or promotional efforts or informal channels of information dissemination, such as "word of mouth" promotion by practitioners or patient support groups. In addition, the OIG considers the provision of free goods or services to existing customers who have an ongoing relationship with a provider likely to influence those customers' future purchases.

Beneficiaries. Section 1128A(a)(5) of the Act bars inducements offered to Medicare and Medicaid beneficiaries, regardless of the beneficiary's medical condition. The OIG is aware that some specialty providers offer valuable gifts to beneficiaries with specific chronic conditions. In many cases, these complimentary goods or services have therapeutic, as well as financial, benefits for patients. While the OIG is mindful of the hardships that chronic medical conditions can cause for beneficiaries, there is no meaningful basis under the statute for exempting valuable gifts based on a beneficiary's medical condition or the condition's severity. Moreover, providers have a greater incentive to offer gifts to chronically ill beneficiaries who are likely to generate substantially more business than other beneficiaries.

Similarly, there is no meaningful statutory basis for a broad exemption based on the financial need of a category of patients. The statute specifically applies the prohibition to the Medicaid program—

a program that is available only to financially needy persons. The inclusion of Medicaid within the prohibition demonstrates Congress' conclusion that categorical financial need is not a sufficient basis for permitting valuable gifts. This conclusion is supported by the statute's specific exception for non-routine waivers of copayments and deductibles based on individual financial need. If Congress intended a broad exception for financially needy persons, it is unlikely that it would have expressly included the Medicaid program within the prohibition and then created such a narrow exception.

Provider, Practitioner, or Supplier. Section 1128A(a)(5) of the Act applies to incentives to select particular providers, practitioners, or suppliers. As noted in the regulations, the OIG has interpreted this element to exclude health plans that offer incentives to Medicare and Medicaid beneficiaries to enroll in a plan. (*See* 65 FR 24400 and 24407.) However, incentives provided to influence an already enrolled beneficiary to select a particular provider, practitioner, or supplier within the plan are subject to the statutory proscription (other than copayment differentials that are part of a health plan design). *Id.* In addition, the OIG does not believe that drug manufacturers are "providers, practitioners, or suppliers" for the limited purposes of section 1128A(a)(5), unless the drug manufacturers also own or operate, directly or indirectly, pharmacies, pharmacy benefits management companies, or other entities that file claims for payment under the Medicare or Medicaid programs.

ADDITIONAL REGULATORY CONSIDERATIONS

Congress has authorized the OIG to create regulatory exceptions to section 1128A(a)(5) of the Act and to issue advisory opinions to protect acceptable arrangements. (*See* sections 1128A(i)(6)(B) and 1128D(b)(2)(A) of the Act.) While the OIG has considered numerous arrangements involving the provision of various free goods and services to beneficiaries, for the following reasons the OIG has concluded that any additional exceptions will likely be few in number and narrow in scope:

- Any exception will create the activity that the statute prohibits—namely, competing for business by giving remuneration to Medicare and Medicaid beneficiaries. Moreover, competition will not only result in providers matching a competitor's offer, but inevitably will trigger ever more valuable offers.

- Since virtually all free goods and services have a corresponding monetary value, there is no principled basis under the statute for distinguishing between the kinds of goods or services offered or the types of beneficiaries to whom the goods or services are offered. Attempting to draw such distinctions would necessarily result in arbitrary standards and would undermine the entire prohibition. Congress has provided no further statutory guidance on the bases for distinguishing and evaluating potential exceptions.

Despite these serious concerns, the OIG is considering soliciting public comment on the possibility of regulatory "safe harbor" exceptions under section 1128A(a)(5) for two kinds of arrangements:

- ***Complimentary local transportation.*** The OIG is considering proposing a new exception for complimentary local transportation offered to beneficiaries residing in the provider's primary catchment area. The proposal would permit some complimentary local transportation of greater than nominal value. However, the exception would not cover luxury or specialized transportation, including limousines or ambulances (but would permit vans specially outfitted to transport wheelchairs). The proposed exception may include transportation to the office or facility of a provider other than the donor; however, such arrangements may implicate the anti-kickback statute insofar as they confer a benefit on a provider that is a potential referral source for the party providing the transportation.

- ***Government-sponsored clinical trials.*** The OIG may propose a new exception for free goods and services (possibly including waivers of copayments) in connection with certain clinical trials that are principally sponsored by the National Institutes of Health or another component of the Department of Health and Human Services.

The OIG is reviewing its pending proposal (65 FR 25460) to permit certain dialysis providers to purchase Medicare supplemental insurance for financially needy persons in the light of the principles established in this Bulletin.

While the OIG does not expect at this time to propose any additional regulatory exceptions related to unadvertised waivers of copayments and deductibles, the OIG recognizes that such waivers occur in a wide variety of circumstances, some of which do not present a significant risk of fraud and abuse. The OIG encourages the industry to bring these situations to our attention through the advisory opinion process. Instructions for requesting an OIG advisory opinion are available on the OIG Web site at http://oig.hhs.gov/advopn/index.htm.

Finally, the OIG reiterates that nothing in section 1128A(a)(5) prevents an independent entity, such as a patient advocacy group, from providing free or other valuable services or remuneration to financially needy beneficiaries, even if the benefits are funded by providers, so long as the independent entity makes an independent determination of need and the beneficiary's receipt of the remuneration does not depend, directly or indirectly, on the beneficiary's use of any particular provider. The OIG has approved several such arrangements through the advisory opinion process, including the American Kidney Fund's program to assist needy patients with end stage renal disease with funds donated by dialysis providers. (*See, e.g.,* OIG Advisory Opinion No. 97-1 and No. 02-1.)

CONCLUSION

Congress has broadly prohibited offering remuneration to Medicare and Medicaid beneficiaries, subject to limited, well-defined exceptions. To the extent that providers have programs in place that do not meet any exception, the OIG, in exercising its enforcement discretion, will take into consideration whether the providers terminate prohibited programs expeditiously following publication of this Bulletin.

The Office of Inspector General (OIG) was established at the Department of Health and Human Services by Congress in 1976 to identify and eliminate fraud, abuse, and waste in the Department's programs and to promote efficiency and economy in departmental operations. The OIG carries out this mission through a nationwide program of audits, investigations, and inspections.

The Fraud and Abuse Control Program, established by the Health Insurance Portability and Accountability Act of 1996 (HIPAA), authorized the OIG to provide guidance to the health care industry to prevent fraud and abuse and to promote the highest level of ethical and lawful conduct. To further these goals, the OIG issues Special Advisory Bulletins about industry practices or arrangements that potentially implicate the fraud and abuse authorities subject to enforcement by the OIG.

[Dated: August 8, 2002.
Janet Rehnquist,
Inspector General.]

Appendix G

Advisory Opinion Materials: Anti-Kickback Statute and Stark Self-Referral Law[1]

Editor's Note: New in this print Supplement: Appendix G-2, Topical Index (Cumulative) and Summaries of the OIG Anti-Kickback Statute Advisory Opinions (Years 2001 through August 11, 2004).

All Advisory Opinion materials in **Appendix G** in the Main Volume are on the accompanying disk in the folder **ADVOPS.** The Anti-Kickback Statute Advisory Opinion documents are in the subfolder **ANTIKICK.** The Stark Law Advisory Opinion documents are in the subfolder **STARK.**

File names for the individual documents on disk are shown on the right under the column "File Name."

Appendix		*File Name*	*Main Volume*	*Supplement*
G-1	**Anti-Kickback Advisory Opinion Regulations (42 C.F.R. Part 1008)**			
	Folder:			
	ADVOPS\ANTIKICK	KICKREGS	disk	App. B-3
G-2	**Summary and Topical Index of Anti-Kickback Statute Advisory Opinions: 1997–2000**			
	Folder:			
	ADVOPS\ANTIKICK	OP_INDEX	disk	—
	(*Source:* The Bureau of National Affairs, Inc.)			

---

[1] Readers may wish to check the OIG or the CMS website for updates or further information on topics of interest: oig.hhs.gov and www.cms.gov.

---

[2]Web addresses are subject to change.

Appendix G-2

Topical Index (Cumulative) and Summaries of OIG Anti-Kickback Statute Advisory Opinions: Years 2001–August 11, 2004 [New][1]

[*Editor's Note:* This Topical Index cumulates all advisory opinions through August 11, 2004. This Summary of Advisory Opinions updates Appendix G-2 in the Main Volume (on disk) and covers opinions from January 11, 2001, through August 11, 2004. Full text of the advisory opinions is available at the Office of Inspector General, Department of Health & Human Services website: http://oig.hhs.gov/fraud/advisoryopinions/opinions.html.]

CUMULATIVE TOPICAL INDEX OF OIG ADVISORY OPINIONS REGARDING THE ANTI-KICKBACK STATUTE

Academic medical centers	02-11, 00-6
Advertising	02-12, 99-10
Ambulance arrangements	00-7
• Ambulance restocking	02-3, 02-2, 01-5, 00-11, 00-9, 99-5, 98-14, 98-13, 98-7, 98-3, 97-6
• Coinsurance waivers	04-06, 04-02, 03-14, 03-11, 03-9, 02-15, 02-8, 01-18, 01-12, 01-11, 01-10, 99-1
• Exclusive arrangement with second responder	04-10
• Free heliopad	03-14
Ambulatory surgical centers	03-5, 03-2, 01-17, 98-12
Bundling	02-10, 01-8, 99-3
Charitable contributions	02-11, 01-19, 01-9, 01-2, 00-6
Clinical trials	04-01
Coinsurance waivers	

---

[1]*Abstracted from* W. Bradley Tully, Federal Anti-Kickback Law, BNA's Health Law & Bus. Series WP Doc. 9 (Portfolio No. 1500 2004).

CUMULATIVE TOPICAL INDEX OF OIG ADVISORY OPINIONS
REGARDING THE ANTI-KICKBACK STATUTE (*CONTINUED*)

CUMULATIVE TOPICAL INDEX OF OIG ADVISORY OPINIONS
REGARDING THE ANTI-KICKBACK STATUTE (*CONTINUED*)

• Pharmacy services	98-15
• Hospital programs	03-8, 03-2
Marketing arrangements	04-03, 99-12, 99-10, 99-8, 99-3, 98-10, 98-4, 98-1
Medicare Part B premium payments	03-3, 02-7, 02-1, 01-15, 98-17, 97-2, 97-1
Patient transportation arrangements	00-7
"Pay-to-play" arrangements	99-5
Physician recruiting arrangements	01-4
Preventive health programs	00-4
Referral potential required for violation	00-1, 99-4
Referral services	00-8
Refunds	02-6
Reorganizations	03-15, 02-5
Remuneration from on-site equipment	02-4
Splitting medical group	02-5
Swapping	03-7, 03-6, 01-18, 99-13, 99-3, 99-2
Telemedicine consultations	04-07, 99-14, 98-18

SUMMARIES OF ADVISORY OPINIONS: YEARS 2001 AND 2002

Advisory Opinion No. 01-1
  Issued Jan. 11, 2001, posted Jan. 18, 2001
  Hospital proposed arrangement whereby it would pay group of cardiac surgeons responsible for 85% of its cardiac admissions 50% of the first year cost savings directly attributable to specific changes in their operating room practices.
  Conclusion: Although proposed arrangement would violate statutory gainsharing prohibition, the OIG would impose neither CMP nor anti-kickback sanctions because sufficient safeguards are in place to protect against patient and program abuse through verifiable cost savings attributable to specific actions, including: surgeons would share in gainsharing distributions on per capita, rather than per-referral or cost-savings activity basis; arrangement would be disclosed in writing to patients; financial incentives are reasonably limited in duration (one-year), amount (aggregate cap), and scope (cost savings from any one action limited by prior-year utilization levels); participation is limited to cardiac surgeons already on the surgical staff.

Advisory Opinion No. 01-2
  Issued Mar. 20, 2001, posted Mar. 27, 2001
  Tax-exempt health care system proposed to solicit and accept proceeds from a charitable-funding event (golf tournament) in which some of the system's vendors and suppliers will participate as sponsors and registrants.

Advisory Opinion No. 01-3
  Issued May 3, 2001, posted May 10, 2001
  Indian tribe proposes arrangement whereby local hospital would discount the Medicare copayment and deductible charges by 10% of the hospital's actual charge for services paid by the Indian Health Service Contract Health Services (CHS) program, resulting in a 50% reduction of copayment amounts.
  Conclusion: Although proposed arrangement would potentially violate the anti-kickback statute as a routine waiver of a portion of the Medicare copayment, the OIG would not impose sanctions because: (1) the federal government receives the benefit of the discount since IHS is responsible for tribe members' copayments; (2) there is no unfair competition because tribe is willing to enter same arrangement with any willing hospital provider; (3) there is no substantial risk of swapping since Medicare or Medicaid beneficiaries comprise only 25% of the patient pool; (4) there are ample safeguards against overutilization since patients may seek only services not available at the tribe's health center and all nonemergent services are subject to preauthorization; and (5) the arrangement, arising in the context of the unique relationship between the government and Indian nations, is consistent with federal policy encouraging prudent purchases of CHS-covered services.

Advisory Opinion No. 01-4
Issued May 3, 2001, posted May 10, 2001

Tax-exempt hospital, located in a medically underserved area (MUA) with a shortage of otolaryngologists and head and neck surgeons, proposes to recruit such a specialist by making interest-bearing loans to a recent medical school graduate during a five-year residency program in those specialties to pay his medical school loans and other educational costs in exchange for a three-year commitment to establish a full-time private specialty practice nearby; maintain staff privileges, accept patients while on-call, and for up to 20 hours per month assist in the hospital's educational, physician-recruitment, and fund-raising programs. The hospital proposes to forgive one-third of the debt for each year the physician fulfills his obligations, with the outstanding balance coming due if the physician defaults on his obligations.

Conclusion: Although the proposed arrangement would not fall within the 42 C.F.R. §1001.952(n) recruitment safe harbor and would potentially violate the anti-kickback statute, the OIG would not impose sanctions because the arrangement: (1) poses minimal risk of abuse because there is a documented shortage of these specialists, the loan amount and duration (although exceeding the three-year safe harbor threshold) have a reasonable, documented basis, the benefit would go directly to the physician, and upon relocation the physician would not have a steady stream of referrals; (2) provides sufficient safeguards because it would not be substantially renegotiated or vary with the volume or value of the physician's referrals to the hospital and would not restrict the physician from working with other entities; and (3) benefits the MUA through increased access to health care services.

Advisory Opinion No. 01-5
Issued May 18, 2001, posted May 23, 2001

Tax-exempt supporting foundation of hospital proposes to enter separate five-year arrangements to lease cardiac diagnostic equipment which enables electrocardiograms to be sent from ambulances to receiving hospitals to four area EMS providers for $1 per year.

Conclusion: Although the arrangement would potentially violate the anti-kickback statute, no sanctions would be imposed because the arrangement involves only emergency services, which poses minimal risk of overutilization; would not change the preexisting referral pattern between EMS providers and area hospitals—based on state and local regulatory protocols—to steer patients to hospital; involves local EMS system in oversight of the arrangement; and would have positive impact on quality of patient care.

Advisory Opinion No. 01-6
Issued May 22, 2001, posted May 29, 2001

Group purchasing organization, a limited partnership consisting of entities affiliated with various health care systems that make substantial purchases of health care products through the GPO, entered written agreements whereby purchasers acknowledge GPO will receive specified group purchasing organization fees quarterly from vendors in connection with such purchases.

Conclusion: The arrangement satisfies criteria of group purchasing organizations safe harbor at 42 U.S.C. §1320a-7b(b)(3)(C) and 42 C.F.R. §1001.952(j).

Advisory Opinion No. 01-7
Issued July 2, 2001, posted July 3, 2001

Tax-exempt cardiology specialty teaching hospital which has a history of providing substantial free and charity medical care, does not bill patients for copayments, regardless of patient's financial need, reason for admission, DRG code or outpatient procedure, length of hospital stay, or treating physician. Instead it receives payment equal to the amount of the waived coinsurance from a related tax-exempt foundation that provides the hospital with substantial financial support. The majority of hospital care is provided by physicians who are full-time hospital employees practicing exclusively at the hospital, but the hospital also has granted hospital staff privileges to private practice physicians.

Conclusion: Waiver of copayments for Medicare Part A hospital inpatient services meets the 42 C.F.R. §1001.952(k) safe harbor. Although waiver of copayments for Medicare Part B and non-inpatient Part A services provided by full-time hospital-employee physicians would potentially violate the anti-kickback statute, the OIG would not impose sanctions because the policy (1) originates from an institutional charitable mission that predates the Medicare and Medicaid programs and (2) poses minimal risk of overutilization because the annual salaries of full-time-employee physicians are predetermined and unrelated to the volume or value of the services that the physicians perform, and since they maintain no outside practices they are not in a position to refer patients. The OIG refused to protect waivers for patients under the care of private practice physicians because this would confer a competitive advantage on the hospital and the private practice physicians over other area hospitals that provide the lucrative cardiology services.

Advisory Opinion No. 01-8
Issued July 3, 2001, posted July 10, 2001

A company proposed to market to nursing facilities (SNFs) a three-year program to manage pressure ulcers. These services were potentially reimbursable under Part A. The program involved the discounted sale of therapeutic mattresses and other support surfaces with limited replacement warranties; a prospectively fixed, per resident/per diem payment for skin and wound care products; and a limited warranty for certain liabilities resulting from skin or wound care deficiencies.

Conclusion: The program did not fall within the discount safe harbor because its pricing arrangement bundles several items and services, and did not technically qualify for the 42 C.F.R. §1001.952(g) warranty safe harbor because its warranty covers "services" as well as "items." Nevertheless, sanctions would not be imposed because: (1) the program covered all beds and residents and pricing was uniform, regardless of the resident's payor; (2) the bundling presented little risk of abuse since SNFs are reimbursed primarily by a global, all-inclusive rate and the value of items or services that could be separately billed was less than 1% of the program's price; (3) there was no risk of swapping because the program would be the only financial arrangement between the company and the SNF; (4) the services component under warranty did not significantly increase the risk of fraud and abuse because the items were the "linchpin" of the program; and (5) if the program worked as intended, patients and the Federal health care programs would benefit.

Advisory Opinion No. 01-9
Issued July 19, 2001, posted July 26, 2001

A city-owned, self-supporting teaching hospital that provided 70% of the uncompensated care in its community proposed to provide support for a nonprofit community health center (CHC), funded under Public Health Service Act §330, that operated as a federally qualified health center under Medicare. The CHC's physicians had admitting privileges in the hospital. The CHC was to assume the operation of primary and urgent care and support services that the hospital had provided at a loss at an off-site clinic in a medically underserved area. The hospital would provide such support by making grants to and leasing portions of the clinic at fair market value to the CHC. The hospital would make three annual grants to CHC to be used, without other restriction, for uncompensated services to the community, with the CHC returning to the hospital annually any funds in excess of actual costs of uncompensated care. In addition, the CHC and the hospital would purchase from each other clinical services and support services for medical education, respectively, at fair market value.

Conclusion: Sanctions would not be imposed because the grant would: (1) ensure continuity of care for the hospital's patients; (2) further the shared charitable mission of the CHC and hospital of making health care services available for underserved persons; (3) indirectly relieve the burden on the federal fisc since the hospital would defray costs that CHC grant funds would normally cover; (4) pose minimal risk of fraud and abuse since the grant amount was not related to the volume or value of referrals between the parties and any potential benefit from insured referrals might be offset by uninsured referrals; (5) the lease met the requirements of the space and equipment rental safe harbors at 42 C.F.R. §1001.952(b) and (c); and (6) patients would be advised in writing of their freedom to choose providers.

Advisory Opinion No. 01-10
Issued July 20, 2001, posted July 26, 2001

A state fire district that operated an ambulance service proposed to bill residents of the district or their insurers (including federal health care programs) only to the extent of their insurance coverage, and to treat operating revenues received from local taxes as payment of the copayments and deductibles due from residents.

Conclusion: Sanctions would not be imposed because the arrangement would not constitute prohibited remuneration under CMS Carrier Manual §2309.4, which specifies that facilities owned and operated by political subdivisions which waive copayments and deductibles from bona fide residents are not to be denied reimbursement on the ground that they have provided free services.

Advisory Opinion No. 01-11
Issued July 20, 2001, posted July 26, 2001

A municipal fire district that operated an ambulance service passed an ordinance that would require district residents to pay for ambulance services to the extent of their insurance coverage and proposed to treat operating revenues received from local taxes as payment of the residents' copayments and deductibles.

Conclusion: Sanctions would not be imposed because arrangement would not constitute prohibited remuneration under CMS Carrier Manual §2309.4, which specifies that facilities owned and operated by political subdivisions which waive copayments and deductibles from bona fide residents are not to be denied reimbursement on the ground that they have provided free services.

Advisory Opinion No. 01-12
Issued July 20, 2001, posted July 26, 2001

An exclusive contract between a city and a nonprofit corporation to provide emergency medical services for city residents prohibited the corporation from billing out-of-pocket copayments and deductibles to bona fide city residents.

Conclusion: Sanctions could be imposed because by requiring the company to bill residents "insurance only" and then failing to reimburse the company for the copayments, the city effectuated a routine waiver that implicated the anti-kickback statute and False Claims Act. The OIG distinguished between the voluntary copayment waivers by local government-owned ambulance companies approved in Advisory Op. No. 01-10 and Advisory Op. No. 01-11 from the requirement that a private company bill insurance only as a condition of obtaining the city's EMS business.

Advisory Opinion No. 01-13
Issued Aug. 17, 2001, posted Aug. 24, 2001

An agreement between a not-for-profit corporation licensed as a community-rated, state-regulated commercial HMO and skilled nursing facilities participating in the HMO's provider network included a coordination of benefits provision, which had been in use for 10 years and was expressly permitted by state insurance regulations, that resulted in a waiver of Medicare coinsurance amounts when Medicare was the primary payor (the situation for fewer than 5% of the HMO's enrollees) if the Medicare reimbursement amount was higher than the HMO's fee schedule amount for SNF reimbursement. Advisory Op. No. 98-5 (issued Apr. 24, 1998) disapproved of the very same COB provision.

Conclusion: The OIG would not impose sanctions because: (1) any potential to manipulate the COB provision for the HMO's benefit was limited, given the regulatory requirement of community rating, and the overwhelming majority of non-Medicare enrollees served by the HMO; (2) the HMO's ability to influence referrals was attenuated; (3) any adverse financial impact on Medicare was limited by the prospective reimbursement methodology for, and low risk of overutilization of, Part A skilled nursing care services; and (4) the COB provision would not increase the likelihood that SNFs would stint on services provided to Medicare enrollees since the SNFs received the same payment for non-Medicare patients they served. OIG Advisory Op. No. 98-5 was accordingly modified.

Advisory Opinion No. 01-14
Issued Aug. 27, 2001, posted Sept. 4, 2001

A nonprofit hospital, as part of an outreach program to encourage use of a satellite center serving a majority uninsured community, waived all charges for uninsured patients and all out-of-pocket expenses for insured patients for breast and gynecological cancer screenings performed at the center and for certain follow-up services performed at other hospital facilities. The center was financed by federal and state grants, private donations, and annual grants from the hospital.

Conclusion: The OIG would not impose sanctions under beneficiary inducement CMP or anti-kickback statute because: (1) given the uninsured status of the large majority of the beneficiaries, it was unlikely the waiver policy would generate substantial remunerative services for the hospital; (2) the receipt of services by some insured patients did not alter the basic charitable nature of policy; and (3) although the follow-up services were outside the 42 U.S.C. §1320a-7a(i)(6) preventive care exception, they were limited to those necessary to confirm the initial screening results and merely effectuated the screening services.

Advisory Opinion No. 01-15
Issued Sept. 19, 2001, posted Sept. 26, 2001

A tax-exempt managed care organization proposed to use its direct community benefits investment funds to subsidize, to the extent a state Medicaid agency did not, the M+C premiums and copayments of enrollees who were dually eligible for Medicare and Medicaid. The MCO used monthly Medicaid eligibility as the criteria for qualifying for the subsidy.

Conclusion: Although the proposed subsidies were functionally indistinguishable from premium and copayment waivers, the OIG would not impose sanctions since the monthly Medicaid-eligibility determinations by state agencies served as a reasonable and reliable substitute for individualized determinations of financial need.

Advisory Opinion No. 01-16
   Editor's Note: Advisory Op. No. 01-16 does not address issues under the anti-kickback statute.

Advisory Opinion No. 01-17
   Issued Oct. 10, 2001, posted Oct. 17, 2001
   An ambulatory surgical center was owned indirectly by a hospital and five ophthalmologists (each meeting the "one-third practice income test" under the surgeon-owned ASC safe harbor) in two group practices. The ophthalmologists' direct investments were in limited liability companies that in turn owned the LLC that was the actual investor in the joint venture. Physicians employed by the hospital and its affiliated entities would not make referrals directly to the ASC, although they might refer patients to the ophthalmologists or their group practices. The hospital, which would annually notify all hospital-affiliated physicians of these measures, would not encourage or require its physicians to refer patients to the ASC, the ophthalmologists, or their group practices, would not track such referrals, and would not relate physician compensation to the value or volume of such referrals. The joint venture also involved two ancillary agreements: (1) a lease and partial lease-back agreement between the ASC and hospital and (2) a medical director agreement between the ASC and an investing ophthalmologist.
   Conclusion: Although the arrangement did not fit within the 42 C.F.R. §1001.952(r)(4) safe harbor for hospital/physician ASCs because the hospital was a potential source of referrals to the ASC and the ophthalmologists had invested indirectly through LLCs, the OIG would not impose sanctions on the ASC or hospital. The measures the hospital would implement relating to referrals by hospital-affiliated physicians would significantly constrain its ability to direct or influence referrals and the use of "pass-through" entities rather than direct ownership did not substantively increase the risk of fraud or abuse since each ophthalmologist would receive a return on investment that was directly proportionate to his or her investment in the ASC. The ancillary agreements also did not increase the risk of abuse since the lease fell within the 42 C.F.R. §1001.952(b) space rental safe harbor and, although the medical director agreement was not within the 42 C.F.R. §1001.952(d) personal services and management contracts safe harbor, it set a specified hourly rate, consistent with fair market value, subject to a monthly cap, that was paid only if there was written documentation.

Advisory Opinion No. 01-18
   Issued Oct. 31, 2001, posted Nov. 7, 2001
   Rural county with a large indigent population awarded an exclusive two-year contract to respond to all emergency calls to an ambulance provider that billed all patients and insurers but, in lieu of collecting out-of-pocket coinsurance payments from county residents, received from the county an annual subsidy, computed as a percentage of the annual per-household EMS fees the county collected from

residents. In addition to performing services for federal program and providing patients, the ambulance company provided services for indigent and uninsured patients for which the county was the responsible payor at reduced rates.

Conclusion: The nonbilling of residents was not a routine waiver of coinsurance that would implicate the anti-kickback statute because the subsidy reasonably approximated the coinsurance obligation and the county collected from, and paid coinsurance on behalf of, its residents. Although the tying of indigent business to the paying business through the exclusivity provision raised anti-kickback concerns, the OIG did not impose sanctions because: (1) the effect on federal program costs, if any, would be minor since utilization is determined by patient "911" calls; (2) the putative prohibited remuneration (the county's avoided costs for indigent and uninsured transports) inured to the public; (3) the county's decision to provide EMS transport through a private provider was within its traditional police powers; and (4) there was no adverse impact on competition.

Advisory Opinion No. 01-19
Issued Nov. 14, 2001, posted Nov. 21, 2001

A tax-exempt hospital proposed to donate the office space it leased to a charity, which was funded solely by donations, that provided free non-medical assistance to patients with terminal illnesses, their families, and the community. The charity's patients, many of whom received medical equipment from the hospital's DME company and items and services from the hospital, did not need to waive their rights to Medicare-funded curative treatment to receive the charity's services because the charity was not a Medicare-certified hospice.

Conclusion: The OIG would not impose sanctions because the charity provided valuable community services without charge, and the hospital had a longstanding relationship with the charity and shared a common charitable mission with it. In addition, because the terminally ill patients had their own physicians, the charity's ability to affect medical items and services orders in the course of providing non-medical assistance was substantially diminished.

Advisory Opinion No. 01-20
Issued Nov. 14, 2001, posted Nov. 21, 2001

A Medicare-certified hospice and nursing facility entered an arrangement for services provided to nursing facility residents who were dually eligible for Medicaid and Medicare hospice benefits whereby the hospice paid the nursing facility the full Medicaid nursing facility per diem rate for non-hospice patients (which covers at least some pharmacy services), plus a separate payment for drugs used for the patients' terminal illnesses.

Conclusion: The arrangement might involve prohibited remuneration that could induce the nursing facility, which collects the full Medicaid per diem payment without having to provide the pharmacy benefit typically covered by the payment, to refer patients for hospice services. Lacking an adequate accounting of the drugs for which separate payment was made that would enable it to evaluate the magnitude of the potential benefit to the nursing facility, the OIG declined to approve the arrangement.

Advisory Opinion No. 01-21
Issued Nov. 16, 2001, posted Nov. 26, 2001

A physician-owned LLC that operated a free-standing ASC entered a series of agreements with a health system whereby: (1) the health system exercised an option to purchase a 15 percent equity interest at fair market value; (2) the ASC purchased management services from the physicians' professional corporation and facilities support from the health system under contracts that did not meet the personal/management services safe harbor because they allowed termination for cause without prohibiting renegotiation within one-year of termination; and (3) the ASC leased space from the health system under a safe harbor lease.

Conclusion: The OIG would not impose sanctions because there were sufficient safeguards in the arrangement in its entirety to minimize risk: (1) the health system would inform its physicians annually that it will not encourage referrals to the ASC or the physician-investors, and will not track or base physician compensation on such referrals; and (2) the termination and renegotiation provisions were strictly limited to commercially reasonable and well-defined contingencies and the requestors certified that any renegotiation would be for fair market value and not more often than annually. The fact that profits and losses were distributed based on each investor's equity ownership, rather than directly proportional to each's capital investment, as would be required for safe harbor protection, did not increase risk of fraud or abuse, since there was a reasonable basis for the different prices which were paid per-unit of investment.

Advisory Opinion No. 02-1
Issued Apr. 4, 2002, posted Apr. 11, 2002

A tax-exempt charity that provided grants to subsidize health insurance premiums and copayments payable by financially needy, privately insured or uninsured patients suffering from chronic illnesses or rare disorders proposed to provide similar financial assistance to Medicare and Medigap beneficiaries, using the same eligibility criteria and grant procedures. Grants would be awarded for a fixed period on a first-come, first-served basis based on financial need, using a preset sliding scale to determine the amount of assistance. Patients selected their providers before applying and the charity did not make referrals to any donor or provider. The charity, which received substantial contributions earmarked for patients with specified diseases from manufacturers of drugs used to treat diseases covered by the program, agreed to inform the donors of the aggregate number of applicants and patients accepted in the donor's designated disease category. About half of grant recipients were referred by donors. The identity of the referral source was not considered in making grants.

Conclusion: Donor contributions to the charity would not be grounds for CMPs under the statute prohibiting remuneration likely to influence Medicare beneficiary's choice of provider because they could not be construed as payments to Medicare beneficiaries; the design and administration of the arrangement interposed an independent charitable organization between donors and patients, provided sufficient insulation so that the charity's subsidy of copayments and deductibles would not be attributed to any donor, and appeared unlikely to influence a beneficiary's selection of a particular provider since patients selected their own providers and were free to change providers at any time. The OIG also would not impose sanctions under the CMP statute because the charity's subsidies for copayments, deductibles and Medigap premiums was not likely to influence any beneficiary's selection of a particular provider and would instead expand beneficiaries' freedom of choice.

Advisory Opinion No. 02-2
Issued Apr. 4, 2002, posted Apr. 11, 2002

A nonprofit state-licensed ambulance company, which used each of its ambulances on average at least three times per week for emergency runs, also provided non-emergency and scheduled transports to two nonprofit hospitals that restocked certain drugs and supplies used during emergency transports without charge to all ambulance companies within their region on a uniform basis, in compliance with detailed regional protocols established by the county medical authority and state EMS rules. The hospitals documented the items restocked and provided copies to the ambulance company, which would maintain them for five years and make them available to HHS upon request. The ambulance company certified that there would be no duplicate billing for restocked drugs or supplies, that the arrangement would not take into account the volume or value of referrals, and that the parties would comply with all federal, state, and local laws regulating ambulance services.

Conclusion: The arrangement satisfied the "general replenishing" safe harbor for ambulance restocking arrangements under 42 C.F.R. §1001.952(v)(3)(i).

Advisory Opinion No. 02-3
Issued Apr. 4, 2002, posted Apr. 11, 2002

A quasi-governmental state agency responsible for planning, implementing and monitoring the development of the EMS system proposed a formal, written, region-wide ambulance restocking program applicable to all ambulance providers in its jurisdiction whereby participating hospitals receiving emergency transport patients would restock the ambulance at no charge.

Conclusion: The arrangement satisfied the "general replenishing" safe harbor for ambulance restocking arrangements under 42 C.F.R. §1001.952(v)(3)(i).

Advisory Opinion No. 02-4
  Issued Apr. 19, 2002, posted Apr. 26, 2002
  A DME company proposed to enter written agreements with hospitals and clinics by which it would place portable oxygen equipment on-site for distribution to patients whose physicians ordered the equipment for home use and who elected to obtain the equipment from the company. The company certified that it would not pay the hospitals and clinics for use of "consignment closets" and, accordingly, that they would receive no remuneration. To protect patient freedom of choice, the company would provide a list of local DME suppliers and encourage the hospitals and clinics to give the list to their patients. The DME company would bill the patient or insurer.
  Conclusion: The OIG would not impose sanctions because no remuneration would flow from the DME company to its potential referral sources—the hospitals and clinics, acting as distributors.

Advisory Opinion No. 02-5
  Issued May 7, 2002, posted May 14, 2002
  A radiation oncology group practice providing both professional and technical radiation therapy services proposed to restructure into two separate legal entities. The reorganized company, which would continue to own and operate radiation therapy equipment, would provide technical radiation therapy services and bill the technical component. The newly formed entity would be a professional organization providing and billing the professional component. The two physician-owners, each owning one-half of the existing company, would each own one-half of the reorganized company and one-half of the new professional organization.
  Conclusion: The OIG would not impose sanctions because the mere reorganization of an existing, unified group practice into separate legal entities did not create a substantial risk of fraud or abuse where the ownership of both reorganized entities was identical to the original entity and the ongoing operations of the reorganized entities were substantially the same as the original entity.

Advisory Opinion No. 02-6
  Issued May 12, 2002, posted May 22, 2002
  A manufacturer and seller of equipment for filtering blood in the treatment of rheumatoid arthritis proposed to refund the purchase price of the equipment to a hospital if a fiscal intermediary denied payment for treatments made with the equipment. For each purchasing hospital, the refund offer expired on the earlier of the 120th day after the first delivery or the hospital's first receipt of notice of a denial by the FI. To qualify for a refund: (1) the treatment must meet the criteria set out in a CMS National Coverage Decision (NCD); (2) the payment denial must be sustained through the first level of appeal; (3) the patient must be a registered out-patient whose primary insurer is Medicare; and (4) the hospital must submit to Medicare all necessary documentation for the claim. If the company refunded the purchase

price, the hospital would be required to report the refund to all payors, refund collected deductibles and copayments to the patient and/or adjust statements to payors to reflect the refund, and upon request, provide the company with proof of these actions and federal and state health care officials with information about the refund program.

Conclusion: The OIG would not impose sanctions because the following safeguards reduced the risk of fraud and abuse: (1) the manufacturer reported the existence of the refund program on the initial invoice to each hospital; (2) the reimbursement guarantee was limited in time to the initial delivery of the equipment or payment denial and in amount to the purchase price of the equipment (no patient care expenses were reimbursed); (3) the guarantee was limited in scope to treatments for outpatients who met the NDC coverage conditions and to Medicare claims through the first level of appeal: and (4) the hospitals agreed to reporting and refunding obligations.

Advisory Opinion No. 02-7
Issued June 5, 2002, posted June 12, 2002

A Medicare-certified (but *not* Medicaid-certified) provider of portable X-ray and other services proposed to waive Part B coinsurance amounts for the X-ray services provided to Full Dual Eligibles who reside in nursing facilities, but would continue to bill and collect X-ray copayments from nursing facility residents who are Qualified Medicare Beneficiaries and from patients who reside in other locations. The state Medicaid program pays the Part B cost-sharing amounts for Qualified Medicare Beneficiaries, but not for Full Dual Eligibles, because portable X-ray services are not state Medicaid benefits. The provider argued that the proposed waiver would reduce the administrative burden on nursing facilities because without the waiver Full Dual Eligibles would be required to pay their Part B copayments for portable X-ray services, which would then require the facilities to do to a monthly, rather than annual, adjustment of the amount residents must pay toward their nursing facility costs (the residents' net available monthly income).

Conclusion: The OIG did not approve the proposed waiver because it presented significant anti-kickback concerns that could not be resolved without a determination of the parties' intent, which is beyond the scope of the advisory opinion process. Significant problems precluding the issuance of a favorable opinion were: (1) the waiver was not based upon an individualized, good faith assessment of a beneficiary's financial need, nor applied uniformly to all of the provider's customers since it would be offered to some beneficiaries in some locations for some services; (2) the waiver would benefit nursing facilities, which are potential referral sources for the provider, by increasing their cash flow and reducing the paperwork necessary to recalculate the NAMI; and (3) the waiver, by giving the provider a competitive advantage in seeking business from nursing homes, would exert pressure on competitors to make similar waivers

Advisory Opinion No. 02-8
  Issued June 12, 2002, posted June 19, 2002
  An ambulance district, a publicly funded, political subdivision of a county, that is the sole provider of 911 emergency medical treatment and transportation for county residents, proposed to bill residents or their insurers (including federal health care programs) only to the extent of their insurance coverage, and to treat operating revenues received from local taxes as payment of the copayments and deductibles due from residents.

  Conclusion: Sanctions would not be imposed because the arrangement would not constitute prohibited remuneration under CMS Carrier Manual §2309.4, which specifies that facilities owned and operated by political subdivisions which waive copayments and deductibles from bona fide residents are not to be denied reimbursement on the ground that they have provided free services.

Advisory Opinion No. 02-9
  Issued June 14, 2002, posted June 21, 2002
  A physician, who is a member of a group practice and derives at least one-third of his medical practice income from all sources from endoscopic procedures that he performs in his office or at a local hospital, proposed to become the sole investor in and sole owner of a surgical center that will own and operate a freestanding, Medicare-certified, endoscopy ASC. He certified that (1) fees for endoscopic procedures he performs anywhere will be distributed solely to him; (2) the surgical center's operating and recovery room space will be dedicated exclusively to the ASC; (3) he will inform referred patients of his investment interest; (4) neither the ASC nor the group practice will loan funds to or guarantee a loan for the physician if any part of the loan will be used to obtain his investment interest; (5) all ancillary services for federal health care program beneficiaries performed at the ASC will be directly and integrally related to primary procedures performed at there, and will not be separately billed to Medicare or another federal health care program; and (6) the ASC and physician will treat patients receiving benefits under any federal health care program in a nondiscriminatory manner.

  Conclusion: The proposed arrangement fits within the 42 C.F.R. §1001.952(r)(2) safe harbor for investment interests in single-specialty ASCs

Advisory Opinion No. 02-10
  Issued July 30, 2002, posted Aug. 7, 2002
  A seller of dialysis equipment and supplies proposed two discount arrangements: (1) Discount A, a uniform discount based on aggregate annual purchases by the purchaser of any and all dialysis equipment and supplies; and (2) Discount B, a discount based on total annual purchases of certain items (which the requestor did not identify) or all items if the purchaser buys a minimum quantity of one or more certain items.

Conclusion: Although the proposed discounts did not fit the 42 C.F.R. §1001.952(h) discount safe harbor because dialysis equipment and services are reimbursed under three different Medicare methodologies, the OIG would not impose administrative sanctions with regard to Discount A because the following safeguards limited the risk of fraud and abuse: (1) the different Medicare payment methodologies result in almost identical payments for discounted equipment and supplies; and (2) the seller certified that it will meet all of the discount safe harbor requirements for sellers. With regard to Discount B, the OIG concluded that it could potentially impose sanctions because of the potential for abuse inherent in "bundling"; it could not determine whether dialysis goods would be supplied at a reduced charge to induce the purchase of other products nor whether the federal health care programs would share appropriately in the discounts.

Advisory Opinion No. 02-11
Issued Aug. 12, 2002, posted Aug. 19, 2002

Pursuant to its legislative mandate to support the state university academic medical center, the state hospital authority (the AMC component responsible for operating the teaching hospital) proposed to make a substantial charitable contribution to the university endowment association (an independent nonprofit corporation that secures and manages funds donated to support university activities) to implement the AMC's cardiovascular services program. The grant was not subject to requirements as to the operation of the cardiovascular services program or referrals to the hospital. The university certified that: (1) total compensation paid by all AMC components to faculty physicians and physicians employed by the hospital authority was set in advance; and (2) it did not require or encourage any physicians to refer patients to the hospital, track referrals made by faculty physicians, or tie faculty physician compensation to the volume or value of referrals.

Conclusion: Although the proposed grant was a substantial donation by a hospital to a major referral source (the university was a referral source for the hospital authority, because the university employs and is affiliated with the faculty physicians who make referrals to the hospital), the OIG would not impose administrative sanctions because: (1) the grant was consistent with the shared public and charitable mission of the AMC components and the state legislation establishing the hospital authority; and (2) there were safeguards in place to insulate physician judgment and income from pressure to refer to the hospital.

Advisory Opinion No. 02-12
Issued Aug. 12, 2002, posted Aug. 19, 2002

A company proposed to contract with MCOs and employer-based health plans to operate an Internet-based incentive system that encourages individuals' compliance efforts with pharmacologic and behavior modification regimens prescribed by their physicians by awarding them "points" for taking desired actions. Physicians who participated at the election of their patients earned points for reviewing monthly patient information and compliance results but not for prescribing items or services. "Points" were redeemable only for goods and services that are not reimbursable by federal health care programs. To generate additional revenue, the company proposed to sell banner ads on its Web site for a fixed, predetermined amount to health care and non-health care advertisers, limiting pharmacy advertisers to those participating in the MCOs' networks. Participating pharmacies could include hyperlinks to their own Web sites in their ads for an additional, per-click fee, and may sponsor chat rooms and interactive forums a fixed, predetermined fee. Ads, sold at fair market value, must comply with the "Health on the Net Foundation Code of Conduct." Visitors could not link to a pharmacy Web site without affirmatively clicking on the hyperlink or effect purchases on a pharmacy Web site without affirmatively electing the purchase and having an opportunity to review it.

Conclusion: The behavior modification drug compliance services did not implicate the anti-kickback statute because these services were not generally reimbursable under federal health care programs. Incentive awards to patients and physicians, although remuneration, did not implicate either the anti-kickback or beneficiary inducement statutes because they are not redeemable for items or services reimbursable by a federal health care program.

In addition, the OIG would not impose sanctions in connection with either the fixed or per-click advertising fees, as long as the fees represented fair market value and did not vary based on the volume or value of business generated from the advertising, nor in connection with the chat-room sponsorship fees. Given the "ubiquity of paid advertising" and the safeguards implemented for hyperlinks, viewers should be able to distinguish paid advertising from a substantive recommendation.

Advisory Opinion No. 02-13
Issued Sept. 27, 2002, posted Oct. 4, 2002

A pharmaceutical company proposed to establish and completely fund a nonprofit, tax-exempt foundation whose sole purpose is to subsidize Medicare Part B beneficiaries' copayment for one of its drugs. The company planned to advertise the financial assistance program to physicians. The charity would determine a patient's eligibility based on financial need without considering the identity of the referring person or physician and provide partial or full subsidization for up to three years.

Conclusion: The OIG did not approve the arrangement because it implicates the anti-kickback statute and poses a substantial risk of federal health care program and patient fraud and abuse because (1) the waiver of the copayment was unlike that of a provider's unadvertised, non-routine waiver based on financial need; (2) physicians would receive full payment for prescribing the drug (i.e., 80% from Medicare, 20% from the foundation); (3) the company would obtain a financial advantage because the incentive to use competing drugs, even if less expensive, would decrease; (4) by increasing the sale price of the drug and reporting a corresponding increase in the drug's average wholesale price (by which Medicare reimbursement is calculated), the company would be able to consistently maintain profits at the expense of the Medicare program; and (5) the company could further profit at Medicare's expense by making sure the drug's sale price exceeds the company's marginal variable cost plus copayment.

Advisory Opinion No. 02-14
Issued Sept. 30, 2002, posted Oct. 7, 2002

A for-profit provider of infusion therapy services proposed to give free personal safety equipment (e.g., helmets, kneepads, medical alert bracelets, tourniquets, cold packs, emergency contact folders, carrying cases for medications) to hemophilia patients and provide free electronic pagers and pager service to parents of pediatric patients. The retail value of the pager and pager service was estimated at $5–$15 per month.

Conclusion: Because the program created an improper inducement to beneficiaries and did not fall within the exceptions to CMPs for delivery of preventative care to asymptomatic persons or provision of goods of nominal value ($10 per item, $50 in the aggregate annually), the OIG would not protect the program. However, the OIG would not impose sanctions under the anti-kickback or CMP statute, provided the annual benefits to any particular beneficiary do not exceed $10 per item and $50 in the aggregate.

Advisory Opinion No. 02-15
Issued Sept. 30, 2002, posted Oct. 7, 2002

A fire district organized as a municipal corporation that is the exclusive EMS provider for county resident proposed to bill residents or their insurers (including federal health care programs) only to the extent of their insurance coverage, and to treat revenues received from local taxes as payment of the copayments and deductibles due from residents.

Conclusion: Sanctions would not be imposed because the arrangement would not constitute prohibited remuneration under CMS Carrier Manual §2309.4, which specifies that facilities owned and operated by political subdivisions that waive copayments and deductibles from bona fide residents are not to be denied reimbursement on the ground that they have provided free services.

Advisory Opinion No. 02-16
Issued Dec. 23, 2002, posted Jan. 3, 2003

A nationwide supplier of blood glucose testing products proposed to enter an agreement with a drug manufacturer by which it would purchase self-monitored blood glucose supplies from the manufacturer and distribute the supplies to patients participating in a clinical trial of patients with Type II diabetes and coronary heart disease initiated by the National Institutes of Health (ACCORD). The supplier, in accordance with NIH historical practice, would waive Part B copayments for the supplies.

Conclusion: Although the waiver of copayments without regard to financial hardship implicates both the anti-kickback and CMP statutes, the OIG would not impose sanctions because the arrangement reasonably accommodates the needs of an important, government-sponsored scientific study without posing a significant risk of fraud and abuse. Specifically: (1) the ACCORD scientific study was initiated, organized, funded, and managed exclusively by an NIH institute; (2) unlike many privately sponsored clinical trials, the study is not intended to develop or benefit any specific commercial product; and (3) NIH believes AC-CORD is likely to have significant consequences for the treatment of all affected patients, including Medicare beneficiaries.

YEAR 2003

Advisory Opinion No. 03-1
Issued Jan. 13, 2003, posted Jan. 21, 2003
Editor's Note: Advisory Op. No. 03-1 did not address issues under the anti-kickback statute.

Advisory Opinion No. 03-2
Issued Jan. 13, 2003, posted Jan. 21, 2003
A nonprofit, tax exempt hospital proposed to acquire an ownership interest in an orthopedic ASC organized as an LLC that is indirectly owned by a physician group practice through a wholly owned holding company in exchange for capital contributions and loans. The proposed arrangement included ancillary agreements: (1) a management service agreement with the group at a fixed annual fee; (2) a facility support agreement with the hospital providing quality assurance and utilization management procedures, shared purchasing for supplies and services, gas services, and code team services for the surgical center; (3) leases between the ASC and the hospital and the group and the hospital; and (4) a noncompetition agreement. The management service and facility support agreements met the safe harbors of 42 C.F.R. §1001.952(d) except for the minimum one-year term requirement, and C.F.R. §1001.952(r)(4) except for the requirements that (1) the hospital not influence referrals; (2) the physicians' interests be held directly by those who meet all the safe harbor requirements; and (3) anything provided by the hospital must comply with a safe harbor.

Conclusion: Although the proposed arrangement did not qualify for safe harbor protections under 42 C.F.R. §1001.952(r), the OIG would not impose sanctions under the anti-kickback statute because the arrangement provides safeguards that constrain the hospital's ability to direct or influence the referrals of its hospital-affiliated physicians to the ASC. The safeguards included: (1) hospital-affiliated physicians will not make referrals directly to the ASC, the group, or the group shareholders, nor will the hospital encourage or track such referrals,

(2) physicians' compensation would not be based on the value or volume of referrals made, and (3) the hospital would inform its physicians of the foregoing measures annually. In addition, neither the deviations from the personal services/management agreement safe harbor requirements nor the noncompetition agreement posed increased risk of fraud or abuse.

Advisory Opinion No. 03-3
Issued Feb. 3, 2003, posted Feb. 12, 2003

A pharmaceutical company manufactures and markets branded self-administered immunosuppressive drugs that a patient must use for the rest of his or her life after an organ transplant. Starting in 2000, Medicare Part B removed a 36-month limit on coverage (effectively creating lifetime coverage) and paid dispensing pharmacies at 95% of the average wholesale price (AWP) of the lowest-cost similar product, which resulted in a patient cost-sharing amount in excess of $1,200 per year. Before the removal of the 36-month limit on coverage, the company's patient assistance program (PAP) provided the drugs at no cost to financially needy, uninsured patients meeting income criteria, including Medicare beneficiaries who had exhausted their coverage. The company proposed to modify its PAP to reimburse the copayment amounts of financially needy Medicare transplant patients who buy the drug from any pharmacy.

Conclusion: The proposed arrangement would not implicate the CMP statute because the company is not a provider, practitioner, or supplier within the meaning of 42 U.S.C. §1320a-7a(a)(5) and, because the beneficiary may buy the drugs at any pharmacy, the arrangement is not likely to influence the selection of a particular supplier. However, depending on intent, the proposed arrangement could be grounds for administrative sanctions under the anti-kickback statute because: the company would pay beneficiaries who use its product, which, for an expensive drug for a chronic condition, can result in considerable profit for the company despite the patient subsidy; the subsidy provides the drugs with a financial advantage over competing drugs; insulating beneficiaries from financial liability can increase Medicare costs; and there are non-abusive alternatives for assisting needy patients (*see, e.g.,* OIG Adv. Op. Nos. 02-1, 97-1, 98-17). In contrast to permissible non-routine copayment waivers by the pharmacy supplying the drugs based on individual financial need, the pharmacy would receive the full payment (80% from Medicare, 20% from the patient) under the arrangement and the availability of assistance would be advertised to transplant physicians, patient advocacy groups, and others.

Advisory Opinion No. 03-4
Issued Feb. 3, 2003, posted Feb. 12, 2003

A for-profit provider of home health care services proposed to provide its homebound patients free medical alert pagers and pager monitoring services to facilitate a rapid response to those who need emergency assistance. The benefit is worth between $20 and $30 per month and $240 to $360 per year.

Conclusion: Although the value of the proposed benefit exceeded the threshold of $10 per item and $50 in the aggregate, per patient, per year set for free services, the OIG would not impose administrative sanctions under the anti-kickback or CMP statute. Given CMS's express encouragement of innovative telehealth technologies in the delivery of home health care (HIM 201.13, interpreting 42 U.S.C. §1395fff(e)(1)), the OIG concluded that provision of the benefit would not be an impermissible inducement. Because the benefit ensured prompt emergency assistance and potentially forestalled the need for more expensive services, it was reasonably related to the delivery of home health services and the fostering of efficiency and quality of care.

Advisory Opinion No. 03-5
Issued Feb. 6, 2003, posted Feb. 13, 2003

A company was formed as an LLC by an acute care hospital, which owns 49%, and a multi-specialty group, which owns 51%, to operate an ASC. The ASC, which maintains an open medical staff, was located on hospital land and leased to the ASC under a written lease. The group has 52 shareholders who are physicians and employees of the group, which also employs other health care professionals. Most of the group physicians are not surgeons. The group physicians' compensation did not take into account referrals to the ASC or the volume of surgical procedures the physicians performed. The hospital employs 42 physicians. Physicians employed by the group perform approximately 25% of the surgeries at the hospital.

Conclusion: The proposed arrangement could generate prohibited remuneration and because the arrangement does not fall within the group practice safe harbor, 42 C.F.R. §1001.952(r)(3), the OIG could impose sanctions under the anti-kickback statute. Safe harbor protection is limited to physician-investors who use the ASC on a regular basis as part of their practices or who practice the same specialty as other physician-investors; the majority of the group physicians fit neither category. The proposed arrangement poses the same risks as an ASC owned directly by surgeons and primary care physicians in the same community and the indirect ownership through a multi-speciality group practice does not reduce the risk the venture may be used to reward referrals.

Advisory Opinion No. 03-6
Issued Mar. 19, 2003, posted Mar. 26, 2003

In response to a county's request for proposal, a medical center proposed to enter into a two-year written agreement: (1) to be the exclusive provider of physician services to a county-owned women's health clinic for a below-fair-market-value fee and (2) to provide inpatient hospital services for the clinic's primarily indigent and low-income patients at no charge. The medical center agreed to move its OB/GYN residency program to the clinic and accept as full payment for its services an amount equal to the additional costs it incurred over the costs of its existing residency program, including paying its medical director for an additional morning per week and a "cushion" for costs not calculated or calculable. The medical center had been formed as the result of a merger between a county hospital and a nonprofit corporation, and, as a result of the merger, the medical center had an obligation to provide care to indigent patients. Approximately 22% of the clinic's patients had Medicaid coverage, while approximately 66% were self-pay indigent patients who would pay on a sliding scale basis.

Conclusion: Although the OIG believed that the proposed arrangement raised potential anti-kickback issues because the medical center may have offered a below-fair-market-value fee for physician services at the clinic to gain access to, or control over, referrals of inpatient obstetrical services payable by Medicaid, the OIG would not impose administrative sanctions absent undisclosed aggravating factors (e.g., overutilization, inappropriate higher costs to federal programs) because: (1) although below-fair-market-value, the medical center's fee was not unreasonable, as it was sufficient to cover the medical center's costs and the arrangement would strengthen the medical center's OB/GYN residency program by exposing residents to a broader range of medical conditions; (2) the opportunity to generate referrals to the medical center's hospital was offset by its agreement to provide inpatient hospital and physician services for clinic patients regardless of their ability to pay; (3) the putative prohibited remuneration (the county's avoided costs for physician services at the clinic) inured to the public benefit; (4) there was no adverse impact on competition because the county used an open competitive bidding process and the arrangement was for only two years; and (5) overutilization or increased cost to federal health care programs was unlikely because the clinic would generate mostly labor and delivery hospital business, which is reimbursed by the state's Medicaid program on a prospective fixed fee basis.

Advisory Opinion No. 03-7
Issued Mar. 19, 2003, posted Mar. 26, 2003

A hospital district and a Medicare-certified end stage renal dialysis provider proposed to enter a competitively bid one-year contract under which the ESRD contractor would: (1) provide acute hemodialysis service to the hospital district's inpatients at fair market value; (2) purchase the hospital district's 10 hemodialysis machines at fair market value; (3) provide chronic hemodialysis service regardless of ability to pay to 19 indigent patients currently grandfathered under the hospital district's program; and (4) accept referrals of all other patients needing chronic hemodialysis services who do not currently qualify for treatment under the hospital district's program.

Conclusion: Although the proposed arrangement raised potential anti-kickback issues because it could result in the hospital district referring federal health program business to the contractor in exchange for free services to indigent patients that the hospital district would otherwise have to fund, the OIG would not impose administrative sanctions because the following factors mitigated the risk of fraud or abuse: (1) the cost to the federal government would not increase because criteria for qualifying for chronic hemodialysis are well established and generally sufficient to deter unnecessary services; (2) any possible putative remuneration (avoided costs for providing chronic hemodialysis to the indigent and uninsured) inured to public, not private, benefit; (3) there was no adverse impact on competition since the hospital district employed an open competitive bidding process and the arrangement was for only one year; (4) it was unclear whether the hospital district could influence referrals for the type of services involved and any influence was likely to be greatest for indigent patients; and (5) because some of the free hemodialysis services would be provided by community ESRD facilities that were not involved in the proposed arrangement or affiliated with the contractor, the effort to provide free services to the grandfathered and other indigent patients could be characterized as a shared effort of the local community of ESRD facilities.

Advisory Opinion No. 03-8
Issued Apr. 3, 2003, posted Apr. 10, 2003

A company proposed to enter into agreements with general acute care hospitals whereby it would develop and manage each hospital's "distinct part" inpatient rehabilitation unit in exchange for a monthly management fee calculated on a per-patient-per-day basis. The manager would provide all patient care personnel (other than nurses, who would be provided by the hospital) and a leadership team consisting of a program director, community outreach coordinator and medical director (who might have a private practice and who might refer patients to the unit). The medical director agreement would be protected under the safe harbor for personal services and management contracts, 42 C.F.R. §1001.952(d). The leadership team would interact with physicians, hospital discharge planning personnel, and third-party payors' utilization review personnel (who might have the ability to make or influence referrals). The company would not directly solicit Medicare and Medicaid beneficiaries or other patients. Approximately 70 percent of the patients in the managed units would be Medicare beneficiaries whose care would be paid for under the PPS system.

Conclusion: The arrangement did not qualify for safe harbor protection under 42 C.F.R. §1001.952(d) because the compensation paid under the management agreement was calculated on a per-patient-per-day basis, and its aggregate amount therefore was not set in advance. The OIG declined to grant protection because there were insufficient safeguards to limit the risk of overutilization: (1) while the PPS payment methodology offset concern about excessive lengths of stay, it did not reduce the risk of overutilization since the company and hospital had an incentive to fill all beds; (2) the OIG was not in a position to determine whether the criteria for admission for the specified conditions for which the company would manage care could be manipulated; (3) the hospital-employed nurses working in the units would share the company's goal of making the program a success; (4) the medical director would be in a position to generate patients for the unit; (5) the company would perform community outreach, including marketing; and (6) the per-patient-per-day fee might also cloak a success fee.

Advisory Opinion No. 03-9
Issued Apr. 17, 2003, posted Apr. 25, 2003
A municipal fire district that was the exclusive provider of emergency medical services for residents of its service area proposed to bill residents, including those covered by federal health care programs, only to the extent of their insurance coverage and to treat revenues received from local taxes as payment of any applicable copayments and deductibles (i.e., institute "insurance-only" billing). Employees of property-tax-paying businesses located in the district would be treated as residents while working on the business premises.

Conclusion: The OIG would not impose sanctions because, under CMS Carriers Manual §2309.4, municipal fire districts that waive copayments and deductibles from their residents are not viewed as furnishing free services, and may therefore receive Medicare payments. According to CMS, §2309.4 also applies to waivers of cost-sharing amounts for employees of property tax-paying businesses located in the fire district while they work on the business premises.

Advisory Opinion No. 03-10
Issued May 8, 2003, posted May 15, 2003
A non-SELECT Medigap insurer proposed to contract with a PPO to include its policyholders in the PPO's hospital network. Under the contract, the insurer would receive a discount (of up to 100 percent) from a network hospital on the Medicare Part A deductible incurred by a policyholder for an inpatient stay at the hospital. (The insurer would otherwise have been obligated to its insureds to pay the deductible under its Medigap policies.) In exchange, the insurer would pay the PPO a fee (e.g. $50) each time the insurer received a discount. The insurer would return a portion of the savings to its policyholders who had an inpatient stay by providing them a $100 credit toward their next renewal premium. This feature would be announced in the Medigap plan materials given to policyholders and in the insurer's marketing materials. The insurer would continue to pay the full deductible for policyholders admitted to non-network hospitals.

Conclusion: Despite the fact that this type of arrangement was expressly denied safe harbor protection, the OIG concluded that it would not impose sanctions under the anti-kickback statute as a result of the discounted deductibles. The OIG believed that the discounts, in combination with Medigap coverage, presented a low risk of fraud or abuse because: (1) they would not affect per service Medicare payments since Part A payments for inpatient services are fixed and unaffected by beneficiary cost-sharing; (2) they would not increase utilization since the patients had already purchased supplemental insurance; (3) hospital competition would not be unfairly affected since PPO membership was open to any hospital; and (4) the arrangement would not affect professional medical judgment since physicians would receive no remuneration and patients could go to any hospital without incurring additional out-of-pocket expense. For similar reasons, the OIG would not impose anti-kickback sanctions based on the premium credits given to the insureds. Although the premium credits implicated the CMP statute by encouraging policyholders to choose network hospitals, the OIG would not impose sanctions because the credits were similar to the differentials in cost-sharing amounts that are allowed when made as part of a health plan design by 42 U.S.C. §1320a-7a(i)(6)(C).

Advisory Opinion No. 03-11
Issued May 21, 2003, posted May 28, 2003

A nonprofit corporation provided emergency ambulance services on a subscription basis. Individuals and businesses paid a fixed annual subscription fee ($20 for individuals; subscription fees for businesses were proportionate to their size). The corporation did not collect Part B cost-sharing amounts from subscribers (other than supplemental insurance coverage amounts), but collected such amounts from nonsubscribers through its contracted billing agent.

Conclusion: The OIG indicated that it would not impose sanctions if either: (1) subscription revenue for all subscribers exceeded the cost-sharing amounts reasonably expected to be waived for all subscribers; or (2) subscription revenues from Part B beneficiaries exceeded the cost-sharing amounts reasonably expected to be waived for subscribing Part B beneficiaries. Because both tests were satisfied, the subscription plan was not viewed as a disguised waiver of Part B cost-sharing amounts.

Advisory Opinion No. 03-12
Issued May 22, 2003, posted May 29, 2003

A medical center and a holding company formed by six radiologists who were the sole shareholders of a professional association meeting the 42 C.F.R. §1001.952(p) group practice safe harbor proposed to own and operate an outpatient open MRI facility. Profits and losses would be split 51 percent/49 percent in accordance with the medical center's and radiology group's capital contributions. The facility would be the only open MRI facility in the medical center's service area. Under ancillary agreements, the radiology group would be the exclusive provider of professional radiology services and would bill patients and their third-party payors directly for the professional component, the medical center would provide clerical staff and technicians in exchange for payment equal to the medical center's payroll expense for those employees, and the group would sublease equipment and assign a lease for space to the facility. Referrals from the medical center and its affiliated physician would be less than 10 percent of all referrals.

Conclusion: Although the proposed arrangement did not satisfy the 42 C.F.R. §1000.952(a)(2) small entity investment safe harbor because it failed to meet the "60-40" tests, the OIG approved the arrangement because only a small portion of referrals would come from the medical center and its affiliated physicians, and, unlike most hospital-physician joint ventures, the investing radiologists were not referral sources for the MRI facility or medical center. Other favorable features included (1) annual notification of all medical center affiliated physicians that the medical center would not encourage or track referrals to the facility and would not base compensation on such referrals, and (2) returns on investment that were proportional to capital investments (not to referrals). The ancillary agreements would not increase the risk because the radiologists billed patients directly, no payments flowed from the facility to the radiology group under the personal services agreement, and the medical center staffing and the equipment and space leasing agreements would require the facility to pay only the actual expenses incurred by the medical center and radiology group.

Advisory Opinion No. 03-13
Issued June 16, 2003, posted June 23, 2003

An MRI center in a federally designated rural area that was not a medically underserved area (MUA) had been owned by a limited partnership since 1990. To raise capital, the partnership proposed to offer limited partnership interests to all members of its local medical community, regardless of hospital affiliation, and to all former members of the boards of the area hospitals on the same terms, regardless of ability to refer patients to, or generate business for, the MRI center. Return on investments was directly proportional to the investor's capital contribution. A local nonprofit hospital leased space to the center, and its supporting foundation, which was the venture's managing partner, owned approximately 30% of the partnership. Various other parties in a position to generate referrals or provide items or services owned approximately 30% of the units, and community members and physicians not in a position to refer owned 40%. The hospital, its foundation, and physician-investors generated 37% of the center's revenues; referrals from disinterested parties generated more than 60%. The center had a management agreement with a radiology group (none of whose members were investors in the center).

Conclusion: Although the arrangement did not meet the 60/40 or MUA investment safe harbors under 42 C.F.R. §1000.952(a), the OIG approved the arrangement because: (1) the center was a bona fide business venture as demonstrated by the same opportunity to invest being offered to both physicians and non-physicians; return on investment being directly proportional to the investor's capital contribution; and because less than 40% of the revenue was derived from business generated by interested investors; (2) the joint venture's structure had none of the suspect characteristics addressed in the OIG's Special Fraud Alert: Joint Venture Arrangements (*see* §1500.06.A.2.); (3) the arrangement was a community-oriented effort to provide MRI services in the rural area, with 85% of patients coming from the area; and (4) the center certified that safe harbors protected the management agreement (42 C.F.R. §1001.952(d)) and space lease (42 C.F.R. §1001.952(b)).

Advisory Opinion No. 03-14
Issued June 26, 2003, posted July 3, 2003

A for-profit ambulance company and a nonprofit hospital serving a 17-county rural area in which trauma victims experienced higher mortality and disability rates than other parts of the state proposed to provide for 24-hour emergency transport of trauma victims. The ambulance company would purchase, operate, staff, manage, and maintain a helicopter equipped with a mobile intensive care unit, and the hospital would provide a landing pad adjacent to its facilities, modest crew quarters, and related utility and security services that could be used by any ambulance company. The destination hospital for area trauma victims was based on predetermined, objective criteria established by regional trauma advisory councils (RACs).

Conclusion: The OIG approved the arrangement because it presented a minimal risk of program abuse while providing significant community benefit. Because the arrangement related only to EMS, it posed little risk of overutilzation and would not steer patients to the hospital since there were extensive regulatory protocols for the trauma care system. Functioning in the context of a state-supervised, coordinated EMS effort, the arrangement would be overseen by the RACs and would likely have a positive impact on the quality of patient care by providing fast and effective pre-hospital trauma care.

Advisory Opinion No. 03-15
Issued Dec. 11, 2003, posted Dec. 18, 2003

A medical group practice and a hospital the group had owned before donating it to a nonprofit corporation in 1963 proposed to reunite as follows: (1) the group would transfer its assets (including its nursing and technical support workforce) to the hospital in exchange for a payment equal to the amount necessary to satisfy all encumbrances related to the transferred assets; (2) the hospital would give the group "meaningful representation" on the hospital's board of directors (the IRS having privately ruled that the proposed restructuring would not affect the hospital's tax-exempt status); and (3) the hospital would buy the office building owned by the trustee of the group's retirement plan and the group would relocate to space the hospital would provide at its clinic. The hospital and group would enter: (1) a 10-year professional services agreement (PSA) whereby the group would be the exclusive provider of professional services in the hospital's outpatient clinic and emergency department in exchange for a fee that would provide substantially the same compensation for the group's physicians as they currently received; and (2) an administrative and support services agreement whereby the hospital would provide services to the group. All agreements would be consistent with fair market value in arms'-length transactions.

Conclusion: The OIG approved the proposed arrangement. Because the transfer of the group's assets to the hospital flowed in the same direction as the most obvious referral pattern, i.e., the physicians' referrals of their patients to the hospital, it generated little kickback concern. In addition, the ancillary PSA, administrative services and building purchase agreements were unlikely to generate prohibited remuneration from the hospital to the group because the agreements were at fair market value, any remuneration would be offset by the group's transfer of assets to the hospital, and the reintegration of the businesses was unlikely to generate measurable new business.

YEAR 2004

Advisory Opinion No. 04-01
  Issued Jan. 21, 2004, posted Feb. 9, 2004
  A nationwide supplier of blood glucose testing products proposed to waive Part B patient cost-sharing obligations for self-monitored blood glucose supplies used by Medicare beneficiaries who participate in the Bypass Angioplasty Revascularization Investigation 2 Diabetes clinical trial (BARI 2D) sponsored by the National Heart, Lung, and Blood Institute (NHLBI) (an institute of NIH), the National Institute of Diabetes and Digestive and Kidney Diseases, and the Centers for Disease Control and Prevention. Neither the supplier nor manufacturer were involved in developing the clinical protocol. NHLBI believed waiving cost-sharing obligations would promote patient participation throughout the study. The supplier also would waive cost-sharing obligations for privately insured participants and provide the supplies free of charge to uninsured participants.

  Conclusion: The OIG approved the proposed arrangement, despite the potential illegal inducement under the CMPL law and prohibited remuneration under the anti-kickback statute. The proposed arrangement reasonably accommodated the needs of an important government sponsored study without posing a significant risk of fraud and abuse because: (1) the NIH-sponsored scientific study was initiated, funded, and managed by NHLBI, which selected the study's clinical centers; (2) BARI 2D, neither a commercial study nor a product-oriented or product-specific study, was not intended for the development of any commercial product; and (3) NHLBI believed the public health and clinical issues addressed would be likely to have significant consequences for the treatment of all patients, including Medicare beneficiaries.

Advisory Opinion No. 04-02
  Issued Mar. 1, 2004, posted Mar. 8, 2004
  A fire department (a political subdivision of a municipality) that is the exclusive provider of EMS within the city limits proposed to im-

plement an ordinance that would fund EMS services through billing for services and a monthly utility fee on residents' water bills. The fire department would bill residents or their insurers (including federal health care programs) only to the extent of their insurance coverage and would treat the revenues received from the utility fee as payment of the copayments and deductibles due from residents.

Conclusion: The OIG would not impose sanctions because the insurance-only arrangement would not constitute prohibited remuneration under CMS Medicare Benefit Policy Manual §50.3, which provides that facilities owned and operated by a state or political subdivision that waive copayments and deductibles from bona fide residents are not treated as providing free services and are entitled to Medicare payment.

Advisory Opinion No. 04-03
Issued May 21, 2002, posted June 1, 2004

An independent marketing company contracted with pharmaceutical companies to survey physicians on their drug labeling and product information preferences. The surveys, which are printed on the back of one dollar checks payable to the responding physician, made a few product-specific statements, asked the physician to respond to four to six questions rating the importance of including the information in the product information, and provided limited information on services and materials available from the pharmaceutical company. The pharmaceutical companies provided targeted lists of physicians to survey. The marketing company ensured no physician would receive more than 12 surveys per year. The marketing company provided the pharmaceutical company with aggregate survey data that could not be tied to an individual physician and forwarded physician requests for product information to the pharmaceutical company's fulfillment mailing facility without information about the physician's survey responses. The marketing company had no patient contact and no contact with physicians other than through the surveys.

Conclusion: Although the arrangement could generate prohibited remuneration under the anti-kickback statute, the OIG would not impose sanctions because the risk of fraud and abuse is mitigated by the following: (1) the $12 annual limit on compensation to physicians reduced the risk the physician payments were intended to induce referrals; (2) the aggregation of survey responses made the surveys an unlikely vehicle for identifying physicians who would be willing to accept improper payments; (3) the limited scope and nature of the survey questions reduced the likelihood the survey was intended to influence physicians' prescribing practices; (4) the marketing company, not being a health care provider or supplier, had no discernible ability to influence referrals to the pharmaceutical companies; and (5) the placement of the survey questions on checks physicians must endorse to deposit enhanced the integrity of the survey program by guarding against individuals other than physicians completing the surveys.

Advisory Opinion No. 04-4
  Issued May 26, 2004, posted June 2, 2004
  An association of state, student, and armed forces optometric associations proposed to provide free vision screening for infants, some of whom may have been covered by Medicaid. The association and a related charity would bear the administrative costs. A licensed optometrist serving on the association's board volunteered to direct the program. Participating association members would agree to screen infants for amblyopia ("lazy eye") free of charge, not condition the free screening on any other services, and, if they recommend additional examination or treatment, inform the infants' parents verbally and in writing of their freedom to choose any practitioner. The association would maintain a registry of participating optometrists on the internet or by calling a toll-free number, but would not recommend a particular optometrist. The program, developed under a memorandum of understanding with HHS as part of HHS's Healthy People 2010 initiative, would be promoted through the association and its affiliated state optometric associations, county health and related departments, and participating optometrists, who may contact their patients to inform them of the program.
  Conclusion: The OIG concluded that because the proposed program would satisfy all requirements of the 42 U.S.C. §1320a-7a(i)(6)(D) preventive care exception, it would not involve prohibited remuneration under the CMP law, and the following safeguards should ensure that the preventive care services would not be impermissibly tied to other Medicare- or Medicaid-reimbursable services: (1) the participating optometrists would agree not to condition the free services on the receipt of any other services and would inform the parents of their freedom to choose other providers for any recommended follow-up care; (2) the potential nexus between the screening and other services would be tenuous because the vast majority of infants will screen negative and the next recommended screening is more than one year after the free screening; (3) parents would select an optometrist from a list of all participants based on factors important to the parents and the association would not recommend particular optometrists for screening or follow-up care; (4) because few infants will require follow-up care, financial gain from subsequent paid visits would be offset by the cost of furnishing the free screenings; (5) payment of the administrative costs by the association and its charity would reduce optometrists' incentive to recommend follow-up care to recoup costs; and (6) free vision screening would confer a public benefit, furthering the charity's mission and HHS's Healthy People 2010 initiative. For similar reasons, the OIG would not impose administrative sanctions under the anti-kickback statute.

Advisory Opinion No. 04-5
  Issued June 2, 2004, posted June 9, 2004
  A laboratory partially owned by several pathologists proposed to participate in a charitable project that provided medical services for

low-income, uninsured county residents who were not eligible for any governmental assistance. The lab would provide services at no charge for project patients referred by the project's volunteer physicians. No remuneration would be made to volunteer physicians, the lab, pathologists performing the laboratory services, or the charitable project. Some physicians who volunteered in the project have made referrals to the lab outside the scope of the project for services payable by a federal health care program.

Conclusion: The OIG concluded that the proposed arrangement would not generate prohibited remuneration under the anti-kickback statute and would not be grounds for sanctions. The arrangement would pose no apparent risk of fraud and abuse because the charitable project would result in no economic value to any party in a position to refer federal health care program business to the lab, and the economic benefit of the lab's participation inures to the public good by increasing availability of services for an underserved population.

Advisory Opinion No. 04-06
Issued June 4, 2004, posted June 14, 2004
A fire district organized as a municipal corporation that supplied and billed for emergency ambulance services it provided through a closely related municipal fire department proposed to establish a fee schedule for emergency medical services. The proposed fee schedule included a base transport rate from which residents would receive a reduction, in consideration of the taxes they paid to support these services, consistent with applicable cost-sharing amounts otherwise due from them; i.e., residents would pay for ambulance services to the extent of their insurance coverage and operating revenues received from local taxes would be treated as payment of any other cost-sharing amounts due from the residents.

Conclusion: The OIG would not impose sanctions because the arrangement would not constitute prohibited remuneration under CMS Benefit Policy Manual Chap. 16, §50.3, which specifies that facilities owned and operated by political subdivisions that waive copayments and deductibles from bona fide residents are not to be denied reimbursement on the ground that they have provided free services.

Advisory Opinion No. 04-07
Issued June 17, 2004, posted June 24, 2004
An integrated nonprofit health care delivery system that operated a school-based health center program for low-income children in rural counties since 1992 added a telemedicine network to link the school-based centers with some of the health system's departments, a family medicine residency training program, a behavioral health center, and the community health department (the "hub sites"). Nurses seeing the students at the school-based centers (the "spoke sites") conducted screening tests and consulted with physicians at the hub sites about treatment and follow-up care. If the screening tests and

teleconsultations indicated students required treatment, they were referred to their regular primary care providers, or if they did not have one, school nurses provided lists of the primary care providers in the students' community. Many students were eligible for Medicaid or Children's Health Insurance Program benefits, which do not reimburse for telemedicine services. Neither the health system nor reimbursement from a federal health care program for teleconsultations or other services provided through the network.

Conclusion: Although the arrangement conferred benefits on three potential referral sources (the school-based health center "spoke" sites that obtained free telecommunications equipment and subsidized line charges; the consulting practitioners at the "hub" sites, who might receive additional opportunities to earn professional fees; and the patients), the OIG would not impose sanctions under the anti-kickback statute because the referral procedures provided sufficient safeguards to reduce the risk the remuneration would generate appreciable referrals of federal health care program business to the consulting practitioners. The OIG also concluded that the provision of the nonreimbursable screening services, which were not tied in any way to the provision of services reimbursable by a federal health care program, did not implicate the CMP prohibition on inducements to beneficiaries and noted the obvious public benefit in facilitating better access to screening services for low-income children in rural areas.

Advisory Opinion No. 04-08
Issued June 23, 2004, posted June 30, 2004

A physician group, a professional corporation comprised of five physicians, three of whom held an ownership interest in the PC, proposed to form an LLC to establish a comprehensive physical therapy center that would lease space, equipment, and the services of a staff therapist to the group's physicians and other physicians (collectively, the lessees). The center, located in the same building as all the lessees, will be open six days a week for eight hours a day and available to the lessees on an unlimited, first-come, first-served basis. The LLC will not bill Medicare, Medicaid, or third-party payors for services provided in the center; each lessee will bill insurers for services rendered to their patients at the center. The lessees will enter a one-year lease with the LLC, paying a monthly rental fee for unlimited use. Lessees using the staff therapist pay a higher rent than those providing their own therapists. The rent paid by each lessee (which does not include charges for the staff therapist) will be calculated at the beginning of the lease term by dividing the total of the fair market value of the monthly rent of all space, equipment, and administrative services by the total number of lessees; thus, each lessee would pay the same amount regardless of actual usage.

Conclusion: The OIG concluded that it could potentially impose administrative sanctions under the anti-kickback statute because the proposed arrangement did not qualify for any safe harbor and posed more than a minimal risk of fraud and abuse. The OIG treated the leases as multiple, overlapping, part-time leases that did not meet the safe harbor requirement that periodic, sporadic, or part-time leases must specify precisely the timing and duration of the rental periods and the compensation charged for each rental period. The proposed arrangement also failed to satisfy the provisions of the space, equipment, and personal services and management contracts safe harbors (42 C.F.R. §1001.952(b), 42 C.F.R. §1001.952(c), and 42 C.F.R. §1001.952(d)) requiring aggregate compensation to be set in advance, consistent with fair market value in an arms-length transaction. The structure of the overlapping, as-needed leases made fair market value difficult to monitor and document; increased the risk some physicians will pay more or less than fair market value; and, depending on the direction of referrals between the group and the lessees, created a risk that these above- or below-fair- market-value payments could be remuneration for referrals. Finally, basing rents on the total rental value of the center's equipment, space, and personnel services (rather than the usage) appeared to permit the LLC (and ultimately the group) to guarantee a desired maximum income stream and create a risk that the guaranteed income stream could be compensation in exchange for referrals.

Advisory Opinion No. 04-09
Issued July 15, 2004, posted July 22, 2004

A professional service corporation comprised of physicians who treat nursing home patients proposed to employ the primary care physicians who treated the patients before they were admitted to the nursing home as "consulting physicians" under an employment agreement requiring consulting physicians to be on call and available for telephone consultations 24 hours per day, seven days per week to respond to the treating physician's inquires in exchange for a payment of $50/hour based on the number of patients, capped at $750 per month for 15 hours of service provided for 20 or more patients. The IRS previously ruled privately that the consulting physicians were bona fide employees of the PSC. The PSC did not bill costs incurred for the consulting services to any patient, federal health care program, or other third-party payor.

Conclusion: Assuming the consulting physicians are bona fide employees under the IRS definition, the proposed arrangement qualified for the statutory exception and regulatory safe harbor for employee compensation (42 U.S.C. §1320a-7b(b)(3)(B), 42 C.F.R. §1001.952(i)) because compensation will be paid to the consulting physicians under an employment agreement for the furnishing of covered items and services. The OIG noted, however, that a similar arrangement with independent contractor physicians would not be protected.

Advisory Opinion No. 04-10
Issued August 4, 2004, posted August 11, 2004

A county that provides first responder services proposed to use an open competitive bidding process to award an exclusive two-year contract to an ambulance company for providing second responder services in connection with the county's emergency response system. Under the proposed arrangement, the second responder was required to to dispatches for ambulance transportation services and pay the county on a per-response basis for the providing first responder services. The second responder, which could bill payors (including Medicare and Medicaid) for the ambulance services and retain all collections, would be at substantial risk for nonpayment. The contract was awarded to the bidder offering to reimburse the county the highest per-response amount. The county certified that it expects the payments from the second responder to be less than the cost of its first responder services.

Conclusion: Although the county's solicitation of payment for first responder services in exchange for an exclusive contract to provide nearly all emergency secondary response ambulance transportation in the county implicates the anti-kickback statute, the OIG declined to impose sanctions based on the following factors: (1) the per-response fees were only one part of a comprehensive regulatory scheme to deliver EMS services: (2) the per-response fees were only partial compensation for the actual cost of delivering first responder services, so the winning bidder did not overpay for the source of referrals; (3) although the aggregate payment varied with the volume of referrals, it was unlikely to increase the risk of overutilization in the context of EMS services; (4) the contract exclusivity did not have an adverse impact on competition under a competitive bidding system; and (5) the putative prohibited remuneration (the county's receipt of the per-response fee) inured to the public benefit.

Appendix I

Office of Inspector General Compliance Materials and Related Industry Documents

Editor's Note: New in this print Supplement: Appendix I-3.1, the Compliance Program Guidance for Pharmaceutical Manufacturers, and Appendix I-3.2, the PhRMA Code on Interactions With Healthcare Professionals.

All Office of Inspector General compliance materials in **Appendix I** in the Main Volume are on the accompanying disk in the folder **OIGCOMPL**. The Compliance Program Guidance documents are in the subfolder **CPG**. The Corporate Integrity Agreement document is in the subfolder **CIA**.

File names for the individual documents on disk are shown on the right under the column "File Name."

Appendix		*File Name*	*Main Volume*	*Supplement*
I-1	**OIG Compliance Program Guidance for Hospitals** (63 Fed. Reg. 8987–8998 (Feb. 23, 1998))			
	Folder:			
	OIGCOMPL\CPG .... (*Source:* oig.hhs.gov/authorities/ docs/cpghosp.pdf)[1]	CPG_HOSP	disk	—
I-2	**OIG Compliance Program Guidance for Individual and Small Group Physician Practices** (65 Fed. Reg. 59,434–59,452 (Oct. 5, 2000))			
	Folder:			
	OIGCOMPL\CPG .... (*Source:* oig.hhs.gov/authorities/ docs/physician.pdf)	CPG_PHYS	disk	—

---

[1] Web addresses are subject to change. Readers may wish to check the OIG website for updates or further information on topics of interest: oig.hhs.gov.

---

[2]Vencor, Inc. has changed its name to Kindred Healthcare, Inc.

Appendix I-3

OIG Compliance Program Guidance
for Pharmaceutical Manufacturers
and PhRMA Code on Interactions
With Healthcare Professionals
[New Appendix]

Appendix I-3.1

OIG Compliance Program Guidance for Pharmaceutical Manufacturers (Apr. 2003) [New]

Source: Office of Inspector General, Department of Health & Human Services, 68 Fed. Reg. 23,731 (May 5, 2003), *available at* http://oig.hhs.gov/fraud/docs/complianceguidance/042803pharmacymfgnonfr.pdf

OFFICE OF INSPECTOR GENERAL'S COMPLIANCE PROGRAM GUIDANCE FOR PHARMACEUTICAL MANUFACTURERS

I. INTRODUCTION

The Office of Inspector General (OIG) of the Department of Health and Human Services is continuing in its efforts to promote voluntary compliance programs for the health care industry. This compliance guidance is intended to assist companies that develop, manufacture, market, and sell pharmaceutical drugs or biological products (pharmaceutical manufacturers) in developing and implementing internal controls and procedures that promote adherence to applicable statutes, regulations, and requirements of the federal health care programs[1] and in evaluating and, as necessary, refining existing compliance programs.

This guidance provides the OIG's views on the fundamental elements of pharmaceutical manufacturer compliance programs and principles that each pharmaceutical manufacturer should consider when creating and implementing an effective compliance program. This guide is not a compliance program. Rather, it is a set of guidelines that pharmaceutical manufacturers should consider when developing and implementing a compliance program or evaluating an existing one.

---

[1]The term "Federal health care programs," as defined in 42 U.S.C. 1320a-7b(f), includes any plan or program that provides health benefits, whether directly, through insurance, or otherwise, which is funded directly, in whole or in part, by the United States government or any state health plan (e.g., Medicaid or a program receiving funds from block grants for social services or child health services). In this document, the term "federal health care program requirements" refers to the statutes, regulations and other rules governing Medicare, Medicaid, and all other federal health care programs.

For those manufacturers with an existing compliance program, this guidance may serve as a benchmark or comparison against which to measure ongoing efforts.

A pharmaceutical manufacturer's implementation of an effective compliance program may require a significant commitment of time and resources by various segments of the organization. In order for a compliance program to be effective, it must have the support and commitment of senior management and the company's governing body. In turn, the corporate leadership should strive to foster a culture that promotes the prevention, detection, and resolution of instances of problems. Although an effective compliance program may require a reallocation of existing resources, the long-term benefits of establishing a compliance program significantly outweigh the initial costs.

In a continuing effort to collaborate closely with the pharmaceutical industry, the OIG published a notice in the *Federal Register* soliciting comments and recommendations on what should be included in this compliance program guidance.[2] Following our review of comments received in response to the solicitation notice, we published draft compliance guidance in the *Federal Register* in order to solicit further comments and recommendations.[3] In addition to considering the comments received in response to that solicitation notice and the draft compliance guidance, in finalizing this guidance we reviewed previous OIG publications, including OIG advisory opinions, safe harbor regulations (including the preambles) relating to the federal anti-kickback statute,[4] Special Fraud Alerts, as well as reports issued by the OIG's Office of Audit Services and Office of Evaluation and Inspections relevant to the pharmaceutical industry. (These materials are available on the OIG web page at http://oig.hhs.gov.) In addition, we relied on the experience gained from investigations of pharmaceutical manufacturers conducted by OIG's Office of Investigations, the Department of Justice, and the state Medicaid Fraud Control Units. We also held meetings with four groups of industry stakeholders—Pharmaceutical Research and Manufacturers of America (PhRMA) and pharmaceutical manufacturer representatives; health plan and health plan association representatives; representatives of pharmacy benefit managers (PBMs) and representatives of the American Medical Association (AMA) and its member organizations.

A. Benefits of a Compliance Program

The OIG believes a comprehensive compliance program provides a mechanism that addresses the public and private sectors' mutual goals of reducing fraud and abuse; enhancing health care provider operational functions; improving the quality of health care services;

---

[2]*See* 66 FR 31246 (June 11, 2001), "Notice for Solicitation of Information and Recommendations for Developing a Compliance Program Guidance for the Pharmaceutical Industry."

[3]*See* 67 FR 62057 (October 3, 2002), "Draft OIG Compliance Program Guidance for Pharmaceutical Manufacturers."

[4]42 U.S.C. 1320a-7b(b).

and reducing the cost of health care. Attaining these goals provides positive results to the pharmaceutical manufacturer, the government, and individual citizens alike. In addition to fulfilling its legal duty to avoid submitting false or inaccurate pricing or rebate information to any federal health care program or engaging in illegal marketing activities, a pharmaceutical manufacturer may gain important additional benefits by voluntarily implementing a compliance program. The benefits may include:

- a concrete demonstration to employees and the community at large of the company's commitment to honest and responsible corporate conduct;
- an increased likelihood of preventing, or at least identifying, and correcting unlawful and unethical behavior at an early stage;
- a mechanism to encourage employees to report potential problems and allow for appropriate internal inquiry and corrective action; and
- through early detection and reporting, minimizing any financial loss to the government and any corresponding financial loss to the company.

The OIG recognizes that the implementation of a compliance program may not entirely eliminate improper conduct from the operations of a pharmaceutical manufacturer. However, a good faith effort by the company to comply with applicable statutes and regulations as well as federal health care program requirements, demonstrated by an effective compliance program, significantly reduces the risk of unlawful conduct and any penalties that result from such behavior.

B. Application of Compliance Program Guidance

Given the wide diversity within the pharmaceutical industry, there is no single "best" pharmaceutical manufacturer compliance program. The OIG recognizes the complexities of this industry and the differences among industry members. Some pharmaceutical manufacturers are small and may have limited resources to devote to compliance measures. Conversely, other companies are well-established, large multi-national corporations with a widely dispersed work force. Some companies may have well-developed compliance programs already in place; others only now may be initiating such efforts. The OIG also recognizes that pharmaceutical manufacturers are subject to extensive regulatory requirements in addition to fraud and abuse-related issues and that many pharmaceutical manufacturers have addressed these obligations through compliance programs. Accordingly, the OIG strongly encourages pharmaceutical manufactures to develop and implement or refine (as necessary) compliance elements that uniquely address the areas of potential problems, common concern, or high risk that apply to their own companies (or, as applicable, to the U.S. operations of their companies).

For example, although they are not exhaustive of all potential risk areas, the OIG has identified three major potential risk areas for pharmaceutical manufacturers: (1) integrity of data used by state and federal governments to establish payment; (2) kickbacks and other illegal remuneration; and (3) compliance with laws regulating drug samples. The risk areas are discussed in greater detail in section II.B.2. below. The compliance measures adopted by a pharmaceutical manufacturer should be tailored to fit the unique environment of the company (including its organizational structure, operations and resources, as well as prior enforcement experience). In short, the OIG recommends that each pharmaceutical manufacturer should adapt the objectives and principles underlying the measures outlined in this guidance to its own particular circumstances.[5]

II. COMPLIANCE PROGRAM ELEMENTS

A. The Basic Compliance Elements

The OIG believes that every effective compliance program must begin with a formal commitment by the pharmaceutical manufacturer's board of directors or other governing body. Evidence of that commitment should include the allocation of adequate resources, a timetable for the implementation of the compliance measures, and the identification of an individual to serve as a compliance officer to ensure that each of the recommended and adopted elements is addressed. Once a commitment has been undertaken, a compliance officer should immediately be chosen to oversee the implementation of the compliance program.

The elements listed below provide a comprehensive and firm foundation upon which an effective compliance program may be built. Further, they are likely to foster the development of a corporate culture of compliance. The OIG recognizes that full implementation of all elements may not be immediately feasible for all pharmaceutical manufacturers. However, as a first step, a good faith and meaningful commitment on the part of the company's management will substantially contribute to the program's successful implementation. As the compliance program is implemented, that commitment should filter down through management to every employee and contractor of the pharmaceutical manufacturer, as applicable for the particular individual.

At a minimum, a comprehensive compliance program should include the following elements:

(1) The development and distribution of written standards of conduct, as well as written policies, procedures and protocols that verbalize the company's commitment to compliance (*e.g.,* by including adherence to the compliance program as an element

---

[5] In addition, the compliance program elements and potential risk areas addressed in this compliance program guidance may also have application to manufacturers of other products that may be reimbursed by federal health care programs, such as medical devices and infant nutritional products.

in evaluating management and employees) and address specific areas of potential fraud and abuse, such as the reporting of pricing and rebate information to the federal health care programs, and sales and marketing practices;

(2) The designation of a compliance officer and other appropriate bodies (*e.g.*, a corporate compliance committee) charged with the responsibility for developing, operating, and monitoring the compliance program, and with authority to report directly to the board of directors and/or the president or CEO;

(3) The development and implementation of regular, effective education and training programs for all affected employees;

(4) The creation and maintenance of an effective line of communication between the compliance officer and all employees, including a process (such as a hotline or other reporting system) to receive complaints or questions, and the adoption of procedures to protect the anonymity of complainants and to protect whistleblowers from retaliation;

(5) The use of audits and/or other risk evaluation techniques to monitor compliance, identify problem areas, and assist in the reduction of identified problems;

(6) The development of policies and procedures addressing the non-employment or retention of individuals or entities excluded from participation in federal health care programs, and the enforcement of appropriate disciplinary action against employees or contractors who have violated company policies and procedures and/or applicable federal health care program requirements; and

(7) The development of policies and procedures for the investigation of identified instances of noncompliance or misconduct. These should include directions regarding the prompt and proper response to detected offenses, such as the initiation of appropriate corrective action and preventive measures and processes to report the offense to relevant authorities in appropriate circumstances.

B. Written Policies and Procedures

In developing a compliance program, every pharmaceutical manufacturer should develop and distribute written compliance standards, procedures, and practices that guide the company and the conduct of its employees in day-to-day operations. These policies and procedures should be developed under the direction and supervision of the compliance officer, the compliance committee, and operational managers. At a minimum, the policies and procedures should be provided to all employees who are affected by these policies, and to any agents or contractors who may furnish services that impact federal health care programs (*e.g.*, contractors involved in the co-promotion of a manufacturer's products).

1. *Code of Conduct*

Although a clear statement of detailed and substantive policies and procedures is at the core of a compliance program, the OIG recommends that pharmaceutical manufacturers also develop a general corporate statement of ethical and compliance principles that will guide the company's operations. One common expression of this statement of principles is the code of conduct. The code should function in the same fashion as a constitution, *i.e.*, as a document that details the fundamental principles, values, and framework for action within an organization. The code of conduct for a pharmaceutical manufacturer should articulate the company's expectations of commitment to compliance by management, employees, and agents, and should summarize the broad ethical and legal principles under which the company must operate. Unlike the more detailed policies and procedures, the code of conduct should be brief, easily readable, and cover general principles applicable to all employees.

As appropriate, the OIG strongly encourages the participation and involvement of the pharmaceutical manufacturer's board of directors, CEO, president, members of senior management, and other personnel from various levels of the organizational structure in the development of all aspects of the compliance program, especially the code of conduct. Management and employee involvement in this process communicates a strong and explicit commitment by management to foster compliance with applicable federal health care program requirements. It also communicates the need for all employees to comply with the organization's code of conduct and policies and procedures.

2. *Specific Risk Areas*

This section is intended to help prudent pharmaceutical manufacturers identify areas of their operations that present potential risk of liability under several key federal fraud and abuse statutes and regulations.[6] This section focuses on areas that are currently of concern to the enforcement community and is not intended to address all potential risk areas for pharmaceutical manufacturers. Importantly, the identification of a particular practice or activity in this section is not intended to imply that the practice or activity is necessarily illegal in all circumstances or that it may not have a valid or lawful purpose underlying it.

This section addresses the following areas of significant concern for pharmaceutical manufacturers: (1) integrity of data used by state and federal governments to establish payment amounts; (2) kickbacks and other illegal remuneration; and (3) compliance with laws regulating drug samples.

This guidance does not create any new law or legal obligations, and the discussions that follow are not intended to present detailed or

---

[6] In addition, pharmaceutical manufacturers should be mindful that many states have fraud and abuse statues—including false claims, anti-kickback and other statues—that are not addressed in this guidance.

comprehensive summaries of lawful and unlawful activity. Rather, these discussions should be used as a starting point for a manufacturer's legal review of its particular practices and for development of policies and procedures to reduce or eliminate potential risk.

a. *Integrity of Data Used to Establish or Determine Government Reimbursement*

Many federal and state health care programs establish or ultimately determine reimbursement rates for pharmaceuticals, either prospectively or retrospectively, using price and sales data directly or indirectly furnished by pharmaceutical manufacturers. The government sets reimbursement with the expectation that the data provided are complete and accurate. The knowing submission of false, fraudulent, or misleading information is actionable. A pharmaceutical manufacturer may be liable under the False Claims Act[7] if government reimbursement (including, but not limited to, reimbursement by Medicare and Medicaid) for the manufacturer's product depends, in whole or in part, on information generated or reported by the manufacturer, directly or indirectly, and the manufacturer has knowingly (as defined in the False Claims Act) failed to generate or report such information completely and accurately. Manufacturers may also be liable for civil money penalties under various laws, rules and regulations. Moreover, in some circumstances, inaccurate or incomplete reporting may be probative of liability under the federal anti-kickback statute.

Where appropriate, manufacturers' reported prices should accurately take into account price reductions, cash discounts, free goods contingent on a purchase agreement, rebates, up-front payments, coupons, goods in kind, free or reduced-price services, grants, or other price concessions or similar benefits offered to some or all purchasers. Any discount, price concession, or similar benefit offered on purchases of multiple products should be fairly apportioned among the products (and could potentially raise anti-kickback issues). Underlying assumptions used in connection with reported prices should be reasoned, consistent, and appropriately documented, and pharmaceutical manufacturers should retain all relevant records reflecting reported prices and efforts to comply with federal health care program requirements.

Given the importance of the Medicaid Rebate Program, as well as other programs that rely on Medicaid Rebate Program benchmarks (such as the 340B Program[8]), manufacturers should pay particular attention to ensuring that they are calculating Average Manufacturer

---

[7] The False Claims Act (31 U.S.C. 3729-33) prohibits knowingly presenting (or causing to be presented) to the federal government a false or fraudulent claim for payment or approval. Additionally, it prohibits knowingly making or using (or causing to be made or used) a false record or statement to get a false or fraudulent claim paid or approved by the federal government or its agents, like a carrier, other claims processor, or state Medicaid program.

[8] The 340B Program, contained as part of the Public Health Services Act and codified at 42 U.S.C. 256b, is administered by the Health Resources and Services Administration (HRSA).

Price and Best Price accurately and that they are paying appropriate rebate amounts for their drugs.[9]

In sum, pharmaceutical manufacturers are responsible for ensuring the integrity of data they generate that is used for government reimbursement purposes.

b. *Kickbacks and Other Illegal Remuneration*

A. *General Considerations*

Pharmaceutical manufacturers, as well as their employees and agents, should be aware of the federal anti-kickback statute and the constraints it places on the marketing and promotion of products reimbursable by the federal health care programs, including, but not limited to, Medicare and Medicaid. In the health care sector, many common business activities, including, for example, sales, marketing, discounting, and purchaser relations, potentially implicate the anti-kickback statute. Pharmaceutical manufacturers and their employees and agents should be aware that the anti-kickback statute prohibits in the health care industry some practices that are common in other business sectors. In short, practices that may be common or longstanding in other businesses are not necessarily acceptable or lawful when soliciting federal health care program business.

The anti-kickback statute is a criminal prohibition against payments (in any form, whether the payments are direct or indirect) made purposefully to induce or reward the referral or generation of federal health care business. The anti-kickback statute addresses not only the offer or payment of anything of value for patient referrals, but also the offer or payment of anything of value in return for purchasing, leasing, ordering, or arranging for or recommending the purchase, lease, or ordering of any item or service reimbursable in whole or part by a federal health care program. The statute extends equally to the solicitation or acceptance of remuneration for referrals. Liability under the anti-kickback statute is determined separately for each party involved. In addition to criminal penalties, violators may be subject to civil monetary sanctions and exclusion from the federal health care programs. Under certain circumstances, a violation of the anti-kickback statute may give rise to liability under the False Claims Act.

Although liability under the anti-kickback statute ultimately turns on a party's intent, it is possible to identify arrangements or practices that may present a significant potential for abuse. Initially, a manufacturer should identify any remunerative relationship between itself (or its representatives) and persons or entities in a position to generate federal health care business for the manufacturer directly or indirectly.

---

[9] 42 U.S.C. 1396r-8. Average Manufacturer Price and Best Price are defined in the statute at 42 U.S.C. 1396r-8(k)(1) and 1396r-8(c)(1), respectively. CMS has provided further guidance on these terms in the National Drug Rebate Agreement and in Medicaid Program Releases available through its web site at www.hcfa.gov/medicaid/drugs/drug.mpg.htm.

Persons or entities in a position to generate federal health care business include, for example, purchasers, benefit managers, formulary committee members, group purchasing organizations (GPOs), physicians and certain allied health care professionals, and pharmacists. The next step is to determine whether any *one* purpose of the remuneration may be to induce or reward the referral or recommendation of business payable in whole or in part by a federal health care program. Importantly, a lawful purpose will not legitimize a payment that also has an unlawful purpose.

Although any arrangement satisfying both tests requires careful scrutiny from a manufacturer, the courts have identified several potentially aggravating considerations that can be useful in identifying arrangements at greatest risk of prosecution. In particular, manufacturers should ask the following questions, among others, about any problematic arrangements or practices they identify:

- Does the arrangement or practice have a potential to interfere with, or skew, clinical decision-making? Does it have a potential to undermine the clinical integrity of a formulary process? If the arrangement or practice involves providing information to decision-makers, prescribers, or patients, is the information complete, accurate, and not misleading?

- Does the arrangement or practice have a potential to increase costs to the federal health care programs, beneficiaries, or enrollees? Does the arrangement or practice have the potential to be a disguised discount to circumvent the Medicaid Rebate Program Best Price calculation?

- Does the arrangement or practice have a potential to increase the risk of overutilization or inappropriate utilization?

- Does the arrangement or practice raise patient safety or quality of care concerns?

Manufacturers that have identified problematic arrangements or practices can take a number of steps to reduce or eliminate the risk of an anti-kickback violation. Detailed guidance relating to a number of specific practices is available from several sources. Most importantly, the anti-kickback statute and the corresponding regulations establish a number of "safe harbors" for common business arrangements, including personal services and management contracts, 42 CFR 1001.952(d), warranties, 42 CFR 1001.952(g), discounts, 42 CFR 1001.952(h), employment, 42 CFR 1001.952(i), GPOs, 42 CFR 1001.952(j), and certain managed care and risk sharing arrangements, 42 CFR 1001.952(m), (t), and (u). *Safe harbor protection requires strict compliance with all applicable conditions set out in the relevant safe harbor.* Although compliance with a safe harbor is voluntary and failure to comply with a safe harbor does not mean an arrangement is illegal, many arrangements can be structured to fit in safe harbors, and we recommend that pharmaceutical manufacturers structure arrangements to fit in a safe harbor whenever possible. Other available guidance includes special fraud alerts and advisory bulletins issued by the OIG identifying and discussing particular practices or issues of concern and OIG advisory opinions issued to specific parties about their particular business arrangements. Parties may apply for an OIG advisory opinion using the procedures set out at 42 CFR part 1008. The safe harbor regulations (and accompanying *Federal Register* preambles), fraud alerts and bulletins, advisory opinions (and instructions for obtaining them), and other guidance are available on the OIG web site at http://oig.hhs.gov.

B. *Key Areas of Potential Risk*

The following discussion highlights several known areas of potential risk. The propriety of any particular arrangement can only be determined after a detailed examination of the attendant facts and circumstances. *The identification of a given practice or activity as "suspect" or as an area of "risk" does not mean it is necessarily illegal or unlawful, or that it cannot be properly structured to fit in a safe harbor.* Nor does it mean that the practice or activity is not beneficial from a clinical, cost, or other perspective. Rather, the areas identified below are those areas of activity that have a potential for abuse based on historical law enforcement experience and that should receive close scrutiny from manufacturers. The discussion highlights potential risks under the anti-kickback statute arising from pharmaceutical manufacturers' relationships with three groups: purchasers (including those using formularies) and their agents; persons and entities in a position to make or influence referrals (including physicians and other health care professionals); and sales agents.

(1) Relationships with Purchasers and their Agents

(a) *Discounts and Other Remuneration to Purchasers*

Pharmaceutical manufacturers offer purchasers a variety of price concessions and other remuneration to induce the purchase of their products. Purchasers include direct purchasers (*e.g.,* hospitals, nursing homes, pharmacies, some physicians), as well as indirect purchasers (*e.g.,* health plans). Inducements offered to purchasers potentially implicate the anti-kickback statute if the purchased products are reimbursable to the purchasers, in whole or in part, directly or indirectly, by any of the federal health care programs. Any remuneration from a manufacturer provided to a purchaser that is expressly or impliedly related to a sale potentially implicates the anti-kickback statute and should be carefully reviewed.

Discounting arrangements are prevalent in the pharmaceutical industry and deserve careful scrutiny particularly because of their potential to implicate the Best Price requirements of the Medicaid Rebate Program. Because the Medicaid Rebate Program in many instances requires that states receive rebates based on the Best Price offered by a pharmaceutical manufacturer to other purchasers, manufacturers have a strong financial incentive to hide *de facto* pricing concessions to other purchasers to avoid passing on the same discount to the states. Because of the potential direct and substantial effect of such practices on federal health care program expenditures and the interest of some manufacturers in avoiding price concessions that would trigger rebates to the states, any remuneration from a manufacturer to a purchaser, however characterized, should be carefully scrutinized.

Discounts. Public policy favors open and legitimate price competition in health care. Thus, the anti-kickback statute contains an exception for discounts offered to customers that submit claims to the federal health care programs, if the discounts are properly disclosed and accurately reported. *See* 42 U.S.C. 1320a-7b(b)(3)(A); 42 CFR 1001.952(h). However, to qualify for the exception, the discount must be in the form of *a reduction in the price* of the good or service based on an arms-length transaction. In other words, the exception covers only reductions in the product's price. Moreover, the regulations provide that the discount must be given at the time of sale or, in certain cases, set at the time of sale, even if finally determined subsequent to the time of sale (*i.e.,* a rebate).

Manufacturers offering discounts should thoroughly familiarize themselves, and have their sales and marketing personnel familiarize themselves, with the discount safe harbor at 42 CFR 1001.952(h) (and, if relevant, the safe harbors for price reductions in the managed care context, 42 CFR 1001.952(m), (t), and (u)). In particular, manufacturers should pay attention to the discount safe harbor requirements applicable to "sellers" and "offerors" of discounts. Under the safe harbor, sellers and offerors have specific obligations that include (i) informing a customer of any discount and of the customer's reporting obligations with respect to that discount, and (ii) refraining from any action that would impede a customer's ability to comply with the safe harbor. To fulfill the safe harbor requirements, manufacturers will need to know how their customers submit claims to the federal health care programs (*e.g.,* whether the customer is a managed care, cost-based, or charge-based biller). Compliance with the safe harbor is determined separately for each party.

Product Support Services. Pharmaceutical manufacturers sometimes offer purchasers certain support services in connection with the sale of their products. These services may include billing assistance tailored to the purchased products, reimbursement consultation, and other programs specifically tied to support of the purchased product. Standing alone, services that have no substantial independent value to the purchaser may not implicate the anti-kickback statute. However, if a manufacturer provides a service having no independent value (such as limited reimbursement support services in connection with its own products) in tandem with another service or program that confers a benefit on a referring provider (such as a reimbursement guarantee that eliminates normal financial risks), the arrangement would raise kickback concerns. For example, the anti-kickback statute would be implicated if a manufacturer were to couple a reimbursement support service with a promise that a purchaser will pay for ordered products only if the purchaser is reimbursed by a federal health care program.

Educational Grants. Pharmaceutical manufacturers sometimes provide grant funding for a wide range of educational activities. While educational funding can provide valuable information to the medical and health care industry, manufacturer grants to purchasers, GPOs, PBMs and similar entities raise concerns under the anti-kickback statute. Funding that is conditioned, in whole or in part, on the purchase of product implicates the statute, even if the educational or research purpose is legitimate. Furthermore, to the extent the manufacturer has any influence over the substance of an educational program or the presenter, there is a risk that the educational program may be used for inappropriate marketing purposes.

To reduce the risks that a grant program is used improperly to induce or reward product purchases or to market product inappropriately, manufacturers should separate their grant making functions from their sales and marketing functions. Effective separation of these functions will help insure that grant funding is not inappropriately influenced by sales or marketing motivations and that the educational purposes of the grant are legitimate. Manufacturers should establish objective criteria for making grants that do not take into account the volume or value of purchases made by, or anticipated from, the grant recipient and that serve to ensure that the funded activities are *bona fide.* The manufacturer should have no control over the speaker or content of the educational presentation. Compliance with such procedures should be documented and regularly monitored.

Research Funding. Manufacturers often contract with purchasers of their products to conduct research activities on behalf of the manufacturer on a fee-for-service basis. These contracts should be structured to fit in the personal services safe harbor whenever possible. Payments for research services should be fair market value for legitimate, reasonable, and necessary services. Post-marketing research activities should be especially scrutinized to ensure that they are legitimate and not simply a pretext to generate prescriptions of a drug. Prudent manufacturers will develop contracting procedures that clearly separate the awarding of research contracts from marketing. Research contracts that originate through the sales or marketing functions—or that are offered to purchasers in connection with sales contacts—are particularly suspect.

Pharmaceutical manufacturers sometimes provide funding to their purchasers for use in the purchasers' own research. In many cases, the research provides valuable scientific and clinical information, improves clinical care, leads to promising new treatments, promotes better delivery of health care, or otherwise benefits patients. However, as with educational grants, if linked directly or indirectly to the purchase of product, research grants can be misused to induce the purchase of business without triggering Medicaid Best Price obligations. To reduce risk, manufacturers should insulate research grant making from sales and marketing influences.

Other remuneration to purchasers. As already noted, any remuneration from a manufacturer provided to a purchaser that is expressly or impliedly related to a sale potentially implicates the anti-kickback statute and should be carefully reviewed. Examples of remuneration in connection with a sale include, but are not limited to, "prebates" and "upfront payments," other free or reduced-price goods or services, and payments to cover the costs of "converting" from a competitor's product. Selective offers of remuneration (*i.e.,* offers made to some but not all purchasers) may increase potential risk if the selection criteria relate directly or indirectly to the volume or value of business generated. In addition, manufacturers may contract with purchasers to provide services to the manufacturer, such as data collection services. These contracts should be structured whenever possible to fit in the personal services safe harbor; in all cases, the remuneration should be fair market value for legitimate, reasonable, and necessary services.

(b) Formularies and Formulary Support Activities

To help control drug costs while maintaining clinical appropriateness and quality of patient care, many purchasers of pharmaceutical products, including indirect purchasers such as health plans, have developed drug formularies to promote rational, clinically appropriate, safe, and cost-effective drug therapy. Formularies are a well-established tool for the effective management of drug benefits. The formulary development process—typically overseen by a committee of physicians, pharmacists, and other health care professionals—determines the drugs that are covered and, if tiered benefit levels are utilized, to which tier the drugs are assigned. So long as the determination of clinical efficacy and appropriateness of formulary drugs by the formulary committee precedes, and is paramount to, the consideration of costs, the development of a formulary is unlikely to raise significant issues under the anti-kickback statute.

Formulary support activities, including related communications with patients and physicians to encourage compliance, are an integral and essential component of successful pharmacy benefits management. Proper utilization of a formulary maximizes the cost-effectiveness of the benefit and assures the quality and appropriateness of the drug therapy. When provided by a PBM, these services are part of the PBM's formulary and benefit management function—a service provided to its customers—and markedly different from its purchasing agent/price negotiator role. Most importantly, the benefits of these formulary support activities inure directly to the PBM and its customers through lower costs.

To date, Medicare and Medicaid involvement with outpatient drug formularies has been limited primarily to Medicaid and Medicare managed care plans. In light of the safe harbors under the anti-kickback statute for those managed care arrangements, the financial arrangements between health plans and pharmaceutical manufacturers or, where the pharmacy benefit is managed by a PBM, the arrangements among the three parties, have received relatively little scrutiny. However, as federal program expenditures for, and coverage of, outpatient pharmaceuticals increase, scrutiny under the anti-kickback statute has also increased. Several practices appear to have the potential for abuse.

- *Relationships with formulary committee members.* Given the importance of formulary placement for a manufacturer's products, unscrupulous manufacturers and sales representatives may attempt to influence committee deliberations. Any remuneration from a manufacturer or its agents directly or indirectly to person in a position to influence formulary decisions related to the manufacturer's products are suspect and should be carefully scrutinized. Manufacturers should also review their contacts with sponsors of formularies to ensure that price negotiations do not influence decisions on clinical safety or efficacy.

- *Payments to PBMs.* Any rebates or other payments by drug manufacturers to PBMs that are based on, or otherwise related to, the PBM's customers' purchases *potentially* implicate the anti-kickback statute. Protection is available by structuring such arrangements to fit in the GPO safe harbor at 42 CFR 1001.952 (j). That safe harbor requires, among other things, that the payments be authorized in advance by the PBM's customer and that all amounts actually paid to the PBM on account of the customer's purchases be disclosed in writing at least annually to the customer. In addition, arrangements with PBMs that assume risk may raise different issues; depending on the circumstances, protection for such arrangements may be available under the managed care safe harbors at 42 CFR 1001.952 (m), (t) and (u).

- *Formulary placement payments.* Lump sum payments for inclusion in a formulary or for exclusive or restricted formulary status are problematic and should be carefully scrutinized.

In addition, some manufacturers provide funding for purchasers' or PBMs' formulary support activities, especially communications with physicians and patients. While the communications may indirectly benefit the manufacturer, the primary economic beneficiary is typically the formulary sponsor. In other words, the manufacturer's dollars appear to replace dollars that would or should be spent by the sponsor. To the extent the manufacturers' payments are linked to drug purchases directly or indirectly, they potentially implicate the anti-kickback statute. Among the questions that should be examined by a manufacturer in connection with these activities are: Is the funding tied to specific drugs or categories? If so, are the categories especially competitive? Is the formulary sponsor funding similar activities for other drug categories? Has funding of PBM activities increased as rebates are increasingly passed back to PBM customers?

(c) *Average Wholesale Price*

The "spread" is the difference between the amount a customer pays for a product and the amount the customer receives upon resale of the product to the patient or other payer. In many situations under the federal programs, pharmaceutical manufacturers control not only the amount at which they sell a product to their customers, but also the amount those customers who purchase the product for their own accounts and thereafter bill the federal health care programs will be reimbursed. To the extent that a manufacturer controls the "spread," it controls its customer's profit.

Average Wholesale Price (AWP) is the benchmark often used to set reimbursement for prescription drugs under the Medicare Part B program. For covered drugs and biologicals, Medicare Part B generally reimburses at "95 percent of average wholesale price." 42 U.S.C. 1395u(o). Similarly many state Medicaid programs and other payers base reimbursement for drugs and biologicals on AWP. Generally, AWP or pricing information used by commercial price reporting services to determine AWP is reported by pharmaceutical manufacturers.

If a pharmaceutical manufacturer purposefully manipulates the AWP to increase its customers' profits by increasing the amount the federal health care programs reimburse its customers, the anti-kickback statute is implicated. Unlike *bona fide* discounts, which transfer remuneration from a seller to a buyer, manipulation of the AWP transfers remuneration to a seller's immediate customer from a subsequent purchaser (the federal or state government). Under the anti-kickback statute, offering remuneration to a purchaser or referral source is improper if one purpose is to induce the purchase or referral of program business. In other words, it is illegal for a manufacturer knowingly to establish or inappropriately maintain a particular AWP if one purpose is to manipulate the "spread" to induce customers to purchase its product.

In the light of this risk, we recommend that manufacturers review their AWP reporting practices and methodology to confirm that marketing considerations do not influence the process. Furthermore, manufacturers should review their marketing practices. The conjunction of manipulation of the AWP to induce customers to purchase a product with active marketing of the spread is strong evidence of the unlawful intent necessary to trigger the anti-kickback statute. Active marketing of the spread includes, for example, sales representatives promoting the spread as a reason to purchase the product or guaranteeing a certain profit or spread in exchange for the purchase of a product.

(2) Relationships with Physicians and Other Persons and Entities in a Position to Make or Influence Referrals

Pharmaceutical manufacturers and their agents may have a variety of remunerative relationships with persons or entities in a position to refer, order, or prescribe—or influence the referral, ordering, or prescribing of—the manufacturers' products, even though the persons or entities may not themselves purchase (or in the case of GPOs or PBMs, arrange for the purchase of) those products. These remunerative relationships potentially implicate the anti-kickback statute. The following discussion focuses on relationships with physicians, but the same principles would apply when evaluating relationships with other parties in a position to influence referrals, including, without limitation, pharmacists and other health care professionals.

Manufacturers, providers, and suppliers of health care products and services frequently cultivate relationships with physicians in a position to generate business for them through a variety of practices, including gifts, entertainment, and personal services compensation arrangements. These activities have a high potential for fraud and abuse and, historically, have generated a substantial number of anti-kickback convictions. There is no substantive difference between remuneration from a pharmaceutical manufacturer or from a durable medical equipment or other supplier—if the remuneration is intended to generate any federal health care business, it potentially violates the anti-kickback statute.

Any time a pharmaceutical manufacturer provides anything of value to a physician who might prescribe the manufacturer's product, the manufacturer should examine whether it is providing a valuable tangible benefit to the physician with the intent to induce or reward referrals. For example, if goods or services provided by the manufacturer eliminate an expense that the physician would have otherwise incurred (*i.e.,* have independent value to the physician), or if items or services are sold to a physician at less than their fair market value, the arrangement may be problematic if the arrangement is tied directly or indirectly to the generation of federal health care program business for the manufacturer. Moreover, under the anti-kickback statute, neither a legitimate purpose for an arrangement (*e.g.,* physician education), nor a fair market value payment, will necessarily protect remuneration if there is also an illegal purpose (*i.e.,* the purposeful inducement of business).

In light of the obvious risks inherent in these arrangements, whenever possible prudent manufacturers and their agents or representatives should structure relationships with physicians to fit in an available safe harbor, such as the safe harbors for personal services and management contracts, 42 CFR 1001.952(d), or employees, 42 CFR 1001.952(i). *An arrangement must fit squarely in a safe harbor to be protected.* In addition, arrangements that do not fit in a safe harbor should be reviewed in light of the totality of all facts and circumstances, bearing in mind the following factors, among others:

- *Nature of the relationship between the parties.* What degree of influence does the physician have, directly or indirectly, on the generation of business for the manufacturer? Does the manufacturer have other direct or indirect relationships with the physician or members of the physician's group?

- *Manner in which the remuneration is determined.* Does the remuneration take into account, directly or indirectly, the volume or value of business generated (*e.g.,* is the remuneration only given to persons who have prescribed or agreed to prescribe the manufacturer's product)? Is the remuneration conditioned in whole or in part on referrals or other business generated? Is there any service provided other than referrals?

- *Value of the remuneration.* Is the remuneration more than trivial in value, including all gifts to any individual, entity, or group of individuals?[10] Do fees for services exceed the fair market value of any legitimate, reasonable, and necessary services rendered by the physician to the manufacturer?

- *Potential federal program impact of the remuneration.* Does the remuneration have the potential to affect costs to any of the federal health care programs or their beneficiaries or to lead to overutilization or inappropriate utilization?

- *Potential conflicts of interest.* Would acceptance of the remuneration diminish, or appear to diminish, the objectivity of professional judgment? Are there patient safety or quality of care concerns? If the remuneration relates to the dissemination of information, is the information complete, accurate, and not misleading?

These concerns are addressed in the PhRMA Code on Interactions with Healthcare Professionals (the "PhRMA Code"), adopted on April 18, 2002, which provides useful and practical advice for reviewing and structuring these relationships. (The PhRMA Code is available through PhRMA's web site at *http://www.phrma.org.*) Although compliance with the PhRMA Code will not protect a manufacturer as a matter of law under the anti-kickback statute, it will substantially reduce the risk of fraud and abuse and help demonstrate a good faith effort to comply with the applicable federal health care program requirements.

The following paragraphs discuss in greater detail several common or problematic relationships between manufacturers and physicians, including "switching" arrangements, consulting and advisory payments, payments for detailing, business courtesies and other gratuities, and educational and research activities.

---

[10] In this regard, pharmaceutical manufacturers should note that the exception for non-monetary compensation under the Stark law (42 U.S.C. 1395nn; 42 CFR 411.357(k)) is not a basis for protection under the anti-kickback statute.

"Switching" arrangements. As noted in the OIG's 1994 Special Fraud Alert (59 FR 65372; December 19, 1994), product conversion arrangements (also known as "switching" arrangements) are suspect under the anti-kickback statute. Switching arrangements involve pharmaceutical manufacturers offering physicians or others cash payments or other benefits each time a patient's prescription is changed to the manufacturer's product from a competing product. This activity clearly implicates the statute, and, while such programs may be permissible in certain managed care arrangements, manufacturers should review very carefully any marketing practices utilizing "switching" payments in connection with products reimbursable by federal health care programs.

Consulting and advisory payments. Pharmaceutical manufacturers frequently engage physicians and other health care professionals to furnish personal services as consultants or advisers to the manufacturer. In general, fair market value payments to small numbers of physicians for *bona fide* consulting or advisory services are unlikely to raise any significant concern. Compensating physicians as "consultants" when they are expected to attend meetings or conferences primarily in a passive capacity is suspect.

Also of concern are compensation relationships with physicians for services connected directly or indirectly to a manufacturer's marketing and sales activities, such as speaking, certain research, or preceptor or "shadowing" services. While these arrangements are potentially beneficial, they also pose a risk of fraud and abuse. In particular, the use of health care professionals for marketing purposes—including, for example, ghost-written papers or speeches—implicates the anti-kickback statute. While full disclosure by physicians of any potential conflicts of interest and of industry sponsorship or affiliation may reduce the risk of abuse, disclosure does not eliminate the risk.

At a minimum, manufacturers should periodically review arrangements for physicians' services to ensure that: (i) the arrangement is set out in writing; (ii) there is a legitimate need for the services; (iii) the services are provided; (iv) the compensation is at fair market value; and (v) all of the preceding facts are documented prior to payment. In addition, to further reduce their risk, manufacturers should structure services arrangements to comply with a safe harbor whenever possible.

Payments for detailing. Recently, some entities have been compensating physicians for time spent listening to sales representatives market pharmaceutical products. In some cases, these payments are characterized as "consulting" fees and may require physicians to complete minimal paperwork. Other companies pay physicians for time spent accessing web sites to view or listen to marketing information or perform "research." All of these activities are highly suspect under the anti-kickback statute, are highly susceptible to fraud and abuse, and should be strongly discouraged.

Business Courtesies and Other Gratuities. Pharmaceutical companies and their employees and agents often engage in a number of other arrangements that offer benefits, directly or indirectly, to physicians or others in a position to make or influence referrals. Examples of remunerative arrangements between pharmaceutical manufacturers (or their representatives) and parties in a position to influence referrals include:

- entertainment, recreation, travel, meals, or other benefits in association with information or marketing presentations; and
- gifts, gratuities, and other business courtesies.

As discussed above, these arrangements potentially implicate the anti-kickback statute if any one purpose of the arrangement is to generate business for the pharmaceutical company. While the determination of whether a particular arrangement violates the anti-kickback statute depends on the specific facts and circumstances, compliance with the PhRMA Code with respect to these arrangements should substantially reduce a manufacturer's risk.

Educational and Research Funding. In some cases, manufacturers contract with physicians to provide research services on a fee-for-service basis. These contracts should be structured to fit in the personal services safe harbor whenever possible. Payments for research services should be fair market value for legitimate, reasonable, and necessary services. Research contracts that originate through the sales or marketing functions—or that are offered to physicians in connection with sales contacts—are particularly suspect. Indicia of questionable research include, for example, research initiated or directed by marketers or sales agents; research that is not transmitted to, or reviewed by, a manufacturer's science component; research that is unnecessarily duplicative or is not needed by the manufacturer for any purpose other than the generation of business; and post-marketing research used as a pretense to promote product. Prudent manufacturers will develop contracting procedures that clearly separate the awarding of research contracts from marketing or promotion of their products.

In addition, pharmaceutical manufacturers also provide other funding for a wide range of physician educational and research activities. Manufacturers should review educational and research grants to physicians similarly to educational and research grants to purchasers (described above). As with grants to purchasers, the OIG recognizes that many grant-funded activities are legitimate and beneficial. When evaluating educational or research grants provided by manufacturers to physicians, manufacturers should determine if the funding is based, in any way, expressly or implicitly, on the physician's referral of the manufacturer's product. If so, the funding plainly implicates the anti-kickback statute. In addition, the manufacturer should determine whether the funding is for *bona fide* educational or research purposes. Absent unusual circumstances, grants or support for educational activities sponsored and organized by medical professional organizations raise little risk of fraud or abuse, provided that the grant or support is not restricted or conditioned with respect to content or faculty.

Pharmaceutical manufacturers often provide funding to other sponsors of continuing medical education (CME) programs. Manufacturers should take steps to ensure that neither they, nor their representatives, are using these activities to channel improper remuneration to physicians or others in a position to generate business for the manufacturer or to influence or control the content of the program.[11] In addition, manufacturers and sponsors of educational programs should be mindful of the relevant rules and regulations of the Food and Drug Administration. Codes of conduct promulgated by the CME industry may provide a useful starting point for manufacturers when reviewing their CME arrangements.

(3) Relationships with Sales Agents

In large part, a pharmaceutical manufacturer's commitment to an effective fraud and abuse compliance program can be measured by its commitment to training and monitoring its sales force. A pharmaceutical manufacturer should: (i) develop a regular and comprehensive training program for its sales force, including refresher and updated training on a regular basis, either in person or through newsletters, memoranda, or the like; (ii) familiarize its sales force with the minimum PhRMA Code standards and other relevant industry standards; (iii) institute and implement corrective action and disciplinary policies applicable to sales agents who engage in improper marketing; (iv) avail itself of the advisory opinion process if it has questions about particular practices used by its sales force; and (v) establish an effective system for tracking, compiling, and reviewing information about sales force activities, including, if appropriate, random spot checking.

In addition, manufacturers should carefully review their compensation arrangements with sales agents. Sales agents, whether employees or independent contractors, are paid to recommend and arrange for the purchase of the items or services they offer for sale on behalf of the pharmaceutical manufacturer they represent. Many arrangements can be structured to fit in the employment or personal services safe harbor. Arrangements that cannot fit into a safe harbor should be carefully reviewed. Among the factors that should be evaluated are:

- the amount of compensation;
- the identity of the sales agent engaged in the marketing or promotional activity (*e.g.*, is the agent a "white coat" marketer or otherwise in a position of exceptional influence);
- the sales agent's relationship with his or her audience;
- the nature of the marketing or promotional activity;
- the item or service being promoted or marketed; and
- the composition of the target audience.

---

[11] CME programs with no industry sponsorship, financing, or affiliation should not raise anti-kickback concerns, although tuition payments by manufacturers (or their representatives) for persons in a position to influence referrals (*e.g.*, physicians or medical students) may raise concerns.

Manufacturers should be aware that a compensation arrangement with a sales agent that fits in a safe harbor can still be evidence of a manufacturer's improper intent when evaluating the legality of the manufacturer's relationships with persons in a position to influence business for the manufacturer. For example, if a manufacturer provides sales employees with extraordinary incentive bonuses and expense accounts, there may well be an inference to be drawn that the manufacturer intentionally motivated the sales force to induce sales through lavish entertainment or other remuneration.

c. Drug Samples

The provision of drug samples is a widespread industry practice that can benefit patients, but can also be an area of potential risk to a pharmaceutical manufacturer. The Prescription Drug Marketing Act of 1987 (PDMA) governs the distribution of drug samples and forbids their sale. 21 U.S.C. 353(c)(1). A drug sample is defined to be a unit of the drug "that is not intended to be sold . . . and is intended to promote the sale of the drug." 21 U.S.C. 353(c)(1). Failure to comply with the requirements of PDMA can result in sanctions. In some circumstances, if the samples have monetary value to the recipient (*e.g.,* a physician) and are used to treat federal health care program beneficiaries, the improper use of samples may also trigger liability under other statutes, including the False Claims Act and the anti-kickback statue.

Pharmaceutical manufacturers should closely follow the PDMA requirements (including all documentation requirements). In addition, manufacturers can minimize their risk of liability by: (i) training their sales force to inform sample recipients in a meaningful manner that samples may not be sold or billed (thus vitiating any monetary value of the sample); (ii) clearly and conspicuously labeling individual samples as units that may not be sold (thus minimizing the ability of recipients to advertently or inadvertently commingle samples with purchased product); and (iii) including on packaging and any documentation related to the samples (such as shipping notices or invoices) a clear and conspicuous notice that the samples are subject to PDMA and may not be sold. Recent government enforcement activity has focused on instances in which drug samples were provided to physicians who, in turn, sold them to the patient or billed them to the federal health care programs on behalf of the patient.

C. Designation of a Compliance Officer and a Compliance Committee

1. Compliance Officer

Every pharmaceutical manufacturer should designate a compliance officer to serve as the focal point for compliance activities.[12] This

---

[12] It is also advisable to designate as a compliance officer an individual with prior experience or knowledge of compliance and operational issues relevant to pharmaceutical manufacturers.

responsibility may be the individual's sole duty or added to other management responsibilities, depending upon the size and resources of the company and the complexity of the task. If the individual has additional management responsibilities, the pharmaceutical manufacturer should ensure that the individual is able to dedicate adequate and substantive time and attention to the compliance functions. Similarly, if the compliance officer delegates some of the compliance duties, he or she should, nonetheless, remain sufficiently involved to fulfill the compliance oversight function.

Designating a compliance officer with the appropriate authority is critical to the success of the program, necessitating the appointment of a high-level official with direct access to the company's president or CEO, board of directors, all other senior management, and legal counsel. The compliance officer should have sufficient funding, resources, and staff to perform his or her responsibilities fully. The compliance officer should be able to effectuate change within the organization as necessary or appropriate and to exercise independent judgment. Optimal placement of the compliance officer within the organization will vary according to the particular situation of a manufacturer.[13]

Coordination and communication with other appropriate individuals or business units are the key functions of the compliance officer with regard to planning, implementing or enhancing, and monitoring the compliance program. The compliance officer's primary responsibilities should include:

- overseeing and monitoring implementation of the compliance program;[14]

- reporting on a regular basis to the company's board of directors, CEO or president, and compliance committee (if applicable) on compliance matters and assisting these individuals or groups to establish methods to reduce the company's vulnerability to fraud and abuse;

- periodically revising the compliance program, as appropriate, to respond to changes in the company's needs and applicable federal health care program requirements, identified weakness in the compliance program, or identified systemic patterns of noncompliance;

---

[13] The OIG believes it is generally not advisable for the compliance function to be subordinate to the pharmaceutical manufacturer's general counsel, or comptroller or similar financial officer. Separation of the compliance function helps to ensure independent and objective legal reviews and financial analysis of the company's compliance efforts and activities. By separating the compliance function from the key management positions of general counsel or chief financial officer (where the size and structure of the pharmaceutical manufacturer make this a feasible option), a system of checks and balances is established to more effectively achieve the goals of the compliance program.

[14] For companies with multiple divisions or regional offices, the OIG encourages coordination with each company location through the use of a compliance officer located in corporate headquarters who is able to communicate with parallel compliance liaisons in each division or regional office, as appropriate.

- developing, coordinating, and participating in a multifaceted educational and training program that focuses on the elements of the compliance program, and seeking to ensure that all affected employees and management understand and comply with pertinent federal and state standards;

- ensuring that independent contractors and agents, particularly those agents and contractors who are involved in sales and marketing activities, are aware of the requirements of the company's compliance program with respect to sales and marketing activities, among other things;

- coordinating personnel issues with the company's Human Resources/Personnel office (or its equivalent) to ensure that the List of Excluded Individuals/Entities[15] has been checked with respect to all employees and independent contractors;

- assisting the company's internal auditors in coordinating internal compliance review and monitoring activities;

- reviewing and, where appropriate, acting in response to reports of noncompliance received through the hotline (or other established reporting mechanism) or otherwise brought to his or her attention (*e.g.*, as a result of an internal audit or by corporate counsel who may have been notified of a potential instance of noncompliance);

- independently investigating and acting on matters related to compliance. To that end, the compliance officer should have the flexibility to design and coordinate internal investigations (*e.g.*, responding to reports of problems or suspected violations) and any resulting corrective action (*e.g.*, making necessary improvements to policies and practices, and taking appropriate disciplinary action) with various company divisions or departments;

- participating with the company's counsel in the appropriate reporting of any self-discovered violations of federal health care program requirements; and

- continuing the momentum and, as appropriate, revision or expansion of the compliance program after the initial years of implementation.[16]

---

[15] As part of its commitment to compliance, a pharmaceutical manufacturer should carefully consider whether to hire or do business with individuals or entities that have been sanctioned by the OIG. The List of Excluded Individuals and Entities can be checked electronically and is accessible through the OIG's web site at: http://oig.hhs.gov.

[16] There are many approaches the compliance officer may enlist to maintain the vitality of the compliance program. Periodic on-site visits of regional operations, bulletins with compliance updates and reminders, distribution of audiotapes, videotapes, CD ROMs, or computer notifications about different risk areas, lectures at management and employee meetings, and circulation of recent articles or publications discussing fraud and abuse are some examples of approaches the compliance officer may employ.

The compliance officer must have the authority to review all documents and other information relevant to compliance activities. This review authority should enable the compliance officer to examine interactions with government programs to determine whether the company is in compliance with federal health care program reporting and rebate requirements and to examine interactions with health care professionals that could violate kickback prohibitions or other federal health care programs requirements. Where appropriate, the compliance officer should seek the advice of competent legal counsel about these matters.

2. Compliance Committee

The OIG recommends that a compliance committee be established to advise the compliance officer and assist in the implementation of the compliance program.[17] When developing an appropriate team of people to serve as the pharmaceutical manufacturer's compliance committee, the company should consider a variety of skills and personality traits that are expected from the team members. The company should expect its compliance committee members and compliance officer to demonstrate high integrity, good judgment, assertiveness, and an approachable demeanor, while eliciting the respect and trust of company employees. These interpersonal skills are as important as the professional experience of the compliance officer and each member of the compliance committee.

Once a pharmaceutical manufacturer chooses the people who will accept the responsibilities vested in members of the compliance committee, the company needs to train these individuals on the policies and procedures of the compliance program, as well as how to discharge their duties. The OIG recognizes that some pharmaceutical manufacturers (*e.g.,* small companies or those with limited budgets) may not have the resources or the need to establish a compliance committee. However, when potential problems are identified at such companies, the OIG recommends the creation of a "task force" to address the particular issues. The members of the task force may vary depending upon the area of concern. For example, if the compliance officer identifies issues relating to improper inducements to the company's purchasers or prescribers, the OIG recommends that a task force be organized to review the arrangements and interactions with those purchasers or prescribers. In essence, the compliance committee is an extension of the compliance officer and provides the organization with increased oversight.

---

[17]The compliance committee benefits from having the perspectives of individuals with varying responsibilities and areas of knowledge in the organization, such as operations, finance, audit, human resources, legal, and sales and marketing, as well as employees and managers of key operating units. The compliance officer should be an integral member of the committee. All committee members should have the requisite seniority and comprehensive experience within their respective departments to recommend and implement any necessary changes to policies and procedures.

D. Conducting Effective Training and Education

The proper education and training of officers, directors, employees, contractors, and agents, and periodic retraining of personnel at all levels are critical elements of an effective compliance program. A pharmaceutical manufacturer must take steps to communicate effectively its standards and procedures to all affected personnel by requiring participation in appropriate training programs and by other means, such as disseminating publications that explain specific requirements in a practical manner. These training programs should include general sessions summarizing the manufacturer's compliance program, written standards, and applicable federal health care program requirements. All employees and, where feasible and appropriate, contractors should receive the general training. More specific training on issues, such as (i) the anti-kickback statute and how it applies to pharmaceutical sales and marketing practices and (ii) the calculation and reporting of pricing information and payment of rebates in connection with federal health care programs, should be targeted at those employees and contractors whose job requirements make the information relevant. The specific training should be tailored to make it as meaningful as possible for each group of participants.

Managers and employees of specific divisions can assist in identifying specialized areas that require training and in carrying out such training. Additional areas for training may also be identified through internal audits and monitoring and from a review of any past compliance problems of the pharmaceutical manufacturer or similarly situated companies. A pharmaceutical manufacturer should regularly review its training and, where appropriate, update the training to reflect issues identified through audits or monitoring and any relevant changes in federal health care program requirements. Training instructors may come from outside or inside the organization, but must be qualified to present the subject matter involved and sufficiently experienced in the issues presented to adequately field questions and coordinate discussions among those being trained. Ideally, training instructors should be available for follow-up questions after the formal training session has been conducted.

The pharmaceutical manufacturer should train new employees soon after they have started working. Training programs and materials should be designed to take into account the skills, experience, and knowledge of the individual trainees. The compliance officer should document any formal training undertaken by the company as part of the compliance program. The company should retain adequate records of its training of employees, including attendance logs, descriptions of the training sessions, and copies of the material distributed at training sessions.

The OIG suggests that all relevant personnel (*i.e.,* employees as well as agents of the pharmaceutical manufacturer) participate in the various educational and training programs of the company. For example, for sales representatives who are responsible for the sale and marketing of the company's products, periodic training in the anti-kickback statute and its safe harbors should be required. Employees should be required to have a minimum number of educational hours per year, as appropriate, as part of their employment responsibilities.

The OIG recognizes that the format of the training program will vary depending upon the size and resources of the pharmaceutical manufacturer. For example, a company with limited resources or whose sales force is widely dispersed may want to create a videotape or computer-based program for each type of training session so new employees and employees outside of central locations can receive training in a timely manner. If videos or computer-based programs are used for compliance training, the OIG suggests that the company make a qualified individual available to field questions from trainees. Also, large pharmaceutical manufacturers may find training via the Internet or video conference capabilities to be a cost-effective means of reaching a large number of employees. Alternatively, large companies may include training sessions as part of regularly scheduled regional meetings.

The OIG recommends that participation in training programs be made a condition of continued employment and that failure to comply with training requirements should result in disciplinary action. Adherence to the training requirements as well as other provisions of the compliance program should be a factor in the annual evaluation of each employee.

E. Developing Effective Lines of Communication

1. Access to Supervisors and / or the Compliance Officer

In order for a compliance program to work, employees must be able to ask questions and report problems. Supervisors play a key role in responding to employee concerns and it is appropriate that they serve as a first line of communications. Pharmaceutical manufacturers should consider the adoption of open-door policies in order to foster dialogue between management and employees. In order to encourage communications, confidentiality and non-retaliation policies should also be developed and distributed to all employees.[18]

Open lines of communication between the compliance officer and employees are equally important to the successful implementation of a compliance program and the reduction of any potential for fraud and abuse. In addition to serving as a contact point for reporting problems and initiating appropriate responsive action, the compliance officer should be viewed as someone to whom personnel can go to get clarification on the company's policies. Questions and responses should be documented and dated and, if appropriate, shared with other staff so that

---

[18] In some cases, employees sue their employers under the False Claims Act's *qui tam* provisions after a failure or apparent failure by the company to take action when the employee brought a questionable, fraudulent, or abusive situation to the attention of senior corporate officials. Whistleblowers must be protected against retaliation, a concept embodied in the provisions of the False Claims Act. *See* 31 U.S.C. 3730(h).

compliance standards or polices can be updated and improved to reflect any necessary changes or clarifications. Pharmaceutical manufacturers may also consider rewarding employees for appropriate use of established reporting systems as a way to encourage the use of such systems.

2. *Hotlines and Other Forms of Communication*

The OIG encourages the use of hotlines, e-mails, newsletters, suggestion boxes, and other forms of information exchange to maintain open lines of communication. In addition, an effective employee exit interview program could be designed to solicit information from departing employees regarding potential misconduct and suspected violations of company policy and procedures. Pharmaceutical manufacturers may also identify areas of risk or concern through periodic surveys or communications with sales representatives about the current marketing environment. This could provide management with insight about and an opportunity to address conduct occurring in the field, either by the company's own sale representatives or those of other companies.

If a pharmaceutical manufacturer establishes a hotline or other reporting mechanism, information regarding how to access the reporting mechanism should be made readily available to all employees and independent contractors by including that information in the code of conduct or by circulating the information (*e.g.*, by publishing the hotline number or e-mail address on wallet cards) or conspicuously posting the information in common work areas. Employees should be permitted to report matters on an anonymous basis.

Reported matters that suggest substantial violations of compliance policies or applicable federal health care program requirements should be documented and investigated promptly to determine their veracity and the scope and cause of any underlying problem. The compliance officer should maintain a detailed log that records such reports, including the nature of any investigation, its results, and any remedial or disciplinary action taken. Such information, redacted of individual identifiers, should be summarized and included in reports to the board of directors, the president or CEO, and compliance committee. Although the pharmaceutical manufacturer should always strive to maintain the confidentiality of an employee's identity, it should also make clear that there might be a point where the individual's identity may become known or need to be revealed in certain instances. The OIG recognizes that protecting anonymity may be infeasible for small companies. However, the OIG believes all employees, when seeking answers to questions or reporting potential instances of fraud and abuse, should know to whom to turn for a meaningful response and should be able to do so without fear of retribution.

F. Auditing and Monitoring

An effective compliance program should incorporate thorough monitoring of its implementation and an ongoing evaluation process. The compliance officer should document this ongoing monitoring, including reports of suspected noncompliance, and provide these assessments to company's senior management and the compliance committee. The extent and frequency of the compliance audits may vary depending on variables such as the pharmaceutical manufacturer's available resources, prior history of noncompliance, and the risk factors particular to the company. The nature of the reviews may also vary and could include a prospective systemic review of the manufacturer's processes, protocols, and practices or a retrospective review of actual practices in a particular area.

Although many assessment techniques are available, it is often effective to have internal or external evaluators who have relevant expertise perform regular compliance reviews. The reviews should focus on those divisions or departments of the pharmaceutical manufacturer that have substantive involvement with or impact on federal health care programs (such as the government contracts and sales and marketing divisions) and on the risk areas identified in this guidance. The reviews should also evaluate the company's policies and procedures regarding other areas of concern identified by the OIG (*e.g.,* through Special Fraud Alerts) and federal and state law enforcement agencies. Specifically, the reviews should evaluate whether the: (1) pharmaceutical manufacturer has policies covering the identified risk areas; (2) policies were implemented and communicated; and (3) policies were followed.

G. Enforcing Standards Through Well-Publicized Disciplinary Guidelines

An effective compliance program should include clear and specific disciplinary policies that set out the consequences of violating the law or the pharmaceutical manufacturer's code of conduct or policies and procedures. A pharmaceutical manufacturer should consistently undertake appropriate disciplinary action across the company in order for the disciplinary policy to have the required deterrent effect. Intentional and material noncompliance should subject transgressors to significant sanctions. Such sanctions could range from oral warnings to suspension, termination or other sanctions, as appropriate. Disciplinary action also may be appropriate where a responsible employee's failure to detect a violation is attributable to his or her negligence or reckless conduct. Each situation must be considered on a case-by-case basis, taking into account all relevant factors, to determine the appropriate response.

H. Responding to Detected Problems and Developing Corrective Action Initiatives

Violation of a pharmaceutical manufacturer's compliance program, failure to comply with applicable federal or state law, and other types of misconduct threaten the company's status as a reliable, honest, and trustworthy participant in the health care industry. Detected but uncorrected misconduct can endanger the reputation and legal status of the company. Consequently, upon receipt of reasonable indications of suspected noncompliance, it is important that the compliance officer or other management officials immediately investigate the allegations to determine whether a material violation of applicable law or the requirements of the compliance program has occurred and, if so, take decisive steps to correct the problem.[19] The exact nature and level of thoroughness of the investigation will vary according to the circumstances, but the review should be detailed enough to identify the root cause of the problem. As appropriate, the investigation may include a corrective action plan, a report and repayment to the government, and/or a referral to criminal and/or civil law enforcement authorities.

Reporting

Where the compliance officer, compliance committee, or a member of senior management discovers credible evidence of misconduct from any source and, after a reasonable inquiry, believes that the misconduct may violate criminal, civil, or administrative law, the company should promptly report the existence of misconduct to the appropriate federal and state authorities[20] within a reasonable period, but not more than 60 days,[21] after determining that there is credible evidence of a violation.[22] Prompt voluntary reporting will demonstrate the pharmaceutical manufacturer's good faith and willingness to work with governmental authorities to correct and remedy the problem. In addition, reporting such conduct will be considered a mitigating factor by the OIG in determining administrative sanctions (*e.g.*, penalties, assessments, and exclusion), if the reporting company becomes the subject of an OIG investigation.[23]

---

[19] Instances of noncompliance must be determined on a case-by-case basis. The existence or amount of a *monetary* loss to a federal health care program is not solely determinative of whether the conduct should be investigated and reported to governmental authorities. In fact, there may be instances where there is no readily identifiable monetary loss, but corrective actions are still necessary to protect the integrity of the health care program.

[20] Appropriate federal and state authorities include the OIG, the Criminal and Civil Divisions of the Department of Justice, the U.S. Attorney in relevant districts, the Food and Drug Administration, the Federal Trade Commission, the Drug Enforcement Administration and the Federal Bureau of Investigation, and the other investigative arms for the agencies administering the affected federal or state health care programs, such as the state Medicaid Fraud Control Unit, the Defense Criminal Investigative Service, the Department of Veterans Affairs, HRSA, and the Office of Personnel Management (which administers the Federal Employee Health Benefits Program).

[21] In contrast, to qualify for the "not less than double damages" provision of the False Claims Act, the provider must provide the report to the government within 30 days after the date when the provider first obtained the information. 31 U.S.C. 3729(a).

[22] Some violations may be so serious that they warrant immediate notification to governmental authorities prior to, or simultaneous with, commencing an internal investigation. By way of example, the OIG believes a provider should report misconduct that: (1) is a clear violation of administrative, civil, or criminal laws; (2) has a significant adverse effect on the quality of care provided to federal health care program beneficiaries; or (3) indicates evidence of a systemic failure to comply with applicable laws or an existing corporate integrity agreement, regardless of the financial impact on federal health care programs.

[23] The OIG has published criteria setting forth those factors that the OIG takes into consideration in determining whether it is appropriate to exclude an individual or entity from program participation pursuant to 42 U.S.C. 1320a-7(b)(7) for violations of various fraud and abuse laws. *See* 62 FR 67392 (December 24, 1997).

When reporting to the government, a pharmaceutical manufacturer should provide all information relevant to the alleged violation of applicable federal or state law(s) and the potential financial or other impact of the alleged violation. The compliance officer, under advice of counsel and with guidance from the governmental authorities, could be requested to continue to investigate the reported violation. Once the investigation is completed, and especially if the investigation ultimately reveals that criminal, civil or administrative violations have occurred, the compliance officer should notify the appropriate governmental authority of the outcome of the investigation, including a description of the impact of the alleged violation on the operation of the applicable federal health care programs or their beneficiaries.

III. Conclusion

In today's environment of increased scrutiny of corporate conduct and increasingly large expenditures for prescription drugs, it is imperative for pharmaceutical manufacturers to establish and maintain effective compliance programs. These programs should foster a culture of compliance that begins at the executive level and permeates throughout the organization. This compliance guidance is designed to provide assistance to all pharmaceutical manufacturers as they either implement compliance programs or re-assess existing programs. The essential elements outlined in this compliance guidance can be adapted to the unique environment of each manufacturer. It is the hope and expectation of the OIG that the resulting compliance programs will benefit not only federal health care programs and their beneficiaries, but also pharmaceutical manufacturers themselves.

Appendix I-3.2

PhRMA Code on Interactions With Healthcare Professionals (July 2002) [New]

Source: Pharmaceutical Research and Manufacturers of America, Code on Interactions With Healthcare Professionals (effective July 2002), *available at* http://www.phrma.org/publications/policy//2002-04-19.391.pdf. *See generally* PhRMA's website—www.phrma.org—for further information.

PhRMA CODE ON INTERACTIONS WITH HEALTHCARE PROFESSIONALS

Preamble

The Pharmaceutical Research and Manufacturers of America (PhRMA) represents research-based pharmaceutical and biotechnology companies. Our members develop and market new medicines to enable patients to live longer and healthier lives.

Ethical relationships with healthcare professionals are critical to our mission of helping patients by developing and marketing new medicines. An important part of achieving this mission is ensuring that healthcare professionals have the latest, most accurate information available regarding prescription medicines, which play an ever-increasing role in patient healthcare. This document focuses on our interactions with healthcare professionals that relate to the marketing of our products.

Effective marketing of medicines ensures that patients have access to the products they need and that the products are used correctly for maximum patient benefit. Our relationships with healthcare professionals are critical to achieving these goals because they enable us to—

- *inform healthcare professionals about the benefits and risks of our products,*
- *provide scientific and educational information,*
- *support medical research and education, and*
- *obtain feedback and advice about our products through consultation with medical experts.*

579

*In interacting with the medical community, we are committed to fol-
lowing the highest ethical standards as well as all legal requirements.
We are also concerned that our interactions with healthcare professionals not be perceived as inappropriate by patients or the public at
large. This Code is to reinforce our intention that our interactions with
healthcare professionals are to benefit patients and to enhance the practice of medicine. The Code is based on the principle that a healthcare
professional's care of patients should be based, and should be perceived
as being based, solely on each patient's medical needs and the healthcare professional's medical knowledge and experience.*

*Therefore, PhRMA adopts, effective July 1, 2002, the following vol-
untary Code on relationships with healthcare professionals. This Code
addresses interactions with respect to marketed products and related
pre-launch activities. It does not address relationships with clinical investigators relating to pre-approval studies.*

PhRMA Code on Interactions with Healthcare Professionals

1. BASIS OF INTERACTIONS

    Our relationships with healthcare professionals are intended to
    benefit patients and to enhance the practice of medicine. Inter-
    actions should be focused on informing healthcare professionals
    about products, providing scientific and educational information,
    and supporting medical research and education.

2. INFORMATIONAL PRESENTATIONS BY OR ON BEHALF OF
    A PHARMACEUTICAL COMPANY

    Informational presentations and discussions by industry represen-
    tatives and others speaking on behalf of a company provide valu-
    able scientific and educational benefits. In connection with such
    presentations or discussions, occasional meals (but no entertainment/
    recreational events) may be offered so long as they: (a) are modest
    as judged by local standards; and (b) occur in a venue and manner
    conducive to informational communication and provide scientific or
    educational value. Inclusion of a healthcare professional's spouse
    or other guests is not appropriate. Offering "take-out" meals or
    meals to be eaten without a company representative being present
    (such as "dine & dash" programs) is not appropriate.

3. THIRD-PARTY EDUCATIONAL OR PROFESSIONAL MEETINGS

    a. Continuing medical education (CME) or other third-party scien-
        tific and educational conferences or professional meetings can
        contribute to the improvement of patient care and therefore, fi-
        nancial support from companies is permissible. Since the giving
        of any subsidy directly to a healthcare professional by a company
        may be viewed as an inappropriate cash gift, any financial sup-
        port should be given to the conference's sponsor which, in turn,
        can use the money to reduce the overall conference registration

fee for all attendees. In addition, when companies underwrite medical conferences or meetings other than their own, responsibility for and control over the selection of content, faculty, educational methods, materials, and venue belongs to the organizers of the conferences or meetings in accordance with their guidelines.

b. Financial support should not be offered for the costs of travel, lodging, or other personal expenses of non-faculty healthcare professionals attending CME or other third-party scientific or educational conferences or professional meetings, either directly to the individuals attending the conference or indirectly to the conference's sponsor (except as set out in section 6 below). Similarly, funding should not be offered to compensate for the time spent by healthcare professionals attending the conference or meeting.

c. Financial support for meals or receptions may be provided to the CME sponsors who in turn can provide meals or receptions for all attendees. A company also may provide meals or receptions directly at such events if it complies with the sponsoring organization's guidelines. In either of the above situations, the meals or receptions should be modest and be conducive to discussion among faculty and attendees, and the amount of time at the meals or receptions should be clearly subordinate to the amount of time spent at the educational activities of the meeting.

d. A conference or meeting shall mean any activity, held at an appropriate location, where (a) the gathering is primarily dedicated, in both time and effort, to promoting objective scientific and educational activities and discourse (one or more educational presentations(s) should be the highlight of the gathering), and (b) the main incentive for bringing attendees together is to further their knowledge on the topic(s) being presented.

4. CONSULTANTS

a. It is appropriate for consultants who provide services to be offered reasonable compensation for those services and to be offered reimbursement for reasonable travel, lodging, and meal expenses incurred as part of providing those services. Compensation and reimbursement that would be inappropriate in other contexts can be acceptable for bona fide consultants in connection with their consulting arrangements. Token consulting or advisory arrangements should not be used to justify compensating healthcare professionals for their time or their travel, lodging, and other out-of-pocket expenses. The following factors support the existence of a bona fide consulting arrangement (not all factors may be relevant to any particular arrangement):

- a written contract specifies the nature of the services to be provided and the basis for payment of those services;
- a legitimate need for the services has been clearly identified in advance of requesting the services and entering into arrangements with the prospective consultants;

- the criteria for selecting consultants are directly related to the identified purpose and the persons responsible for selecting the consultants have the expertise necessary to evaluate whether the particular healthcare professionals meet those criteria;
- the number of healthcare professionals retained is not greater than the number reasonably necessary to achieve the identified purpose;
- the retaining company maintains records concerning and makes appropriate use of the services provided by consultants;
- the venue and circumstances of any meeting with consultants are conducive to the consulting services and activities related to the services are the primary focus of the meeting, and any social or entertainment events are clearly subordinate in terms of time and emphasis.

b. It is not appropriate to pay honoraria or travel or lodging expenses to nonfaculty and non-consultant attendees at company-sponsored meetings including attendees who participate in interactive sessions.

5. SPEAKER TRAINING MEETINGS

It is appropriate for healthcare professionals who participate in programs intended to recruit and train speakers for company sponsored speaker bureaus to be offered reasonable compensation for their time, considering the value of the type of services provided, and to be offered reimbursement for reasonable travel, lodging, and meal expenses, when (1) the participants receive extensive training on the company's drug products and on compliance with FDA regulatory requirements for communications about such products, (2) this training will result in the participants providing a valuable service to the company, and (3) the participants meet the criteria for consultants (as discussed in part 4.a. above).

6. SCHOLARSHIPS AND EDUCATIONAL FUNDS

Financial assistance for scholarships or other educational funds to permit medical students, residents, fellows, and other healthcare professionals in training to attend carefully selected educational conferences may be offered so long as the selection of individuals who will receive the funds is made by the academic or training institution. "Carefully selected educational conferences" are generally defined as the major educational, scientific, or policy-making meetings of national, regional, or specialty medical associations.

7. EDUCATIONAL AND PRACTICE-RELATED ITEMS

a. Items primarily for the benefit of patients may be offered to healthcare professionals if they are not of substantial value

($100 or less). For example, an anatomical model for use in an examination room primarily involves a patient benefit, whereas a VCR or CD player does not. Items should not be offered on more than an occasional basis, even if each individual item is appropriate. Providing product samples for patient use in accordance with the Prescription Drug Marketing Act is acceptable.

b. Items of minimal value may be offered if they are primarily associated with a healthcare professional's practice (such as pens, notepads, and similar "reminder" items with company or product logos).

c. Items intended for the personal benefit of healthcare professionals (such as floral arrangements, artwork, music CDs or tickets to a sporting event) should not be offered.

d. Payments in cash or cash equivalents (such as gift certificates) should not be offered to healthcare professionals either directly or indirectly, except as compensation for bona fide services (as described in parts 4 and 5). Cash or equivalent payments of any kind create a potential appearance of impropriety or conflict of interest.

8. INDEPENDENCE OF DECISION MAKING

No grants, scholarships, subsidies, support, consulting contracts, or educational or practice related items should be provided or offered to a healthcare professional in exchange for prescribing products or for a commitment to continue prescribing products. Nothing should be offered or provided in a manner or on conditions that would interfere with the independence of a healthcare professional's prescribing practices.

9. ADHERENCE TO CODE

Each member company is strongly encouraged to adopt procedures to assure adherence to this Code.

Frequently Asked Questions

a. **Question**

Under the Code, may items such as stethoscopes be offered to healthcare professionals?

Answer

Yes, because these items primarily benefit patients, so long as the items are not of substantial value and are only occasionally offered to the healthcare professional. Items that are of more than minimal value and do not primarily benefit patients are also not permitted even if they bear a company or product name.

b. **Question**

Under the Code, may golf balls and sports bags be provided if they bear a company or product name?

Answer

No. Golf balls and sports bags, even if of minimal value, do not primarily entail a benefit to patients and are not primarily associated with the healthcare professional's practice, even if they bear the name of a company or product.

c. **Question**

Under the Code, may healthcare professionals be provided with gasoline for their cars if they are provided with product information at the same time?

Answer

No. Items intended for the personal benefit of a healthcare professional should not be offered.

d. **Question**

The Code says that informational presentations and discussions may be accompanied by occasional, modest meals. What types of presentations and meals would this include?

Answer

An informational presentation or discussion may be accompanied by a modest meal provided that the venue and manner of presentation/discussion is conducive to a scientific or educational interchange. For example, if a medical or scientific expert (who is a consultant to or employee of the company) is providing information about recently obtained study data to an audience of healthcare professionals, this could be done over lunch or dinner at a quiet restaurant providing the meal was of modest value as judged by local standards.

Following the same logic, if a sales representative is providing substantial scientific or educational information regarding a company's products to one or a few healthcare practitioners, this could also be done during a modest meal which could be at or outside of a physician's office.

However, if the nature or location of the meal would not facilitate communication of the information, then a meal would not be appropriate. Further, the use of modest meals on more than an occasional basis would not be appropriate.

e. **Question**

A representative of Company X provides pizza for the staff of a medical office. Is this consistent with the Code?

Answer

This would be consistent with the Code if the representative will provide an informational presentation to the medical staff in conjunction with the meal of modest value, so long as the location of the presentation is conducive to a scientific or educational communication. Merely dropping off food for the office staff, however, would not be consistent with the Code.

f. **Question**

A representative of Company X invites physicians to meet to hear a scientific and educational presentation about a new drug at the café at a nearby bookstore. Coffee and cake are provided by the representative and, following the presentation (which is in small groups), each physician is given a gift certificate for books in the amount of $30. Does this conform to the Code?

Answer

No. While the presentation may present scientific or educational information and the coffee and cake may appropriately be provided, an open-ended gift certificate is a cash equivalent. A medical textbook, a book on patient care, or a gift certificate redeemable solely for a medical textbook or book on patient care could be provided if it is not of substantial value.

g. **Question**

Company C invites 30 physicians to a corporate suite at a professional baseball game for a 45-minute scientific and educational presentation followed by a buffet and the three-hour game. Does this conform to the Code?

Answer

No. A modest buffet meal accompanying a scientific or educational would be acceptable. However, the provision of entertainment and/or recreational activities, including entertainment at sporting events in connection with an educational or scientific presentation or discussion, is inconsistent with the Code.

h. **Question**

Under what circumstances would the Code permit a company to provide entertainment or recreational activities directly to healthcare practitioners?

Answer

Companies may provide modest entertainment or recreational activities to healthcare practitioners in a context where those practitioners are providing a legitimate service to the companies, such as when they act as bona fide consultants on an advisory board or are trained at a speaker-training meeting.

Companies should generally not provide entertainment or recreational activities to healthcare practitioners. Thus, companies should not invite healthcare professionals to sporting events, concerts, or shows, or provide them with recreational activities such as hunting, fishing, boating, ski trips, or golf outings, even if those entertainment events or recreational activities are used to facilitate informational interchanges between the company representative and the healthcare professional. Similarly, it would be inappropriate to provide these types of entertainment and recreational events in conjunction with promotional scientific presentations by medical experts.

i. **Question**

Company A retains a small group of 15 nationally known physicians regarding a therapeutic area relevant to company A's products to advise on general medical and business issues and provide guidance on product development and research programs for those products. These physicians are paid significant fees, but those fees are typical of the fees paid to thought leaders in this therapeutic area. They normally meet once or twice a year at resort locations to discuss the latest product data, research programs and Company plans for the product(s). Does this comply with the Code? If it does, is it appropriate to pay for the spouse of the healthcare professional to attend, as well?

Answer

This arrangement appears to comply with the Code. The number of advisors seems reasonably small. The advisors seem to have been selected based on their expertise in the areas where advice is needed. While the consultants are paid significant fees, these appear to be reasonable under the circumstances. Finally, while holding consultant meetings at resort locations is not prohibited, the facilities chosen should be conducive to the services provided as well as reasonable and appropriate to the conduct of the meeting.

It would not be appropriate to pay for the cost of the spouse of the advisor. If the spouse attends, it should be at the cost of the advisor.

j. **Question**

Company A invites 300 physicians/consultants to a two-day and one-night speaker-training program at a regional golf resort. All attendees are compensated for their participation and their expenses are reimbursed. Prospective speakers are selected based on recommendations of the Company's district managers and an assessment of their qualifications by the Company's medical or scientific personnel. Each of the attendees is required to sign an agreement in advance covering the services they will provide. They are educated by a faculty on the full range of data surrounding the disease state and the Company's drug product, on presentation skills, and on FDA regulatory requirements. The Company plans to use at least 280 participants as speakers over the coming year, and it needs to train 300 speakers in order to ensure that 280 will actually be available when needed. Training sessions take both days, and the Company provides for a few hours of golf and meals. Does this program conform to the Code? If so, is it appropriate to pay for a spouse of the healthcare professional, as well?

Answer

This arrangement appears to comply with the Code. Speaker training is an essential activity because FDA holds companies accountable for the presentations of their speakers. In this case, the participants undergo extensive training that will result in a valuable service being provided to the company, and the arrangement meets reasonable indicia of a bona fide consulting relationship. While resort locations are not prohibited, the Company may want to consider whether it would be more appropriate to hold the training session at a non-resort location. In this case, the number of speakers being trained is important; if significantly more participants were trained than were to be used as speakers, this arrangement would not comply with the Code.

The amount of time spent training speakers should be reasonable in relation to the material that has to be covered. The compensation offered to prospective speakers, including the value of any entertainment, should be evaluated to assure that it is reasonable compensation for that time.

It would not be appropriate to pay for the cost of the spouse of the healthcare professional. If the spouse attends, it should be at the cost of the healthcare professional.

k. **Question**

A sales representative invites a physician out for a round of golf and lunch following the golf. The physician is very busy and is difficult to see in her office. The cost of the golf and the lunch combined are $65. Does this comply with the code?

Answer

No. It is inconsistent with the Code to provide entertainment or recreational activities such as golf.

Table of Cases

*References are to chapter and footnote number (e.g., **8:** 5, 69 refers to footnotes 5 and 69 in Chapter 8). Chapters 2 and 9 are new in the Supplement.*

Index

*References are to section numbers in the Supplement (e.g., **5:** IV.K.2 refers to section IV.K.2 in Chapter 5). App. indicates Appendix. Chapters 2 and 9 are new in the Supplement.*

A

Abbott Laboratories, 1: I.A
Academic medical centers (AMCs)
Stark law exception, **2:** III.B.3, VI.J, X; **5:** IV.I
    evidence of affiliation, **2:** X.D
    faculty practice plans, **2:** X.C; **5:** IV.I
    nonprofit support organization as part of, **2:** X.D
    referring physicians, **2:** X.B; **5:** IV.I
    single legal entity, qualification of, **2:** X.D; **5:** IV.I
    teaching hospitals, **2:** X.A
Accreditation organizations. *See* Joint Commission on Accreditation of Healthcare Organizations (JCAHO)
Acknowledgment of accuracy of Medicare diagnoses, 5: III.D
Adjusted community rate proposals (ACRPs)
follow-up to verify correction of problems, **6:** II.B.22
Administrative remedies
federal, **4:** IV.E. *See also* Civil money penalties (CMPs)
state, **4:** IV.F. *See also* State enforcement
Advisory bulletins. *See* Alerts and advisory bulletins
Advisory opinions
anti-kickback statute, **1:** II.A.4
    Topical Index (Cumulative) and Summaries (2001 to Aug. 11, 2004), **App.** G-2
specialty hospitals subject to moratorium on physician ownership, **1:** II.B.3
Stark law, **1:** II.B.3; **2:** XVII
    community need for services, **2:** III.B.3
Alerts and advisory bulletins
Appendix F on disk with the Main Volume contains reprints of the alerts and bulletins.
anti-kickback statute, **1:** II.A.5
concierge physician practices, **1:** II.A.5
Contractual Joint Venture Bulletin, **1:** II.A.5

discount drug card programs, **1:** II.A.5
gainsharing, **1:** II.D.4
gifts, **1:** II.A.5; **App.** F-18
hospitals
    incentives to referring physicians, **5:** IV.K.2
    uninsured or underinsured charges, **1:** II.A.5
malpractice insurance subsidies, **1:** II.A.5
misuse of HHS words and symbols, **1:** II.A.5
Telemarketing By Durable Medical Equipment Suppliers (Special Fraud Alert), **1:** II.A.3
uninsured or underinsured, hospital charges for, **1:** II.A.5
Allegheny Health Education Research Foundation, 8: III.E.2
Ambulances
restocking arrangements, safe harbor for, **1:** II.A.2; **App.** A-2
suppliers, Compliance Program Guidance for, **1:** IV.A; **7:** III.B, III.B.10; **8:** IV.B
Ambulatory surgery centers
Stark law exception
    implantation of devices at, **2:** XI.A
American Bar Association, Health Law Section
comments on Stark II regulations, Phase I and II, **2:** II.C.4.a
American Stock Exchange, 8: II.C
Anti-kickback statute
42 U.S.C. §1320a-7b(b) is reprinted in Appendix A-1; the regulatory safe harbors, 42 C.F.R. §1001.952, are reprinted in Appendix A-2.
advisory bulletins and other guidance documents, **1:** II.A.5
advisory opinions, **1:** II.A.4
    Topical Index (Cumulative) and Summaries (2001 to Aug. 11, 2004), **App.** G-2
defense strategies, **4:** XII.D.2
    kickbacks as false claims, **4:** XII.D.2.a
    statutory exceptions and safe harbors, **4:** XII.D.2.b